D0859631

# CIVIL WAR JOURNAL™

# The Legacies

# CIVIL WAR

*edited by*

WILLIAM C. DAVIS, BRIAN C. POHANKA AND DON TROIANI

# JOURNAL™

Published in Nashville, Tennessee, by Rutledge Hill Press®, 211 Seventh Avenue North, Nashville, Tennessee 37219. Distributed in Canada by H. B. Fenn and Co., Ltd., 34 Nixon Road, Bolton, Ontario L7E 1W2. Distributed in Australia by The Five Mile Press, 22 Summit Road, Noble Park, Victoria 3174. Distributed in New Zealand by Tandem Press, 2 Rugby Road, Birkenhead, Auckland 10. Distributed in the United Kingdom by Verulam Publishing, Ltd., 152a Park Street Lane, Park Street, St. Albans, Hertfordshire AL2 2AU.

Typography by Compass Communications, Inc., Nashville, Tennessee.



**Library of Congress Cataloging-in-Publication Data**

Civil War journal / edited by William C. Davis, Brian C. Pohanka, and Don Troiani.
p. cm.
Fifty-two edited scripts from the television program Civil War journal.
Includes bibliographical references and index.
Contents: [2] The Legacies
ISBN 1-55853-439-3
1. United States—History—Civil War, 1861–1865. I. Davis, William C., 1946- . II. Pohanka, Brian C., 1955- . III. Troiani, Don. IV. Civil War journal (Television program)
E468.C6247 1997
973.7′8—dc21 97-6861
CIP

Printed in the United States of America.
1 2 3 4 5 6 7 8 9 — 04 03 02 01 00 99

# Contents

*Preface* vii
*Acknowledgments* ix
*Contributors* x

1. Slavery 2
2. Divided Families 38
3. First Ladies, North and South 62
4. Civilians in the War 92
5. Women at War 116
6. Zouaves! 140
7. Immigrants and the War 168
8. Reporting the War 196
9. Mathew B. Brady 224
10. Alexander Gardner 256
11. The Spies' War 292
12. Banners of Glory 322
13. Artillery 350
14. Trains at War 380
15. Battlefield Medicine 408
16. Prison Camps 436
17. Arlington 470

*Bibliography* 496
*Illustration Credits* 498
*Index* 503

# Preface

THE LEGACIES OF the Civil War are profound and continue to affect Americans today. The economic, social, and political changes due to the abolition of slavery are obvious examples, but as the chapters in this book indicate, the war changed how Americans think and go about their business in many ways. The four bloody years in the 1860s were a watershed for all American people.

The war, for instance, pushed medical science beyond old limits. Doctors developed and refined techniques that would not have been attempted if they had not been challenged. The details are frequently gruesome, but the Civil War changed medicine forever.

The Civil War was the first conflict to be thoroughly photographed, allowing citizens to see the atrocities of war first hand. Mathew Brady and Alexander Gardner developed the concept of photojournalism and, at the same time, changed the way Americans thought about war. The relationship between the press and the government and the issue of censorship was first defined during the war, establishing the basis for future reporting and photojournalism.

Similarly, there were few principles of espionage before the Civil War. Spies tended to be amateurs, and their intelligence of limited value. By war's end America had a tradition of effective information gathering, and established the foundations for future sophistication in clandestine warfare.

Railroads were just approaching maturity in 1860. The war gave trains an opportunity to prove their effectiveness at determining the outcome of many battles and ultimately influencing the course of the war itself.

The Civil War divided families and the nation, opened a door to greater freedom and enlarged roles for all women, provided a means by which immigrants could forge a strong allegiance to their new homeland, and left a legacy of examples of bravery, dedication, and patriotism that still inspire us.

The topics selected for this book are those chosen for the History Channel's *Civil War Journal*. This is the third volume in the three-volume series; the first two discuss *The Leaders* and *The Battles* of the Civil War. The text for each chapter was taken from the script for the corresponding episode of the television series. An effort was made to maintain the voice, nuance, and inflection conveyed by the many experts who made this a distinctive body of work. Their words are set off in the text with superscript bullets; open bullets (°) mark the beginning of a speaker's words and solid bullets (•) indicate the conclusion. Attribution is indicated by initials in the left margin, and those initials are indentified on the first page of each chapter.

Unlike the two earlier volumes, however, in which the subject matter was well suited to the characteristics of effective television, there is a greater departure from the scripts in this volume because television does not handle concepts as effectively as it does stories. Nevertheless, we have sought to be true to the original script while providing a text that effectively makes use of the characteristics of effective printed communication.

An understanding of the Civil War is an important part of understanding who we are as Americans. It is our purpose to contribute to that understanding.

William C. Davis
Brian C. Pohanka
Don Troiani

# Acknowledgments

MANY PEOPLE were involved in the creation of this book. Each chapter started with a script for the television episode. The writers and producers of each episode are Martin Gillam ("Slavery" and "Immigrants and the War"), Linda Fuller ("Divided Families" and "The Spies' War"), Laura Verklan ("First Ladies, North and South" and "Women at War"), Greg Goldman ("Civilians in the War," "Alexander Gardner," and "Trains at War"), Richard Jones ("Zouaves!"), Noah Morowitz ("Reporting the War"), Authur Drooker ("Mathew B. Brady" and "Arlington"), Rob Kirk ("Banners of Glory"), Rob Lihani ("Artillery"), Dennie Gordon ("Battlefield Medicine"), and Kellie Flanagan ("Prison Camps"). The text was adapted for print by Clint Johnson, Ed Curtis, and Lawrence M. Stone. The captions were written by Milton Bagby, Dana B. Shoaf, and Heidi Campbell-Shoaf and edited by Alice Ewing. Devereaux Cannon consulted on "Banners of Glory."

Of course an adaptation such as this would not have been possible without the assistance of Craig Haffner and Donna Lusitana of Greystone Communications. Similarly, Thomas Heymann and Jonathan Paisner of A&E Television Networks have been invaluable in their guidance.

A book such as this is dependent on the willingness of archives, museums, historical societies, universities, and private collectors to allow us access to their collections for photographs. We cannot be profuse enough in our thanks to the many people and institutions involved. The list of photograph credits appears on pages 498 and following. Of particular help has been Martin Baldessari, JoAnna McDonald, Jennifer Greenstein, and Ralph Eubanks and Blaine Marshall of the Library of Congress.

We have enjoyed working with the editors of Rutledge Hill Press in the production of this volume.

# The Contributors

One of the distinctive elements of *Civil War Journal: The Legacies* is the authority conveyed by the sixty-five scholars, historians, curators, and descendants who infused each topic with something of themselves, bringing the leaders alive for a television audience. Their comments have been marked throughout the text, with an open superscript bullet ( °) indicating the beginning and a solid superscript bullet (•) marking the conclusion of direct quotations from the television script. Initials appear in the left margin designating attribution. Each chapter's opening page includes a list in the lower right hand corner of the experts whose voices can be heard on the pages that follow. Their names are reproduced here in two lists, one arranged by last name and another by initials (page xii).

| | |
|---|---|
| AA | *Alan Axelrod,* historian and author of *The War between the Spies* |
| JB | *Jean Baker,* professor of history, Goucher College |
| CB | *Crickett Bauer,* costume historian |
| ECB | *Edwin C. Bearss,* chief historian and special assistant to the director for military sites, National Park Service |
| JB | *Joseph Bilby,* author and historian |
| SDB | *Scott D. Breckinridge,* Breckinridge descendent |
| FLB | *Frank L. Byrne,* professor of history, Kent State University |
| JC | *Joan Cashin,* professor of history, Ohio State University |
| TYC | *Thomas Y. Cartwright,* curator and historian, The Carter House, Franklin, Tennessee |
| EC | *Elwood Christ,* historian, Adams County Historical Society, Gettysburg, Pennsylvania |
| TGC | *Thomas G. Clemens,* professor of history, Hagerstown Junior College |
| CC | *Catherine Clinton,* historian and author, Harvard University |
| EJC | *Earl J. Coates,* historian |
| GAC | *Gregory A. Coco,* historian, author, and professor, Gettysburg College |
| GC | *Gordon Cotton,* curator, Old Court House Museum, Vicksburg, Mississippi |
| MPC | *Mary P. Coulling,* author and historian |
| LLC | *Lynda Lasswell Crist,* editor, Jefferson Davis papers |
| GED | *Gordon E. Damman,* chairman, National Museum of Civil War Medicine |

WCD *William C. Davis,* historian and author
PJD *Peter J. D'Onofrio,* president, Society of Civil War Surgeons
EFG *Elizabeth Fox-Genovese,* historian, author, and professor, Emory University
WAF *William A. Frassanito,* historian and author
DWG *David Winfred Gaddy,* military historian and author
GWG *Gary W. Gallagher,* professor of history, Pennsylvania State University
WPG *Walter P. Gray,* California State Railroad Museum
WWG *William W. Gwaltney,* historian and author
JPH *John P. Hankey,* historian
SH *Steven Hill,* Massachusetts State House Flag Project
JJH *John J. Hennessy,* historian and author
HH *Harold Holzer,* author, historian, and vice president for communications, Metropolitan Museum of Art, New York City
BJ *Brooks Johnson,* curator of photography, The Chrysler Museum
JCK *James C. Klotter,* state historian, Kentucky Historical Society
LK *Lawrence Kohl,* historian, University of Alabama
JL *Juanita Leisch,* author
HMM *Howard Michael Madaus,* curator, Cody Firearms Museum (BBHC)
JFM *John M. Marszalek,* professor of history, Mississippi University
WM *William Marvel,* author of *Andersonville: The Last Depot*
MJM *Michael J. McAfee,* curator of uniforms, West Point Museum, U.S. Military Academy
IM *Ian McCulloch,* military historian, Black Watch of Canada
JMM *James M. McPherson,* professor of history, Princeton University
EGM *Edna Greene Medford,* historian, Howard University
WM *Warren Motts,* photo historian, Gettysburg battlefield guide
AM *Agnes Mullins,* curator, Arlington House
CN *Chris Nelson,* historian and journalist
NIP *Nell Irvin Painter,* historian and author of *Sojourner Truth: A Life, a Symbol*
MP *Mary Panzer,* curator of photography, National Portrait Gallery
BP *Brian Pohanka,* historian
BPR *Barry Pritzker,* historian and author
GAR *Gerald A. Regan,* journalist
JIR *James I. Robertson, Jr.,* Alumni Distinguished Professor of History, Virginia Tech, Blacksburg, Virginia
GR *Grant Romer,* director, museum studies, The George Eastman House
TLS *Thomas L. Sherlock,* historian, Arlington National Cemetery
NS *Nina Silber,* professor, Boston University
PSS *Paul S. Sledzik,* National Museum of Health and Medicine
CS *Cindy Small,* author and historian
CWS *Charles W. Smithgall,* artillery specialist
WFS *William F. Stapp,* senior curator of photography, The George Eastman House
DT *Don Troiani,* artist and historian
LT *Linda Turner,* co-author of *Mary Todd Lincoln: Her Life and Letters*
DLV *David L. Valuska,* professor of history, Kutztown Unversity
JAW *James A. Ward,* historian

| | |
|---|---|
| AA | Alan Axelrod |
| AM | Agnes Mullins |
| BJ | Brooks Johnson |
| BP | Brian Pohanka |
| BPr | Barry Pritzker |
| CB | Crickett Bauer |
| CC | Catherine Clinton |
| CN | Chris Nelson |
| CS | Cindy Small |
| CWS | Charles W. Smithgall |
| DLV | David L. Valuska |
| DT | Don Troiani |
| DWG | David Winfield Gaddy |
| EC | Elwood Christ |
| ECB | Edwin C. Bearss |
| EFG | Elizabeth Fox-Genovese |
| EGM | Edna Greene Medford |
| EJC | Earl J. Coates |
| FLB | Frank L. Byrne |
| GAC | Gregory A. Coco |
| GAR | Gerald A. Regan |
| GC | Gordon Cotton |
| GED | Gordon E. Damman |
| GR | Grant Romer |
| GWG | Gary W. Gallagher |
| HH | Harold Holzer |
| HMM | Howard Michael Madaus |
| IM | Ian McCulloch |
| JAW | James A. Ward |
| JB | Jean Baker (chapters 2,3) |
| JB | Joseph Bilby (chapter 7) |
| JC | Joan Cashin |
| JCK | James C. Klotter |
| JFM | John M. Marszalek |
| JIR | James I. Robertson, Jr. |
| JJH | John J. Hennessy |
| JL | Juanita Leisch |
| JMM | James M. McPherson |
| JPH | John P. Hankey |
| LK | Lawrence Kohl |
| LLC | Lynda Lasswell Crist |
| LT | Linda Turner |
| MJM | Michael J. McAfee |
| MP | Mary Panzer |
| MPC | Mary P. Coulling |
| NIP | Nell Irvin Painter |
| NS | Nina Silber |
| PJD | Peter J. D'Onofrio |
| PSS | Paul S. Sledzik |
| SDB | Scott D. Breckinridge |
| SH | Steven Hill |
| TGC | Thomas G. Clemens |
| TLS | Thomas L. Sherlock |
| TYC | Thomas Y. Cartwright |
| WAF | William A. Frassanito |
| WCD | William C. Davis |
| WFS | William F. Stapp |
| WM | Warren Motts (chapter 9) |
| WM | William Marvel (chapter 16) |
| WPG | Walter P. Gray |
| WWG | William W. Gwaltney |

# CIVIL WAR JOURNAL™

# The Legacies

# SLAVERY

The ABOLITION OF SLAVERY, OF ALL OF the legacies of the American Civil War, is the most far-reaching and perhaps the most difficult to address objectively. For those whose ancestors were slaves, the issue has a heightened emotional dimension because their forebears suffered under an economic and social system that viewed and treated them as property rather than people. For those whose ancestors were not slaves, the issue is less personal and more difficult to understand in human terms. As well as being an emotional issue, the abolition of slavery also involved political, economic, and moral aspects.

Politically, in mid-nineteenth-century America abolition was at the heart of the battle over the right of individual states to determine their own destiny. It was this aspect of abolition that led to the Civil War. Most Northern soldiers did not go to battle to free the slaves in the South, but to put down the insurrection among the rebelling states and restore the Union. Likewise, most Southern soldiers did not take up arms to preserve the institution of slavery, but to continue the fight for the freedom to choose their own destiny begun in the American Revolution. In 1776 the American colonies revolted against a system of government in which they had no representation but which assessed taxes and made laws concerning matters about which it had no firsthand knowledge. In 1861 the South rose up against a government that it believed was on the verge of destroying its way of life, which included the enslavement of more than one-third of the region's population.

| | |
|---|---|
| **WCD** | William C. Davis |
| **WWG** | William W. Gwaltney |
| **EGM** | Edna Greene Medford |
| **NIP** | Nell Irvin Painter |
| **JIR** | James I. Robertson Jr. |

*Although Congress outlawed the slave trade in 1808, the law was poorly enforced and African slaves continued to be brought into the United States until the start of the Civil War. Slavery was not abolished in Puerto Rico until 1873, in Cuba until 1886, and in Brazil until 1888. Drawn in the 1870s, the illustrations above show typical slave trading transactions. The lucrative slave trade encouraged African rulers to sell Africans from other tribes whom they captured as prisoners of war in return for European-made cloth, guns, and iron (above left). From the 1500s until the 1800s European slave traders brought up to 10 million slaves to North and South America from Africa's west coast between Senegal and Angola. About one-half million slaves came to the United States and Canada. Before making a purchase, the traders inspected their potential "merchandise" as they would livestock (above right). After the Civil War, a former slave, when asked about his propensity for stealing from his master, replied, "White folks stole de niggers, . . . jes' like you'd go get a drove of horses and sell 'em."*

Economically, slavery was the necessary ingredient that fueled the agrarian way of life in the South through a dependence on cash crops such as rice, tobacco, and cotton. In 1860 cotton accounted for an astounding 57 percent of the value of all American exports. The South, however, lacked the kind of industrial infrastructure that was booming in the North. Nevertheless, the South had confidence that just as it had succeeded in bartering cotton for goods and luxuries from the Continent for the first half of the 1800s, it would easily continue to do so as an independent country in the latter half of the nineteenth century. Of course, for the Southern cotton empire to succeed, it had to maintain its monopoly on European markets and it had to retain an enslaved labor force. Abolition threatened to destroy the economic strength of the South, wrecking this agrarian way of life and promoting the cultivation of cotton in Egypt and India to which Europe would turn when American cotton disappeared from its market.

Morally, slavery debased an entire people and cataloged them as property to be bought and sold like most farm animals, with no regard for familial ties. Except for abolitionists, most free persons in the mid-nineteenth century did not view slavery in the same moral terms as people do at the turn of the twenty-first century. Those who were not abolitionists usually accepted the legal determination that slaves were property—not human beings—and because they were property their owners could do what they wanted with them. Even some free blacks were slave owners and evidently saw nothing morally wrong with it. Whether a slave owner was benevolent toward his slaves or treated them harshly, such types of slave owners viewed human beings as property, a legal conclusion that had tragic moral consequences. The abolition of slavery was a moral issue, but it took abolitionists who were regarded as fanatics at the time to make this point.

*Unimaginable horrors cascaded on the captive Africans as they were forced from their homeland and placed aboard ships for the "Middle Passage" across the Atlantic to a U.S. port. Shackled with heavy chains for much of the trip, the miserable slaves often lay for days in their own excrement and vomit. When they were released for periods of exercise, some desperately ended their terror by leaping to their deaths in the ocean. This nineteenth-century illustration served to instruct the captain of a slave ship how best to use his storage space to maximize his cargo load and profit.*

By the mid-nineteenth century, the United States was one of the few Western countries still practicing slavery. Britain, France, Spain, and other countries outlawed slave trading in the late 1700s and early 1800s. The legal prohibition of slavery itself occurred in Britain in the 1830s, in France in the 1840s, in Portugal in 1858—although it did not fully take effect until 1878—and in Holland in 1863. At the time of the Civil War, slavery was still actively practiced only in the southern United States, Cuba, and Brazil. In the American South, the white community vowed to do anything necessary to preserve slavery, even if it meant civil war.

For decades the South had heard northern politicians warn that slavery must end one day. In 1855 Abraham Lincoln, an obscure congressman from Illinois, pronounced: "As a nation we began by declaring that all men are created equal. We now practically read it, all men are created equal except Negroes." Not long afterward, in a senatorial race, Lincoln began a traveling series of debates with Stephen A. Douglas over the future of slavery in the new territories.

While those in power debated the future for politically powerless slaves, the slaves in the South knew exactly what they wanted. Anthony Bingham, one of these slaves, confessed, "I never saw the day since I knew anything that I didn't want to be free."

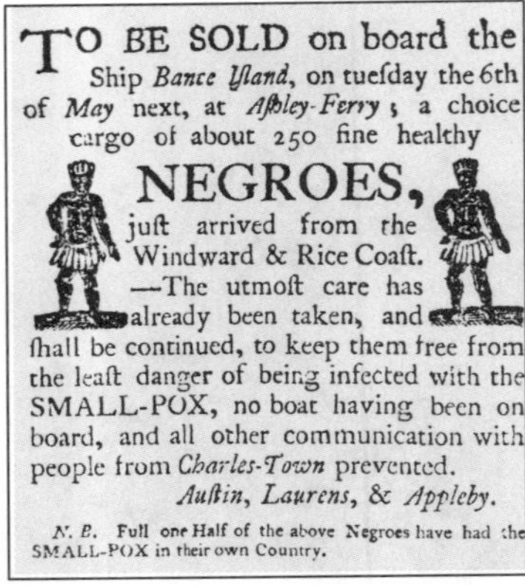

TO BE SOLD on board the Ship *Bance Yland*, on tueſday the 6th of *May* next, at *Aſhley-Ferry*; a choice cargo of about 250 fine healthy

NEGROES,

juſt arrived from the Windward & Rice Coaſt. —The utmoſt care has already been taken, and ſhall be continued, to keep them free from the leaſt danger of being infected with the SMALL-POX, no boat having been on board, and all other communication with people from *Charles-Town* prevented.

*Auſtin, Laurens, & Appleby.*

*N. B.* Full one Half of the above Negroes have had the SMALL-POX in their own Country.

*A broadside (above) advertising a slave auction aboard ship assures potential buyers that the cargo is free of smallpox. Willis Cofer, a former slave, said that bidding at such auctions would start at two hundred fifty dollars for a young, strong man. "A good young breedin' 'oman brung two thousand dollars easy, 'cause de marsters wanted . . . plenty of strong healthy chillun. Cyarpenters and bricklayers and blacksmiths brung . . . from three thousand to five thousand dollars. . . . A good field hand brung 'bout two hundred dollars."*

*An 1861 engraving (below) from* Harper's Weekly, *a Northern periodical, linked the "Southern rebellion" with slavery by depicting an auction beneath the first national banner of the Confederacy.*

The first slaves had arrived in America in 1619 when a Dutch ship docked at the Jamestown, Virginia, colony with twenty blacks for sale. The colonists, feeling overworked carving out a living in the new frontier, quickly purchased the men and readily accepted the institution of slavery.

Within a few decades the practice of owning human beings was accepted by all thirteen colonies. Slaves were trained to work on farms, in factories, and as craftsmen, such as blacksmiths and carpenters. Skilled slaves built the houses of George Washington at Mount Vernon and Thomas Jefferson at Monticello. Few whites found anything wrong with a custom that many believed was sanctioned by the Bible.

EGM °In fact, when the nation was founded in 1776, freedom for the slaves was crossed out of the Declaration of Independence. When the federal government was created in 1789, slavery was sanctioned by the Constitution• through the three-fifths compromise, which enumerated three-fifths of a state's slave population for purposes of representation and taxation.

Only in the 1820s and 1830s did slavery begin to disappear in the northern states, not because of moral considerations, but rather economics. Instead of using African-born slaves in the region's rapidly emerging factory-based economy, the North drew on the vast numbers of European immigrants whose cultural heritage was similar to the existing population's and whose assimilation was impeded only by language. To be sure, immigrants were paid such low wages that they were little more than slaves, but they were free to marry, free to read, free to associate with whom they wanted, and once they had paid their debts to the company store, free to move on to a better life.

Most of the blacks in the South did not have the freedom to move. The southern economy, based on crops that were exchanged for manufactured goods from the North and Europe, needed WCD them. °Remove what was believed to be cheap labor—like slaves—from the South, and the cotton industry and other agricultural commerce might very likely have collapsed.•

Although slavery had been accepted as a fact of life in the colonies, by the beginning of the nineteenth century even some citizens in the South had begun to question its value. In fact, there were more slaves in the South at one point in the late 1790s than there was work for them to do on the farms and plantations. Thus many slave owners freed their slaves because owning and caring for them had become unproductive. Ultimately, laws were enacted to protect elderly slaves from being turned off the plantations when they could no longer work in the fields.

Some slaves bought their freedom with wages they had earned while hired out to others, a practice exploited by many slave owners who needed ready cash between crop sales. An owner kept most of the slave's wages but gave him a portion as an incentive to do good work. At one point in the early 1790s, more than 10 percent of the South's black population was free; most of these lived in the Upper South where cotton was no longer grown. Some free blacks even purchased slaves themselves to help them operate their own farms, demonstrating how widely accepted slavery was as a social institution.

In 1793 schoolteacher Eli Whitney helped to revive the languishing institution of slavery in the South by making it essential to the southern economy and southern existence. While tutoring some children on a Georgia plantation, Whitney noticed a number of slaves laboriously picking out the seeds from the cotton bolls so the bolls could be baled and shipped for final processing. He returned home to New Haven, Connecticut, and within months developed and refined a machine he called a cotton engine through which raw cotton was deseeded. What had once been a time-consuming task that significantly limited the availability of southern cotton was streamlined. Slaves who had

*Before being brought to the auction block, slaves were herded into holding cells or pens, like this one of the Alexandria, Virginia, firm of Price, Birch and Company. One slave remembered that the pens were covered with cloth sheets, a tactic that stimulated buyer anticipation by preventing them from seeing the "stock" too soon. At the appointed time, an overseer would lift the curtain, and the bidders would begin crowding around the pen, eyeing their potential purchases. Such dank cells were often the last places slaves saw family members before they were sold to different owners and transported to various parts of the country.*

*Out of concern for their economic investment, most owners attempted to provide crude but adequate housing for their slaves. Such living quarters were often similar to the slave cabins pictured at right, usually sixteen by eighteen feet with dirt or plank floors and with fireplaces used for both cooking and heating. Census and plantation records from the antebellum era indicated that the most common living arrangement in such cabins was a single-family unit of five to six people. In some instances, much more crowded conditions existed, although southern agricultural magazines and most planters decried overcrowding as "unhealthy" and the cause of "immorality between the sexes." Small slave children had plenty of playmates in "the quarter."*

spent days deseeding cotton could return to planting, cultivating, and harvesting the crop.

The sudden new importance of slaves can be seen in the accelerated levels of cotton production between 1790 and 1810. In 1790 the South produced only a few thousand bales of cotton; twenty years later production had increased to nearly a quarter million bales. By 1860 several million bales of cotton were sold to the North and abroad, representing approximately 57 percent of the value of all American exports. As one southern politician boasted, in the South cotton was king.

In 1808 the international slave trade was abolished, but if any slaves had hoped that the need for their labor would diminish, such hope disappeared with the appearance of Whitney's cotton gin. By the 1850s there were nearly four million slaves in the South, comprising one-third of the southern population. In portions of Virginia, South Carolina, Florida, and Mississippi, slaves vastly outnumbered the free population. Slavery, which had almost ebbed, took off like a great flood, even creating a forced migration of slaves from the Upper South to the Lower South, where richer land could be found.

While most southerners believed slavery was necessary for the region's economic survival, many understood that slavery was also a convenient social tool. EGM ○Even if the South had decided that it could afford to end slavery for economic reasons, the southerners were concerned with how they would control the large number of African Americans once they had their freedom.•

The owners' control of their slaves went beyond just sending the black workers into the fields at dawn and making sure they were in their cabins at night. Slaves could not travel, marry, or even learn to read without their owner's permission. Owners were restricted in JIR what they could do with their slaves. ○A number of states passed laws against educating slaves because reading stimulated ideas, and ideas ultimately led to demands for changes in the social structure. Ignorance became a powerful weapon in the hands of a southern aristocracy that needed to subjugate a lower class.•

Control was maintained through discipline, which could be extreme, but whipping was more the exception than the rule. Harsh punishment was reserved for

*Despite the overall desperate nature of human slavery, slaves, particularly those on large plantations, often recognized that their master's financial well-being rested upon their efforts in planting, nurturing, and harvesting the cash crop. In turn, the slaves were sometimes able to demand an infrequent day off or extra food and clothing from their owners. One historian has described this as a system whereby slaves could force owners to use "positive inducements" rather than harsh discipline in return for work. A South Carolina planter named James Henry Hammond, for example, attempted to limit the amount of time his slaves had off for Christmas. He wrote in his diary, however, that he was "persuaded out of my decision by the Negroes." This image of plantation slave quarters on Port Royal Island, South Carolina, was photographed by Timothy O'Sullivan in 1862.*

JIR recalcitrant slaves and perpetual runaways. °Masters did not go out into the fields late in the afternoon and beat their slaves. They could ill afford to damage the people who were producing their crops and generating their
NIP income.• °Daily violence on the plantations might include something as common as cuffing slaves when they failed to do the work they were supposed to do or for some minor offense such as not smiling. Some owners, however, turned violent when they were annoyed or tired or drunk.•

Violence was prevalent early, during slavery's introduction into the colonies, when the white masters sometimes viewed the Africans as subhuman. As the institution grew more familiar over the decades, most owners began to think of the slaves as "their people," childlike creatures who needed to be fed, clothed, and housed in exchange for labor. There was little cruelty, and a few plantation owners even allowed their slaves to organize their own system of justice and punishment to deal with minor offenses against the master or fellow slaves.

The greatest cruelty slaves faced was not the whip but the breakup of slave families. Slaves were always afraid
NIP of being sold, and °approximately one-third of slave

*Before the war, Savannah, Georgia, was a city that owed its prosperity to cotton, and cotton brought with it slavery. In 1848 forty-one percent of Savannah's population were slaves and the city became a target for those who wanted to report on the mistreatment of African Americans. One ardent abolitionist, reporting on an 1859 slave auction, said, "The Negroes were examined with as little consideration as if they had been brutes indeed: those slave-drivers pushing the women about, pulling their lips apart to see their teeth, pinching their limbs to find how muscular they were, and, oh! Hardest, cruelest of all, tearing apart parents and children, brother from brother, sister from sister, loving heart from loving heart." The picture at right is of the slave cabins at the Hermitage Plantation in Savannah where slaves were raised to sell at the market.*

families were broken up by sale. It could happen at any time. The field hands might return to their cabins one night and discover that their owner had died and his property had to be settled through a sale.• That property of course included all the slaves owned by the estate. If the owner was behind in his taxes or if the farm was heavily in debt, slaves were assets that could be liquidated easily to bring in cash. Such sales, however, created horrific scenes. "My mother," recalled a young slave, Cy Henson, "half distracted, fell at the owner's feet and clung to his knees, entreating him to buy her baby as well as herself. He kicked her away."

*As Union soldiers began to move into Southern territory, they encountered large groups of slaves like the one pictured above on a plantation in South Carolina. Although many Northern troops never acknowledged blacks as their equals, their firsthand look at the conditions of human servitude caused them to hate the system as an evil affecting all Americans. In an 1862 letter to his wife written from Tennessee, Indiana soldier Walter Gresham penned that while he was "no abolitionist," the more he saw "of slavery in all its enormity" the more he became convinced that it was a "curse to . . . [the] country."*

Slaves were frequently the most valuable assets on a farm, their value driven up by the outlawing of the slave trade. A strong farm hand could fetch up to fifteen hundred dollars in the 1850s. A healthy slave girl might bring five thousand dollars based on her ability to bear children, who would inherit her slave status, thus perpetuating the labor force.

EGM This led to °one of the many tragedies and abuses of slavery: African-American women could not protect themselves. They could not look to their husbands, their brothers, or their fathers for protection either. Any white man felt it was his right to accost a slave woman if he chose to.•

Owners often did not ponder the morality of owning other people. Most argued that slavery benefited the slave. They believed that taking the blacks out of the African jungle and transporting them to the South had given them a much better life by working in the cotton fields than by continually fighting each
WCD other in tribal wars. °It was a very paternalistic attitude based on the belief of the inferiority of the slaves.• In the owners' view, without someone to provide food and shelter in exchange for labor, the slaves would be lost in the world.

Racial lines were drawn and supported by the science of the day. "Negroes consume less oxygen than

*Beginning in the 1830s, the abolitionist movement, spearheaded by people like William Lloyd Garrison and Theodore Dwight Weld, grew into an organized crusade aimed at the "immediate and universal emancipation of all slaves." Although actual membership in abolitionist societies never amounted to more than a handful of the northern public, there is little doubt that abolitionists did serve to keep the issue of slavery topical and controversial throughout the antebellum period. This beseeching and poignant 1837 poster is just one example of how abolitionists attempted to publicize the plight of American slaves.*

the white, thus it is a blessing to Negroes to have persons in authority set over them to take care of them," wrote Dr. Samuel Cartwright of Louisiana University, a scientist in the 1850s who theorized that blacks had different circulatory and nervous systems from whites. From examining the facial features of slaves, he deduced they were more closely related to monkeys rather than being in the same species as Caucasians.

As proof that slaves were happy with their lot, owners frequently cited the fact that they were always singing. What the masters did not know was that those songs, frequently sung in tribal languages, were sometimes coded
EGM to mean something only to other slaves. ○There were many messages in the songs. In some instances they made fun of the slave owner. In other instances they sang songs about freedom. Had the owner listened closely enough, he would have understood that his slaves were not at all happy.•

For example, one slave song was titled "Follow the Drinking Gourd," a slow, melodic song that mentioned rivers and men "who will carry you to freedom." While owners may have thought the steady beat of the song helped the slaves hoe the cotton better, they must have overlooked the lyrics. The drinking gourd referred to the Big Dipper constellation, which has at its tip the North Star. The song told escaping slaves how to find their way north and suggested they look for men along the big rivers, like the Ohio, who would row them across to freedom.

Far from always being happy, slaves found numerous ways to express their unhappiness with their owners whenever work demands were unreasonable or mem-
EGM bers of their community were sold. ○They intentionally broke tools,• for instance, by slamming hoes into the ground and breaking their handles. They would injure mules to keep from plowing and engage in other work
EGM slowdowns. ○Some more daring slaves might grind up glass and put it in their owner's food.•

The most dangerous course for both slave and master was armed resistance. The first instances occurred within a couple of decades of the initial importation of slaves. Violent outbreaks happened in nearly all the colonies, with the largest in the eighteenth century being the

Stono Revolt in 1739 near Charleston, South Carolina. Several dozen slaves banded together and killed a number of whites before a vigilante force captured and executed them.

*Master and slave frequently battled each other over religious autonomy on the plantations. Although this image depicts slaves praying with a black minister in a black church, many owners forbade their slaves to conduct their own church services. Instead, they had to attend meetings conducted by white preachers who told their audiences, said Alice Sewell, to "be good servants," and to help "Old Marse and Old Miss." After the approved ceremony, where the slaves sat in a balcony or other segregated part of the church, they might have their own secretive prayer meeting in a cabin where they would "set fer hours . . . an' praise de Lord."*

Nearly one hundred years later, in August 1831, a much larger slave revolt took place, sending waves of fear throughout the white South. Ironically, it occurred within forty-five miles of Jamestown, Virginia, the site where slavery was introduced into the New World. The revolt was led by a slave named Nat Turner, a self-educated slave preacher who became convinced after witnessing a solar eclipse that the Lord had spoken directly to him with orders to slay his enemies in preparation for the Second Coming of Christ. Turner and several followers hacked his master's family to death, starting a two-day, plantation-to-plantation killing spree that recruited seventy
WCD slaves into joining the violence. °Turner seemed to have had no particular plan in mind. The rampage was, if anything, a spontaneous outburst of rage and resistance against remaining a slave any longer.•

The extreme violence of Nat Turner's revolt enraged
JIR those who had to quell it. °Turner's master had been decapitated, and his wife's throat had been cut. The small band of slaves moved from home to home throughout the county, butchering the whites as they went. In all, fifty-nine whites were killed.•

WCD °Turner and the slaves who followed him were very quickly tracked down. Almost all the participants were later tried and executed, but this revolt generated fear throughout the entire South.• Slave owners hundreds of miles away who learned of the revolt through newspaper accounts began to look at their slaves warily.

NIP °Owners felt they could not trust their slaves because they knew they had imposed a false happiness on them. On one hand, the owners appreciated the sense of diffidence in their slaves; on the other hand, they were afraid of the mask.•

In addition to the fear that their slaves would revolt, slave owners also feared that northern politicians were planning a political revolt in the halls of Congress. They believed the Yankees were plotting to end slavery and with it the southern way of life.

WHILE THE South based its economy on plantation farming and imported almost all manufactured goods from the North or overseas, the North built its wealth in cities and on manufactured foods made in its own factories. Yankees were able to oppose slavery because they did not need slavery, but most northerners were not anxious to embrace blacks as equals. The North had abolished slavery, not racism. By the 1850s there were 325,000 free blacks living in the North, but many of the 20 million white northerners would have preferred that they lived elsewhere. WWG °There was much feeling among Americans, North and South, that if the slaves should be free, they could not live in a society designed by and for white Americans.•

The American Colonization Society was founded in 1816 with a generous grant from Congress and the goal of sending freed slaves back to Africa. Through its efforts, fifteen thousand black Americans, many of whom had been born in this country, were persuaded to move to West Africa and settle a new colony called

*Slaves young and old gather for a portrait in front of their Virginia quarters. The peaceful nature of the image belies the havoc that slavery brought to families. In addition to the strains caused by forced breeding and constant work, slave owners could on a whim tear apart family units and marriage unions by selling or renting children or a husband or wife to a distant plantation. This potential threat was foreshadowed by the owners' amending their properties' marriage vows to end with the ominous phrase, "'till death or distance do us part."*

WWG Liberia. °Colonization was a way to salve one's conscience; the slaves could be sent back to the continent from which they had come and the situation among the states would be settled.• The American colony in Liberia eventually collapsed due to disease and economic problems, but Liberia itself became an independent country in 1848.

Eli Whitney's invention of the cotton gin in 1793, a machine that quickly and efficiently separated seeds from cotton bolls, allowed southern cotton planters to increase the size and profitability of their cotton crops. This led to an increasing demand for slave labor. The Florida field hands above engaged in the backbreaking work of manually harvesting cotton were photographed after the war. Census records from 1790 indicate that approximately 700,000 slaves lived in the United States. By 1810, after the advent of the cotton gin, this figure had surged to 1.2 million. Northerners as well as southerners benefited from the increase in slave labor because the bountiful crops produced in the South's cotton fields made many New England textile mill owners very wealthy.

While concerned wealthy northerners were shipping blacks overseas, the government in Washington was struggling with what to do about blacks and slavery within the country. In 1857 the U.S. Supreme Court ruled that slaves were not citizens. The case concerned a slave whose owner, an army surgeon, had taken him into the western territories and free states where slavery was not legally recognized. The slave's name was Dred Scott, and he believed that his being within the borders of these free states made him a free man, and so he sued for his freedom. There was little surprise that the Court denied Scott's freedom, but the grounds for the decision shocked most northern sensibilities.

Eighty-year-old Chief Justice Roger Taney, himself a former slave owner, delivered the Court's opinion. "They are beings of inferior order. So far inferior they have no rights which the white man is bound to respect," he wrote. As an inferior being, Scott could not be a citizen nor did he have the right to sue. Furthermore, the chief justice announced, the Constitution afforded slavery an ironclad protection. The seven-to-two majority decision of the Court not only rejected Scott's claim to freedom but underscored the nature of slaves as property, granting that an owner could do with that property as he pleased.

Emboldened by the Supreme Court decision, southerners began to press for stricter enforcement of the Fugitive Slave Act of 1850, which required northerners to assist in returning runaway slaves to their southern owners. This act, a stronger version of a law originally passed in 1793, called for a one-thousand-dollar fine

*Slave women were responsible for cooking both simple and elaborate meals for their owners, and their culinary efforts were often praised in contemporary accounts. Sarah Williams, a white New Yorker visiting the South in 1853, wrote home of the "famous 'barbecue' of the South," that consisted of "roasted pig" which the slaves "dressed with red pepper and vinegar." African traditions regarding the use of spices were brought to America by the first slaves to arrive and were passed on to future generations through oral recipes. In the slave quarters women adeptly used various peppers and herbs to make palatable dinners of animal parts snubbed by their masters, such as boiled pig intestines, or chitterlings.*

and six months' incarceration for anyone aiding a slave to escape. The law was written broadly and interpreted the provision of food or shelter to a runaway as punishable offenses. In effect, the law demanded that the entire population of the country become a slave-catching militia.

JIR °Only the most minimal description was required of a slave for him to be "identified" and returned to slavery. One notable incidence of the effect of this law was a black man in Indiana who was returned to a Mississippi plantation nineteen years after he had escaped.•

Not all northerners complied with the law. Some religious groups, such as the Society of Friends, or Quakers, had been opposed to slavery in the colonies for
NIP more than 150 years. °These were people who read their Bibles and believed that the example of Jesus was that all people were human and equal.• At first they organized protests, wrote tracts, and founded schools for free blacks. They took active roles in hiding runaway slaves on their way to Canada where U.S. laws could not reenslave them. As the numbers of antislavery activists grew, the movement spread into other religious groups and took on a broadly based name: abolitionist.

The most vocal abolitionist of the time was William Lloyd Garrison, a Massachusetts publisher and founder of the American Anti-Slavery Society, who believed the immediate emancipation of the slaves was a moral matter. Considered a radical even by northern standards, Garrison once publicly burned copies of the U.S. Constitution because it sanctioned slavery. On another occasion he walked out of a meeting with women abolitionists when chauvinist male abolitionists objected to the females' taking on men's work. On several occasions Garrison was beaten by northerners unsympathetic to his cause.

"I will not equivocate, I will not excuse, I will not retreat, and I will be heard," Garrison said in 1831, the same year as the Nat Turner slave revolt in Virginia. Some southerners, ignoring that slaves were forbidden to know how to read, feared that Garrison's newspaper, the *Liberator,* might inspire other blacks to rise up. They threatened to arrest him if he ever ventured south and placed a price on his head.

Although abolitionists remained a minority group, they continued to attract both black and white followers, including a runaway slave who would become the most famous black orator of his time. Frederick Douglass, a runaway slave from Maryland who was inspired to activism himself after attending one of Garrison's lectures, held audiences spellbound with his command of the language. In 1842 he stood before an antislavery society and proclaimed: "I appear this evening as a thief and robber. I stole this head, these limbs, this body from my master and ran off with them."

EGM °Douglass was extraordinarily important in persuading blacks and whites in the North to join the antislavery cause because he was a man who had himself been enslaved. He described firsthand what slavery was like to audiences that heretofore had heard only from white abolitionists who had no firsthand idea what life as a slave was like.•

The abolitionists did more than make speeches. Some helped slaves to escape to the North through the so-called Underground Railroad, a network of safe houses and hiding places spread from the Deep South into the North. The railroad was run by "conductors" EGM sympathetic to the cause of black freedom. °Runaway slaves would travel at night and hide during the day in private homes, barns, secret cellars, churches, or wherever they could find someone to help them along the way.•

Many Quakers took an active role in the Underground Railroad. Men such as Levi Coffin in North Carolina organized their neighbors and fellow church members. Coffin once stayed up all night serving whiskey to a man searching for his runaway slave. While the man was getting drunk, the fugitive slave was being escorted from Coffin's house to another hiding place. When the hungover man awoke the next day, he felt so

*Lucy Edwards served as a slave nurse, or "mammy," to the children of her Virginia master. Her healthy and well-dressed appearance indicates the high status such bondswomen could obtain, for owners became dependent on them and trusted such nurses to raise and nurture their sons and daughters. "My baby . . . is a great deal fonder of her Mammy than she is of me," white Louisianan Laura Tibbals confided to a relative. "She nurses her and it would be a great trial to go without her." The formation of such powerful white-black bonds was one of the many ironies of the institution of slavery.*

*While their parents worked the fields, slave children were often left in the care of older women no longer capable of physically demanding tasks. Former slave Robert Shepherd remembered that a woman named "Aunt Viney tuk keer of us . . . while dey mammies was at wuk in de fields." Aunt Viney would blow a horn to let her charges know dinner was ready, and at this sound, said Shepherd, the "chillun come a-runnin from evvy which way [to] a great long trough what went plum 'cross de yard, and dat was whar es et." Shepherd claimed that the infants had to eat with their hands the meals of vegetables and broth poured over crumbled corn bread.*

bad, he went back home, forgetting about the escaped slave.

Two Quaker boys from the same community spent much of their youth driving wagons of hay or firewood back and forth to Indiana, a distance of more than five hundred miles. It was a journey that could easily take a month or more. The wagon had a false bottom under which as many as eight runaway slaves could hide. The two boys began their missions of mercy when they were twelve.

The most famous conductor on the Underground Railroad was Harriet Tubman, a runaway slave from Maryland, who came to be known as Moses after leading so JIR many people to freedom. °She went south at least nineteen times,• even into the coastal regions of South Car- EGM olina. °Legend has it that she never allowed anyone to look back during an escape. If a runaway decided to turn back, Tubman would hold a gun to his head and make him continue.•

How many slaves escaped through the Underground Railroad will never be known because the conductors and their allies rarely recorded anything in case they were questioned by local authorities. The best guess is that during thirty years, forty thousand escaped, or about 1 percent of the total held in bondage. Those who did escape between 1830 and 1860 helped to raise the northern consciousness about slavery when other freed slaves joined Douglass behind the speaker's podium.

Yet it was not the issue of runaway slaves or religious abolitionists who polarized the issue of slavery for the North. Land and power did that. The question centered on what was going to happen with the new western territories that would one day become states. Would they enter the Union as free states or slave states? The answer EGM to that question would dictate °who was going to control Congress, and by extension the country. Northerners wanted every new state to enter the Union free, but the South wanted each new state to be slave.•

Battle lines were drawn around the Kansas Territory. Illinois Sen. Stephen A. Douglas proposed the Kansas-Nebraska Act of 1854, which allowed the issue to be decided by a vote of the settlers as to whether the new state would be free or slave. The act superseded the Missouri Compromise of 1820 that forbade slavery in any state made from the Louisiana Purchase that was geographically north of Missouri's southern border.

Since this bit of gerrymandering kept the southern regions of the western territories open to slavery and cotton growing, the cotton politicians did not object to Douglas's proposal as long as there was a balance of power between slave and free states. That balance,

*This 1859 Eastman Johnson painting,* **Negro Life at the South, or Old Kentucky Home,** *presents an idealized, bucolic view of slavery. Contented blacks relax to the tunes of a softly plucked banjo as the kind-faced white woman enters the yard at right to visit "her folks." The scene was the backyard of Johnson's father's house in Washington, D.C., and the white woman at the right was Johnson's sister Mary.*

*A southern tobacco merchant used as a product label this scene taken directly from Eastman Johnson's* Negro Life at the South, *shown on page 19. The advertisement attempted to depict slavery as a gentle system to northern and foreign consumers, one that allowed slaves a measure of dignity and that produced contented "darkies." Despite this economic propaganda, the illustration does allude to black contributions to American culture, for African-American James Bland wrote the song "Carry Me Back to Ol' Virginny," a popular hit in the nineteenth century.*

however, was threatened by the debate over the admission of Kansas and Nebraska as states.

Kansas became a battleground as settlers moved in and clustered in proslavery and antislavery towns. Bands of Missourians crossed into Kansas to intimidate the Free Soilers (as the antislavery party was known), raid abolitionist towns, and cast illegal ballots. Before long both the pro- and the antislavery sides sent in their own ruffians to swing the vote their way. They were not above shooting, stabbing, and beating each other to death to influence the outcome. Finally, on May 21, 1856, the Free Soil settlement of Lawrence was sacked by proslavers, and the nation first heard the name of John Brown.

Fifty-six-year-old Brown was an itinerant tanner who had been raised as an abolitionist by fanatically religious parents. He had failed at every business venture he tried because he was focused on one goal—the abolition of slavery. In 1855 he followed one of his sons to Kansas with a determination to wipe out proslavers wherever he found them.

When Brown was prevented from marching on Lawrence by the army's occupation of the town, he returned to his camp at the Osawatomie settlement determined to strike a retaliatory blow. A short time later, when he heard that Massachusetts Sen. Charles Sumner, the leading abolitionist voice in the Senate at the time, had been assaulted on the floor of the Senate by South Carolina Congressman Preston Brooks, Brown decided to avenge Lawrence and Sumner immediately.

On the night of May 24, 1856, Brown gathered his sons and a small group of followers and set out for the cabin of James Doyle, near Pottawatomie Creek. Doyle and his two sons had been active in the proslavery party. Brown's men assaulted the cabin and dragged the three men outside. There, while the wives and children of their victims looked on in horror, Brown and his men hacked the three men to death with artillery broadswords.

*In August 1831 slave preacher Nat Turner led nearly eighty slaves on a bloodthirsty, disorganized rampage through Southhampton County, Virginia. Turner, who claimed he had been inspired by visions of heaven running with blood, and his band hacked to death about sixty whites—many of whom were women and children—before local militia quelled the rebellion. The aftermath of the revolt was also bloody. One hundred slaves were executed for complicity in the scheme, although most of those killed were innocent. Turner's rebellion horrified white southerners and led to the implementation of additional laws governing slave conduct.*

The Pottawatomie massacre triggered guerrilla warfare throughout Kansas, and Brown went into hiding and eventually left the area. JIR °The Kansas Territory came to be known as Bleeding Kansas, and for four years the proslavers and antislavers fought it out.• Ultimately, Kansas was admitted as a free state, but only after five constitutions had been drafted and at least two hundred lives had been lost.

Three years later Brown struck again. Having grown a white, Moses-like beard to disguise himself, he went to Harpers Ferry, Virginia, in October 1859 with the intention of starting a nationwide slave uprising. Brown's attack on the town failed; his slave revolt never materialized. He was captured by a contingent of marines commanded by Lt. Col. Robert E. Lee and turned over to the state of Virginia for trial. Convicted of treason, Brown was sentenced to hang. As he was leaving the jail for the short ride to the gallows, he turned to one of his attendants and handed him the last words he wrote from his jail cell. They proved to be prophetic: "I John Brown am now quite certain that the crimes of this guilty, land: will never be purged away; but with Blood. I had as I now think: vainly flattered myself that without much bloodshed; it might be done."

As events unfolded, Brown predicted and played a leading role in bringing on the coming war. After his execution, North-South tensions were close to a breaking point. JIR °Brown had done things that could not be overlooked. Southerners might ignore the propaganda

*The slave of a U.S. Army surgeon, Dred Scott sued for his freedom after the death of his master, basing his case on the fact he had resided in areas where the Missouri Compromise of 1820 forbade slavery. By 1857 the case had reached the U.S. Supreme Court. In a shocking decision that exacerbated tensions between the North and South, the Supreme Court ruled that the Missouri Compromise was unconstitutional and that blacks were not citizens and thus could not sue for their freedom. This precedent gave legal sanction for slaveholders to take their slaves anywhere in the United States. A sympathetic white family finally bought and emancipated Scott.*

of the abolitionists, but the revolt that Brown tried to incite brought the two sections close to war.•

In the North a new political party sprang up. The Republicans were dedicated to preventing slavery from expanding into the new territories, but the party and its presidential candidate in 1860 were careful not to oppose slavery in the South. That candidate was Lincoln, and he had been speaking out publicly against the spread of slavery for more than four years, including the Lincoln-Douglas debates of 1858. Yet Lincoln went to great pains to explain to his listeners that he was not an abolitionist.

NIP °Lincoln was not against slavery where it already
existed; he was opposed to the expansion of slavery,
which was the Republican Party's stand. He himself was
not particularly comfortable around African Americans;
he was very much a midwesterner of his time.• For the
southern states, however, any opposition to slavery was
WWG too much. °Because Lincoln had been outspoken in his
criticisms of slavery for almost twenty years, including
many statements that could be interpreted as antislavery,
he was not trusted by the South.• Thus, several states
threatened to leave the Union if Lincoln were elected.

Despite winning almost no votes in the southern states, Lincoln carried the 1860 election. With his election, however, seven southern states—South Carolina, Mississippi, Alabama, Georgia, Florida, Louisiana, and Texas—began seceding in December 1860 and then convened a convention in February 1861 to form the Confederate States of America.

Lincoln was silent from the day of his election until he departed Springfield, Illinois, for Washington and his inauguration. When he did speak to groups along the train route to the capital, he tried to reassure the South that he had no intention of becoming an abolitionist. After taking the oath of office on March 4, he addressed the seceded states with these words: "I have no purpose, directly or indirectly, to interfere with the institution of slavery in the States where it exists. I believe I have no lawful right to do so, and I have no inclination to do so."

JIR There is little question that °Lincoln saw slavery as an evil, but not an evil to the extent in 1861 of shatter-

*In 1852 abolitionist Harriet Beecher Stowe published* Uncle Tom's Cabin, *a novel that inflamed passions regarding slavery throughout America. Although many slave owners saw her book as an attack upon their way of life, Stowe considered slavery a stain upon the moral fabric of the entire country, and she castigated northerners and southerners alike in her tale of the struggles of Uncle Tom and his fellow slaves. The novel, from which the illustration at the left was taken, had sold an astounding seven million copies worldwide by the outbreak of the Civil War and contributed to the division between the North and the South. The story is told that when Abraham Lincoln was introduced to Stowe, he said, "So you're the little lady who caused this big war."*

ing the Union. When criticized in the fall of 1862 for not emancipating the slaves, Lincoln expressed his beliefs in an open letter to Horace Greeley in the *New York Tribune:* "My paramount object in this struggle is to save the Union, and is not either to save or to destroy slavery. If I could save the Union without freeing any slave I would do it, and if I could save it by freeing all the slaves I would do it; and if I could save it by freeing some and leaving others alone I would also do that."•

The South did not want to take chances on the promises of a man it believed wanted to destroy slavery and therefore its way of life. The new Southern Confederacy fired on a holdout garrison of U.S. soldiers inside Fort Sumter in Charleston Harbor, South Carolina, on April 12, 1861. Sectional tension had given way to war, and in the near future, slavery would become one of Lincoln's targets.

To the consternation of abolitionists and free black leaders in the North, Lincoln and his administration did not make the abolition of slavery in the South a war goal. All through 1861 and most of 1862 Lincoln repeated that the United States was a union of all the states and the preservation of that Union was his goal in fighting, winning, and ending the war. He never mentioned slavery.

Slavery had been a hotly debated political issue for most of the first half of the nineteenth century. In 1861 it became a military issue as well. Many of the North's prominent leaders and generals had little interest in the fate of slavery. Except for a handful of abolitionist

*In this romanticized print, escaping slaves struggle over an icy landscape as white Underground Railroad conductors lead them northward. However, it has been proven that the concept of northern whites leading slaves from checkpoint to checkpoint has been much overstated. In reality, it was most often free blacks who risked their lives to help escapees flee bondage. The number of slaves who made it to freedom was relatively small. Even such a successful conductor as Harriet Tubman claimed to have helped liberate only about three hundred slaves on the nineteen tension-filled trips she made into the South.*

officers, the vast majority of Lincoln's generals publicly stated that they had no use for blacks except as laborers, which was how they were viewed already in the South. A politically appointed general from Illinois, Lincoln's own home state, Maj. Gen. John "Black Jack" Logan, threatened to take his men home if the war turned into a battle to free the slaves.

As the war dragged on, Lincoln found himself under fire from the Democrats for not finding a general who could win the war and from the voters for the seemingly endless casualty lists. In September 1862, after a marginal Federal victory at the battle of Antietam in Maryland, the president decided to change the focus of the war. He unveiled the Emancipation Proclamation to his cabinet. The decree would take effect January 1, 1863, and it declared that most slaves then in Confederate territory would be free. Lincoln appeared to have taken the moral high ground, but he was also motivated by other considerations.

JIR °The practical reasons the president had for emancipation were purely military. The four million slaves in the South were a tremendous labor base, and they were sustaining the Southern Confederacy to a great degree by building forts and planting and harvesting crops. Enticing slaves to flee to the Union lines in return for their freedom would be a tremendous blow to the South.• Lincoln also portrayed this new policy in moral terms: "In giving freedom to the slave, we assure freedom to the free. We shall nobly save or meanly lose the last best hope of earth."

Lincoln was not quite honest in his declaration of "freedom" for the slaves. The Emancipation Proclamation freed only those slaves in the states then in rebellion against the United States. Those slaves in states still loyal to the Union—Kentucky, Delaware, Missouri, and Maryland—would still belong to their owners. In further demonstrating the political nature of the act, the president named specific counties in states under partial Federal control, like Louisiana and Virginia, where the slaves were "left precisely as if the Proclamation were not issued."

*Henry "Box" Brown engineered one of the more fantastic slave escapes. Sympathetic helpers sealed Brown into a packing crate in Richmond, Virginia, and shipped him to Philadelphia, Pennsylvania. As this lithograph indicates, Brown's successful and daring venture made him a darling to abolitionist societies and hot copy in northern newspapers. Brown used his sudden change of status from that of slave to that of free celebrity to his advantage by telling his thrilling story to spellbound predominately white audiences. The resourceful Brown even used his famous shipping crate as a prop during these performances.*

Even as he signed the proclamation, Lincoln agonized. For one thing, he still favored colonization, and he told black leaders so. "Our white men are cutting one another's throats and but for your race among us, there could not be war. It is better for us both, therefore, to be separated," he said in August 1862 when he first discussed the issue with black leaders.

"The tone of frankness and benevolence which he assumes in his speech is too thin a mask not to be seen through," remarked a disappointed Frederick Douglass.

NIP °In the first years of his presidency, Lincoln sent people to investigate if blacks should move to Honduras or Haiti or other parts of the New World.• He gave some investors money from the Federal treasury to start colonies of freed slaves only to discover too late that he had been duped.

EGM °Politically, Lincoln was worried that efforts to emancipate all slaves might send the four Border Slave States into the welcoming arms of the Confederacy.• Southern sympathizers in Missouri, Kentucky, Maryland, and Delaware had discussed leaving the Union, and all but
JIR Delaware had regiments fighting for the South. °The critical nature of the Border States was summed up by the president in the first months of the war when he said, "I hope God is on our side, but I've got to have Kentucky." He had to have the loyalty of the Border

*To celebrate his seventy-fifth birthday in 1857, South Carolina planter James Rembert had a photographer record images of his family and his slaves gathered at the "Big House." Class and racial distinctions are easily discerned, as only white people are pictured at the front door (above). In contrast, Rembert's slaves were posed at the back of the house (on facing page). They were organized by status: a trusted female cook and male driver—a slave who assisted the white overseer—stand closest to the camera; house servants follow; and lowly field hands form the last row.*

States to help contain the South. With that in mind, Lincoln exempted Union-held areas from freeing their slaves. Thus the popular image of Lincoln's wielding his pen and shattering the chains of four million slaves in the South is not entirely true. The Emancipation Proclamation directed freedom only for those slaves Lincoln could not touch.•

Lincoln's ambiguous stance was not lost on many world observers. "Where he has no power, Mr. Lincoln sets the Negroes free. Where he retains power, he will consider them as slaves," wrote the London *Times* in a critical editorial when it was still unclear if England would choose sides or stay out of the war.

EGM There is little doubt that °the president was a reluctant emancipator. He issued the proclamation as a military measure, hoping to throw the South into chaos.•
JIR He also hoped it would °prevent Europe, which was antislavery, from supporting the South. Lincoln succeeded first on this second point, successfully executing a diplomatic coup.•

The proclamation sparked a wave of criticism led, of course, by the South. "It is the most execrable measure in the history of guilty man," said Confederate President Jefferson Davis. He further denounced it as an attempt to stir up the slaves to insurrection and called the proclamation another reason why the South had to fight for its independence.

There were plenty of proclamation critics in the North, too. In several cities there were riots. Factory workers feared the newly freed slaves would come north
JIR and take their jobs. °No one knew what was going to happen with this great influx of black people into Northern society.•

So widespread was the backlash that at one point Lincoln considered revoking the proclamation. Hannah Johnson, a runaway slave's daughter, spoke to the president in late 1863: "They tell me you will take back the Proclamation. Don't do it. In a thousand years that action of yours will make the angels sing your praises. I know it."

While Northern politicians worried about getting reelected and Northern workers worried about job security, the Emancipation Proclamation had an electric effect on free blacks in the North. Many were former slaves, and the proclamation cleared the way for them to join the Union army, something black leaders had been pressuring Lincoln to allow since the beginning of the war.

EGM °From the very beginning, African Americans saw the war as one of liberation for the slaves in the South, and so they were quite willing to put their lives on the line to help free those who were still enslaved.• Frederick Douglass was in the forefront of those advocating the recruitment of black soldiers. At a recruiting rally he called on his fellow men of color, saying, "Liberty won by white men would lose half its luster. I urge you to fly to arms. The war is now invested with sanctity."

WCD °The thought of black soldiers in the Union army sent a jolt of outrage through much of the conservative Northern population who felt betrayed on two counts: Lincoln had not only turned the war into a war to free the slaves, whom they did not care about, but he was now making their white sons fight alongside black soldiers. What if one of their sons died because the black soldier standing next to him did not do his duty?•

While the general impression of the Emancipation Proclamation was that Lincoln wanted to free the slaves, the president was also looking at the logistics necessary to win the war. Thousands of white Northern soldiers had been killed in 1862 at Shiloh, Second Manassas, Antietam, and Fredericksburg. The Union army needed more manpower to overwhelm the South. By adding black troops to the Federal cause, Lincoln hoped to tip the balance of the war.

EGM °LONG BEFORE the whites saw it as such, the slaves in the South viewed the Civil War as the path that would lead

*Many Civil War-period illustrations cast Abraham Lincoln as a "great emancipator," paternal and benevolent toward slaves. Modern scholarship has revealed a more complex view of Lincoln. Like most white Americans of his era, Lincoln initially had little faith in the ability of African Americans, although he did not approve of slavery. As he came into contact with educated and distinguished people like Frederick Douglass, Lincoln's opinion of blacks rose, but he may never have considered them his true equals. Nonetheless, his Emancipation Proclamation, despite technically freeing only the slaves behind Confederate lines, was a critical step in ensuring the legal abolishment of involuntary servitude in the United States.*

to their liberation. This war was their chance for freedom.• WWG °They knew they would finally be free at some appreciable level if they went north or just reached the Union lines.•

As soon as the war broke out, slaves began running away from their masters. Many headed for Virginia's Fort Monroe at the tip of the peninsula between the James and York rivers across from Norfolk, a section of the state that had remained under Union control. Early in the war three runaway slaves were granted asylum in the fort by Union Maj. Gen. Benjamin Butler. JIR °The next day, under a flag of truce, the Confederate colonel who owned the slaves demanded their return under the Fugitive Slave Law. Butler promptly refused, pointing out that the Fugitive Slave Law applied only to states within the Union, which Virginia was not since it had seceded. Butler then pronounced these slaves to be "contraband of war."•

Besides coining the term *contrabands* for runaway blacks that would be used by Union soldiers for the rest of the war, Butler's action turned the trickle of runaway slaves into a river. The Emancipation Proclamation then turned the river into a flood. JIR °Wherever a Union army marched, slaves tried to run to it, seeking the freedom that this document seemed to promise.•

Yet not all Southern slaves and free blacks ran toward the Federal soldiers seeking freedom. Some stood alongside Southern soldiers and fought the invading Union army. Although most Southern states proscribed blacks from carrying arms, wartime pressures allowed field commanders to ignore the laws. Many Confederate officers had brought their body servants along and sometimes gave them weapons to protect themselves. Some Rebel regiments had full-blooded free blacks, mulattoes, and quadroons standing shoulder to shoulder with white Rebels against all-white Northern regiments who refused to integrate their forces. Early in the war, several hundred free blacks in Louisiana offered to form their own regiments to fight the Union invaders, but they were turned down. When the Northern army occupied New Orleans in April 1862, the offer of the free blacks was tendered to the Federals and this time accepted.

Most slaves relied not on Federal proclamations or decrees but on their own initiative to gain their freedom. When a Union force ventured into a region of the South, slaves fled to the protection of the blue-coated soldiers. Such escapees were classified by the national government as "contraband of war," or "contrabands" for short. Once inside the Yankee lines, African Americans usually could find work, like these former slaves employed at a supply base on Virginia's James River. Unfortunately, most contrabands quickly discovered that freedom did not mean equality. They were often forced to endure racist and shabby treatment at the hands of their Northern "liberators."

For much of the war, blacks both free and enslaved seemed to be more welcome in the Southern army than they were in the Northern army. The use of contrabands was controversial, especially since many in the North were not comfortable with the idea of fighting to free the slaves as opposed to the original war aim of fighting to repair the Union.

"The army hates to think that we are fighting for the Negro. They are lazy and don't know what freedom means," said Charles Johnson of the Sixteenth Massachusetts. "I believe the greatest part of the army would hiss old Abe out of camp if he came down here," said Sam Fisher of the Fourth New Jersey after he had heard about the Emancipation Proclamation. This was not just the opinion of the common soldier. In 1861 Gen. George B. McClellan, elevated to command of the Union army, announced: "Help me to dodge the nigger. We want nothing to do with him. I am fighting to preserve the integrity of the Union."

Whether they were welcomed or not behind Union lines, runaway slaves continued to come. Gradually they were accepted and were given work as laborers, spies, sailors, and later as soldiers.

Many slave owners could not understand why their slaves ran away. "The Yankees have excited the foulest demonic passions of the Negro, hitherto so peaceful and happy," wrote Emma Holmes, a slave owner. NIP °Repeatedly, the word *ungrateful* comes up in slave owners' accounts as if they had expected their slaves to be grateful to them for being enslaved.•

In the spring of 1863 the Union army reluctantly began accepting black men into the ranks, although the men were segregated into all-black units instead of being incorporated into existing regiments. Near Beaufort, South Carolina, the first two Federal black regiments in the country, the First and Second South Carolina Volunteers, were made up of freed slaves from the sea island cotton plantations. They trained on a former plantation that was the site where the

Emancipation Proclamation was first read in public to a group of freed slaves.

In the North, free black men formed their own state-supported regiments, determined to prove to the skeptics that they could fight. Yet even the president had reservations. As early as 1861 Lincoln had said, "If we arm them I fear that in a few weeks the arms would be in the hands of the Rebels."

One of the first all-black regiments formed in the North was the Fifty-fourth Massachusetts, made up of elite free black men from the Northeast. Their ranks included so many highly educated men that the Fifty-fourth's literacy rate was higher than most white Northern regiments. Two sons of Frederick Douglass were among its volunteers.

The Fifty-fourth shipped out for South Carolina in 1863. It was led by Col. Robert Gould Shaw, a twenty-six-year-old Harvard-educated son of a prominent white abolitionist family. While Shaw had his doubts about the intelligence and abilities of the men under his command, he wanted them to have a chance to show their valor. He did not have long to wait.

After training for a few days near Beaufort, the Fifty-fourth was transported to James Island, South Carolina, southeast of Charleston. Without giving the men a chance to rest, sleep, or eat, the white commanders ordered the black regiment to Morris Island where a Confederate earthwork called Fort (or Battery) Wagner protected the northern end of the island. To attack Charleston, the Federal army had to take Wagner. After a naval bombardment had failed to destroy the Confederates, the Union commander chose to assault the flank of the fort, requiring his men to run down a narrow, sandy beach, through a water-and-obstacle-filled moat, and up the steep sides of the fort. During every moment of the onslaught, the attacking Union soldiers would be under the guns of the Confederates.

Although Shaw's regiment had not slept for two days and had had very little

*Ox carts filled with meager belongings of a contraband family halt in a shallow section of Virginia's Rappahannock River. This photograph was taken in August 1862 by Timothy O'Sullivan. Slave Felix Haywood remembered that when Union "Soldiers, all of a sudden, wuz everywha'" on the grounds of his plantation, spontaneous expressions of joy swept through the slave cabins. "Everyone went wild. . . . We wuz free! Just like that, we wuz free," said Haywood. In short order, all the "colored folks" gathered their belongings and "started on the move. They seemed to want to get closer to freedom, so they'd know what it wuz—like it was a place or a city. Me and my father stuck as close as a lean tick to a sick kitten."*

to eat, the Fifty-fourth was offered the chance to lead the attack. Shaw realized his regiment was being given an opportunity to sacrifice itself, but he did not object. He knew what the commanders of the other white regiments were thinking.

One of these was the field commander, Brig. Gen. Truman Seymour, who had been with Robert Anderson at Fort Sumter at the beginning of the war. In the planning for the assault on Wagner, Seymour told his general officers: "I guess we'll put those damn niggers in the advance. We may as well get rid of them, one time as another."

The Fifty-fourth led the charge on Wagner and lost nearly half of its men, 281 out of 600. Shaw was killed on the parapet. None of the white regiments succeeded in overcoming the fort's defenses, and later congressional investigation of the attack concluded that it should never have been made. Still, the bravery of the men of the Fifty-fourth in the face of the Confederate guns proved that African Americans could be solders.

The *New York Tribune* reported, "General Seymour was not in the advance, but he is now an admirer of Negro troops." Yet in February 1864, seven months after the disastrous attack on Battery Wagner, Seymour again misused black troops and the Fifty-fourth at the battle of Olustee, Florida. The outcome was an even worse debacle than Wagner. Nearly one-third of the five thousand mostly black Union troops were killed, wounded, or captured, one of the worst Union defeats of the war based on percentages. The only bright spot in the battle was the performance of the Fifty-fourth Massachusetts. While other white and black regiments crumbled and ran from withering Confederate musket and cannon fire, the Fifty-fourth held steady and covered the Union retreat. As they neared Jacksonville, the regiment came upon a train loaded with wounded. The train's locomotive had broken down, and so the Fifty-fourth hooked ropes to the cars loaded with wounded and pulled them to safety.

More than 180,000 black troops fought for the Union; 37,000 died and 22 were awarded the Medal of Honor, most for defending their unit's flag or capturing

*From Civil War battlefields in the trans-Mississippi, to eastern and western theaters, to those in the Deep South, black troops fought to advance the cause of their race. All the while, the U.S. Colored Troops endured racism and prejudice within their own army and the searing hatred of their foes, who sometimes slaughtered African-American soldiers after they had surrendered. At times, however, the bravery of black soldiers even evoked a grudging respect from the Confederates. After the 1863 Battle of Milliken's Bend, Louisiana, for example, Rebel Brig. Gen. Henry E. McCulloch wrote in his report that the "Negro portion of the enemy's force [fought] with considerable obstinacy, while the white or true Yankee portion ran like whipped curs almost as soon as [our] charge was ordered."*

*In 1866 artist Thomas W. Wood completed this trio of paintings showing the rise of an African-American man from tattered contraband fresh from slavery to proud soldier and then to disabled veteran eligible for a government pension. Nearly two hundred thousand black soldiers fought for the North and actively helped secure the freedom of all black Americans. James H. Gooding of the famous Fifty-fourth Massachusetts Infantry spoke for many blacks of the era when he wrote that his "people" realized that they had to fight and "forego comfort, home, [and] fear" so that "the civilized world" would see former slaves as "something more than hewers of wood and drawers of water."*

JIR an enemy flag. °One might conclude that this huge number of blacks was the difference in the final Union triumph of the war.• In August 1864, Lincoln admitted, "Without our black troops we would be compelled to abandon the war in three weeks."

The Southerners, however, were outraged that they
WWG had to fight African Americans. °The North had done something that heretofore had been unthinkable in the South: they had armed large numbers of blacks. This insult was answered with the threat of death should any of these black soldiers be captured.•

The most controversial atrocity of the war occurred on April 12, 1864, in Tennessee at Fort Pillow, an earthen fort on the Mississippi River about forty miles north of Memphis. The garrison of 295 white Unionist Tennesseans and 262 black soldiers under the command of Maj. Lionel F. Booth was attacked by 1,500 Confederates led by Maj. Gen. Nathan Bedford Forrest. After surrounding the fort and fighting for several hours, Forrest demanded the fort's surrender.

The Federal commander refused, despite warnings from Forrest that he could not be responsible for what would happen if his men were forced to attack again. Still the Federal commander refused. When Forrest's men attacked, they did so with a vengeance.

Union soldiers testified before the U.S. Congressional Committee on the Conduct of the War that the

*Some U.S. Colored Troops benefited from educational opportunities offered them by considerate white commanders and civilian aide workers. Here, teachers and officers stand behind a class of black troops, several of whom are holding textbooks. In other cases, however, shortsighted, racist white commanders applied racial stereotypes to their African-American soldiers and treated them as "simple" and "docile" inferiors. One soldier in the Forty-third U.S. Colored Infantry regretted that his officers would "strike the men with their swords and jog and punch them in their side to show them how to drill."*

attacking Confederates shouted racial epithets and murdered the fort's black soldiers who had dropped their weapons and surrendered. Confederates countered that the black soldiers were the fiercest defenders of the fort and did not make any effort to throw down their arms.

EGM °Almost two hundred men—black and white—were killed at Fort Pillow. Some were begging for their lives and were not allowed to surrender. Forrest later reported that the river was colored by the blood of the slaughtered for two hundred yards.• Forrest, a prewar slave trader, denied that his men had massacred the black troops. He said the battle was a typically vicious fight that escalated because of the refusal of the Federal commander to surrender.

As the North gradually gained the upper hand in the war, the South debated using slaves as soldiers. Some popular generals such as Maj. Gen. Patrick Cleburne, an Irish immigrant who had never owned slaves, supported the idea, but the proposal met fierce resistance from the plantation owners. "If slaves make good soldiers, our whole theory of slavery is wrong," said Maj. Gen. Howell Cobb, a Georgian who had served as chairman of the committee that organized the Confederacy.

JIR °The political position of the South was that blacks were an inferior race that had to be treated as children. The region's system of slavery was based on that rationale.• In early 1865, however, a desperate Confederacy authorized black troops. By then it was too late, and even then the idea was not welcomed by many citizens.
WWG °A company of black men was drilling without arms in

*In this post-Civil War image, Christian A. Fleetwood of the Fourth U.S. Colored Infantry proudly wears the Medal of Honor he received for his bravery during the desperate and bloody September 29, 1864, battle of Chaffin's Farm, also known as New Market Heights, a strongpoint in the Confederate lines protecting Richmond and Petersburg. During the unsuccessful attack, Sergeant Major Fleetwood snatched his regiment's flag after two previous color-bearers had been gunned down and carried it throughout the rest of the battle. The Fourth suffered 178 casualties in the fight. Overall, twenty-nine black soldiers were awarded the Medal of Honor, America's most coveted military decoration, for heroism in Civil War engagements.*

Richmond, Virginia. For their trouble they were pelted with mud by the citizens.•

By early 1865 Lincoln knew the North was about to win the war. To capitalize on that, he proposed amending the Constitution to ban slavery forever and said: "This is a king's cure for all the evils. Live or die, I give my heart and hand to this measure."

In late January the Thirteenth Amendment passed Congress, making it the law of the land that "Neither slavery nor involuntary servitude except as punishment for crime shall exist within the United States." Indiana Congressman George Julian, a Quaker abolitionist and political reformer who had pestered Lincoln for four years to promote such an amendment, recalled: "Members shouted, some embraced, others wept. I felt I was in a new country." Among those cheering the passage of the amendment were African Americans who just one year earlier had not been allowed in the congressional gallery.

EGM °By the end of the war Lincoln realized that there was no way the country could go back to being half-slave and half-free. He came to that realization because African Americans had forced him to that point. In a way, the blacks were liberating themselves; they did not wait for Lincoln.•

Proposing the Thirteenth Amendment and later passing it before the war was over did not, however, cure the North of its own racism. In October 1864 Union Maj. Gen. William T. Sherman began his March to the Sea from Atlanta with sixty-five thousand soldiers. Along the way he burned plantations and freed as many as twenty-five thousand slaves.

EGM °These slaves were in fear of reenslavement so they kept close to the Union troops. Sherman saw them as a nuisance. They ate his food, and they were in the
JIR way.• °He had no liberal feelings toward the blacks and once made the statement, "A nigger is not a white man and no amount of psalm singing is going to change that fact."•

As Sherman's army moved within thirty miles of Savannah, it came to Ebenezer Creek. The commander of the last corps of men, Union Maj. Gen. Jefferson C. Davis, asked the runaway slaves following the army to stand to one side so his men could get across the pontoon bridge spanning the creek. The obedient freed slaves, assuming they could cross once the army had passed, watched as their white protectors marched ahead. Once his men were across the creek, however, Davis had the pontoon bridge taken up, stranding the blacks on the other side of the creek, which was swollen from recent rains.

*Slaves sit outside of their cabins in this Civil War-era image. Many slaves in the more isolated regions of the South did not see a Federal army soldier or gain their freedom until the last days of the war. In the meantime, they continued to work as usual for their masters. Katie Phoenix recollected that her owner, a Mrs. Harris, had her convinced the union armies were akin to evil, nightmarish "spider[s]" that were "going to come and wipe away the house." "Everythin' was like a tangled dream," shuddered Phoenix, "jus' opposite to what I found out later it was."*

The former slaves panicked. They knew, as Davis did, that Confederate cavalry were following Sherman's army. If they were captured, they would be sent back to their plantations. Scores, perhaps hundreds, dove into the creek attempting to swim across. No one knows how many died in the attempt. The hundreds of slaves who could not get across the creek were captured and returned to their former owners.

Once he reached the Atlantic coast, Sherman surprised everyone by offering thousands of acres of confiscated sea island plantations to the slaves following him. JIR While °this was considered a benevolent move on Sherman's part, it was probably more likely that he was trying to rid himself of the slaves as he continued his military campaign into North Carolina.• A Republican congressman tried to formalize the policy later, dubbing it "forty acres and a mule," as a commitment the nation would make to the former slaves.

When the war ended with the surrender at Appomattox, the newly freed slaves hoped that Lincoln, their emancipator in war, would be their champion in peace. Those hopes, however, ended on Good Friday, April 15, 1865, at the hands of an assassin.

In an assessment of the president, Frederick Douglass said: "From an abolitionist point of view, Mr. Lincoln seemed tardy, cold, dull, and indifferent. But measuring him by the sentiment of his country, he was swift,

zealous, radical, and determined." For these reasons,
EGM °Lincoln was a hero to the former slaves.• During his
NIP presidency, their lives had changed forever. °They were
free.• Yet their changed lives were not as complete as they
EGM had hoped. °Many who had been granted land soon lost it as the new president, Andrew Johnson, ordered the property returned to its former owners. Most former slaves were left with nothing except their freedom.•

WCD Those who had been °master and slave before the war became employer and employee after the war, often on terms that were not as good for the free blacks as they had been for the slaves before the war. Now the owner, who was no longer a master, had no obligation to provide housing, medical care, or care for the elderly.•

Partly to help former slaves start their new lives in the postwar transition, Union troops were kept in the South. A federal agency, the Freedmen's Bureau, was created and headed by a former Union general, Oliver O. Howard, to help freed slaves adjust to self-sufficiency. Much of the real power, however, was still in the hands of the statehouses, and they were still run by southern whites.

WCD °Southern politicians in 1865 and 1866 tried to behave as if the war had never been fought. While they had lost the war, they returned to treating the blacks as they had done before, except now they called them free rather than slaves.•

*This lithograph signed by Edward W. Clay and published by A. Donnelly in 1841 presents an idealized depiction of contented slaves and benevolent masters. The caption that accompanies the lithograph has the slaves saying, "God bless you massa! You feed and clothe us. When we are sick you nurse us, and when too old to work, you provide for us!" The masters reply, "These poor creatures are a sacred legacy from my ancestors and while a dollar is left me, nothing shall be spared to increase their comfort and happiness."*

Because many whites resented the northerners' patronizing blacks in the South, new southern regulations, the so-called Jim Crow laws, were created that severely restricted black citizens' rights in voting, housing, and traveling. These laws led to a segregation of the races and were meant to keep the blacks out of the political and social systems that emerged after the war.

WWG °African Americans could vote if they could pass a literacy test. If the literacy test was completed successfully in English, it might be resubmitted to the potential black voter in Latin. In the South, blacks were not seen as citizens; they were seen as problems. Since Lincoln had ultimately made blacks the foremost cause of the war, they were blamed for all the reversals that had taken place in the South.•

JIR °Thousands of blacks headed north to a so-called free land of opportunity. When they arrived they found neither free land nor a land of opportunity. There was nothing for them there, just as there was nothing for them in the South. As a freed race, the blacks had to scratch and claw to find a future.•

Freedom for the slaves had come at a cost of four years of civil war and more than six hundred thousand
NIP American lives; however, °freedom could not have come to them in any other way. Throughout the early nineteenth century all the political compromises had provided temporary solutions, and efforts to satisfy all sides
WCD had failed.• Finally both sides realized that °some issues in national affairs cannot be compromised. Sadly, the only remaining resort was the arbitration of the sword.•
EGM °The Civil War was not begun to liberate African Americans, but that was the end result.•

Although the war ended the institution of slavery in America, it did not end inequality between the races. For black Americans a long struggle for civil rights still lay ahead. Even so, four years of war had brought changes that few people, black or white, would have thought possible when it first began. Ultimately, the war had turned slaves into soldiers and property into persons.

*After the Civil War, northern agents of the Freedmen's Bureau, a federal agency that attempted to help newly freed slaves and poor southern whites, distributed photographs such as this one in order to publicize their efforts. While the generation represented by Isaac and Rosa, "emancipated slave children," knew little slavery, it was their lot to endure the tribulations of the Ku Klux Klan in Reconstruction America and the Jim Crow segregation laws adopted in the late 1800s. They bore such indignities with as much grace as possible, calling upon the memories of their parents' struggles to guide them, In turn, proud African Americans like Issac and Rosa imparted to their descendents the strength necessary to fight the civil rights battle of the twentieth century.*

# DIVIDED FAMILIES

*When* THE FIRST SHOT OF THE CIVIL War arced over Charleston Harbor toward Fort Sumter on April 12, 1861, the young nation was put to its greatest test. The war did not just set state against state or North against South, it forced people to choose sides within their own families. It broke hearts and created divisions that sometimes never healed.

On April 14, 1861, as he surrendered Fort Sumter and lowered the battle-stricken American flag, Maj. Robert Anderson, a southerner by birth, said: "Our southern brethren have done grievously wrong. They have rebelled and have attacked their fathers' house and their loyal brothers. They must be punished and brought back, but this necessity breaks my heart."

WCD °Anderson was the first person whose loyalty was tested by the war. He was a Kentuckian of Virginia ancestry, and his wife was from Georgia. Anderson had been a slave owner, but he did not believe slavery was an issue over which the nation should go to war. He was a believer in the Union, and when the call went out for southern officers to defend their states, Anderson continued to wear the Union blue that he had pledged long ago to defend.•

In 1860 Secretary of War John B. Floyd, a Virginian, appointed Anderson to the command of the federal forts in Charleston because he believed the choice of a southerner might soothe the growing tensions in South Carolina since Anderson's sympathies were perceived to be entirely with the South. Yet the new commander's sympathies were not to be confused with his loyalties.

| | |
|---|---|
| **JB** | Jean Baker |
| **SDB** | Scott D. Breckinridge |
| **CC** | Catherine Clinton |
| **MPC** | Mary P. Coulling |
| **WCD** | William C. Davis |
| **JCK** | James C. Klotter |
| **BP** | Brian Pohanka |
| **JIR** | James I. Robertson Jr. |

*In 1861 Robert Anderson, a Kentuckian of Virginia ancestry whose wife was from Georgia, was a thirty-six-year veteran of the U.S. Army. Although a southerner, he did not leave the Union army when Southern states began to talk of secession and was made commander of Fort Sumter, a position he held when the attack on Sumter came that initiated the Civil War. Anderson's health was ruined by the tragic events in Charleston Harbor, and his doctors even forbade him to write a report of the bombardment, fearing that such a painful recounting would cause his condition to further deteriorate. In 1863 Anderson retired from the military, although he still performed occasional administrative duties for the Union. At war's end he had the honor of being asked to raise the U.S. flag over Sumter. He was so weak, however, that he could do little more than clutch the flagstaff while others raised the banner. Anderson later went to France in an effort to recoup his health. He died there in 1871.*

Anderson later explained: "The selection of the place in which we were born was not an act of our own volition. But when we took the oath of allegiance to our government, it was an act of our manhood and that oath we cannot break."

WCD °Anderson was regarded as a traitor by most Southerners. In the North, however, most people regarded him as a hero, not just because he had held out bravely at Fort Sumter, but because he was a Southerner who had remained loyal to the Union.•

Appointed a general for his actions in Charleston, Anderson did little of note during the balance of the
WCD war. His actions, however, cost him °the good will of his family. Because he had been forced to choose sides against the section, the people, and many of the institutions that he had grown up revering, he was a casualty of the war even though he outlived it.•

JIR °Civil wars do not begin with a huge explosion. They start as a list of grievances that accumulate until one party finally takes a position that cannot be compromised.• Tensions between North and South had been simmering at least since 1820 when the Mis-
JIR souri Compromise was passed. °Southerners viewed the North as an abolitionist camp bent on eliminating something that was none of their business. Northerners viewed the South as a land of tyranny, where vast numbers of pathetic people were enslaved. A picture was created of two despicable enemies when that was not the case at all. While there were abolitionist fervor and abuses of slavery, neither was the norm throughout either section. The news media and public spokesmen for both sides, however, charged the atmosphere with hostility. Their distortions of reality had as much to do with the coming of the Civil War as did slavery.•

When pro-Union candidate Abraham Lincoln was elected president in 1860, a sense of doom filled the air. In local communities and homes in the South, secession was debated. Could states choose to leave the country? Could they form a separate nation? On the observance of Washington's birthday in February 1861, meetings were held across the South to question the makeup of the nation. Was one's loyalty to one's state? to the Union? to one's family?

BP °Those who ultimately turned against their families and their states were ostracized. Their letters were burned or not answered. They were shunned on the street. They were reviled as traitors to their people and to their kind. This was the great test of loyalty, not just the concept of state versus the national government, but the choice of loyalty between one's family or country. Could a man turn his back on his family? Could a man renounce his blood, his kin, his loved ones? Many did choose loyalty to their country or state over loyalty to their family, and in those instances the Civil War became a blood feud.•

Divided loyalties affected not just the common soldier, but the leaders and generals as well. Lincoln's wife, Mary, was estranged from her family during the war, as was Jeb Stuart's wife, Flora. Percival and Thomas Drayton were brothers who fought against each other at Port Royal Sound, South Carolina. Robert E. Lee's family was divided by the war but found reconciliation after the conflict ended. Union Gen. George H. Thomas and Confederate legend Stonewall Jackson were estranged from their sisters and never reconciled. The war also divided the Crittenden and Breckinridge families of Kentucky and the Terrill family of Virginia. Recounted here are a few stories chosen from among thousands.

*The prestige and power of America's highest political office did not shield the Lincolns from the tension of divided loyalties within their family. Of the first lady's thirteen brothers and sisters, eight supported the Confederacy including three half brothers who joined the Confederate army. The tragedy of divided loyalties was particularly acute in the border states like Kentucky, Delaware, Maryland, and Missouri, and it was not uncommon for towns in such states to produce both Union and Confederate regiments.*

### *The Lincolns and the Todds*

LINCOLN SEEMED to sense this issue of family versus family three years before the war started. In 1858 in the first paragraph of his opening speech in the series of senatorial campaign debates he had with Stephen A. Douglas, Lincoln identified the tension that would dominate the American people for the next seven years: "A house divided against itself cannot stand. I believe this government cannot endure permanently, half-slave and half-free. I do not expect the Union to be dissolved—I do not expect the house to fall—but I do expect it will cease to be divided."

*Mary Todd Lincoln's life in the White House was full of emotional turmoil. Her favorite son, twelve-year-old Willie, died of disease in 1862. Charges of disloyalty were made against her because of her Southern connections. She was devastated by the death in battle of her brother-in-law Confederate Gen. Benjamin Helm. Thus it may be understandable that she desperately wanted to protect her eldest son, Robert (above). After graduating from Harvard he was finally allowed to join the army over her protests—with a safe assignment on General Grant's staff. Many years later it was Robert who felt it necessary to commit his mother to a mental institution.*

Once the war had begun, not even the White House was immune to the intra-family conflict. The first lady, Mary Todd Lincoln, strongly supported the Union cause despite the fact that she feared for her eldest son, Robert. She tried to protect him by encouraging his education at Harvard University, but Robert persuaded his father to allow him to join the army. He eventually served as a staff officer under Ulysses S. Grant, who obliged the Lincolns by keeping their son far from the fighting.

While the first lady's son was safe, she was in emotional turmoil because three of her half-brothers—Sam, David, and Alexander—joined the Confederate army. Of her thirteen siblings, eight supported the South and five the North. Her problems were compounded when tragedy struck her younger sister Emilie.

JIR °The Lincolns loved Emilie and looked on her almost as a daughter. Her husband was Benjamin Hardin Helm,• a thirty-year-old 1851 graduate of West Point who had resigned from the army after a year's service to become a lawyer and later a Kentucky legislator. In 1856 he married Emilie, and she introduced him to her brother-in-law in 1858, who at that time was becoming famous for the campaign debates he was conducting with Sen. Stephen A. Douglas. Helm and Lincoln probably debated something of slavery between themselves, but their common ties to Kentucky and the two sisters who loved each other overcame whatever disagreements they had.

Lincoln was elected president, and Kentucky, a slave state, wavered over which side it would join officially. WCD °The Northern president offered his favorite brother-in-law a major's commission in the Federal army. Instead, Helm joined the Confederacy and raised the First Kentucky Cavalry. Despite frequent absences from service due to sickness, Helm was elevated in rank to brigadier general and commanded a division in the western theater. He was killed in action at the battle of Chickamauga in September 1863.

Upon hearing the news of Helm's death, Lincoln was seen in tears, saying that he felt like David of old in the Bible when he lost his son Absalom.• It was not the first time the war had hit close to home for Lincoln's family. In June 1861 a young lawyer whom Lincoln considered almost like a son, Elmer Ellsworth, had been killed in a raid on Alexandria, Virginia. In October of the same year Sen. Edward Baker, a close friend after whom Lincoln had named a son, had been killed at Ball's Bluff, Virginia. Now his favorite brother-in-law was dead.

JIR °Emilie Helm left Atlanta for her home in Kentucky, but she was detained by Union officials. She appealed to the White House, and Lincoln sent a message ordering her release and directing that she come to Washington.• The widowed Todd sister and her three sons visited the White House in early December 1863.

For a while the Lincolns tried to keep Emilie's visit a secret, but her presence in the Executive Mansion created a problem as she was CC °the grieving wife of a fallen Confederate general. She was offended by some of the pro-Union talk of some guests to the White House, and thus Emilie became a political embarrassment to the first family.• One evening the Lincolns were entertaining two Union generals, one of whom was Daniel E. Sickles, who had lost a leg at the battle of Gettysburg. Sickles was no stranger to scandals, but he was taken aback to find a Confederate living in the home of the president. Emilie was hardly one to sit idly by as others vilified the cause for which her husband had died. After one such comment, she angrily responded to Sickles, "If I had twenty sons, they would all be fighting yours." CC °She eventually had to leave the Lincolns because her defending her Confederate loyalties was an embarrassment for the first family.•

Emilie Helm ignored her sister's pleas to take an oath of loyalty to the Union because the Union had killed her husband. In mid-December Lincoln finally ordered her home to Kentucky without the pledge. Although she was gone, the Lincolns had not heard the last of her.

JCK °Back in Lexington, Emilie wrote to Lincoln the following fall asking for his help by allowing her to sell six hundred bales of cotton so she could support herself. Lincoln refused, calling her a Confederate sympathizer who would not pledge her loyalty to the Union. Emilie wrote back and expressed her anger in no uncertain

*Capts. David Todd (above) and Alexander Todd (below), half-brothers of Mary Todd Lincoln, gave their lives for the Confederate cause in 1863. Alexander, who served on the staff of his brother-in-law, Gen. Benjamin Helm, died by friendly fire near Baton Rouge, Louisiana, when, in the darkness of night, Southern infantry mistakenly fired at a returning column of Confederate cavalry. Frantic officers finally managed to halt the ill-advised shooting, but not before a round struck Todd and he toppled dead from his horse.*

*In 1856 Benjamin Hardin Helm, a West Point graduate and a former dragoon officer, married Emilie Todd, the half-sister of Mary Todd Lincoln. The picture of the couple above was taken in 1857, when Helm was serving his native state of Kentucky as a commonwealth attorney. During the prewar period, Helm and Abraham Lincoln often enjoyed each other's company. A brigadier general in the Confederate army, Helm (near right below) was killed in action on the second day of the battle of Chickamauga in 1863. After he heard the news of Helm's death, Lincoln was seen in tears, saying that he felt like David in the Bible when he lost his son Absalom. One of Helm's fellow officers wrote to his wife, Emilie (shown far right below, years after Helm's death), lauding the dead general as "a patriot and a hero."*

terms,• blaming Lincoln for the deaths of her siblings and her husband. She concluded, "I also remind you that your JCK minié bullets have made us what we are." °When the first lady saw the letter, she became furious.•

JB °Emilie Todd Helm and Mary Todd Lincoln never reconciled and never saw each other again. The first lady had so absorbed the idea that she and her husband represented the Union that it was impossible for her to see what she considered her sister's disloyalty as anything but a permanent scar on their relationship.•

Nor did the first lady ever see her brother Alexander again. He was mortally wounded in the battle of Baton Rouge, Louisiana, in 1862, but she did not grieve for her dead sibling. Mary Lincoln rather noted: "I have just heard one of my brothers was killed in the war. Since he chose to be our deadly enemy, I see no reason why I should bitterly mourn his death. Why should I sympathize with the Rebels? They would hang my husband tomorrow if it was in their power."

JIR °Another of Mary Todd Lincoln's sisters was Martha Todd White, a resident of Selma, Alabama, when the war broke out. Hearing of Emilie's visit, Martha wrote the president requesting a pass to come north to "recruit my health, to replenish my wardrobe, and to take for my own use articles not now obtained in the South." She came to Washington amid rumors that by the time she departed, her trunks would be filled with

*Scheming Martha Todd White (far left) journeyed from Alabama to Washington during the Civil War, determined to take advantage of her relationship to her famous sister and brother-in-law. Martha's efforts failed for the most part, but not before she generated more negative press critical of Mr. and Mrs. Lincoln's Southern associations.*

*Elody Todd (near left), another of Mary Lincoln's sisters, also lived in Alabama, married a Confederate officer during the war, and supported the Confederate cause. Just as the Northern press often irresponsibly accused Mary Todd Lincoln of harboring Southern sentiment, Elody frequently found herself under the unjustified suspicion of being a closet Lincolnite and supporter of the Union cause.*

quinine—a drug desperately needed by the hard-pressed Confederacy—and destined for the black market in the South.• Martha stayed at the Willard Hotel and behaved so obnoxiously, according to Mary Lincoln, that the first lady refused to see her. Martha, however, told everyone she was Mary's sister and then elaborated on the virtues of the Confederacy.

JB °Martha never saw the Lincolns, who perceived her as an adventurer out to exploit the family relationship, and Mary and Martha never saw each other after the Civil War. The situation differed from that with Emilie in that there was little question that Martha had wanted to exploit the Lincolns and had embarrassed both the president and the first lady.•

Just as the Lincolns' Southern relatives were something of an embarrassment, those same Southerners experienced a measure of humiliation regarding their
WCD relation to the Yankee president. °Lincoln, they pointed out, was not blood; he had married into the family.•

Mary Todd Lincoln's third sister, Elody Todd, lived in Selma, Alabama, and was a highly visible and vocal participant in the secession ceremonies, perhaps to show the public her rejection of the election of her brother-in-law. Nevertheless, in 1861 she claimed, "I never go in public that my feelings are not wounded."
CC °To prove that she was a Southern loyalist, Elody gave

*James Ewell Brown (Jeb) Stuart, pictured below left in his pre-Civil War U.S. Army uniform, was the great Confederate cavalry general whom General Lee called "the eyes of the army." His father-in-law, Philip St. George Cooke (below right), was also a West Point graduate and had been Stuart's first commanding officer, but he remained with the Union. On at least two occasions the two engaged each other on the battlefield. An undistinguished brigadier general, Cooke is remembered especially for what became of his family. His son, John Rogers Cooke, gave up a commission in the U.S. infantry, eventually becoming a Confederate general. It was years after the war before father and son tried to make peace with each other. Two of Cooke's daughters were Southern sympathizers, although a third remained loyal to the Union. The bitterness in the family was extreme. Jeb and Flora Stuart had named their son after Flora's father, but in 1861 they changed his name.*

a Confederate banner to her fiancé while he organized a regiment. She married him during the war, becoming Mary Todd Lincoln's third sister to wed a Confederate officer.•

As the war dragged on, the loss of contact with her BP family became a burden for the first lady. °The torment of the divided Todd family became more and more painful as Mary Lincoln saw the war claim close friends and relatives. These developments were torturous to her because she internalized all slights and grievances as being directed specifically at her. She was so shaken by some of these losses that frequently Lincoln doubted her sanity. The fact that the White House could be so disturbed by the war indicates the pain and trauma that the country as a whole endured during this time.•

### *The Stuarts and the Cookes*

In 1861 all Americans faced the challenge of taking a stand and then backing up their conviction with action.

For many, these decisions were not clear-cut, not even within their own families.

One case in point is that of James Ewell Brown "Jeb" Stuart and his wife's family, the Cookes. Shortly after the outbreak of hostilities, Stuart wrote his wife, Flora: "My darling wife, I am extremely anxious about your Pa and your brother. I do hope both will resign at once. How can they serve Lincoln's diabolical government?"

Stuart was a Virginian who resigned from the U.S. Army to join the Confederacy as a cavalry officer, and within months his leadership skills had put him in charge of the entire Southern cavalry. He had no trouble choosing sides, but it created problems within his family. His father-in-law was also a Virginian and had been Stuart's first commanding officer after his graduation from West Point, but Philip St. George Cooke decided to remain loyal to the Union. Regarding that decision, the flamboyant Stuart commented: "I have felt great mortification at Colonel Cooke's course. He will regret it but once and that will be continually."

Flora was forced to face an agonizing choice: to side with her husband or her father. BP ○Even though her father had been in the army for thirty-four years, and army life was all Flora had known, she decided to support her husband. That disappointed the senior Cooke, but to compound his problems he had a son, John Rogers Cooke, who had been educated at Harvard and then entered the U.S. Army. The younger Cooke was an officer in the infantry but gave up his commission to join his brother-in-law and the Confederacy. Philip St. George Cooke would have to fight both his daughter's husband and his own son.• Only one of his daughters stayed loyal to the Union.

The bitterness between the two families over the split went to extremes. JIR ○Stuart and his wife had named their son after Flora's father, but in 1861 they changed the child's name.

On at least two occasions Cooke and Stuart met face to face on the battlefield.• Their most memorable meeting was during the Peninsula campaign in June 1862. Stuart was sent on a mission to determine the size of the Union army, and he led his command entirely

*Philip St. George Cooke's daughter Flora (above) married Jeb Stuart and supported the Confederacy, even after her husband was mortally wounded in 1864.*

*Cooke's son John Rogers Cooke (below) was also in opposition to his father and battled for much of the war with Robert E. Lee's Army of Northern Virginia. Considered one of the best brigadier generals in Southern service, the younger Cooke incurred more than half a dozen wounds. After Appomatox he helped establish Richmond's Confederate Soldiers Home.*

around the Federals. Some of the troops Stuart encountered during the last leg of that first ride around the Federal army were from Cooke's command.

The two men never saw each other again. Stuart was killed in May 1864 at Yellow Tavern, Virginia. Cooke's son, John, was wounded seven times and became one of the most skilled generals in Robert E. Lee's army. John Cooke survived the war, but it took years before the son and father tried to make peace with each other.

*While Thomas Drayton (below left) became a brigadier for the Rebel army, his brother Percival (below right) overlooked his family's South Carolina heritage and served as a commander in the U.S. Navy. The Yankees got the better of the deal, for Percival made a fine naval officer, serving as the captain of several warships and partcipating in attacks along the coast of his native state as well as in the battle of Mobile Bay. He died from disease in August 1865. Thomas Drayton never achieved distinction on the battlefield, although he remained in service throughout the war, perhaps because of his friendship with Confederate President Jefferson Davis. He survived his brother by nearly thirty years.*

### *The Brothers Drayton*

TWO BROTHERS from South Carolina truly made the conflict a brothers' war. Percival Drayton, a commander in the U.S. Navy, had lived in the North so long that he never had any doubts as to his loyalties. In

October 1861 he commanded the lead ship that attacked the Confederate forts protecting Port Royal Sound, South Carolina. His guns were aimed at his older brother, Confederate Brig. Gen. Thomas Drayton, who commanded a fort on the grounds of the Drayton family plantation on Hilton Head Island. The Confederates under Thomas Drayton were inexperienced gunners, and they did not successfully defend the sound. The Federal gunners, coached by Percival Drayton, were better shots. The accurate fire on the forts from the younger Drayton soon forced the older Drayton to surrender.

Percival went on to a distinguished naval career that included blockade duty and the unsuccessful 1863 attack on Charleston. His career climaxed in 1864 when he was appointed David Farragut's fleet captain at the battle of Mobile Bay. He died only months after the war ended.

Thomas led one of James Longstreet's brigades at Second Manassas, South Mountain, and Antietam, unfortunately proving himself to be an inept field commander. During the final two years of the war he served in the Trans-Mississippi District. After the war he took up farming in Georgia, then moved to North Carolina and became an insurance agent.

*Virginian George H. Thomas stayed in Federal blue when the Civil War began and went on to render distinguished service on many contested fields. His decision to fight for the North brought him the lasting animosity of his sisters. In addition, many of Thomas's Northern peers distrusted him, and even President Lincoln supposedly bypassed Thomas for a promotion in part because of his Old Dominion ties. However, this seems an odd position for the chief executive to take considering his own Kentucky heritage. Thomas bore such circumstances with dignity and was eventually rewarded with the rank of major general and the command of the Army of the Cumberland. He also became one of only thirteen Union officers to receive the Thanks of Congress.*

### *The Thomases*

UNION MAJ. GEN. George H. Thomas from Southampton County, Virginia, seemed to catch distrust from both sides. His colleagues expected him to leave the U.S. Army when Virginia seceded, but he remained in blue and drew the ire of his family, particularly his sisters.

CC °Thomas was very close to his sisters, and they
expected that he would follow his family and join the
Confederacy. He did not, and he never explained how
JIR or why he made the decision.• °His sisters, who lived

*Citing loyalty to his family and Virginia, Robert E. Lee refused command of the Union army, resigned his commision, and became a general in the new army of the Confederate States of America. Throughout the war, across many bloody battlefields, Lee faced old comrades from his days at West Point and his service in the Mexican War. Following Appomattox, Lee refused to let bitterness and grudges, common among defeated people thoughout history, affect his life. He became an icon for the South, and his attitude of peaceful acceptance and reconciliation was an important example. He rejoined his family and retired to civilian life, becoming head of Washington College in Lexington, Virginia, which was later renamed Washington and Lee in his honor.*

in the family home, did not just disown him, they declared that he never existed. They turned his picture to the wall and refused to have any contact with him. One legend claims that in their last letter to him they asked that he change his name and leave the Thomas family.

Instead Thomas went on to a highly distinguished career. In September 1863 he won the nickname Rock of Chickamauga for a brilliant rear-guard stand covering the retreat of the Union army after it lost the field to Braxton Bragg and James Longstreet. The following year, in the last major battle of the western theater, Thomas was given another name, the Hammer of Nashville, for his routing of the second largest Confederate army and John Bell Hood.•

Yet, though Thomas had demonstrated his loyalty time and time again, he was never fully trusted by the Union high command. Sherman and Grant, both native Northerners, did not trust him and expected him to show Southern sympathies.

The war's end did not end the animosity Thomas's sisters felt for their brother, however. WCD °When they were almost destitute, he tried to help them, but they refused his aid. Even then, to them their brother no longer existed.•

JIR °The family's rejection must have troubled Thomas deeply, and it may have contributed to his early death in 1870 at the age of fifty-four. After the war he gained a great deal of weight and died of a stroke while at a duty post in San Francisco. Instead of being taken back to his native Virginia for burial, he was laid to rest in Troy, New York, his wife's home.•

### *The Lees*

BP °THOMAS WAS a stalwart steeped in the dignity of the old regular army. In this way he was very much like another Virginian, Robert E. Lee. Both men faced a similar dilemma. Did the Union have the strongest claim to their loyalty? Did the army, which had given them so many opportunities and rewarded them with rank and respect among their peers, have the greater claim? Did their state have the greatest pull? Thomas chose to remain within the ranks; Lee made an agonized decision to give his loyalty to Virginia.•

*The Civil War splintered many family trees, and the venerable Lee family was not immune to such terrible effects. Samuel Phillips Lee, only five years younger than his relative Confederate Gen. Robert E. Lee, chose to remain a U.S. naval officer. A veteran of the Mexican War, Samuel Lee was commanding the Vandalia at Cape Town, South Africa, when the war broke out. Under his own initiative, Lee sailed his ship back to the U.S. in order to help quell the rebellion. He distinguished himself on blockade duty both in the Atlantic and on the Mississippi. In 1864 Lee's riverine fleet helped George H. Thomas repel the advance of Confederate Gen. John Bell Hood. By 1870 Lee had attained the rank of full rear admiral.*

To his sister, on April 20, 1861, Lee explained his rationale: "I had to meet the question whether I should take part against my native state. With all my devotion to the Union and the feeling of loyalty and duty of an American citizen, I have not been able to make up my mind to raise my hand against my relatives, my children, my home."

Lee, son of a Revolutionary War hero, had been a career army officer since graduating from West Point in 1829. He had been a hero during the Mexican War, had been superintendent at West Point, and was serving with distinction in the elite Second U.S. Cavalry in Texas when war seemed likely. He reported to Washington on orders from Gen. Winfield Scott and was promoted to full colonel and then offered command of the Federal army.

All night Lee paced the floors of the Arlington mansion, considering what his loyalty to the Union would mean to his family of seven children. At dawn he returned to Scott's office and tendered his resignation.

Mary Custis Lee, Lee's wife, was pained by Virginia's secession and by her husband's resignation. As the great-granddaughter of Martha Washington, Mary Lee took pride in the family's heritage. To one of her children she wrote: "With a sad, heavy heart, my dear child, I write, for the prospects before us are sad indeed, as I think both parties are wrong in this fratricidal war. There is nothing comforting even in the hopes that God may prosper the right, for I see no right in the matter. We can only pray that in his mercy he will spare us."

MPC °Although the family had owned some slaves before the war, they were not proslavery. They were Unionists, but Virginia was the primary allegiance for all of them.• Yet even in a family so instilled in the South as the Lees, there was turmoil. One of Lee's nephews fought for the North under Gen. John Pope. A cousin also remained loyal to the North. Unlike many families, however, the end of the war brought healing for the Lees.

MPC °Lee would not have anything to do with grudges after the war. Mary Lee took up again with her nephew and his wife and their cousins, who frequently visited the general and his wife at his college post in Lexington, Virginia. Once the war was over, the Lee family put it aside and accepted that this was once again a united country.•

*When Thomas J. "Stonewall" Jackson made the choice to ally with the South, it did not meet with the same acceptance within his family as did Robert E. Lee's decision. Jackson's sister, who had lent a sympathetic and loving ear when others had called him such epithets as "Tom Fool Jackson" and "Old Blue Light" because of his odd personality, turned her back on him when he accepted a commission in the Confederate army. Although little is known about Jackson's feelings about his sister's ire, he did state he "regretted that his sister entertained Union sentiments." The general continued to inquire after his sister's well being until his death, which came as a result of wounds he received during the battle of Chancellorsville in May 1863.*

### *The Jackson Siblings*

For every story of reconciliation, however, there are
JIR many stories of unresolved, hard feelings. °One of the saddest of these concerns the legendary Thomas Jonathan "Stonewall" Jackson and his sister, Laura. They had been orphaned at an early age and were raised by different members of the family, but for each the other was all that truly remained of family. Beginning in 1842, brother and sister began a steady correspondence, and for almost nineteen years they kept in constant touch. They clung to the other, facing each other's cares and problems.•

Through their writings, Laura helped her brother survive his loneliness at West Point, and in the following decade Thomas helped her buttress a shaky religious faith. One example of their closeness can be found in Jackson's January 28, 1844, letter to Laura: "Dear, Sister, I received with much pleasure, your letter and was highly gratified to hear that your health is improving. I ever remain yours with high esteem. If I had one wish it would be to see you as soon as you see this." His last words to her were written on April 6, 1861, a week before the bombardment of Fort Sumter. He primarily addressed a problem of faith, but there was also a hint of parting in his words: "When a cloud comes between you and the sun, do you fear that the sun will never appear again? I am well satisfied that you are a child of God, and that you will be saved in heaven, there forever to dwell with the ransomed of the Lord."

When Jackson cast his lot with the Confederacy, Laura was enraged. Despite the fact that her husband, Jonathan, and her neighbors in Beverly, a small town in northwestern Virginia, were Confederate sympathizers, Laura was an adamant supporter of the Union. As the war progressed she allegedly claimed that she "could take care of the wounded Feds. as fast as brother Thomas could wound them."

*Although a stong family resemblance can be seen in the face of Laura Jackson Arnold, the sister of Stonewall Jackson, the similarity did not extend to political ideology. Laura, who lived in the town of Beverly in present-day West Virginia, became enraged when she heard that her only brother had cast his lot with the Confederacy, a stance made even more remarkable by the fact that her husband was pro-Confederate. A staunch Unionist, she loathed what her brother had done and was not shy in expressing her feelings about his actions. She openly nursed wounded Northern troops in her home and proclaimed that she "could take care of the wounded Feds. as fast as brother Thomas could wound them." Even the tragic death of her brother did not soften her disgust.*

JIR °A one-sided schism developed between the two orphans. Laura became such an active Unionist that she castigated and criticized her brother, even to the point of making up stories about him. She accused him of cheating on his West Point entrance examination and would not allow anyone to mention his name in her presence. For his part, Jackson always inquired about her whenever he encountered travelers who had been through Beverly. Only once did anyone hear him comment about her, and this lifelong friend recalled Jackson's voicing his regrets that Laura "entertained Union sentiments, but his expressions about her were kind but brief."

This schism between brother and sister was never resolved. Jackson died on May 10, 1863, and Laura Jackson Arnold never recanted the way she felt.• Her outspoken Unionism estranged her from the Jackson family for the rest of her life. She divorced her husband in 1870, and due to poor health, took up residence in a private sanitorium near Columbus, Ohio, from 1881 to

1910. Laura died in 1911 in the home of her daughter-in-law in Buckhannon, West Virginia.

*The outbreak of the Civil War formed a troubling capstone to the distinguished political career of Kentucky-born Sen. John J. Crittenden. Throughout the antebellum era, Crittenden had spoken against both the expansion of slavery and of abolitionism, hoping that slavery would die out on its own. When war clouds formed after Lincoln's 1860 election, Crittenden tried to placate the troubled American populace with his Crittenden Compromise, an act that limited the spread of slavery and proposed that new states should use popular sovereignty to decide if they would be slave or free. Both North and South were already girded for combat, however, and the compromise was defeated. Troubled by his country's future, Crittenden left office in 1861 and watched in sadness as his two sons joined opposing armies. The elder Crittenden died in 1863 and never knew the outcome of the war.*

### *The Crittenden Family*

SOMETIMES THE stories of well-known families were played out on the national stage. Celebrity status, however, did not lessen the pain. One of these was the Crittenden family of Kentucky. The patriarch of the family, John J. Crittenden, had begun a political career in 1809 and served as state legislator, secretary of state, U.S. senator, U.S. district attorney, attorney general under William Henry Harrison and Millard Fillmore, and governor of Kentucky.

Crittenden was a strong advocate of compromise. He was also a southerner who hoped slavery would die out as impractical and expensive, but he reluctantly supported the South fearing that efforts to abolish slavery would lead to war. In December 1860, he proposed a compromise that would protect slavery where it existed and allow future states to decide the issue for themselves. When it failed to pass the Senate, Crittenden knew war was imminent.

JCK °Some of the urgency behind his efforts could be attributed to his trying to save his family. If there were a war, the Crittenden family would most likely be fractured.•

Crittenden had two sons. The older, George, a West Point graduate, was serving in the regular army when the war started. He resigned his commission to join the Confederacy and was made a major general in hopes that he could sway Kentucky toward the Southern fold. Crittenden's younger son, Thomas, a lawyer, remained loyal to the Union and also became a major general. George's decision, however, devastated his father.

JCK °The elder Crittenden tried to keep George from leaving the Federal army by reminding him that this was the nation under which he had grown up; this was the nation he had to support. Nevertheless, George became a Confederate, and his father wrote that George's decision filled him with shame and sorrow.• On April 30, 1861, the aging statesman wrote to his Rebel son: "It becomes you to be vigilant, very vigilant and with all your energy and courage that need be to resist every attempt of treachery or rebellion against the Rebels. It is my anxiety alone that prompts me to write to you."

Neither brother proved to be very effectual in his military endeavors. George lost his first major battle at Mill Springs, Kentucky, in January 1862, possibly attributable to the fact that WCD °he had a problem with drink. He was not cashiered, but late in 1862 George was forced to step aside. He finished the war in a minor position.

Yankee Thomas Crittenden rose to corps command and was a fairly prominent man until the battle of Chickamauga in September 1863, where his Twenty-first Corps was overrun. He never had a field command again.•

As was the case with many divided families, Confederate George Crittenden never had the opportunity to resolve his differences with his father; JCK °John J. Crittenden died in July 1863. Both sons survived the war and were eventually buried in the same cemetery as their father. Like so many in families divided by the war, they found at least in death the peace that they lacked in life during the war.•

For many families the peace that normally came with reconciliation or compromise remained elusive. Fighting seemed to be the only answer. Such is the nature of a civil war, JIR °which is basically a family feud on a national scale. Regardless of what causes a war—whether it be religious, political, or social—civil wars tend to shatter families and end tragically. This was certainly the case with the American Civil War and particularly with families living in the Upper South and Border States like Virginia, Maryland, Kentucky, and Missouri.•

The Border States were politically aligned North or South but emotionally divided. For example, JCK °there were eighteen Kentucky regiments on the battlefield at Shiloh, Tennessee, in April 1862; thirteen carried the Union flag and five the battle flag of the Confederacy.

*The sons of Sen. John J. Crittenden did not live up to their father's high reputation. A U.S. Army major general, Thomas L. (above) was one of several officers held accountable for the Union rout at Chickamauga. Although a military court absolved him, his career was blighted. He remained in the army until 1881.*

*A Confederate major general, George B. (below) was a heavy drinker and was accused of being drunk while in command of the Southern forces when they were defeated at Mill Springs. He resigned his command but served in unofficial capacities throughout the war.*

Like John J. Crittenden, Robert J. Breckinridge was the patriarch of an influential and powerful Kentucky family that was rent asunder by the firing on Fort Sumter. Although he owned slaves, the elder Breckinridge supported the Union and felt that civil war would only bring destruction and ruin to the South and its economy. He was distressed and embittered when two of his sons and his nephew chose to fight for the Confederacy. He wrote: "My sons have disobeyed their father and betrayed their country. It only remains for them to denounce their God." Even though they lived in the same city, his daughter-in-law refused to let him see his grandchild throughout the war because of the harsh words he had uttered against the Confederate cause.

That meant the soldiers looking down their gun barrels at each other might see a friend, a relative, a brother, or a father. This was truly a brother's war for these people in these areas. People could not remain neutral; they had to take sides despite knowing that eventually their own families would suffer losses and hardships beyond anything they could imagine. No one wanted that, but they all had to face it.•

### *The Breckinridges*

WHILE THE war ravaged many families like the Crittendens, other Kentuckians were also hit hard. Few families were as damaged by their split loyalties as were the Breckinridges of JCK Kentucky, °perhaps the prototype of the divided family in the nation and in Kentucky particularly. Robert J. Breckinridge was sixty-one years old at the start of the war. Professionally, he had been everything: a lawyer, a minister, head of the Presbyterian Church, a college president, and later an architect of the Kentucky public school system. He supported the Union wholeheartedly, but he was a slaveholder• who believed in gradual emancipation and recolonization.

His nephew, John C. Breckinridge, had served as a U.S. congressman, senator, and James Buchanan's vice president. He had run for president in 1860, finishing WCD second to Lincoln in the four-man contest. °In 1861 John was a U.S. senator who by year's end was a Confederate general, appointed more for his well-known Kentucky family name than for his military skills. Breckinridge never believed in the Confederacy or secession, but because of his loyalty to his state and his belief in states' rights, he was forced to turn his back on the oath he had taken as a vice president.•

SDB °Robert Breckinridge supported his nephew John when he ran for the presidency against Lincoln. In Robert's mind preservation of the Union was foremost. Once the Union had been preserved, the question of slavery could be solved. Although uncle and nephew split in principle, they never split personally.•

The elder Breckinridge not only grieved because his nephew chose the Confederacy, he was distressed that two of his sons also chose to fight for the South. As an embittered old man he wrote: "My sons have disobeyed their father and betrayed their country. It only remains for them to denounce their God."

His sons had not found the decision easy, however. Robert Jr. was the first to leave and wrote a farewell note to his father on July 4, 1861, concluding: "I have no money, no business now and few friends. I can but try and commence life anew. Be, if you please, sir, as lenient as possible in your thoughts of me."

JCK °A year later, another son, Willie, decided to join the South and wrote his father, telling him that no matter what happened, he would love his father forever because he had raised Willie and loved him. Willie asked that his father not take the decision to join the Confederacy as a personal insult to his beliefs. Willie slipped away, borrowed a saddle, got on a horse in the dark of night, rode to the top of a hill, then looked back at his father's house. Tears filled his eyes, but he rode off to join his brother. He fought a battle that same day, still outfitted in civilian clothes.• Late in 1862 Willie wrote his father again: "Please, sir, be kind in your thoughts to me. Don't tell me that I've been wrong. Love me for what I am, your loving son, not for the cause that I support."

Ultimately two of the Breckinridge brothers, Joseph and Willie, faced each other across the line of battle at JCK Atlanta in 1864, and Yankee Joseph was captured. °When Willie Breckinridge heard of his brother's capture, he rode all night to where Joseph was being held. Willie gave him some gold coins so he would have some money when he went to a prison camp. He then rode back to his command so he could fight again the next day.

The good news about the Breckinridge family was that those family ties remained intact.• Despite his own bitter disappointment, Robert Breckinridge did whatever he could to help his Confederate sons during the

*Robert Breckinridge Jr., eldest son of Robert Breckinridge Sr., was the first to depart for Confederate service, leaving his father a farewell note that concluded: "Be, if you please, sir, as lenient as possible in your thoughts of me." He became a captain of the Second Kentucky Infantry, a regiment in the famous Orphan Brigade. He was captured and faced possible execution as a spy, but it is thought his father—an outspoken supporter of Lincoln—used his influence with the president to save his son's life. Margaret Breckinridge, a relative from New Jersey, became a Union nurse and agent for the Christian Commission. She was assigned to work on a steamboat on the Mississippi River, ministering to the spiritual needs of Ulysses S. Grant's army during the siege of Vicksburg. She contracted typhoid fever and died in late July 1864.*

*The most famous Breckinridge was Robert Breckinridge Sr.'s nephew, John C. (above). He had been vice president of the United States under James Buchanan and a serious contender for president against Abraham Lincoln. A Confederate major general and secretary of war, he fled abroad at war's end until a general amnesty was declared.*

*His cousin Willie (below), the senior Breckinridge's second Rebel son and a Confederate cavalry colonel, faced his Yankee brother Joseph across the line of battle at Atlanta in 1864.*

SDB war. °His older son, Robert Jr., was taken prisoner, and there was a chance that he might be executed as a spy. Nothing happened to him, however, and he was held as the only Southern prisoner in a prison in Columbus, Ohio. Many believed that Robert Sr.—the emancipationist, the Unionist, the outspoken supporter of Lincoln—had used his influence with the president to ensure his son's life.•

Even though he continued to help his family, Robert Breckinridge Sr. never stopped preaching against the Confederacy. As late as 1864, he wrote, "We must maintain the Constitution, and with undoubted certainty put to death anyone who undertakes to trample it under foot." He, nevertheless, paid a high personal price for his denouncements of the Confederacy.

JCK °Breckinridge's daughter-in-law, Melissa DeShay Breckinridge, refused to let Robert Sr. see his grandchild, even though they lived in the same city, because of the harsh words that he had uttered against the Confederate cause. The only time he saw his granddaughter was when she was in the care of a servant. Robert Sr. put the little girl on his lap and said: "God bless the child. She's the prettiest thing I ever saw." After that she was taken away, and he did not see her again for the duration of the war.•

It took four years for the deep wounds to heal, but ultimately Robert Breckinridge Sr. saw his grandchildren. His nephew, John C., however, was not as fortu-
JCK nate. °John C. had been a Confederate leader in Kentucky. He was a Southern general, and in the last months of the war he had been the Confederate secretary of war. He had helped negotiate the surrender of one of the last large Confederate armies in the field at Durham Station, North Carolina. Afraid he would be pursued as a war criminal, John C. escaped to Florida where he battled heat and starvation, living off of turtle eggs and rotten fruit before sailing the Florida Straits in an exposed rowboat to Cuba. From there he made his way to Europe and later to Canada where he lived for three years until taking advantage of a general amnesty. He returned home to Kentucky in 1869 and found some of the familial wounds had finally healed.• John C. practiced law for a while, but a lung infection kept

him severely ill for the last two years of his life. When he died in 1875 he was only fifty-four years old, a shadow of the strong man he had once been.

### *The Terrill Family*

SOMETIMES FAMILY divisions transcended contention and ended tragically. Such was the case of the Terrill family of Virginia, who lived near the mountainous western counties that broke off and formed the Unionist state of West Virginia in 1863.

JIR °William Terrill Sr. was a well-known and prosperous attorney and a member of the Virginia General Assembly. His oldest son, William Jr., had graduated from West Point in 1853. When the war began, the son came home and informed his father that he felt his duty was with the North.• As a concession to his father and his own feelings, William vowed that he would not fight against Virginia. He would ask to be assigned to regions that would not bring him into contact with old friends or his home state.

A younger brother, James B. Terrill, chose a different path. As a graduate of the Virginia Military Institute, James believed he owed his allegiance to his home state and joined the Confederacy.

BP °When the war began, these two brothers were diametrically opposed on the issue of secession. Their father supported James and professed that Virginia needed them both.• He told his elder son: "Can you be so recreant and so unnatural as to aid in the bad attempt to impose a yoke of tyranny upon your kith and kin? Do so and your name shall be stricken from the family records. . . . If you renounce your family, we will remove your name from the family records. It's as if you never existed."

The end result for each brother was the same.
WCD °William died at the battle of Perryville, Kentucky, in October 1862 when a Confederate shell fragment struck him in the chest. Rather than return his body to Virginia, Federal officials sent it to West Point. James was killed in May 1864 near Richmond, Virginia, the day before his commission as brigadier

*The tale of Virginia-born brothers William R. and James B. Terrill aptly summarizes the painful experience of many U.S. households from 1861 to 1865. William (near right) went to West Point, graduating in 1853. After Fort Sumter, he chose to stay in the Federal army but requested that he be sent west so that he would not have to fight in Virginia. William's fine service as an artillery officer at Shiloh led to his promotion to brigadier general, a rank he held when he was killed at the October 1862 battle of Perryville.*

*James (far right) attended the Virginia Military Institute, receiving his diploma in 1858. By 1861, he was fighting in Confederate gray at Manassas as an officer in the Thirteenth Virginia Infantry. Dependable and brave, he gained a commission to brigadier general, but before learning of his promotion he died while battling elements of the Union Army of the Potomac on May 30, 1864. Thus in one family there were two bothers, two causes, two deaths, and two tragedies—an all too common legacy of the American Civil War's divided families.*

general came through. Instead of sending his body through the lines, Union soldiers buried him where he fell.•

William Sr. survived both his sons but never had the chance to bury either of them in the family cemetery.
BP Instead he °erected a monument to them on which he had the following inscription carved: "God alone knows which was right." William Sr. was heartbroken. He had renounced his elder son and never had the chance to reconcile, to embrace him again. The tragedy of the Civil War was that passions ran so high and there were cases where family members never had the chance to speak to each other again.•

JIR °Civil wars are always different from other wars because they are family feuds, and there is nothing more vicious than a family feud. When both sides know each other, speak the same language, have the same likes and dislikes, share a common heritage, then hate becomes more intense than would be the case in fighting another nation.•

One Southern woman wrote in her memoirs: "I never fully realized the fratricidal character of the conflict until I lost my idolized brother Dave of the Southern army one day, and was nursing my Northern husband back to life the next."

WCD °What else in American life could force men and women to choose to fight against their own family? The trauma caused by those kinds of decisions is so deeply rooted in us that inevitably we are drawn back over and over and over again to look at these people who had to choose where their loyalties lay and to empathize with them and to try to understand them.•

BP °No matter what their loyalty, every person had to consciously consider what he was going to do and what the issues were that caused him to fight. Thus these stories of divided families and divided states make the point that the fate of this country hung in the balance in the mid-nineteenth century. The war could have gone either way because people sincerely believed with all their heart and soul both of these diametrically opposed philosophies, and they fought just as strongly for the Confederacy and for the Union.•

The entire nation paid a heavy price for the Civil War. Everyone sacrificed and everyone suffered, but perhaps none sacrificed more or lost more than those whose families were divided by the war. Once divided, the wounds suffered almost never healed.

# FIRST LADIES, NORTH AND SOUTH

*Married* TO THE TWO MOST powerful men in America during the Civil War, Mary Todd Lincoln and Varina Howell Davis were both controversial and oftentimes misunderstood. Both were reluctantly in the public eye. Both were the victims of political hostilities, bitter criticism, and malicious gossip. Both endured similar tragedies that struck their families. Mary Lincoln was the wife of Abraham Lincoln, the president of the United States, and Varina Davis was the wife of Jefferson Davis, the president of the Confederate States of America.

While the popular image of the two presidents is that of two men desperately fighting a war alone, concentrating so much on victory that they had little time for anything else, the truth is that both Lincoln and Davis depended on their wives and families to give them a respite from the daily pressures of war. In short, the two men loved and needed their wives.

In 1862 Lincoln commented, "My wife is as handsome as she was when she was a girl and I, a poor nobody then, fell in love with her and what is more, I have never fallen out." In 1865 Davis, writing to Varina about his consultations with his generals and cabinet members and telling her of his realization that the war was lost, wrote, "Dear wife, this is not the fate to which I invited you when the future was rose-colored to us both, but I know you will bear it even better than myself, and that of us two, I alone will ever look back reproachfully on my past career."

| | |
|---|---|
| **JB** | Jean Baker |
| **GC** | Gordon Cotton |
| **LLC** | Lynda Lasswell Crist |
| **JC** | Joan Cashin |
| **WCD** | William C. Davis |
| **LT** | Linda Turner |

*Mary Todd Lincoln's father, Robert S. Todd (top), was a Lexington, Kentucky, bank president who served for a time in the Kentucky senate. Like many in his state, Todd owned slaves—house servants—but he became a proponent of gradual emancipation. A forward thinking father, he took pains to ensure that all of his children received a good eduction. Mary's mother, Eliza Parker, died when Mary was a child. Unable to see eye-to-eye with her stepmother, Elizabeth Humphries Todd (below), Mary made a fateful decision to live with a sister in Springfield, Illinois, where she met her future husband.*

JC There were many °similarities between the two first ladies. Both were southerners. Both were intelligent. Both married complicated men. Both shared the burdens of a desperately harassed husband. Both were caught in the political undertow of animosities within their husbands' administrations. Both contended with the prejudices and prerogatives of a Congress, one in Washington and one in Richmond. Both endured unprecedented publicity from a large and aggressive press. In the end, both of them saw their lives forever changed by the Civil War.•

One first lady, Varina Howell Davis, became a symbol of reconciliation between the North and South. The other, Mary Todd Lincoln, is remembered as the most despised and misunderstood woman in American history. Yet for four years Mary Lincoln and Varina Davis led parallel lives in two separate White Houses.

Mary Lincoln, the better-known first lady of the two since the North was more populated, was the more complicated and the more unstable. She was a woman who absorbed everything that happened in her life, allowing events large and small to erode her personal well-being. For all her strengths and contributions to her husband's administration, Mary Lincoln's nerves were fragile and the effect on her personality was cumulative. Her behavior became increasingly neurotic and included many angry public outbursts as well as erratic spending sprees that plunged her deeper and deeper in debt. Her spurts of eccentric behavior seemed to validate the fabricated rumors that were spread about her.

LT °She had the ability to be an outstanding first lady under almost any conditions, but she came to the White House at the most tragic, difficult moment in the country's history.• Nevertheless, she presided over the president's home with skill, looking after her husband's political interests by conciliating some of his strongest opponents in Congress and widening the circle of friends who influenced him. She also looked after his health by encouraging him to eat and sleep when he was inclined to do neither. Except when she was trapped by one of her violent headaches or irrepressible rages, she kept the White House cheerful and their children happy. Despite the many criticisms of her contemporaries, Mary Lincoln was a good manager of the domestic affairs of the White House, a congenial hostess, and a compassionate first lady.

*The Todds owned a large, well-appointed home on Lexington's Main Street, the thoroughfare pictured here in 1860. This city where Mary was born on December 13, 1818, was the cultural and political hub of Kentucky during her youth. Mary's education was further enriched by contact with esteemed statesmen like Henry Clay. Abraham Lincoln was also born and lived for a time in Kentucky; but in contrast to his wife, he lived an impoverished, isolated, and rural existence during his childhood. Both the Todd house and the site of Lincoln's birthplace have been preserved and are open to the public.*

The road to the White House for Mary Lincoln began in Lexington, Kentucky. She was born Mary Ann Todd in 1818 into a prominent family of merchants and Revolutionary War heroes. In a time when women's education was not universally accepted as necessary and many women were expected to be seen and not heard while men made the tough decisions, Mary Todd was the exception.

JB °She was intelligent and very well schooled, but she also had two sides to her personality. She could be loyal and loving and also tempestuous. Many biographers have underlined the fact that the Todds of Kentucky were renowned for their tempers.• That sort of combination made Mary Todd a natural politician, or at least a young woman who would make a good wife for a good politician.

LT °Whig Party politics captivated her even as a child. Henry Clay, the Speaker of the House of Representatives and later U.S. senator from Kentucky, was a friend of the Todd family, and Mary often sat next to him at her father's table and hung on his every word as he described Washington and the congressional debates.• At an age when most children were playing with dolls and make-believe, Mary Todd was interested in politics and seemed to sense which politicians were the most effective, such as Clay who tried for decades to stave off
LT civil war. °As a young woman, she seemed interested in men who would one day develop into presidential timber, and she tended to choose as her beaux those who had political aspirations.•

In 1839, at age twenty-one, Mary Todd's life changed forever when she moved to Springfield, Illinois, to live with her eldest sister, Elizabeth Edwards. It was there she met Abraham Lincoln, a thirty-year-old self-taught

*These 1846 daguerreotypes of Mary and Abraham Lincoln were made less than four years after they were married. Abraham's political fortunes had risen since their marriage in 1842, and he was serving as an Illinois congressman at the time these images were made. The handsome photograph of Mary at age twenty-eight captures the essence of the intelligent, engaging personality that so captivated Abraham. In contrast, many of the images taken later in her life show a woman worn down by the strains of war and personal tragedy.*

lawyer who shared a law practice with her cousin. Lincoln had already been in the Illinois legislature and was in the third year of his law practice. He showed no ambition to go much further politically than he had already been.

JB °Their meeting was hardly a case of love at first sight, only the start of a long, somewhat difficult courtship. While they must have been mutually attracted, they were very different.•

Lincoln was the son of a poor Kentucky farmer and rough around the edges. He had little formal schooling, but the persistent teaching of his stepmother gave him a love of education and the background to educate himself. He took manual labor jobs to buy books and found a job as a postmaster, a natural setting for him to meet people and share the humorous tales he collected. Using his wit, he ran for the state legislature in 1834 and lost but came back two years later and won. In 1836 he borrowed some law books and taught himself the practice, becoming a circuit-riding lawyer until settling down in Springfield. It was then, perhaps Lincoln's first opportunity to settle down, that Mary Todd entered his life.

Mary saw something in the six-foot-four-inch-tall Lincoln, who towered over the average man's five feet six inches and over her at just over five feet. She set her goal to marry him. After a stormy courtship, a modest wedding ceremony was held on a rainy day in Springfield on November 4, 1842. After exchanging vows, Lincoln slipped on Mary's finger a ring, which he had had inscribed "Love Is Eternal."

*In 1856 Mary Lincoln urged her husband to renovate the small home they had bought as newlyweds in 1844 and shared with three sons and an Irish maid. Carpenters transformed the cramped accommodations into the spacious frame dwelling seen in this image taken during the 1860 presidential campaign. Much of the renovation took place when Abraham was away arguing cases. Once upon returning to town and seeing the changes wrought to his home, he jokingly asked a friend, "Do you know where Lincoln lives?" Mary did much of the interior decorating herself, picking tastefully patterned carpets and wallpaper for the various rooms. One guest applauded the home's air of "quiet refinement." The only home that Lincoln ever owned, this is now the property of the National Park Service and open to the public.*

THE NEXT year and several hundred miles south of Springfield, another presidential marriage was in the making. In 1843 seventeen-year-old Varina Howell, an educated woman born and reared in Natchez, Mississippi, was introduced to Jefferson Davis, a thirty-five-year-old West Point–educated lawyer and owner of a prosperous Mississippi cotton plan-
LLC tation called Brierfield. °The meeting had been engineered by Jefferson's older brother, Joseph, who was a close friend of Varina's father. Joseph had decided it was time for Jefferson to remarry after ten years of being a widower.•

Davis had been a virtual recluse since his ill-fated 1835 marriage to Sarah Knox Taylor, the daughter of his former dragoon regiment's commanding officer, Zachary Taylor, who would later be a general, a war hero, and president of the United States. Taylor did not approve of his daughter's plans to marry and much less with Davis's plan to resign his commission and take his frail daughter to Mississippi during the hot summer "fever" months.

Three months after their wedding, Sarah contracted malaria and died. Devastated at her death, for which he blamed himself, Davis virtually withdrew from public life, rarely leaving his plantation until he met Varina.

GC °He was twice her age, but Davis admired her wit, her spunkiness, and her attitude, and he certainly had an eye for beauty. She was quite lovely,• with long black hair and delicate features. Varina also had a good education that allowed her to form her own opinions.
LLC She first noticed their differences and °wrote her

mother: "Would you believe it, he is refined and cultivated, and yet he is a Democrat!" The Howell family was very strongly Whig in its political affiliation, and Whigs always thought themselves more sophisticated than Democrats.•

Like Mary Todd, Varina had an ability to read instantly a man when she met him. In a letter to her mother, she said: "He impresses me as a remarkable kind of man, but of uncertain temper, and has a way of taking for granted that everybody agrees with him when he expresses an opinion, which offends me; yet he is most agreeable and has a peculiarly sweet voice and a winning manner of asserting himself. The fact is, he is the kind of person I should expect to rescue one from a mad dog at any risk, but to insist upon a stoical indifference to the fright afterward."

Despite their differences in age and politics, on February 26, 1845, Jefferson and Varina were married. On that day, Varina Howell became the second Mrs. Davis and mistress of Davis's plantation, and Davis emerged from his ten-year depression. A few months later he was nominated for a seat in the U.S. House of Representatives. In September 1845 he began his campaign, and Varina caught a glimpse of what political life might hold for her. She recalled in her memoirs, "Then I began to know the bitterness of being a politician's wife, and that it meant long absences, pecuniary depletion from ruinous absenteeism, illness from exposure, misconceptions, defamation of character; everything which darkens the sunlight and contracts the happy sphere of home."

In November 1845 Davis was elected to the House, and he and Varina set out for Washington. In the years that followed she was an eyewitness to the momentous events that occurred in Washington during the fateful years before the Civil War and would be an observant friend or critic of many national leaders. She was fascinated by the debates in Congress and found the Senate filled with the giants of the land: Daniel Webster, Henry Clay, Thomas Hart Benton, Sam Houston, and John C. Calhoun. Her Whig loyalties, however, tarnished her perceptions of James K. Polk, and she was

*Eighteen-year-old Varina Howell posed for this portrait about the time she met her future husband. While Jefferson Davis appears thin and haggard in his wartime images, he appears here as a handsome, debonair man who caught Varina's eye prior to their 1845 wedding. In 1846 he left for the Mexican War, commanding a regiment of men known as the Mississippi Rifles—named for the accurate weapons they carried. Under Davis's leadership, the Rifles' deadly shooting crumpled several Mexican attacks at the battle of Buena Vista.*

critical of Sarah Polk's Presbyterian strictures on White House entertaining.

The pleasant life the Davises enjoyed in the nation's capital, where Varina delighted in entertaining, was interrupted in May 1846 by the Mexican War. The couple quarreled over Davis's decision to seek a military role in the conflict, and the argument jeopardized the delicate balance between their battle of wills, abated only by Varina's subordinating her judgment to Davis's absolute decisions. They returned to Brierfield, and in mid-July Davis departed for his regiment. The tension between husband and wife was never greater than during this period. Following victories at Monterrey and Buena Vista, the Mississippi regiment returned home in early June 1847. Davis had been wounded, and so he returned pale, thin, and on crutches. Polk offered him a brigadier's commission, but Davis declined. A greater offering was before him, and a few weeks later he accepted an appointment from the governor to fill a vacated seat in the U.S. Senate. Yet he did not take Varina with him to Washington. The two were quarreling almost constantly, and Davis felt they would not be able to conceal their difficulties from Washington society. He believed the marriage was breaking down and there was a need for a separation. On December 6, 1847, he entered the Senate and took the seat next to John C. Calhoun.

*These photographs (right) show Jefferson and Varina Davis after Jefferson had returned as a hero from the Mexican War. He served as U.S. Senator from Mississippi until the state ordered him to leave the Senate after Lincoln's election. The Davises returned to their plantation, but in 1861 Jefferson was elected president of the new Confederate States of America.*

*The Davises lived in the White House of the Confederacy (below) in Richmond from the summer of 1861 until 1865. The structure served as both a residence and an office for President Davis, although he had little time to escape his professional burdens and relax with his wife. Varina sometimes found herself serving as "first nurse" to the Confederacy, caring for her overworked and stressed husband when he suffered from one of his frequent bouts of fever or migraine headaches. It was also in the White House that Varina mourned the death of her father and her youngest son, Joseph. The house has been restored to its Victorian opulence, with many of its original furnishings, and is open to the public.*

Husband and wife wrote frequently, but Davis was adamant in demanding that Varina be subservient, not question him or his actions and motives, and be what a wife should be—"kind and peaceful." Finally, her letters reflected a gradual change, an acceptance of what he saw her role to be in their marriage, or more directly, subservience. That summer he visited Varina at Brierfield and found that she had progressed in conforming her behavior to his wishes. The two devoted their attentions to the construction of a new home on the property, and neither ever mentioned the separation again.

Varina returned to Washington in the spring of 1850 and adapted to the more challenging role demanded of her as a senator's wife. She missed few debates in the Senate, and her husband's friendship with Zachary Taylor allowed the Davises access to the White House, even though president and senator were of opposing parties. They left Washington again in 1851 when Davis ran for governor of Mississippi and lost.

For the next two years Davis and Varina settled down for the longest and happiest stay they would enjoy at Brierfield. In addition to refurbishing the plantation, Varina gave birth to a son on July 30, 1852, and he was named

Samuel after Jefferson's father. When Franklin Pierce was elected president in 1852, he consulted Davis regarding cabinet appointments. Against Varina's wishes, Davis returned to Washington and accepted the post of secretary of war. It was a position that appealed to him and one for which he was ideally suited. When Varina returned to the capital, it was not long until she became one of Jane Pierce's closest friends and the unofficial White House hostess.

Tragedy struck the Davis family when twenty-three-month-old Samuel died of an unknown illness in June 1854. Varina subsequently gave birth to a daughter, Margaret, in February 1855, two years later to another son, named after his father, and two years later to another son, named after his uncle, Joseph. Pierce failed to win reelection, but Davis returned to the Senate in 1857.

The political scene in Washington in the late 1850s was becoming increasingly difficult for Davis. The issue of slavery was dividing the nation in two. When it looked as if Lincoln would be elected, Davis tried to moderate the southern response, to maneuver for time so that several states might act in unison, which he believed would accomplish a peaceful and permanent withdrawal from the Union. While he attended a meeting in Jackson, Mississippi, called by the governor to plan the state's course of action, Varina wrote from Washington that a "settled gloom [hung] over everyone here. . . . Everyone is scared, especially [President] Buchanan." Davis returned to Washington at Buchanan's request for his input on the upcoming State of the Union address, but neither side responded positively to Buchanan's address. Davis himself vacillated between secession and remaining in the Union.

Although she probably kept her opinions to herself, Varina was much opposed to secession. She told her

Montgomery Ala.
Feb. 20. 1861
My dear Wife,
I have been so crowded and pressed that the first wish to write to you has been thus long deferred
I was inaugurated on monday having reached here on saturday night. The audience was large and brilliant upon my weary heart was showered smiles plaudits and flowers, but beyond them I saw troubles and thorns innumerable. We are without machinery without means and threatened by powerful opposition but I do not despond and will not shrink from the

*The selection of Jefferson Davis as the Confederate president signaled the beginning of extremely stressful years for Varina. Often separated by the exigencies of war, she and Jefferson tried to maintain contact by mail, although at times even this proved difficult. In the above letter, written two days after his February 20, 1861, inauguration, Jefferson complained to Varina: "I have been so crowded and pressed that the first wish to write to you had been thus long deferred." The worried president also confided that, although the favorable reception he had received in Montgomery had cheered his "weary heart," he "saw troubles and thorns immeasurable" on the horizon. The South is "threatened by powerful opposition but I do not despair."*

*"Mrs. Davis does not like her husband being made president," claimed a companion of the Southern first lady, because "people are hard to please." Until the bombardment of Fort Sumter, Varina had desired reconciliation between the North and the South, hoping a compromise could be achieved that would spare the country and her family the upheaval of a civil war. As early as 1860, she reportedly wore a badge in Washington proclaiming "Jeff Davis no seceder." Nevertheless, she worked hard at being a congenial hostess in the Confederate White House, although she missed her Mississippi friends and found "playing Mrs. President" too often to be tedious and "slow work." The photograph above was taken of Mrs. Davis in 1860 or 1861.*

mother in a letter in the winter of 1860–61 that the South simply could not win a war, that the region lacked the manpower and the manufacturing capacity to wage war successfully.•

At the same time that Davis was doing his best in the Senate to defend slavery and the South, Lincoln was stepping into the political arena as the Republican presidential candidate with an antislavery
LT platform. °He would have made his mark one way or another without Mary or with no wife at all, but with Mary he was almost certain to have a good chance at being president of the United States because of her particular background. Her acquaintance with politicians and previous presidential candidates gave her some insights into the makeup of a candidate, and she was no doubt able to counsel Lincoln on how to act like a president.•

Mary's aspirations for her husband became a reality in November 1860 when Lincoln was elected the sixteenth president of the United States. It was more than a victory for
LT him. °On election day he left the telegraph office in Springfield and went home and stood in the front yard and shouted, "Mary, Mary, we've won!" That "we" was not mere courtesy. Lincoln had enormous respect for his wife's opinions, and he freely consulted her.•

South Carolina, Mississippi, Florida, Alabama, Georgia, and Louisiana responded to Lincoln's election by seceding from the Union and calling for a convention to meet in Montgomery, Alabama, to form a new government. To southerners, Lincoln's election was a declaration of war. The man who had spoken out against slavery for years had won. That was the only message they needed.

Davis and his colleagues from Florida and Alabama decided to submit their resignations and formally leave the Senate together on January 21, 1861. He was the last of the five to speak. Davis spoke of those with whom he had worked in the Senate chamber, he addressed states' rights in the context of the nation's founding documents, and he apologized to those he had offended in debate. He concluded: "In the presence of my God I wish you well: and such, I am sure is the feeling of the people whom I represent toward those whom you represent. . . . It remains for me to bid you a final farewell."

He and Varina returned to Brierfield. "I found much to be done and have entered upon me the most agreeable of all labors planting shrubs and trees and directing the operations of the field," Davis wrote a week after his arrival. He seemed overly concerned for Varina's garden, which had been ruined by the floods of the 1850s. The two of them spent hours tending the flowers and vegetable plants. Politics seemed almost forgotten. Davis expected a military appointment by the government that was being formed in Montgomery at the time. What happened was not what he expected.

*Mr. and Mrs. Jefferson Davis entertain a group of Confederate officers at their Richmond home. The clean-shaven president is seen speaking with a woman guest. The dark-bearded officer in the center facing the viewer is G. W. Custis Lee, Robert E. Lee's eldest son. Varina entertained often in Richmond. In her diary on May 20, 1961, Mary Boykin Chesnut wrote: "Lunched at Mrs. Davis's. . . . Everything so nice to eat. . . . And she was as nice as the luncheon. When she is in the mood, I do not know so pleasant a person. She is awfully clever—always."*

A rider approached the Davises as they were pruning roses and handed Davis a telegram. Although he had not attended the convention, Davis had been elected president of the Confederate States of America. Varina's first impression, based on her husband's countenance, was that tragedy had again struck the family. When he informed her of his election, she wrote that he spoke "as a man might speak of a sentence of death." To some friends, she confided, "I felt his genius was military, but that as a party manager, he would not succeed."

As would become obvious as the Civil War progressed, she was wrong on the first count, but right on the second. Davis continually offered his military opinions to his generals, and they ignored them the best they could. As the chief of the army he frequently appointed old West Point and Mexican War friends to high office without regard for their abilities. As president, he never wavered from Varina's first assessment of her husband; he always believed he was right and was suspicious of anyone who questioned his opinions. That might have made him a good king, but his arrogance kept him constantly at odds with the Confederate Congress and his own cabinet members. Even his vice president, Alexander Stephens of Georgia, rarely spoke to him and, in fact, spent much of the war at his home in Georgia.

In February 1861 Varina Davis became the first lady of the Confederacy, occupying a house temporarily in Montgomery, Alabama. The government was then moved to Richmond, and Varina followed late in the summer of 1861 and moved into a three-story house on Clay Street that was dubbed the White House of the Confederacy. She was delighted with the mansion's large, airy rooms, which the women of Richmond had furnished elegantly if not practically. The work of the decorating committee spared Varina the temptation to indulge in extravagant spending during wartime, and so she avoided the criticism that befell Mary Lincoln later.

In March 1861 Mary Lincoln became first lady of the United States and moved into the White House, just ninety miles north of the Confederate capital. She was surprised to find the mansion rundown and began to redecorate it immediately. Mary was determined to make the White House a properly elegant home for the president and his family as well as a showcase of her own taste and refinement.

WCD °**W**HEN THE two presidents took office, and the two first ladies moved into their respective executive mansions, there was no well-developed notion of what a first lady was supposed to be. Almost anything Varina Davis did would set a precedent. As the first lady of the beleaguered nation, she tried to set an example for the women of the Confederacy by taking part in relief work, charitable organizations, and what were called starvation parties.•

LLC °Davis always praised Varina for upholding him during his many long periods of illness. His eyesight was limited, and he was prone to constant headaches. She helped by writing correspondence and reading dispatches and books to him.• Although he had professional secretaries who did much of the official work of the Confederacy, Varina often filled the role of personal secretary.

JB °Mary Lincoln's greatest contribution to the role of the first lady was to challenge the stereotypes and the conventions of being the president's wife. She was the first woman to be called first lady. Most of her predecessors were unknown to the public, and with the exception of the flamboyant Dolley Madison, few citizens even knew the names of the wives of the presidents. Mary Lincoln refused to be limited to the upstairs family quarters of the White House. She chose to play a role in her husband's administration, and she set up a salon and invited important American literary figures and politicians like Charles Sumner of Massachusetts to discuss the events of the day.•

*Critics accused Mrs. Lincoln of being such a doting mother that she was unable to discipline her often rambunctious boys. During an 1866 interview, however, Mary claimed that her husband condoned her soft-hearted handling of the children, and that the president had told her it gave him "pleasure" to see the lads, "free, happy and unrestrained by parental tyranny. Love is the chain whereby to lock a child to its parent." Sadly, the loving parents had to endure the death of Edward, their second child, in 1850 and of Willie, their third, in 1862. Tad, the youngest son, died in 1871. Here Willie (left) and Tad (right) pose with their mother.*

During 1861 Mary Lincoln redecorated the White House in the style befitting European royalty and regularly held court in the Blue Room for visitors. Such extravagant behavior at a time when hundreds of thousands of men were sleeping under thin blankets in the Maryland and Virginia countryside did not go unnoticed by the eastern press. The eastern newspapers, most of them owned by Democrats, were disappointed that a crude westerner had won election to the highest office in the land. They did not appreciate his little southern-born wife either. One newspaper called her "the Republican queen."

LT °Mary Lincoln entertained lavishly. She gave parties. She dressed in a certain style. She had a view of the White House as the centerpiece of a great democratic nation, the first time that concept was given over to reality. In her eyes, the members of the president's family were more than just individuals; they were symbols of the country.• The White House too was more than just a residence; it was a symbol of the nation.

*From the moment Mary Lincoln came to Washington in 1861, members of the city's high society looked askance at the Kentucky native, considering her a boorish product of an unsophisticated frontier upbringing, a criticism that had no basis in fact. At the same time, Northern newspapers sneered at Mary's well-planned receptions and her efforts to rehabilitate the drab interior of the White House as frivolous and unnecessary expenditures in wartime. She was greatly distressed by this cruel paradox, and it haunted her the rest of her life. During a postwar conversation with an acquaintance, she stated that whenever she asked the president for anything, he would reply, "'You know what you want—go and get it': he [never] asked me if it was necessary."*

Mrs. Lincoln's image began to deteriorate as the numbers of reporters began to grow. Between battles the press had little to write about. With no fighting to observe, they turned to the house on Pennsylvania Avenue and the president's family. Mary Lincoln's distinctive style made her a celebrity and a target of their writing. To be sure, there was a side to the first lady that craved this attention, and she found a certain satisfaction in reading about herself in the newspapers, even if she did not always like what she read. She could discount her critics as narrow-minded commentators of a male-dominated society, and there was no doubt that reporters exaggerated and frequently were wrong in what they reported. What was maddening to Mary was that they were fickle, one day complimentary of her, the next critical.

At first some reporters took to her. "All eyes were turned on Mrs. Lincoln, whose admirable ease and grace won compliments from thousands," wrote William Howard Russell, a reporter for the *Times* of London in 1861 in a time when the newspapers were still sizing up the new administration. As the war dragged on past the ninety days politicians and generals had originally predicted it would last, Mary Lincoln generated more negative news. She went on lavish shopping trips to New York, and she hired a personal seamstress, Elizabeth Keckley, a former slave who had once worked for Varina Davis.

Elizabeth Keckley became Mary's confidante in the White House. Mary was comfortable around Elizabeth, who seemed to know or sense what the first lady wanted, and they became close friends, so much so that Elizabeth observed many intimate moments in the Lincoln White House. Writing in 1862, Keckley noted: "Mr. and Mrs. Lincoln discussed the relations of cabinet officers and gentlemen prominent in politics in my presence. Her intuition about the sincerity of individuals was more accurate than that of her husband."

Mary was sensitive to the patronage practice of the time. She believed she had an intuitive sense of who would serve her husband well in the cabinet, and she was not above writing letters to various politicians to encour-

*Born in 1843, Robert (left), the eldest child of the Lincolns, appears as he did when he attended Harvard during the Civil War years. Of all the Lincoln children, Robert seemed the most distant from his parents. Tad (center), whose proper name was Thomas and the baby of the family, was only seven years old in 1860. He enjoyed playing soldier by dressing in a lieutenant colonel's uniform and was known to give "orders" to the White House staff and to pay visits to Union soldiers while wearing the clothes of his "rank." Studious Willie (right) seemed to be the favorite of both his parents. His fever-racked death shattered the Lincolns, and those who knew Mary well claimed she never got over his untimely passing.*

age them to support one or another patronage seeker.• At
WCD the same time, °Mary was inordinately susceptible to flattery. As a result, she was often manipulated by people who wanted something from her husband.

Varina Davis, on the other hand, was not vulnerable to flattery, and men did not seek her out to get the president's ear. Instead there was a widespread notion that the Confederate first lady exploited her influence on her husband throughout the war. Officers who fell afoul of her soon found themselves dealt with harshly by Davis.•

While politics and patronage were not unfamiliar to her, Varina's primary duties as first lady were always focused on her children. By 1862 she had one daughter
JC and three young sons. °Of course she was required to attend certain public functions, but she was scrupulous in managing her schedule to allow sufficient time to be with her children.•

Mary Lincoln was equally devoted to her three children: Robert, Tad, and Willie. Like her Confederate counterpart,
LT Mary had also lost a son before the war. °She was

*Although Mary posed with a smile for this Mathew Brady photograph, her years as the first lady of the splintered nation brought her more sorrow than joy. In addition to her other problems, Mrs. Lincon was involved in a serious carriage accident on July 2, 1863. The incident occurred when the driver's seat came loose, frightening the horses which took off in a mad gallop. Mary pitched headlong from the runaway vehicle, striking her skull on a rock. At first it seemed that she had suffered only bruises and slight cuts, but the incisions became infected, and for three weeks she lay feverish and bedridden. The wounds healed, but Mary appeared to have more frequent headaches after this occurrence, and her son Robert later believed the mishap contributed to her mental decline.*

a wonderful mother to her sons and doted on them, treating them as equals.•

In February 1862 the first of many unending tragedies began to take their toll on the Lincolns. While they were hosting a lavish ball on the first floor of the White House, Willie was upstairs with a fever that developed, it was thought, when Mary had allowed him to ride during a rain. More likely he had contracted typhoid by drinking water from the Potomac River, which was polluted from the camps of thousands of soldiers stationed around Washington. °Willie was the son most like his father—gentle and kind. If Mary had been asked who her favorite was, like most mothers she would not have answered but secretly she would have thought it was Willie.• Two weeks after the ball the Lincolns lost their eleven-year-old son.

°After Willie died in the White House, in Mary's eyes the mansion lost its aura as a glorious home and Washington lost its sense of wonderfulness. To her, both were places of death, destruction, misery, and despair.• She never again entered Willie's bedroom or the room in which he was embalmed for burial.

Mary was not alone in her grief. Lincoln had trouble sleeping but had happy dreams of being with Willie, only to wake up to the sad recognition of his lost son. Unlike Mary, the president would lock himself in Willie's room for a few moments every Thursday, to mourn his son and observe the day of the week on which he had died. Complicating matters even more, Tad developed the same illness in the weeks that followed Willie's death, and both parents found some comfort in caring for him. For nearly a year all social activities at the Executive Mansion were suspended. Finally, Mary came out of her depression and said, "If I had not felt the spur of necessity urging me to cheer Mr. Lincoln, whose grief was as great as my own, I could never have smiled again."

*Accustomed to fine clothing, Mary often ran up large bills buying exquisite gowns. Her taste for such finery drew the ire of her husband's political opponents and Washington society women who thought Mrs. Lincoln's habiliments proved too thin a veneer to hide her "crude" western manners. One Democratic paper commented scathingly that Mary was "a fool—the laughing stock of her town, her vulgarity only the more conspicuous in consequence of her fine carriage and horses and servants in livery and fine dresses, and her damnable airs."*

LT °Yet she could not resign herself to Willie's loss and sought comfort in spiritualism. Spiritualism was prevalent in the nineteenth century because so many young lives were taken so suddenly without a chance for loved ones to say good-bye. Many people consulted spiritualists to contact the dead. Mary began attending séances and hosted a few at the White House, which Lincoln himself attended
JB once or twice to please his wife.• °This was further evidence of the strength of their marriage: Lincoln as a husband was not embarrassed by the fact that his wife was having séances in the White House and even supported her.•

Spiritualists comforted Mary through her period of mourning, but the White House séances merely added fuel to the press's mounting war of words against the first lady. She was not alone in this, because the Richmond press scrutinized Varina, too. Criticizing and satirizing political leaders had been a time-honored tradition by the press, but attacking their wives was something new. The burden of living in the public eye was almost too much for both women to bear.

WCD °This was one of the unfortunate precedents set during the Civil War. Mary Lincoln was attacked for her extravagant spending and her fancy ball gowns. Varina Davis was attacked for what some perceived to be a rather bumpkinish, country way about her, when she should presumably be more dignified. Yet Varina was also condemned for having an imperious manner. Like her Northern counterpart, a newspaper dubbed her queen too, "Queen Varina."•

MARY LINCOLN was particularly susceptible to criticism as the war dragged on into its third year. "The people scrutinize every article I wear with critical curiosity. The very fact of having come from the west subjects me to more searching observations," she wrote in 1864.

As the war intensified, newspapers accused Mary Lincoln of being a Southern sympathizer because of her Kentucky heritage and the fact that three of her brothers and a brother-in-law fought with the Confederacy. Such LT charges were made with no basis in fact. °She was no Southern sympathizer even though three of her brothers were killed. Their deaths saddened her, but she depersonalized her sorrow as only she could by saying, "They would destroy our country and they would kill my husband if they could."•

In December 1863 Mary Lincoln's loyalty came under scrutiny again when her Rebel sister Emilie Todd LT Helm was a guest at the White House. °Emilie's husband, Brig. Gen. Benjamin Hardin Helm, had been killed at the battle of Chickamauga. Soothing grieving widows was nothing new for the Lincolns, but Helm had been a Confederate general, a man who had turned down a major's commission in the Union army from Lincoln. After her husband's death, Emilie wanted to return to her family in Lexington, Kentucky. Union authorities, however, would not let her pass through Federal territory unless she swore an oath of loyalty to the Union. Angry at the Union that had killed her husband, she refused. When the case was brought to the president's attention, Lincoln told the officers, "Send her to me." The defiant, angry, aggrieved Rebel widow ended up in the White House. The newspapers were astounded.• She stayed for two weeks and then left for Lexington, steadfastly refusing to take a loyalty oath to the government that had killed her husband.

While she was trying to cope with public criticism just as Mary Lincoln was, Varina Davis lost a second JC child, just as Mary Lincoln had. °Five-year-old Joseph was playing on the balcony of the Confederate White House, probably climbing on the railing at the far left corner. He lost his footing and fell almost twenty feet to the brick pavement below, breaking his neck. His death devastated his parents.• Davis was in his office when he received the news. When other messengers arrived with news from the front, he said: "I cannot do it. I cannot. I cannot." He went upstairs and stayed all night in a vigil over his lost son. While Varina was heard shrieking in

Northern politicians and military leaders—including General Grant, who stands right of center with his right hand on his hip—surround President and Mrs. Lincoln at a White House reception celebrating the surrender of the South's Army of Northern Virginia. In the brief interim between this and John Wilkes Booth's desperate act, Mary and Abraham seemed to find a reawakened interest in one another. They went for relaxing walks and carriage rides, during which they discussed travel plans and the future of the children. Mary remembered that during this time her husband was once again "cheery—funny [and] in high spirits."

agony, he was heard pacing back and forth overhead. The next morning he was back at his desk, doing what he had to do as the Confederate president. Two months after Joseph's death, Varina's grief was assuaged when she gave birth to her sixth and last child, Varina Ann, nicknamed Winnie.

As the conflict dragged into the fourth year, the physical and emotional burdens of the war had taken its toll on both presidential families. °Mary Lincoln was truly interested in the progress of the war and followed it, but when the news was too depressing, too frightening, too morbid, she found release in her séances and her shopping. Lincoln withdrew from her and stopped confiding in her, which shocked her. The change had nothing to do with loss of affection; it was simply his preoccupation with the conduct of the war.• Lincoln consoled himself with the belief that once the war was over, he and Mary would rebuild what they had once had.

°On the last day of his life, they took a carriage ride together, as they frequently did. She remembered his saying, "We must be more cheerful, between the war and the loss of our darling Willie, we have both been very miserable."• The Lincolns discussed their hopes for the future. The war was all but over. The killing had stopped. Lincoln looked forward to rebuilding the country.

*This portrait of Mary was painted by Francis Bicknell Carpenter in 1865 before the assassination of President Lincoln. The beginning of that fateful year seemed to hold a brighter promise for Mrs. Lincoln, as the Confederacy was in its death throes and Mary had finally begun to put Willie's death behind her. The horrifying crash of a madman's derringer, however, dashed forevermore Mary Todd Lincoln's hopes for a happy future.*

THE EVENING of April 14, 1865, was supposed to be a time of celebration for the Lincolns, and they chose to attend a play at Ford's Theatre, *Our American Cousin,* with Maj. Henry Rathbone and Clara Harris. The Grants had been invited to accompany the Lincolns, but Julia Grant was weary of Mary Lincoln's erratic behavior and the couple declined.

°The Lincolns enjoyed the theater, and this was the first play they had attended since the war began. At one point Mary leaned toward her husband, put her arm through his, smiled up at him, and whispered, "What will Miss Harris think of me hanging on to you so?"

The president whispered back, "She won't think a thing about it."•

Those were his last words. Moments later a shot rang out, and the president collapsed in his chair with a bullet from a single-shot pistol lodged in his brain. The assassin, John Wilkes Booth, an actor and Confederate sympathizer, vaulted to the stage and fled.

Lincoln was rushed across the street to a house owned by William Petersen, a merchant-tailor, and put in bed as doctors rushed to the scene. Mary watched as they carried him out and wailed, "Oh, my God, and have I given my husband to die?"

°She straggled across the street to the Petersen house and sat in the parlor, wringing her hands, weeping, and crying.• Once allowed into the bedroom to see him, she became uncontrollable and was removed from the room. Lincoln's cabinet officers gave orders not to let "that woman" return. They, however, crowded around him although they could do nothing for the president other than witness his last hours.

°Lincoln never regained consciousness; his brain had been virtually destroyed. He made no sound apart from wracking breaths. As dawn came, he died.•

Millions of mourners watched the funeral train take the president's casket to his burial site in Springfield, but Mary Lincoln was prostrate in the White House, unable to pull herself together to attend. As was the custom of the time, bereavement became the occasion to demonstrate one's deepest emotions. Elizabeth Keckley, the first lady's seamstress, recalled the scene: "The wails of a broken heart, the unearthly shrieks, tempestuous outbursts of grief from soul."

In May 1865 the widowed first lady descended the White House steps for the last time, and Washington society heaped one final cruelty upon her. Now that the president was dead, the cabinet members, congressmen, and senators saw no need to say anything comforting to his widow. Their political loyalties had already shifted, and they had no time for an emotionally disturbed woman whom they had never liked. She said good-bye to Elizabeth Keckley, then she and Tad embarked by train for Chicago. She could not bear to return to their former home in Springfield. Keckley commented: "There was scarcely a friend to tell her good-bye. The silence was almost painful."

A month earlier the first lady of the Confederacy had also left her White House in Richmond, but under much different circumstances. Before the war's end, Varina Davis and her family had fled south through the Carolinas. With the Federals slowly surrounding Richmond, she feared what would happen to her husband. Davis finally caught up with his family in Georgia. With a handful of guards, they hoped to cross the Mississippi and possibly enter Mexico.

By this time Lincoln had been assassinated, and Davis was wanted for his alleged part in the conspir-
JC acy. °Federal cavalry combed the countryside looking for the Confederate president and co-conspirator.• On the morning of May 19, 1865, Union horse soldiers surrounded the Davis camp in Irwinville, Georgia. The fugitive president was arrested and sent to Fort Monroe in Virginia, while Varina and the children were put under house arrest in Savannah, Georgia.

LLC °Davis's prison years were Varina's finest hour. From the moment he was captured, she began considering ways to have him released. She wrote to everyone she knew and had known in Washington, begging them to intervene in his behalf, including President Andrew Johnson, with whom Davis had feuded quite often when the two of them served in the House and Senate together before the war.•

*On April 14, 1865, John Wilkes Booth entered a side door at Ford's Theatre and walked up a flight of stairs to a position behind the seats occupied by President Lincoln and his wife. Booth then pulled a small pistol from his coat and fired a bullet into Abraham Lincoln's brain. "They have shot the president! They have shot the president!" Mary screamed as she struggled to hold her bleeding spouse and prevent him from slumping over in his chair. Throughout the night, an anguished, inconlsolable Mary kept vigil for her dying husband, at times begging him to regain consciousness and speak to her. Her remonstrations were in vain, and Mary was forced to don mourning clothes as pictured above.*

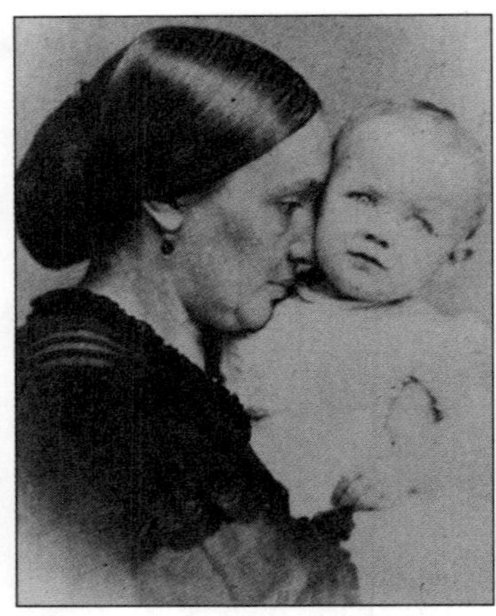

*Varina caresses her youngest daughter, Varina Anne, or "Winnie," (above) who was born in 1864. After the war, Southern veterans christened Winnie the "Daughter of the Confederacy" because of her wartime birth. They nearly revoked the title when Winnie became engaged to the grandson of a famous abolitionist. Varina disliked his weak finances and forbade the wedding. Winnie never married and died in 1898 from complications brought on by malaria.*

*Varina's sister Margaret "Maggie" Graham Howell (below), stayed in Richmond for much of the Civil War. She was known for her good humor, and one contemporary considered Maggie a "bright spot" in the often "somber-tinted" atmosphere that pervaded Richmond at that time.*

"How can honest men and gentlemen from your country stand idly by to see a gentleman maligned, insulted, tortured, and denied the right of trial by the usual forms of law?" Varina wrote in 1865 in the first of many pleading letters. She was not exaggerating. Davis was at first kept shackled in a cell. A light was kept on in his cell constantly, and a guard stayed near him at all times but was not permitted to speak to him. To Varina, such poor treatment was horrible for a man who had simply acted on his political beliefs.

In 1867 pressure grew in Washington to release Davis, and a number of wealthy northerners, including Cornelius Vanderbilt, offered to pay his bond. Following a pro forma hearing, Davis was released, but in the years ahead he was never tried. As for the assassination of President Lincoln, John Wilkes Booth and eight other conspirators were found guilty. Four of them, including the mother of one of the conspirators, were hanged. No evidence was ever found implicating Davis or any member of the Confederate government in Booth's plot.

For Davis, freedom left him and his family with an
LLC unsettled future. ○They traveled abroad for some years, and he eventually took a job with a life insurance company in Memphis, Tennessee.• In 1876 he began work on his memoirs, *The Rise and Fall of the Confederate Government*. He was still without a career position that would help him provide for his family. A wealthy southern widow, Sarah Dorsey, learned of Davis's situation and invited him to live and write on her plantation, Beauvoir, in Biloxi, Mississippi. Davis accepted immediately, without telling Varina.

LLC ○Varina had left the country to see a doctor in England because she thought she might have a heart condition. When she read about Davis's moving to the widow's Mississippi home in the English newspapers, she was humiliated.• She returned to Memphis but refused to join her husband in Mississippi and live under another woman's roof. In 1877 she wrote her husband: "I do not desire ever to see her house. When people here ask me what part of your book she is writing, I feel aggravated nearly to death."

*Like Mary Lincoln, Varina Howell Davis also wore the black clothes of mourning (above left) and knew too well the pain of losing children. Only one of her six offspring, her daughter Margaret, outlived her.*

*The Davis brood (above right) was photographed in 1867. Jefferson Jr. (left) was born in 1857 and died in 1878 of yellow fever. Next to him is Margaret, the oldest surviving child at the time. William (third from left), born in 1861, stands next to Margaret and stares at the camera with a bemused expression. He died in the 1870s from disease. Winnie, the baby of the family, is at the far right. The eldest child, Samuel, had died in 1854 at age two; and Joseph, born in 1859, had fallen to his death from a veranda of the Confederate White House in 1864.*

LLC °Davis's relationship to Sarah Dorsey was the subject of much gossip, with some people guessing that Dorsey had a romantic interest in the former Confederate president, but there is no evidence there was any kind of intimacy between them. Varina lived apart from her husband for almost a year before she finally capitulated and joined him at Beauvoir.•

MARY LINCOLN was having her own problems adapting to postwar America. After spending several years in Chicago, she and Tad went to live in Europe, seeking refuge from what she called "the vampire press." They returned in 1871, and eighteen-year-old Tad became seriously ill. While his doctors were not sure of the problem, it was later diagnosed as intractable pleurisy,
LT °the formation of fluid in the sacks around the lung. There was no cure. Mary maintained a death vigil over him until he died. She then began another series of spiritualist encounters,• endless visits to health spas, and occasional panics on the anniversaries of the deaths of her husband and children.

JB °According to Robert Todd Lincoln, her eldest and now only surviving son, his mother's behavior became increas-

*Fearful of being cast as a coward, the Lincoln's oldest son, Robert, wanted to join the Union army after he received his degree from Harvard in 1864. Mary, however, adamantly opposed the idea, fearful she would lose yet another son. "I know that Robert's plan to go into the Army is manly and noble . . . ," Mary beseeched her husband, "but oh! I am frightened he may never come back to us." Robert, though, kept after his father to obtain him a comission. Eventually, his pressure paid off, and he served in the Army of the Potomac as a captain on General Grant's staff. Grant ensured that Robert spent the majority of his time in quiet rear areas and never faced any serious danger.*

ingly aberrant. She was buying things she did not need, like ten pairs of gloves and fourteen scarves, and she was spending more and more time with spiritualists. Robert decided that his mother should be institutionalized.•

LT °His actions have been described as despicable. Robert hired Pinkerton detectives to trace her movements and carefully rounded up doctors, hotel maids, waiters, and store clerks to testify about her unusual behavior. He swore out a warrant for her arrest as a lunatic, "for her benefit and the safety of the community." Robert then avoided his mother until they saw each other in court. He even hired a defense attorney for her, a longtime family friend, with the strict injunction that he not offer a defense.•

On May 19, 1875, the former first lady was brought to a courtroom in the massive Cook County Courthouse. She endured a three-hour description of her unsoundness of mind from seventeen witnesses. The first five were doctors who in one voice stated Mary Lincoln should be institutionalized, even though they had never interviewed her and had only heard of her peculiar behavior from Robert and his lawyers.

JB °The most devastating testimony was that of a doctor who happened to be a friend of Robert's. He had heard Mary Lincoln say that she had headaches and the headaches felt as if someone was pulling strings out of her brain.•

Several hotel employees testified next and reported that Mrs. Lincoln "was not like ladies in general." She was terrified of being alone and often paid one of them to spend the night in her room. Some days she spoke of hearing voices through the walls. She also believed that someone watched her through the small window in her bathroom. One day she claimed the South Side of Chicago was on fire and had the hotel manager send her trunks to Milwaukee for safety.

Salesclerks related stories of her extravagant taste and purchases in quantity. One had sold her three watches, and the next day she returned two. Another had sold her several sets of lace curtains that remained unopened in her room. A last reported that she haggled with him over the price of gloves and handkerchiefs.

Robert was the final witness. He related several stories of difficult moments with his mother and then condemned her to an asylum by saying: "I have no doubt my mother is insane. She has long been a source of great anxiety to me. She has no home and no reason to make these purchases."

JB °Mary Lincoln's attorney said nothing in her defense and simply agreed with the witnesses that Robert had organized.• While the jury deliberated the "evidence," Robert approached his mother and tried to take her hand. Mary cried aloud, "Oh, Robert, to think that my son would do this to me." Within ten minutes the all-male jury returned with the verdict that the former first lady was insane. The following day she was committed to Bellevue Sanitarium, near Chicago, in the town of Batavia.

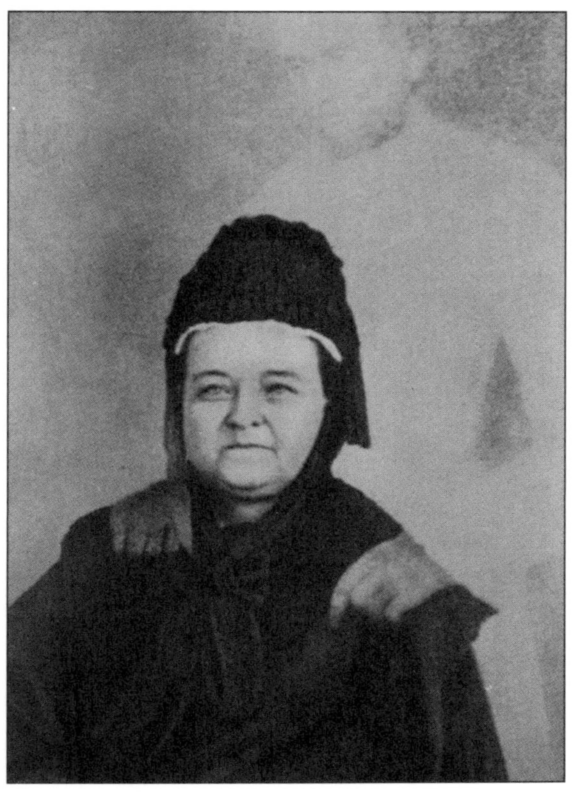

*Mary turned to spiritualism in a sad effort to keep in touch with her dead sons and husband. She once told a friend that the spirit of Willie visited her "every night," and he would stand at the "foot of [my] bed with the same sweet adorable smile" he had when he was alive. "Sometimes," said Mary, "Little Eddie" would be with his brother. In 1872 a photographer who claimed he could capture the "essence" of dead relatives took this image purporting to show Mary in the presence of her husband's protective ghost. Mary was far from alone in her interest in contacting deceased relatives. The high infant mortality rate of the nineteenth century caused many Americans to try to communicate with dead children, and several spiritualist fads swept the country during that time.*

Mary Lincoln stayed in Bellevue only three months and three weeks. During that time she was a model patient and required no medication or restraint. Through the intervention of one of the few women attorneys in the country, Myra Bradwell, she gained her release.

LT °Bradwell accepted Mary's case as a cause for women's rights because Mary Lincoln was not the only woman of the day railroaded into a mental hospital when she became hysterical or troublesome. That her case was typical was one of the sad features of Victorian society.• "Mary Lincoln is no more insane than I am," said Bradwell in 1872.

JB °Although freed from the institution, Mary Lincoln carried the burden of having been once judged insane. She more likely was highly neurotic, which was inconvenient for her son, Robert.• His motives in institutionalizing his mother were never clear. He may have been protecting his own political career by trying to distance himself from his mother and by stopping the constant attention being paid to her by the press. He had begun a bureaucratic career in which he played various roles in the administrations of several presidents—including

*Robert Todd Lincoln (above), the couple's only child to reach adulthood, served two presidents as secretary of war, was U.S. minister to great Britain, and president of the Pullman Railroad Car Company. Though his successes accrued him wealth and a handsome Vermont estate, Robert remained continually troubled by the demeanor of his suffering mother. On one occasion, Robert wrote a biographer of his father, pleading with him not to "mention" his mother in the text, contending "it would not be pleasant for her . . . to be made public property . . . in that way."*

two more assassinated presidents, James A. Garfield and William B. McKinley.

Mary Lincoln never forgave her only surviving son for his actions. On July 16, 1882, she suffered a stroke and died in her sister Elizabeth's home in Springfield. She was sixty-four years old when she was finally reunited with her martyred husband at Oak Ridge Cemetery in Springfield. One pastor spoke of two pines that had grown so close their roots were intertwined. When one was struck by lightning, the other wasted away. "With the one that lingered, it was only a slow death from the same cause. When Abraham Lincoln died, she died," the Reverend James A. Reed eulogized.

VARINA DAVIS outlived Mary Lincoln by twenty-four years. She also survived her husband, who died in 1889, and except for her eldest daughter, Margaret, she outlived all her children.

When Varina arrived at Beauvoir, Sarah Dorsey relinquished to her the role of Davis's secretary. In February 1879 Dorsey was stricken with cancer and moved to New Orleans to be near her doctors. She wanted the Davises to stay at Beauvoir and offered to sell it to them for $5,500 to be paid in three installments. Davis made one payment of the three before Dorsey died. In her will she bequeathed the estate to him.

In the spring of 1880 Davis completed his book, *The Rise and Fall of the Confederate Government.* It was not a financial success, and Davis rationalized that he had not written it for profit but to "set the righteous motives of the South before the world."

For the next decade the Davises found a sense of serenity and peace at Beauvoir. Old friends, including some northerners, came to visit, and Davis proved to be a genial host, positioning chairs near the window of the parlor or taking his guests onto the verandah to enjoy the sea breezes and chat. With Varina's help, he continued to write short pieces for various magazines.

Davis fell ill after a routine trip to Brierfield. He returned only as far as New Orleans, where Varina joined him and watched over him until he died on December 6, 1889. Following his death, she took an active role in securing his place and that of the Confederacy in history. She made sure southern museums had artifacts from the Davises, including letters she and her husband had written to each other. Yet she also recognized that she had her own life to live.

GC ○She did not want to stay on the Mississippi Gulf Coast with nothing to do. Publishing friends encouraged her to write her memoirs, which resulted in a history and defense of the Confederacy, a biography of Davis, and an autobiography of Varina. When the writing was finished, Varina moved to New York to work on the proofs for the book and decided to stay permanently. She worked for the rest of her life writing articles for various newspapers under an arrangement with Joseph Pulitzer. Many southerners were infuriated that Varina had abandoned the South for the North, but she believed she could heal some of the lingering sectional wounds. She forgave the North; the North did not have to forgive her.•

One surprising friendship that developed during her years in New York was with Julia Grant, the widow of U. S. Grant. They met when Varina visited West Point in June 1893. Varina wrote a tribute to

*The former president of the Confederacy and his wife posed for this picture in 1868, not long after his release from Fortress Monroe. During Jefferson's imprisonment, Varina worked diligently to free her husband. The strain the Davises had undergone is evident on their faces.*

*Deeded to them by an admirer, Beauvoir (below left) was the last home of Jefferson and Varina Davis. Shaded by live oak trees and facing the Gulf of Mexico, the dwelling provided them with a sense of security. Here the Davises wrote their memoirs. After Jefferson's death, Varina donated Beauvoir to the state of Mississippi and it became a home for Confederate veterans. Now restored as it was when the Davises lived there, Beauvoir is open to the public in Biloxi, Mississippi.*

*Throughout her life, Varina Davis sought respite from the turmoil of political life in her children, and she relished her roles as mother, grandmother, and great-grandmother. Varina's daughters Margaret (left) and Winnie (right) are shown striking a teatime pose (right).*

*In the photograph below, an aged Varina sits surrounded by the progeny of her daughter Margaret. The former Confederate first lady is holding her great-granddaughter, Varina Margaret Webb; her granddaughter, Mrs. Varina Howell Hayes Webb, stands wearing the light-colored dress; Margaret is seated to her right.*

Grant for the *New York World* and was a guest at the dedication of Grant's Tomb in Riverside Park in 1897. Four years later she wrote a second tribute for the paper, which included a notation: "Mrs. Jefferson Davis has been living in New York City for several years, respected by men and women of both North and South and dearly beloved by all who are privileged to know her personally."

On October 16, 1906, eighty-year-old Varina Davis, who was suffering from pneumonia, died. The U.S. Military Band played "Dixie" as she was laid to rest next to her husband in Richmond's Hollywood Cemetery. The *Richmond News Leader* reported her death and commented, "She was one of the last living mementoes of the Confederate government, one of the last of all to die."

THE TWO first ladies of the Civil War passed away without ever meeting. Neither woman had ever written or spoken about the other. Yet Mary Lincoln and

Varina Davis shared a lifetime of common tragedies and each left her own legacy.

JC °Varina Davis in the end had become a citizen of a united country again. She had diffused, perhaps, some of the criticism the people had made of her earlier in her life. Mary Lincoln did not have the same kind of attention and tribute when she
LT died.• Instead, °she had the worst reputation of any first lady, which she did not deserve. Instead of seeing her as an eccentric, history should look at her as a misunderstood victim of her times. She did have a profound influence in that she changed the attitude of the public toward the president's wife. No longer was it sufficient for Mrs. President to hide in the shadows. Ever after, for good or for ill, significant attention has been paid to the wife of the president.•

*After the death of her husband in 1889, Varina Davis moved to New York City, another controversial act in a controversial life. Newspaper magnate Joseph Pulitzer—a relative by marriage—helped her become a writer for various periodicals, thus ensuring her financial stability during her last years. This image was taken shortly before her death of pneumonia on October 16, 1906. The courage and fortitude Varina exhibited during her life and her efforts to achieve national reconciliation after the war make her a model of what a first lady should be.*

The whims of history played curiously with these two women. Mary Lincoln saw the war end in glorious victory, and five days later her world was shattered when her husband was mortally wounded in a darkened theater. Varina Davis suffered the humiliation and hardships of defeat, became a fugitive, saw her husband's capture, incarceration, and vilification. Yet she went on to become a symbol of national reconciliation and ended her days honored in the North as well as the South.

# CIVILIANS IN THE WAR

*Prior to* THE AMERICAN CIVIL War, wars were fought mostly by professional soldiers organized into large armies. Battles were staged on plains particularly suited for the maneuvering of thousands of men. Towns that might be in the way of the armies were often occupied but did not usually become part of the battlefield itself.

When war broke out between the American states in 1861, most civilians never expected to be in harm's way. They contributed their sons and husbands to the war effort and possibly anticipated helping the cause by rolling cartridges or bandages or manufacturing munitions. Americans expected to read about the war in their newspapers, dreading only the days when casualty lists were published.

The Northern population especially believed it was safe. Awakening one morning to the sight of smoke on the horizon and the roar of cannon in the distance was something most likely to happen in the South. Yet for some Northerners the murderous conflict trespassed upon their very doorsteps. In this way the Civil War engulfed everyone and everything in its path, including the occasional desperate human tide of noncombatants, such as fifteen-year-old Tillie Pierce, twenty-year-old Jennie Wade, and sixty-nine-year-old John Burns of Gettysburg who endured the horrors of the battle that raged around them. In the South, however, the hardships inflicted on the population were lengthy and merciless. Those who survived had been tested with fire. "If this war has developed some of the most brutal, bestial

| | |
|---|---|
| EC | Elwood Christ |
| CC | Catherine Clinton |
| GAC | Gregory A. Coco |
| WCD | William C. Davis |
| BP | Brian Pohanka |
| CS | Cindy Small |

*Support for the Confederacy and its secession was not universal south of the Mason-Dixon Line. One strong pocket of Unionist sympathy was in the northwestern portion of Virginia, and by the end of 1861 more than twelve thousand men from that region, such as these in Morgantown, had joined the federal army to fight for "Union and Liberty." The strength of this pro-Northern sentiment culminated in the formation of the Reorganized Government of Virginia, which officially joined the Union in 1863 as the state of West Virginia.*

and devilish qualities lurking in the human race, it has also shown how much of the angel there is in the best men and women," wrote Mary Livermore in 1863.

For those towns that became battle zones, the war's approach followed a tragic pattern. The first hint of trouble usually came in the form of rumors. WCD °Stories would circulate that an army was marching toward an area. If an army was following a road that led past a town, sooner or later it would be in that town. The first visual sign of an approaching army would be skirmishers and scouts reconnoitering the advance. Hours before the army's arrival, there would be a sudden increase in the number of deer and small animals running through the fields around the town.• Animals scurrying through Federal camps had given advanced warning of Confederate surprise attacks at Shiloh in 1862 and at Chancellorsville in 1863, although many of the city-bred Union soldiers failed to interpret the wildlife activity correctly.

Although it took time for the Federal and Confederate armies to amass at Gettysburg in 1863, the mammoth confrontation began with the same pattern of rumor and encroachment. The townspeople had plenty of warning that a Southern army was heading their way. On June 28, 1863, a force of Confederates under Maj. Gen. Jubal Early arrived at the small Pennsylvania crossroads. The advance cavalrymen rode through the town square shooting their pistols in the air and looting some stores. Early ordered the town's merchants to provide him with clothing and money or he would put the town to the torch. After gathering some supplies, the Rebels departed. Farther north several farmers near Harrisburg, the state capital, fled into the city to escape the approach of Maj. Gen. Richard Ewell's men who threatened to capture and burn the capital.

Anyone who could read a map and suspected that the Union army would be in pursuit of the Confederates would have recognized the danger in which Get-

*In East Tennessee Union sympathies were not as prevalent as they were in northwestern Virginia and divergent loyalties split apart neighborhoods and families. Tennessee was the last state to secede from the Union, but its mountainous eastern third remained largely pro-Union, except for Knoxville, the largest city in the region. For a short while after the war started, the opposing factions there coexisted well enough to hold rival recruiting rallies beneath their respective flags at opposite ends of the same street as seen in this drawing. However, in May 1861 gunfire broke up a pro-Union gathering, and in June a statewide plebiscite voted for secession. The East Tennessee counties tried to leave the state and remain in the Union, but Confederate military occupation squelched the effort. Some Union supporters moved away and others conducted guerrilla-type activities. Disagreements between Unionists and Confederates in East Tennessee continued long after the war was over.*

tysburg found itself—eleven roads intersected the town. If a Rebel force scattered to the west, north, and northeast was trying to concentrate its numbers in the face of a Northern army advancing from the south, it was obvious that the two opposing forces would meet near Gettysburg.

Strangers, possibly Southern spies, had been in and around the town for several days. On June 30, a brigade of Federal cavalry took a position to the west of the town.

Being trapped between two armies transformed the lives of civilians, throwing them into living from moment to moment. Their peaceful lives were shattered by the almost surreal sight of savage fighting on the same fields and streets they had used for years. Women became widows, children became orphans, and families unraveled as the maelstrom of war destroyed everything in sight.

The war was terrifying enough for civilian adults, but for children the drawing of battle lines must have been even more of a shock. Just days before the war's most important battle, fifteen-year-old Tillie Pierce, daughter of Gettysburg's butcher, led a nearly idyllic existence in this quiet Pennsylvania town. In 1886 thirty-eight-year-old Tillie Pierce recorded her memories of the battle in *At Gettysburg: Or What a Girl Saw and Heard of the Battle,* beginning with a pleasant reminiscence of life before the battle: "Gettysburg is my native place. It is most pleasantly located in a healthful region of the country,

*In the early years of the Civil War Southern women were as enthusiastic about the prospects of the Confederacy as their menfolk. The romance and drama of war caught the imagination of both sexes as can be seen in the photograph above of a young woman posing proudly beside her dashing soldier. As the conflict wore on, however, women of the South such as in the family pictured below keenly felt the absence of their husbands and fathers, many of whom fell under the hails of musketry and shellfire.*

near the southern border of Pennsylvania. Fondly do I cherish the scenes of my childhood. There, our merry peals of laughter mingled with the sweet warbling of birds. What pleasant times were ours."

During the course of three days of battle, the conflict changed and matured Tillie Pierce. Her honest account of these wartime experiences presents a unique perspective of the engagement. °She was not one of the generals trying to make excuses thirty years later in a book written to make him look good. Nor was she a soldier trying to inflate her own experience for some reason. Nor was she trying to gain political office. She was just a resident of Gettysburg who, as a teenager, witnessed these horrific events.•

Tillie Pierce's initiation to the killing fields started in earnest on July 1, 1863, the first day of the battle. Early that morning a Confederate division under Maj. Gen. Henry Heth approached the town from the west. He was under orders from Robert E. Lee not to bring on a "general engagement," and Heth believed the only opposition he might face would be militia, the same men who had run from Early's soldiers a week earlier. Heth's men, however, stumbled into two brigades of Union cavalry under Brig. Gen. John Buford.

When Tillie's parents realized that the immediate area west of town was engulfed in full-scale fighting, they decided to send her to what they hoped would be a safe place far from the shooting. With a neighbor, Henrietta Schriver, and Schriver's two children, Tillie started out on foot from downtown Gettysburg by way of Baltimore Street toward the farm of Jacob Weikert, Mrs. Schriver's father. The Weikert farm, several miles away, lay beyond the south end of Cemetery Ridge, a low ridge that ran behind the town. The Weikerts lived near two small wooded hills at the end of Cemetery Ridge that were known as Big and Little Round Top.

Tillie described the beginning of the journey: "About one o'clock we started out on foot, the battle still going on. They told us to hurry as fast as possible, that we were in great danger of being shot by the rebels. As we looked toward the Seminary Ridge [west side of town], I could see and hear the confusion of the battle—

troops moving hither and thither, smoke of conflict arising from the fields, shells bursting in the air. These things, beheld for the first time, filled my soul with the greatest of apprehensions."

The small entourage took the Taneytown road, which was one of the routes being used to rush Union reinforcements into action. Although Schriver, Tillie, and the children were walking away from the fighting, Federal casualties began appearing along the roadside, having been sent back from the fighting in McPherson's Woods and along Willoughby Run to the west and from Oak Hill in the north.

*John Minor Botts, shown here with his family, pushed the limits of free speech in the Confederacy. A Union sympathizer, he did not hesitate to criticize the new government in Richmond and oppose the right of Virginia to secede from the Union. Botts was summarily arrested for his views in 1862. Released after agreeing not to berate the Confederacy in its own capital, Botts moved with his family to an estate named Auburn in Culpeper County, Virginia. Ironically, this placed him at one of the crossroads of the war, where he faced the same trials as other farmers of the area. Following a cavalry review hosted by Confederate Gen. J. E. B. Stuart that trampled much of his corn crop, Botts personally lodged his complaint to Stuart. A camp servant reported that "Mr. Botts ripped and rarred and snorted but Genrul Stuart warn't put out none at all." Stuart listened to the disgruntled gentleman but made no move to compensate or apologize for the damage.*

"While traveling along," Tillie recalled, "we were overtaken by a wagon in which was the body of a dead soldier. Some of the men told us that it was the body of General [John] Reynolds, and that he had been killed during the forenoon in battle."

Forty-three-year-old Maj. Gen. John Reynolds of Lancaster, Pennsylvania, was one of the rising stars in the Union army and commanded a wing of the army consisting of the First, Third, and Ninth Corps. He was personally placing regiments in the line in McPherson's Woods when a Confederate felled him, killing him instantly.

Danger seemed to mount for the young women as they moved farther from the fighting. One soldier, realizing their peril, stopped a passing wagon and helped them to board it. As the battle intensified, it became more expedient to get the refugees down the Taneytown road and to the relative safety of the Weikert farm. "What a ride!" Tillie remembered. "I will never forget it. The wagon had no springs, and as the driver was anxious to put the greatest distance between himself and the battle in the least time possible, the jolting and bumping were brought out to perfection. At last, we reached Mr. Weikert's and were gladly welcomed into their home."

The little group of women had unknowingly moved to one of the battle's next hot spots. The Weikert farm

*Civilian life in the South quickly became one of anxiety and fear. Rumors of impending battles kept many Southerners on edge. When it appeared that Savannah, Georgia, would be attacked in 1861, panic gripped the city's citizens (above left). The news turned out to be false. However, frequently throughout the four-year struggle, civilians, many of whom were women and children, were caught in or near battles.*

*Unable to feel safe in their homes, some Union sympathizers in the South packed their belongings and fled the Confederacy. The engraving by Thomas Nast (above right) appeared in the September 19, 1863, edition of* Harper's Weekly *and evokes the fear and uncertainty these refugees felt. However, fleeing the loathing glances and harassment meted out by former friends and neighbors as well as the prospect of confiscation of their property by the Confederate army appeared to be the only chance for survival for these families.*

was on the eastern side of Little Round Top, one of the highest points along the high ground of the battlefield. During the second and third days of the battle the Round Tops would be one of the anchoring points of the Union line and the scene of fierce fighting.•

When Jacob Weikert sensed the danger, he also realized there was no use in abandoning the farm; finding a safer location seemed impossible. For her part, Tillie tried to make herself useful.

"The infantry began coming," she recalled. "I was not long in learning what I could do. Obtaining a bucket, I hastened to the spring, and carried water for the moving column."

GAC The soldiers appreciated Tillie's efforts. °Many of them probably had sisters her age. From her perspective it must have been a fascinating sight—the officers on horseback and the men moving along in a wave of blue. Tillie began doing what she could to aid and comfort them.• This contact with the soldiers pro-
EC foundly affected her; °she saw things a fifteen-year-old would normally never see. The wounded were sights that few people anticipated. At first Tillie saw them coming back from the fighting with their arms in slings. Later she saw them as they were brought in by ambulances and stretchers.•

Looking back from almost twenty-five years, she wrote: "Now the wounded began to come in greater numbers, some limping, some with their heads and arms in bandages, some crawling. It was a truly pitiful gathering. Before night, the farm was filled with shattered and dying heroes. Nothing before in my experience has ever paralleled this sight. There were the groaning and crying, struggling and dying, crowded side by side while attendants sought to aid and relieve them as best they could." For all of Gettysburg's residents, the following days would turn into a waking nightmare, one from which there was no escape.

FOR TILLIE the second day of the battle "dawned bright and clear." She remembered: "The hot rays of the July sun soon fell upon the landscape. About ten o'clock, many pieces of artillery and large ammunition trains came up. Regiment after regiment continued to press forward."

Outwardly, Tillie controlled her emotions during the ordeal, but inwardly—like everyone caught in battle—she struggled with problems over which she had no control. She began to absorb the sights, smells, and sounds of a battlefield. As she saw how

*The parents of fifteen-year-old Tillie Pierce (above) thought they were sending her away from the dangers they knew were coming to their home in Gettysburg. But their plan backfired when Tillie found herself near one of the most hotly contested areas of the Gettysburg battlefield. Tillie traveled down the road out of town (below left) to the farm of her neighbor's father, Jacob Weikert. Here, as the battle raged around Little Round Top and on Cemetery Ridge, she witnessed firsthand the gore and death of combat. She saw bullet wounds, amputated limbs, and dead soldiers—sights that most teenage girls in the North would never see. Sadly, many youngsters in the South could tell of similar experiences as the armies crisscrossed their land.*

*The influx of wounded soldiers traumatized the citizens of towns near Civil War battlefields and sorely strained their already limited supplies. In this engraving civilians in Richmond provide aid to wounded Confederates following the 1862 battle of Seven Pines. Constance Cary Harrison described the scene: "Early next morning the whole town was on the street. Ambulances, litters, carts, every vehicle the city could produce, went and came with a ghastly burden. . . . Men in every stage of mutilation lying on the bare [floor] boards, with perhaps a haversack or an army blanket beneath their heads—some dying, all suffering keenly, while waiting their turn to be attended to. To be there empty-handed and impotent nearly broke our hearts."*

terrible the fighting was becoming, she began to have doubts that she or anyone else could survive it: "How often my thoughts were fixed on my dear ones at home. Were they well? Were they alive? Did I still have a home? These and many other silent inquiries sprang to my mind without any hope of an answer."

She was an acute observer of the soldiers, even getting caught up in the morbid humor exhibited by men on the edge: "In the forenoon, my attention was called to numerous rough boxes which had been placed along the road, just outside the garden fence. Ominous and dismal as was the sight presented, it did not prevent some of the soldiers from passing jocular expressions. One of the men nearby, being addressed with the remark that there was no telling how soon he would be put in one of them, replied, 'I will consider myself lucky if I get one.'"

Many of the conflict's key players passed by the Weikert farm, and Tillie was an eyewitness. One such encounter allegedly involved the commander of the Army of the Potomac himself, Maj. Gen. George Gordon Meade. At the time, all Tillie knew was that three men on horseback had asked for water: "He kindly requested me to give them a drink. I asked him to please excuse the tin cup I then held in my hand. He replied, 'Certainly, that will be alright.' After he drank, he thanked me very pleasantly and rode rapidly away. I asked a soldier, 'Who did he say that officer was?' He replied, 'General Meade.'"

The young Gettysburg schoolgirl became such a familiar and popular face to the soldiers at the Weikert house that some of them allowed her into their confidence. She was busy trying to comfort them, not hiding or cowering in the basement. She was outside, in the open, just as they were. The soldiers, especially the wounded, greatly appreciated this fresh, innocent fifteen-year-old girl unscarred by the war.•

Tillie's curiosity eventually led her to some officers who were trying to follow the progress of the battle through field glasses: "By and by, they asked me if I would like to look. Having expressed my desire to do so, they gave me the glasses. The country for miles and miles around seemed to be filled with troops, artillery moving here and there, as fast as they could go, long lines of infantries forming into position, officers on horseback galloping hither and thither. It was a grand and awful spectacle, and impressed me as being some great view."

Finally, death trespassed on the Weikert farm, and Tillie was there to see it: "Shortly before noon, I observed soldiers lying on the ground just back of the house, dead. They had fallen just where they had been standing. I was told that they had been picked off by Rebel sharpshooters who were up on Big Round Top."

Until then Tillie had not seen what war was like, just the results of it. When Federal artillery was brought into the Weikert yard, the battle was closer to her than ever: "Toward the middle of the afternoon, heavy cannonading began just back of the house. This was so terrible and severe that it was with great difficulty we could hear ourselves speak. It began very unexpectedly, so that we were all terror-stricken and hardly knew what to do. It seemed as though the heavens were sending forth peal upon peal of terrible thunder directly over our heads, while at the same time, the very earth beneath our feet trembled."

The number of casualties continued to rise. Tillie described an encounter with a wounded soldier and his friend, who was keeping a bedside vigil: "He was watching over a wounded soldier, who was lying upon the floor. I talked to the wounded man. The poor man looked so earnestly into my face, saying, 'Will you promise me to come back in the morning to see me?' I replied, 'Yes, indeed.' He seemed so satisfied, and faintly smiled. The sun was high in the heavens when I awoke the next day. The first thought that came into my mind was my promise of the night before. I hastened down to the little basement room, and as I entered, the soldier lay there dead. His faithful atten-

*Although child soldiers such as the one above were not common and were most often treated as regimental pets, some did distinguish themselves in battle. Twelve-year-old Orion P. Howe, a drummer with the Fifty-fifth Illinois, helped resupply the soldiers fighting around Vicksburg, Mississippi, on May 19, 1863. Running through a barrage of musket balls and canister fire while taking cartridges to the men at the front, he was shot in the leg. Unable to continue his task, he found Maj. Gen. William Tecumseh Sherman and shouted, "General Sherman, send some cartridges to Colonel Malmborg; the men are all out. . . . They shot me in the leg, sir; but I can go to the hospital." This heroic deed earned Howe a glowing recommendation from Sherman, a place in the hearts of the men of the Fifty-fifth, and several laudatory poems in the pages of popular magazines.*

*While the average age of a Union army soldier was eighteen, boys much younger, often orphans or runaways, sought the excitement and camaraderie of the real army. William Black (above) with his arm in a sling, is believed to be the youngest soldier to be reported wounded in battle. Nine-year-old Johnny Clem (below), was mustered in as a musician with Company C of the 22nd Michigan in 1863 after he had tagged along with various Union regiments since 1861. Captured once and wounded twice, he was mustered out in 1864. Denied entrance into West Point due to lack of education, Johnny Clem was commissioned as a lieutenant in 1871 and after serving in the Army for thirty-five more years, resigned in 1916 at the rank of major general.*

dant was still at his side. The attendant looked up to me and asked, 'Do you know who this is?' I replied, 'No, sir.' He said, 'This is the body of General [Stephen] Weed,' a New York man."

Thirty-two-year-old Brig. Gen. Stephen Weed had been a career artillerist since graduating from West Point in 1854. He had commanded batteries in all of the major battles of the East and had shown such skill that he was shifted from commanding the artillery of the Fifth Corps to a brigade command of four infantry regiments. Weed rushed his men to the defense of Little Round Top not far from the Weikert farm and personally saw to it that four cannon were wrestled to the top of the rocky knob to defend it against further Confederate infantry attack. While organizing the batteries, he was shot through the chest and taken down to the Weikert farm.

Tillie likely heard the tremendous fighting that took place just a few hundred yards away as several thousand Confederates failed in their attempt to capture Little Round Top. She must have seen hundreds of casualties, but on the third day of battle, she witnessed the most gruesome view of wartime experience: "By this time, amputating benches had been placed about the house. I saw them lifting the poor men upon them, and the surgeons sawing and cutting off arms and legs. Some of the soldiers fairly begged to be taken next, so great was their suffering. To the south of the house, I noticed a pile of limbs higher than the fence. It was a ghastly sight. I could have no other feeling than that the whole scene was one of cruel butchery."

Almost as quickly as it had come, the nightmare of Gettysburg began to subside: "Twilight had now fallen. Another day had closed, with the soldiers saying that they believed on this day the rebels were whipped, but at an awful sacrifice."

It was several days later that Tillie dared to return to her parents' home in Gettysburg. First, she climbed Little Round Top to get the best view of the battlefield. Her description of the quiet battlefield was as graphic as the fighting itself: "We gazed upon the valley of death. It was an awful spectacle—dead soldiers, bloated horses,

*When men went to fight, women were left to support the war as civilians. Many did so by joining the work force. Even though women earned much less than men for the same or similar jobs, one hundred thousand Northern women found factory work. Others organized local societies—the largest of which was the U.S. Sanitary Commission—that provided blankets, clothing, medicine, and other necessities for the soldiers. The women at left, for instance, are making havelocks to protect the necks of Union soldiers. The engraving is from* Harper's Weekly *and was made from a drawing by Winslow Homer.*

shattered cannon and caissons, thousands of small arms. The stench arising from the fields of carnage was most sickening. The whole landscape had been changed, and I felt as though we were in a strange and blighted land. With such surroundings, I made my journey home. The terrors of war are fully known only to those who have seen and heard them. It was my luck to see only part, but it was sufficient."

TILLIE WOULD have been considered a young woman by Civil War standards, but thousands of innocent children were swept up in the holocaust of the war as well. At first, they were protected far behind the battle lines in their homes. The war seemed far away. It was something to dream about, something to act out on the playground.

WCD °The children wanted a role in this war, especially the boys who from age five and six were conscious that the war was going on. They dressed in military uniforms; they played with toy guns; they marched in toy battalions. Lincoln's son Tad ran all over the White House in a special uniform made for him. To them war was a grand adventure.•

In the South, children were taught from an early age to hate Yankees. Even school textbooks hammered hate messages. An 1864 elementary mathematics book taught multiplication with examples like: If one

Confederate soldier kills ninety Yankees, how many Yankees can ten Confederate soldiers kill?

Some children, particularly orphans who had no one to watch over them, joined the army. Boys as young as ten enlisted on both sides primarily as drummers, fifers, or helpers around the cook fires.

The most famous child in uniform was Union drummer John Clem, a nine-
BP year-old from Ohio. °He ran away from home and was turned down by two regiments—the Third Ohio and the Twenty-second Michigan—but attached himself to the Twenty-second and refused to go home. Although he was not officially enrolled as a soldier, he performed regular duties around the camp and the officers donated enough money to pay him the customary thirteen dollars a month. To the men he was a combination regimental mascot and patriotic symbol.•

Clem fought at the battle of Shiloh where he first attracted the attention of the press when his drum was shattered by a cannonball. In an article on "The Drummer Boy of Shiloh" he was dubbed Johnny Shiloh.

*The patriotic desire to help the boys in uniform led to the formation of aid organizations such as the Sanitary Commission (above) and the U. S. Christian Commission (below), two of the largest. Raising money through contributions and, in the case of the Sanitary Commission, large fairs, these groups distributed millions of dollars worth of supplies to soldiers in the field. Services ranged from providing medical care to letter writing materials. As the war wore on, the drain on donors sometimes became too great. In 1864 Miss E. S. Denroche wrote to Mrs. Helen W. Marshall of the Sanitary Commission explaining why she could not contribute more to the commission's cause: "I am shut in school from $8^{1}/_{2}$ until 4 P.M. every day. I have all my own house keeping to do and we have no baker here. . . . I have an acre and three quarters of land to take care of out of school and in winter all my wood to saw and split at least I had to . . . until . . . I found it was injuring my health. . . . You must see I have not much leisure."*

During the Federal retreat in September 1863 following the battle of Chickamauga, legend claims that Clem felled a Confederate officer, using a musket that had been cut down to fit his small stature. Between Shiloh and Chickamauga he was enrolled in the service legitimately and began drawing his own pay as a courier. Clem was wounded twice and stayed in the army after the war. He failed to gain admission to West Point, but a personal appeal to President Ulysses S. Grant, his commander at Shiloh, won him a second lieutenant's appointment. He eventually rose to the rank of major general, retiring in 1916 after a military career of more than fifty-five years.

*Older men, like young boys, endeavored to make a contribution to their country's war effort. Although the upper age limit for soldiers in both North and South was about forty-five, men even in their fifties and beyond managed to enlist. At age sixty Pvt. George Taylor of the Sixtieth Virginia Infantry earned the nickname "father of the regiment" and received recognition for his gallantry at the battle of Frayser's Farm. Recognizing they were too old to bear arms, many men administered the various relief organizations and worked on farms and in factories to help produce needed war supplies. John Burns (above), said to be a veteran of the War of 1812, picked up his old flintlock and joined the fight near his hometown of Gettysburg.*

The elderly were also pulled into service during the war. They were often called on to return to work or to raise the children and head the households in place of their absent sons and daughters. Some even went into combat like sixty-nine-year-old John Burns of Gettysburg, whom some believe was a veteran of the War of 1812. With the passage of time and the notoriety Burns received following the battle of Gettysburg, the legend of the man has become so intertwined with the truth that the distinction between fact and fiction has been lost.

EC What is known about Burns is that °he was a cantankerous elderly gentleman who had been constable and an officer of the court in Gettysburg.• In July 1863 he was making his living as a shoemaker. When the battle started on the morning of July 1, Burns was determined to enter the fray.

GAC He was an outspoken patriot, and °when the Confederates appeared, Burns found an opportunity to demonstrate his patriotism and fight against the evil that had invaded his state just as he had fought the British when they had invaded the country fifty years earlier.• Patriot or not, Burns certainly did not look like a soldier. In the accounts that circulated about him, all of them point out that nearly everything about him was

*As Federal troops moved through the South, slaves sought freedom and protection behind Union lines. Generally, military commanders used their own discretion in dealing with them. Some set up camps for these "contrabands of war" and tried to care for the fugitives as best they could, although lacking funds to carry out extensive relief programs. On occasion refugees were given land and tools to raise cotton for government use. Many contrabands, however, were crowded into unhealthy camps where they died of exposure, disease, and malnutrition. Others voluntarily returned to their masters. Men often worked as laborers for the army and, when permitted in 1863, joined the army. The problem of what to do with the contrabands was a chronic headache for Federal officers who felt their mission was to wage war. Pictured above is an 1863 contraband camp in Baton Rouge, Louisiana, similar to what one Union officer described as "innumerable huts of contrabands in the vicinity of the camps and fortifications . . . a nuisance besides being an expense to the Government."*

antiquated. His weapon was believed to have been an out-of-date flintlock. His clothes were equally out of GAC style in that °he wore a long black coat, probably a white shirt, a vest, and a stovepipe hat.•

Rushing toward the sound of the fighting, Burns went up Seminary Ridge seeking to join the 150th GAC Pennsylvania Volunteers. °He approached the first officer he saw, probably Lt. Col. Thomas Chamberlain, and offered his services. While Chamberlain was talking to Burns, Col. Langhorne Wister came over. Both officers saw that Burns was serious, but they were not willing to put him in line with their men. Instead, they told him to seek the cover of the woods.

Burns did as he was told and encountered one of the Iron Brigade regiments, probably the Second or Seventh Wisconsin. The midwesterners were dressed in long blue frock coats that reached their knees and distinctive black hats with tall crowns. Ironically, Burns was dressed similarly with his long black coat and stovepipe hat.

Once he was accepted by the soldiers, Burns traded his old flintlock for a discarded Enfield or Springfield EC and joined the ranks.• °Some of the men taunted him about his age, but once in battle he seemed to gain GAC their respect.• °Some witnesses claimed Burns was a good shot and that he took down two Confederates. By the end of the afternoon, however, the old man had received at least three minor wounds. The last one took him out of the battle when either his leg or ankle was hit. Burns was carried back to his house for treatment and recuperation. His story was recorded by several reporters, and he became a national sensation. His fame spread so far so quickly that in November 1863, when the president came to dedicate the national cemetery, Lincoln asked to meet him.• The elderly veteran died in 1872.

CIVILIANS KEPT in touch with their soldiers through letters. On November 16, 1863, Mary Culver wrote her husband: "Oh, Frank, do you think I can come to you? I will sell the cow and everything else I have to pay my expenses." Her husband replied: "My dear wife, I know it would be a lasting pleasure to both of us could you come, but God, I believe, wills it otherwise. I can give you no assurance of coming home, but trust in God that in His good time He will allow us to meet. Give my love to all the family."

WCD °The correspondence between soldiers in the field and their wives, their parents, their sweethearts, and friends back home was staggering in its proportions. The soldiers wrote about whatever they saw, about what their friends were doing, and about the battles they survived, but most of all they

*Civilians living near besieged locales became helpless and defenseless witnesses to a deadly test of will between opposing forces. In 1863 the residents of Vicksburg, Mississippi, and the Confederate forces defending the city came under siege by the Union army. From May 19 to July 4, 1863, the city was bombarded with artillery fire.* Frank Leslie's Illustrated Newspaper *published the engraving at left showing women refugees camped near Vicksburg during the siege. A Confederate cavalryman brings them news from the town. During this ordeal the inhabitants endeavored to maintain normal day-to-day lives, because, as one woman explained, to simply "sit and listen as if waiting for death in a horrible manner would drive me insane." The noted illustrator Howard Pyle painted the scene above of women and soldiers cowering during a bombardment.*

*War spread even into the frontier towns of the plains states, taking many civilians by surprise. In their effort to further the Confederate cause, guerrilla bands known as bushwhackers often raided Unionist settlements. The attack of William Clarke Quantrill, a notorious outlaw turned bushwhacker, on Lawrence, Kansas, on August 21, 1863, shocked and horrified the North. He and his men hunted down and slaughtered every male inhabitant of the town they could find, about 150 men and boys. They also destroyed $1.5 million worth of property. Kansas Gov. Thomas Carney wrote, "No fiend in human shape could have acted with more savage barbarity."*

wrote of their homesickness. Sometimes they wrote of premonitions of death. The home news could include stories of their children and how the farm was running. Their writing was an attempt to maintain some semblance of ordinary, everyday contact that men and women, men and their families had between each other, and it was incalculably important in maintaining the morale of the armies.•

One of the most unusual and heartbreaking stories of the war involved twenty-year-old Jennie Wade. The first day of the battle of Gettysburg found Jennie and her mother caring for Jennie's sister, Georgia McClellan, who had just given birth. There were no men in the house, just two boys—Jennie's younger brother Harry and a handicapped boarder. The house stood on Baltimore Street, which was the scene of constant fighting, and a continual stream of tired and hungry Federal troops passed by it. Jennie began serving the soldiers bread and water, oblivious to the fact that Confederate and Federal sharpshooters were exchanging shots near the house.

CS °She never gave a second thought to whether she should stay or flee the turmoil. Her family was quite patriotic, and a sense of duty spurred her into action. Wounded soldiers were laid out all around the house. Their moans, groans, and cries for help moved Jennie to do whatever she could for them. She gave them food and water, she was cheerful, and she gave them spiritual comfort.•

Jennie likely sympathized with the soldiers she was serving. They reminded her of two childhood friends, Wesley Culp and Jack Skelley. Culp had been a wagon maker in Gettysburg before moving south. When the war broke out, he joined the Confederate army.

Skelley was Culp's best friend, although they had not seen each other for several years. Jennie was Skelley's girlfriend and had also grown up with Culp. The three had often played together as children on the Culp farm on Culp's Hill behind Gettysburg.

CS °Just two weeks before the battle of Gettysburg, Skelley was wounded at the battle of Second Winchester. Culp was also in the battle and heard through a friend that Skelley had been wounded and taken prisoner. He visited Skelley, and they talked about home and about friendships.• GAC °The wounded Federal gave Culp a written message to deliver to his family and possibly a message for Jennie Wade.•

*In response to the depredations inflicted by William C. Quantrill's bushwhackers, Union Gen. Thomas Ewing issued Order No. 11 requiring the evacuation of four Missouri counties thought to contain Southern sympathizers who harbored the guerrillas. The inhabitants had fifteen days to leave and violators would be executed. Outraged by this move, artist George Caleb Bingham vowed, "I will make you infamous with pen and brush as far as I am able." Rendered in the late 1860s, Order No. 11 reflects Bingham's signature use of color and light. The melodramatic scene shows a stern, almost evil looking, Union officer enforcing the order for the people to evacuate and for all grain and hay in the region to be burned, illustrated by the red glow in the background. In contrast, Bingham portrays the civilians in an almost holy light, pleading for their homes.*

CS °Family members believe that Culp was carrying a message from Skelley that was going to announce his engagement to Jennie, which would take place on his expected furlough in September. Other theories are that Skelley was sending his dying wishes home to his mother.•

Jennie was unaware of her friends' conversation and the message. CS °Across from the home where she tried to comfort her sister and the wounded Union soldiers was the Wagon Hotel, and behind it was an orchard. Union sharpshooters had infested the orchard and had targeted several buildings along Baltimore Street where Confederate sharpshooters were positioned in the upper floors. By the end of July 2, 150 bullets had struck the McClellan home.•

Ignoring the danger, Jennie continued to help the soldiers who came to the door, EC °doing whatever she could to be helpful.• On the evening of July 2, Confederate John Wesley Culp entered his hometown and briefly visited with relatives, but he did not have time to deliver Jack Skelley's message, promising he would do so in the morning.

The message was never delivered. The next day at 8 A.M. Culp was the only man in his regiment killed in the fighting on Culp's Hill, land owned by his cousin. It was the very ground on which he had played as a child with his friends.

Less than an hour later, fate caught up with Jennie Wade. CS °She was standing at her biscuit dough tray while her mother was starting the fire at the stove. At

*Sherman's March to the Sea was designed to demoralize the South by inflicting his concept of total warfare upon the civilian population. "Like demons they rushed in," Dolly Sumner Birge charged. "Like famished wolves they come breaking locks and whatever is in their way." Taking no supply trains with him, Sherman ordered his men to live off the land, to forage "liberally." With this vague license to pillage—not just for food—the troops began stealing silver, breaking dishes, cutting paintings from their frames, smashing pianos, and generally engaging in wanton destruction of property. Surprisingly, very few civilians were killed or injured. Nevertheless, the swath he cut from Atlanta to the sea remained seared into the minds and hearts of Southerners. The illustration above shows Georgia refugees in flight before Sherman's army. Ironically, the Federals believed that those who fled were sympathetic to the Confederate cause. Thus their homes were often looted and sometimes burned, while the homes of those who stayed were sometimes left unscathed.*

about 8:30 a bullet pierced the outer door on the north side of the home. It penetrated the inside door in-between the parlor and the kitchen, then hit Jennie in the back, just below her left shoulder blade, piercing her heart instantly and settling in the corset in the front of her body. She fell dead to the floor.•

It is believed that the fatal shot was a stray bullet, fired by a Confederate rifleman who could not have seen Jennie through the closed door. Jennie Wade became the only civilian casualty of the battle of Gettysburg.

Jennie's body was taken to the basement of the house. In her apron her mother found a photograph of Jack Skelley, the man whose message had never reached her. Nine days later, Skelley himself died of the wounds he received at Winchester. All three of the childhood friends were dead.

Word of Jennie's sacrifice and patriotism spread, and she became one of the heroes of the battle of Gettysburg and °a symbol of what the civilian community had lost to the war. The death of a healthy, attractive woman underlined the tragedy of Gettysburg. The townspeople could claim to have suffered too, not because their homes and shops were ravaged by the battle, their crops were destroyed, or their fields were littered with the corpses of soldiers and animals, but because the war killed an innocent person caught in the crossfire.•

OTHER WOMEN came to know war well, and it often made them angry and determined. One British visitor observed: "I'd question whether either ancient or modern history can furnish an example of a conflict which was so much a woman's war as this. The bitterest, most vengeful of politicians in this controversy are the ladies."

This was particularly true in the South where the women were among the most ardent supporters of the

Confederacy. They stood up to the invading Yankees and cursed them. They urged their men to leave home, go to the front, and drive the Yankees from the South. Antagonized by the poor treatment they received from Southern women, Union CC soldiers countered with °apocryphal tales, such as the Southern woman who used the skull of a Northern soldier on her dressing table to hold her jewelry.•

*These stark, silent monoliths, chimneys of once grand residences, attest to the destruction of war. In reporting on his army's actions in Georgia in 1864, Sherman listed that the men had destroyed three hundred miles of railway and seized five thousand horses, four thousand mules, and thirteen thousand head of cattle. In addition, they took 9.5 million pounds of corn and 10.5 million pounds of fodder for their animals. Eliza Frances "Fanny" Andrews witnessed the destruction caused by Sherman's troops: "The dwellings that were standing all showed signs of pillage, and on every plantation we saw the charred remains of the gin-house and packing screw, while here and there lone chimneystacks, 'Sherman's Sentinels,' told of homes laid in ashes."*

As the South's fortunes declined, perhaps no group of civilians suffered more than the women. Few could have predicted the depths to which they would be plunged by supporting a losing cause. Mary Chesnut, the great diarist of the war, noted: "There are nights here with the moonlight cold and ghostly, when I could tear my hair and cry aloud for all that has passed and gone."

WCD °The war visited hardships on women North and South, but in the end it was much harder for the women of the Confederacy. They suffered far greater losses among their men who went away to war and never came home again. They saw so much devastation visited on their homeland.• For many, it seemed like the war would never end.

Northern towns like Gettysburg were invaded only once by Southern armies, but in the South invasion BP became a way of life. °The ordeal that the women of Gettysburg faced, of two armies fighting and destroying their town, was faced by countless Southern women countless times. Cities like Winchester, Virginia, changed hands two dozen times during the course of the war. Alexandria, Virginia, was occupied by Federal troops in the first weeks of the war and was under Union control for four years.•

With their men off fighting the war, Southern women felt helpless at the hands of Union scavengers. During William T. Sherman's March to the Sea, Mary Mallard of Georgia reported: "I see my house broken open, threatened to be burned to ashes. I'm refused food in order to be starved to death. I'm told that I should be humbled

*Many factors contributed to the shortages experienced by Southerners during the Civil War. Manufactured goods became scarce as Union blockades of Southern ports stopped the flow of imported goods. Even food, which could be grown at home, was seized by passing armies and fell victim to the destruction of battle. The engraving above left, published in* Harper's Weekly *in 1864, shows a destitute farm family grating hard corn for cornmeal after their supply of wheat flour had given out. As early as 1862, however, the reliability of this locally grown staple already showed ominous signs of strain in North Carolina as one farmer wrote, "The corn crop is wretched. . . . The prospect is far worse than it's been since Columbus discovered America."*

*Looting pushed some householders to the breaking point. Even in the prosperous Shenandoah Valley, the breadbasket of the Confederacy, losses were felt keenly by the populace. In this late nineteenth century rendering (above right), James E. Taylor illustrated the frustration and anger that many civilians felt over the depredations of the passing armies. A Southern woman scolds the men around her for not intervening against the federal foraging.*

in the very dust I walk upon. I'm cursed and reviled as a rebel, a hypocrite and devil."

The concept of total war was applied nowhere as completely as it was by Sherman in the March to the Sea. While his army was to live off the land, foraging as necessary, Sherman officially opposed plundering, but in practice pillaging and looting created the kind of terror he wanted to instill in the civilian population. The more havoc he could cause, the less hope these people would have and the less trust they would place in their government and in their army. Civilians were not innocent bystanders; to Sherman, they were the enemy, too. During the March to the Sea, he put into practice his long-held views of collective responsibility. He once explained to an aide, "In war everything is right which prevents anything. If bridges are burned I have a right to burn all houses near it." Should a Southern civilian complain that his home was torched, "if they find that their burning bridges only destroys their own citizens' houses they'll stop it."

Sherman claimed there was no other way to achieve his goal short of the South's surrender. To a friend he wrote: "I pledge you that my study is to accomplish peace and honor at as small a cost to life and property as possible . . . [and] that I will take infinitely more delight in curing the wounds made by war than by inflicting them." To his wife, Ellen, he confessed: "I know I grieved as much as any man when I saw pain and sorrow and affliction among the innocent and distressed and when I saw burning and desolation. But these were incidents of war, and were forced upon us."

*Acts of civilian defiance to enemy armies became legendary and were celebrated in art, poetry, and prose. In this drawing, Mrs. Mary Miller of Martinsburg, West Virginia, is draped in a U. S. flag, valiantly standing her ground in front of the threatening guns and bayonets of Confederate soldiers. Another incident of defiance was immortalized by John Greenleaf Whittier in his poem "Barbara Fritchie." Ninety-six-year-old Fritchie allegedly waved the Stars and Stripes in front of Confederate troops under the command of Gen. "Stonewall" Jackson passing through her hometown of Frederick, Maryland. Although the incident never occurred, the legend created by Whittier's poem added Fritchie to the pantheon of brave, stouthearted civilians who remained true to their beliefs in the face of war.*

In Georgia, Sherman's foragers had been selective in their violence against property; they showed no such restraint in South Carolina. Sherman's army as a whole blamed the Palmetto State for the war and were determined to punish the people accordingly. Sherman told one of his generals: "You need not be so careful there about private property. . . . The more of it you destroy the better it will be. The people of South Carolina should be made to feel the war, for they brought it on and are responsible more than anybody else for our presence here. Now is the time to punish them." To Washington he reported: "I almost tremble for her fate but feel that she deserves all that seems in store for her." In the end Sherman not only terrified Southerners, he traumatized them, and they remained stunned long after the war was over.

Many women lost their livelihoods to the Northern
WCD invaders. °They might still have their house, their children, many of their belongings, but the surrounding fields might be destroyed. If the crops had already been harvested, they would be taken. If not, they were probably destroyed in the field. All of their rolling stock, their wagons and anything else like that, would have been taken or burned. Any livestock would have been taken to feed the invader.• The most the women of the South could do was rely on each other.

They fought back with whatever they could, sometimes using their children. When Federal troops entered Baton Rouge, crowds of ragged boys unmercifully pursued and harassed them on the streets. In New Orleans, the ire of the Southern women became out-

*The destruction caused by Northern and Southern armies remained for years as a reminder of the terrible conflict. The homes of many once prosperous families, like this desolate ruin, were usually demolished, forever changing the landscape of the South. Those Confederate soldiers fortunate enough to survive the war, returned home to find weary, depressed families and the challenge of trying to rebuild a life and livelihood. It was a formidable task and the South, proclaimed to be the nation's "number one economic problem" by President Franklin D. Roosevelt, remained desperately poor well into the twentieth century.*

right hostility against the Northern WCD troops occupying the city. ○They would not walk past Yankees on the sidewalk but would cross the street to avoid them entirely. When they had no alternative, rather than return a Federal's greeting, they would turn their faces away, hide behind a fan, or return an icy stare. In a few cases, some women spat on them and some emptied their chamber pots onto passing soldiers.

Union Maj. Gen. Benjamin Butler, the commander of occupied New Orleans, quashed these hostilities by issuing an order—General Orders No. 28—that any women of New Orleans who behaved in this fashion toward the Northerners would be regarded as "women of the city [i.e., prostitutes] plying their trade." The South was outraged by Butler's pronouncing these patriots to be prostitutes. It was the worst possible violation of the exaggerated Southern code of honor to accuse a woman of being a whore. Butler had essentially made war on Southern women.• As insulted as the women of New Orleans claimed to be, the insults directed at Federal troops stopped.

Sometimes civilian refugees became a problem in the South. With so many people being run off their land, the major cities of the Confederacy became refugee centers, teeming with destitute women and hungry children. A Charleston man was not alone in his sentiment: "I dread to hear the doorbell ring. The refugees eat up pretty much everything that is raised in the neighborhood."

BP Nevertheless ○these people had to find someplace to live. Cities like Atlanta and Richmond became overcrowded with refugees. In later years, as the war came to these cities, the people discovered there was no escape from this war.•

With no chance for employment and little hope, many Southern women grew desperate. Prostitution was considered disgraceful, as witnessed by the uproar over

Butler's order in New Orleans, but some women became prostitutes to stay alive, especially in towns that cc had large populations of occupying Union soldiers. °For many it was the only way to support themselves and their families during times of famine, deprivation, and hardship.

The lack of virtue of women was something that soldiers frequently commented on. Union Maj. W. J. Ninns was stationed in eastern Tennessee and complained to his wife: "Female virtue, if it ever existed in this country, seems now almost a perfect wreck. Prostitutes are thickly crowded through mountain and valley and hamlet and city."•

After so much suffering and degradation for both civilians and soldiers in the South, the war's end came as a blessing. They had fought far beyond anyone's expectations and sacrificed far beyond the call of duty.

WCD °The Confederacy failed for a variety of reasons in the end. It could no longer sustain its armies in the field. It could no longer keep Yankee armies from marching wherever they chose. Eventually, the final nail in the South's coffin was the destruction of the will of the Confederate people themselves to continue to support the war. That the Confederacy lived as long as it did, that its armies stayed in the field as long as they did, achieving the miracles that they did, was largely due to the support they had from the people at home.•

The contributions of civilian heroes to the war effort often rivaled those of the men who fought on the battlefields, for with food, bandages, and prayers, they exemplified the compassionate side of America, an all-important national virtue that was almost lost when the house divided.

# WOMEN AT WAR

Common PERCEPTIONS OF THE roles men and women played in the Civil War portray the men in uniform, marching gallantly off to fight for freedom and honor, while the women stayed at home, venturing out only as far as the picket fence to wave tear-stained handkerchiefs gaily after their brave husbands, beaux, and sons. Heroism and devotion, however, were demonstrated not only by those in uniform, but by women as well. This war that eventually focused on the freedom of an enslaved people also became a crucial turning point for women in terms of their determining the roles they would play in the future.

JIR °Prior to the Civil War, society had dictated that women were supposed to stay at home, prepare the meals for their household, bear children, and be seen
NS and not heard.• °They were clearly regarded as inferior, an attitude implicit in the era's ideal of womanhood, called the "cult of domesticity," which maintained that women's natural abilities were limited to the home and that they certainly lacked the aptitude for political
JIR issues.• °The war changed that by forcing women into roles that had been vacated by the men who were fighting it. Meeting this challenge increased women's experiences and moved them toward equality.• The letters, books, and diaries many of them left behind reveal the other side of the war—the women's war.

Previously concerned only with domestic matters while their husbands ran the household business, women were now forced to take on the responsibilities

| | |
|---|---|
| CB | Crickett Bauer |
| CC | Catherine Clinton |
| EFG | Elizabeth Fox-Genovese |
| JL | Juanita Leisch |
| EGM | Edna Greene Medford |
| NIP | Nell Irvin Painter |
| BP | Brian Pohanka |
| JIR | James I. Robertson Jr. |
| NS | Nina Silber |

*Even though women were faced with managing home, work, and family alone during the war, they encouraged their husbands, brothers, and sweethearts to fight for the cause. Southern women, here urging their men to the recruiting station, were known to be particularly fervent in supporting the war effort in the early years of the conflict. Note the woman below the stairway berating her reluctant husband for not going off to war with his fellow townsmen.*

and the work the men left behind. They farmed. They bought and sold goods. Those with slaves worked with the overseers to keep the plantations operating. Hands that had known only cooking and needlework became blistered and calloused as they performed the work formerly done by men. JIR °Women hitched themselves to the plows since the horses had been confiscated. Many were employed by the government as clerks and stenographers, a field that was new to them. Large numbers of them entered the factories for the first time.•

Clara Barton, the founder of the American Red Cross, was one of the first to explore this change in women's roles. In 1861 she wrote: "This conflict is one thing I've been waiting for. I'm well and strong and young enough to go to the front. If I can't be a soldier, I'll help the soldier." At the time Barton worked as a copyist in the U.S. Patent Office, holding a menial job like so many women of the time. Within a few months she left that job to organize an independent organization of nurses. She found notoriety at Antietam, and by the end of the war she had become so well known that politicians were asking her opinion on how to improve battlefield medicine.

Women, particularly Southern women who often had to confront invading Yankees face-to-face without weapons, had strong feelings about the war. Their frustrations were recorded in their diaries, such as Sarah Morgan wrote in 1864: "If I was a man. Oh, if I was only a man! For two years, that has been my only cry. Blood, fire, desolation—rather than submit we should light our own funeral pyre as a memorial to our sorrow and suffering."

The Civil War affected all women—North and South, black and white, rich and poor, free and slave. They seemed to understand more fully than men the plight of slaves. As early as the 1830s a few northern women, white and black, stepped into the public arena as abolitionists and lashed out against slavery, even though they faced stern opposition for speaking out in public. Many male abolitionists believed that the women should let them lead in freeing the slaves. Even some brave women in the South—such as the Grimké sisters—spoke out against the practice. In 1851 Angelina Grimké denounced slavery and said: "I appeal to you, my friends, as a mother. Are you willing to enslave your children?"

In her 1857 autobiography, *Incidents in the Life of a Slave Girl,* Harriet Jacobs, a black abolitionist, wrote: "I do earnestly desire to arouse the women of the North to a sense of the condition of two million women of the South still in bondage, suffering what I suffered, and most of the time far worse."

EGM °It was only logical that abolitionism and feminism would merge. Over a period of time abolitionist women realized that they needed to campaign for the extension of their own rights as well, and so the two movements blended. Black women, North and South, understood that the war was about the preservation of the Union, but unlike white women, they hoped that the war would lead to emancipation for the slaves in the South. Those who were already free hoped that the war would expand their liberties.•

JIR °Most slave-holding women in the South were vehement in defending their way of life. They quickly pointed out that the Founding Fathers did not think slavery was illegal when they drafted the Constitution.•
EFG °They understood perfectly well that their social position was intertwined with slavery. To emancipate the slaves would mean that they would have to perform the tasks the slaves did in the home.•

NS °Some white women in the North opposed slavery because the free labor asked of slaves competed with salaried workers for jobs. In that sense, the women believed that the presence of slavery hurt them economically. Other white women in the North were abolitionists who opposed the institution of slavery for moral reasons.•

EGM °Over a period of time, abolitionist women realized that they needed to campaign not for freedom for the slaves, but for the extension of their own rights as well.• Following the Seneca Falls Convention of 1848,

*Born a slave in New York around 1797, Sojourner Truth fled her master in the 1820s and, along with other slaves of the Empire State, became legally free with the ratification of the New York Emancipation Act of 1827. In 1843 she changed her name from Isabella Van Wagener to Sojourner Truth and embarked on a life of itinerant preaching. Later the same year, she was introduced to the abolitionist cause and became one of its most eloquent speakers, drawing large crowds throughout New England and the Midwest. She also championed the women's suffrage cause. Upon the outbreak of the Civil War, she solicited supplies for black volunteer regiments and in 1864 Abraham Lincoln received her in the White House, a notable honor for a woman who never learned to read or write.*

*Harriet Beecher Stowe (above) and Harriet Tubman (below), notable for disparate accomplishments, shared the common bond of abolitionism. Stowe's* Uncle Tom's Cabin *influenced northern readers' perception of slavery and intensified the disagreement between the North and the South that led to the Civil War. Harriet Tubman, a former slave, was a major conductor on the Underground Railroad, leading several hundred slaves to freedom in the 1850s. She was touted by abolitionists and reviled by slaveholders who offered rewards for her capture that eventually totaled close to forty thousand dollars.*

abolitionists and women's rights advocates joined forces to champion their cause for equal rights for African Americans and women. It was after this meeting of the so-called radicals that women began to address the issues publicly. "Herein is a woman more fully identified with a slave than a man can possibly be, for she learns the misfortune of being born an heir to the crown of thorns," said Elizabeth Cady Stanton, an abolitionist, in 1860.

As more white women took the stage, so too did black women. Sojourner Truth, a free slave from New York, became one of the most influential black abolitionists and feminists of her time. When a white abolitionist complained that women were weaker than men, she responded: "Look at my arm! I have plowed and planted and gathered into barns and no man could head me! And ain't I a woman?!" She underlined her point by adding that she had given birth to thirteen children, most of whom had been sold into slavery.

NIP °Truth began her public career as an itinerant preacher, later addressing the issues of antislavery and feminism. She made the link between slavery and families because she had lost children to slavery.• With evangelistic fervor, she announced, "A woman set the world wrong by eating the forbidden fruit, and now she was gonna set it right."

While many women abolitionists used the podium, others used the pen. In 1852 Harriet Beecher Stowe, daughter of a prominent New England preacher, wrote *Uncle Tom's Cabin,* a novel of slavery and oppression. Since she had never been South to observe slavery firsthand, she drew on her experience with the black domestic workers her family had hired from slave owners. She never maintained that the novel was an accurate depiction of slavery but a call to arms to end the practice. "The object of these sketches is to awaken sympathy and feeling for the African race, to show their wrongs and sorrows under a system so necessarily cruel," she explained in 1852 after the novel had sold three hundred thousand copies in the first year.

NS °*Uncle Tom's Cabin* made a lot of northerners feel the tragedy of slavery more deeply and experience it more

directly. Without question, it was the most influential novel ever written in America.• EFG °Abraham Lincoln himself is reputed to have greeted Stowe by saying, "So you're the little lady who caused this big war."•

In the decade before the Civil War a former slave, Harriet Tubman, began a career of leading runaway slaves to freedom through the Underground Railroad. NIP °She was an extraordinary woman. Known as Moses or General Tubman, she made several trips to the South to bring out her family and then others. She may have helped as many as two or three hundred slaves find freedom in the North.• Tubman once claimed, "I was a conductor of the Underground Railroad for eight years, and I can say what most conductors can't say: I never ran my train off the track, and I have never lost a passenger."

While abolitionist Harriet Beecher Stowe had written the most popular prewar novel, another abolitionist woman wrote the most popular battle song. Julia Ward Howe was inspired one night by the glow of hundreds of Union campfires around the national capital to compose the lyrics to "The Battle Hymn of the Republic." Her words inspired patriotism in the sol-

*As men formed themselves into armies, women created organizations of their own. In both North and South, women banded together to aid the soldiers from their respective states. Soon women were shipping boxes filled with newly sewn shirts, hand-knitted socks, jars of preserves, and more to grateful regiments. The caption on the illustration below left reads: "Great Meeting of the Ladies of New York at the Cooper Institute on Monday, April 29, 1861, to organize a society to be called Woman's Central Association of Relief to make clothes, lint, bandages, and to furnish nurses for the soldiers of the Northern Army." The U.S. Sanitary Commission served as an umbrella organization for distribution of the supplies collected by dozens of local groups in Northern communities, such as the Women's Central Association of Relief in New York City (above). The idea of a sanitary fair originated in Chicago in 1863. Crowds thronged to the fairgrounds to buy items ranging from turnips to handmade lace. Abraham Lincoln donated the original draft of the Emancipation Proclamation, which was auctioned for three thousand dollars. Soon such fairs were being held throughout the North, and approximately $4.3 million was raised. The sanitary fairs provided a public expression of unity and patriotism when national morale was low.*

*First organized in New York City in 1861 by the YMCA, the U.S. Christian Commission coordinated with the U.S. Sanitary Commission to minister to the physical well-being of soldiers at the front. The primary focus of the Christian Commission, however, was on spiritual well-being. Many men, away from home for the first time, fell prey to drink, gambling, and prostitution that were ever present in the army camps. Lunch and coffee wagons were dispatched to compete with the sutlers who sold whiskey. Bibles were distributed. In the more permanent installations, reading rooms were set up and stocked with religious literature, magazines, and hometown newspapers. After the Christian Commission disbanded in 1866, a grateful federal government estimated that it had raised and spent $6 million to help the soldiers. Shown above are a Sanitary Commission camp (left) and a Christian Commission camp (right). Both gave women the opportunity to travel and to contribute to the war effort while reinforcing traditional female roles as caretakers and moral guides.*

diers who marched off to battle as well as in the women they left behind.

CC °THE OUTBREAK of war was something that women could support patriotically, but in reality they were forced to confront the division of their household and splits
NIP within the family.• °The greatest wartime contribution women made was probably the most difficult to see: They kept things going at home. They did jobs that their husbands had done before they went to war. Women took responsibilities they were denied earlier, but now the war forced them to accept them. Sometimes they were able to combine skills they already knew with commerce and the war effort.•

CB °Women made a singularly significant contribution to the war effort as a result of their skills as seamstresses. They sewed hundreds of thousands of uniforms and were largely responsible for clothing both armies.•

Women in the North and in the South also mobilized soup kitchens and relief societies that rolled bandages and bedding. More daring women worked in ammunition factories, rolling cartridges and filling them with black powder. Sometimes the women paid with their lives for their new freedom to choose where they worked.

BP °A horrible explosion rocked the Washington arsenal in June 1864, killing twenty-three women. The next day, at their mass burial in the Congressional Cemetery, President Lincoln was on hand to honor them. His concern showed that while their work was not glamorous, it was important work.•

For Union women, no effort helped save more soldiers' lives than the U.S. Sanitary Commission, which worked to help the wounded and to prevent the spread of disease in camps. JL °The Sanitary Commission was organized around local chapters reporting to the national organization. It sponsored huge fairs in Philadelphia, New York City, and other cities to raise money for medical supplies for the organizations in the field with the troops. In four years the fairs raised more than $4 million.•

Although Northern women were expected to sacrifice in the name of patriotism, the first lady, Mary Todd Lincoln, was criticized for not setting a good example. A former Kentucky belle who had several family members fighting in the Confederate army, she was accused of having alleged Confederate sympathies and was pilloried for her wartime extravagances.

CB °At a time when all the North's resources were needed to field an army, the first lady insisted on redecorating the White House and expanding her wardrobe in ways befitting a president's wife. This seeming indifference to the war effort fueled a long-running feud with a critical press. Many people wanted to view Mrs. Lincoln as a role model, but she did not behave that way.•

*Ladies of the Christian and Sanitary Commissions gained invaluable experience in organizational management and public speaking while working within accepted societal roles for women. Shown here are women and men of the Sanitary Commission at Fredericksburg in 1864 where they distributed supplies and cared for the sick.*

*Not only did the Sanitary Commission lighten the soldier's lot through handing out delicacies from home, it worked to improve the sanitation of camps and hospitals in an effort to stem the spread of disease that killed and weakened thousands of fighting men. It also protected dependent families of sick and wounded soldiers and helped discharged soldiers with pension claims. Commission members served without pay, while hired workers received small salaries. With headquarters in Washington, the commission oversaw more than seven thousand local aid societies. Its efforts were financed by donations and by funds raised at sanitary fairs. During the war it distributed donated supplies valued at $15 million.*

Criticism of the first lady probably could not have
NS been avoided. °The Civil War occurred at a time when
there were very strict ideas about what was proper
for men and proper for women. The war changed
those conventions.•

As the war intensified and casualties mounted,
women found themselves entering the nursing profession, which had previously been performed only by
JIR men. °Few American women had ever entered a hospital and subjected themselves to the sights, the sounds,
or the stench that marked such buildings. Yet as the war
continued, there were not enough male nurses to
handle the load. On both sides, the call went out for
women volunteers.•

In 1862 Confederate nurse Kate Cumming noted:
"The foul air from this mass of human beings at first
made me giddy and sick. We have to walk in blood and
JL water, but we think nothing of it." °Another woman
told of finding maggots already grown into the wound
of one soldier. She claimed to have pulled a full pint of
worms out of this particular wound.•

The sights were no less severe in the North. Louisa May Alcott reported after her first day as a nurse: "Legless, armless occupants entering my ward admonished me that I was there to work, not to wonder or weep." Thirty-year-old Alcott described the horrible scenes she encountered in the Northern hospitals.

Of all Union nurses, none gained more respect than Mary Anne Bickerdyke, a forty-four-year-old widow

*The Confiscation Act of 1862 declared all slaves taking refuge behind Union lines to be captives of war who were to be set free. This clarified matters for Union field commanders who were confused over their obligations to the refugees. However, when thousands of these slaves suddenly became freedmen, they found liberation brought frightening uncertainties. Northern relief societies started collecting food and clothing for them and began sending teachers to educate them. Laws in the Southern states forbade teaching slaves to read and write because of fear that education would foment dreaded insurrections. In 1862 the New England Freedman's Aid Society began operating schools in South Carolina like the one on Edisto Island (below, left) where teachers and students pose in the doorway. The Northern women who went south to teach the former slaves were a dedicated and idealistic group. A faculty of black and white teachers (below, right) is shown posing at Norfolk, Virginia, in 1865.*

*A team of women from the Michigan State Relief Association (left) cooks outdoors for wounded Federal soldiers at White House Landing, Virginia. Obviously, they are providing cheeful companionship as well. State-based groups focused specifically on the boys from their home states, whereas the U.S. Sanitary and Christian Commissions ministered to soldiers from all states of the Union.*

NS from Ohio when the war started. °She may have gotten the nickname Mother Bickerdyke because so many of the soldiers on the battlefield were looking for a maternal figure, or she may have been dubbed that by some officers who were at times amazed and irritated at her take-charge, no-nonsense nature, which frequently clashed with military protocol.

After the February 1862 battle of Fort Donelson, she appeared on the battlefield at midnight looking for wounded soldiers. The story was picked up by several newspapers, and she was portrayed as a miraculous relief worker who came to the soldiers in their hour of need.• After the war she refused to write her memoirs but told anyone who asked that she had been in nineteen battles, as many as most soldiers. "By God, man! Mother Bickerdyke outranks everyone. Even Lincoln," said Gen. Ulysses S. Grant in 1862 when someone complained about the way the widow was running roughshod over military regulations.

BP °Very few nurses actually ventured onto the battlefields under fire, but one who did was Clara Barton. At the September 1862 battle of Antietam, she was tending to a soldier when a bullet passed under her arm and killed him.• When she was interviewed after the battle, she said: "I did not wait for reporters and journalists to

*All the aid groups had to deal with the logistics of getting personnel and supplies to the sites where they were most needed. To do this, they employed creative strategies to raise the necessary cash. Among the most successful fundraisers were fairs where trinkets, war-related memorabilia, and battlefield artifacts enticed ticket holders to buy souvenirs or donate money. The photo below of three young women posing in nurses' costumes was sold in New York. Fairs held at New York and Philadelphia each raised one million dollars for the U.S. Sanitary Commission.*

tell us that a battle had been fought. I went in while the battle raged."

Medicine was very much a man's profession in the 1860s, but one woman overcame the odds to serve. °Mary Edwards Walker was one of the few women in the country at that time who had a medical degree.• Considered a militant eccentric by everyone, including her own family, Walker left her medical practice to go to war. She treated the wounded of both sides and in 1864 was captured and held for four months in a Confederate prison. °Walker wore a uniform like the male surgeons, but she sometimes wore a skirt over the trousers.• °Most descriptions of her focus on her dress and gloss over her accomplishments as the only woman doctor in the army during the war.•

*Among the women who responded to the cries of the wounded were Clara Barton (above) and Mary Anne "Mother" Bickerdyke (below). Called the "Angel of the Battlefield," Barton, the future founder of the Red Cross, had to overcome gender resistance, but in 1864 she was appointed superintendent of nurses for the Army of the James. When someone complained about the way the middle-aged widow Bickerdyke flaunted military regulations to help the wounded, General Grant replied, "By God, man! Mother Bickerdyke outranks everyone. Even Lincoln."*

Walker came under fire at the battles of Fredericksburg and Gettysburg, and after much lobbying on her part in 1865 she was awarded the Medal of Honor, the only woman to receive such esteem. She spent the next forty years lobbying for various women's causes so rudely that her own family disowned her. °In 1917 a federal review board revoked nine hundred awardings of the Medal of Honor, including Walker's, for lack of War Department documentation. Walker refused to return the medal and died two years later (the medal was officially restored in 1977). Although she was a genuine eccentric, her service as a surgeon could not be denied, and she paved the way for other women.•

IN THE mid-nineteenth century, women represented civility and a certain quality of life. As the war dragged on, those qualities were magnified. Writing from the field in early 1865, Confederate soldier Henry Seller confessed to his wife: "I do look rough, my dear beauty. Too rough to be your mate. I would, were it not for honor and country, leave it tomorrow." Rather than counsel desertion, his wife, Sally, responded: "More than one time today I have stolen to our room alone and as near to you as possible. All tears would unbiding start, and now, I cannot see to write."

As the months of separation turned into years, many women took advantage of any opportunity to visit their

*War fever infected both men and women in 1861. Unable to enlist in the army, women turned to nursing as one way to express their support for the cause and to partake in some of the adventure experienced by their male counterparts. The engravings on this page reflect the naiveté with which some of the volunteers approached the duty of nursing. Although mid-nineteenth century hospitals were far from clean, sterile environments, the orderly scene (left) showing future nurses visiting a New York City hospital in 1861 is a far cry from the chaotic, fetid field hospitals established after battles in barns and homes.*

husbands in camp. Even if they knew nothing about nursing and there were no wounded to help, women wanted to be near their men, work around them whenever possible, and do whatever they could to bolster morale. BP °Women brought a sense of civilization into the camps. The letters and diaries of the soldiers often described how things became calmer when women visited. They symbolized everyone's family, everyone's mother, everyone's sister.•

Yet not everyone believed that women should be allowed to visit the camps. JL °Some officers were strongly opposed to their presence, feeling that it undermined or destroyed discipline and order. Most officers, however, encouraged wives to visit their husbands, believing that whatever was good for the morale of the troops made the troops better.•

An Indiana soldier, David Bean, wrote home in 1861 about how spirits were raised in camp following such a visitation: "Quite an excitement has been raised among the boys. There was a woman in the camp with hoops on! You must know we've not seen but one woman here for six weeks or more."

Most women who stayed at the Union camps were cooks and laundresses. Contrabands, or escaped slaves, were hired for these jobs, too. EGM °Susie King Taylor was one of the most well known of the black women in the Federal camps in South Carolina because she could read and

*The cartoon below from* Harper's Weekly *pokes fun at a civilian nursing volunteer by picturing "a sick and wounded, but good-looking solider and an anxious lady nurse in search of a subject." The Lady Nurse says, "My poor fellow, can I do anything for you?" "No, ma'am! Nothin'," the soldier replies emphatically. Lady Nurse: "I should like to do something for you. Shall I not sponge your face and brow for you?" Soldier (despairingly): "You may if want to very bad; but you'll be the fourteenth lady as has done it this blessed mornin'."*

*Working without pay for the four years of the war, Dorothea Lynde Dix served as the Federal government's superintendent of women nurses, with total authority over the selection and management of all women nurses employed by the armies but under the "control and direction" of the medical officers in charge at each hospital. She developed an efficient operation in spite of resentment and petty jealousy shown her by many army doctors. When the government did not provide the stores she wanted, she procured them as donations from private citizens.*

write. She was a cook, nurse, and a teacher to the troops, later marrying one of the men.• He, in turn, taught her a valuable skill, about which she bragged, "I learned to handle a musket very well while I was in the regiment, and could shoot straight and often hit the target."

Some women were not content to be with their husbands only in training camp. They wanted to see what the war was about, and so they followed their men off to war. Kady Brownell was one of these, and she was made an unofficial mascot of the First Rhode Island. She claimed to have carried a flag at First Manassas and later at the battle of New Bern, North Carolina. When her husband was wounded in North Carolina, she nursed him back to health. When he was discharged for his wound, she went with him, ending her brief military career.

CC °Many women found themselves stranded, cut off from the men who had supported them previously. They had to support themselves and their children, and
BP so some turned to prostitution.• °Prostitutes managed to get to the front, too. One of these was an orphaned teenager named Anna Jones, who allegedly became a companion to two Union cavalry officers—Maj. Gen.

*A group of Confederate officers, their wives, and children pose in a formal portrait (right) in camp near Richmond, Virginia. Throughout the war, officers were permitted to have their wives join them in camp, most often during the winter cessation of hostilities. While some officers opposed the presence of women, most believed their visits improved morale and brought a sense of civilization into camp. Letters and diaries of the soldiers described how things became calmer when women visited. They symbolized everyone's mother and everyone's sister.*

Judson Kilpatrick and Brig. Gen. George Armstrong Custer.• In 1862 she noted, "When I joined General Kilpatrick's command and went to the front as the friend and companion of General Custer, General Kilpatrick became very jealous of General Custer's attentions to me."

Of all the female adventurers who went to war, none were more respected among the troops than the vivandières—women unofficially attached to a regiment who performed various camp and nursing duties. °They were modeled after a centuries-old French army tradition that allowed a woman to dress in a stylized uniform similar to her regiment. Her primary responsibility was to bolster the soldiers' morale, but she was not a prostitute. She carried food and sometimes a small keg of liquor.• In 1864 an officer of the Eighth Ohio described the exploits of a vivandière marching with his unit while the air was filled with Minié balls: "She was wonderfully courageous, or else she didn't understand the danger."

°The most famous of the American vivandières was French-born Marie Tepe (or Tebe), known throughout the Army of the Potomac as French Mary. Her husband was a soldier in the 114th Pennsylvania Zouaves, but

*Mary Edwards Walker was one of the few women to serve during the war as an assistant surgeon with the Union army. She was also the only woman to be awarded the Medal of Honor for gallantry. Dr. Walker attended the wounded on both sides, being captured while treating a Confederate soldier and imprisoned for four months. An early advocate of dress reform, she wore a modified surgeon's uniform but usually wore a skirt over her trousers.*

*In the early years of the conflict, the wives of even enlisted men were permitted to stay in winter camp. This family (left), connected with the Thirty-first Pennsylvania Infantry Regiment, set up housekeeping out of a small military-issue A-frame tent. It is possible that the woman also took in laundry to supplement her husband's army pay. By the close of 1862, the lengthening war, mounting casualties, and the need to take care of their homes caused most women to remain away from the camps.*

*Some women were attached to regiments as vivandières and performed various camp and nursing duties. Marie Tepe, dressed here in a blue Zouave jacket and a red-trimmed skirt over red trousers, also made money by selling tobacco, cigars, hams, and contraband whiskey to the troops of the 114th Pennsylvania Volunteers, Collis's Zouaves. She served with this regiment from August 1862 until the war's end in the eastern theater and was awarded a medal for gallantry at Chancellorsville where, with her uniform riddled with bullets, she brought water to the wounded on the battlefield.*

her life is shrouded in mystery. There is no doubt, however, about her bravery under fire. Wherever the 114th went, be it on the march or in battle, French Mary was there. She was wounded in the heel at Fredericksburg. After Chancellorsville, where she took water to the men on the battlefield, she was decorated with a Kearny Cross, one of the few medals for valor that existed at the time.• Forty years after the war, crippled by the pain from her war wound, Tebe committed suicide, becoming another casualty of war.

WHILE THE vivandières came under fire, they did not fight. Combat was still primarily a male exclusive, but not all soldiers who marched into the line of fire were men. Untold numbers of women, North and South, disguised their gender to fight in a war that only wanted men. Women's rights activist Susan B. Anthony pointed out to her audiences in the late nineteenth century: "Hundreds of women marched steadily up to the mouth of a hungered cannon. Through all this, women were sustained by the enthusiasm born of love of country and liberty."

CC °After the war, a member of the Sanitary Commission estimated that four hundred women had served as soldiers during the war. They became soldiers for as many reasons as men did. Some wanted to accompany sweethearts. Some were not interested in marriage, families, or traditional women's roles. They sought the life of independence and freedom that a soldier's life afforded them.•

BP °While it seems difficult to believe that a woman could successfully pass herself off as a man and not be discovered, it was possible in the nineteenth century,• particularly since so many soldiers were not yet old enough to shave. These younger soldiers were roughly the same size as young women. Women bound their breasts, cut their hair short, deepened their voice, and wore men's clothing to pass the cursory examinations that generally did not include much more than a recruiting officer's brief questioning regarding the recruit's
BP health. °The time was also one in which people demonstrated a great deal of modesty and expected privacy.•

The memoirs of a handful of women describe their life in the military, proving that they fought in the war. They were usually discovered when they were wounded or hospitalized. At least six women in uniform delivered babies.

Solomon Newton of the Tenth Massachusetts wrote home concerning the discovery of a woman in the regiment: "There was an orderly in one of our regiments, and he and the corporal always slept together. Well, the other night, the corporal had a baby, for the corporal turned out to be a woman! She'd been in three or four fights!"

There exist only a few well-documented cases of women soldiers. Malinda Blalock from Grandfather Mountain, North Carolina, did not want to be apart from her husband, Keith, and so she cut her hair and enlisted in the Twenty-sixth North Carolina as Keith's sixteen-year-old brother, Sam. When her husband was discharged from the army for disease, Malinda revealed herself and was discharged at the same time.

Edwin Wakeman aka Lyons Wakeman of New York State was actually Sarah Rosetta Wakeman. Dressed as a man, she left home in early August 1862 to find work in Binghamton, New York. With no apparent expectation of marriage and knowing that her income would be limited as a woman, Rosetta decided she could earn more as a man. Her reasons for leaving home included a desire to help the family out of debt and an inability to get along with some family members.

In Binghamton she eventually took a job as a boatman on a coal barge. After her first trip upriver, soldiers from the 153d New York encouraged her to enlist. The $152 bonus for signing up was irresistible. On August 30, 1862, she joined the regiment as Lyons Wakeman.

The 153d remained in the area until it filled its quota of volunteers and entered government service on October 17, 1862. The unit arrived in Washington in late October. For the next nine months the New Yorkers performed police and guard duty in Alexandria, Virginia, protecting the perimeter of Washington.

*As companies began to form to march off to war, they often adopted a mascot of sorts, a "Daughter of the Regiment." While most daughters were for show and merely marched with the regiment in parades dressed in a fanciful military-inspired "uniform," a few, like Kady Brownell, continued to march all the way to the battlefield. Attached to the First Rhode Island Infantry, a three-month's regiment in which her husband was an orderly sergeant, she carried the colors during parade and trained with the rest of the men in marksmanship. She and her spouse reenlisted in the Fifth Rhode Island in August 1861 where Brownell served until returning home with her wounded husband after the battle of New Bern.*

*Serving as vivandières was as close to soldiering as most women could get without disguising themselves as men. Malinda Blalock, shown here holding a picture of her husband, chose to cross the barrier between the sexes to fight in the army. One of the few known women to serve in the Confederate army, Blalock enlisted in the Twenty-sixth North Carolina as her husband's brother "Sam." She was not detected and only revealed her true identity when her husband was discharged from the army because of disease and she asked to be discharged also.*

Rosetta's first field duty occurred in late February 1864, when the 153d marched almost seven hundred miles to join the Red River campaign in Louisiana. Private Wakeman encountered her first actual combat experience on April 9, 1864. Although the unit's first engagement successfully repelled the Confederates, the army had to retreat.

Near the end of the campaign, Rosetta and many of her fellow soldiers were stricken with dysentery. She entered the regimental hospital at Alexandria, Louisiana, on May 3 and was transferred to the Marine Hospital in New Orleans on May 22. She died on June 19, 1864, with no record of her having been revealed as a woman.

Rosetta's identity remained undiscovered for more than a century until her letters were discovered by descendants. CC °She left behind a ring, which was engraved with her regiment and her name, that testifies to the veracity of the account of her service. It was sent to her family in New York; she is buried in Louisiana in a grave marked Lyons.

Wakeman wrote long, poignant letters to her family about the life of a soldier.• In one of her last letters, she wrote: "Dear Father and Mother, it would make your hair stand out to be where I've been. How would you like to be in the front and have the rear rank load and fire their guns over your shoulders? Goodbye from your Lyons Wakeman, or Rosetta Wakeman, 153rd New York Volunteers."

CC °Serving in the Red River campaign alongside Lyons aka Rosetta Wakeman was Albert Cashier, who was really Jennie Hodgers.• Hodgers, an Irish immigrant, served for three years in the Ninety-fifth Illinois. Her alias is inscribed on the Illinois monument at Vicksburg along with the names of all the other soldiers from her state who fought there. After the war Hodgers continued living as a man and took up farming. She attended several postwar veterans conventions as Cashier, and her fellow soldiers remembered that the little man could keep up as well as anyone. Her secret was only discovered in 1911 when she was struck by an automobile and taken to a hospital where it was discovered that she was a women. During a Pension Bureau investigation, a former comrade admitted his failure to identify Cashier as a woman but remarked that the regiment had often discussed the fact that Cashier had no beard. Cashier-Hodgers was also described as "the shortest man in the company" and "a brave little soldier." When she died, she was buried in a Union uniform.

The Second Michigan Infantry enlisted the services of Pvt. Franklin Thompson. "He" was actually a Canadian named Sarah Edmonds who had dressed as a boy since childhood and had used the name Franklin Thompson years earlier to break into the business of selling Bibles. "I thank God that I am permitted in this hour of my adopted country's need to express a tithe of gratitude which I feel toward the people of the Northern states," wrote Edmonds aka Thompson in 1861. Her regiment participated in the Peninsula campaign and the battles of First Manassas, Antietam, and Fredericksburg. In April 1863, she contracted malaria and deserted, fearing hospitalization would reveal her gender.

Soldiers in the brigade with Private Thompson referred to "him" as "Our Woman" because of "his" feminine mannerisms and "ridiculously small boots." Despite these clues, her fellow soldiers asserted in testimony after the war that they never doubted "he" was anything but a male.

Edmonds spent the remaining years of the war as a nurse and a spy, passing herself off as a man or a woman as necessary. She claimed to have known other women posing as men and said she buried one after the battle of Antietam. She survived the war and wrote a book about her exploits in 1865 titled *Nurse and Spy in the Union Army.* While many women claimed to have served as men, Edmonds could prove it. She showed up at a convention of her regiment after the war and revealed to them for the first time that she was a woman. She was the only woman officially to join the Grand Army of the Republic, the Union veterans organization.

There are numerous accounts in letters and even occasionally in official reports that refer to stories of women

*Sara Rosetta Wakeman served under the name Lyons Wakeman in the 153d New York. Her charade began before she became a soldier when she astutely realized that she could earn more money working as a man than as a woman, thus providing more help to her struggling family. She signed up with the 153d partly for the $152 bonus, and found herself in the Red River campaign in 1864. Wakeman contracted dysentery on the campaign and died from complications on June 19, 1864. She left behind a ring (below) engraved with her regiment and name, a photograph, and a cache of wartime letters written to her family.*

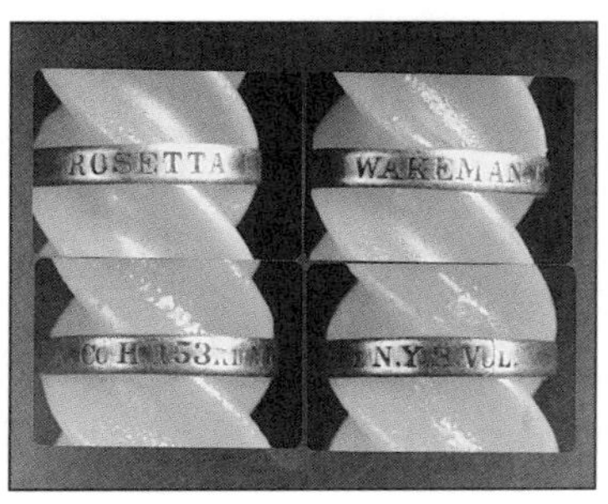

*In three years of hard service, Pvt. Albert Cashier (right) followed the flag of Company 6, Ninety-fifth Illinois Infantry into battle at such places as Vicksburg, Nashville, and Mobile. After discharge in 1865, Cashier made a living as a farmhand and attended Grand Army of the Republic conventions where fellow soldiers recalled the slight veteran as a good soldier who handled a rifle with skill and kept up on long marches. An automobile accident in 1911 revealed the fact that Cashier was a woman, Jennie Hodgers. When she died in 1915, she was buried in her U.S. Army uniform. Hers was the only documented case of a woman fulfilling an army enlistment.*

*Sarah Emma Evelyn Edmonds (below), donned a blue uniform as Franklin Thompson of Company F, Second Michigan Infantry. In addition to fighting in the battles of Blackburn's Ford and First Bull Run and in the Peninsular campaign, she was able to breach Confederate lines to gather intelligence "disguised" as a woman. Upon contracting malaria in 1863, Franklin Thompson deserted the army in fear of being discovered. Edmonds regained her health and worked with the Christian Commission at Harpers Ferry until the end of the war. In 1884 she was granted a pension of twelve dollars a month and the Forty-ninth Congress removed the charge of desertion from her record.*

dressed as soldiers being found dead on the battlefield. One Confederate woman was found dead in front of the stone wall after Pickett's Charge at Gettysburg.•

Gen. Philip H. Sheridan wrote in his memoirs of discovering two women in his ranks when they became drunk and fell into a river, almost drowning. Sheridan went down to see the novelty for himself and found one mannish-looking woman, a teamster, smoking a corncob pipe. He described the other woman, a soldier, as being almost too attractive to have pulled off the deception. Sheridan put both of them in dresses and shipped them north. He did not record their names.

ALTHOUGH THE blue and the gray did not recruit women as soldiers, they did recruit them as spies. JIR °Spying was very easy for women because they were above suspicion; men did not expect them to take up this dangerous work.•

CC °Espionage was important to both sides. Young girls would go for horseback rides all night to pass along valuable information, such as troop movements, then return before sunrise. Society women sewed coded messages into the linings of dresses and cloaks. Some used dressmakers' patterns to pass information back and forth from household to household.• Some spies operated in plain sight of the other side.

*Many factors contributed to a convincing disguise of a woman as a male soldier, not the least of which was a "manly" look. As seen in these photographs of Frances L. Clalin in hoopskirt and in uniform, she had little problem passing as a man, although there is no confirmation of her service. In another instance, it was recorded in June 1861 that "Mary W. Dennis, a stately damsel of six feet two inches, was chosen first lieutenant of the Stillwater Company in the first regiment raised in Minnesota." The account continues by saying that it was no wonder she could pull off the charade as "It is not unlikely, when we consider her unusual height, the physician never supposed that such a stately girl existed outside the walls of a museum."*

Elizabeth Van Lew of Richmond, nicknamed Crazy Bet, was considered one of the most effective spies for the Union. CC °She was an eccentric before the war, and so she overemphasized her behavior as part of her act. She dressed in old clothes, messed up her hair, and then walked the streets, talking to herself to make sure no one believed she had a cogent thought in her head. She convinced a freed slave, Mary Bowser, to return to Richmond and take a job as a maid at the Confederate White House. When Jefferson Davis would leave his orders and other important papers on his desk, Bowser, a supposedly uneducated, illiterate slave, would straighten them up, read them, and pass the information along to Van Lew, who would send the data through the lines.• Ulysses S. Grant called Van Lew's spy network his most reliable source of information, and in appreciation as president after the war, he named her postmistress of Richmond. Of course, after the war, when the people of Richmond learned of her deceptions, Van Lew was shunned socially.

One of the most notorious Southern spies lived in the Northern capital. JIR °Rose O'Neal Greenhow was a Washington socialite who entertained almost nightly at her home at the start of the war. Her guest lists included prominent senators, military officers, and cabinet

*As the conflict wore on, women of the South increasingly felt the effects of war raging on their home soil. The Union blockade of Southern ports, combined with the needs of the Confederate army and the foraging of the Federal army, drained the previously abundant resources of the South. The faces of these North Carolina women exhibit the self-confidence and determination needed to persevere through the hardship of war and the difficult process of Reconstuction. Women devised ingenious substitutes and methods of stretching what supplies were left to them. One woman in Alabama, in need of sugar, used what she had at hand—watermelons. She scooped out the pulp and let the juice drip through a sack into a tub. "She built her fire, boiled the juice slowly . . . and was rewarded with syrup of a flavor as fine, or even finer, than that made from sugar-cane. . . . The balance of her melon crop was converted into sugar and syrup."*

members. The wine flowed copiously each evening during the meal so that the conversation would be less guarded. At the conclusion of every meal, a servant would deliver the information to a contact in northern Virginia.•

Greenhow, nicknamed Wild Rose, ran a spy ring of forty-eight women and two men that continued to function even after she was discovered and placed under house arrest. Although facing the CC threat of hanging, ○she still managed to smuggle coded messages to her Confederate contacts until Federal authorities confined her to the Old Capitol Prison with her daughter. After considering hanging her, which was rejected since a trial would be scandalous to the administration, she was deported. Greenhow was given a heroine's welcome in Richmond and commended by Jefferson Davis for her role in the victory at Manassas.•

In 1862 Davis sent her to Europe to rally support for their cause, but her return voyage in October 1864 ended in tragedy off Fort Fisher near Wilmington, CC North Carolina. ○She was bringing back several important documents and a vast amount of gold when her ship was cut off by a Union blockading ship. Greenhow tried to make it to shore in a rowboat, but the boat capsized and she drowned. She was laid in state on the Wilmington dock, given a heroine's burial, and treated as one of the great martyrs of the Confederacy.•

Most women never expected the conflict to last as long as it did, but as the years passed, the physical and emotional burden became almost too much for them to JIR bear. ○If anything, women dwelled in a world of anxiety.• Mary Chesnut observed, "Grief and constant anxiety kill nearly as many women as men die on the JIR battlefield." ○The great diarist described numerous instances when a woman would finally hear that her husband had been killed, and she would go upstairs, get in her bed, turn her face to the wall, and die. She had simply lost the will to live.• Many were as frustrated as Sarah Morgan in March 1864 when she learned of the deaths of her brothers: "Dead, dead, both dead! Oh, my brothers! What have we lived for except you? We who would so gladly have laid down our lives for yours are left desolate to mourn."

In 1864 Union Gen. William Tecumseh Sherman and his sixty-three-thousand-man army foraged liberally across the Georgia countryside from Atlanta to Savannah. After a few weeks' rest they moved from Savannah into the Carolinas, not intent on battling any Confederates as much as laying waste to the land itself, burning barns, killing livestock, and destroying crops. Their only opposition were the Southern women intent on maintaining their property as their husbands had left it. For these women, the war had come to their doorsteps.

*For the women of the South, the war was fought literally in their back yards. Randolph Stevenson, who worked in Columbia, South Carolina, when Sherman marched into the state, reported on the fugitives from the Federal soldiers. "Scarcely had General Sherman's forces crossed the Savannah River into South Carolina, when a free license was given to the soldiers to plunder and pillage to their utmost desire. . . . The roads were lined with fugitives. Long trains of wagons with women and children . . . were flying by thousands before the destroying hosts. . . . They knew not whither they were going; . . . leaving their homesteads to be destroyed by the pursuing foe. . . . I had occasion to pass by one of these camps. I noticed sitting at the foot of an old pine-tree a woman, with the corpse of an infant on her lap. . . . She told me that her husband was in the army, and that her child, eighteen months old, had fallen sick on the road and had died a few hours since. . . . Her old patriarchal father was then engaged in digging a grave in the sand a few yards from the road, in which to deposit the remains of her little cherub."*

NS °Southern white women felt the effects of the war in ways that Northern white women never did. For the people of the South, the war meant shortages and sacrifice, and the women of the Confederacy were focused on survival, which counters the legend of Southern women as willing to do anything for the cause.• When Sherman's soldiers arrived, the desperate situation took a turn for the worse.

BP °Mills, crops, foodstuffs, and livestock were either destroyed or confiscated. By and large, the homes were left standing, but when discipline broke down, Union soldiers ransacked these looking for money and valuables.•

A quarter of a million Southern white women became refugees of war, fleeing from the invading Yankee army. Newly freed Southern black women also became refugees of war.

EGM °Slaves were fleeing the plantations in droves even before Lincoln issued the Emancipation Proclamation. African-American women generally were sent to contraband camps where they had to deal with the squalor there. About 25 percent of the camps' popu-

lation died from starvation, disease, and exposure.•

Northern women understood some of the horrors of war. Although not as often as the South, their home fronts sometimes became the battlefront. At Gettysburg, Jennie Wade was killed by a stray bullet that ripped through her sister's home while she was baking bread. Although she was the only civilian casualty of the battle, the women of the town had to deal with tens of thousands of dead, dying, and wounded men after the battle.

BP °Gettysburg is the best known example of what could happen to a town when war passed its way. The townspeople were devastated by the carnage, the unburied dead, and the terrible stench of the battlefield. They had no choice but to deal with this, and the vast majority of those who had to deal with it were women.•

In addition to the hundreds of thousands of men who died in the war, untold numbers of women lost their lives to disease, starvation, and battle. For the survivors, the grieving would not end quickly, but amid their sorrow emerged a legacy of independence and free-

*Shown here are two views of Southern women in wartime. A group of women, perhaps the wife and daughters of a farmer, gather outside their home (above) near the battlefield of Cedar Mountain, Virginia. The scene below right shows the mistress of a plantation waiting on her columned porch with her daughters as Federal soldiers arrive. The slaves exhibit joy at their liberation. After the Yankees came, the lives of all these women changed. Although many middle-class Southern farmers did not own slaves, they benefited from the largesse of the slave owner and the ability to "rent" or "borrow" slaves to help with planting and harvesting.*

NIP dom. °The greatest change for American women occurred for black women who had been slaves; they went from slavery to freedom.•

JIR °American women as a group, however, came into their own, although it took a war to accomplish that. In the course of those four years, they increased their presence in industry and business and established the field of nursing in this country.•

EGM °If nothing else, the war forced America to come to terms with enlarged roles for women in society. Many men may not have been pleased with the fact that women were moving beyond the household domain, but they had no choice but to accept women in the public arena.• Septima Collis, in her wartime memoirs, added: "During this four years' drama, I was sometimes in the audience, once or twice upon the stage itself. When the curtain fell at last, they stamped their impression upon my young life. They strengthened me for undertakings for which I otherwise would have lacked nerve and endurance, and gave me a fonder longing for the comforts of peace."

The women who endured the Civil War left a legacy of greater freedom for all women than had ever existed before. Old stereotypes were weakened, and women emerged from the wreckage and carnage of the war into a society where a woman's place was not confined to the home as often.

*The Civil War brought death and grief to homes regardless of social status, political persuasion, or race. Women anxiously read casualty lists published in newspapers after military engagements, desperately hoping not to find the name of a loved one. In this sketch made by A. R. Waud in 1866, a woman who has traveled from afar finds the name of her beloved soldier inscribed on a wooden grave marker erected on a now peaceful battlefield. For years after the conflict, women from the North and the South repeated this tragic scene as they attempted to come to terms with the tremendous carnage and human suffering occasioned by the Civil War.*

# ZOUAVES!

The PRACTICE OF WARFARE IN THE nineteenth century was no less awful, gory, or violent than it had been at any other time, yet the people of the Victorian era saw it as romantic adventure. They chose to focus on the most colorful and elegant aspects of their military traditions—the proud English Guards, the Scottish Highlanders, and the French Chasseurs and Zouaves—and ignored the ignoble common soldier. Only the most visible, vivid, and idealist aspects of soldiering were celebrated. Of these idealized and romantic images of soldiering, none affected the United States more than the exotic image of the Zouaves.

In the years before the Civil War, a fascination with
WCD Zouaves swept America, °capturing the imagination of both northerners and southerners. The colorful uniforms, the performance of the drill, and the pomp and ceremony attached to them was a way of expressing an inner exuberance that societal convention repressed in most Americans of the mid-nineteenth century.• Yet the story of the Zouaves is practically lost to history. Many either know nothing of them or entertain a distorted view of their role in the Civil War.

BP °The Zouave legacy and uniform had its origins in a North African tribe, the Zouaoua, which had been pacified by the French and then recruited into the French army that invaded Algeria in the 1830s. Over the next two decades the French began to dress recruits in the Zouave uniform—baggy red trousers, short blue jacket with red piping, and a tasseled fez. These elements of the uniform were associated with Algeria and Morocco,

| | |
|---|---|
| EJC | Earl J. Coates |
| WCD | William C. Davis |
| JJH | John J. Hennessy |
| MJM | Michael J. McAfee |
| BP | Brian Pohanka |
| DT | Don Troiani |

*The colorful array of uniforms worn by Zouave regiments is indicated by these illustrations. On the far left, a private in the Seventy-sixth Pennsylvania Keystone Zouaves stands at guard bayonet. This regiment fought bravely in the vicinity of Charleston in the summer of 1863 and participated in the operations around Petersburg the following summer.*

*The Zouave second from the left wears the distinctive light blue, yellow-trimmed garb of the 146th New York with leather cuffs or greaves, called* jambières, *to protect the upper portion of the white gaiters. The regiment was issued this uniform in June 1863 and continued to wear it through the end of the war.*

*The Zouave third from the left is a member of the 165th New York Infantry or Second Battalion of the Duryée's Zouaves.*

*Not all Zouaves wore fezzes or turbans as the kepi-wearing Thirty-third New Jersey infantryman on the far right attests. He is shown as he would have appeared during the Chattanooga campaign. Called the "red tape men" by their more plainly clad comrades, these men wore out their Zouave-style uniforms during the Atlanta campaign and were then issued regulation Union blouses and trousers.*

but the deeds of the French Zouaves in the Crimean War of 1853–56 and in every campaign of the armies of Napoleon III made them the best-known, most-written-about soldiers in Europe. Their accomplishments captured the attention of military men and civilians alike. Six battalions of Zouaves were sent to the Crimea. There they scaled the heights of the River Alma by boosting one another up on each others' shoulders. A Zouave regiment also stormed and captured the Malakoff, the strongest Russian fortress at Sebastopol. When that war ended, France was perceived as the preeminent military power in Europe and the model for the armies of the world.•

The U.S. Army noted the Zouave phenomenon in an 1855 report by Capt. George B. McClellan, who was among the U.S. observers allowed to visit both sides during the latter part of the Crimean War. He wrote: "They are selected from among the old campaigners for their fine physique and tried courage, and have certainly proved that they are what their appearance would indicate—the most reckless, self-reliant, and complete infantry that Europe can produce. With his graceful dress, soldierly bearing, and vigilant attitude, the Zouave at an outpost is the beau-ideal of a soldier."

DT In the United States °the Zouave look became a celebrated fashion that contributed to American society's unrealistic and highly romanticized view of war. Patriotic song sheets were garnished with depictions of Zouaves in action. Women adopted Zouave dress with short garibaldi-style jackets and embroidered skirts. Children ran around in little Zouave outfits, complete with fezzes.• Ultimately, the Zouave look was introduced into several communities when the style was adopted by local militia units.

EJC °These Zouave units were the equivalent of exclusive men's clubs and satisfied the desire for adventure that swept the country in the late 1850s. The popular reading of the time was filled with the tales of adventurers traveling across the plains and fighting the native tribes to earn a portion of land to farm, but not everyone was willing to give up the security of their home, join a wagon train, and face the rigors of the western frontier. There was less risk in joining a Zouave unit and wearing an impressive uniform that might attract feminine attention.•

As events unfolded and war between the states seemed inevitable, men began enlisting in Zouave companies with the belief that these would be the premier fighting units certain to see action in what they assumed would be a short war. While the elite seemed
WCD to be drawn to the Zouaves, the groups °ironically also seemed to attract the lowest elements.

Some of the roughest, rowdiest types in the cities signed up with the Zouave units. They were not looking for adventure necessarily, but becoming a Zouave pulled them out of the gutter, kept them out of jail, and gave them an extraordinary uniform and better pay than most of them had ever seen.•

WCD Despite the popularity of the Zouave sensation, °it was not until 1859 that the first widely publicized American Zouave unit was formed. The United States Zouave Cadets was founded by twenty-three-year-old lawyer Elmer Ephraim Ellsworth of Chicago. Although the name was something of a misnomer since all the "cadets" were from Chicago, Ellsworth combined the flashy Zouave uniform with a precision high-speed

*Inspired by the tales of Zouaves he heard from a retired French army surgeon, Elmer Ellsworth left his legal practice to form the U.S. Zouave Cadets in 1859. The handsome, athletic Ellsworth looked as if he were born to wear a uniform, and he personified military ideals to the pre-Civil War northern public, attaining a level of fame similar to that accorded to sports heroes today. Ironically, Ellsworth had wanted to attend West Point but could not get an appointment to the academy.*

march and weapons gymnastics that had not been seen in other American units.•

Ellsworth's Zouaves, as they came to be known, MJM became more than a drill team. °The young visionary saw Zouaves as ideal soldiers and imposed strict moral discipline on the cadets, turning his organization into a physical-cultural movement. He insisted that his men be not only in good physical condition but that they be morally upright. They were not allowed to drink, gamble, or play billiards, which was different from many other Zouave units. They could not patronize brothels or act in any way "unbecoming to a gentleman." They were to be proper Victorians.•

Quickly Ellsworth's men became the undisputed champions at local drill competitions. Confident in his men's abilities and being ambitious himself, Ellsworth issued a nationwide challenge in September 1859 to "any company of the Militia or regular Army of the United States or Canada" to compete with his Zouaves MJM "for a stand of Championship Colors." °To his surprise, no one responded to the invitation.

In 1860 Ellsworth decided to seek out competitions and arranged a tour of several eastern cities through which he could exhibit the prowess of his cadets. He raised funds for the tour by selling his own property, soliciting donations, and getting free passes from the railroads. His fund-raising allowed him to take fifty hand-picked men throughout most of the Northeast, visiting eighteen cities between July 2 and August 14. The tour was not just successful, it was a sensation. The high

*In the summer of 1860, Ellsworth heightened America's Zouave mania when he took his cadets on a journey through the Midwest and Northeast. Ellsworth's Zouaves performed their intricate maneuvers for excited crowds on dozens of dusty streets and fairgrounds in Michigan, Ohio, New York, Pennsylvania, Maryland, Missouri, and Illinois. They returned to their native Chicago in mid-August having achieved national renown, and dozens of new Zouave companies formed to emulate the flashily dressed soldiers. In the image below the Zouaves, accompanied by a band, are arrayed in front of a hardware store while on their tour. Ellsworth stands in front of his men, holding his sword with its point*

point occurred in New York City in mid-July, and the coverage in several illustrated weekly newspapers spread the fame of Ellsworth's Zouaves even farther. Photographs were taken wherever they performed, and Ellsworth became a celebrity.•

The grand tour also spawned dozens of Zouave companies. °Almost as soon as Ellsworth's company had departed a city where the local militia unit had been humbled, that local unit chose to refit as a Zouave unit.•

*As the Zouaves visited various cities, the leaders of existing militia units eagerly sought to have their photo taken with Ellsworth. The smartly dressed Ellsworth is second from left, striking a suitably martial stance as he poses with officers of the Sixth New York State Militia. The two men at the far right were subordinates of Ellsworth in the Zouave Cadets. The officer standing at right, Joseph R. Scott, became Colonel of the Nineteenth Illinois and was mortally wounded at the battle of Stones River, Tennessee.*

Shortly after the grand tour, Ellsworth disbanded his Zouave Cadets; they had served their purpose. Ellsworth had made a name for himself and, most importantly to a young man with bigger things on his mind, it had afforded him the chance to meet the Republican presidential candidate, Abraham Lincoln, in Springfield. The two men became close, and Ellsworth joined Lincoln's law practice. It was not long before the young Zouave master followed the new president to Washington, but as they did so, the country stood on the brink of war.

Although Americans clamored for war °in 1861, they were deluded by a naive notion of what war was going to be like, and the legacy of Zouaves was no small factor in that illusion. Many people believed that combat would be like the Zouaves—colorful, dashing, and devil-may-care. The message that became entangled with the Zouave fever which swept the country was that the war was going to be fun, no one would die, and everyone would be a hero.•

THE PREWAR martial demonstrations by the Zouaves had brought them into prominence, but when the war broke out many wondered if more traditional militia units might overshadow the flashy Zouaves. Ellsworth again decided to prove the superiority of Zouaves by showing that those who could meet his specifications would indeed be the finest and the bravest soldiers in the army. He managed to rally public support, but not in the way he had intended.

Shortly after shots were exchanged across Charleston Harbor and the war commenced, Ellsworth abandoned his plan to create a militia bureau within the government WCD °and moved to New York City, where he organized a new regiment of Zouaves from the men of the New York City Fire Department. They were called the Fire Zouaves and were constituted according to Ellsworth's notion that firemen were already disciplined men accustomed to performing dangerous duty during a crisis situation; therefore, they would make good soldiers. Ellsworth's Fire Zouaves, also known as the Eleventh New York Volunteers, were brave and athletic men in some ways that Ellsworth could appreciate. What he had not counted on, however, was that New York City firemen mostly came from the city's rowdier elements. These firefighters were accustomed to doing as they pleased and did not respond well to anyone's ordering them around.•

MJM °Ellsworth never tamed his men, but he gained their affection and loyalty. They arrived in Washington on May 2, 1861. Far from their homes—and former bosses in New York City—the Fire Zouaves became an undisciplined group of rowdies. Camped in the House of Representatives, they roamed wherever they chose, including swinging on the ropes and scaffolding of the unfinished Capitol dome. They visited bars and restaurants, charging elaborate dinners to the government or to Jefferson Davis, president of the Confederacy. According to one account, Ellsworth paid for the damages done by his men out of his own pocket. Nevertheless, their brazenness terrorized women on the streets. There were many complaints at first, but thanks to one deed of heroism, the Fire Zouaves quieted all of Washington.•

Before daybreak on May 9, a fire broke out in downtown Washington that threatened to burn down the Willard Hotel, the most distinguished hotel in the capital. In addition to alerting the city's fire department, the military governor called on Ellsworth's Fire Zouaves. Ellsworth tried to take a few of his firemen to quash the blaze, but the whole regiment overpowered the pickets assigned to keep them in camp and rushed to the scene. Ellsworth took command from the Washington fire

chief, and his men heroically extinguished the fire after a two-hour battle. The hotel management hosted the regiment to breakfast, after which the Zouaves sang "Dixie" and marched back to their barracks in perfect order. A purse of five hundred dollars was collected and later given to the New Yorkers.

The rescue of the Willard Hotel salvaged the perception of the Fire Zouaves among the civilians, but the War Department still had reservations about the undisciplined New Yorkers. Officers desired discipline and respect from their soldiers, and the Fire Zouaves lacked both.

Tensions around Washington in early May were heightened in anticipation of the ratification of Virginia's secession by popular vote on May 23. When that happened, Union troops were scheduled to occupy Alexandria immediately as part of the defense of the national capital. Ellsworth politicked that his regiment, being the first volunteer regiment sworn into government service, should have a significant role in the anticipated movement, the first true Union military action of the war.

*An unidentified Zouave regiment leads the Army of the Potomac down Pennsylvania Avenue in Washington, D.C., in 1861. The unfinished dome of the U.S. Capitol dominates the far skyline. Such reviews helped induce recruitment and built Northern support for the burgeoning war effort, easy tasks in the days before huge casualty lists dominated newspaper columns. Zouave regiments, with their colorful uniforms and swaggering soldiers, often led such parades, ducking floral bouquets tossed to them by cheering adoring females. All too soon, however, the men would be eluding projectiles of a far more deadly sort on countless battlefields, and the cheers would be replaced by the screams of wounded comrades.*

The nighttime occupation of Alexandria would amount to a peaceful invasion of northern Virginia. Ellsworth received the assignment he desired, possibly with Lincoln's assistance. The young colonel informed his troops that they would embark via steamer for Alexandria: "All I can tell you is to prepare yourselves for a nice little sail, and, at the end of it, a skirmish." The townspeople allegedly had asked that the Zouaves not be sent to occupy their city. To this, Ellsworth told his men: "Act as men; do nothing to shame the regiment; show the enemy that you are men, as well as soldiers, and that you will treat them with kindness until they force you to use violence. I want you to kill them with kindness."

BP ○Perhaps sensing something about the danger he faced, Ellsworth penned a moving letter to his parents that last evening in camp:•

> The regiment is ordered to move across the river to-night. We have no means of knowing what reception we are to meet with. I am inclined to the opinion that our entrance to the city of Alexandria will be hotly contested, as I am just informed a large force has arrived there to-day. Should this happen, my dear parents, it may be my lot to be injured in some manner. Whatever may happen, cherish the consolation that I was engaged in the performance of a sacred duty; and to-night, thinking over the probabilities of the morrow and the occurrences of the past, I am perfectly content to accept whatever my fortune may be, confident that He who noteth even the fall of a sparrow will have some purpose even in the fate of one like me.

MJM ○Ellsworth dressed in his finest uniform and took the small gold badge that the city of Baltimore had given him saying, "We do this not for ourselves but for our country," and placed that on the breast of his uniform. The regiment marched out of Washington and into Alexandria. It was assumed this would be a quiet,

*After Fort Sumter, Ellsworth was concerned that the nation's capital faced immediate danger from a Rebel force, and so he ventured to New York City to raise a Zouave regiment. He targeted New York's firemen, stating, "They are sleeping on a volcano at Washington and I want men who can go into a fight now." Before the end of April 1861, Ellsworth had raised the Eleventh New York, also called Ellsworth's Fire Zouaves.*

*The firemen-turned-soldiers trooped out of New York City late in the month, arriving in Washington a few days later where they were given a heroes' welcome and assigned quarters in the U.S. Capitol. Before long, though, their welcome wore thin as the district's residents became dismayed by the Fire Zouaves' tendencies for drinking and truculent behavior. Two of Ellsworth's Zouaves are posed in a tintype wearing the red shirts and blue fezzes of the Eleventh. The right-hand soldier's beltplate is stamped SNY for the State of New York, although it reads in reverse due to the format of the original image.*

nonviolent occupation of the city since the Confederates had recognized their vulnerability so close to the U.S. capital and had evacuated. Ellsworth met no resistance, which might have disturbed him since he had no chance to act bravely on the battlefield, nor demonstrate his men's training.

As they marched through the town in the early morning hours, they passed a hotel that had a huge Confederate flag flying from its roof. It was the same flag Ellsworth knew was visible from the White House across the Potomac in Washington.•

BP ○"Boys, we must have that flag!" he announced. He took a party of seven men into the lobby of the hotel then went upstairs. Ellsworth himself went through the attic, onto the roof, and cut down the flag.

He was coming down the stairway when James W. Jackson, the innkeeper, stepped out of the shadows with a double-barreled shotgun. Just before he reached the landing, Cpl. Francis Brownell saw Jackson and tried to knock his weapon aside, but Brownell lost his balance and his rifle slid off the shotgun. At that point, Ellsworth turned the corner on the landing, and Jackson pulled the trigger. One barrel discharged into Ellsworth's chest, striking the gold badge he wore over his heart and driving it into his chest, killing him almost instantly.

Brownell recovered, turned, and fired a shot at Jackson, striking the innkeeper in the face. As Jackson fell back, the second barrel of the shotgun discharged, and the shot crashed into the upper part of the door just above Brownell's head. Brownell thrust his bayonet through Jackson to finish him off as he fell.•

Jackson became the first martyr of the Confederacy, a man who died defending his home against what the South saw as foreign invaders. Ellsworth, the handsome, skilled Zouave who was already famous, thanks to his national drilling tour just less than a year earlier, became the first martyr of the Union and the first Union officer killed.

*At three o'clock in the morning, recalled Pvt. Harrison Comings, the frantic ringing of alarm bells and "a cry of fire" awakened the drowsing Fire Zouaves. Willard's Hotel, a Washington social institution, was threatened by a fire next door, and the firemen instinctively responded and raced from their bivouac toward the imperiled hostelry "to fight the element of destruction." By eight that morning the fire had been subdued, and the Willard had been saved. The Eleventh was once again in the good graces of the citizens of Washington, and they were feted with speeches and a free breakfast from the hotel's grateful manager. A few days later President Lincoln treated the Eleventh to a review.*

*Throughout the morning hours of May 24, 1861, Union troops left the District of Columbia and moved into Virginia in the North's first excursion onto the soil of the Confederate states. While most Yankee regiments crossed the Potomac on bridges, Ellsworth's New Yorkers traveled from their encampment in Washington (above) to Alexandria by steamboat, landing near dawn. The Eleventh quickly formed and hastened into Alexandria, taking possession of a railroad depot and cutting telegraph lines to Richmond. The movement went smoothly and with little incident until Ellsworth fatefully spied a large Confederate banner snapping in the breeze over the Marshall House Hotel.*

MJM °Ellsworth's death shocked the nation. Lincoln also was grieved because the young man had become almost like a son to him. He arranged for Ellsworth's body to lie in state in the White House.•

BP °The Zouave colonel's death spawned several songs and even the formation of a regiment, the Forty-fourth New York Infantry, which was also known as Ellsworth's Avengers. Like many things raised in the heat of the moment, however, enthusiasm waned.• With Ellsworth's death, the Fire Zouaves suddenly lost their luster. Another Zouave regiment, Duryée's Zouaves, the Fifth New York, become the first Zouave heroes of the war.

BP °The Fifth New York was founded by Abram Duryée, a wealthy mahogany importer in Manhattan. For more than a decade he had been colonel of the Seventh New York, which was considered the finest militia unit in New York State. Duryée had seen Ellsworth's hand-picked cadets perform in New York City in July 1860 and decided that he would organize his own Zouave regiment.•

Duryée believed that if he could not best Ellsworth on the drill field, he could at least beat him in the dressing room. The uniform worn by the Fifth New York was much closer to that of the true French Zouave pattern with billowy red pantaloons, short blue jackets with red trim, and red fezzes that sported braided tassels. The uniform of Ellsworth's Fire Zouaves was less striking: gray pants and jacket and red shirts and caps.

Perhaps the greatest difference between Duryée and Ellsworth rested in the officers each chose for his respective regiment. Ellsworth had chosen his from among the BP firemen; Duryée °made sure that his officers were hand-picked from among the best soldiers he could find. He chose many veterans of the Seventh New York, his former regiment, and he selected several West Pointers. From the beginning he insisted that his officers enforce strict military discipline and deportment.

The Fifth New York under Duryée's command participated in the first land engagement of the Civil War, the battle of Big Bethel, Virginia, on June 10, 1861, more than a month before Bull Run.• It was not an auspicious beginning. The Federals were divided into two columns, trying to surprise a Confederate force in the early morning. Instead, one Federal column mistook the other for Confederates and fired on it. The Southerners, still in camp, were alerted by the clash of the two Federal columns. The Yankees lost eighteen men, the Rebels one.

MJM °Although it was more like a skirmish than a small battle, Northern newspapers—especially *Harper's Weekly*—portrayed Big Bethel as a grand battlefield with waves of Zouaves attacking fortified Confederate positions that did not exist.• The press, enamored with Zouaves, overplayed the events at Big Bethel because the drawings of colorful regiments helped sell papers.

DT °The Confederate newspapers called the Federal Zouaves "demons incarnate." They portrayed the Yankees in red shirts with horns sprouting around their fezzes. Some worried Southerners thought the Zouaves might be the secret weapon of the war and wondered if any soldiers could stand up to men who had been so well trained.•

On July 21, 1861, the Eleventh New York, Ellsworth's Fire Zouaves, received the chance to prove themselves at the first major engagement of the war—the battle of BP First Manassas. °They marched into northern Virginia behind Lt. Col. Noah Farnham, a veteran executive of the New York City Fire Department. The Fire Zouaves were eager for the fray, full of bombast and braggadocio of how they would defeat the Confederacy single-handedly. Meanwhile, as they marched to the front, the heat, dust, and humidity preyed on them just as it did on the other Federal volunteers.•

*Seconds after Marshall House proprietor James W. Jackson gunned down Ellsworth, Cpl. Francis E. Brownell shot and bayoneted Jackson to death. Brownell became a celebrity in the North, receiving the nickname "Ellsworth's Avenger." In honor of his actions, Brownell was given a lieutenant's commission in the Eleventh U.S. Regular Infantry, a position he held until leaving the army in 1863. In 1877 Brownell received the Medal of Honor for killing the "murderer of Colonel Ellsworth." The uniform Brownell wore at the Marshall House and in the above pose is today displayed in the visitor center of the Manassas National Battlefield Park.*

*Inspired by Ellsworth's 1860 tour, Abram Duryée (above left) formed his own Zouave regiment, Duryée's Zouaves, or the Fifth New York. Outfitted with stunning red and blue uniforms and led by experienced militia officers, the Fifth rapidly gained a reputation for military prowess. Federal newspapers kept close tabs on the regiment during the opening battles and campaigns of the Civil War, reporting its exploits to an eager Northern public. Duryée eventually became a brigadier general and commanded a brigade at Second Manassas and Antietam. Having suffered five combat wounds, he resigned from the military in 1863. The drawing above right captures the Fifth New York at Federal Hill, Baltimore, engaged in bayonet drill, a flashy, specialized exercise at which it excelled.*

The Eleventh New York was still undisciplined and just as inexperienced in battle as everyone else at Manassas. Once the battle was joined, confusion reigned, and the Eleventh New York found itself caught under Confederate fire on top of Henry Hill. DT °The reality of battle for the Fire Zouaves was that they faced opposing troops much like themselves. Drawing fire from the Rebels, they encountered walls of incoming lead. What training they could remember did not count for anything anymore, nor did their uniforms help. In fact, dressed in bright red shirts, the Fire Zouaves attracted enemy fire.• The New Yorkers tried to return the fire as best they could and finally retreated.

JJH °As they reached the bottom of the hill, another horror descended upon them: Confederate Col. James Ewell Brown Stuart's First Virginia Cavalry. Stuart, who had at first mistook the advancing Union Zouaves for Confederate Zouaves who were retreating, slashed into the New Yorkers with sabers and pistols. The Virginia cavalrymen rode right through the Fire Zouaves and left them in total chaos. The Eleventh New York reformed and went back into the fight, but the unit remained shaky.•

BP °Stuart's cavalry charge planted the seeds of demoralization in the Fire Zouaves. When another volley of gunfire crashed into their flanks, the New Yorkers began to give way. That collapse soon turned into a full-scale rout. At first, no one seemed to notice that the "bravest of the brave" had run from the Manassas battlefield.

For a time the Fire Zouaves were touted in the newspapers and highlighted in engravings that portrayed them heroically. Eventually the truth of what had happened at Manassas was revealed. Not only was the battle a disaster for the Union, it was an utter humiliation for the Fire Zouaves who were swept away in the rout along with all of the rest of the Union army.•

The Eleventh New York never recovered from that shame, and the regiment was sent back to New York for reorganization and never again saw combat. While the career of the Fire Zouaves was over, other Zouave units were far from finished.

As THE war ground on, it became painfully clear just how brutal the fighting was going to be and that it could only get worse. Although the Zouaves were not exempt from the mounting numbers of dead and wounded, there were plenty of men ready and anxious to enlist as Zouaves.

DT °Part of the reason so many joined Zouave regiments was marketing by recruiters who promised to make all of them heroes. One enlistment poster for the Seventy-second Pennsylvania—comprised of Philadelphia firemen—showed a Zouave with an American flag in one hand, a Bowie knife in the other hand, and his foot on the chest of a Confederate pleading for mercy.•

Yet no matter how impressive the uniforms were, once the parades were over and the regiment had moved to the front, the Zouaves' lives as soldiers began. No recruiting poster told the dashing recruits the whole story about being soldiers. EJC °Even for Zouaves, latrines had to be dug, brush had to be cleared, guard duty had to be stood, and other soldier duties had to be done. Just being Zouaves did not exempt them from regular duty. Zouaves might have thought of themselves as something special, but they were just

*The Fifth's baptism by fire at the battle of Big Bethel was less than auspicious. The inexperienced troops initially caused themselves harm by trading shots with a supporting Union column which caused thirty-one casualties, seven of them fatal. Alarmed by this tragic mishap, Duryée argued to cancel the attack, but his superior overruled him. The Fifth then gamely tried to overrun an enemy position, attacking over a marshy landscape that further hampered its efforts. Their futile attacks were repulsed at the cost of nineteen casualties.*

*On the porch of a plantation house near Hampton, Virginia, sharply attired officers of the Fifth (below) mimic the act of reconnoitering enemy positions for a photographer. The officer peering through the telescope is the regiment's lieutenant colonel, Gouverneur K. Warren, who later gained fame for his role in helping to reinforce Little Round Top at the battle of Gettysburg. Colonel Duryée stands with his right hand on the map table.*

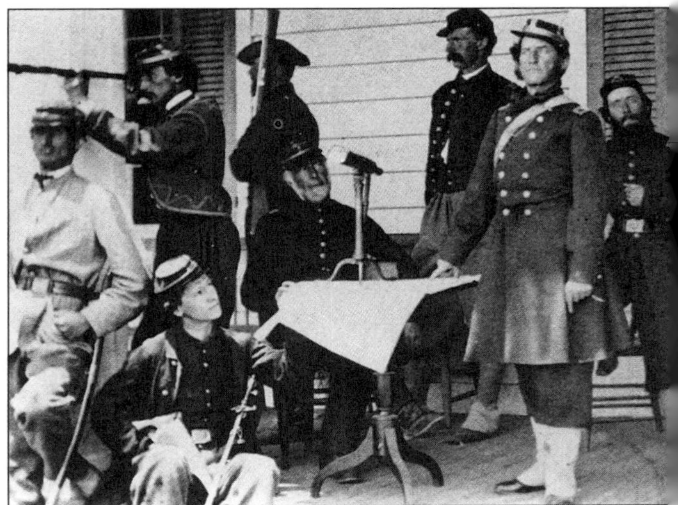

*The battle of First Manassas was a sobering experince for America. The casualty lists resulting from the fight shocked people in the North and South, as did the thought of loved ones incarcerated in faraway prisons. At right are members of the Eleventh New York Fire Zouaves captured at Manassas. They have hand-lettered the sign proclaiming a cell at Charleston's Castle Pinckney prison to be* Hotel de Zouave. *Overall the Eleventh incurred 188 casualties in the engagement along Bull Run.*

*Frederick Smart (below) had his picture taken while the Fifth New York was serving garrison duty in Baltimore. Smart posed in full marching order, with a knapsack topped by a rolled blanket or overcoat on his back. The private's red-and-blue-trimmed sash is also clearly visible. Zouave sashes were wound around the waist several times and worn under the waistbelt; they served no real purpose other than decoration.*

soldiers, and they were expected to do everything soldiers were supposed to do.•

That which differentiated one Zouave regiment from another was not so much the subtle variation in uniforms, but the quality of the regiments' leadership. Good regiments were formed and led by capable and ambitious men, such as Lew Wallace, better remembered as author of *Ben-Hur.*

Wallace was involved in the formation of the Eleventh Indiana, also called Wallace's Zouaves. Compared to their eastern counterparts, Wallace's Zouaves looked tame, largely because Wallace believed less garish colors were more appropriate to Christians than the Moslem-inspired original. Officers wore gray jackets and white pants while the men wore sky blue pants and dark blue jackets with sky blue trim.

The Ninth New York, also known as Hawkins's Zouaves, wore more traditional Zouave garb—dark blue pants, a dark blue short jacket with red trim, and a red
DT fez. The regiment's colonel, °Rush C. Hawkins, was a part of the New York intelligentsia. He was a collector of medieval books and, before the Civil War, a leader in the militia. Hawkins organized the Ninth New York to be an exemplary regiment in every respect. His men were generally educated, well trained, and well dressed (their uniforms were tailored at Brooks Brothers).•

Hawkins, like Ellsworth and Duryée, was sensitive to publicity. At the battle of Roanoke Island, North Car-

*Rush Hawkins, the dapper colonel of the Ninth New York Zouaves, stands second from the left in the photo at left. His hands are clasped on the hilt of his sword and he is accompanied by his fellow regimental officers.*

*Below is a fierce member of the Ninth, or Hawkins's Zouaves, whose most noteworthy action came at the September 1862 battle of Antietam. The New Yorkers participated in the final Federal attack and were driving on the Confederate right flank when they were hit by Rebel Gen. A. P. Hill's counterattack. Finding themselves flanked, the bloodied men of the Ninth, who had driven farther than any other Union regiment, reluctantly retreated to the bluffs overlooking Antietam Creek. They paid a high price for their bravery, adding 240 men—64 per cent of the number who began the attack—to the casualty tally of America's bloodiest day.*

olina, in February 1862, Hawkins led his Zouaves in what he described afterward as a gallant charge against a Confederate fort. The fort, however, had been abandoned and was manned by other Union regiments when Hawkins's men came running up, shouting "Zou! Zou! Zou!" The fact that the Ninth New York had little role in capturing the fort did not deter its colonel from initiating a campaign in New York City to have medals struck for his Zouaves' bravery. The fund-raising campaign, however, fell apart when the New Yorkers heard that Hawkins had torched a North Carolina town whose citizens had offended him.

While that was the low point for Hawkins's Zouaves, DT °the high point occurred during the September 1862 battle of Antietam where they charged the right side of the Confederate line after crossing Antietam Creek at Snavely's Ford, south of the Burnside Bridge, near the end of the day and almost succeeded in breaking through. Of all the Union regiments fighting that day, Hawkins's Zouaves came the closest to reaching Sharpsburg and threatening Lee's headquarters, but they were practically annihilated in the charge.•

The North was not alone in organizing Zouave companies. BP °Similar units were founded in the South, but they comprised a smaller segment of the Confederate army. The Zouave phenomenon had not swept through the South because Ellsworth had not included the region in his famous 1860 tour. Most Southern units

*Burly, hard-drinking Maj. C. Roberdeau Wheat (below), founder of the First Louisiana Special Battalion best known as Wheat's Tiger Zouaves, was a perfect match for his rowdy soldiers. Before the Civil War, Wheat had taken advantage of his wealth to live the life of a soldier of fortune. He left law school to serve the United States in the Mexican War, fought with several filibustering expeditions in Latin America, and then became an officer in the Mexican Army. Wheat was warring in Italy when he returned to Louisiana to fight for the*

that were formed as Zouaves came from Louisiana, which had a strong and proud French heritage. The most famous of these was the First Louisiana Special Battalion, also called Wheat's Tigers, after its leader, Maj. Chatham Roberdeau Wheat.•

Wheat was an impressive-looking man who stood more than six feet four inches tall and weighed nearly three hundred pounds. He had fought in the Mexican War, campaigned at times in Latin America, and joined a company of English volunteers fighting with Giuseppe Garibaldi's revolutionaries in Italy. Between wars he practiced law in New Orleans and served in the state legislature.

One company of Wheat's battalion was comprised of former convicts, ruffians, and Irishmen who dubbed themselves the "Tiger Rifles." The name came to be used for the entire battalion. A wealthy citizen, A. Keene Richards, provided uniforms for the battalion, but the Tigers' costume was not nearly as colorful as those of the Union Zouaves. Wheat's men wore blue-and-white striped pants tucked into white leggings, a scarlet skullcap with a long tassel, a red shirt, and an open blue Zouave jacket.

Wheat's Tigers arrived in Virginia in time for the battle of First Manassas and were positioned on the left side of the Confederate line. During the fighting, Wheat

*South. Shortly before being shot in the head and killed at Gaines's Mill, Wheat reportedly had a drink with another officer and said, "Something tells old Bob that this is the last drink he'll ever take in this world."*

*Few images of Wheat's Tigers exist. The soldiers above belong to another Zouave organization from Louisiana, Coppen's Zouaves. They were perhaps even rowdier and tougher than Wheat's Tigers.*

and about two hundred Tigers found themselves facing several thousand Yankee soldiers across Bull Run Creek. The Rebel Zouaves attacked, splashing across the creek while they fired their muskets and, rather than stopping to reload, waved their Bowie knives at the Yankees. The Federals pulled back at the strange sight of these knife-wielding men chasing them.

During the charge, Wheat was shot through both lungs. A surgeon somberly told him he was dying, but the well-traveled soldier of fortune replied, "I don't feel like dying just yet," and recovered. He lived another year before being killed while leading his Tigers at the battle of Gaines's Mill during the spring 1862 Peninsula campaign. After Wheat's death, no one could control his Tigers. The battalion was broken up and the men transferred to other Louisiana commands.

DT °Another unit with an equally bad reputation but an excellent battle record was Gaston Coppens's Zouaves, officially the First Battalion, Louisiana Zouaves, who also were mostly from New Orleans. It was made up of French Creoles, and some of the men had served in Zouave units of the French army before the Civil War. While most Zouaves wore fezzes or turbans as headgear, Coppens's men wore red sacks with ends that were tossed over their shoulders.

*During the first engagement of the Seven Days' battles, the battle of Gaines's Mill fought on June 27, 1862, the Fifth New York suffered heavy casualties as it stood its ground against numerous Rebel assaults. One private in the Fifth remembered sadly, "Our boys fell in heaps," as the Zouaves became engulfed in musket fire from the Southern forces. This painting depicts the moment that Sgt. John H. Berrian stepped forward with the Fifth's regimental color, soon to be joined by national standard bearer Sgt. Andrews B. Allison. Their intrepid actions galvanized the battered Empire State solders to launch yet another counterattack that temporarily checked their onrushing gray-clad foes.*

While en route to Virginia by train, several of Coppens's undisciplined men cavorted about the cars and even danced on the roofs of the boxcars. Although warned by the conductors, they continued to dance until the train was jolted and several Zouaves fell between the boxcars and were killed.•

Coppens's Zouaves were one of the few Zouave regiments during the Civil War to have vivandières, women who wore a uniform modeled on that worn by the Zouaves with a few feminine modifications. In the French army, each battalion had at least one vivandière who accompanied them in the field and served alongside the soldiers in Algeria and the Crimea. Seeing a woman on the battlefield in the United States, however, was a bit of a rarity.

Some Northern Zouave regiments had vivandières as well. The vivandière of the 114th Pennsylvania, also known as Collis's Zouaves, was Marie Tepe, a French woman married to one of the soldiers. Nicknamed French Mary, she accompanied her regiment in many hard-fought campaigns. She was wounded at the battle of Fredericksburg and

received the Kearny Cross for her bravery under fire at Chancellorsville.•

THE SOLDIERS in the regular army held varying opinions of the Zouaves. Some believed their colorfully garbed colleagues were all show and no substance, and many resented the fact that the press emphasized the Zouaves in their drawings and stories when the exotically attired soldiers had played a small or insignificant part in a battle or campaign.

WCD °Contrary to what many newspaper correspondents wrote and what the public believed, no Zouave regiment played a decisive role in any battle. There were too few of them to accomplish such a goal. Zouave regiments were generally scattered throughout the armies rather than grouped together. In a brigade of five regiments, one might be a Zouave unit, which was far too few men to form an effective, singular fighting force.•

Yet while Zouaves made up less than 5 percent of the fighting forces during the war, individual regiments performed admirably in some battles. MJM °While Zouaves have been treated like a footnote in the war, many good regiments were Zouaves, and the Civil War was fought on a regimental level. Their performance during individual battles shaped the outcome of the engagement and, by extension, the war.•

The Fifth New York, Duryée's Zouaves, was one unit that ennobled the Zouave image during the war. In campaign after campaign the men proved willing to risk

*Not all Zouaves experienced the glory of victory during battle. The soldiers above and below belonged to a Rhode Island unit christened the "Burnside Zouaves" in honor of Gen. Ambrose Burnside, who lived in the state before the war. The Burnside Zouaves entered Federal service in May 1862 and were promptly sent to garrison the forts protecting Washington, D.C. They kept this assignment until they were mustered out in September of the same year, having lost only three men to disease in their short term of service. The Burnside Zouaves wore light blue jackets and red pants; the noncommissioned officers wore unusual white kepis.*

*The Tenth New York, or National Zouaves, was one of four Zouave regiments raised in New York City in the first two months of the Civil War. The other units were the Fifth (Duryee's Zouaves), the Ninth (Hawkins's Zouaves), and the Eleventh (Ellsworth's Fire Zouaves) New York. The Tenth re-formed as a battalion after its first term of service expired in May 1863. The National Zouaves then fought at Gettysburg and throughout Gen. Ulysses S. Grant's grueling overland campaign in the spring and summer of 1864. By the time the remnants of the Tenth saw the Army of Northern Virginia surrender at Appomattox Court House, 201 of their comrades had died by Southern gunfire or the complications of disease.*

everything to accomplish their mission. Early in the war the Fifth New York was stationed in Baltimore for several months, guarding that city, which was pro-Confederate. This duty gave the Zouaves time to improve their martial skills, and they became experts at the bayonet drill. These drills with the fearsome bayonet gave the soldiers a great deal of confidence in facing hand-to-hand fighting.

The Fifth New York was called upon to test these skills at Gaines's Mill, Virginia, on June 27, 1862, in the bloodiest battle of the Seven Days' campaign waged on Virginia's Peninsula to blunt the Federal campaign pressing toward Richmond. George B. McClellan's army began to lose the initiative at Gaines's Mill, and the Fifth New York was ordered up to provide rearguard duty and cover the Union retreat.

When three Confederate regiments fell on them, the New Yorkers launched a bayonet charge, "like demons through the wood with a bayonet," one soldier recalled. A Southern soldier described it as "the most desperate charge I ever witnessed."

The Fifth New York drove back a South Carolina regiment, inflicting losses of 60 percent. Other Confederate units rushed forward, forming along the edge of some woods to the right of the Zouaves and opening fire. The Fifth New York lost as much as a third of its men in the exchange and almost collapsed.

Suddenly the regimental color-bearer, Sgt. John H. Berrian, enraged after seeing his brother killed beside him, grasped the flag and carried it thirty paces forward, planting the blue banner firmly in the ground. He was joined by the national color-bearer, Sgt. Andrew B. Allison, an English immigrant and veteran of the Crimean War.

The officers ordered the pair back into the line, but Berrian and Allison refused and the rest of the regiment was inspired by this show of bravery. The Zouaves charged the Confederates in the woods and drove them back at bayonet point.

The exploits of the Fifth New York at Gaines's Mill convinced many doubters that Zouave regiments could live up to their uniform. Many regular army men in the Army of the Potomac concluded that the Fifth New York

*Ignoring the pleas of an officer, wounded and exhausted members of the Fifth New York Zouaves (left) stream to the rear at Second Manassas as Confederate Gen. John B. Hood's attack virtually surrounds their position and begins to shatter their regiment. In the background, other troops of the Fifth continue to fire upon the horde of Rebels driving relentlessly on their position. When the regiment left Federal service on May 14, 1863, many of the survivors still had time to serve on their personal enlistments and were placed in the 146th New York.*

was the equal of the best-drilled regular soldiers with whom they shared the field that day.•

The regiment lost more than 169 of its 450 men at Gaines's Mill, and two months later it was thrown into JJH the fray again at the battle of Second Manassas. °There the regiment was commanded by Capt. Cleveland Winslow. This was his first battle at the head of a regiment, and his effectiveness as a commander was diluted because he was a pretentious martinet. One New Yorker complained that Winslow had bugle calls for everything except the calls of nature, and the soldier surmised that Winslow lay awake at night devising new calls for that.•

During the battle of Second Manassas, on the far left of the Federal line, everything seemed quiet on the afternoon of August 30, 1862, until suddenly the Fifth New York found itself in the path of James Longstreet's JJH massive Confederate counterattack. °The New Yorkers were lounging on the ridge line and at 4 P.M. heard the rustle of brush as six companies of skirmishers from the Tenth New York came running back toward them.

The Fifth New York formed into a line of battle facing the woods, with the remaining four companies of the Tenth New York on its left. Before they could level their rifles to fire, three regiments of the Confederate Texas Brigade—which also included Georgians and

*Captain Cleveland Winslow (below), a brave man but a pretentious martinet and unpopular with his men, commanded the regiment at Second Manassas. That afternoon every officer of the Fifth was either killed or wounded, except Winslow, who left the field unharmed even though his horse had been shot from under him.*

*A young man during the Civil War, Winslow Homer was employed by* Harper's Weekly *as a free-lance illustrator to depict military scenes. His work often focused on intimate moments of human interest as opposed to clashing armies. Later he translated many of his drawings to canvas. Shown above is his* Brierwood Pipe *in which a private whiles away idle hours by carving a pipe bowl as his partner, clutching his own smoldering pipe, looks on and provides advice. Gnarled briarroot, the project's raw material, lies at the soldiers' feet. Homer's skilled composition brings an air of tranquility and peace to the scene.*

BP

South Carolinians—fired on them. Pvt. Andrew Coats of the Fifth said it sounded like "an immense flock of partridges" taking off as the bullets ripped through the foliage. Pvt. Alfred Davenport described the sound of the volley as sort of "a continual hiss and sluck, with the last sound telling that the bullet had gone into some man's body."

The Fifth tried to return fire, but the skirmishers of the Tenth were still rolling out of the woods and into the line of the Fifth, blocking the field of fire toward the Southerners. As the Confederate bullets ripped into the Union line, Private Coats said, "There we stood like statues. We could not see the enemy—but we saw streaks of smoke drifting between the trees."•

Caught in the open with no clear view of the Rebels, the Fifth New York held its ground until the men of the Tenth had cleared the line. Finally the men of the Fifth stood in the open in their brilliantly colored uniforms and fired a long volley into the woods from which the Texans also fired. As bullets tore into the Union line, a few new recruits began to break. The Southerners cleared the woods and rushed the New Yorkers. The order was given for the Zouaves to fall back, but no one heard it in the noise of battle.

°The disciplined Fifth New York held its ground, even though the Texans seemed to fold around them. Coats observed: "Where the regiment stood that day was the very vortex of Hell. Not only were men wounded, or killed, they were riddled." The color guard was all but wiped out; both of the color-bearers and seven of the eight men in the color guard were killed, but the banners were not lost.

Sergeant Allison carried the national flag just as he did at Gaines's Mill. He was killed, and the flag draped over him as he went down. Several men tried to pick up the Stars and Stripes, but they were all shot down

*The Seventy-second Pennsylvania, one of the Keystone State's Fire Zouave regiments, wore its Zouave-style clothing when it helped defend the Angle against Pickett's Charge at the battle of Gettysburg. The Seventy-second was sometimes referred to as Baxter's Zouaves, after DeWitt Clinton Baxter, the unit's organizer. Images taken late in the war seem to indicate the regiment had been issued standard Federal uniforms, although they also continued to wear their Zouave outfits. Another Pennsylvania regiment, the Ninety-fifth, wore an identical jacket, but with a dark blue vest instead of the sky blue variety worn by infantrymen of the Seventy-second.*

before they could get it off the ground. Finally, a young corporal, Lucien B. Swain, dashed up and pried the flag out of Allison's hands and removed it safely from the field.

As the drama unfolded with the national colors, Sgt. Francis Spelman, the man carrying the regimental flag, the New
JJH York flag, was mortally wounded• ○and bleeding profusely from the side. At the moment he saw a friend running toward the rear and called out to him: "Chambers! Chambers! Don't let them get my flag!" William H. Chambers ran back, grabbed the flag from Spelman, and carried it off the field. Spelman died where he lay. Many marveled that when he had the opportunity to call for help, he did not call for someone to help him, but for someone to take the flag off the field.•

The charging wave of Rebels became too much, and the New Yorkers broke and ran for their lives down the hill, across a small creek, and up the hill beyond, leaving behind their dead and wounded. Joe Joskins of the Fifth Texas noted that the creek "ran blood" and that the Federals had "completely dammed it up with their dead and dying bodies." Another Texan, looking upon the scene later, recalled that the bodies of the colorfully uniformed Zouaves lay so close together as to give "the appearance of a Texas hillside when carpeted in the spring by wild flowers of many hues and tints."

When the retreat was over, more Fifth New Yorkers had died in those few minutes than did any other Union infantry regiment in any other battle of the war. The regiment lost 328 of its 500 men—118 were killed or mortally wounded. Every officer of the Fifth was either dead or wounded that afternoon, except one, Cleveland Winslow. Even though his horse was shot out from under him, Winslow managed to leave the field unharmed. For many of his wounded men, however, the ordeal was just beginning.

BP ○The aftermath of battle was always horrible, and the aftermath of Second Manassas was made even more horrible for the hundreds of wounded Zouaves lying on the Virginia hillside because they lay on that field amid the dead and the dying for nearly a week without medical assistance. The battle had passed them by, and the war had moved on. Some men were robbed and brutalized by the victorious Rebels, but other Confederates had compassion on the New Yorkers.

James Whytal's right arm was shattered above the elbow, and he was slowly bleeding to death. Near him lay a wounded Texan. The two dragged themselves together under the trees, and as other men groaned and died around them, they did what they could to help one another though they were enemies. The Confederate took the Zouave's turban and used it to bind their wounds, and Whytal survived his wound as a result of the kindness shown him by this enemy.•

A WIDELY held misconception about the Zouaves is that they faded from view by the middle of the war. Southern Zouaves, like the Eufaula Zouaves of Alabama, the Chichester Zouaves of South Carolina, the Richmond Zouaves of Virginia, and the Maryland Guard Zouaves, WCD ○did not last long because of chronic supply problems in the South. The Confederate government had enough

*On the hot afternoon of May 5, 1864, the 140th New York took part in the opening actions of the horrific battle of the Wilderness. After deploying in an open area known as Saunders's Field that lay astride the Orange Turnpike, the Zouaves hurtled toward the Confederate line awaiting them in the thick woods to the west. When George Ryan, the 140th's colonel, lost his horse to enemy gunfire, he continued to lead his men on foot. When he lost his sword, Ryan then brandished his hat and raced through the pelting gunfire at the head of the regiment, the scene depicted here. After reaching the enemy position and engaging in a bitter hand-to-hand contest, the New York Zouaves were pushed back and retreated across the bloody field. Somehow Ryan managed to emerge unharmed from the fight, but 274 of his men had become prisoners of the enemy or lay wounded or dead under the Virginia sun.*

*At Gettysburg the 114th Pennsylvania had the misfortune to be in the path of the assault launched by Southern Gen. James Longstreet on July 2. After a supporting infantry gave way, the 114th's left flank was subjected to what the regiment's battle report called a "murderous fire." Unable to withstand the withering Rebel volleys, the 114th's battle line disintegrated, its ranking officer was captured, and the Pennsylvanians became separated from the rest of their brigade. A captain managed to lead those who remained off the battlefield, but the 114th did not rejoin its brigade until the next day. In honor of its sacrifice, the 114th became the headquarters guard of the Army of the Potomac in 1864. This photograph was taken while the 114th was serving in this capacity during the siege of Petersburg.*

problems keeping its soldiers fed and armed without keeping Zouave units in exotic baggy pants, braided jackets, fezzes, and turbans. The Southern Zouaves were absorbed into the already undersupplied and ill-equipped Confederate army by 1863.•

Conversely, supply was no problem in the North. Not only did the Union quartermaster supply Zouave uniforms, but recruiters maintained a steady flow of new recruits to fill their ranks. New units continued to form and distinguish themselves in battle, and thus Zouaves remained within the ranks of the Federal armies throughout the war.

EJC °One of these was the 114th Pennsylvania, also known as Collis's Zouaves, a regiment formed in Philadelphia and named after Charles H. T. Collis. In addition to the usual Zouave accouterments, the 114th Pennsylvania was distinguished by a wrapped turban that was generally larger than those worn by any other Zouave units. This elaborate headwear, however, was reserved for formal occasions.

The 114th Pennsylvania's most notable engagement occurred on the second day at Gettysburg, on the Emmitsburg road where they were in the path of the Mississippi Brigade under Brig. Gen. William Barksdale. The Zouaves held their ground until Barksdale's men overwhelmed them. In the annals of the French army there was no more glorious, no more hard-fighting example of a Zouave unit than Collis's at Gettysburg.•

*Bearing tattered battle flags, proud Union veterans of the 165th New York Zouaves, survivors of engagements in Louisiana and the Shenandoah Valley, parade down New York City's Riverside Drive in this image made about 1900. By the time this photograph was taken, colorful military uniforms like those of the Civil War's Zouave regiments were nearly obsolete. Khaki and olive drab dominated the armies of the twentieth century.*

BP °Federal Zouave regiments fought throughout the war. An entire brigade, including the 140th and 146th New York Regiments—superb Zouave units—served with Ulysses S. Grant as he battled Lee's army from the summer of 1864 through the April 1865 battle of Five Forks. On the morning on which Grant and Lee met to negotiate the surrender of the Army of Northern Virginia, the last Union soldier killed at Appomattox was fifteen-year-old Pvt. William Montgomery, a Zouave, serving in the ranks of the 155th Pennsylvania. Thus, some have pointed out that the first Union officer to die in the war was a Zouave—Elmer Ellsworth, and the last soldier to die at Appomattox was a Zouave.•

WCD °When the Civil War ended, Zouaves virtually disappeared from the American military because Americans North and South, civilian and military, no longer viewed warfare as an idealized adventure for brightly costumed soldiers. Zouaves personified something that had never been—glorious war—and the romantic ideal of the Zouave soldier as the bravest of the brave died as the Civil War became history.•

Nevertheless, some vestiges of once glorious Zouaves remained in America's postwar years. Many veterans still proudly wore their red-and-blue uniforms in parades, and a few Zouave-inspired militia units appeared for a time. In the late nineteenth century the public even enjoyed a

*The French Zouaves pointing a machine gun in 1915 were almost an anachronism, and the last time Zouaves fought was in the trenches of World War I. Their type of warfare had become outdated, and the idealized, glamorized image of the fearsome men in exotic, vividly colored garb was no longer seen on the battlefield.*

resurrected Zouave precision drill team known as Deblin's Zouaves as part of Buffalo Bill's Wild West Show.

In Europe, Zouaves remained part of the French army, serving in the Franco-Prussian War and even up to World War I. There, in the trenches, Zouaves finally MJM faded into history. °New technologies had unleashed tremendous firepower on the battlefield, and survival for the foot soldier demanded concealment. The fact that soldiers no longer fought in the open and charged into the enemy as they had during the nineteenth century meant that the Zouaves and that type of warfare were obsolete. The idealized, glamorized image of the fearsome man in the red pants was removed from the battlefield.•

Zouaves were the personification of a misconception of war as adventure. True nobility could not be found in battles that left masses of men scarred and mutilated. The colorful garb that tinted the romantic view of soldiering and human conflict was nothing more than a cruel mirage. The Zouaves had a romantic view of soldiering and of human conflict that now seems unenlightened, almost foolhardy. Yet for four years, despite tremendous losses, Zouaves had captured the imagination of America and generated a legacy of bravery and bluster that few have overshadowed.

# IMMIGRANTS AND THE WAR

With ITS FIRST SETTLERS BEING THE Spanish in Florida, the English in Jamestown, and the Dutch in New York, the land that became the United States has always been one of immigrants. In the 1840s and 1850s emigrants from Europe arrived by the millions, coming to America to escape revolution and famine. For decades these newcomers thought their greatest challenge would be finding work and raising families in the new land. Those who arrived in the 1850s, however, found themselves caught up in the national crisis of regional differences that had been brewing for fifty years and threatening civil war—a war that was not of their making. Nevertheless, the newcomers felt a strong allegiance to the states where they had begun their new lives. If their states needed them to fight, then fight they would.

Immigrants played a vital role on both sides just by filling out the ranks. Of the three million men under arms, 20 percent had been born in countries other than the United States. At first immigrant soldiers were not welcomed into the ranks by men who were themselves
BP only a generation or two removed from Europe. °A great deal of bigotry was directed toward these newer immigrants by everyone and reinforced by their depictions in the daily and weekly newspapers. The Irish were caricatured as apes and the Germans as dour, pipe-
WCD smoking, stupid people.• °Immigrants were looked down upon because they were largely an unmoneyed class coming to American shores and competing with Americans for jobs.•

| | |
|---|---|
| **JB** | Joseph Bilby |
| **TYC** | Thomas Y. Cartwright |
| **WCD** | William C. Davis |
| **LK** | Lawrence Kohl |
| **IM** | Ian McCulloch |
| **BP** | Brian Pohanka |
| **DLV** | David L. Valuska |

*America has always been a nation of immigrants. Europeans like these Irish peasants left for the New World for a variety of reasons. Famine, poor treatment from social superiors, and an inability to better their conditions were all factors that caused the Irish and other emigrants to leave extended families and familiar surroundings for the shores of the United States. Unhappily, many immigrants experienced similar prejudices and economic hardships when they arrived in America. Still, the fast-growing, bustling country offered them a better life than they had known in the Old World. The outbreak of the Civil War provided an excellent opportunity for many immigrants to serve in the Northern or Southern military, thereby gaining acceptance and respect and, in some cases, a promise of citizenship.*

Lincoln had courted the foreign-born population in 1860, and when the war began he rewarded its leaders with military appointments. They responded eagerly when the call went out for volunteers to quash the rebellion and actively recruited their countrymen. Companies of German, Irish, Scandinavian, and French organized quickly, elected officers, and were mustered into government service. Xenophobic prejudice, however, hampered many regiments, especially when they received such criticism as that of Harvard-educated Maj. Henry Abbott: "The more foreign a regiment is, the more cowardly it is. The French and Italians are incapable of showing any pluck at all."

In the decade before the war, nearly three million immigrants arrived in America, and 85 percent of them
WCD settled in the North. °They were attracted to the North because there were jobs there and land was cheap, but they were also attracted by a political identification with the ideals of freedom and representative government.• Many who immigrated to the South—primarily through port cities like New Orleans, Charleston, Wilmington, and Savannah—followed family members and nationalities who were already there, such as the Scots and the Irish.

### *The Irish*

THE LARGEST numbers of emigrants came from Ireland, with more than one million coming to America in the 1840s to escape starvation at home caused by a potato
TYC famine that the British rulers had made worse. °Ireland grew enough food to feed the Irish four times over, but by law all food was sent to England.•

Angered by England's indifference to the famine and years of control by a government removed from Ireland's shores, many Irish immigrants to America dreamed of returning home one day to drive out the British. Some prepared for that future invasion by joining militia companies in the United States. One such unit was the Sixty-ninth New York.

When the Prince of Wales visited New York in 1860, the Sixty-ninth's commander, Col. Michael Corcoran, an Irishman whose father had once served in the British army, refused to parade the regiment before the LK man he considered an invader of Ireland. °He was adamant that no Irishman, American citizen or not, should show respect or do any favors for the British royal family.• In response to his insubordination, Corcoran was court-martialed and faced imprisonment when the Civil War began. The Federal authorities, however, realized the Sixty-ninth was vital to the Union cause, and so Corcoran was released and the incident forgotten.

Accompanied by the cheers of thousands, Corcoran marched off with his regiment of Irish immigrants to defend the Union. They had no reservation about fight- LK ing for the Union because °they felt a sense of gratitude to the country for providing them asylum from the desperate straits that Ireland experienced in the mid-nineteenth century.•

In their first battle at Manassas in July 1861, Corcoran's Sixty-ninth New York was among the few Northern regiments to be praised for their courage. While most of the Federal units crumbled, the Sixty-ninth WCD retreated under control, °proving to the rest of the

*As the war escalated and more recruits were needed to fill the ranks, both sides, but particularly the North, curried the favor of their immigrant populations. This engraving shows Northern recruiters pitching the benefits of military service to a recently arrived band of Irish and German immigrants. Many new arrivals found the enticements of cash bounties irresistible, and they joined the Union army by the thousands. Southerners often derided such soldiers as "Lincoln's hirelings," although many such men overcame the barriers of language and custom to perform bravely and well on numerous battlefields.*

*When Michael Corcoran refused to have his men of the Sixty-ninth New York submit to a review by England's Prince of Wales, he became a hero among America's Irish community. A song entitled "The Irish Volunteer" was written to celebrate the occasion. One verse claimed:*

*When the Prince of Wales came over here, and made a hubbaboo,*
*Oh, everybody turned out, you know, in gold and tinsel too;*
*But then the good old Sixty-ninth didn't like these lords or peers—*
*They wouldn't give a damn for kings, the Irish volunteers!*

*The Sixty-ninth New York later proved its courage and ability to fight at Manassas and attained the rank of brigadier general.*

country that while some Irishmen might be poor and illiterate, they could fight and were dependable.•

Corcoran, however, was captured and almost became a martyr. When the Union threatened to hang some captured Confederate seamen as pirates, the South responded that they would hang a captured Union officer in retaliation. Corcoran drew the short lot. The Yankees backed down, and Corcoran remained alive. He was exchanged in April 1862, promoted to brigadier general, and formed a brigade of Irish-Americans called the Corcoran Legion. Corcoran, however, died ingloriously when his horse fell on a slippery winter road in December 1863.

With Corcoran lost, the leadership of the Sixty-ninth fell to former Irish revolutionary Maj. Thomas Francis Meagher. The British had once banished him for life to Tasmania because of a speech he gave on overthrowing British rule in Ireland. He escaped from the island and fled to California. From there he moved to New York City, where he practiced law. Although he became an American citizen, he still hoped he would return one day to a free Ireland.

BP Meagher was a gifted orator. °His speeches could move men to tears or whip them into a fury to scream for vengeance and blood.• To the men of his command, he promised: "Today it is for the American Republic we fight. Tomorrow it will be for Ireland."

Following the battle at Manassas, Meagher formed an entire Irish brigade, a unit of several regiments numbering several thousand native sons of Ireland, which would become a symbol to the 150,000 Irish soldiers in blue. Starting with the core 69th New York, Meagher recruited the 63d and 88th New York, and later added the 28th Massachusetts, and the 116th Pennsylvania. The units of the Irish Brigade adopted their own distinctive flags, a green banner emblazoned with an Irish harp. It also adopted its own battle cry, "Clear the Way!" shouted in the ancient Gaelic language.

Even though the soldiers were Irish-Americans now, that did not mean they did not long to be Irishmen again. Many Irish joined the Fenian brotherhood, which was planning Ireland's liberation. This revolutionary organization held weekly meetings in Union camps throughout the war. BP °If the leaders of Great Britain knew about the meetings, they did not voice any official objections to the Northern authorities. Still, the United States ran the risk of offending British sensibilities by allowing these gatherings of revolutionaries.• Had the Yankee government's tolerance toward revolutionary Irishmen been widely known, the English would have had another reason for supporting the South.

*Father William Corby, one of the more famous Catholic clerics to accompany an Irish contingent during the Civil War, is seated right front in this July 1862 image of men in the Irish Brigade. Corby often administered to their spiritual needs before they entered a fight. The most singular example of this occurred when Corby gave absolution to his flock of warriors just before they stormed into the Wheat Field on the second day of the battle of Gettysburg. A soldier in a Pennsylvania regiment saw the incident and recorded that "The Irish Brigade . . . was first assembled in a solid mass, and their . . . priest performed some religious ceremony . . . while the men stood, undisturbed by bursting shells, with bowed heads in reverent silence."*

The Irish dreams, however, stretched across enemy lines. TYC °Confederate Irish would meet Union Irish to swap lies, whiskey, and tobacco and discuss the liberation of Ireland.• LK °Of course, when they faced each other in battle they fought without discrimination.• Such was the situation at Antietam where many Southern Irish clashed with Meagher's Irish Brigade at the Sunken Road.

WCD °Meagher's philosophy of fighting was stereotypically Celtic: Get in close, fight hard, and do as much damage as possible.• BP °The Confederates huddled in the Sunken Road poured volley after volley into the advancing Irish, who fell in piles but would not retreat. Meagher's men saw their friends, brothers, and comrades shot down around them. Yet they charged fearlessly toward the Sunken Road, graphically renaming the site Bloody Lane.•

Amid the wholesale carnage at Antietam, the Irish Brigade lost more than five hundred men, but it won the admiration of the rest of the Union Army of the Potomac. Before they could recover their losses, worse was to come.

Three months later, at Fredericksburg, Virginia, the Irish Brigade was ordered to assault the Confederate position at the stone wall at the foot of BP °Marye's Heights, an almost impregnable position, similar to the Sunken Road at Antietam. The ridge allowed Rebel artillery and riflemen to sweep every inch of the ground in front of them.• For the better part of a day, wave

Although Thomas Francis Meagher (above)—pronounced Marr—and his famed Irish Brigade received much of the publicity accorded to Irish units, many other regiments full of men of Irish descent also served the Northern cause well.

The Ninth Massachusetts Infantry, part of which is pictured below outside of a humorously named tent, was composed largely of Irishmen from Boston. From June 1861 until its muster out in June 1864, the Ninth served the Union cause, taking part in many of the large battles fought by the Army of the Potomac. Its heaviest losses came at the battle of Gaines's Mill, where the regiment lost 57 men killed and 174 troops wounded and missing.

after wave of Federal soldiers had been cut down by the deadly fire, and no one came closer than one hundred feet to the stone wall.

LK °One of the Irishmen went up to his regimental chaplain, William Corby, and asked incredulously, "Father, they're not going to make us assault those positions?" The chaplain replied, "Don't worry, son, the generals aren't that stupid."• The Federal commander, Ambrose E. Burnside, might not have been stupid, but he was single-minded, and he was determined his men would take those heights.

Because the brigade's green regimental flags had been damaged at Antietam, Meagher had his soldiers place sprigs of boxwood in their hats to identify themselves
BP and to remind them of Ireland. °Then he led his men forward and up the slopes toward the stone wall that sheltered half of Lee's army. The cheers went up from the Federals waiting in support: "Go in boys! Give it to them, boys!" The Irish moved forward, but men fell every step of the way.•

The Irish advance was so fearless even the Confederates behind the wall applauded and cheered as they
LK fired on the men in the blue overcoats. °George Pickett, who would lead his own hopeless charge later in the war, wrote his wife that cheers went up among the Irish

*Father Scully, the Catholic priest of the Ninth Massachusetts Infantry, prepares to deliver a sermon at a camp on Arlington Heights, Virginia. The adherence many Irishmen had to the Catholic faith was one of the factors that made them stand out in both the Federal and Confederate armies, which were dominated by Protestant soldiers. Since America's colonial era, Catholics had been scorned and feared as papists who, it was thought, would unquestioningly follow the orders of a foreign pope. Although such prejudice began to melt away as blue- and gray-clad Catholics demonstrated their allegiance to their respective sides, it was still present in American politics as late as 1960 when John F. Kennedy, a Catholic, was elected president.*

behind the wall—Irishmen from Georgia. They cheered the valor of the Yankee Irish attacking the wall.•

The assault ground to a halt well short of the stone wall. More than 12,500 Union soldiers lay dead and wounded on the slope before Marye's Heights. Of the 1,200 members of the Irish Brigade who advanced against the wall, slightly more than 200 returned.
LK °The Confederates said after the battle that the bodies closest to the stone wall all had sprigs of boxwood in their hats.•

JB °After the attack the division commander was reviewing the Eighty-eighth New York when he saw a man standing by himself. The general ordered, "Soldier, stand with your company!" The soldier replied, "I am my company."• Such losses inspired Maj. Lawrence Reynolds to praise the Irishmen in verse: "Mourn ye the blood on this steel rusted blade. / 'Tis all that is left of the Irish Brigade."

The Irish Brigade was forced to fill in its ranks with non-Irish recruits, and it was never the same to
BP Meagher, who could not bear to lead it again. °He had seen his men wasted in two terrible battles and it affected him in such a way that he resigned his command but stayed in the army. Although he remained in uniform the rest of the war, Meagher's heart was never
WCD again in the fighting.• °He took to hard drinking, trying to forget the brave, Irishmen, now dead, he had talked

*Within a span of four months in the fall and winter of 1862, the Irish Brigade suffered withering casualties at the September battle of Antietam and the December engagement of Fredericksburg. At Antietam, the Hibernians followed their green flags into crashing volleys fired by Rebels hiding in the Sunken Road. The field in front of the road was strewn with the bodies of brave Irishmen (left). The brigade was called upon at Fredericksburg to once more assail an entrenched Confederate line. During this attack, Irish Brigade troops fell dead and wounded by the score as they pushed toward the Southern infantry dug in below the Marye House (right).*

into joining the army. In 1867, while serving as acting governor, he accidentally drowned in Montana.•

The Confederate army also had Irish soldiers, but only one quarter as many as the Federal. Unlike the recent surge of immigrants in the North, most of the South's Irish had been in the country for several generations. Although their numbers were smaller, the South laid claim to the greatest Irish-American general of the war: Patrick Cleburne.

TYC °Cleburne was born on Saint Patrick's Day 1828 in County Cork, Ireland. After studying as a pharmacist, he joined the British army and served until 1849, when he immigrated to the United States. Cleburne was working in Helena, Arkansas, as a pharmacist and also reading law when the war started. He enlisted as a private but was elected colonel of his regiment. By March 1862 he was a general and won his first fame at Shiloh the following month. During the coming months he advanced in command, and his men developed a reputation as the best-drilled troops in the Army of Tennessee.•

Like most Irish Confederates, Cleburne possessed a heartfelt loyalty for his new homeland. He fought for
JB the South for the same reasons that most of °the Southern Irish took up arms for their adopted country: The situation paralleled the British oppression of Ireland—

that is, a larger nation trying to impose its will on a smaller country.•

Cleburne should have been promoted to command of the Army of Tennessee, but in 1864 he suggested the South should use slaves as soldiers in return for their freedom. Southern leaders were horrified at the idea of hundreds of thousands of freed, armed slaves among TYC them. As a result, °the Confederate high command passed over Cleburne's promotion four times. He was killed at the November 1864 battle of Franklin, Tennessee, leading a hopeless charge over open ground toward an entrenched Union army.• It was an attack he knew would fail, one that he knew would probably kill him, but he went anyway because he believed in the Confederate cause as much as he believed it was his duty. Weeks after his death, the Confederate Congress finally agreed to arm the slaves, but it was too late to have any effect.

The loss of so many veteran soldiers was a sad blow to those who cherished hopes of Irish freedom. After the war some Irish-Americans did attack the British in both Ireland and Canada, but both campaigns were hopeless failures. Former Union Brig. Gen. Thomas Sweeny—a one-armed veteran and staunch Irish patriot although he had been in the United States for more than thirty-five years—was arrested for leading the attack into Canada.

*Two years of fighting had reduced the Sixty-ninth Pennsylvania, which had been recruited from working-class Philadelphia Irishmen, from its original one thousand men to a mere 258. On a hot July 3, 1863, at Gettysburg, they were barraged for two hours by Confederate fire. When the artillery stopped, the sons of Ireland were startled to see 12,000 Confederates marching toward them. The Sixty-ninth's Col. Dennis O'Kane urged his men not to fire on the Southerners until they "could distinguish the whites of their eyes." When the men of the Sixty-ninth finally did fire, there was a terrible slaughter, but the Southerners kept coming. Colonel O'Kane and thirty-one other Irishmen were killed in the ensuing hand-to-hand combat.*

*Orphaned at age fifteen, Confederate Gen. Patrick Cleburne had served as a corporal in the British army before he left his native Ireland to come to America in 1849. By 1863, he held the rank of major general and the command of one of the divisions in the Army of Tennessee. Cleburne died during the ill-advised Southern assault at the battle of Franklin, on November 30, 1864. Reports stated that his body had been found about forty yards from the Federal earthworks. A Yankee Minié ball had ripped into his chest, just below his heart, and his hand still tightly clasped his sword. Sadly, Cleburne had recently become engaged to a woman named Susan Tarleton. Her handkerchief, a token of her love, was found in the pocket of his blood-stained uniform.*

The Irish, however, did win a postwar victory in the United States. Their sacrifice and heroism during the war helped to break down the prejudice against them.

### *The Germans*

IN 1848 the loose confederation of German states was engulfed by revolution and many failed attempts to overthrow the aristocracy. Thousands of political refugees fled to the United States to escape both the fighting and the revenge DLV of the German rulers. ○They came with a sense of total commitment and found America's representative government to be what they had wanted to establish in their old country, and so they embraced this new homeland without reservation.•

Most Germans settled in the northern states; only a small number went south BP because ○they were not comfortable with slavery. Slavery ran counter to what the Germans had aspired to in their homeland, and at least in their minds, slavery seemed to be a corruption of the American ideal.•

When the North went to war, nearly two hundred thousand German immigrants enlisted, making one of every eight Union soldiers German. They knew what they DLV were fighting for. ○The *Cincinnati Zeitung* had encouraged the German immigrants to do all they could to save America from the Americans, pointing out that Americans lacked the German perspective on despotism.•

Like the Irish, the Germans were defending a country BP that often mocked them. ○They were called Dutchmen from a corruption of *Deutsch,* the German word for *German*. To American ears it sounded like the word WCD *Dutch.*• ○When Germans spoke English, they stuttered and emphasized guttural sounds. Many unsympathetic Americans equated these efforts at mastering a second language as stupidity.•

For Germans living in the South, prejudice sometimes went beyond name calling. Although many

*Unlike the mass of Irish immigrants, who were often poor and uneducated, German émigrés most often fled their homeland because of political unrest and thus came from a mix of social and economic levels. Many Germans became prosperous farmers, while others settled in urban areas, opening shops or other small businesses. Some cities, like Milwaukee and Saint Louis, had large, successful German populations. Nonetheless, such relative prosperity did not prevent the newly arrived "Dutch" from being loathed by "native" white Americans. This painting depicts a German family preparing to depart for the United States.*

Germans fought for the Confederacy, others were victimized. °Since few Germans were slave owners, they were often suspected of being spies or agitators. At Gainesville, Texas, in 1862, more than a dozen German settlers were hanged for not doing enough to aid the Confederate war effort. There was little evidence they had spied against the Confederacy; they simply had not been outspoken enough in their support of the South.•

Germans in the North had demonstrated their pro-Union feelings early in the war when German militia in St. Louis helped to prevent one of the largest arsenals in the country from falling into Confederate hands. °Lincoln, seeking ethnic political support for future congressional and presidential elections, turned to prominent German citizens and offered command positions in return for their votes and loyalty.•

Carl Schurz had been part of the German revolutionary movement and had settled in Wisconsin, where he became a politically influential Republican. He had supported Lincoln's nomination and delivered the German vote in the election of 1860. In appreciation, Lincoln appointed Schurz minister to Spain, but Schurz preferred a military posting. He returned from Spain in

*Carl Schurz was a graduate of the University of Bonn and was esteemed for his intellectual prowess. Fluent in English, he often lectured in public before the war regarding the evils of slavery. Desirous of obtaining the support of the large German population in the North, the Lincoln administration granted Schurz the rank of brigadier general in 1862. His first action came when troops under his command were badly routed at Freeman's Ford on the Rappahannock River in a skirmish that presaged the battle of Second Bull Run. Schurz continued to rise in rank regardless of his uneven military record and ended the conflict a major general. After the Civil War, Schurz served a term in the U. S. Senate from Missouri.*

WCD

January 1862 and resigned his office. The president responded by naming Schurz a brigadier of volunteers in April 1862.

Despite not having any military training, Schurz proved to be a competent general, garnering the respect of professional soldiers and popularity with the German troops he commanded. His first action was to command the rear guard during the withdrawal after the battle of Second Manassas. At Gettysburg he commanded a division of the Eleventh Corps, after which he and his men were transferred to the western theater. Schurz arrived in Chattanooga just in time to hurl back Bragg's army and lay the groundwork for Sherman's Georgia campaign. Schurz left the army briefly in mid-1864 to work for Lincoln's reelection.

°At the same time, one of Lincoln's worst military appointments was Franz Sigel.• A graduate of Karlsruhe Military Academy, Sigel had fled Germany after the unsuccessful 1848 revolution in Prussia. He taught school in St. Louis and played an influential role among the German community in Missouri. Lincoln appointed Sigel a brigadier general in August 1861.

His first action was at Wilson's Creek that same month. The battle was going well for the Federals until a Confederate counterattack routed Sigel's men and drove them from the field. Sigel abandoned his half of the command and returned to his hotel room in Springfield, Missouri. When he yielded the field, the remaining Union force fell back to Springfield. Lacking sufficient supplies, the Southerners chose not to pursue and pulled back. Even so, Sigel remained popular with his German troops, and a recruiting song—"I'm Going to Fight mit Sigel"—was written that helped to add more German soldiers to the Federal rolls.

Sigel's finest performance came at the March 1862 battle of Pea Ridge, Arkansas, where he commanded two divisions and personally directed the Federal artillery in demoralizing and shattering a Confederate force under Gen. Earl Van Dorn. He was transferred to the eastern theater where he engaged Stonewall Jackson in the Shenandoah and commanded the First Corps under John Pope at the battle of Second Manassas.

*Pandemonium reigns as Federal troops flee before a crushing Rebel attack at the battle of Second Bull Run. In the midst of the debacle, Carl Schurz was ordered to use his division to form a rear guard to try to stop the rout. Much like the officer pictured in this sketch, Schurz rode into the midst of the panicked bluecoats, who, he said, were in a very "shattered condition" and "in full retreat." Although he admitted his efforts to reform the "straggling soldiers met with very small success," the brave Schurz did manage to convince a Union battery to resume firing upon the hard-driving Confederates. The cannon blasts helped to check the Southern advance until a more formidable battleline could be cobbled together.*

In May 1864 Sigel's military usefulness ended at New Market, Virginia, where a company of cadets from the Virginia Military Institute spearheaded a charge that broke through the center of his line, which caused the entire Federal force to collapse and withdraw. Sigel was relieved of duty and never given another field command. His record was an odd mix of ineptitude and ability, and his military service was not much better than mediocre.

DLV ○Lincoln kept Sigel on through the 1864 elections. The ethnic vote was not as critical as it had been four years earlier, but Sigel was still able to rally the German immigrants to support the Republican administration.•

Schurz and Sigel both served in the Union Eleventh Corps, which in the early years of the war was more than half-German. The corps commander was Maj. Gen. Oliver O. Howard, a devoutly religious, stiff-mannered Yankee from Maine with little respect for immigrants
BP but with a special feeling for blacks and slaves. ○Howard lacked a sensitivity for the men in the ranks and did not come across to them as one who cared particularly about them.•

Together Howard and the Germans made history, although it would not be something they would especially enjoy. At the May 1863 battle of Chancellorsville, the Eleventh Corps was camped in the spot where Stonewall Jackson's twenty-eight thousand Confederates made their surprise attack on the Union right flank. Howard had made the mistake of not anchoring his line with any geographical feature, such as a stream or wood line. Instead, his flank was in the air.

DLV °Schurz was the first to be aware that something was happening. He informed Howard that reports were coming to him that a Rebel force was approaching around his right flank. Howard ignored him until Jackson's men came charging through the forest at dusk.•

BP °The twilight attack took the Eleventh Corps by surprise. Some regiments fought back and suffered terrible losses; others offered little resistance and fell back.•
WCD °Howard's corps was routed, but it had been caught unaware, and any soldier in either army would have reacted in the same way without feeling ashamed or disgraced.• Many soldiers, however, particularly those who had not faced Jackson's attack, believed that the rout of the Eleventh Corps confirmed their prejudice. Darwin Cody, a Union gunner, voiced his frustration after the battle: "The Germans ran without firing a gun. I say damn the Dutch!"

*Franz Sigel was one of the most conspicuous Germans to have fought for the North. Unfortunately, much of his notoriety stems from his failures on the battlefield. David Hunter Strother, a staff officer under Sigel in 1864, said that at the battle of New Market, "Sigel seemed in a state of excitement and rode here and there . . . jabbering in German. . . . He seemed to forget his English entirely." Strother did admit, though, that Sigel was personally brave and recalled that as "shells flew over and burst" nearby, Sigel "snapped his fingers at them and whistled an imitation of them, thus to show his contempt of the danger."*

BP °The Eleventh Corps was dubbed "The Flying Dutchmen" for fleeing the fight, and the Germans were viewed as reluctant fighters. Yet they were not defeated because they were Germans; they were defeated because their corps commander—Howard—and their army commander—Joseph Hooker—did not respond to the situation. The generals ignored reports that the Confederates were moving against their flank, and that resulted in high casualties among the German-American ranks.•

Two months later history repeated itself at Gettysburg. On the first day of the fighting, Schurz placed the Eleventh Corps on Oak Ridge, north of the town. His men were barely in place before they were attacked by
BP two Confederate divisions. °They were hit, flanked, crushed, and pushed back toward the town, and

Schurz's men broke and ran just as they had at Chancellorsville. Even though their regiments fought hard and suffered significant losses, the prevailing view among the Army of the Potomac was that the "Dutchmen" had run away again.•

The criticism leveled at the Germans was so strong that the War Department transferred the entire Eleventh Corps to the western theater, perhaps hoping that Generals Grant and Sherman would have better luck with
BP the Dutch. °With its past several hundred miles behind it, the Eleventh Corps did perform better. It fought well at Chattanooga, where the men charged up Lookout Mountain and captured the height.• The Eleventh Corps, however, would never redeem its image completely. It later merged with the Twelfth Corps and lost its ethnic identity.

Many German units served heroically in the western
DLV theater—outfits like the Thirty-second Indiana. °The Thirty-second was immortalized by Lew Wallace in his novel *Ben-Hur.* His recollection of the Thirty-second at Shiloh served as the model for his descriptions of the Roman legions marching into Rome.•

The old Eleventh Corps veterans never resolved their hard feelings over their treatment by the Army of the
BP Potomac. °For years after the war they would refight the battles of Chancellorsville and Gettysburg, trying to prove

*German-Americans of the Forty-first New York, some of the troops that went to "Fight mit Sigel," relax in a fortification in Virginia. Also referred to as the "Second Yager Regiment," the Forty-first fought in the largely German Eleventh Corps and saw action in many of the Army of the Potomac's engagements. The language barrier sometimes hampered German soldiers like these, for many of them had arrived in America so recently that they could not yet speak English. During combat, communication problems seriously hampered the effectiveness of "Dutch" regiments and often led to unnecessary casualties or improper movements.*

*Brig. Gen. Julius Stahel, who was born and raised in Hungary, was an officer with a checkered military career. Removed from various commands when his troops failed to perform satisfactorily, he fought well in the battle of Piedmont and was awarded the Medal of Honor.*

that they did not flee the fighting, trying to expunge the charges of cowardice made by their fellow soldiers.•

WCD °Although the German community had given their lives for their adopted country, it was difficult to win approval from Americans. Every time they spoke, they called attention to the fact that they were not native-born Americans. They had a long way to go before they would be accepted as citizens without qualification.•

### *Soldiers of Fortune*

WHILE SOME Americans viewed immigrant soldiers with suspicion, many were impressed easily by foreign-born officers. Several Europeans presented themselves in full uniform before their recruiters and created such an impression as to be welcomed into the service as officers. In the field, however, the commanders who inherited these foreign officers had no way of knowing how good they were until they came under fire.

BP °Both North and South tended to view their armies as bumpkins in uniform or, at best, as armed rabbles. It had been fifteen years since the country had fought a major war. In the meantime Europe had seen fighting throughout the 1850s, and most of the tactics and strategies that influenced the conduct of the Civil War were based on those Continental wars. Thus Europeans were considered the leading experts on modern warfare.•

The great Italian revolutionary hero Guiseppe Garibaldi was courted by both sides. On behalf of the North, Theodore Canisius, once Lincoln's partner in the *Illinois Staats-Anzeiger* and American consul to Vienna during the war, initiated negotiations on his own to offer a command in the Union army to Garibaldi.

Meanwhile, Washington filled with European officers, all offering their credentials to the War Department. WCD At the time °there were no personnel to check the backgrounds of these men. Such procedures were too long and too difficult to determine if those enlisting were as skilled as they claimed to be.•

Not everyone in the country was convinced these soldiers of fortune were real. Early in 1861 the *New York*

*Times* warned, "It is unwise to accept an inability to speak English as evidence of military experience."

○Many of these men were frauds. One was Col. Lionel Jobert D'Epineuil, who claimed to have a distinguished record in the French army and to have been decorated by the emperor, Napoleon III.• D'Epineuil expected to raise a regiment of Zouaves from the French immigrants in New York City, but most of those who were qualified had already enlisted. By November 1861 he had assembled the Fifty-third New York from various ethnic backgrounds, but his officers were all of Gallic heritage. Almost immediately the regiment began to fall apart. D'Epineuil quarreled with his officers, discipline collapsed, and desertions increased. The Fifty-third was assigned to accompany an expedition against North Carolina, but its transport ship failed to rendezvous with the other elements of the expedition. ○By the time the bedraggled soldiers arrived they were in a state of mutiny, and D'Epineuil more or less suffered a breakdown. In the ensuing confusion, D'Epineuil's regiment was sent to Annapolis, where it was discovered that he had never served in the French army and all his other claims were also fraudulent. Charges were drawn up, and D'Epineuil resigned. The regiment was broken up and disbanded in disgrace.•

Alfred N. A. Duffié, another Frenchman, was a minor aristocrat who talked his way into an appointment as a colonel of Federal cavalry. He had been educated at Saint Cyr and decorated for his service in the Crimean War, but Duffié was promoted beyond his abilities. ○He fought through most of the war, but he was criticized regularly for being slow to join the action. Duffié looked the epitome of a French cavalier, but he was overcautious, egotistical, and a poor commander. His tardiness helped lose the June 1863 cavalry battle at Brandy Station.• Still he managed a promotion to brigadier.

The Frenchmen's superiors were secretly delighted when he was captured by the Confederates during Philip H. Sheridan's Shenandoah campaign in 1864. Duffié was seized while riding in the back of an ambulance wagon within sight of the Union camp. His commander did not demand his return. Sheridan's report included

*Little-known Brig. Gen. Albin Schoepf (above) was born of Polish and Austrian parents and was a captain in the Austrian army before coming to the United States in 1851. He fought in several battles in Kentucky before being transferred to superintend the Northern prison at Fort Delaware.*

*Maine-born Oliver O. Howard (below) was a poor choice to lead the heavily German Eleventh Corps. Howard had little understanding of his foreign troops, and they in turn distrusted Howard. Although foreign subordinates like Carl Schurz had warned Howard of the impending Rebel attack at Chancellorsville, he failed to take appropriate defensive measures that could have saved his command.*

*The flight of the Eleventh Corps at Chancellorsville brought a deep, and largely undeserved, stain to the reputations of German-American troops. Afterwards, "American" troops jeered at their German compatriots, "[You] fights mit Sigel but runs mit Schurz, you tam cowards." The non-German officers of the Eleventh Corps also berated their own troops after the battle. "You can imagine my disgust and indignation at the miserable behavior of the Eleventh Corps. You know I have always been down on the Dutch and do not abate my contempt now," scoffed Francis Barlow, commander of the Corps's First Division. A disheartened captain wrote, "The Eleventh Corps is composed primarily of New York Dutch . . . They have never stood fire and I suppose never will."*

the assessment that his brigadier was "a trifling man and a poor soldier. He was captured by his own stupidity."

No soldier of fortune, however, was more celebrated than England's Sir Percy Wyndham, who was made a colonel of the First New Jersey Cavalry. Wyndham had the background and looked the part of a soldier. He had fought with Garibaldi in Italy, and when he came to the United States, he sported one of the largest mustaches on the continent: two huge, thick brushes that jutted out at least six inches from each side of his face.

Early in the war Wyndham boasted that he would capture Col. Turner Ashby, Stonewall Jackson's head of cavalry and a man who was fast becoming a legend for his horsemanship. Instead, on June 6, 1862, an amused Ashby captured the brash Englishman just south of Harrisonburg when Wyndham recklessly charged Ashby's rear guard. In addition to capturing the mustachioed soldier of fortune, Ashby's men left thirty-six Union horsemen on the field and captured another sixty-three.

JB ○As Wyndham was being led through the Confederate lines, he encountered Col. Roberdeau Wheat of the Louisiana Tigers. They greeted each other warmly and enjoyed a brief reunion; both had fought for Italian independence in 1860.•

Wyndham was exchanged within a few months
BP and ○rejoined his regiment in time to lead a thunder-

ing cavalry charge at Brandy Station in June 1863. His brigade went up Fleetwood Hill and crashed into the Rebels with the Englishman in the forefront of the attack.•

By the end of the war Wyndham had established a fine military reputation, but he did not carry that success into civilian
JB life. °He left the army and was involved in a number of business ventures, including a military school and a failed oil refinery that exploded. He then went to India to recoup his fortunes.•

Wyndham ended up giving hot air balloon rides in a badly worn craft.
BP °One of his potential customers pointed this out, and Wyndham replied, "Why, I've taken them up with a hole so big you could drive a wagon through it." Just to show this customer that he was being far too apprehensive, he took the balloon up. It promptly came back down into a lake, and that was the end of Wyndham.•

*Some foreign officers came to the United States to observe the strategy and tactics of the North and South and report their findings to their armies back home. These British officers were photographed at a Union camp near Yorktown, Virginia, in 1862. The officer standing at the far right is in mufti—or civilian—dress. One such foreign observer was Arthur J. L. Fremantle, an English colonel who spent a good deal of time with Gen. Robert E. Lee's army. At Gettysburg, Fremantle recalled that he had a hard time convincing locals he was "an English spectator and a non-combatant." He also "observed that Southern Irishmen make excellent 'Rebs,' and have no sort of scruple in killing as many of their Northern brethren as they possibly can."*

### *The Canadians*

DURING THE Civil War, America's northern neighbor was not yet called Canada; it was still officially British North America. Although officially neutral, like Britain, more than fifty thousand Canadians fought in the war, primarily for the North because many Canadians living in and near the United States strongly believed that slavery
WCD was morally wrong. °Slavery had never existed in Canada; thus, Canadians could side with the Union on humanitarian grounds.•

The cash bounties being offered to join the Federal
IM army and navy were also significant inducements. °At the outset of the war, the Union navy was small, which forced the government to look to British North America's maritime provinces in search of crews for the expanding fleet.• As a result, Canadian sailors were with David Farragut in August 1864 when he sailed into Mobile Bay, Alabama. When Farragut's flagship was

*Lt. James Bumgardner of the Fifty-second Virginia Infantry remembered that after Sir Percy Wyndham (above) was captured in 1862, he was indignant and angry. Wyndham "was very tall, elegantly dressed," wrote Bumgardner, "wearing every ornament permissible under regulations. His low-topped boots had gold tassels hanging out in front. As he passed by . . . [a guard] called out: 'Look yonder boys; there is a Yankee colonel!' . . . He, a titled Englishman . . . called a Yankee by a . . . ragged Rebel!" Wyndham, continued Bumgardner, responded to his tormentors "with a . . . look of scorn, [and] said: 'I am not a Yankee, you . . . Rebel fool.'" Wyndham's retort was met with laughter, causing him to fill the air with curses and oaths.*

struck, Canadian William Pelham helped save the ship. IM ○He cleared the decks of debris, ensured the wounded were taken below, and organized the remounting of guns as necessary and returning them to action. He was subsequently awarded the Medal of Honor for his efforts.• Four other Canadians won Medals of Honor at Mobile Bay, and twenty-four more received it by the war's end.

Canada had become a final destination for runaway slaves on the Underground Railroad during the decades that the Fugitive Slave Act required northerners to aid in their apprehension. Thus many African Americans in Canada were keen to return to the country of their birth and fight for the Union.

When the Emancipation Proclamation was promulgated in January 1863, African Americans in Canada returned to U.S. borders to join the Union army. IM ○Young blacks enlisted en masse in Michigan and traveled as far as Massachusetts so they could enroll in the Fifty-fifth Massachusetts Infantry, a black regiment being formed after the battle-proven successes of the famous Fifty-fourth Massachusetts.•

Canadians in Yankee uniforms were not restricted IM in gender. ○Franklin Thompson of the Second Michigan fought at the September 1862 battle of Antietam and was in fact Canadian Sarah Edmonds. She had been dressing as a boy since growing up on her father's farm and had run away when she did not like the man her father had chosen for her husband. She took the name of Franklin Thompson to sell Bibles, and when the war started "Thompson" joined the Union army. While no one discovered her secret, several men in her company noted that "he" was different and nicknamed "him" the "hairless boy." Thompson aka Edmonds did not reveal her gender until 1884 at a reunion of the Second Michigan.•

While Canadian participation helped in the Union victory, it ultimately had a greater effect on the Canadian territory itself. IM ○Many of the British North Americans who fought in the war developed a greater understanding of nationhood, and two years after the war, Canada became an independent nation.•

*Paris-born Alfred Alexander Duffié (above right) proudly wears the four medals he received during the Crimean War while fighting in the French army. His mediocre command record in the Federal Cavalry Corps and his haughty attitude won him few friends within the Union ranks where he served.*

*During the 1864 Shenandoah Valley campaign, the Confederate partisan ranger John Mosby captured Duffié as he rode in a Federal ambulance (above left). One of Mosby's men quipped that as they bore down upon the lurching ambulance, he saw the "general and his aide tossing from one side to the other over the top of each other—Hats off! Now down—then up! Every few minutes a shell would burst close to the carriage, and down their heads would duck to the bottom of the carriage."*

### *The French*

VERY FEW British Canadians fought for the South, but many French Canadians fought alongside their Louisiana Cajun cousins. One study of the birthplaces of the seven thousand Confederates from Louisiana found only twenty-three hundred had been born in the state. Almost as many had been born abroad in such places as France, Ireland, Germany, Switzerland, Canada, Scotland, Poland, and Brazil. °Of all the foreign nationalities that came to the United States to fight, more people of French descent fought for the Confederacy than for the Union.•

The French Zouave, however, influenced both sides. Zouaves represented an elite fighting force; they were reputed to be the bravest of the brave. That conception permeated the North much more than the South because the immediate prewar years saw city and state militias in the North model themselves after the Zouaves. °Zouave uniforms also added a sense of dash and bravado to young men on the adventure of a lifetime—glorious war—and the image was very popular with impressionable young women.• Zouave influence in the South was largely limited to the French heritage of Louisiana, where many former Zouaves of the French army had immigrated over the decade prior to the war.

Among the Louisiana French soldiers were the infamous Coppens's Zouaves, formally known as the First

*One of the few Frenchmen to fight for the Confederacy, Prince Camille Armand Jules Marie de Polignac (above) began his Southern service as a lieutenant colonel and rose to the rank of major general.*

*The French noblemen (below) were observing Union Gen. McClellan's Peninsula campaign: the comte de Paris (center of the group); his brother, the duc de Chartres (far left); their uncle, the prince de Joinville (second from left). The comte de Paris kept a journal of his experiences and observations in America.*

Battalion, Louisiana Zouaves, organized by Gaston WCD Coppens. °One Confederate commander said Coppens's Zouaves was composed of the gutter sweepings of New Orleans. Some of the men in Coppens's company enlisted so they could continue doing what they had been doing in private life, namely, brawling, and be paid for services rendered.• In every town near which they camped, robberies and burglaries increased to the point that the towns begged the army to move the Louisianians.

The adventures of Coppens's Zouaves began on the BP train that was supposed to take them to Virginia. °The enlisted men uncoupled the car carrying their officers at a stop while the officers were eating, then they hijacked the rest of the train while a number of them cavorted on the roofs of the cars.• At one point the train was jolted, and some of the men fell from the tops of boxcars and were crushed. Another Zouave standing on one of the cars did not see a low bridge. The train stopped in Montgomery, Alabama, where the Zouaves ran amuck, searching for alcohol. Several hours later TYC °the officers caught up with the battalion and pistol-whipped the men onto another train.• By the time Coppens's Zouaves reached the Virginia front, nine of the beaten, bloody men had died from their escapade.

In battle the Zouaves showed the same WCD reckless abandon, °proving to be vicious soldiers. Indeed, like most Confederate Zouave regiments, Coppens's Zouaves were so aggressive on the battlefield they BP virtually bled themselves to death.• °By the time the Confederate army reached Antietam in September 1862, there were very few Southern Zouaves remaining. After Antietam—where their commander died—Coppens's regiment ceased to exist.•

Another Frenchman in Confederate colors was the aristocratic Prince Camille Armand Jules Marie de Polignac. His family was one of the most distinguished families of France, and he had served in the French army during the Crimean War.

He was in South America, studying plant life, when the Civil War broke out, and he offered his services to the Confederacy. In July 1861 he was made a lieutenant colonel of infantry and then served as chief of staff to P. G. T. Beauregard at the April 1862 battle of Shiloh.

WCD °Polignac's men had great difficulty pronouncing his last name, much less his full name, and so they called him Polecat. The Frenchman was more amused than insulted, especially since he, unlike many foreign officers, proved to be an excellent general.•

By January 1863 Polignac was a brigadier serving in the western theater of the war. He distinguished himself in the defense against the Federals' Red River campaign and at the battle of Mansfield, Louisiana, in April 1864. His performance during the latter action led to his advance in rank to major general.

TYC °In March 1865 Polignac went to France to seek aid for the Confederacy, but the surrender at Appomattox made his mission pointless.• Rather than return to the United States, he retired to his family's estates and wrote several articles on the Civil War. When he died in Paris in 1913, Polignac was the last surviving major general of the Confederacy.

BP °In the Federal army the most successful French-born officer was Phillippe Régis Dénis de Keredern de Trobriand. He had a career as an author, poet, novelist, philanderer, and duelist before he met an American heiress. The couple were married in Paris in 1843, moved to Venice, and then settled in New York in 1847. There de Trobriand was editor of the *Revue de nouveau monde* and a contributing writer to *Le courier des Etats-Unis*.•

When the war began, de Trobriand enlisted and was made colonel of the Garde Lafayette, a French militia unit
IM that formed the nucleus of the Fifty-fifth New York. °The unit had more than a Gallic look to it; the Garde Lafayette also had the flavor as well, taking along renowned chefs and cooks for the officers' mess. The Garde were quickly nicknamed Les Gardes des Fourchettes, which translated means "Guards of the Forks."•

BP °American regiments were surprised to see de Trobriand's red-trousered Fifty-fifth New York chasing

*Born into a wealthy French family in 1816, Régis de Trobriand was the descendent of a father and uncle who fought with Napoleon Bonaparte. A Renaissance man who enjoyed painting, writing, and the study of the law, de Trobriand had a particular love for the life of a soldier. He entered Union service as the colonel of the Fifty-fifth New York and ended the war as a major general. The pose above shows him as a brigadier general. As the Fifty-fifth prepared to parade out of New York City, de Trobriand wrote: "I took a long look at that double line of brave men, gayly marching to meet the hazards of the field of battle, where many must shed their blood and many must loose [sic] their lives. . . . At the command, Forward! March! the noise of the drums was for an instant drowned by a rousing hurrah! The die was cast, the Fifty-fifth was on the road to the front."*

*Fancy uniforms alone did not make a good regiment as in the case of Col. Lionel Jobert D'Epineuil's Zouaves, the Fifty-third New York Infantry. Its brief, doleful history began in the late summer of 1861, when D'Epineuil attempted to raise a regiment from the French populace of New York City. He soon found, however, that most of the area's Frenchmen were already in Federal service, and so he had to accept a mix of nationalities and men of questionable character into the unit. A poor disciplinarian, D'Epineuil allowed the morale of the Fifty-third to deteriorate to the point where the regiment became more trouble than it was worth. Gen. George B. McClellan, who was then commanding the Army of the Potomac, personally ordered the unit disbanded after only two months of service.*

frogs through swamps, taking them back to camp, and eating them.• They relinquished their forks, however, long enough to impress their fellow regiments in battle, including a daring charge at Fair Oaks during the 1862 IM Peninsula campaign. °Toward the end of that particular engagement one of the soldiers said, "They can call us Les Gardes des Fourchettes any time they want."•

De Trobriand served gallantly as a brigade then division commander from Gettysburg to Appomattox Court House. His bravery and skill demonstrated to native-born Northern soldiers that not all immigrants were to be looked down upon.

### *Multinational Regiments*

Of all the foreign regiments, none was more foreign than the Thirty-ninth New York, also called the Garibaldi Guard. The regiment was named for Guiseppe Garibaldi, the Italian patriot and general who succeeded DLV in unifying his country in 1861. °Seven different ethnic groups were found in this regiment of nine hundred men, including Hungarians, Italians, Poles, Germans, Czechs, Spaniards, and Portuguese.•

In such a diverse regiment as this, the problem of WCD communicating orders was enormous. °An order might have to go through three or four translations. For instance, "Tell Stavo to attack the right flank" would have to be translated from German to Polish and from Polish to Italian and from Italian to Czech to reach all of the officers. Yet when the order finally reached the men, it might be announced as something like "My sweater's too tight."•

The Thirty-ninth's Hungarian colonel, Frederic BP D'Utassy, did understand the language of money. °His career ended rather quickly when it was discovered that he was selling government horses to civilians and pocketing the money. He was prosecuted and imprisoned.• D'Utassy's deputy, Italian Alex Repetti, ran afoul of military justice and was court-martialed.

WCD °The French-inspired Zouaves were not the only regiments of provocatively dressed soldiers in the Union army. Scotsmen of the Seventy-ninth New York Highlanders began the war wearing kilts. That did not go over well with Yankees accustomed to seeing men in pants.• The editors of the *New York Military Gazette* criticized the look as, "Short petticoats and bare knees, in poor taste and barbarous."

Fashionable or not, kilts were not practical. Before their first battle, many in the Seventy-ninth had retired their kilts, except for one officer. En route to Manassas Junction, the officer BP °chased a pig under a fence. When the officer tried to jump over the fence, his kilt snagged on a rail. He hung there helpless for a few moments while his men and others laughed at him as they marched past. He changed to trousers before the unit reached Bull Run.•

*Col. Waldimir Kryzanowski, a native of a Polish region of Europe, was a brave and competent leader, although his record is often overshadowed by the fact that he fought for most of the war in the ill-fated Eleventh Corps. At Gettysburg Kryzanowski's superiors ordered his brigade to move forward in a compact mass of columns, a formation that made them ripe for incurring heavy casualties by artillery fire. One of Kryzanowski's men wrote that the Confederate "shells plunged through our solid squares, making terrible havoc." Kryzanowski was himself hurt when his horse was shot and he was thrown off the stricken animal. The injured Polish officer managed to recover sufficiently to lead his regiments to the safety of Cemetery Hill.*

Of all the diverse nationalities among the Union general officers, there was only one Russian. Ivan Vasilovitch Turchinoff was a graduate of the Imperial Military School in St. Petersburg. He advanced quickly in the ranks from an ensign in the horse artillery to a colonel of the imperial guard. Turchinoff fought in Hungary and the Crimea and was praised for designing the coastal defenses of Finland. He and his wife immigrated to the United States in 1856; he Americanized his name to Turchin and worked for the Illinois Central Railroad.

When war broke out, he was made colonel of the Nineteenth Illinois, which he drilled into a hard-fighting unit. His wife accompanied him, serving as a nurse and mother figure for the regiment. The Nineteenth saw action in Missouri, Kentucky, and Alabama. TYC °The capture of Huntsville, Alabama, earned Turchin the nicknames "the Russian Thunderbolt" and "the Mad Cossack."

Turchin practiced the Continental theory of war, a version of total war that prompted him in May 1862 to raze the city of Athens, Alabama, after some of the townspeople fired on his brigade.• JB °He did not order the town burned, but he said he would shut his eyes to whatever looting his men desired for an hour. When he learned the town had not been torched, he announced that he would shut his eyes for an hour and a half. His men finally understood, and they burned the town.•

Don Carlos Buell, Turchin's field commander, was incensed at the burning of Athens and ordered the Russian court-martialed and dismissed from the service. JB °Turchin's persuasive wife took the case to Washington and appealed personally to President Lincoln. The Russian officer was not only reinstated but also promoted from colonel to brigadier general.•

Turchin went on to lead his brigade at Chickamauga, Chattanooga, and throughout the Atlanta campaign. His failing health, however, forced him to resign in October 1864.

The Union army had a Latin flavor, too. Brothers Federico and Adolfo Cavadra had a Cuban father and a Philadelphia-born mother; the brothers became distinguished Union officers. BP °After the war, both brothers went to Cuba to fight for the freedom of their country, which was still under the rule of Spain.• DLV °Both became involved in running weapons and supplies into the island to aid the insurrectionists, and both were given the rank of general in the insurrectional army.• BP °The two brothers were arrested and suffered tragic fates: Federico was executed by firing squad and Adolfo died of disease.•

*The officers of the multinational Thirty-ninth New York (below), the Garibaldi Guard, had resplendent, opulent uniforms. The wide-brimmed hats, trimmed with green cockades, worn by some were modeled on the uniform of the famous Bersaglieri, the elite Italian infantry troops. Although Hungarian Frederick D'Utassy (above), the first colonel of the regiment, left the army under a cloud of scandal, the Thirty-ninth continued to fight until the end of the war and teamed with other regiments at Gettysburg to push back a Confederate assault on July 2.*

MORE THAN half a million immigrants fought in the Civil War and helped determine the outcome. Whether they fought for the North or the South, they earned the right to call themselves Americans with their blood. BP °The fact that immigrants fought with such bravery on both sides meant that their acceptance by the typical American had come a long way from those days before the war when they were treated as less than human beings.•

There was no better illustration of why these immigrants fought than Union soldier James McKay Rorty, who brought his whole family, one by one, from Ireland to New York. When his father pleaded with him not to fight, Rorty wrote the reason why he must: "The separation of this Union would close forever the wide portals through which the pilgrims of liberty have sought and found it. Our only guarantee is the Constitution, our only safety is in the Union, one and indivisible." Rorty was twenty-six years old when he died commanding a New York battery at Gettysburg.

The end of the Civil War sparked the greatest tide of immigration in American history. During the next fifty years, twenty-five million Europeans came to America. The fact that the United States still existed as one nation was due in no small part to the sacrifices made in the Civil War by earlier immigrants.

The friction that had dominated the immigrant soldiers' experience when the war began dissipated as it dragged on, and foreigners came to be respected for their martial qualities and battlefield successes. The Irish regiments especially were noted for their reckless courage in battle, having received more decorations and casualties than any other regiments in the Union army. Soon, courage in battle became the mark of a man, and the soldier who proved his bravery was no longer disparaged for peculiarities of speech or custom.

*John Basil Turchin came to the United States from Russia only five years before the outbreak of the Civil War. An experienced soldier who had fought in the czar's Imperial Guard, Turchin became the colonel of an Illinois regiment in 1861. Schooled in European-style warfare in which the looting of hostile towns was considered a matter of course, in February 1862 Turchin told his troops, "I will shut mine eyes for von hour," so that they could pillage and burn Athens, Alabama, after some of the townspeople had fired on his brigade. Although this tactic would later become common, Turchin was at first denounced for his conduct, and only a personal plea by his wife to Abraham Lincoln saved him from a dishonorable discharge. The Russian later gained a promotion to brigadier general and fought with distinction at the battles of Chickamauga and Missionary Ridge before failing health drove him to leave the army in October 1864.*

PHILADA
N.Y. AND
BALTIMORE
PAPERS.

# REPORTING THE WAR

The NATION FIRST LEARNED OF FORT Sumter, Manassas, Shiloh, Gettysburg, and Appomattox from the reporters who ventured onto these battlefields with the armies that fought there. Their descriptions of these events revolutionized the industry, one that had already gone through tremendous change in the twenty years before the war. In spite of the changes that had already taken place in newspaper publishing, all aspects—reporting, editing, circulation, printing, advertising, and illustration—were affected by the Civil War. transforming newspapers from a messenger of editorial opinion into a conduit of information upon which individual opinion could be based. At the same time, the course of the war was affected by the way in which the news of the conflict was dispensed to the American public, generating largely wide-based support and participation for the war effort.

Almost 150 years later, the memories and emotions of the battlefield and the home front can be known due to the effort of these pioneering newspaper and magazine reporters, artists, and photographers. During the war, they were the primary avenue by which the public learned what was happening to their loved ones in harm's way.

Three factors influenced drastic changes in the press in the years prior to the Civil War. First, the literacy rate in America increased, and more publications were made available. The Civil War, in fact, was the first war in

| | |
|---|---|
| WCD | William C. Davis |
| JJH | John J. Hennessy |
| HH | Harold Holzer |
| JFM | John F. Marszalek |
| CN | Chris Nelson |
| BP | Brian Pohanka |
| GAR | Gerald A. Regan |
| JIR | James I. Robertson Jr. |

*Born into poverty, William Lloyd Garrison went to work as a printer to help support his family and became enthralled with the power of newspapers to communicate ideas. Many people came to hate Garrison for his strong support of abolitionism, and on one occasion he had to hide from a gang of white laborers who wanted to lynch him. Nevertheless, Garrison fearlessly used his newspaper, the* Liberator, *to expound his opposition to the slave system, stating, "I am in earnest—and I will not equivocate—I will not excuse—I will not retreat a single inch—and I will be heard." Although his paper had a fairly small circulation, Garrison is credited with keeping the abolition of slavery a topical issue throughout the antebellum era. In 1866 Garrison stepped down from his role with the* Liberator *after the ratification of the Thirteenth Amendment formally abolished involuntary servitude.*

which the average soldier could be reasonably expected to read and write. Second, editors began to emphasize news gathering. Previously, newspapers printed whatever news came their way. Systematic efforts at seeking the news did not exist until the second quarter of the nineteenth century. The first Washington correspondent, for instance, began covering news of the nation's capital in the 1820s and 1830s. He was James Gordon Bennett, who later established the *New York Herald.* In 1848 six leading New York papers formed a cooperative, the forerunner of the Associated Press, "to procure foreign news by telegraph" from Boston from the ships arriving from Europe. The telegraph itself, which was developed in 1844, revolutionized news gathering by allowing news to be transmitted instantaneously. Third, dramatic developments occurred in the technology of printing. In the early 1800s most newspapers were printed on hand presses, but by the outbreak of the Civil War, papers were using cylinder presses capable of making up to twenty thousand impressions an hour.

These drastic changes led to a dramatic increase in the influence of the press, which was seen in the significant role it played in events leading up to the Civil War. Abolitionists, for example, promulgated their cause through independent newspapers, the best known being William Lloyd Garrison's *Liberator* in Boston. Although it was influential, the *Liberator* never had more than three thousand subscribers. The *Liberator* caused such violent reaction among its readers that Amos Kendall, himself a journalist, believed that Garrison should be gagged. As postmaster general, Kendall allowed abolitionist papers to be removed from the mail going into the South.

Because of such censorship, freedom of the press became an important issue in addition to freedom from slavery for the abolitionists, who were frequently persecuted. James G. Birney, for instance, was mobbed when he began printing the *Philanthropist* in Cincinnati, and Elijah Lovejoy, editor of the *Saint Louis Observer,* was murdered, becoming a martyr for the abolitionist cause.

The abolitionist theme was picked up by leading newspapers of the day, including Horace Greeley's *New York Tribune,* which had a circulation of its weekly edition of two hundred thousand in the 1850s. Greeley felt so strongly about abolition that he helped form the new Republican party. Abraham Lincoln read the *Tribune* regularly and was an admirer of "Uncle Horace." Joseph Medill's *Chicago Tribune* was also strongly against slavery, but more moderate papers, such as the *New York Herald* and the *Springfield (Ill.) Republican*, were opposed to the abolitionists.

The public believed what they read. Newspaper editors knew the weight of the written word and often allowed rumor and exaggeration to be printed as fact. Perhaps the most glaring example of this gullibility occurred during the decade preceding the war, when newspapers in the South insisted that a slave revolt was imminent. They carried reports that the slaves were being incited by white infiltrators and outside agitators. Ultimately, the papers claimed that the blacks were going to murder their masters on the day Lincoln was inaugurated as president. Slave armies would then take over the cities of Montgomery, Natchez, and New Orleans so they could set up black kingdoms in the South.

All of this was nonsense, growing out of fear and rumor that was exaggerated by the press, but it panicked the South. The fear, however, was real, dating back to the most recent slave revolt in 1831, which was led by Nat Turner in Virginia and had left fifty-five whites

*Horace Greeley, one of the most influential editors in American journalism, went to work at age fourteen for a small newspaper in his native New Hampshire. A few years later he moved to New York City and became heavily involved in Whig politics, starting his famous* New York Tribune *in 1840 as a vehicle for that party's message. Greeley was an idealist who believed that the political and material wealth of the United States should be shared by the common man. The secret of the popularity of Greeley and his paper was his commitment to his readers. During the Civil War, many Union soldiers resented Greeley's daily headline "Forward to Richmond," which was felt to be the opinion of a civilian who knew little of the horrors of battle. Crusty and often disheveled, Greeley remained an influential and respected journalist until he died in the 1870s.*

*The massive printing press pictured at left was one of three used by the* Tribune *in 1861. The rotary press revolutionized newspaper distribution. In 1800 newspapers were printed one sheet at a time. By 1860, however, rotary presses could print more than 20,000 sheets per hour.*

*The grand and imposing buildings of several newspapers in New York City's "Printing House Square" underscore the importance the press held in nineteenth-century America. The offices of the* Sunday Times *are at far left, and immediately adjacent is the headquarters of Horace Greeley's* New York Tribune. *Many famous people passed the threshold of this edifice, including Karl Marx, whom Greeley employed for a time as a foreign correspondent. The large structure that houses the* New York Times *stands at the center of the sketch. In addition to these papers, the city was home to the* New York Herald, *the* Journal, *the* Evening Post, *and many others.*

dead. The panic during the 1850s led to hundreds of slaves being whipped and lynched as punishment for their involvement in the phantom conspiracy.

When the war broke out, people in both the North and the South wanted whatever news they could get. Out of this chaotic cauldron, daily newspapers and weekly magazines carried desperately needed news that might contain some element of hope that the end of the strug-
BP gle was in sight. ○The public wanted to know if their loved ones were at the front and if they were in danger. They wanted to know what was happening to the army in which their husband or brother or son marched.•

Common soldiers such as Sam Watson, a veteran of the Confederate Army of Tennessee, articulated their experiences as best they could, which were sometimes put into print: "Are these things real? . . . Did I see those brave and noble countrymen of mine laid low in death and weltering in their blood? Did I see our country laid waste and in ruins? Did I see soldiers marching, the earth trembling and jarring beneath their measured tread? Did I see the ruins of smouldering cities and deserted homes? . . . Surely they are but the vagaries of mine own imagination. . . . But, hush! I now hear the approach of battle. That low, rumbling sound in the west is the roar of cannon in the distance."

WCD ○Both North and South possessed a tremendous sense of involvement and patriotism. People bought newspapers and kept them for the entire war, building a

personal archive of the news of what was happening day by day, week by week, year by year. Their concern for family members in uniform was expressed by a ravenous appetite for news.•

Most of the news was accumulated and distributed in the North. Except for the early months of the war, the journalists who covered the struggle for Northern newspapers had no counterparts in the South, where the lack of manpower and resources hobbled the Confederate press. As early as May 23, 1861, the *New York Herald* noted that many Southern papers had been reduced to half-sheets, and by the spring of 1863 this was also true of every daily paper in Richmond.

When the war broke out, the South lacked a metropolitan press. In 1860 Richmond's population was only thirty-eight thousand, but as the community of the Confederate capital increased during the war, the *Richmond Dispatch,* the city's largest paper, developed a circulation of almost eighteen thousand, but even that was hardly enough to support a significant news staff. New Orleans was the only city in the South to have more than one hundred thousand residents, but the Crescent City was occupied by Union forces in April 1862. Before that date, the *Daily Picayune* groaned that all of its reporters had enlisted.

Enterprising Southern editors organized a cooperative, the Press Association of the Confederate States, to pool their war news, which they gathered from official reports, occasional contributors (usually staff officers), and the

*Publishing a pro-Southern newspaper in the North could be dangerous during the Civil War. An angry mob (above left) streams from the office of such a paper, the* Haverhill (Massachusetts) Democrat, *bearing the tarred and feathered publisher on a rail. The image above right shows the ransacked office of the anti-Union* Bridgeport (Connecticut) Farmer. *In addition to such informal and violent repression of the press, the Federal government sanctioned the suppression of twenty newspapers during the war. President Lincoln pursued a shrewd course regarding the infringement of freedom of the press. Publicly, he condoned such action, thereby satisfying the extreme element of his Republican Party. Privately he fretted that suppression could actually galvanize more opposition to his administration and the war effort. In one case, Lincoln wrote a general who had arrested the publisher of a Saint Louis paper that he "regret[ed] to learn" of the incident. The president then suggested the officer avoid "the trouble this is likely to bring" by freeing the prisoner.*

*Two influential Southern editors were William Tappan Thompson (above) of the* Savannah Morning News *and Col. John Forsyth (below), who served dual roles for the Confederacy as the mayor of Mobile and the editor of the* Mobile Advertiser and Register. *The Mobile paper was staunchly pro-secession, and helped keep the city's citizens behind the Southern cause until the last bitter days of the conflict.*

Northern papers. The latter was used so frequently that Northern reporters could be said to have reported the war for both sides. On the whole, the Press Association served its forty-three-member daily papers well. It made an effort to report no opinions or comments on events and the resulting objectivity of its stories has been regarded as constituting a revolution in journalistic writing.

This loose framework of news-gathering was not limited to the South. CN °While in many ways the Civil War was a modern war, the Federal government lacked a sophisticated reporting network. The Lincoln administration was often in the dark as to what was happening to the armies in the field and relied on newspaper reporters as much as anybody. The president himself frequently visited the telegraph office near the White House between midnight and 2 A.M.—nightly during active campaigning—for some word of the war. Sometimes his first information on an engagement came from an enterprising journalist submitting his story via telegraph.•

During the early months of the war, much of the reporting was highly patriotic and wildly inaccurate. WCD °Yankee newsmen covering the Federal army usually reported that the men fought bravely and the generals led brilliantly. If the battle was lost, it was because the army succumbed to overwhelmingly superior numbers and the enemy had fought in a cowardly, craven fashion. This was what the people at home wanted to hear, and the newspaper reporters gave it to them.•

JIR °It took a while for the journalists to begin to portray the real carnage, the human debris, the absolute hell of the battles they reported. Initially, their reports could only occasionally allude to the human sacrifice on the battlefield without going into too much detail.•

The men who reported the war in the East for the Northern newspapers were a unique breed. CIN °They called themselves "Bohemians" because they were proud of being raffish and nonconformist. After their first battle, they called themselves the Bohemian Brigade. They kept a common headquarters in the field, where they wrote their stories and drank together.• They lived the adventure of a lifetime and placed their own peculiar stamp on some of the most tedious tasks.

*The* Atlanta Daily Intelligencer, *one of four papers published in that city, kept residents informed of General Sherman's approach throughout the frightening summer and fall of 1864, advising the populace to "stand firm." When the fall of Atlanta became inevitable, the paper left its office (left) for a safer location.*

*New York Herald* reporter George Alfred Townsend turned the grim duty of compiling casualty lists into a lark: "I went to and fro obtaining the names of killed, wounded, and missing. These I scrawled upon bits of newspaper, upon envelopes, upon the lining of my hat, and finally upon my shirt wristbands. I was literally filled with notes, and if I had been shot, endeavors to obtain my name would have been extremely difficult."

WCD °When the people at home knew that a battle was being fought, they swarmed the newspaper office. After the first news came in, the publisher would run off a special broadside and post it outside his door, highlighting what had happened at the battle and listing the initial casualties.• Those in the front ranks of the crowd would generally call out the news to the people behind.

WCD °The War Department tried to discourage the printing of casualty lists. Such news was depressing, especially when it appeared in the newspaper week after week, month after month, year after year.•

Knowing that the public was desperate for news of the front lines, the Bohemians competed intensely,
CN and the "scoop" was born. °When the reporters for the city newspapers had a scoop, it meant an extra sixty or seventy thousand newspapers in sales. This was an era when five thousand papers sold in a day would be the average circulation, and so a boost of sixty-five thousand copies was extremely profitable to the newspaper owners.

*Newspapers were a welcome diversion from the monotony of military life and important factors in keeping morale high. This painting by William Ludwell Sheppard shows entrenched Confederate troops eagerly devouring the contents of a paper. When possible, soldiers would use "appropriated" printing presses to put out camp or regimental newspapers, often applying colorful names to them. Confederates published the* Mule, *the* Wood Chuck, *and the* Rapid Ann, *the last a somewhat ribald turn on the name of Virginia's Rapidan River. Union makeshift publishers printed the* Buck and Ball, *the* Camp Kettle, *and the* Unconditional S. Grant.

Sometimes the New York reporters, who had large expense accounts, would charter a train for themselves alone. They would write their stories on the train on the way back home from a battle. The charter might cost five hundred dollars, an unbelievable amount of money at the time, but it was a sum the newspaper owners were willing to spend to beat their competition on the streets.•

Americans everywhere came to rely on the New York newspapers, whose editors were the most outspoken. One editor towered above the others: Horace Greeley of the *New York Tribune.* °He had become one of the most important people in America during the decade prior to the war. People subscribed to the *Tribune* all over the country, North and South, because, love him or hate him, they wanted to know what Greeley thought about every issue, including the war.•

In June 1861, before any significant battles had been fought, Greeley believed the Federal volunteers could easily conquer Richmond and end the war. Day after day his *Tribune* thundered with headlines of "On to Richmond!" Thousands of young volunteers, particularly those from New York State, massed in Washington eager to crush the Rebels.

Amid the hysteria rose one dissenting voice, London *Times* correspondent William Howard Russell, a man who had seen war firsthand in the Crimea and who saw that the Union volunteers were woefully unprepared for the fight ahead of them. In the weeks before the battle of First Manassas he wrote: "I heard occasional dropping shots in the camp. To my looks of inquiry, an engineer said quietly: 'They are volunteers shooting themselves.' The number of accidents and the carelessness of the men is astonishing. In every day's paper, there is a count of deaths and wounded caused by the discharge of firearms in the tents."

Greeley and the *Tribune* continued to rouse public opinion and forced Lincoln to act prematurely. For a brief time the press controlled the operations of the military. The war cries "On to Richmond!" "Forward to Richmond!" "End the Rebellion Now!" propelled the Union army under Gen. Irvin McDowell out of Washington and into battle with the Confederate army of Gen. P. G. T. Beauregard at Manassas.

The rush to arms proved reckless. The confused Federal forces suffered a disastrous defeat at the battle of First Manassas in July 1861. *Boston Journal* reporter Charles C. Coffin described the battle in words the country was not yet ready to read: "Men fall. They are bleeding, torn and mangled. The trees are splintered as if smitten by thunderbolts. There is smoke, dust, wild talking, shouting, hissings, howlings, explosions. It's a strange, new, unanticipated experience to the soldiers of both armies."

As soon as that battle ended, Greeley, who had clamored long and hard for the move against Richmond because he felt victory was easily attainable, became a prophet of doom. He immediately became an outspoken critic, calling upon Lincoln to end the war: "If the Rebels are not to be beaten, then every drop of blood henceforth shed in this quarrel will be wantonly,

*As in today's newspapers, editorial cartoons in the nineteenth century either supported or took jibes at prominent political figures. This one appeared during the 1864 presidential election and portrays the Democratic candidate Gen. George McClellan as Shakespeare's Hamlet. He is holding the head of Abraham Lincoln, who fills the role of "poor Yorick" in the play. The cartoon also takes a potshot at the Irish, casting a son of the Emerald Isle as the grinning, ghoulish gravedigger.*

**Frank Leslie's Illustrated Newspaper** *and* **Harper's Weekly,** *whose mastheads are shown above on this and the facing page, were two of the most popular weekly national papers during the Civil War era. Although they were printed in the North, both Union and Confederate soldiers eagerly read these papers when they could. Frank Leslie, the editor and owner of his self-named paper, was one of the first publishers to use a production system that could quickly engrave copies of photographs for publication. His process allowed his paper to print images of incidents that had occurred within the same week, providing an exciting immediacy previously unknown.* **Leslie's Illustrated** *put into print approximately three thousand war-related engravings between 1861 and 1865.*

wickedly shed. It is best for the country and for mankind that we make peace with the Rebels at once, and on their own terms. Do not shrink even from that."

Ignoring Greeley's advice, Lincoln issued a call for another one million men to fight the Rebels. The president had learned two valuable lessons: The fight to preserve the Union would be long and hard, and for as long as it lasted, he would suffer at the hands of a powerful press.

DESPITE THE Bohemians, the Northern newspapers lacked the manpower to cover the war along a ten-thousand-mile front. To compensate, they drew on the soldiers themselves and filled their columns with letters from the camps. The result was a peculiar combination of current news from the front that the newspapers would not otherwise have had and an effective way for soldiers to communicate with their families and friends that the men in uniform would not have had otherwise. These letters provided a candid picture of what the war
CN was like for the ordinary foot soldier. °Many of the smaller newspapers relied especially on these "special correspondents," soldiers in the ranks or officers writing home or composing specific reports for the newspapers.• Thus, at times, those who fought the war and those who reported it were one and the same.

JIR The men who had enlisted in 1861 had °entered the army with great excitement, great exuberance, and

unbridled patriotism. When the war did not end after one battle and six months of service, they began to wonder, and the drudgery, dreariness, and loneliness of camp life began to set in.• In the meantime, the people at home were admonished by the newspapers to remember their loved ones in the army. The *Herkimer County Journal* in 1861 carried one such solicitation: "Father, Mother, and Friends: Remember your loved ones are exposed not only to the dangers, but also to the vices and temptations of camp. Let your communications be long and frequent, so their minds may be turned to their homes and kindred scenes of the past."

JJH °Letters from the front carried news of casualties in personal terms that were genuine and heartfelt.• For example, an 1861 issue of the *Addison Advertisor* included the notice: "William W. Noble was taken sick, and the next we heard of him, Captain Baldwin had a letter informing us of his death. The news struck upon our ears like a thunderbolt. We have lost a kind friend and a brave comrade. It seems yesterday he was with us but is cold and mute in a coffin today."

As regimental casualties mounted, support from the folks at home might lag, and so °the newspapers often carried pleas from soldiers written to entire communities. Occasionally the open letter would be signed by several officers or soldiers in a regiment asking the people to bear up in support of the war and not to forget the men in the field.• In 1862 the Forty-fourth New York addressed its hometown through the *Rochester Democrat:* "When we came to the field, we came with your blessing. Will you now join with those worse-than-

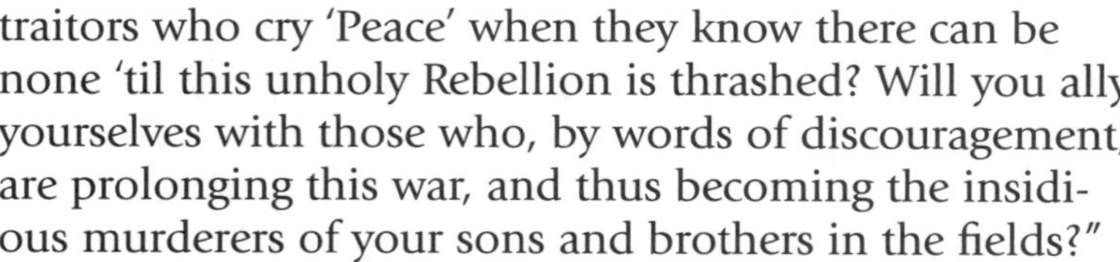

traitors who cry 'Peace' when they know there can be none 'til this unholy Rebellion is thrashed? Will you ally yourselves with those who, by words of discouragement, are prolonging this war, and thus becoming the insidious murderers of your sons and brothers in the fields?"

Writing with brutal honesty, many letters described the transformation from father, son, or sweetheart into killing machine. In 1861 a soldier wrote in the *Winona Republican:* "With your first shot, you become a new man. The dead and dying around you, if they receive a passing thought, only serve to stimulate you to revenge. You become cool and deliberate and watch the showers of bursting shells as they rake their murderous channels through the ranks with a feeling so callous that your soul seems dead to every sympathizing thought."

JJH °As more lives were lost and more men were wounded or mangled and sent home from the front, the need to justify those sacrifices grew, too.• No one wanted to believe that their friends had died in vain. Having already given so much, the men in the ranks were eager for signs of progress and signals of victory.

BP °Starved for information and lacking any reliable information on what their generals were planning, soldiers would often meet between the lines either surreptitiously or during informal truces to trade newspapers
JIR and talk.• °This fraternization occurred throughout the war. If there was a swimming hole in no-man's-land, it was quite natural for the soldiers to negotiate an informal truce so both sides could bathe, although the generals tried to discourage the practice. Both sides had enough in common to integrate moments of civility into tense confrontations, and afterward both sides readily attacked the other when orders were given.•

*Unlike many of his Bohemian Brigade peers, Charles Coffin of the* Boston Journal *indulged in neither alcohol nor tobacco. Publishing his columns under his middle name, Carleton, Coffin covered the Union defeat at First Bull Run and many other wartime events. Gen. Ulysses S. Grant, it is said, particularly appreciated Coffin's direct manner of questioning and honest reporting. Before the war ended, he began to publish books based on his experiences at the front.* My Days and Nights on the Battlefield *(1864) and* Following the Flag *(1865) were two such titles. After the war Coffin remained popular. He traveled abroad and wrote* Our New Way Around the World *in 1869.*

DURING THE war the North had to learn to balance the need for national security with the public's right to know. It was a problem the country had never faced, but the power of the press, the effectiveness of the railway post and the telegraph in disseminating information, and the uncertainty military authorities had of the purpose of censorship all created a situation where the problem of balancing national security with freedom of the press had to be addressed.

There were three stages in the development of censorship during the Civil War. The first began with the post office's refusing to send messages into enemy areas. On July 8, 1861, Gen. Winfield Scott issued an order forbidding telegraph companies from transmitting any information of a military nature. There was a need for some restriction on the flow of information because without such the enemy would obtain valuable military intelligence. In 1862 official government censorship was placed under the direction of Secretary of War Edwin Stanton who ordered correspondents to submit their news copy to provost marshals for approval before transmitting it. Deletions would be made only on military matters. These guidelines at least gave reporters an idea of what they could expect from the military censors.

*Journalists seek the shade of the field headquarters of the* New York Herald *during a hot afternoon in August 1863. War correspondents, like the armies on which they reported, often endured sweltering weather or pouring rain, days of bad food and long marches, and other hardships in their quest to help their readers understand the course of the conflict. Many of the men pictured here had probably helped to cover the battle of Gettysburg. While observing Confederate positions at this battle, Whitelaw Reid, who wrote under the pen name "Agate" for the* Cincinnati Dispatch, *reported that he was "startled by the buzzing hiss of a well-aimed Minié" fired at him by the "foes" of the Union.*

The second period of censorship was marked by the poor administration of Stanton's guidelines and capricious censorship by ambitious military leaders. The difficulties reporters experienced during this period are illustrated by the actions of Gen. William Tecumseh Sherman. He hated the press because it tried to expose the truth about his army. When a reporter for the *Cincinnati Commercial* attempted to interview him, he meant to deflect Sherman's suspicions by saying, "But, General, the people are anxious. I'm only after the truth." Sherman responded, "We don't want the truth told about things here—that's what we don't want! Truth, eh? No, sir! We don't want the enemy any better informed than he is!"

JFM Because of his suspicions about reporters, °Sherman tried to exclude reporters from his army. When he could not exclude them he tried to censor them. The result was that the correspondents retaliated against Sherman. Whenever they could, the Bohemians would

*The Civil War was the first conflict in which photographers, aided by advances in photographic equipment, took to the field to record the events of the conflict. Not every "Dag-type artist," as the soldiers sometimes called photographers, recorded images for journalistic purposes. Many traveled to army camps to photograph individual soldiers, who then sent their images home. The photos above show wagons for hauling developing chemicals and glass negative plates. The negatives were exposed into actual pictures under shrouds like those draping the wagon above right. The field darkroom in the photograph above left belonged to Sam A. Cooley who worked with the Union Tenth Corps in Florida and Georgia.*

"write him down," as they called it. Their ultimate revenge came in Kentucky in late 1861 when Sherman was going through a period of depression. A Cincinnati newspaper editorial claimed that Sherman was insane, and the "news" was picked up by newspapers all over the country as a way of striking back at the general who hated newspapermen.•

The third phase of censorship, from 1864 until the end of the war, was a relatively successful one. By this time the Federal government had come to a better understanding of the balance between the competing needs and freedoms, and the press was more cooperative.

During the war the Northern press scrutinized the country's leaders with a vengeance. As would be
JFM expected, Lincoln was frequently °lambasted at the hands of the press. The president, however, paid little attention to those things. He believed if he were successful in preserving the Union, the people would respond to his leadership. On the other hand, if he lost the war, it would matter little what the newspapers said because there would be no nation.•

Wise enough to ignore his critics, Lincoln was also crafty enough to appreciate the importance of projecting a strong image through the media. He knew how to get the attention of the press and, through it, how to reach
HH the American people. °For a man who was supposedly shy, modest, and even embarrassed about his appearance, Lincoln managed to visit the Washington photography studios often. His growing a beard projected a more

fatherly image. Afterward he was more frequently called "Uncle Abe" or "Father Abraham" instead of "Honest Abe."

Lincoln's press consciousness influenced him to wear certain clothing and appear in a certain way. He wore the tallest stovepipe hats he could find to accentuate his height. Standing more than six feet four inches, the president was already one of the tallest men in any city he visited, but with the hat, he seemed almost seven feet tall. He knew the hat would make him stand out regardless of where he was.•

WCD °The president's face showed much of his character. In photographs it seemed to show kindness and humanity, but pictures of Lincoln taken between 1861 and 1865 also reveal the dreadful physical and emotional toll that the war took on him. He was wearing out year by year.• HH °The last series of studio portraits made in February 1865, however, showed for the first time in four years the slight hint of a smile on his haggard face. He could finally glimpse the end of the long and bloody trial; it was inevitable that the South would surrender during the coming months.•

*The top-hatted editor of the* Pittsburgh Dispatch, *Joseph S. Lane, is precariously perched on the far right window ledge of his paper's office building, on June 9, 1862. He watches the crowd in the street below, which had assembled to read the latest news concerning Gen. George B. McClellan's efforts to take Richmond during the Peninsula campaign. Similar gatherings occurred in towns large and small, North and South, as people anxiously waited for newspapers to post casualty lists on billboards like the one hanging below the editor. In such a public fashion, many relatives received the devastating news that a loved one had been killed or wounded in battle.*

No two people were more responsible for the smile on Lincoln's face than Generals Sherman and Ulysses S. Grant. Partners in reuniting America with continuous victories in the West under Sherman and the constant wearing down of Lee in the East by Grant, the two generals had very different experiences with the American press.

JFM °Sherman distrusted the press like no other general in the war. He viewed all reporters as Confederate spies. He contended that whether intentional or not, by generating stories about what his army was doing, the correspondents were giving strategic information to the enemy.•

WCD °Reporters occasionally accurately published the strength of units in the field by saying that a specific brigade mustered five thousand men, although it

*Two British correspondents covering the Civil War were Frank Vizetelly (above) of the* Illustrated London News *and William Howard Russell (below) of the* Times *(London). Vizetelly first reported from the Northern side and then moved to the Southern to gain better perspective. Russell returned home after he was banned from accompanying the Union Army of the Potomac because of his unflattering dispatches about its retreat after Second Bull Run. He was nicknamed "Bull Run" Russell.*

JFM

would be expressed more colorfully, such as "five thousand of the bravest and truest ever . . ." Sherman did not mind "the bravest and truest" part of the description, as that was a morale booster for the people at home, but knowing that a specific unit had five thousand soldiers would be of interest to the enemy.• In addition to informing the Rebels of troop strengths, newspaper stories might also reveal when a unit had arrived or when it would be leaving an area.

His unmitigated suspicion never faltered. "To every army and almost every general," Sherman said, "a newspaper reporter goes along filling up our transports, swelling our trains, reporting our progress, picking up dropped expressions, inciting jealousy and discontent, and doing infernal mischief. If the press can govern the country, let them fight the battles."

In December 1862, *New York Herald* correspondent Thomas Knox wrote a story criticizing Sherman's defeat at Chickasaw Bluffs, below Vicksburg, Mississippi, and violated military censorship regulations. Incensed, Sherman ordered that Knox, a civilian, undergo a military court-martial for treason. In a letter to Adm. David D. Porter, he announced, "I am going to have the correspondent of the N.Y. Herald tried by a court martial as a spy, not that I want the fellow shot, but because I want to establish the principle that such people cannot attend our armies, in violation of orders, and defy us, publishing their garbled statements and defaming officers who are doing their best."

After fifteen days the court convicted Knox of a lesser charge and permanently banned him from Sherman's army. Both sides appealed: Sherman to Grant, and Knox and his brother Bohemians to Lincoln. Grant chose to do nothing, but Lincoln set aside the verdict and referred the matter to Grant, sending Knox to his headquarters, where he could stay or, if Grant chose, be sent back to Sherman's army. The president's action tacitly affirmed the right of the media to accompany the army, and Sherman's action established the precedent that correspondents must be acceptable to the commander in the field.

°Sherman's action intimidated the reporters into being more careful. The best situation for him, however, was to keep them away from his army altogether, which he did during his March to the Sea in October 1864.• While that assuaged Sherman's suspicions of spies in his midst, it also meant that Washington had no way of knowing what was happening to his army of sixty-two thousand. As soon as Sherman and his men entered the Georgia heartland, all communication was cut off.

What the Northern editors did not know was that while Sherman hated them, he loved the Southern press and used it to terrify the Georgians. When he declared, "War is nothing but cruelty," the message was unmistakable. CN °He said things that he knew the Confederate editors would reprint and enlarge upon as proof that the Yankees really were devils and that they were going to burn everything. Rebel newspaper editors thus helped Sherman disseminate the fear that he planned to use as a weapon to demoralize the South.•

Sherman's news blackout during the March to the Sea also raised tensions in the North. JFM °Northerners were very uneasy about the sudden disappearance of a Federal army in the Deep South. Southern papers claimed that Sherman was lost in the swamps of Georgia, and no one in the War Department could confirm or deny that. Finally Sherman emerged in Savannah just as he had planned and sent Lincoln a telegram offering the captured city as a Christmas present. The news erupted all over the North.•

*A relatively new technology, the telegraph, was used extensively by both armies, giving generals the best communication system in the history of warfare until that time. In 1861 only one wire had just been strung to span the continent. By 1864 the U.S. Military Telegraph Service was using more than 6,500 miles of wire. In most cases the wire would be hung on poles cut for the purpose, but sometimes it was simply draped over accommodating bushes or tree limbs. The field station pictured below was near City Point, Virginia, and kept General Grant apprised of the effort to capture Petersburg. During his drive on Atlanta, Gen. William T. Sherman also used the telegraph effectively. At the battle of Kennesaw Mountain, Sherman was able to get progress reports from his subordinates during the fight.*

As Sherman was capturing Savannah, Grant was strangling the Army of Northern Virginia at Petersburg. Were it not for the prudent actions of a war correspondent—Sylvanus Cadwallader of the *Chicago Times*—two years earlier, Grant most likely would have been nowhere near Petersburg in 1865 and might not even have been in uniform.

CN °Grant's weakness was that he drank when he was lonely and missed his wife and children. According to Cadwallader's postwar memoirs, on a steamboat trip on the Mississippi River in June 1863, Grant managed to break into the boat captain's liquor supply. Cadwallader came across Grant before anyone else saw him drunk,

Alfred R. Waud, shown above on the Gettysburg battlefield, was one of the best "special artists" of the war. His drawings, which were turned into engravings for the *New York Illustrated News* and *Harper's Weekly*, are works of art in their own right. His battle scenes convey the immediacy of deadly combat almost as well as modern stop-action photography. Waud was known to carry a bowie knife and revolver tucked into his belt, and earned the respect of the soldiers he drew both for his bravery as well as for his attention to detail. His sketch below shows Federal cannoneers in action at Gettysburg's Cemetery Hill.

and he maneuvered him into a cabin. The newsman locked the door and then threw the liquor out the window. Grant ordered him out, but Cadwallader ignored him.• He kept Grant in the cabin and away from prying eyes until the general was sober.

GAR °Cadwallader never said anything about the incident, and the episode never made it into the papers. Nevertheless, Grant was anxious about the matter, waiting to see whether Cadwallader would submit the story to his editors. When it appeared the incident would pass unreported, Grant rewarded Cadwallader's discretion.•

The reporter entered into a pact with Grant's staff to CN keep the general away from liquor and °saved Grant's career. From that moment on, Cadwallader was treated like a member of the general's staff.• His tent was pitched and struck for him by headquarters orderlies, his rations and feed for his horse were provided, and passes were given to him like no other news reporter CN had ever known. °He could go anywhere he wanted, get any story he wanted, and his dispatches were sent back to the New York press without being reviewed by the military censors. Grant would say, "It's Cadwallader; send it on through."•

Cadwallader gained extraordinary access to momentous events and was the only reporter present when Lee surrendered to Grant at the Wilmer McLean House in Appomattox. By putting patriotism above journalism, Cadwallader had served both masters and played a part in saving the Union.

JUST AS they devoured their daily newspapers, Americans hungered for visual depictions of the war. The technology of reproducing photographs in print had not yet been perfected, and so daily newspapers offered mostly articles with occasional illustrations. For pictures of the war, the public turned to illustrated BP journals such as °*Harper's Weekly* and *Frank Leslie's Illustrated Newspaper.* Both magazines sold for six or eight cents a copy, expensive in those days, but they were the only media that printed images of the battlefields and the generals whose troops were involved in the action.•

The illustrated journals sent sketch artists into the field to record their impressions of battles and soldiers. These drawings were then reproduced as woodcuts that could be printed in the weeklies and then mass produced as popular prints for home use.

HH °The style of the day called for walls to be decorated heavily, and so people were always looking for affordable illustrations. Images of the war also made a statement about the loyalty of a family. Anyone hanging a print of Lincoln's reading the Emancipation Proclamation subtly informed neighbors and visitors that he supported the war and even the liberation of slaves.•

The first hint of the demand for this kind of art came following the May 1861 shooting of Col. Elmer Ellsworth, who had been killed by an Alexandria, Virginia, innkeeper after Ellsworth had removed a Confederate flag from the roof of the inn. Within weeks, dozens of drawings of the dashing young colonel hung in thou-
HH sands of Northern homes. °For many families, Ellsworth symbolized the frightening prospect of the loss of a son, and eventually he came to symbolize all the North's sons. Families knew if a celebrity such as Ellsworth—he was renowned across the North as a popularizer of Zouave drill teams from 1860 until his death—could be lost so quickly and tragically, anyone could be killed. Ellsworth's death generated a sense of foreboding that manifested itself in a huge demand for his portrait.•

Some artists created works that served both the commercial demands of patriotic readers and satisfied their own perspective of the war. Among these, the best was
BP Winslow Homer. °His sketches for *Harper's* were published within weeks of their creation, and they were positive, heroic, and pro-Union. His private sketches were used in later paintings, and these reveal graphically the boredom, the dirt, and the depressed lot of the soldier in the field.•

Developments in photography, however, allowed
WCD soldier life to be captured as never before. °It has been estimated that at least one million photographs were taken during the war. The overwhelming majority of these

*One of the most important of all American artists, Winslow Homer said of his method, "When I have selected the thing carefully, I paint it exactly as it appears." This was as true of the Civil War drawings he made for* Harper's Weekly *as of his later paintings. He first depicted Gen. George B. McClellan's Army of the Potomac in 1861 and then covered the Peninsula campaign as a "special artist." Unlike most artist-correspondents, Homer's scenes often dealt with everyday camp life rather than fighting. His subjects, which appear deceptively simple, reflected man's humanness in the face of an indifferent or hostile universe. In later years Homer painted many breathtaking seascapes.*

*One of the best special artists of the Civil War was Thomas Nast, who worked mainly for* Harper's Weekly. *An immigrant from Germany, Nast began drawing illustrations for New York papers when he was only fifteen years old. After the war he became an editorial cartoonist, pioneering the tradition of pointed political cartoons. He is credited with being the first to use the elephant and the donkey as the symbols of the Republican and Democratic parties. A champion of the antislavery cause, Nast's works generally favored President Lincoln and his policies. Apart from the war, Nast's drawings of Santa Claus almost single-handedly defined the look of jolly Old Saint Nick in American popular culture.*

were individual portraits photographed in temporary studios set up in the camps and sold for twenty-five cents apiece.• The men posed while the photographer adjusted his camera and checked the lighting. Ordinarily, enlisted men leaned on their muskets and officers sat with their legs crossed and their sword hilt turned toward the camera. Zouaves ballooned the fullness of their trousers, and men in distinctive uniforms posed facing the camera to call attention to the detail of their costumes. Each man usually purchased many copies for his mother, sisters, and wife or sweetheart.

Mathew Brady, one of the country's best-known photographers, pondered making a photographic record of the war, and in June 1861 the American Photographic Society proposed the idea to the War Department. The society failed to get an endorsement, but Brady persisted. He hoped to find government funding for the project or, failing that, considered that sufficient sales of the images afterward would underwrite the task. His immediate problem was gaining permission to take photographs within the army. In July 1861 Gens. Winfield Scott and Irvin McDowell gave their blessings, and Brady began training assistants and gathering equipment, supplies, and vehicles needed for the work in the field.

Before the war, sketches and paintings of battles depicted masses of brave soldiers achieving glorious victories. Photographs, however, presented a realistic image
BP of what war was. °Images of bloated horses and mangled corpses were quite a contrast alongside paintings of charging soldiers with fixed bayonets and flags flying in the sunshine. Photography began to show that war was horrible, and it was during this conflict that warfare was presented honestly to the public for the first time.•

At the same time, battlefield photographers faced a myriad of physical and technical challenges to create these images. They had to carry portable darkrooms,
WCD because °an image had to be developed almost immediately after the negative was exposed. Photographers could not make several exposures and then develop them later; each photograph had to be developed within a few minutes or the image was lost.•

The process was tedious, requiring the subject to remain still at least six seconds because any movement would blur the image. Usually photographers took pictures of static scenes. Yet their prints of battle carnage were so evocative, sketch artists used them as the basis for many drawings. The publication of these images forever changed how Americans thought of war.

WCD °One famous photograph showed a dead Confederate with his hand blown off, lying beside him, and his entrails spilling out of his shirt. That was an entirely different picture than most Victorians would have wanted to believe war was like.

While some Americans tried to forget, a number of exposures from 1862 had burned themselves into the national consciousness. When Lee's army invaded Maryland in September 1862, both sides waited anxiously for news of the outcome. After Lee's army had retreated into Virginia and George B. McClellan had claimed a victory for the Union. The JIR °news continued to occupy American newspapers for weeks. There were not enough words to describe the single day of battle with more than twenty-three thousand casualties.•

HH °The fighting at the Cornfield and the Sunken Road could not be sketched. When artists tried to draw that bloody farm road filled with Confederate dead, it seemed

*The engraving at left of an Army of the Potomac sharpshooter on picket duty sighting on a target was prepared from one of Winslow Homer's field sketches. To produce such an illustration, an engraver would carve a mirror image copy of the artist's drawing onto a piece of wood. Ink would then be applied to the woodblock copy, and it would be pressed onto newsprint, creating the positive image.* Harper's Weekly *published more than thirty-five wood engravings from Homer's sketches during the war.*

*Appreciative of Thomas Nast's talents, the editors at* Harper's Weekly *often published the artist's renderings in large single- or multi-page formats. This example of Nast's work, entitled* The Press on the Field, *conveys the variety of experiences faced by journalists covering the armies. The large panels at left and right, labeled "Contraband News" and "Reliable Information," depict the sometimes questionable sources of information with which reporters had to contend. Other vignettes include artists and reporters at work while under fire, a facsimile of the interior of a sketchbook, and a family—note the absence of a military age male—anxiously poring over the pages of the latest edition of a newspaper.*

cartoonish because it was so improbable that so many men could be killed in such a crowded space. People needed the reality of the photographic lens to lend credence to the casualty lists that were almost too grisly to believe.•

It took a photographer, Alexander Gardner, to capture the unbelievable carnage at Antietam. His photographs, credited to Brady, his employer, shocked America when they were exhibited in New York a month after the battle. The reviewer for the *New York Times* assessed the poignant effect of the exhibit: "Mr. Brady has done something to bring home to us the terrible reality and earnestness of war. If he has not brought home bodies and laid them in our own door yard and along our streets, he has done something very like it. These pictures have a terrible distinctiveness." Gardner later published the photographs in a book, the first time that such a documentation of warfare had been done.

WCD °This graphic nature of Civil War photographs made them unpopular in the years immediately following the war. They were brutal reminders of something that had happened which many people wanted to forget.•

The worst of the war brought out the best of the war coverage. The many stories of the Bohemian Brigade were diverse, dashing, and sometimes humorous. Two of the most interesting tales include the experiences of George Smalley at Antietam and Samuel Wilkeson at Gettysburg.

At Antietam, reporter George Smalley of the *New York Tribune* became part of the story he was covering. CN °During the battle he found himself next to Maj. Gen. Joseph Hooker, one of the Union field commanders. All of Hooker's staff were on other duties for the general, and so Hooker turned to Smalley and asked who he was and what he was doing. Smalley identified himself as a correspondent, and Hooker asked him to carry a message for him. Smalley spent the day running through the lines on his horse delivering messages while under fire.• Afterward Hooker complimented the newsman in his report: "In all the experiences which I had of war, I never saw the most experienced and veteran soldier exhibit more tranquil fortitude and unshaken valor than was exhibited by that young man."

In his role as messenger for Hooker, Smalley endured Confederate bullets and various Union officers, including a colonel who initially refused to accept instructions from a reporter.

GAR °Smalley said, "Well, then, shall I convey to General Hooker that you decline to obey his order?"

The rattled man replied: "Lord, no. Don't do that. The Rebels are too many for us, but I'd rather face them than General Hooker." The colonel then immediately dispatched his men to the front.•

*While employed by* Frank Leslie's Illustrated Newspaper, *artist-correspondent Edwin Forbes witnessed the campaigns of the Army of the Potomac from 1861 to 1864. An example of his work,* Newspapers in Camp, *appears at left. Forbes's wartime illustrations received an award at the 1876 Centennial Exposition in Philadelphia. The same year General Sherman, who harbored a well-known dislike for the press, bought a set of original Forbes sketches and donated them to the U.S. government. With the help of his wife, Forbes compiled and published the majority of his drawings in* Thirty Years After, An Artist's Story of the Great War.

Newspaper vendors, like the one pictured below, were welcomed by news-starved soldiers who also depended on relatives to send them their favorite papers. On April 29, 1862, Francis A. Donaldson of the Seventy-first Pennsylvania wrote and thanked his brother for mailing a copy of the "Philada. Inquirer" with its "account of the capture of New Orleans by our glorious Navy." Donaldson then related that an officer had dug up an unexploded Confederate cannonball, and "put into it a copy of the New York Herald . . . and fired it back . . . to the enemy . . . where I presume it has been received and contents noted."

After the battle, an exhausted Smalley raced to New York by train to file his story. He composed it along the way, staying awake all night to file his account in time for the next day's edition. CN °The typesetters had it in print within hours of Smalley's arrival. It was considered one of the great scoops of the war. Sixty to seventy thousand extra papers were sold, and most importantly from the government's standpoint, it proclaimed a very important Union victory:• "Battlefield of Sharpsburg, Wednesday evening, September 17, 1862. Fierce and desperate battle between 200,000 men [more accurately, the combined armies approximated 120,000] has raged since daylight. It is the greatest fight since Waterloo contested with an obstinacy equal even to Waterloo. The dead have strewn so thickly that as you ride you cannot guide your horse's steps too carefully. Pale and bloody faces are everywhere upturned. Sad and terrible."

Ten months after Antietam, the nation bore the news of the killing fields of Gettysburg. JIR °The difficulty the press faced was in convincing the nation that a battle of such magnitude had occurred. Three days of fighting had yielded more than fifty thousand casualties. Gettysburg had a population of approximately twenty-four hundred, but by July 4 there were approximately twenty-two thousand wounded men inside the town.•

There, on the Pennsylvania countryside, one reporter faced his greatest challenge. CN °Sam Wilkeson of the *New York Times* was an excellent reporter known for his passion to report the war accurately and for his support of the Union cause. His eldest son, Bayard, was an officer in the Fourth U.S. Artillery at Gettysburg.•

When he arrived at the front, the father learned that his son had been gravely wounded, his leg shattered by a cannonball. The young officer was behind enemy lines, and his condition unknown.

GAR °In spite of the stress of not knowing what had happened to his son, Wilkeson went about compiling the information he needed to prepare his account of the battle.• JJH °His writing went beyond reporting the news; it was a record of sensations and feelings. He had no time to interpret the event, no time to understand it. He was simply trying to describe the spectacle, the horror, the feeling of what it was like to be near the battle: "Every size and form of shell known to British and American gunnery, shrieked, whirred, moaned and whistled and wrathfully fluttered over our ground. . . . Soldiers in federal blue were torn to pieces in the road and died with the peculiar yells that blend the extorted cry of pain with horror and despair."

Only after the guns were silent did Wilkeson discover Bayard's fate. The young man had amputated his own leg with a penknife, but he had died as a prisoner in a Confederate field hospital. When Wilkeson found Bayard's grave, he sat beside it and pulled out his pen: "Headquarters of the Potomac, Saturday night, July 4, 1863. Who can write the history of a battle, whose eyes are immovably fastened upon a central figure of transcendingly important interest—the dead body of an oldest born. Oh, you dead who at Gettysburg have baptized with your blood the second birth of freedom in America. How you are to be envied. I rise from a grave whose wet clay I have passionately kissed, and I look up and see Christ spanning this battlefield and reaching fraternally and lovingly up to heaven. His right hand

*Reporters and photographers pose for this amusing photograph, taken during the Christmas season of 1864. J. Knox of the* Boston Herald *sits second from left. Simon P. Hanscom—with hat in hand—and Frank G. Chapman of the* New York Herald *are to Knox's left. Alfred Waud is second from right, his beard partially obscured by a hat. One can assume the contents of the punchbowl being freely dispensed by the African-American waiters would not meet with the approval of a temperance advocate.*

*A cartoonist depicting Sherman as Santa Claus stuffing Savannah in Lincoln's stocking could not resist making the journalist-hating general look slightly mad.*

*Thomas Knox was the* New York Herald *reporter whose story criticizing Sherman's defeat at Chickasaw Bluffs caused Sherman to order his court-martial. Only Lincoln's intervention prevented it.*

opens the gates of paradise. With his left he beckons these mutilated, bloody, swollen forms to ascend."

While much is made of Gettysburg in any writing on the Civil War, the battle was also the scene of a journalistic first and a testimony to the men who spent four years reporting the war. On the afternoon of July 3, as Lee's legions massed and began the march toward the center of the Union line known as Pickett's Charge, a young Cullen B. Aubrey was riding among the Federal troops selling newspapers. For the first time, soldiers were able to read an account of a battle as they fought it. Aubrey had picked up piles of the *Philadelphia Inquirer* from a train at Westminster and returned to the battlefield to sell the news to the soldiers. "They went like gingerbread at a state fair," he remembered.

After years of bloodletting, North and South found common ground in their mutual misery. Scorching words and searing pictures had invaded homes across the land with images of war. These words touched the nation with fire despite a climate of cynicism, which was best described by the poet Walt Whitman: "The real war will never get in the books. . . . The actual soldier of 1861–5, North and South, with all his ways, his incredible dauntlessness, habits, practices, tastes, language, his fierce friendship, his appetite, rankness, his superb strength and animality, lawless gait, and a hundred unnamed lights and shades of camp, I say, will never be written." Yet, like the nation itself, American journalism had come of age bearing eloquent witness to an unimaginable anguish. Some of the real war did get into the books. Despite bitter divisions, Americans from all walks of life were joined by the enduring memory of shared suffering.

The war would have been won by the North without the press. Newspapers, after all, provided useful information to the enemy, but there can be no doubt that the contribution of the steady flow of news from the Bohemian Brigade was a tremendous influence on Northern morale.

No people in history were more tightly bound by a shared experience than the millions who read these wartime accounts in their newspapers. For the first time ever, an entire country knew what it was about, knew what its leaders were doing, and knew what had happened the day before and might happen a day or two hence.

The idea that the public should look to the press for information regarding public affairs, and thereby make them their own affairs, is deeply rooted in the democratic tradition. In the event of the Civil War, that idea gained shape and meaning it had never had before. Lincoln called the Civil War "a people's war." The Bohemians, reporting the war profusely and constantly, ensured that news of the war was disseminated across the country and helped to underline the people's role in it. Driven by significant pressures in the constantly evolving way in which news was reported to the public, the Bohemians hurdled those restrictions imposed by generals and politicians, learned to deal fairly with military censorship, and established the right of the public to know, thereby highlighting the role of the press in the democratic process.

*Americans owe a great debt to journalists and photographers, like the one above washing his negatives at Cold Harbor, Virginia, or like* New York Times *reporter Samuel Wilkeson (below). While covering the battle of Gettysburg, Wilkeson learned his son Bayard had been hit. Afterwards, he wrote a poignant dispatch while sitting beside his son's grave. Men like these left a rich record in image and text that serve as prototypes for those who have recorded later struggles.*

# MATHEW B. BRADY

WCD ○The OLD ADAGE THAT A PICTURE IS worth a thousand words was proven by approximately two hundred Civil War photographers who worked between 1861 and 1865. The first true photojournalists, these pioneers extensively documented the war and its effects, and their images have, for succeeding generations, become what most people know of the Civil War. Only photographs could bring home to the people of the North and the South what a thousand men in the field looked like or what destruction really meant. The public could read about the events of the war, but there was a great difference between interpreting a description of how occupied Richmond looked in 1865 and seeing the stark, grim photographs that revealed a burned-out, devastated city.•

BP In any discussion ○of Civil War photography, the one name that immediately comes to mind is Mathew Brady.• It was Brady's vision of the documentary importance of photography that changed it from a novelty reserved for the rich and famous to a significant and popular form of visual communication. BPr ○The great misconception about Brady is that he was the one who actually operated the shutter for this vast collection of work. He had been a photographer early in his career, but that changed in 1851 when his eyesight weakened and his role became that of a promoter, following the custom among the better New York photographers of acting as proprietors rather than camera operators.• WAF Thus ○Brady most likely did not take a single photograph during the entire Civil War.•

| | |
|---|---|
| **WCD** | William C. Davis |
| **WAF** | William A. Frassanito |
| **WM** | Warren Motts |
| **MP** | Mary Panzer |
| **BP** | Brian Pohanka |
| **BPr** | Barry Pritzker |
| **GR** | Grant Romer |

*This engraved portrait was made from an 1851 photograph of Mathew Brady. About twenty-seven years old, Brady was already famous, as much as a showman as a photographer. Because printers lacked the technical ability to directly reproduce photographs, an engraving was required. Engravers were highly skilled craftsmen and artists, and the more talented the engraver, the more faithful was the likeness to the original photograph.*

Instead Brady's significance at the time was in the establishment of a brand name that was perceived as a mark of quality in the emerging field of photography. When customers came to Brady's studio to have their portraits made, they most likely did not expect to find Brady himself behind the camera, but they knew their photograph would be made according to a strict standard of excellence by his carefully selected assistants. As was the custom of the day, Brady stamped his name on the photograph's paper jacket, marking it as one from his studio. The photographer, a Brady employee, might have chafed when compliments were extended to the shop owner, but he likely did not complain. Such complaints were not voiced at the time.

Later, particularly as the war began to reach its conclusion, Brady expanded his name-stamping process. By
BPr then his °main enterprise was collecting rather than making Civil War photographs.• Since he paid the photographer for the original, he considered that image his
BPr property and applied the Brady stamp. °It became impossible to distinguish a Civil War photograph that Brady might have taken himself from one taken by a photographer in his employ or from one that Brady simply acquired.•

It would be decades before historians realized that Brady was not the wizard of the camera as he first
MP appeared, and °many were disillusioned to learn that Brady was not the one who operated the shutter but the person who ran the studio and hired the men behind the cameras and the men who finished the pic-
WM tures. While Brady may have gotten the credit,• °he was largely a promoter who knew how to put his name before the public by stamping "Photographed by Brady" on every image in his collection.•

BP While it may be true that °Brady was vain and ambitious, he was also a man with a vision, a true sense of history, and a man who saw the importance of the Civil War. He was also the man most responsible for preserving the images of the war for future generations.•

Ironically, for a man who was one of the most public figures of his time, little is known of Brady the private man. He was born in 1822 or 1823—Brady himself was

BPr not really sure—°in Warren County, New York, to Irish immigrant parents of whom he spoke very little. He left home at the age of sixteen and traveled to Saratoga Springs, a popular resort community of the day. There he met William Page, a portrait painter, and started to study portraiture under Page's tutelage. Both of them traveled to New York City in 1840, where together they studied with Samuel F. B. Morse.•

WM °Morse was already known as an inventor and painter. In 1839 he had traveled to France to patent the telegraph. While there he heard about a new form of art being perfected by Louis Daguerre, a Parisian artist who, in conjunction with Joseph Niepce, had been experimenting with a *camera obscura,* which projected an inverted image onto a piece of canvas so one could create dioramas and drawings in proper perspective.• Wanting to preserve chemically the projected images, MP °Daguerre perfected a process that created a photographic image on a shiny piece of silver-coated copper.• In exchange for revealing the secret for capturing images and then developing them with a combination of chemicals and heat, Daguerre was given a lifetime pension by the French government. The resulting photographs were called daguerreotypes in his honor.

MP °The daguerreotype was an instant sensation because it took image-making out of the hands of artists and made it available to anyone who could operate a BPr camera.• °Morse was fascinated by the process of daguerreotypy after learning the process from Daguerre himself, and when he returned to the United States from France, Morse already had his own camera. Within days he opened a studio to make daguerreotypes and to give lessons in daguerreotypy. Tuition was fifty dollars for several sessions. Among his first students was the teenaged Brady,• who worked part-time in a jewelry shop to generate the necessary funds.

MP °Although the daguerreotype had been invented in France, it very quickly became popular in America, with various early photographers gradually modifying the process. One of the problems was devising a way to develop the images faster so a photographer could produce portraits in a single day.• When first announced,

*In 1826 Joseph Niepce, a Frenchman, had successfully created a photographic image on treated pewter, but the exposure time was eight hours. In the 1830s Louis Daguerre (above), also from France, began experimenting with the process. By using different plates and chemicals, Daguerre reduced the time to five minutes. Other improvements soon followed. The French government awarded Daguerre a lifetime pension, and the first true photographic process would forever bear his name—the daguerreotype.*

*After four years of apprenticeship, Brady opened a gallery in New York City at the corner of Broadway and Fulton Street. Although very young, Brady already possessed two qualities that would forever mark his career: showmanship and a knack for rubbing elbows with the rich, the famous, and—perhaps most importantly—the influential. Located in a prosperous commercial neighborhood, Brady's elegantly appointed salon quickly attracted New York's best people. He soon earned the sobriquet "Brady of Broadway."*

the photographic process could take more than twenty minutes, and so most early daguerreotypes were of still lifes such as plants or buildings. These images were also small, barely an inch across.

BP ○Daguerreotypes were one-of-a-kind images. They were also mirror images, with the image on the plate being reversed from what it was in life. The daguerreotype was usually put in a small case and treated as a work of art since it was one of a kind.•

For the first half of the 1840s, daguerreotypy was a GR fascinating subject to Americans. ○Daguerreotypes were only a step away from actually seeing a person, and that added a magical or spiritual quality to the image. Such uniqueness was valued by the people of the day.•

As a student of Morse, Brady was at the center of BP these developments, and ○in 1844 he opened his first gallery on Broadway in New York City.• Taking a cue from his competitors who preached that a photographer could never have too much light, Brady had skylights installed in the roof of his studio, the first time that had ever been done. This innovation would become standard with all photographers in the years to come.

WITHIN MONTHS Brady, a young man of twenty-one with an unknown past, reinvented himself as Brady of Broadway, soon to be a world-famous photographer. °The transformation did not take long because Brady was energetic.• In his first year of operation he won the silver medal and top honors at the first competitive photographic exhibition sponsored by the American Institute in New York. °For the next four years Brady regularly won the same prize for the technical superiority of his photographs. In 1849 the New York newspapers announced the granting of the annual prize by noting that Brady had won again.•

Throughout his career, Brady paid careful attention to the location of his studios. His first studio was at 205 Broadway, near Saint Paul's Church and City Hall Park, across from the pillared building that housed the business of publisher and art collector Daniel Appleton, steps away from P. T. Barnum's American Museum, and near the city's best hotels. The studio was on the top floor of a three-story building to which Brady had a fourth floor added.

The affable Brady may have received financial assistance from his previous employer, A. T. Stewart, a pioneer department store merchant, and his neighbor, Barnum. Brady's studio had only the finest instruments, and he employed the most highly skilled assistants. Elegant furnishings and expensively framed daguerreotypes appointed the reception room, and the gallery included a private entrance for celebrities. At the time, Brady's was the most attractive and efficient gallery of the ninety-seven professional daguerreotypists in the city, setting the standard for both quality and style.

°It was during this time that photography was quickly transformed from a novelty and curiosity into something people wanted to see and experience themselves. The daguerrean galleries were impressive and became shops that everyone wanted to patronize.• The awards and prizes earned by Brady also brought in customers.

Brady's studio was open from 8 A.M. until 6 P.M., depending on the availability of natural light. Most of the work focused on family portraits, and children posed frequently. The gallery included a dressing room so customers could change into clothes suitable for

*Dolley Madison, former first lady and, at age eighty, the grande dame of Washington society, sat for the above daguerreotype in 1848. Such prestigious portraits were a coup for Brady, who used them to influence other famous Washingtonians to pose for him.*

*Military men were also important subjects for Brady. Winfield Scott (below), hero of the Mexican War, became General-in-Chief of the Federal Army during the Civil War.*

*Brady sought out and photographed well-known entertainers such as singer Jenny Lind, "the Swedish Nightingale."*

photography. Dark jackets and dresses were preferred because light-colored clothing exposed quickly and dominated the final photograph. Brady charged two to five dollars for a portrait, depending on the size of the image. Most other studios charged less.

Brady was a perfectionist who worked tirelessly as long as he had sufficient light. At the same time, his eyesight worsened and the lenses of his glasses thickened. His colleagues regarded him as a shy, reserved man, but the people who endured some of the discomforts of posing recalled him as an Irishman with a penchant for storytelling and an endless supply of anecdotes.

BPr During this time, °Barnum, a circus promoter, and Brady became friends. They shared many ideas about self-promotion and public relations. Brady, who claimed to have made more than twenty thousand exposures in his early years, knew how to attract the public. His artistic background and sense of history combined when he conceived a plan to make portraits of the rich and famous, the eminent citizens of the republic.• Brady titled the project the Gallery of Illustrious Americans.

*Brady's sense that he was recording history is part of what led him to establish a studio in Washington in March 1849. The portrait (below) of Zachary Taylor's cabinet was part of Brady's prodigious effort to capture the face of American government. It was during this period that Brady published* The Gallery of Illustrious Americans.

There was little doubt that these dignitaries and lumi-
BP naries would respond favorably to the project. °Despite his humble origins, Brady came across as a well-dressed gentlemen with polished diplomatic skills. He knew when to cultivate and pander, when to be silent. Most importantly, he knew how to pose his subjects to capture something of their soul with the camera.•

Brady pioneered a host of basic pho-
WM tographic practices. °When he assessed a subject, he looked for the angle that flattered the person most. He noticed physical defects that he could correct. In the case of freckles, he would rub the area until it reddened so the camera would not record them. If a person had sunken cheeks, Brady would put cotton in the cheeks to make them fuller and healthier looking. If a subject had protruding ears, Brady used a waxy substance to make them stick to the head. He became an excellent technician at posing his

GR subjects,• and °this was the basis behind the success of his daguerreotypes—they conveyed something of the character of his subjects.•

WCD °The procedure in making a daguerreotype was complicated. The subject had to be as immobile as possible, which meant shallow breathing and not blinking for as long as thirty seconds, depending on the light. To aid the person being photographed, Brady and other artists used a metal tripod called an immobilizer, which was hidden from sight behind the subject. At the top of the device was a pincer that held a person's head so as to avoid the slightest movement. Once the subject was steady, the shutter cap was removed and the exposure was completed.•

Brady's reputation spread across the country. He captured the sixth president of the United States, John Quincy Adams, not long before Adams died. Brady also photographed Andrew Jackson (or had Jackson photographed and acquired the negative), the seventh president, just weeks before Jackson's death. Martin Van Buren, the eighth president, and John Tyler, the tenth president, likewise posed for Brady. Toward the close of his only term in office, James K. Polk, the eleventh president, opened the doors of the White House to twenty-seven-year-old Brady, who posed the chief executive in the Executive Mansion's dining room. Brady also photographed well-known women such as the most famous first lady of the day, Dolley Madison, the widow of former President James Madison, and Elizabeth Schuyler Hamilton, the widow of Alexander Hamilton, first secretary of the treasury.

He sought out the great men of the time, pleading, begging, and cajoling them to pose for him. Hardly a statesman, politician, writer, scientist, or intellectual failed to respond, especially if Brady did not charge them for sitting for him. In 1848 he traveled to Washington for the inauguration of Zachary Taylor; he returned to New York in 1849 with images of Taylor, the cabinet, most of the members of the Senate, many congressmen, and the justices of the Supreme Court. Brady did not fail to include the most popular politicians of the day: Henry Clay, Daniel Webster, and John C. Calhoun.

*The Mexican War victory of Gen. Zachary Taylor (above) at the battle of Buena Vista in 1847 helped propel him to the White House. As president, his hard-line policies on secession and slavery might have prevented the Civil War, but his sudden death in office ended any such possibility.*

*As U. S. Supreme Court Chief Justice, Roger Brooke Taney (below) spoke for the majority opinion in the Dred Scott case, which returned Scott to slavery. The decision, which caused intense debate, is considered a key milepost on America's road to civil war. Both pictures are by Brady.*

*This view of Gen. Ulysses S. Grant posing in Brady's studio is rare in that it is a documentary picture of the photographic process rather than a portrait of the great general. Grant stands against an immobilizer, a clamp used to keep the subject's head still during the long exposure time, as the slightest movement meant a blurred image. For an actual portrait, the subject and camera would be aligned so that the immobilizer was out of sight. Grant stands on a numbered, segmented platform used for noting a position during the posing stage.*

This desire to photograph the giants of the land was based on more than an urge for fame and profit. Brady understood that he was acting as a historian with a camera and stated in an interview: "From the first, I regarded myself as under obligation to my country to preserve the faces of its historic men and women."

Choosing twenty-four images from his collection, Brady decided to publish an elaborate book using his original daguerreotypes and including brief biographi- MP cal sketches. °At the time, printing technology could not reproduce daguerreotypes directly; instead, a lithographer copied the image onto stone, which was then used to generate copies.• Brady engaged Charles Edwards Lester, former consul to Genoa and one of the foremost art critics of the time, to write the text, and Francis D'Avignon to prepare the lithographs. Lester had praised Brady's work earlier and noted, "So far as the daguerreotype is concerned, we are not aware that any man has devoted himself to it with so much earnestness or expended upon its development so much time and expense as Mr. Brady."

Brady himself underwrote the project and spent five years on the endeavor. When the book was finally published in 1850, it contained only twelve of the originally planned twenty-four images "of the most eminent citizens of the American Republic since the days of Washington": Webster, Clay, Calhoun, Presidents Zachary Taylor and Millard Fillmore, Gens. John C. Frémont and Winfield Scott, Sens. Lewis Cass and Silas Wright, historian William H. Prescott, artist John J. Audubon, and author-minister William Ellery Channing. The publication weighed five pounds and sold for thirty dollars.

*The Photographic Art Journal* observed, "The whole work surpasses in artistic beauty and typographical magnificence anything which has been published in this country or in Europe." The volume received similar accolades from a host of reviewers, but sales were disappointing. Brady viewed it as a critical success but a financial failure. A year or two later he reduced the price BPr by half. °The venture was Brady's first attempt at being the nation's photographic historian. His ideas were not limited to famous men; once he said that he might publish a book documenting the mothers of America's most famous men.• Acclaim for *The Gallery,* however, stimulated business for the studio.

WCD °When people walked past the portraits of Clay, Webster, Polk, and a host of other dignitaries hanging in Brady's studio, they were impressed. They then sat before the same camera that had recorded those images. Such experiences generated a heady feeling of equality for the common man, because everyone was regarded equally by the lens.•

During his sojourn to Washington in 1848 Brady met Julia Elizabeth Handy. The details of their encounter, courtship, and marriage, like so much of Brady's personal life, are not known. One biographer claimed that the romance was set against the backdrop of a Maryland plantation where the photographer first glimpsed the belle at a picnic. In his later years, Brady reminisced that the happiest moment of his life occurred at the Handy plantation the evening Julia and he first waltzed. They were married in Washington in 1850 or 1851.

*This photograph of Daniel Webster appeared as a lithograph in Brady's book* The Gallery of Illustrious Americans. *Talented engraver Francis D'Avignon was paid a fee of one hundred dollars per engraving for his work on the twelve portraits in the book. Catching Webster took patience. Senator, secretary of state, and world-renowned orator, Webster found it impossible to commit to a sitting, yet he became the epitome of charm when Brady finally got him into the studio.*

In the summer of 1851 the Bradys visited Europe. Although the trip was meant to be a vacation and a honeymoon, Brady allegedly planned to see Daguerre and show him his work and also to photograph a number of European personalities. Daguerre, however, died while the Bradys were in transit.

In London, Brady entered a collection of forty-eight portraits of notable Americans in a photographic competition conducted at the International Exhibition at the Crystal Palace. He and two other American daguerreotypists swept the event, with Brady receiving a medal for the overall excellence of his work. The exhibition's official report noted, "On examining the daguerreotypes contributed by the United States, every observer is struck by their beauty of execution, the broad and well tinted masses of light and shade, and the total absence of all glare, which render them so superior to many works in the class."

While in London, Brady may have met Alexander
BP Gardner, a Scottish photographer. °Gardner possessed

*An "illustrious American" who was an even more difficult subject than Daniel Webster was John C. Calhoun. He refused to pose for a "counterfeit portrait" until a mutual friend talked him into a sitting for Brady. This photo as a D'Avingnon lithograph appeared in Brady's* The Gallery of Illustrious Americans. *Lithography involved drawing or painting with a greasy pencil on a flat slab of limestone. Once the stone was wet down with water, a greasy ink was applied which adhered only to the drawing. Printing occurred when paper sheets were rolled across the slab.*

tremendous artistic skills and a solid business aptitude. When he later migrated to the United States in 1856, Brady hired him and installed him as manager of one of his New York galleries.• °Gardner had developed an expertise in the latest photographic evolution of the wet-plate or collodion process, which placed the image on a wet glass plate rather than a metal plate. Since the image was on glass, it was essentially a negative from which copies could be made.•

Brady returned to New York in May 1852, but rather than adopt the wet-plate process, he opened a second gallery in another fashionable New York neighborhood. While he was distracted with the work of opening this gallery, most daguerrists in the city converted to the new process and gained a temporary edge over Brady of Broadway until Gardner arrived in 1856. In addition to converting Brady's studios to the collodion process, Gardner convinced Brady to hire a bookkeeper and implement professional accounting procedures. As a result, Brady became even more prosperous.

Gardner influenced °Brady to embrace the new technology to create magnificent portraits, called imperials, a reference to the size of the negative. These negatives were sixteen by twenty inches or twenty by twenty-four inches, which were capable of making life-size images.• Brady charged between $50 and $750 apiece for imperials, depending on the amount of retouching the portrait required. Enlarged images emphasized wrinkles, blemishes, and other facial defects, and so Brady °retouched these to make the image look more like a painting than a photograph.• He hired resourceful artists to remove imperfections, smooth rumpled clothing, straighten ties, and improve hairstyles. °These imperial prints turned Brady of Broadway the peddler into Brady the artist-photographer.•

In 1858 Brady opened a studio in Washington, named it the National Photographic Art Gallery, and installed Gardner as manager. In 1859 he opened a third gallery in New York near the intersection of Broadway and Bleecker Street, and in 1860 he opened a fourth studio at the intersection of Broadway and Tenth Street, which he named the National Portrait Gallery. By that time he had become one of the most successful photographers in the world.

The rich and famous, with whom Brady had sought to establish himself, now came to him unsolicited to have their portraits taken. Brady's career had reached its zenith. One of his finest moments came on October 13, 1860, when nineteen-year-old Edward, Prince of Wales and heir to the English throne, entered Brady's studio with his entourage during a visit to New York. The prince posed alone and then with the members of his party. Brady took a full-length portrait, three imperials, and a number of portraits for use as card photographs, or cartes de visite.

Many New York photographers had tried WM to arrange the royal sitting, and °as the photographs were being completed, Brady asked the duke of Newcastle why the royal party had chosen his studio. The duke allegedly replied, "Are you not the Mr. Brady who earned the prize nine years ago in London? You owe it to yourself. We had your place of business down in our notebooks before we started."•

*Brady is shown with his wife, Julia (left), and her sister, Mrs. Haggerty (right). Although little is known of their married life, Mathew and Julia lived quietly at New York's Astor Hotel, near Brady's studio, enjoyed carriage rides in the country, and occasionally went out to dinner and the theater. By the standards of the day, Brady's studio was a glamorous spot, and Mrs. Brady liked to drop by, often taking friends with her.*

As distinguished as the royal visit was, on February 27, 1860, Brady made perhaps the most influential photograph of his entire career: his first portrait of Abraham Lincoln. It was taken when the presidential candidate was in New York to deliver an antislavery speech at the Cooper Union.

BPr °At the time Lincoln was not particularly well known east of Illinois, and to the extent that he was known he was looked upon as a bumpkin. When the six-foot-four-inch-tall midwesterner appeared at Brady's gallery, the photographer decided to pose Lincoln standing, with one hand on a book and the other at his side. Dissatisfied with the stance, he asked Lincoln if he could "arrange" his collar. Lincoln smiled, realizing the effect Brady was trying to create, and said, "Ah, I see you want to shorten my neck." Brady replied, "That's just it, Mr. Lincoln."

*Constructed of iron and glass and sprawled over nineteen acres, London's Crystal Palace housed the first true world's fair in 1851. In the daguerreotype competition held as part of the "Exhibition of the Industry of All Nations," Brady's entries won an award for general excellence. While praise of his work poured from the English press in elegant phrases,* New York Tribune *editor Horace Greeley got to the point with typical American verve: "In daguerreotypes, we beat the world!" Knowing the publicity value of a medal such as the one below, Brady wasted no time promoting the awards he won at the exhibition.*

Lincoln's Cooper Union speech was an overnight sensation. As soon as it hit the New York newspapers the next day, the rest of the national press scrambled for images of Lincoln. Of course, Brady had the only recent photograph, and it showed, not a bumpkin, but "Honest Abe," serious, poised, and dignified.

Twelve weeks later Lincoln received the Republican nomination for the presidency. Brady's photograph was used extensively during the campaign. It appeared on the front page of *Harper's Weekly* and innumerable publications. It was duplicated as a card photograph and on banners and buttons. Currier and Ives made lithographs from it. Later, after taking up residence in the White House, Lincoln welcomed Brady and alluded to the power of the photograph when he said, "Brady and the Cooper Union made me president."•

In the years following Lincoln's election, the president became something of an industry for Brady. In addition to photographing Lincoln on numerous occasions, Brady and his operators also recorded the images of his family, close friends, members of the cabinet and Congress, and his enemies. By one count, the president was photographed 126 times, 30 times by Gardner (many before Gardner split with Brady and opened his own studio), 13 times by Anthony Berger (a Brady employee), and 11 times by Brady or likely one of his other operators.

When the Civil War broke out in 1861, Brady resolved to take his cameras out of the studio and onto the rugged terrain of the battlefield. His mission was to create a complete photographic record of the war. The project began as a personal obsession and eventually became a national treasure.

BP °Both Brady and Gardner claimed to have conceived the idea of photographing the war; both were likely telling the truth because they thought alike. Recording the war in photographs was an idea WCD whose time had come,• but °war photography was not a new idea in 1861. The earliest war photographs, daguerreotypes, were taken in Mexico in 1847 or 1848. A few years later, in the Crimea, several British photographers, most notably Roger Fenton, used the wet-plate process to record systematically images of that war. Their output was no more than a few hundred photographs, and they were not widely reproduced, but by 1861 the technical processes had been developed to duplicate photographs. At the same time, the Civil War presented the grandest canvas on which to practice the photographic art.•

*By the time of the Civil War a new photographic method was putting an end to daguerreotypes. Using the wet plate process, a negative was made from which a large number of prints could be created. This remarkable picture shows a photo shop of the period. Sheets of uncut prints hang from the wall. Men and women work together, along with children—this was before child labor laws—in assembly-line fashion.*

As war in the United States became imminent, Brady, like many photographers, began mass producing a new kind WCD of picture, the carte de visite. °The term literally meant visiting card. It was a photograph about the size of a business or a calling card, made from a collodion negative so innumerable copies could be reproduced at low cost. The process was perfectly timed for the Civil War. It was an inexpensive way for soldiers in the field to send their likeness to their loved ones. Every general and a multitude of soldiers sat for their cartes de visite.•

MP °Collecting card photographs was something everyone could do. In addition to collecting photographs of friends and relatives, people wanted images of politicians, clergymen, and other celebrities. Albums were supplied to mount the cards, and a host of photographs were mass produced.• Supply could hardly keep up with demand.

At first Brady disparaged them as cheapened photographs, because they lacked the quality on which he had prided the output of his studios. The cartes de visite sold for twenty-five cents apiece and did not require the skilled touch of an artist. Gardner, while still in Brady's employ, however, recognized the commercial potential and moved quickly to capitalize on the demand.

*In 1860 Brady opened a fourth studio at Tenth Street and Broadway in New York City, which he named the National Portrait Gallery. Lavishly furnished, it had a separate entrance for society ladies so that they would not have to enter through the common areas open to the public.*

Finally, Gardner convinced Brady to allow Edward and Henry Anthony of New York, the largest photographic supply house in the country, to generate the card photographs as orders were received. Brady supplied the Anthonys with his negatives and received a portion of the profits. His financial records show that he received an average of four thousand dollars a year through the arrangement, and of course, the reverse side of every card sold was identified as having been made from a Brady negative. Furthermore, the money earned from the sale of cartes de visite helped subsidize Brady's plan to photograph the war.

WCD °Brady knew that eventually a news-hungry public in the North would want to see scenes of the battlefields where its sons, husbands, and fathers were fighting.•

BP °The first great battle of the Civil War was Bull Run at Manassas, Virginia. It was thought that this one battle would quickly decide the outcome of the war, and so most of Washington society, including the politicians and their ladies, expecting to be entertained by the contest, journeyed into the Virginia countryside to watch the battle.•

Brady followed along in a hastily prepared mobile darkroom he called a "what-is-it" wagon. The canopy was sealed against light, and the wagon was modified with built-in containers for chemicals, shelves, and compartments for cameras, lenses, and other photographic supplies and equipment. He was accompanied by a newspaper reporter and a sketch artist, probably Alfred Waud. "Destiny overruled me! Like Euphorion, I felt I had to go. A spirit in my feet said, Go! and I went," he later wrote.

The battle did not go as anyone in the North expected. Within hours the poorly trained Union army was crushed by the equally poorly trained Confederates. What had started out as a stroll into Virginia became a rout back to Washington.

BP °Brady was caught up in the chaos. His wagon was overturned, but he managed to save some plates that he had made before the battle had started. It took him three days to get back to Washington,• and no photographs by Brady of the battle or its aftermath have ever been seen. He found refuge in the thickly wooded area near the battlefield. When he stumbled upon a company of volunteers from New York, they gave him a sword to protect himself.

WAF °Even though the battle was a Union disaster, it was thrilling for Brady. Despite his lack of professional success in the field, others in the media glamorized Brady's attempt. The *Humphrey's Journal* observed: "Brady has shown more pluck than many of the officers and soldiers who were in the fight."

One of the first things Brady did when he managed to get back to Washington was to have his own picture taken wearing a long white linen duster and his trademark broad-brimmed hat. Outlined under the duster is the scabbard of the sword he had been given. For the first time he had done something that would become a habit throughout the war: he documented the fact that he had been at the battle.•

While other photographers roamed the battlefields and afterward published folios of their work, they frequently depicted barren landscapes and bloated bodies. Gardner's *Photographic Sketchbook of the War* contained one hundred plates, seventy-five of which focused on the scene of battle or views of the countryside, and ten

*On the eve of the Civil War, Brady was wealthy and famous. Nearing forty, his galleries in New York and Washington were at the top of the trade, and the* New York Times *had dubbed him "the Prince of Photographers."*

*In 1860 Edward, Prince of Wales (with top hat in hand, standing amidst his entourage) came to New York. The city pulled out all the stops for the heir to the British throne, including parades and a society ball. When he came for his portrait session, Brady closed the salon to the public at Edward's request. For Brady, photographing Edward was a plum, socially and financially. By the session's end, the crowd of onlookers outside had grown so large that police were called to control it.*

Brady's Gallery
352 Penn. Ave. Wash.
Mr Pres.
Dear Sir
I have repeated Calls every hour in the day for your Photograph And would regard it as a great favor if you Could give me a sitting to day so that I may be able to exhibit a large picture on the 4th. If you Cannot Call today Please Call at your earliest Convenience and very Much oblige
Yours truly
M. B. Brady

-241920

*The letter above is from Mathew Brady to President Lincoln asking Lincoln to sit for a photograph. Brady's unique relationship with Lincoln helped him cover the war in the field. A scrawled note that read "Pass Brady," signed "A. Lincoln," gave the photographer and his operatives access to everything behind Union lines. Brady's second studio in Washington, opened in 1856 and operated by Alexander Gardner, took more pictures of Lincoln than any other individual or firm.*

that might be called portraits, and fifteen that depicted camp life. In Brady's collection, however, these proportions were reversed; fully 75 percent of his images focused on individuals, groups, and regiments.

This emphasis on portraiture was a Brady distinctive. Another distinctive was the numerous photographs that documented Brady's presence in army camps or showed him mingling with significant officers at several important campaigns including Manassas (July 1861), Antietam (September 1862), Gettysburg (July 1863), the Wilderness (May 1864), Petersburg (June 1864), and at City Point with Ulysses
MP S. Grant and Ambrose E. Burnside. °Brady saw himself as a representative of the people, and he wanted the public to see the war through his eyes,• yet it is impossible to chart his movements with certainty.

Concentrating on the men who might find fame in the field gave Brady an excuse to be in the field as well. It freed him from the studio, which was being dominated by the carte de visite trade that did not challenge his sense of skill and artistry, and placed him next to men whose fame was within reach by a battle or two. While he could enrich their reputations with his camera, his reputation was enriched as well.

The studios in Washington and New York were useful for displaying the images from the battlefield and the portraits of the Union army leaders, and Brady's prestige rose when he added portraits of the men people knew only from newspaper descriptions. One reporter noted that George B. McClellan, William T. Sherman, and Grant "are as brilliant but as distant from us as planets; it is a pleasure to have these planets photographed and be upon whispering terms with the Generals who are now to the nation as gods."

Brady knew that he would not be able to photograph everyone and everything that merited remembrance, so
GR °he invested his knowledge, reputation, and connections to organize a group of photographers to go into the field.• During the four years of the war, Brady outfitted twenty photographers, paying them thirty-five dollars a week, and maintained thirty-five bases of operation across the war front at a cost of one hundred

thousand dollars, approximately his entire net worth. This corps of photographers included virtually all of the most talented operators of the day: Gardner, his brother James, Timothy O'Sullivan, George Barnard, James Gibson, David Knox, William Pywell, David Woodbury, John Wood, and John Reekie.

BP Wherever they went, °these field photographers had to carry not only their cameras but also their darkrooms. Using Brady's original what-is-it wagon as a model, they modified their wagons to hold their cameras, chemicals, and glass plates. Even though the wagons made image-taking possible, the most challenging chore was transporting the fragile glass negatives from the scene of the action to Washington or New York. All the photographers had tales of losing some of their most remarkable images when negatives were broken in transit.•

In the field they welcomed conditions that approximated the placelessness of the studio setting. Subjects assumed heroic poses they had learned to hold in the studios with the help of posing stands and tables, but now they supported themselves against trees, camp furniture, and tent poles. While they were not confined by the studios or the reach of interior lighting, groups continued to pose in the same symmetrical clusters they would have assumed had they been in a studio.

Once they arrived at a battle site, the photographers MP faced severe hardships. °The wet-plate process was cumbersome. The photographer had to make the negative, sensitize it, slip it in the camera, and take the picture before the negative had a chance to dry. He had to complete the entire process in one spot without stopping. If any fighting was going on, it was impossible to make photographs. The cameras were incapable of capturing movement since the natural lighting of the day required BPr subjects to be still for several seconds.• °Almost all photographs were posed. Many nonetheless have the look of spontaneity despite the fact the subjects had to remain immobile for the operator to make the shot.•

Even if the exposure was made correctly, something WCD could still go wrong. °Back in the wagon, the workspace was stuffy at best and rank from postbattle odors

*Lincoln posed at Brady's studio in New York before his address at Cooper Union, February 27, 1860. In his speech that night, Lincoln did not call for an overnight end to slavery, but instead proposed that it not be spread into new territories. "Let us have faith that right makes might, and in that faith, let us, to the end, dare to do our duty as we understand it," Lincoln told his Cooper Union audience. Twelve weeks later Lincoln received the Republican nomination for president, and this photograph was used extensively during the campaign. Later, the president received Brady in the White House and said, "Brady and the Cooper Union made me president."*

*Alexander Gardner may have been Brady's most prominent cameraman in Washington, but he wasn't the only one. The photo above of Lincoln with his hair uncharacteristically combed down over his right brow was taken by Thomas Le Mere in April 1863.*

*A year later, on February 9, 1864, in his Washington studio, Brady posed Lincoln and his ten-year-old son Tad (below) looking through a photograph album. Anthony Berger operated the camera. The image was reproduced as a card, an engraving, a lithograph, and a painting.*

at worst. A gust of air, a bit of light, a sudden jolt, the wrong temperature, or insects could spoil an image that had taken the photographer a great deal of time, care, and effort to get.• In spite of these hardships and technical limitations, the images produced by Brady and his photographers not only recorded history but also made history.

BP °GIVEN THE technical limitations of their cameras and the process, no Civil War photographers ventured into the field thinking they were going to capture a battle with their cameras. Instead they recorded thousands of images of soldiers in camp and in the field. Most of these were group shots revealing grizzled veterans, newly arrived reinforcements, and an incredible montage of the men who fought the war. Even more than a century later, their faces continue to evoke a connection with the viewer.• Yet, as suggestive as these photographs are, the images with the most impact were those of the aftermath of battle; the pictures of the dead transcend time.

WCD °The camera revealed the dark side of war that many knew might exist but which few had ever seen.• The first images of the dead to be viewed widely were taken at Antietam in September 1862 by Brady photographers Gardner and Gibson. They began making photographs within hours of the Southern withdrawal into Virginia, focusing on the results of the day's fighting and recording the images of dead soldiers along the Hagerstown pike, the Sunken Road, and the Burnside Bridge. Gardner and Gibson returned to the Washington studio with approximately seventy photographs. Within a month's time Brady placed many of these images on display in his New York gallery. The exhibit drew large crowds and a tremendous response.

The *New York Times* noted that the public had heretofore experienced the war as seemingly endless casualty lists that made the conflict inconvenient, "like a funeral next door. . . . We recognize the battlefield as a reality, but it stands as a remote one." The exhibit in Brady's gallery had "done something to bring home to us the terrible reality and earnestness of war. If [the photographer] has not brought bodies and laid them in our door-yards and along the streets, he has done something very like it." Visitors to Brady's gallery were accustomed to gazing on portraits of the famous, but the *Times* noted that the crowds stared at the photographs with "a terrible fascination . . . that draws one near these pictures and makes him loathe to leave them. You will see hushed, reverend groups standing around these weird copies of carnage, bending down to look in the pale faces of the dead, chained by the strange spell that dwells in dead men's eyes."

*Characteristically, Brady placed himself in the center of this photo of leading artists of the day. Remarkable in its composition, the picture required every participant to be carefully posed as a portrait artist would do. Each member of the ensemble is clearly featured here in a single setting like actors in a stage play.*

WAF °This very important series of photographs enhanced Brady's prestige because they were not credited to the men who actually recorded the photographs. It was this problem over credit that disappointed and irritated men like Gardner, who deserved the praise. Instead, Brady's photographers saw their employer claim all the credit. Shortly after the Antietam exhibit, Gardner broke with Brady to open his own gallery in Washington and quickly attracted several of Brady's best cameramen; they too were irritated with Brady's stamping his name on their photographs.•

Brady, however, was puzzled by his employees' fixa-
GR tion on the credit issue. °In the daguerrean era, the one who owned the studio, who had made the reputation and invested his money in the enterprise, always received credit for the product that came out of that studio. That was the standard practice. By the time of the Civil War, the custom had begun to grind on the pride of the men who felt that they were the artistic contributors who deserved recognition and more of the profit.•

Now rivals, Brady and Gardner set out to outdo each other. Perhaps the greatest contrast between their work can be seen in the way in which each responded to the photographic opportunity following the battle of Gettysburg in July 1863. As soon as Gardner learned of the engagement, he prepared his equipment and journeyed to the Pennsylvania crossroads town with O'Sullivan and Gibson. In his haste, Gardner encountered Jeb

*The wet-plate process made it easier for photography to move outdoors, which Brady did by using darkrooms on wheels, which were nicknamed "what-is-it" wagons. In 1851 British photographer Frederick Scott Archer invented the wet plate method in which a sheet of glass was coated with silver salts and a wet, sticky substance called collodian. Placed in a camera and exposed for eight to twenty seconds, the plate then had to be developed before the emulsion dried. It was a cumbersome and delicate process, but the result—plate glass negatives from which unlimited prints could be made—revolutionized photography.*

Stuart's retreating cavalry and was briefly held captive; he photographed the inn in which he was held prisoner. When the photographers arrived on the battlefield in the late afternoon of July 5, Gardner, O'Sullivan, and Gibson began their work immediately, concentrating on the corpses still on the field. On the next day they focused on significant sites around the battlefield and remnants of the struggle. On July 7 they recorded the appearance of the town itself.

Brady and his photographers did not arrive in Gettysburg until a week after Gardner had returned to Washington. By that time, however, most of the landmarks of the battle had been established, and Brady was able to take advantage of several guides to the battlefield. Brady's people documented Lee's headquarters, McPherson's Woods, Little Round Top, the Lutheran seminary, and several other sites that became part of the story of the battle. They lacked the impact of the death views recorded by Gardner, O'Sullivan, and Gibson, but Brady's images proved to be very popular and were widely circulated in newspapers and magazines.

Although Gardner was no longer a part of it, Brady's Washington studio continued to produce definitive portraits of the war's leading political and military figures. Possibly the best-known photographs of Lincoln were taken there on February 9, 1864. While Anthony Berger operated the camera that day, Brady posed the president. In one series, Lincoln was photographed in profile. These images were later used by sculptor Victor D. Brenner in the design of the Lincoln-head penny. In another group of images, the president was seated, looking pensive. That portrait—which Lincoln's son Robert deemed the best likeness of his father—was adapted by the Treasury Department for the five-dollar bill. In another set, Lincoln's ten-year-old son Tad stood next to his father while the two looked through a photograph album. That image was reproduced as a card photograph, an engraving, a lithograph, and a painting.

The next month, amid rumors that Grant was en route to Washington to be appointed general in charge of all Union armies, Brady received several requests for Grant's picture. Those images that were available were not acceptable to Brady, and so he greeted the general at the train depot on March 8 and invited him to pose. Following his appointment with the president the next day, Grant went to Brady's studio accompanied by the secretary of war, Edwin M. Stanton.

Brady had three cameras ready for the sitting, and the session was going well until passing clouds dimmed the light from the skylights. An assistant went to the roof to adjust the mats used to modulate the light in the studio, and his foot slipped, breaking the skylight and showering the operating room with splinters of glass. A one-inch-thick piece of glass came very close to Grant, but the general seemed not to notice. Stanton, however, turned pale and pulled Brady aside, telling him that no one must know about the accident because the public might think there was a plot afoot to assassinate Grant. Brady promised to say nothing and returned to the session. The resulting images showed a relaxed, well-groomed, calm, even youngish Grant, perhaps the best ever taken of the general.

By 1865 Brady lacked the funds to pursue his project, so he covered fewer and fewer of the war's "prominent events." The loss of Gardner had been a heavy blow financially because Brady found no replacement with Gardner's business aptitude, and his Washington studio ceased to be profitable. He could no longer keep his photographers in the field supplied and paid.

On April 9, 1865, Brady was in Petersburg when he heard the news of Lee's surrender at Appomattox Court House. He immediately left for the small Virginia town but arrived too late to record the meeting of Grant and Lee. His only consolation was that no other photographer had succeeded in capturing the moment either. After taking several photographs of the Wilmer McLean house, site of the surrender, Brady set out for Richmond. He recorded several dramatic images of the abandoned city and the widespread devastation, but his goal was to photograph Lee.

*Brady established his persona as a field journalist visually by always having himself photographed wearing a flat-brimmed straw hat and often a duster. Although he rarely saw a battle while it happened and was under fire only once, and then only by accident at Petersburg, the public accepted Brady's pictures—rushed from the front—as evidence that they were seeing the war with their very own eyes. This portrait was made early in the war after First Bull Run.*

*Brady hired and equipped twenty crews to take photographs in every theater of the war, but his war-zone travels, so far as anyone knows, were limited to Virginia and areas nearby. He included himself in many photos, such as the one above right where he stands to the side as Maj. Gen. Robert B. Potter and his staff solemnly pose in a pine thicket. This made it seem to the public as if Brady were everywhere. He appeared again standing at the right in a photograph taken at Harpers Ferry (above left), the site of the John Brown raid and an important railroad junction. Harpers Ferry was a day's ride from Washington and Brady and his assistant David B. Woodbury took advantage of Federal occupation to photograph the ruins there in October 1862.*

Lee had come to Richmond because his wife was in the city. At first he declined to pose for Brady but eventually yielded. Brady photographed Lee standing and seated and with his son Custis and his chief of staff, WM Walter Taylor. °Lee wore the same uniform he had worn at the surrender. The image shows a proud general with heartache in his eyes as only Brady could have captured him.• The resulting photographs were perhaps the most moving of Brady's war portraits.

When Brady returned to Washington after the war he found that he was no longer the nation's photographer. That honor was now Gardner's. The Scotsman had made the last studio portraits of Lincoln. Gardner now recorded the most important events of the day, such as the trial and hanging of the Lincoln conspirators and the autopsy of John Wilkes Booth.

Brady's Washington studio, meanwhile, became mired in one legal action after another as creditors sought to be paid. In 1868 Brady declared bankruptcy but retained his studio when he was the only person to bid on it at auction.

MP Despite his financial difficulties, °Brady became obsessed with his collection of war photographs.• He expected that the sales of card photographs and other images would generate enough money to pull him out of debt, but the war pictures sold well only for a short time. The public seemed to want to forget.

WCD °Sadly, from 1865 onward, Brady's story was one of
BP almost uninterrupted decline.• °His financial problems

*Brady placed himself in photographs taken at the gatehouse of the Gettysburg cemetery (above left) and at Petersburg (above right), where he stands in the center wearing a straw hat. Brady's arrival at the Gettysburg battlefield a week after the conflict worked to his advantage, since local residents were by then getting over the fright of the battle and becoming expert tour guides. When Brady asked officers of a Federal battery at Petersburg to swing into action for the picture shown above, Confederate gunners mistook the show for real battle and opened fire. The horse pulling Brady's what-is-it wagon bolted, scattering plates and equipment. Brady, unharmed, called the event his closest call of the war.*

extended to his New York studios, and his friendships and connections with the city's power brokers failed to protect him. With assets of less than twelve thousand dollars and debts in excess of twenty-five thousand dollars, he declared bankruptcy again.•

Brady had been a wealthy and famous man at the beginning of the Civil War, but his devotion to the task of documenting the war with pictures led to his financial ruin. With his studios a disaster in New York, he returned to Washington a bad-tempered, quarrelsome alcoholic in his fifties.

MP °In 1870 he tried to sell his photographs to the New-York Historical Society, but the society could not
WCD raise sufficient funds.• °In 1874 the owner of a New York warehouse auctioned off some of Brady's war negatives for nonpayment of storage charges. These were finally acquired by the government through the intervention of Secretary of War William Belknap, who authorized a payment of $2,840 to Brady. Encouraged that the government might be willing to purchase his entire collection of war photographs, Brady offered them for sale to Belknap.

In March 1875 Congress appropriated twenty-five thousand dollars to pay Brady for all his negatives, not just those relating to the war. Eventually, Brady relinquished 5,712 negatives of various sizes. While the payment was hardly close to what the images were worth,• the infusion of cash energized Brady. He remodeled his Washington studio, which once again

*In March 1864 Ulysses S. Grant was promoted to lieutenant general and put in command of all Union armies. After a trip to Washington, during which the portrait above left was made in Brady's studio, Grant reconsidered his plan to direct the war from the West. "When I got to Washington and saw the situation," Grant wrote, "it was plain that here was the point for the commanding general to be."*

*Brady received permission to construct a platform for his camera crew at Lincoln's first inaugural on March 4, 1861. It was feared that the inauguration would be disrupted and so Brady's work, assisted by Alexander Gardner, was done under the watchful eye of Pinkerton's men. Interestingly, the photograph above right records the event, but not the participants. Unlike modern television coverage, there are no close-up images because there were no telephoto lenses available.*

became the studio of choice for the powerful and the popular celebrities of the day. Part of his success lay in the departure of his old competitors, who were now in the West creating a catalog of life on the frontier. Brady's good fortune, however, was short-lived. Photographic technology changed yet again, and Brady could no longer keep up. His Washington studio gradually declined.

Brady's wife, Julia, to whom he had been married for almost thirty years, suffered from a heart condition and was bedridden most of the time. Brady's health too was becoming a serious problem as his sight worsened and arthritis hobbled him.

In 1881 he sold his prized portraits of Webster, Clay, and Calhoun to the government, but he lost his studio in court for nonpayment of an employee's wages. What little work he was able to solicit barely met his needs. In 1887 Julia died, and Brady tried to continue working. He became a "sad little man," according to Lydia Mantle Fox, a manager of a secretarial service in Washington for congressmen with no office staffs of their own. Brady plagued her with requests to contact any politicians who might have an interest in the remaining war photographs he owned, and he regaled her with stories of his golden years as the prince of the New York photographers and his experiences during the war. He also complained to her of his financial woes, his failing health, and his sense of loss over Julia's death.

WCD °In 1895 Brady was badly injured when a horse-drawn streetcar struck him in downtown Washington, leaving him bleeding and unconscious.• He spent several weeks recovering in a hospital and afterward at the home of his nephew. Almost blind and in very poor health, he returned to New York for the last time.

Brady's failing spirits were buoyed when several friends in the Seventh Regiment announced plans to recognize his achievements at a testimonial benefit at Carnegie Hall on January 30, 1896. Although there is little evidence to support the story, according to some family records part of the program was to be a stereopticon show of 135 of Brady's photographs with commentary by Brady himself.

*Brady's photograph (above) of the ruins of its capital, Richmond, Virginia, symbolized the broken Confederacy.*

*Shortly after he surrendered at Appomattox Court House, Gen. Robert E. Lee (below) posed for Brady with his son Custis (left) and his aide Walter Taylor (right) on the back porch of Lee's home in Richmond.*

Whether or not there was a slideshow to accompany MP his presentation, °in his lecture Brady wanted to offer a way of thinking about what had happened to the country during the Civil War. He wanted his presentation to propose a rationale, a logic for a war that was inherently chaotic, difficult, and disorganized. He succeeded in that historians continue to use Brady's pictures over and over in their study of the war.•

In November 1895, as he prepared for this special WCD evening, °Brady collapsed with a painful kidney ailment and was hospitalized. For a while he seemed to improve, and he continued to prepare his presentation from his hospital bed. Shortly after New Year's Day 1896, however, his condition worsened, and Brady died on January 15.• His body was sent to Washington for interment next to Julia in the Congressional Cemetery.

A friend went to Brady's rooms to collect his belongings and found little in the way of worldly goods. His legacy was instead the vast collection of daguerreotypes, stereo views, card photographs, and images produced by his New York and Washington studios, many of which were sold to the public by Anthony and Company during the last quarter of the nineteenth century. The company had kept Brady supplied during the war, and when he could not pay, he offered the firm more than seven thousand negatives. In 1907, after many succeeding buyers, these negatives were obtained by Edward B. Eaton, a Hartford, Connecticut, publisher, and used in several different works, the best-known of which was the ten-volume *The Photographic History of the Civil War* released in 1911–12. After Eaton's death in 1942, the Library of Congress purchased the negatives.

Another collection of several thousand Brady photographs from his Washington studio was inherited by Levin Handy, Brady's nephew. After Handy's death, the Library of Congress obtained these negatives from his two daughters. These included 350 to 400 daguerreotypes of some of the most distinguished personalities of the mid-nineteenth century: the actor Edwin Booth, Stephen A. Douglas, Brigham Young, Daniel Webster, and Brady himself.

Anthony and Company compiled yet another cache of Brady photographs amounting to fifteen to eighteen thousand negatives in wooden storage boxes that were later obtained by Anthony, Scovill, and Company. This collection was purchased in 1902 by Frederick Hill

*Abraham Lincoln's funeral procession on F Street in Washington marked the loss of Brady's once greatest ally and was like a door closing on this chapter of his life. Brady's business in Washington went into a steady decline with the end of the war. Brady had not even made the last portraits of Lincoln. That distinction went to his former associate Alexander Gardner, whose final haunting picture of a wistfully smiling president was taken February 5, 1865.*

Meserve, an amateur historian and dedicated collector of images of Lincoln and the Civil War. Meserve identified most of the negatives and their photographers before his death in 1962. In 1981 the National Portrait Gallery purchased fifty-four hundred negatives from the Meserve family. Thus the largest body of Brady images may be found in the collections of the Library of Congress, the National Archives, and the National Portrait Gallery of the Smithsonian Institution.

BP Despite his financial woes, °Brady's greatest moment came after the Civil War when he realized the importance of the photographs he had collected. While he likely thought he would profit from sales of the images, he also knew the historical value of those prints. Although not many people were willing to listen to Brady during his pitiful last years, he latched on to the idea that the photographic legacy of the Civil War should be preserved, and he persisted in that belief until he died.•

WCD In retrospect, °Brady was a pioneering newsman, artist, and war photographer who changed forever the way Americans viewed war. It was no longer sanitary, no longer distant, no longer glorious, because he showed the public what the hard hand of war could do to the land and the
BPr people.• °He was the first to grasp the significance of the ability of photographs to influence public opinion.•

MP °Brady understood that photography could stop time and replace real events with photographed ones. His images of the Civil War have become the Civil War for succeeding generations. It was his understanding of the way in which photography could supersede reality that sets him apart from everyone else.• His sad demise can never overshadow his glorious contributions to photography and to the nation. His efforts ensured that the country would have a visual record of the defining event in its history.

*The portrait of Brady above was made in 1875 when he was about fifty-three years old, near the time that Congress purchased a majority of his negatives, giving him much needed cash. Although Brady sold the collection for twenty-five cents on the dollar, the money put him back in business, at least for a while. He is shown below in 1888. Despite impoverishment and a loss of prestige, a series of accidents and illnesses, failing eyesight and the death of his beloved wife, Brady never lost touch with Brady the showman.*

*A Gallery of Brady Photographs*

*Clockwise from top of page 252: a group of non-commissioned officers of a New York Infantry regiment in Virginia, 1864; a New York State Militia soldier: George Armstrong Custer, U.S. Cavalry officer, after the war; the Ninty-sixth Pennsylvania Infantry drilling at Camp Northumberland, 1861; Fort Totten, near Rock Creek Church, Washington, D.C., one of sixty-eight forts that encircled the capital; Grapevine Bridge over the Chickahominy River in Virginia, prior to the Seven Days Campaign, 1862; the unfinished United Capitol Building, 1858.*

*Clockwise from right: Col. Ambrose Burnside and officers of the First Rhode Island Volunteers, Camp Sprague, 1861; officers of the 164th New York Infantry relax with a game of chess while their families visit them at Alexandria, Virginia, 1863; (left) servants of Prince de Joinville doing chores at Camp Winfield Scott, Yorktown, Virginia, May 3, 1862; (right) the tent of Johnson the Sutler of the Union Second Division, Ninth Corps; officers of the Fifty-fifth New York Infantry at Fort Gaines, defending Washington, D.C., in the winter of 1861-2; crew members cooking on the deck of a Federal ironclad in the James River, Virginia, July 9, 1862; a soldier of the Fifth New York Zouaves pretends to be injured for the benefit of the camera before leaving on the Chancellorsville Campaign in 1863.*

# ALEXANDER GARDNER

*While* THE NAME MOST COMMONLY associated with Civil War photography is that of Mathew Brady, perhaps the best and most significant photographer of the war was Alexander Gardner, an artist with a camera and onetime Brady employee who—until recently—had somehow slipped through the cracks of history almost unnoticed. It was Gardner's misfortune to have his name and memory eclipsed by that of Brady. Both men were pioneers of American photojournalism and war photography. The two had collaborated for years, beginning in 1856 when Gardner opened and managed Brady's Washington studio before the war and concluding in the weeks that followed the September 1862 battle of Antietam. Like that of every Brady operative, Gardner's work was published under the Brady name, and his photographs, which were used as the basis for newspaper illustrations, were thus identified to the public as Brady photographs, with the implication that Brady himself had created the images. To this day many scholars perpetuate the error, and this oversight has continued to conceal Gardner's genius, with many of his most powerful photographs being credited to Brady.

It was through Gardner's lens that the country first witnessed the dead on the battlefield. Previously, artists had glorified battle, but Gardner's photographs of shattered, bloated bodies revealed the grisly truth about death on the country's killing fields, and for the first time the true nature of war was demonstrated to the American public in graphic detail.

| | |
|---|---|
| WAF | William A. Frassanito |
| BJ | Brooks Johnson |
| MP | Mary Panzer |
| BP | Brian Pohanka |
| WFS | William F. Stapp |

BP °Gardner was arguably the greatest of the Civil War photographers and undoubtedly one of the most important in the history of the art.• His reputation soared during the Civil War, aided particularly by the endorsements of the Washington elite. By the war's end, he had overshadowed his rival and former employer, Brady, but while Gardner came to be better known after the war, two developments eventually buried his name and exalted Brady's. First, Gardner's enterprise expanded after the war, concentrating on the nation's westward movement and leaving the Civil War behind; however, Brady was obsessed with marketing his Civil War collection from the war's end until his death in 1896. Second, Gardner died before his colleague, in 1882, leaving the field to Brady alone.

WAF His journey into photography began °in Scotland, where Gardner was born on October 17, 1821, in Paisley.• Shortly afterward, the family moved to Glasgow, where twin sisters, Agnes and Catherine, were born in 1826 and a brother, James, was born in 1829. Gardner's father, James, most likely died of cholera at about the same time as his last child was born. Alexander excelled at his studies, particularly astronomy, botany, WAF and chemistry, and at the age of fourteen °he was apprenticed to a jeweler.• As a craftsman in a class-conscious society, Gardner was viewed as one of the privileged, but he became concerned about the inequalities, wrongs, and sufferings in society and developed an interest in the plight of the working class. As a Calvinist, he viewed good fortune as the result of hard work, and when he considered the ideals espoused by Robert Owen, a Welsh socialist, Gardner became interested in utopian societies.

Gardner changed careers in 1847, becoming a manager of a discount and loan company. Later that year he became a charter member of the Glasgow Atheneum, which gave him access to a library and opportunities to attend lectures delivered twice a week. Concerned with the exploitation of the working class, he supported the cooperative movement in Scotland and began to envision building such a society in the United States. In June 1850 his future brother-in-law and eight friends and relatives established a cooperative community in Clayton County, Iowa. Gardner oversaw the establishment of the community from Glasgow and maintained and cultivated the community's business interests and investments, recruited new members, and even scheduled the duties of each person in the community.

WAF °In 1851 Gardner changed careers again, becoming the proprietor of the *Glasgow Sentinel,* and used his editorial prerogatives to advocate the rights of workers.• Within three months the *Sentinel*'s circulation reached sixty-five hundred, making it the city's BJ second largest newspaper. °That same year, the Crystal Palace Exhibition was staged in London's Hyde Park, and Gardner possibly may have met Brady, who had received the grand prize medal in the daguerreotype competition.•

*Although he gave Alexander Gardner his start in America, Mathew Brady's custom of not crediting his photographers with their work rankled the hardworking and talented Gardner. It was not unusual for Brady (above) to receive a photo from another photographer and, if he liked it and thought he could sell it, stamp his name on it and put it in his catalog. This practice gave the false impression that Brady himself had made all such pictures. When he broke away from Brady, Gardner promised his photographers that they would receive credit for their work.*

Gardner's newspaper career ended in 1852 when the experimental Iowa community failed and he had to travel to the site where his business acumen was needed to settle the colony's affairs. Most of the members merged into other settlements throughout Clayton County, and Gardner returned to Glasgow.

His interest in chemistry and science most likely influenced Gardner to experiment with photography. The *Sentinel* had reviewed the openings of many daguerreotype studios as well as the Crystal Palace Exhibition. BJ In 1855 the newspaper also reviewed °Roger Fenton's photographs taken during the Crimean War,• although Fenton's photographs failed to capture the great sweep of battle and its tragic costs. The photography of warfare on a large scale was yet to come. Whatever influence these reviews may have had upon Gardner, by December 1855 he had opened a portrait studio and was enticing customers by offering gold watches as a premium for anyone purchasing a calotype portrait and by giving a portrait brooch with the purchase of each collodion print. The jewelry was no doubt what remained from his original apprenticeship.

An editorial in the *Dumbarton Herald* confirmed the veracity of the offer: "Mr. Gardner is practicing among us as a photographic artist and the portraits he has turned out of several well known townsmen entitle

*James Gardner, eight years younger than his brother, came to the United States with the utopian community Alexander Gardner and others founded in Iowa. When the experiment failed in 1852, James returned to Scotland, then immigrated back to New York, along with Alexander's family and their mother, in 1856.*

*James and Timothy H. O'Sullivan (below) were the first employees of Gardner's Washington studio. First hired as an apprentice, O'Sullivan developed into one of the finest photographers of the period.*

him to be considered among the foremost professors of this beautiful art. . . . To congregations who wish a faithful portrait of their minister having all the breadth and vigor of a steel engraving combined with the delicacy and minuteness of the finest daguerreotype, the present opportunity ought not to be lost sight of. . . . The watch and brooch which he purposes making a present of to his finest subscribers we have seen and can truly say they are no sham." By March 1856 Gardner no longer needed to induce customers into his studio with gifts, and by the following month he ceased advertising altogether.

For a man with Gardner's intellectual curiosity, the camera had an enormous attraction, and indeed the
WFS world at large seemed dazzled by the new device. °The camera generated a tremendous degree of excitement and curiosity about its potential. Almost immediately it was viewed as an instrument of documentation without peer.• At the same time, advancements in image processing were being developed, and Gardner was well practiced in the newer techniques when he immigrated to America in the spring of 1856.

Gardner and his family planned to join the survivors of the Iowa colony, but upon their arrival in New York they learned that most of their friends and family members had been stricken with tuberculosis. Leaving his mother, his wife, his brother, and his two children in New York, Gardner visited the former utopian community to make arrangements for his niece, overseeing her adoption by a local attorney. When he returned to New York, weighing the choice of either returning to Scotland or staying in America, he sought out Brady and found a job.

Brady had built his reputation as a portrait artist, one of the best in the world, and his studios were frequented by the country's most famous and powerful personalities. Yet by the time Gardner joined him, Brady had stepped away from the camera. Born nearsighted, Brady's eyes were already failing him by his late thirties, and so he hired men like Gardner to make the images.
MP °Brady was also beginning to enjoy the attentions of New York society and was no longer compelled to

operate the camera at his gallery.• Still, he made sure his name was stamped on every photograph.

In Gardner, Brady found an artist similar in temperament to himself and, given the Scotsman's publishing and administrative experience, someone who could fulfill the studio's commercial commitment while Brady attended to the clientele. As a businessman Gardner was surprised at the poor condition of Brady's bookkeeping. Immediately, he instituted standard business procedures and insisted that Brady engage a professional bookkeeper. At first Brady was annoyed with the formalities but came to appreciate them when he grasped how profitable the business could become.

Gardner also brought with him an expertise in the making of imperial prints, life-size portraits that could be retouched to remove unpleasant wrinkles, unkempt hair, and disheveled clothing. Prices ranged from $50 to $750 depending on the amount of retouching necessary. Brady hired professional artists for the work, essentially transforming a photograph into a painting. One competitor complained that the images had "nothing imperial about them except the price."

Brady had long desired having a studio in Washington, and on January 26, 1858, he formally announced its opening in the *Washington Daily National Intelligencer.* Gardner, his brother, James, and Timothy O'Sullivan, a young apprentice, were given the responsibility of running the studio and looking after Brady's interests.

*A recent innovation when the war started was the carte de visite, or card photograph, which was small, easily reproduced, and inexpensive. Brady disdained the cards, believing they debased the photographer's art, but Gardner regarded them as lucrative for the studio. He ordered a special four-lens camera to quadruple the number of prints from a single pose. The cards soared in popularity as volunteers wanted to be photographed in uniform before they left for war. Shown above are four cartes de visite (left to right): a paroled Confederate prisoner from J. E. B. Stuart's command; an unidentified child; two unidentified soldier-brothers; Hannibal Hamlin, vice-president of the United States during Lincoln's first term.*

*In October 1862 when Lincoln visited General McClellan at the site of the bloody September battle of Antietam, Gardner was there. One of his photographs showed Dr. Jonathan Letterman, medical director of the Army of the Potomac (fifth from left, hatless and coatless) with officers from McClellan's staff. During the recent Peninsula campaign, medical attention had been so lax that some of the wounded remained unattended on the battlefield for as long as a week. Civilians were enraged and in July McClellan appointed Dr. Letterman, who immediately established an ambulance corps which brought the wounded to new "primary stations" near the battlefield, such as tents as seen in the background.*

Gardner arrived in Washington in February 1858, and the quality of his work immediately attracted the public's attention. He was an innovator and never hesitated to acquire any enhancement that might improve his photographs and impress customers. In addition to paying the studio employees a fair wage, Gardner allowed the photographers to pursue outside work but insisted on retaining their negatives. He opposed Brady's practice of luring prospective clients with the promise of complimentary sittings. As long as the shop was profitable, Brady never questioned him, and as long as Gardner had complete control of the studio he was content to work for Brady.

There was a great deal of competition among the Washington photographers, but Gardner's reputation set Brady's studio apart from the rest. In 1859 the carte de visite, or card photograph, became popular, and Gardner viewed the small, easily reproduced, and inexpensive photographs as a lucrative enterprise for the studio. At the least, the cards meant repeat customers. Brady disdained the format, believing that it debased the skill of photographers. Gardner nevertheless ordered a special four-lens camera so as to quadruple the number of prints from a single pose.

During the tense period in which the nation braced for war following Lincoln's election in November 1860, Gardner began preparing for the changes war would bring to the Washington area. He ordered additional carte de visite cameras, expecting that a sudden influx of soldiers might generate a demand for individual portraits in uniform. Anticipating that the war would make a great many heroes and the public would want card photographs of these men, Gardner contracted with E. and H. T. Anthony, the country's largest photographic supply house, to make and distribute card photographs from negatives furnished by Brady and Company and for which Anthony would pay a royalty. In the first year of the agreement, Brady received twelve thousand dollars, and he averaged four thousand dollars per year for the rest of the war.

As artists and businessmen, Gardner and Brady realized the historic opportunity that lay before them in WFS photographing the war. °Both claimed to have initiated the idea. If the idea was not Brady's, he quickly and wholeheartedly accepted it because he understood a one-million-man army would be good business.•

After the outbreak of hostilities at Fort Sumter, Brady set in motion his wartime photographic unit. America had never gone to war on such a massive scale before and neither had the camera. Brady himself tried to BP cover the battle of First Manassas, but °he was caught up in the retreat and returned to Washington without having recorded any images of the battle.• He learned from the experience that war photography demanded a BJ different approach. °He decided to assign the actual work to other men. Even though he would not follow the armies himself, Brady would stamp his name on the photographs taken by his employees in the field.•

WAF °This practice of placing his name on every image he touched so as to have almost every newspaper illustration bear the Brady credit line generated the myth that Brady was everywhere photographing everything. While his employees may not have liked the practice, it was not uncommon. Of course, one of these employees whose photographs were involved was Gardner.•

*Gardner's colleague James F. Gibson took this picture near Fair Oaks, Virginia, in June 1862, during the Peninsula campaign. The men are all officers in Horse Battery A, Second U.S. Artillery. The scene here is half of a stereoview, which was popular at the time. A stereoview tricks the eye into seeing a photograph in three dimensions. This was accomplished by using a camera with two lenses, each lens viewing the scene from a slightly different angle. When viewed through a stereopticon, the eye attempted to reconcile the difference, creating an illusion of depth.*

Brady's clearance to photograph the war ultimately came from Lincoln, and there are many theories of how the photographer's meeting with the president was arranged. The most probable BP conjecture is that either °Brady or Gardner had some influence with Allan Pinkerton, head of the intelligence service that eventually became the Secret Service, and facilitated the encounter.

When Pinkerton was attached to George B. McClellan's staff and the Army of the Potomac in the fall of 1861, he recommended Gardner be made chief photographer under the jurisdiction of the topographical engineers.• This appointment, which also conferred the honorary rank of captain on the Scotsman, essentially ended Gardner's conventional management of Brady's Washington studio in November 1861, but Gardner continued his relationship with Brady and the studio. The appointment, however, served as a cover for a more clandestine role in Pinkerton's service. Gardner had complete access to McClellan's troops and encampments, which Pinkerton exploited to detect spies among the soldiers by analyzing the random group photographs taken by Gardner. The camera was also used to copy maps and charts that were supplied to the field and divisional commands. Photographs of potential battlefields were also studied to acquaint field commanders with the terrain and to inform planners so they could anticipate locations for field hospitals, mess areas, and barracks. The Corps of Engineers also reviewed photographs of bridges, railroads, and other installations it might have to rebuild or enhance.

There is little doubt that the arrangements between Pinkerton and Gardner were acceptable to Brady who viewed the appointment as a way of securing exclusive photographs whose publication he alone would control. The tacit involvement of the Brady organization also allowed Gardner to utilize his colleagues as photographers in the field, including his brother, James, O'Sullivan, James F. Gibson, George N. Barnard, John Wood, David Woodbury, William R. Pywell, David Knox, and John Reekie. The photographers were allowed to copyright their work with the stipulation that Brady would publish it first in his album gallery.

In April 1862 Gardner dispatched Gibson, Barnard, and Wood to accompany McClellan's army in the Peninsula campaign, which focused on Williamsburg, Yorktown, Norfolk, and Richmond. While a Union victory remained elusive, these photographers made significant steps in developing a methodology for documentary war photography by recording images of installations, camps, and field hospitals and portraits of officers and foreign observers.

Brady published the Peninsula campaign photographs in the summer of 1862, and they were critically acclaimed by the press—"exquisite in beauty, truthful as the records of heaven"—and sold well to the public. Gardner had long considered the possible commercial success of the war views and in July 1862 entered a brief partnership with Gibson. Under the terms of the agreement, each shared in the proceeds from the sale of any photographs taken by Gibson; Gardner's role was to publish and market them. The partnership dissolved the following month, but the men worked well together and the basis for a future relationship was established.

Gardner returned to the Virginia Peninsula with Gibson and fulfilled his obligation to Pinkerton. The rest of the Brady photographers were scattered among the ranks, accompanying and photographing the army across the Virginia battlefront. Gardner's epic challenge as a war photographer came after the September 17, 1862, battle of Antietam. Gibson and Gardner arrived on the battlefield near the small Maryland town of Sharpsburg as Lee was withdrawing into Virginia. A caption on one of their photographs claimed that the image had been taken on September 17, but it is most likely the two men arrived on September 18, the day after the battle.

BP °Antietam was the bloodiest single day in American history with more than twenty-three thousand Americans killed, wounded, or missing. It was the most dramatic and important clash of arms to that date on the American continent, and Gardner was determined to record what he could of the human destruction.

The bodies still on the battlefield when Gardner and Gibson arrived were Confederates because the victor usually buried his dead first; thus most of the Union casualties had already been interred. The Southern corpses had been in the sun for two days and were decomposing rapidly. Everywhere the two photographers looked, they saw thousands of human corpses and animal carcasses.• It was also clear that the photog-
BP raphers were in a race with time. °Burial details were at work almost at their heels, adding an element of haste to their task.•

WAF Further complicating the work was the fact that °the wet-plate process was bulky and time consuming; each image required at least ten minutes. The cameras lacked

*In the 1870s Gardner's daughter Eliza posed for this carte de visite photograph. Early in 1863, perhaps as a result of having seen the effects of war on civilian populations, Gardner moved his wife and his then-infant daughter out of harm's way to McGregor's Landing, Iowa, where his brother-in-law Robertson Sinclair had lived since the failure of their utopian community in nearby Clayton County. However, Gardner kept his son Lawrence in school at Emmitsburg, Maryland—a hamlet on the road to Gettysburg.*

*When they went on display at the Brady gallery in New York, photographs of the Antietam battlefield by Gardner and James Gibson changed the way the Northern public perceived the war and the way the press reported it. Clockwise from right: a dead Confederate soldier; a Federal burial detail at work; Confederate dead in front of Dunker Church—one of Gardner's most famous pictures; a haunting photo of a dead horse; dead Louisiana soldiers along the Hagerstown Pike.*

*James Gardner stands next to an artillery wagon near Petersburg, Virginia, in 1864. While Alexander Gardner and his staff were occasionally photographed at the front, Mathew Brady had himself included in many battlefield and camp photos, making him seem almost omnipresent. Brady's talent for self-promotion was a strength of his not shared by the less-promotion-minded Alexander Gardner.*

shutters, and so Gardner and Gibson had to estimate the necessary exposure each subject required according to their experience and knowledge of weather conditions. They would remove the lens cap and estimate if the exposure needed two, five, or ten seconds.•

Gardner and Gibson began by photographing the dead scattered along the Hagerstown pike. On September 19 they focused on the Sunken Road, and on September 21 and 22 they concentrated on the middle bridge on the right side of the Confederate battle line. When they were finished, they had created seventy images of the Antietam battlefield: Gardner took fifty-five stereoviews and eight large-format views and Gibson executed seven stereoviews. While the circumstances were daunting, Gardner knew what he wanted to show.

His skill as an artist and journalist can be seen in an
BP image of a dead horse he took at Antietam. °Hundreds
of dead horses were scattered on the field, but one had fallen to its knees and appeared to be resting. Even in death, it looked as if it were attempting to rise from the ground. Gardner recorded this image, possibly realizing that it symbolized the unreality and cruelty of war.•

With every photograph they took, Gardner and Gibson took significant strides in the maturation of war
MP photography. °They refined techniques still used to
arrange settings, find appropriate landscapes, and create
WAF images to convey substantial information.• °Their only
limitation was their technology and equipment, which precluded any attempts to record combat in the field. Had they tried, they likely would not have captured much. Typically, battlefields were cloaked with a vast fog of white smoke generated by muskets and cannon. Even soldiers on the field could hardly see the details of the battlefield.• Even without combat photographs, Gardner's camera sufficiently captured the horror of war.

Gardner's images of the aftermath of the battle were
WAF in some ways more graphic than the battle itself. °The

photographs of the Confederate dead along the Hagerstown pike were interesting from a historical perspective because they clearly conveyed the intensity of the fighting there. The bodies remained where they fell, and rigor mortis had frozen their arms and hands in midair positions, presenting a grisly tableau of war.•

*Timothy O'Sullivan's photographic wagon is halted on a Virginia roadside during the war. The rolling darkroom was a cramped affair, with barely room for a photographer to stand in the back, his vats of collodion, unmixed chemicals, and fixative baths in front of him. Darkness was essential and so the inside of the wagon was lit with subdued yellow light. The chemical mixtures were all so sensitive, one photographer reported, that "the slightest breath might carry enough poison across the plate . . . to make it produce a blank spot instead of some much desired effect."*

Once Gardner and Gibson had collected the images, they were rushed to New York where they were put on display at the Brady gallery. The carnage on display stunned the public. Despite the element of shock, the *New York Times* enthusiastically praised the exhibit: "The dead of the battlefield come to us very rarely, even in dreams. We see the list in the morning paper at breakfast, but dismiss its recollection with coffee. It is like a funeral next door. It attracts your attention but does not enlist your sympathy. But it is very different when the hearse stops at your own door and the corpse is carried out over your own threshold. Those who lose friends in battle know what battlefields are. . . . Mr. Brady has done something to bring home to us the terrible reality and earnestness of war. If he has not brought home bodies and laid them in our door-yards and along our streets, he has done something very like it. These pictures have a terrible distinctiveness."

The Antietam photographs began to change the way the public perceived the war and the way the press BP reported it. °Here was war with none of its glory and all of its horrors, brought home in such a way that the people knew that what they were looking at was real. Photographs were not fanciful engravings or heroic paintings; they were graphic images of an unretouched battlefield. These were real bloated, mangled bodies, lying in the sunshine unburied. They were somebody's husband, brother, or son.• In response to the Antietam photographs, Oliver Wendell Holmes Sr.—whose son was a junior officer with the Twentieth Massachusetts—articulated one aspect of the public's understanding:

"War is the surgery of crime. What a repulsive, brutal, sickening thing it is, this dashing together of two frantic mobs which we give the name of armies."

The *Times,* however, credited Brady with this insight into the battle, and the labors of Gardner and Gibson were overlooked. In time Gardner's name would come before the public, but in the meantime the Scotsman returned to Antietam in October 1862 when Lincoln visited General McClellan at the battlefield. He took twenty-five exposures: twelve stereoviews and thirteen large-format views. On October 7 he copyrighted eighteen views from this second set of images and the initial photographs of Antietam, listing Brady as the publisher.

In November 1862 Lincoln relieved McClellan of command. In domino fashion, Pinkerton was replaced and Gardner's role as chief photographer of the Army of the Potomac was redefined, which allowed Gardner to rethink his relationship with the Brady studio. Some time in early November he left Brady's employ, taking with him all the negatives of the Peninsula campaign, Second Manassas, and Antietam. The separation was apparently amicable, because both men maintained a respect for the other for the rest of their lives.

*On May 26, 1863, Gardner and his brother James opened their own studio in Washington at 511 Seventh Street, at the intersection with D Street. Gardner's Gallery was in a walkup over Shepard's & Riley's bookstore. In their grand opening announcement, the brothers boasted that, with their new equipment, posing for a carte de visite "rarely exceeds five seconds! Oftener, not more than one or two!"*

*A young man, possibly Gardner's fifteen-year-old son Lawrence, poses in a wide view of the interior of Gardner's new gallery in Washington. Gardner was confident that the lighting in the new studio was designed to eliminate heavy and unnatural shadows under the eyebrows and chin, which was the natural consequence of using light primarily from overhead skylights.*

GARDNER LEFT Brady's studio for the field and joined Gibson, then with Ambrose E. Burnside's command as it was beginning its move on Richmond by way of Fredericksburg. When Joseph E. Hooker replaced Burnside in command in February 1863, O'Sullivan joined Gardner and Gibson as they shadowed the Union army.

That spring, Gardner closed his home in Maryland and sent his wife and infant daughter to McGregor's Landing, Iowa. His fifteen-year-old son, Lawrence, remained at a boarding school in Emmitsburg, Maryland, ten miles from Gettysburg, Pennsylvania.

With James, his brother, Gardner began planning the opening of their own studio in Washington. They chose a location at the intersection of Seventh and D streets and established the business on the top floor of the building, opposite the *Washington Daily National Intelligencer.* Shortly after the gallery was completed, the Gardners hired several of their former Brady colleagues: O'Sullivan, Gibson, Pywell, Knox, Reekie, and W. Morris Smith. Unlike their former employer, Gardner promised his photographers that they would always receive credit for their images.

Gardner had little trouble attracting a clientele since most of Washington society had known him while he managed Brady's studio. Among others, Walt Whitman commented favorably on his technique: "Gardner was a real artist. He had a feel for his work, the inner-feel, if I may say so. He was also beyond his craft. He saw further than his camera, saw more. His pictures are evidence of his endowment."

In addition to running the studio, Gardner continued to venture into the field and to send his own photographers with the army. During the summer of 1863 he was with the Army of the Potomac, which was spread out in northern Virginia between Manassas and Leesburg. On June 25 Gardner returned to Washington. The first news of the battle of Gettysburg reached the

*A portrait of Gardner taken about the time he opened his own studio shows him sitting in the same chair he used for the portraits of virtually every politician and diplomat in Washington, including the photographs of Abraham Lincoln made in November 1863. Gardner's bearing, his full head of unruly hair, and the rumpled lab coat betray his artistic nature.*

national capital on July 3, and Gardner, O'Sullivan, and Gibson gathered their equipment and began the journey to document the fighting. Alarmed and concerned for his son's safety in Emmitsburg, Gardner rushed ahead and was captured there by Jeb Stuart's retreating cavalry. He was detained only briefly and then resumed the trip to the battlefield.

The photographers arrived at Gettysburg on the morning of July 5. They entered via the Emmitsburg road, near the Rose farm, one of the last areas to be cleared of the dead. They took twenty exposures in the area. On July 6 they concentrated on the areas near the Devil's Den and at the base of Big Round Top. Most of these photographs were views of breastworks and scenes of the battlefield. On July 7 they focused on the town and the cemetery.

Gardner was exhilarated to find his team the only group of photographers on the field so soon after the fighting. His WAF excitement was short-lived. °The Gardner team had arrived too soon after the battle for anyone to reconstruct accurately and comprehensively what had happened between July 1 and 3. Gardner moved around the battlefield looking for subjects without the benefit of a guide because no guides were available. A guide might have made no difference to Gardner, because he was more interested in the dead than in photographing the historic sites of the battleground.•

At Antietam, Gardner had developed the concept of carefully composing his photographs with certain elements, and at Gettysburg he improvised another technique: BP manipulating the scene. °One particularly horrific view, probably the most shocking Civil War photograph taken during the war, was Gardner's image of a Confederate soldier who had been disemboweled, possibly by a shell but more probably by wild pigs. Gardner almost certainly laid a musket across the body, probably one that he carried with him as a prop. The photographer also likely repositioned a canteen to add to the composition and possibly adjusted the man's severed hand and lowered the body's arm in such a way that it could be included in the image.•

WAF °Gardner and his colleagues spent nearly an hour photographing another body at Devil's Den. After they left it, they came across what they presumed was a Confederate sharpshooter's position about forty yards away. Gardner saw this as an excellent backdrop for a storytelling photograph of the Rebel sharpshooters who had fired on the Federal positions on Little Round Top. Only one element was lacking that would enhance the drama of this view: There were no dead sharpshooters behind this wall. The photographers decided to use the body they had just finished photographing. They placed it on a blanket, carried it to the site, and laid it behind the wall.•

By later photojournalistic standards, Gardner's moving and posing corpses would be considered inappropriate, but at the time there were no such rules. BP °In Gardner's mind he was reinforcing the power of the experience.• BJ °He was a moralizer, and he wanted this picture to create a compelling image that would make the viewer contemplate how life had ended for this young soldier.•

WAF °Roughly 75 percent of Gardner's Gettysburg photographs were highly salable images of the dead on the field,• capturing the horror of the battle and the image of the conflict as the soldiers remembered it long after they had left the area—bloated corpses, dead horses, open graves, and other scenes of carnage. The death views of Antietam had commanded the public's attention and had sold well, too. Considering the number of death views and the amount of time Gardner and his colleagues expended on them as subjects, it was apparent that Gardner was aware of the commercial value of these pictures. Yet, in so doing, he completely overlooked the landmarks of the battle, such as Lee's headquarters, Pennsylvania College, the Lutheran seminary, and the Union earthworks on Culp's Hill.

When Gardner returned to the capital, he traveled by way of Emmitsburg to pick up his son. A week or so

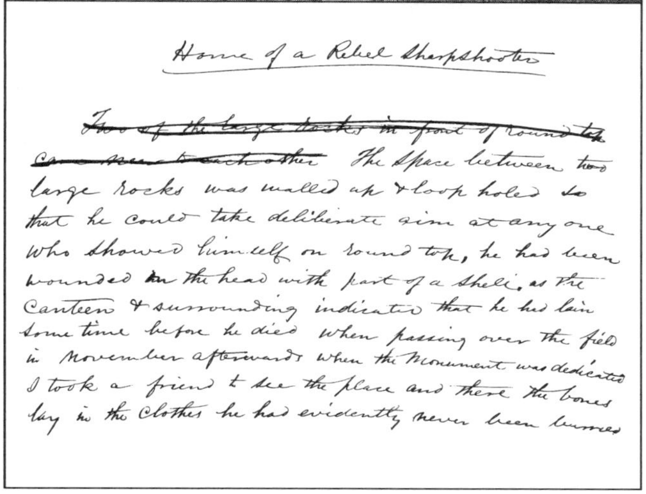

Home of a Rebel Sharpshooter

~~Two of the large rocks in front of round top came near to each other~~ The space between two large rocks was walled up & loop holed so that he could take deliberate aim at any one who showed himself on round top, he had been wounded in the head with part of a shell, as the canteen & surrounding indicated that he had lain some time before he died when passing over the field in November afterwards when the Monument was dedicated I took a friend to see the place and there the bones lay in the clothes he had evidently never been buried

*At Gettysburg, Gardner frequently manipulated the scene to achieve the effect he wanted. Although such manipulation is unacceptable by the standards of modern photojournalism, it did make Gardner's pictures more dramatic. Clockwise from the top of page 274: a dead Confederate soldier with a rifle and canteen which were added by Gardner; Devil's Den with a dead Confederate who was placed in the scene by Gardner—whose handwritten account reconstructing how the young Confederate fought and died behind these rocks is in all likelihood a complete fiction; Union dead on the battlefield at Gettysburg—the picture was titled "A Harvest of Death"; a dead Confederate soldier; Confederate dead near the Rose Woods with Gardner's darkroom wagon in the background.*

*Gardner's colleague James Gibson took this view of the Farmers' Inn at Emmitsburg where Gardner was detained by retreating Confederate cavalry on July 5. At Gettysburg, Gardner had two darkroom wagons, and he, Gibson, and Timothy O'Sullivan worked together to prepare and develop the plates. Credit for the stereoviews they made was evenly divided among them, while O'Sullivan shot most of the large format pictures.*

later Brady ventured to Gettysburg with a team of photographers, probably David Woodbury and Anthony Berger. By that time several guides were available, and the Brady team focused on specific sites that were becoming well known to the public. Although these lacked the dramatic impact of the Gardner views, Brady's photographs were used to illustrate an August 1863 issue of *Harper's Weekly* devoted to the battle. Gardner's Gettysburg images meanwhile appeared in his *Catalogue of Photographic Incidents of the War* in September 1863.

By the time Ulysses S. Grant was appointed general of the Union armies on March 12, 1864, Gardner had placed O'Sullivan in charge of his field operations. Gardner's status with the army was ambiguous at best, leading Grant to require him to submit an application for passes for his photographers. When that was approved, Gardner and his associates received privileges beyond those extended to any other photography firm. In April, Grant issued orders that all civilians—including sutlers, traders, and photographers—would vacate all Federal camps by April 16. Gardner's photographers, however, remained with the army throughout the spring offensive that ultimately stalled on the outskirts of Petersburg that summer.

The cost of maintaining a group of photographers in the field was becoming prohibitive to Gardner. O'Sullivan had been with the army for three months, and the returns from his photograph sales were not commensurate with his expenses. When the army began to lay siege to Petersburg, Gardner started to shuttle his photographers between the front and Washington until September 1864, when he temporarily suspended field operations.

In December 1864 Gardner dispatched O'Sullivan to document the assault on the last Confederate stronghold at Fort Fisher, North Carolina. His photographers did not return to Virginia until after Petersburg and Richmond fell in April 1865.

Gardner himself traveled to Richmond on April 5 and began photographing the city, documenting the destruction that followed the Confederate evacuation. He took more than 150 views between April 6 and 15 and published them under the title *Memories of the War.* His assistant, John Reekie, visited Robert E. Lee's Franklin Street residence, hoping to photograph the general; he had to settle for a view of the house. O'Sullivan was sent to Appomattox Court House to document the site of the surrender and then to Petersburg to record the sight of the Federal positions along the Appomattox River.

After the war, Gardner published *Gardner's Photographic Sketch Book of the War,* containing one hundred photographs by his various cameramen. He organized the images chronologically, accompanying each with a descriptive text that never failed to show his absolute disdain for everything the South had represented. It was the first serious effort to market a book of wartime photographs. Most of the images were the same ones from Antietam and Gettysburg that had aroused the public when they were first exhibited in 1862 and 1863. It was a stirring pictorial record of the war witnessed by Gardner and his employees and became one of the most important publications in the history of photography.•

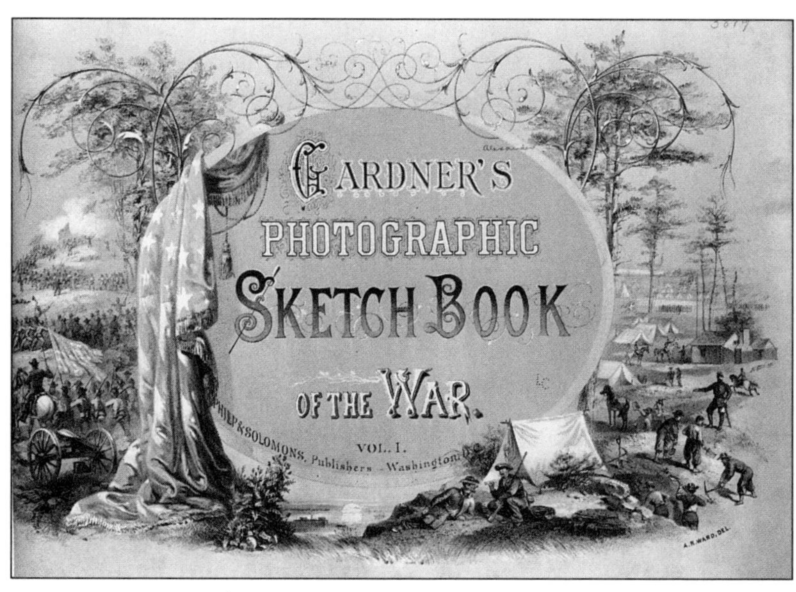


*One of the most important publications in the history of photography is* Gardner's Photographic Sketch Book of the War, *containing one hundred photographs by his various cameramen. It was the first serious effort to market a book of wartime photographs. Shown at left is the title page from the 1866 edition. Gardner organized the images chronologically with descriptive text that invariably showed his anti-Confederate bias. The* Sketch Book *was published by Philp & Solomons, in partnership with whom Gardner had briefly opened a gallery before he had his own Seventh Street studio in Washington. In their advertising circular, the publisher stated, "The eye rests upon these pictured pages with the happy consciousness that they are no fancy sketches, drawn 'out of the artist's head' for the sensational adornment of some pictorial newspaper."*

*In April 1865 fleeing Confederates torched Richmond's riverfront warehouses as Union forces approached. The fires quickly spread out of control and were not contained until Federal troops blew up buildings ahead of the blaze. That portion of the city became known as the "Burnt District" (above left). In the path of the fire, the Gallego Flour Mill (above right) exploded. Photographers rushed to document the fallen capital. The Anthony firm published a number of views made by cameramen other than Gardner or Brady. In all, as many as three hundred pictures of Richmond may have been taken within two weeks of its fall.*

The *Sketch Book* was released in two volumes and in two editions; the 1865 edition was bound in red leather, the 1866 edition in blue leather. Each view in the first edition included the caption "Incidents of the War," the name of the publisher, and the date of the photograph. The second edition omitted these but included the individual plate numbers for each image. The publication sold for $150. No more than two hundred sets were produced; only twenty remain intact.

WITH PHOTOGRAPHY becoming more commonplace, Abraham Lincoln became one of the most photographed presidents of the nineteenth century. Thirty-three photographers on sixty-one occasions generated 127 portraits of the sixteenth president. Of those thirty-three photographers, Gardner photographed Lincoln more than any other. Between February 1861 and March 1865, the Scotsman took thirty-seven photographs of the president, more than twice as many as his nearest competitor, Anthony Berger, who had taken thirteen.

BJ °Gardner first photographed Lincoln in Brady's studio on February 24, 1861, just after the president-elect had arrived in Washington. It was the first photograph of Lincoln with his newly grown beard.• The photographer made five carte de visite views, and these were used by *Harper's Weekly* in its coverage of the inauguration.

Feb. 22, 1861

Mr Gardner—

President Elect Lincoln will visit the gallery on the 24th. Please ready equipment.

M.B. Brady

*Shown above is Mathew Brady's note to Gardner, dated February 22, 1861, telling him that the president-elect would be coming to Brady's studio to sit for a portrait. When Alexander Gardner, who would do the actual photographing, asked artist George Story for his advice on how Lincoln should be posed, the portrait painter—observing the subject's mood—leaned over and whispered to Gardner, "Bring your instrument here and take the picture." That June, Story was commissioned to paint a portrait of Lincoln. The fidgety president could not sit still, and so Story's portrait was based upon Gardner's photographs.*

Artist George Story, a friend of Brady's, was there to offer suggestions on how the president-elect should pose. He recalled watching Lincoln during the first photo session: "When I entered the room, the president was seated in a chair wholly absorbed in deep thought. Lincoln seemed absolutely indifferent to all that was going on about him, and he gave the impression that he was a man who was overwhelmed with anxiety and fatigue and care."

Gardner was behind the camera on March 4, 1861, as Lincoln took the oath of office. Eighteen months later, after the battle of Antietam, Gardner took six photographs of Lincoln on October 3–4, 1862, during his visit with George B. McClellan. En route to the battlefield, Lincoln telegraphed his wife: "General McClellan and myself are to be photographed tomorrow by A. Gardner if we can sit still long enough. I feel General M should have no problem on his end, but I may sway in the breeze a bit."

Lincoln's first visit to Gardner's studio occurred on Sunday, August 9, 1863. He made four cartes de visite and three imperial portraits. Afterward the president thanked Gardner in a note: "My Dear Sir: Allow me to return my sincere thanks for the cards and pictures which you have kindly sent me. I think they are generally very successful. The Imperial photograph in which the head leans upon the hand I regard as the best that I have yet seen." The president returned on November 8, 1863, for five portraits, and on February 5, 1865, for three cartes de visite and two imperial portraits.

WFS ○Gardner became the president's favorite photographer partly because his gallery was within walking distance of the White House. Sometimes Lincoln visited Gardner's studio on a whim. The two men had an excellent rapport, which is evident in the Gardner photographs as Lincoln appears more vulnerable than those made by any other photographer. Gardner's images of the president could have been made only in

*Alexander Gardner made more photographic portraits of President Abraham Lincoln than any other photographer. Clockwise from right: a carte de visite of Lincoln, February 24, 1861; the famous "cracked plate" photo of February, 1865; Lincoln's second inauguration, March 4, 1865; a portrait taken November 8, 1863; a portrait taken August 9, 1863; Lincoln with Gen. George McClellan at Fifth Corps headquarters at Antietam, October 3, 1862.*

*Because Gardner's photographic ties with Lincoln were so strong, he took it upon himself to document the sites involved in the president's assassination, beginning with the exterior of Ford's Theatre, which was draped in black mourning bunting. Earlier Gardner's photographs had helped Allan Pinkerton's Secret Service detect spies among the soldiers in the Army of the Potomac by analyzing group photographs, and so it was natural for him to be called upon to be the official chronicler of the Lincoln conspiracy.*

moments of relaxation or total forgetfulness of the wartime situation. Lincoln understood, consciously or intuitively, that he had a photogenic face, and so he wanted his photographs to communicate and create a sense of his presence with the public.•

Gardner's photographs also show the physical and mental toll the war exacted from the president as he led the nation through its darkest hours. Rarely have a series of photographs taken over a span of so few years shown a man to age faster than Lincoln. The burden of war transformed Lincoln from a vibrant man at his inauguration into a bent, weary man by the war's end.

BJ °The full-frontal portrait of November 8, 1863, has frequently been called the best Lincoln portrait and one of the greatest American photographs ever made. The camera captured him midway through the war. He was not the zestful man he had been in 1861, nor was he the haggard president to be recorded in 1865. He was in a transitional phase.•

Gardner's final images of Lincoln were taken during the president's second inauguration on March 4, 1865. He was one of the few photographers to record both inaugurations.

BJ °The last formal portrait Gardner made of Lincoln was on February 5, 1865, and was made more interesting because Lincoln had brought his son Tad with him. The boy's mischievousness was captured in a view with both father and son leaning on the same table, the president being seated and Tad standing opposite him.• The famous and powerful "cracked-plate portrait" was also produced during this session.

WFS °The glass plate broke because it was picked up incorrectly by a corner and snapped from its own weight. Gardner made one print from it, but technically it was considered a failure because only a small portion of the face was in focus. Yet that focused portion includes Lincoln's left eye, which was closest to the camera. Gardner caught Lincoln in a moment of introspection, when he was unaware of the camera. In that instant the photographer captured a penetrating, moving insight into Lincoln's personality, revealing the emotions he felt about the war and the sacrifice it had required of him, making this an extremely powerful and poignant portrait.•

*Shown above planning the capture of assassin John Wilkes Booth are U.S. Army Col. Lafayette C. Baker (center), Lt. Luther Baker (left), and Lt. Col. Everton J. Congor (right). In his instructions, Colonel Baker said, "There must be no shooting. The villain must be returned alive." However, it did not happen that way. Gardner posed this photograph after Booth's apprehension and death.*

GARDNER'S PHOTOGRAPHIC ties with Lincoln were so strong, they continued even after the president's death. Following Lincoln's assassination at Ford's Theatre, it was through Gardner's camera that the country witnessed the roundup and execution of those involved in the conspiracy.

Gardner took it upon himself to document the sites involved in the assassination. What he created photographically in the days and weeks following Lincoln's death laid the cornerstone for the field of reporting that would later be called photojournalism. °Gardner began by photographing the exterior of Ford's Theatre, which was trimmed in black mourning bunting. He photographed the interior of the theater, including the box in which Lincoln had been shot, and these views show the tear in the flag caused by

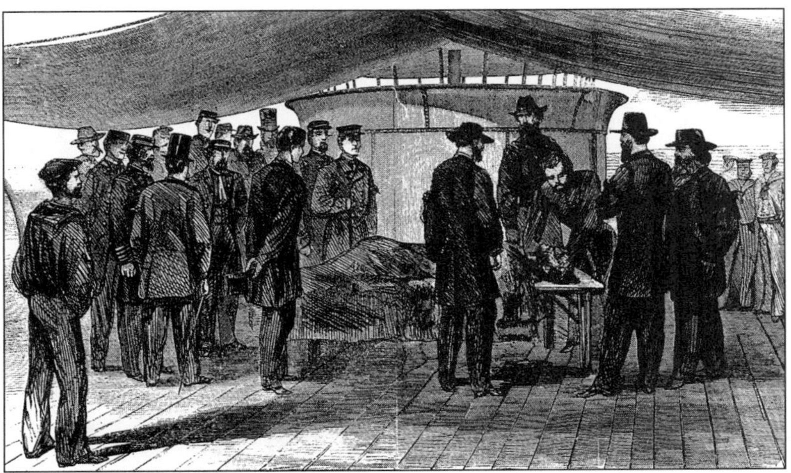

*After his capture, Booth's body was transferred to the ironclad* USS Montauk *for an autopsy and Gardner was brought in to record the scene. The illustration from* Harper's Weekly, *on May 13, 1865, (left) has long been thought to be based on Gardner's post-mortem shot. However, it is known he made only one negative and one print; and government detective James A. Wardell testified that, on orders, he accompanied Gardner the entire time and personally delivered the negative and the print to Colonel Baker at the War Department. Neither has been seen since. Gardner is shown in the illustration standing on the right, meaning either O'Sullivan took the picture or the engraver added Gardner.*

*As Booth's alleged fellow conspirators were rounded up, Gardner and O'Sullivan were brought in to photograph them. Shown above, photographed April 27, 1865, are (from left) David E. Herold, Lewis Paine, Joao M. Celestino (later released), and Samuel Arnold.*

*The view below is of the gallows at the Old Arsenal Prison in Washington where the Lincoln conspirators would be hanged. Gardner and O'Sullivan manned two cameras positioned in the upstairs windows of the building on the left. The* Washington Star *reported on July 7, 1865: "Presently, a window was raised, and forthwith was seen the protruding snout of the camera. . . . Gardner's good-humored face presently was seen over the camera as he took a sight at the gallows, to see that it was focused properly."*

the spur of assassin John Wilkes Booth when he leaped from the box to the stage and escaped.• Gardner photographed the stable where Booth had kept his horse. He also recorded an image of the telegraph office that first broadcast the news of Lincoln's death. Lastly, Gardner went to the Navy Yard Bridge, the route of Booth's escape to Maryland, and photographed it.

Because Gardner had demonstrated his value to the Secret Service during the war, which involved his work with Pinkerton, he was engaged by the agency to duplicate photographs of three of the conspirators—Booth, John Surrat, and David Herold—which were used on a wanted poster and also distributed during the manhunt for Booth.

On April 26, 1865, Booth and Herold were trapped in a tobacco shed near Port Royal, Virginia, by federal troops. Herold surrendered; Booth did not. In the chaos

that followed, the assassin was shot and died on the porch of the nearby farmhouse. His body was transferred to the ironclad USS *Montauk* for an autopsy. Gardner was brought in to photograph the scene.

BJ °Gardner made one plate and one print, both of which have since vanished. It has been assumed that the government confiscated and likely destroyed them to eliminate any chance of Booth's becoming a martyr by living on in the form of a death photograph. The image, however, may have been the basis for an engraving that was reproduced in *Harper's Weekly.* Gardner himself can be seen standing to the right, meaning that either O'Sullivan took the photograph or the engraver added Gardner.•

*The bodies of Surratt, Paine, Herold, and Atzerodt have become still as the crowd of witnesses thins. The conspirators were cut down after thirty minutes. Bottles containing identifying information were placed in each coffin. Under the supervision of Capt. Christian Rath, the ropes and portions of the gallows were cut into small pieces for souvenirs. Outside the prison spectators were served lemonade and cakes. The remaining four conspirators, Samuel Arnold, Edward Spangler, Michael O'Laughlin, and Dr. Samuel Mudd, were given prison sentences.*

As Booth's fellow conspirators were rounded up, they were imprisoned on the ironclad in chains and hooded, BJ and °Gardner and O'Sullivan were brought in to photograph them. All of the suspects, even those who were later released, except for Mary Surratt, were taken on deck and their hoods removed long enough to be photographed.

In making these pictures, Gardner set a precedent for photographing and identifying criminals that is still used today. He photographed each conspirator from a straight-forward, frontal view and then he took a profile view. It was a very simple concept that no one had done before.•

On May 10, 1865, eight conspirators were tried in a military court. A verdict was reached on July 5. Four were sentenced to death—Mary Surratt, Lewis Paine, David Herold, and George Atzerodt—and four were given prison sentences—Samuel Mudd, Samuel Arnold, Michael O'Laughlin, and Edward Spangler.

On July 7, 1865, Gardner and his photographic team recorded the hanging of the four condemned conspirators. They were the only photographers sanctioned for the task by the government, and their documentation of this historic event made history itself. BJ °This was the first time that an event of this type was

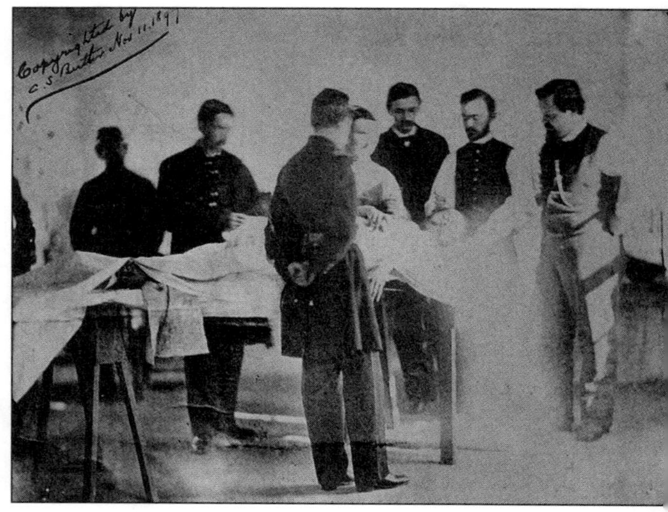

*The noose is placed around the neck of Captain Henry Wirz (above left), the man who ran Andersonville prison. When the officer who read the charges against Wirz told him he deplored this duty, Wirz replied, "I know what orders are . . . and I am being hanged for obeying them." The drop failed to break Wirz's neck. As he slowly strangled, the spectators, including soldiers who had climbed trees outside the prison's walls, chanted, "Wirz, remember Andersonville! Wirz, remember Andersonville!"*

*Like Booth's autopsy picture, the shot of the autopsy of Henry Wirz (above right) was suppressed by order of the War Department. Fortunately, a copy of Gardner's photo turned up in 1952 in the Hay-Nicolay papers held by the Illinois State Historical Society.*

documented as it was taking place. There had been previous photographs that could be termed journalistic, but this was the first sequence of photographs depicting an event as it was happening.•

Adding to the suspense of the hanging was the fact that one of the condemned was a woman. Mary Surratt owned the boarding house where the conspirators met, but it had not been proven that she had a part in the plotting of the assassination. The government had never hanged a woman before, and there was some question whether she would be pardoned at the last minute by officials overcome by their consciences.

BP °Gen. Winfield Scott Hancock was in charge of the military district in which the executions were to take place. He positioned messengers between the Old Arsenal Prison and the White House in case President Andrew Johnson should decide to pardon Surratt at the last minute. No pardon came.

Gardner made no effort to control the scene or to ask the witnesses not to move. His photographs documented the execution as it happened. The death warrant was read by Brig. Gen. John Hartranft. The nooses were positioned around the necks of the four. The photographs convey something of Atzerodt's terror, Paine's defiance, and Surratt's tragedy. The soldiers along the wall looked at the camera and at the scaffold. Below the

*Temporarily closing his Washington gallery, Alexander Gardner took his son Lawrence and a long-time associate, William Pywell, with him to Kansas to document the building of the transcontinental railroad. Gardner's simple and unpretentious pictures of the vast prairies and newly founded towns helped make the West understandable to easterners. The view of Fort Leavenworth, Kansas (left), appeared in his collection* Across the Continent on the Union Pacific Railway.

gallows a man prepared to knock out the support that would drop the conspirators from the scaffold.

The last few photographs show a blurred image as the bodies fell and swayed at the end of the ropes. Another shows the bodies hanging motionless. The coffins were nearby. Finally, the last image shows the soldiers departing and the reporters leaving the scene to get the story to their newspapers.•

On November 10, 1865, Gardner was again commissioned to photograph an execution. Confederate Capt. Henry Wirz, commandant of the Andersonville prisoner-of-war camp in Georgia, was convicted of crimes against humanity and sentenced to hang. Gardner recorded the execution with five photographs: the reading of the warrant, the placement of the noose, the jeering of the soldiers in attendance, the moment the trap was sprung, and Wirz writhing at the end of the rope. An autopsy was performed inside one of the prison buildings and photographed by Gardner. Finally, the body was buried near the graves of the Lincoln conspirators.

With this series of execution photographs, his Lincoln images, and his storied Antietam and Gettysburg series, Gardner established himself as the foremost photographer of the Civil War era. Considering his career, it is unfortunate that history seemed to remember only

*Gardner was photographed in 1868, a year after his appointment as chief photographer of the Union Pacific Railway, Eastern Division, and he began chronicling the settling of the West.*

*Gardner sits upon his camera near the Union Pacific depot at Manhattan, Kansas (above left). He actually followed the line only as far as Hays, Kansas, 580 miles west of Saint Louis, but his contract allowed him to publish photographs from the entire expedition, which crossed New Mexico, Arizona, and California.*

*Entitled "A Rare Specimen Found on a Hill above Fort Riley, Kansas," the photo above right shows Gardner seated on a crate holding the lens of a camera. In the background is his photographic wagon with its stand-up darkroom.*

Brady's name in conjunction with the task of photographing the war. Brady's reputation was established, however, because Gardner died fourteen years before Brady, and because Brady was an excellent promoter who had devoted the last half of his life to collecting and selling images of the Civil War. When a new generation began to study the Civil War toward the end of the nineteenth century, Brady was able to provide them with "his" photographs, following the older practice of claiming all rights to images other than those generated in his studio, including the thousands of images he had purchased from other photographers.

During the postwar years Brady could not sell his war views and endured severe financial hardship as a result. WFS °His studio was eventually broken up and his negatives were dispersed, most of them being sold to the government to pay his debts. These photographs still had his name on them regardless of whether the negatives had been made by him or under his supervision and patronage. The collection also included thousands of the images that Brady had purchased and preserved that had nothing to do with his studio other than the fact that his name was attached to them.

Most of Brady's negatives wound up in the Library of Congress and the National Archives, with the Brady name still attached to them. Only recently has it become obvious that no one man could have generated all that work, and scholars have scrutinized the documents of the period to discover who might have taken each particular image.•

Ironically, history has been generous to the Brady legacy, where life was not to the man. °By the 1880s Brady had lost his studio and was working for other people. By the 1890s he was virtually a pauper, reliving the past, until he died in a charity hospital.•

WAF

As for Gardner, after the war he went from one success to another. He continued to be a Washington photographer, surviving a fire at his studio on September 25, 1865. He finally had the opportunity to photograph Lee and Grant separately in February 1866 when the two generals were summoned to appear before a congressional committee on reconstruction and the conduct of the war.

In 1867 Gardner was appointed the chief photographer of the Union Pacific Rail Way, Eastern Division, and he began chronicling the settling of the West. He temporarily closed his Washington gallery and traveled to Kansas to document the building of the transcontinental railroad. He took countless views of the wide and barren land around him and also documented the newly emerging towns of the West.

An 1865 fire at the Smithsonian damaged or destroyed many paintings of American Indians, and the

*Exceedingly rare unpublished carte de visite portrait of Alexander Gardner in the buckskin outfit of Judge Arney, takin in 1861.*

*After a fire at the Smithsonian Institution damaged or destroyed many paintings of American Indians, it was suggested that the void might be filled by photographing Indian delegations visiting Washington. Gardner was retained to do this. Shown at left is the Sauk and Fox delegation with the Commissioner of Indian Affairs Lewis V. Bogy standing in the center. Gardner traveled to the West to document signing ceremonies as well as individuals and their camps. Today his work is a priceless historical record. In Fort Laramie, as he photographed a treaty negotiation with the Indians of the Northern Plains, Four Bears, an Oglala Sioux, told him bluntly: "You say you will protect us for thirty years, but I do not believe it."*

*At the Fort Laramie conference in 1868, commissioners and Indian leaders posed for Gardner. Native American leaders are (from left) Packs His Drum, Old Man Afraid of His Horses, and Red Bear. The Oglala and Brule people finally signed the treaty in November, but later that month Custer's Seventh Cavalry attacked one of their villages on the Washita. Unimpeded, whites continued to overrun the Black Hills, land considered sacred by the Indians.*

suggestion was made that the void might be filled with photographic portraits of the Indian delegations visiting Washington. Gardner was retained privately to photograph these groups, making images of the representatives of the various tribes. In 1872 he was made the official photographer of the Bureau of Indian Affairs. Gardner photographed treaty conferences, documenting signing ceremonies as well as individual representatives and their camps. He returned to Washington with more than two hundred images. Their historical value was deemed priceless by journalist Raymond J. DeMallie: "Gardner's photographs are the only ones known to have been taken of any of the activities of the 1860s commissions. They are valuable because they document the commissions, but even more so, they are valuable because they are the earliest surviving photographic record of the Indians of the Northern Plains taken in their own territory."

Gardner devoted the rest of his life to his passion to help others, which had influenced him early in his career. In 1875 he volunteered to codify the Washington, D.C., police department's photographic files, making them uniform in size and style. He was interested in assisting the poor by encouraging self-reliance and in 1874 was appointed president of the Masonic Mutual Relief Association, which operated as a type of life insurance company. He later formed the Washington Beneficial Endowment Association, dedicating himself to any plan that might improve the condition of working people and opposing any scheme that was remotely speculative or which might satisfy only the greed of a few. He became president of the Equitable Co-operative Building Association, which aided those wanting to buy a home. Gardner and other like-minded Masons founded Saint John's Mite Association, a Washington-based charity. He formally retired from photography in 1879 to devote his life to the Washington Beneficial Endowment Association and the Masonic Mutual Relief Association.

On December 10, 1882, sixty-one-year-old Gardner died following a two-week illness. He was buried in Washington's Glenwood Cemetery.

Only a portion of Gardner's photographs survived him. In 1882 two photograph collectors, Albert Ordway and Arnold Rand, began gathering material for a comprehensive portrait album of the war. They purchased a collection of Brady negatives from E. and H. T. Anthony and supplemented it with two thousand images made by either Gardner or those in his employ. At one time they tried and failed to sell the negatives to the government, finally selling them in 1885 to John C. Taylor, who peddled prints from the negatives to the public. In 1905 he sold the collection to Edward B. Eaton, president of *Connecticut Magazine*, who utilized the views in numerous publications until 1916. The negatives were warehoused until 1942, when the Library of Congress paid the storage fee and took possession of the entire collection.

A sadder fate awaited another group of Civil War photographs, possibly including a large segment of Gardner images. Charles Bender, a scrap-glass dealer in Washington purchased thousands of wet-plate negatives in 1908 from Moses P. Rice, a longtime Washington photographer. The negatives had been stored in Ford's Theatre under Brady's name and probably included a large portion of Gardner's work. When Bender failed to sell the negatives, he reasoned that if the images had any value, Rice would not have sold them, so he salvaged the glass by stripping the emulsion and retaining the silver. The glass was then sold to photographers and gas meter manufacturers.

Someone said of Gardner that he had no other desire than to search for the best and find the truth. He chose photography as a means to this goal. By his life's end, he had played an instrumental role in the creation of what this century now calls photojournalism. Even though his name was remembered by few, the images Gardner left behind are among the most striking and memorable of any in America's great photographic legacy.

*In 1871 Gardner moved his gallery from Seventh and D Streets to 921 Pennsylvania Avenue. Always an idealist, as evidenced by his youthful involvement with the utopian community in Iowa and the antislavery sentiments which captioned his war photos, Gardner was, in the end, interested mainly in the betterment of the lives of common people. He formed the Washington Beneficial Endowment Association; became the president of the Equitable Co-operative Building Association, which aided those wanting to buy a home; with other like-minded Masons founded Saint John's Mite Association, a Washington-based charity; and was president of the Masonic Mutual Relief Association. Gardner died in 1882 at the age of sixty-one.*

# THE SPIES' WAR

The CIVIL WAR WAS FOUGHT BY NON-professional soldiers and amateur spies. Yet while both armies had a core of professionally trained officers, neither side had an established intelligence service
AA until midway through the conflict. °Spying was left to amateurs because, in the mid-nineteenth-century culture of the U.S. military, espionage was disdained as less than honorable. Few people were attracted to the task, and military planners on both sides preferred not to think about it.• This attitude was part of the legacy of George Washington, who had organized and financed an efficient and effective intelligence operation during the Revolutionary War. Afterward, with an ocean separating the fledgling country from the Continent, the first president counseled his political heirs to avoid European entanglements, and thus there was little need for an intelligence department within the nominal military establishment.

The ideological nature of the Civil War sparked patriotic fervor on both sides, leading those who were not able to bear arms to consider spying. The task was relatively easy in that North and South spoke the same language (regional dialects notwithstanding), professed a common moral code, shared a mutual history, and knew
DWG each other's geography. °Thus the skills most necessary for spies were daring, bravery, and resourcefulness, which imbued the task with a degree of romanticism to offset the severe penalty of death if one were caught. A spy infiltrated an enemy's camp to inspect his works, ascertain his strength and intentions, watch his movements,

| | |
|---|---|
| AA | Alan Axelrod |
| ECB | Edwin C. Bearss |
| CC | Catherine Clinton |
| WCD | William C. Davis |
| DWG | David Winfred Gaddy |
| EGM | Edna Greene Medford |
| NIP | Nell Irvin Painter |
| BP | Brian Pohanka |
| JIR | James I. Robertson Jr. |

*Before the war secret societies with antigovernment agendas conducted occasional undercover operations. In the north, a broad grouping of "Copperhead" societies included the Knights of the Golden Circle, the Order of American Knights, the Sons of Liberty, and in Baltimore the Knights of Liberty. In the midwest, some Copperheads wanted the South out of the Union, while others plotted for a secession of the midwestern states. For supposedly secret societies, all were relatively open and, for the most part, easily infiltrated by Federal agents. For instance, in addition to discovering an early plot to assassinate Lincoln, Allan Pinkerton's operatives broke up a plan by a secret society to invade Washington (its unfinished Capitol is shown above). The leaders of the plot were jailed, putting an end to the Knights of Liberty.*

and secretly communicate the intelligence to the other side.•

°When the information was valuable, it was often not properly channeled to those who could most use it. Even if the intelligence did make it to the right person, neither side had an efficient means for analyzing and interpreting the data. At best, important information was shared with a field commander just before a battle. There was no attempt to coordinate trends, to assess the patterns of action taken by the other side, or to analyze long-term troop movements. No one conceived the value of interpreting this information, allocated funds to do so, or knew how to process intelligence.•

At the outset of the war, Southern spies held several advantages over their Northern counterparts. The Federal bureaucracy had been in place for seventy years, so Confederate agents could be placed through normal hiring opportunities or recruited in place because of their regional sympathies. The Union, however, could not target a government that did not as yet exist. °The Northern capital at Washington was a southern community predominantly populated by Southerners. The average resident could easily spy on the camps that ringed the city and note the frequent parades staged to impress the people and their politicians.• The earliest known Confederate rings in Washington were those of Rose O'Neal Greenhow and Benjamin F. Stringfellow, which were in place before the war began. The Union, however, had no such rings operating in the Confederacy; the organization headed by Elizabeth Van Lew in Richmond was inaugurated on her own initiative. The South also gained valuable information from those officers who took up arms for the South, but there was no similar abandonment of Southern roles for Northern sympathies. There were few safe houses for Federal operatives in the South, but the Confederacy enjoyed an extensive network of safe houses and courier routes that had been established early in the war by Southern sympathizers in the North, primarily in southern Maryland.

AA °These advantages were a blessing and a curse because much of the information that was gathered was poor.• Even when vital information was gathered properly, it was often interpreted poorly by the officers it was intended to help. Typically the generals who had spies reporting to them had no idea what to do with the information that did reach them. They usually did not share it with other officers and frequently did not
AA even pass it up the command chain. °The paucity of Northern spies, however, led one general to say, "We knew more about what was going on in China than we knew what was going on in Richmond."•

BP °Both sides gathered as much information as they could, but neither was adept at discriminating between accuracy and exaggeration. Espionage and interpretation were relegated to subordinate officers who took an interest in such things and encouraged them, whereas higher up the chain of command, information gathered by spies was treated indifferently if it was considered at all. The general tendency was not to trust a spy, although there were some significant exceptions to that practice.•

The disorganized and inefficient nature of spying in the Civil War means that the story of espionage is in fact the story of individuals, brave men and women who risked their lives to give their side whatever advantage they could. Many were unsung heroes who never pursued fame because they never revealed their exploits during or after the war. Some operated at the behest of the government, and others operated on their own initiative.

In the North one man had the trust of the Yankee president and his highest officers: Allan J. Pinkerton. He had immigrated to the United States from Glasgow, Scotland, and found work as an apprentice barrel maker in Illinois. While cutting wood on one of the islands in the Fox River, Pinkerton stumbled across a hideout for counterfeiters. He led a raid on the camp, nabbing the whole gang, and was named deputy sheriff afterward. Later Pinkerton was hired as a deputy by the sheriff of Cook County, Illinois, and then accepted a position with the Chicago Police Department as its first detective. His success in that capacity attracted the attention of several railroad owners whose lines had been struck by a rash of robberies. They convinced Pinkerton to resign from the police force and open his own detective agency and specialize in railroad security.

One of Pinkerton's clients was the Illinois Central Railroad, which had as its president George B. McClellan. An ambitious attorney named Abraham Lincoln handled much of the railroad's legal work.

WCD °Shortly before the war started, several railroad executives grew concerned that Southern sympathizers might sabotage their lines entering Washington. Railroads were an obvious target since they carried men, machinery, animals, foodstuffs, supplies, and information.• Samuel H. Felton of the Philadelphia, Wilming-

*"The Life of a Spy" (below) was drawn by Thomas Nast for* Harper's Weekly, *October 24, 1863. The left side shows the spy "in enemy works," stealing "booty" from a sleeping enemy, and being chased. The far right side shows the spy being challenged, a safe return, and telling of his adventures to an appreciative audience. The center panels, however, show what happened to many spies—their capture and hanging. At the beginning of the war, more spies were imprisoned or exchanged than hanged. As the war dragged on, field officers were more likely to use the rope. Such a fate befell Southerner Lawrence Orton Williams. Passing through Tennessee posing as a Union "inspector," Williams was detained and questioned by Federals at Franklin. When his story didn't add up, he and a fellow officer were promptly hanged.*

ton, and Baltimore Railroad engaged Pinkerton to investigate rumors that his railroad was at risk. Pinkerton operatives infiltrated the Secessionist groups in Baltimore and discovered, not only a plan to obstruct the railroads, but a plot to assassinate Lincoln before the inauguration.

JIR °Maryland was a divided state, containing quite a number of Secessionists and a small group of assassins who believed the murder of the president-elect might boost the Southern cause.• The leader of the plot was Cypriano Ferrandini, an Italian barber at one of the Baltimore hotels and captain of the Constitutional Guards, a Secessionist organization. Pinkerton, under the guise of E. J. Allen, met with Ferrandini and learned the details of the plot firsthand and also that several prominent Baltimore residents were involved, including the police superintendent. "In a week from today," Ferrandini declared, "the North shall want another president, for Lincoln will be a corpse."

Pinkerton intercepted Lincoln in Philadelphia on February 21, 1861, with the news. Within hours his report was corroborated by a separate, congressionally appointed investigator. Lincoln's safekeeping was entrusted to Pinkerton, and the train's schedule was altered so as to arrive in Baltimore—the alleged scene of the assassination—during the early morning hours. Guards were also posted along the route to ensure the
BP safety of the track. °To further foil the conspirators, Pinkerton convinced the president-elect to travel disguised as a common citizen. As a politician, however, Lincoln preferred to be seen en route to the capital; he wanted to be seen waving to the public, acting like their leader, rather than sneaking through Maryland's largest city. Pinkerton was insistent, and Lincoln reluctantly cooperated.•

AA °After arriving in Baltimore at 3:30 A.M., Lincoln's car had to be drawn by horses from one station to another through the city streets so another locomotive could haul the train to its final destination. This was Lincoln's most vulnerable moment and the one in which Pinkerton knew the conspirators planned to attack.• Everything proceeded normally, except the

*The serendipitous discovery of a counterfeiters' hideout started the career in law enforcement of Allan Pinkerton (1819–1884.) Railroad detective Pinkerton's recovery of a large sum of money stolen from the Adams Express Company and his unearthing of the Baltimore plot to kill Lincoln made his reputation and earned him his job at the beginning of the war. Although he was unofficial "Head of the Secret Service," Pinkerton's talents were in police work, not espionage and intelligence.*

*Railroad runners whose lines had been struck by a rash of robberies persuaded Pinkerton to open his own detective agency, which used the logo shown above. It was in this capacity that Pinkerton first met George B. McClellan (below), who was president of the Illinois Central Railroad at the time. When McClellan became a Union general, he called upon Pinkerton. His first assignment for Gen. McClellan took him south to Memphis where he learned of a Rebel plot to "abandon" a wagonload of poisoned whiskey in the path of oncoming Northern troops. At Jackson, Mississippi, he was recognized by a German barber who had shaved him once in Chicago. Pinkerton hotly denied he was any form of Yankee, then took the other customers of the barber shop for a round of drinks.*

locomotive to Washington was an hour behind schedule, and Pinkerton and the presidential-elect party waited on tenderhooks while a drunk on the depot platform sang "Dixie" over and over again.

Lincoln's train pulled into Washington around 6:00 A.M. on February 23. Pinkerton accompanied the president-elect from the train to Willard's Hotel, where Gen. Charles P. Stone assumed responsibility for Lincoln's security. In his postwar memoirs, the detective wrote, "I had informed Mr. Lincoln in Philadelphia that I would answer with my life for his safe arrival in Washington, and I redeemed my pledge."

Pinkerton returned to Chicago and the business of railroad security until he was summoned to Washington in late July 1861 to join the staff of the new commander of the Army of the Potomac, Maj. Gen. George B. McClellan. The detective revived his alter ego, E. J. Allen, and was given the task of establishing an intelligence-gathering organization. Lacking any prior formal agency on which to pattern his activities, Pinkerton simply recreated his detective agency and enlisted the same operatives he had used as railroad security specialists. His results were often mixed.

The primary task Pinkerton faced as McClellan's hand-picked intelligence gatherer was to ascertain the strength of the Confederate forces the Federal army would encounter. Unfortunately, the two men respected each other to the degree that neither questioned the assertions of the other. If McClellan believed he faced one hundred thousand Confederates, Pinkerton directed his people to find the data that would confirm the general's suspicions. Likewise, when Pinkerton presented his findings to McClellan, the general never questioned him. Ultimately, Pinkerton's estimates were always highly inflated.•

WCD °Pinkerton relied on a mystical formula that he devised, which was inaccurate and always gave inflated numbers. Generally, Pinkerton's figures at least doubled the enemy numbers.• Pinkerton's gross miscalculations and ineptitude as a military observer had a devastating effect on McClellan's 1862 Peninsula campaign.
DWG °His information confirmed the general's worst fears only because McClellan wanted his fears reinforced. When Pinkerton estimated that the Union army faced one hundred thousand Confederates, McClellan cautiously called for reinforcements for his one-hundred-thousand-man army, believing that success required an attacking force to outnumber its opponents two to one. In actuality, McClellan already outnumbered the Confederates on the peninsula and around Richmond by nearly two to
AA one.• °As a result, the Peninsula campaign dragged on into a series of battles that ultimately forced the general to withdraw and probably extended the war.•

*Pinkerton's duties also included protecting President Lincoln (above, with Pinkerton on his right and Gen. John A. McClernand on his left at Sharpsburg), a job made more difficult when the Army of the Potomac was in the field. Despite being spread too thin, Pinkerton performed that assignment well. Without Pinkerton's services, Lincoln would have had no protection at all.*

ALTHOUGH PINKERTON proved lacking as an intelligence gatherer, he excelled as a spy catcher. His greatest success was the apprehension of Rose O'Neal Greenhow, a charming fortyish widow and Washington socialite with strong Southern sympathies. Her home was the center of Confederate espionage in the Yankee capital.

She had come to Washington from Maryland in the 1830s to stay with an aunt who kept a boardinghouse in the Old Capitol building. Many of the tenants were congressmen, and chief among these and most admired by the young girl was South Carolina Sen. John C. Calhoun.

At the age of twenty-six, Rose O'Neal married Robert Greenhow, a physician-turned-academician who worked as a translator for the State Department. Greenhow was seventeen years older than his bride, and while he was not a wealthy man, his family name was distinguished

*Soldiers in the U. S. Signal Corps observed enemy movements from towers, ridgetops, and balloons, and then transmitted their findings by semaphore. They are shown at right reconnoitering Confederate operations at Fredericksburg. In the Confederate army, espionage came under the direction of the C.S.A. Signal Corps.*

and he was well placed in Washington society. That and a small brick house were all he left his wife and four daughters when he died in 1854. Taking advantage of her acquaintances, the widow Greenhow helped her friends to find positions and promotions within the government bureaucracy, and they reciprocated by ensuring her well being. She was at the height of her career as capital hostess and power broker during the administration of James Buchanan. In fact, the bachelor president was known to frequent the Greenhow home, although he was by no means the only politician to enjoy the widow's company. Her other callers included Mississippi Sen. Jefferson Davis and New York Sen. William H. Seward.

*Federal spies with the Army of the Potomac pose for the camera. This was before the practice of having one's face recorded was recognized as a liability for a covert agent.*

At the outbreak of the war, Thomas Jordan, an officer on Winfield Scott's staff, began to build a Southern intelligence network in the capital. Most officers with Confederate sympathies resigned their commissions when the war began, but Jordan lingered in Washington for a little more than a month, studying Scott's war plans and organizing a Southern spy ring. One of his acquaintances was the widow Greenhow, and some scholars believe the two were romantically involved. Prior to Jordan's leaving Washington to join P. G. T. Beauregard's staff, he gave the widow a basic cipher for encoding dispatches and arranged a system of couriers to convey her messages into the Confederacy.

Greenhow's Southern sympathies were well known, but that did not prevent several high-level politicians from attending her parties and striving to impress her with their knowledge of the buildup of men and materiél around the capital. Nor was she prevented from visiting AA the Lincoln White House. °Men found her irresistible, and she invited them to her parties. Her guests ranged from lowly lieutenants to senior politicians. One smitten admirer was Massachusetts Sen. Henry Wilson, chairman of the Military Affairs Committee.•

Although it is unknown if Greenhow traded sexual favors for information, the implication exists. In her autobiography, she wrote, "I employed every capacity with which God has endowed me, and the result was far more successful than my hopes could have flattered me to expect." On July 10, 1861, according to Beauregard himself, Greenhow provided the information that Federal forces were being gathered for an advance on Manassas.

ECB °Senator Wilson divulged that Gen. Irvin McDowell's army was preparing to march into Virginia. Greenhow perhaps suspected that she might be under observation, so she enlisted a friend, Betty Duvall,• to deliver a coded message to Beauregard's headquarters. Duvall dressed as a farm girl and entered Virginia where she changed into a more BP stylish riding habit. °When she came across the headquarters of South Carolina Gen. M. L. Bonham in Fairfax, Duvall removed a pouch from her hair and delivered the news:• "McDowell has certainly been ordered to advance on the sixteenth. R.O.G."

The information was corroborated by Northern newspaper stories and a captured Union soldier. Beauregard responded with a request for information on numbers and the disposition of the Union artillery, intelligence that Greenhow provided up until the morning of the battle. Beauregard later claimed, "I was almost as well advised of

*Col. George H. Sharpe (seated at left in the picture below) organized the Union's Bureau of Military Information. Working for Gen. George Gordon Meade at the time of Gettysburg, Sharpe's accurate reports informed Meade of the movement of the Southerners into Pennsylvania as early as four days before the battle. Sharpe's report on Confederate troop strength at the battle of Chancellorsville was accurate to within one-quarter of one percent. When General Grant came east in 1864, he quickly brought Sharpe onto his staff.*

*A Yale-educated lawyer, Maj. William Norris (above) headed the Confederacy's Secret Service bureau, which has been called the most effective military intelligence establishment of the war. Norris had spying operations as far north as Canada.*

*Thomas Nelson Conrad (below), a Confederate spy, was a Georgetown headmaster who was deported after Federals caught his students raising and lowering window shades to transmit messages in code. Returning to Washington, he changed his beard, dress and manner, and lived near the War Department. Clerks sympathetic to the South would leave documents on their desks when they went to lunch. Conrad would slip into the building, read the material, and forward the information to Richmond.*

the strength of the hostile army in my front as its commander." Greenhow's messages even included the route
ECB of the Federal advance, °which convinced Confederate President Jefferson Davis to authorize Joseph E. Johnston to leave the Shenandoah Valley and reinforce Beauregard. The advantage gained by the Southerners facilitated their victory in the first significant battle of the war.•

After the battle, Greenhow traveled from Washington to New York to place her second-eldest daughter, Leila, on a ship to California where she would join her older sister. The youngest daughter, eight-year-old Rose, remained with her mother. When news of the Union defeat reached Manhattan, Greenhow hardly repressed her delight. Within forty-eight hours of the Rebel triumph, she received a message from Jordan: "Our President and our General direct me to thank you. We rely on your further information. The Confederacy owes you a debt." As soon as Greenhow returned to Washington on July 23, she joined in efforts to raise funds for food and clothing for the Confederates taken prisoner during the battle.

Emboldened by her success in gathering and conveying information to her contact behind Rebel lines, Greenhow and her accomplices continued to note troop strengths and dispositions in the belief that a Confederate attack on Washington was imminent. Yet, rather than assume an inconspicuous manner, Greenhow flaunted her Southern sympathies until she finally attracted the attention of the Federal authorities. At first she was denied any further contact with the Confederate prisoners, and then the War Department enlisted Pinkerton's services to place her under surveillance.

While the early months of the war proved to be a time of awkwardness and unsophistication in Union intelligence operations, Pinkerton's surveillance of Greenhow was almost comedic. The detective and two of his men positioned themselves outside the Greenhow house. Noting a lighted window, Pinkerton was hefted on the shoulders of the other two men and peered into the house. He saw no one but heard the footsteps of someone approaching the front door.

*One of the most successful Confederate spies, Rose O'Neal Greenhow, is pictured above in a Mathew Brady photograph with her eight-year-old daughter, Little Rose. The window in the Old Capitol Prison in Washington, D.C., has been boarded up to eliminate contact with the outside world. An impoverished widow, she had moved in the highest political and social circles because of her good looks and charm. Important men who knew important information about the war found her irresistible, and she later wrote, "I employed every capacity with which God has endowed me, and the result was far more successful than my hopes could have flattered me to expect." Detective Allan Pinkerton did not succumb to her charms, however, and was instrumental in her arrest. After Greenhow was paroled to the South, Jefferson Davis sent her to Europe as a courier. She drowned on the return voyage.*

Jumping down, the three detectives scurried under the front porch as the visitor rang the doorbell. After the caller was admitted, the three men ran back to the window and lifted Pinkerton again to see what was happening.

Pinkerton recognized the visitor as one of the senior members of the provost marshal's office and watched him present Greenhow with a map of the Washington defenses. The sudden sound of people from the street sent the three detectives under the Greenhow stoop again. When Pinkerton returned to the window, the officer and Greenhow were out of sight. About an hour later the officer left, and Pinkerton followed him with such haste that he left his shoes behind. After shadowing the man for several blocks, something went wrong and the sock-footed detective was arrested, thrown into a guard house, and later interrogated by the officer he had been following. When Pinkerton refused to answer any questions, he was returned to his cell. There he bribed a guard to convey a message to one of his contacts in the War Department. The next day Pinkerton was taken to the assistant secretary of war, Thomas A. Scott, and he submitted his report on Greenhow's activity. The conspiring officer was arrested, and Pinkerton was instructed to continue the Greenhow surveillance.

Despite whatever caution Pinkerton may have taken in watching Greenhow, the widow knew she was under scrutiny and seemed almost to enjoy the attention. By August 23 Pinkerton decided he had enough evidence to arrest Greenhow. He confronted her outside her home, searched the house, and placed Greenhow under house arrest. Several of her contacts were arrested when they came to the house to deliver their information. A week later the Greenhow house became a detention center for other women suspected of spying for the Confederacy.

An Englishman, Timothy Webster (above), was Allan Pinkerton's most talented operative. His first assignment was to spy on the formation of Confederate units in Kentucky and Tennessee. In Memphis he was able to gather information by convincing Confederate officers he was an ardent Secessionist. After they all downed much bourbon, the Southerners (incorrectly shown in Federal uniforms below left) insisted on buying Webster a "secession chapeau"—Confederate officer's cap. One of his associates said of Webster, "He practically mesmerized you into thinking he was whatever he decided to be."

Confinement, however, did not deter Greenhow. JIR °She continued sending messages through Union lines by exploiting well-meaning jailers who mailed letters for her that were addressed to her contacts behind the Rebel lines, and she allegedly devised a way of communicating through her "tapestry" work, which was hung across the windows from time to time. Finally, on January 18, 1862, Greenhow and another woman were transferred to the Old Capitol Prison,• the same building in which Greenhow's aunt had maintained a boardinghouse and the young Greenhow had been enchanted with John C. Calhoun.

Greenhow remained there with her eight-year-old daughter, imprisoned with Confederate soldiers, spies, suspicious persons, Union deserters, and contrabands (indigent freed slaves who had nowhere else to go). In March she was given a hearing during which a judge, frustrated with her rebuffs of all attempts to forgive her offenses, declared that she was more guilty of mischief than treason. On June 2, 1862, Greenhow was paroled to the South on her promise not to return to the North for the duration of the war.

JIR °Richmond welcomed Greenhow like a hero, and shortly after her arrival she was sent to Europe as a unofficial ambassador for the Confederate government.• She remained in Europe for more than two years and wrote an autobiography, *My Imprisonment and the First Year of Abolition Rule at Washington.*

*For more than one year Webster was a highly effective spy for Pinkerton, traveling throughout the South. On Webster's third trip to Richmond, a squall pushed the boat in which he was riding onto a sandbar one hundred yards from the Virginia shore. He leaped into the water and bravely carried two women passengers and their children to shore (bottom right on page 304). Wet and cold from his exposure, Webster developed rheumatism, which contributed to his downfall.*

*Webster became a mole in the office of Confederate Secretary of War Judah P. Benjamin and faithfully delivered information to Rebel agents in the North—but not before Federal authorities got a look. When his rheumatism flared up again, Webster was confined to his Richmond hotel room. Concerned over not hearing from his agent, Allan Pinkerton sent two other agents to look for him, which led to his betrayal, apprehension, trial, and sentence to death. His only supporter, a woman named Hattie Lawton, pleaded with authorities (left) that he be shot rather than hanged like a felon. The request was denied. The first rope broke and a second noose was prepared. Webster's final comment was, "I die again." Lawton was also a Federal agent, and she was later jailed but not executed.*

JIR °In October 1864 Greenhow was returning from England aboard the blockade-runner *Condor* with gold and dispatches sewn into her dress when the Wilmington-bound ship was discovered near shore by a Union blockader.• While the helmsman battled rough seas and tried to avert the hulk of another blockade-runner that had run aground the night before, the *Condor* ran aground on a sandbar just two hundred yards from Confederate Fort Fisher. Fearing that she might be imprisoned again and against the advice of the captain, Greenhow insisted on reaching shore by the ship's JIR small boat. °Waves immediately swamped the small craft, overturning it. The sailors manning the boat were able to cling to it until they were rescued, but the gold sewn into Greenhow's clothing dragged her down and she drowned in the sea. Her body was recovered the next day, and she was buried with military honors.•

DEATH WAS one of the inherent dangers faced by the men and women who engaged in spying. One who risked his life and lost was Pinkerton's most effective operative of the early war years, Timothy Webster. The forty-year-old Englishman had been the foremost detective in the Pinkerton agency during the ten years before the war, and it was supposedly he who discovered the plot against Lincoln in Baltimore. In his postwar memoirs, Pinkerton recalled: "He, amongst all the force who

*The Northern press mocked the Confederate use of women as spies in this cartoon, calling the "cavalry" rider "General Stuart's New Aid [sic]." However, their Union counterparts who spied on the South achieved results as remarkable as those of the Southern spies. While visiting friends in Richmond, Mrs. E. H. Baker, a Chicago native who worked for Pinkerton, watched the test run of an underwater ram being built at Tredegar Iron Works, which she toured. Her timely report alerted the U.S. Navy and saved Federal ships in the James River.*

*Canadian-born Emma Edmonds darkened her face with silver nitrate, donned a curly wig, and infiltrated the Southern lines posing as a black man. At other times she went as a black mammy or as a fat Irish peddler woman named Bridget O'Shea. She once posed as a young Southerner named Charles Mayberry and worked her way into the Confederate underground at Louisville. Edmonds was so good at her craft that she duped everyone—including the Yankees, who thought she was Pvt. Franklin Thompson of the Second Michigan.*

went with me, deserves the credit for saving the life of Mr. Lincoln, even more than I do."

WCD °If only half of what Pinkerton said about Webster can be believed, he was a remarkable man. He operated repeatedly behind enemy lines, in the Confederacy, gathering information and sending it North. Webster was captured or suspected time after time, but he always managed to talk his way out of trouble.• In Memphis he so impressed a group of Southern officers that, after several rounds of bourbon, they insisted on buying him a "secession chapeau"—a Confederate officer's hat.

DWG °Pinkerton used Webster extensively in the South, because he was able to pass himself off as a trustworthy Southerner. On at least two occasions he was arrested by other Pinkerton men who did not know who he was.•

For more than a year Webster carried out many daring operations and gathered crucial information. On his third trip to Richmond, Webster was aboard a boat with two women and their three children who were joining their husbands, Confederate officers. The boat struck a sandbar, and Webster carried the women and
DWG children ashore. °As a result, he contracted rheumatism. On his fourth trip to Richmond, the recurring rheumatism incapacitated him, and he was confined to his hotel room. Since Webster was out of communication with Washington, Pinkerton became very concerned about him and made the mistake of sending two agents—Pryce Lewis and John Scully—to Richmond to find him.•

AA °Lewis and Scully's arrival in the Confederate capital raised suspicions almost immediately. John Winder, the provost marshal, was alerted and had them followed. They led the Confederates to Webster's hotel room. Webster was placed under surveillance, and the two agents were arrested. Lewis escaped with several other prisoners, but Scully was sentenced to death and saved his life by confessing that Webster was a more important spy. Webster, helpless with rheumatism, was arrested,• tried, and convicted of spying.

On August 29, 1862, Webster was hanged, the first American to be hanged for spying since Nathan Hale and the first spy of the war to be sentenced to death. In his postwar memoirs, Pinkerton sorrowfully observed: "Rebel vengeance was at last satisfied, the appetite for human blood sated. Farewell, brave spirit, thou has suffered in a glorious cause and died a martyr's death."

ALTHOUGH THE penalty for spying was death, that punishment did not deter some women from engaging in
JIR espionage. In many ways °women made excellent spies because the men on both sides tended to underestimate their capacity for gathering information and relaying it, and when women were caught in the act of spying both sides tended to be lenient in their treatment. Women knew this, and so they felt little hesitation in carrying on their activities.• At the same time,
WCD °women viewed spying as slightly naughty, a behind-closed-doors endeavor that could be highly exciting, a little dangerous, very dashing, and even romantic.•
JIR °They were expected to be homebodies with little interest in public affairs, and that presumption only added
WCD to the luster of spying.• °Spying also gave women a sense of doing one's part for the cause, and since women could not enlist in the armies to fight, they could gather information and send it to the other side.•

Women spies had the same handicaps as men in that they were generally untrained amateurs who did not know what information was pertinent and what was
AA useless, but °amateur or not they were nonetheless brave and inventive.• While the results of their work might or might not be used effectively, there was no lack of willing loyalists.

One Southern spy whose exploits generated a great
JIR deal of notoriety was Belle Boyd, also known as °the "siren of the Shenandoah." Boyd was born in 1843 in Martinsburg, Virginia, the daughter of a prosperous merchant. As a teenager at the start of the war, she was
AA vivacious and energetic.• °Although she lived in a stronghold of Union sympathy, Boyd was an ardent

*A Northern journalist who interviewed Belle Boyd (above) wrote, "Without being beautiful, she is very attractive, is quite tall, has a superb figure, an intellectual face, and dresses with much taste." After her arrest in July 1862, she was sent north to Maryland for imprisonment. She waved a Confederate flag from the window of the train at every whistle stop, and then so thoroughly charmed her warden in Baltimore that he personally released her with no more than a warning to behave. She immediately returned to the Shenandoah to resume spying. Belle's conduct, which helped make her one of the Confederacy's most successful spies, scandalized proper Southern ladies. She traveled alone, struck up conversations with soldiers in both blue and gray, and visited officers in their tents. After the war she became a successful actress, enchanting audiences across the nation as "La Belle Rebelle."*

Secessionist and at least four other members of her family were Southern spies. Boyd, however, flaunted her Secessionist sympathies. She wore a Confederate soldier's sash around her waist and a palmetto pin on her bodice, and she decorated her home with Confederate flags.•

By the time Boyd was seventeen years old, she had made the Southern cause her own. "My duties were painful in the extreme!" she later wrote. "But I allowed for one thought to keep possession of my mind—I was doing all a woman could do in her country's cause."

JIR °In 1861 Union troops occupied Martinsburg, and on July 4, while celebrating Independence Day and becoming somewhat drunk, several soldiers decided to visit the Boyd home, remove the Confederate decorations about which they had heard, and raise the Stars and Stripes. One of the Boyd household servants overheard the soldiers and raced ahead of them to remove the Southern banners. When the soldiers arrived and found there were no flags to seize, they decided nevertheless to raise the Union banner. Boyd's mother confronted them, declaring that every member of the household would rather die than have the Yankee flag hoisted over their heads, but the soldiers ignored her and continued to raise the standard. Seventeen-year-old Boyd then produced a pistol and fired into the group, gravely wounding one of the men. The Federal soldiers withdrew with their bleeding comrade, leaving the flag unraised. The man died three days after the incident, but because of her youth, Boyd was not charged with murder. She was tried, reprimanded, and released, but the incident established her reputation immediately.•

When Boyd recalled the incident in her autobiography, she was remorseless: "Shall I be ashamed to confess that I recall without one shadow of remorse the act that I saved my mother from insult and perhaps death?

That the blood I then shed has left no stain on my soul, imposed no burden upon my conscience?"

Boyd was flirtatious with the occupying Yankees, and DWG ○something about her manner captivated the men in uniform• so that they tended to talk very freely when they were in her presence. She was not beautiful, but described as "very attractive. . . . quite tall, has a superb figure, an intellectual face, and dressed with much taste." One Northern paper alleged Boyd was "an accomplished prostitute." Few officers to whom she directed her charms failed to divulge information of troop strength and battle plans. Boyd wrote out the details, frequently without encoding it, and reported it through a number of couriers. Adding to the sheer bravado of her actions, the young girl also stole weapons.

In early 1862 Boyd moved from Martinsburg to Front Royal. Shortly after her arrival, Union troops occupied the town. She tried to return to Martinsburg and was arrested and sent to Baltimore. The authorities in Baltimore, however, were unsure of what to do with her, so they returned her to Martinsburg, where she was placed under surveillance. Boyd ventured back to Front Royal and beguiled a member of Gen. James Shields's staff.

AA ○In May 1862 Boyd achieved the pinnacle of her success when she gathered information about Federal troop movements being planned to support the Union army on the Virginia Peninsula that would leave only a small force to hold Front Royal. She passed the intelligence on to Gen. Thomas J. "Stonewall" Jackson who was campaigning in the Shenandoah Valley to keep several Federal units from joining the campaign that was threatening Richmond.•

During the initial moments of the battle of Front Royal, Boyd saw how the Union soldiers were defending the town and rode across the field of battle and into the Confederate ranks. She reported her latest observations to one of Jackson's aides, possibly Henry Kyd Douglas. The relevance of her report may or may not have influenced the outcome of the battle, but the fact remains that Jackson routed the Federals.

Like Greenhow, Boyd was not good at concealing the fact that she was a spy. The Federals arrested her four

*The Van Lew mansion was headquarters for Union espionage in the Confederate capital of Richmond. Always looking for an advantage, Northern sympathizer Elizabeth Van Lew invited Confederate Libby Prison's new warden and his wife to stay at her home while they searched for permanent quarters. She thereby ingratiated herself to them and paved the way for her visits to the prison, where she both passed and picked up information from Union prisoners.*

more times until she was finally incarcerated on July 29, 1862, in the Old Capitol Prison. Some report that she became the darling of the prison, others that she teased her guards with scandalous glimpses of her bare neck and arms. Boyd was never tried, and after she refused to take the oath of allegiance, she was paroled to the Confederacy in December 1862.

In early 1863 Boyd was apprehended as a courier on the blockade-runner *Greyhound.* She was to be imprisoned in Fort Warren, Massachusetts, but while she was en route Boyd charmed Lt. Samuel Wylde Hardinge, one of the officers of the Federal vessel that had apprehended her, and he helped gain her release. She was deported to Canada, and Hardinge was court-martialed and discharged. Boyd went on to England from Canada
JIR and became a celebrity as a Confederate spy. °She published a book of her adventures as *Belle Boyd in Camp and Prison* and discovered a career on the stage.

Hardinge followed Boyd to England, and in August 1864 they were married.• Apparently, she convinced him to return to the United States and spy for the South, but he was caught and imprisoned and there he died. Boyd, a widow at the age of twenty-one, remained in England
JIR for the duration of the war. °When she returned to the United States, she continued her stage career, emphasizing and exaggerating her experiences as the "Cleopatra of the Secession." To the press she was known as the "Rebel Joan of Arc." She married two more times. In 1900 Boyd died in Kilborn, Wisconsin, just before she was scheduled to perform,• and was buried there.

WCD °Boyd was an example of Southern womanhood who sacrificed much for the cause because she had done what most Confederate women would not dare to do and what many men could not dare to do. For that she was lionized throughout her later years as southerners took pride in her experiences just as they took pride in their generals. Boyd's tales of exciting exploits allowed the people of the South to relive some of the better days of the war and their successes, and women especially lived vicariously through her stage performances.•

*Perhaps the most effective spy on either side, "Crazy Bet" Van Lew is all the more remarkable for having been self-trained in the art of spying. The Van Lews owned a farm outside Richmond, and Elizabeth asked for and received a pass from the Confederates to go through the lines to tend the farm. This short journey was the first leg for any message she was smuggling out in a hollow egg or in a basket with a false bottom. Letters she wrote to relatives in Union-controlled Norfolk were routed to Fort Monroe, where Union Gen. Benjamin Butler dabbed milk on the chatty notes to reveal the real messages written in invisible ink.*

ONE OF the most successful spies of the war was Elizabeth Van Lew of Richmond who spied for the Union. Both of her parents—John and Eliza—were northerners who had met in Richmond in 1818 after he had moved there for his health. The couple had three children and enjoyed all that Richmond society had to offer. Despite treatments for a respiratory condition at the spas in western Virginia, the patriarch of the Van Lew family died in 1843.

AA °Elizabeth was proud of being a southerner, but she was an abolitionist, believing that slavery was evil.• Her attitude toward slavery was influenced by an outspoken governess in Philadelphia in the early 1830s and possibly by a slave trader's daughter whom she met at one of the spas visited by the Van Lews. The girl told Elizabeth about one of her father's sales that separated a slave mother from her child and the mother's anguish and sudden death caused by the separation. The story had a lasting effect on Elizabeth. After her father's death, she convinced her mother to free their nine slaves, and she took part of her inheritance and purchased any relatives of the Van Lew slaves and gave them their freedom.

The abolitionist sentiments of the Van Lews became known throughout Richmond society, and they were excluded subtly from the events and parties of the social calendar. When war broke out, Elizabeth chose to do whatever she could to see the South defeated. She used a route along the James River to funnel information to the Federals at Fort Monroe.

WCD °Information was conveyed by former servants carrying baskets of eggs. One egg in each basket had been drained of its contents, which was replaced with part of a message written on very thin onionskin paper.• Notes were also carried in the soles of the servants' shoes. Van Lew understood that one of her messages might fall into the wrong hands, so she tore them into several parts and sent each by a different courier using separate routes. As additional security measures, Van Lew enciphered every

| 6 | r | n | b | h | t | x |
|---|---|---|---|---|---|---|
| 3 | v | 1 | u | 8 | 4 | w |
| 1 | e | m | 3 | j | 5 | g |
| 5 | l | a | 9 | 0 | i | d |
| 2 | k | 7 | 2 | z | 6 | s |
| 4 | p | o | y | c | f | q |
| | 1 | 3 | 6 | 2 | 5 | 4 |

*The secret cipher used by Elizabeth Van Lew was discovered in her watch-case after her death. It is a simple thirty-six-square grid containing the alphabet and the numbers zero through nine. Crazy Bet's courier system worked so flawlessly that on one occasion she had fresh flowers delivered directly to General Grant. President Grant's appointment of Van Lew to be postmistress of Richmond after the war was one of the few acts of official recognition for the sacrifices she made for the Union.*

message she sent, using a code of her own, and wrote her reports with a colorless liquid that became visible after the paper was dabbed with milk.

JIR °In the early months of the war, Elizabeth and her mother visited Union prisoners in Richmond prisons, bringing them books and food. When Libby Warehouse was converted into a prison in March 1862, Elizabeth made the Yankee officers imprisoned there her special cause. Using books with split spines to conceal notes and dishes with false bottoms, she conveyed information from the prisoners to Fort Monroe.• To allay any AA suspicions, °she took advantage of her reputation as an eccentric, slightly crazy spinster. She let her hair go, wore threadbare clothing, and mumbled to herself and sang nonsensical songs as she walked. Her neighbors began calling her "Crazy Bet," but Van Lew proved to be shrewd and capable.• When the authorities revoked her pass allowing her to visit the prisoners, she appealed to the provost marshal, John H. Winder, an old family friend, and he issued her a pass, seeing no harm in humoring an addled old woman.

Van Lew's greatest achievement was placing one of her former slaves, Mary Elizabeth Bowser, in the Confederate White House, the home of President Jefferson Davis. After she had been given her freedom by the Van Lews, Bowser had been educated in a Quaker school for blacks in Philadelphia. Van Lew persuaded a friend to use Bowser as an assistant whenever she helped at any formal affairs at the mansion. Bowser pretended to be illiterate so as not to raise suspicions. After helping out at several occasions in the executive mansion, the friend suggested to Varina Davis that Bowser might be a servant worth hiring, and from 1863 until the end of the war Bowser worked for the Davis family.

EGM °Bowser was primarily a dining servant, and so she was able to overhear almost every dinner conversation.• WCD Thus °on several occasions she witnessed meetings

between Davis and Robert E. Lee, members of the Confederate cabinet, and other influential people at which EGM policy and strategy were discussed.• °Bowser also cleaned in Davis's office and saw dispatches and orders that were yet to be given to the Confederate commanders.•

One of Bowser's contacts was Thomas McNiven who worked out of the bakery patronized by the Davis family. His memory of the network was recorded by his grandson, Robert W. Waitt, who claimed that Bowser "had a photographic mind. Everything she saw on the Rebel President's desk she could repeat word for word. . . . She made a point of always coming out to my wagon when I made deliveries at the Davis's home to drop [off] information."

In addition to her work as a spy, Van Lew established a network of safe houses to convey escaping prisoners safely from Richmond to Williamsburg and into the Union lines. The close proximity of the Van Lew house to Libby Prison made it a safe house as well. An escape on February 9, 1864, was the most successful in the prison's brief history due in no small measure to the thoroughness of Van Lew's planning. At the same time, it led to one of the most disastrous missions of the war.

Shortly after the February 1864 escape, Van Lew informed Gen. Benjamin F. Butler at Fort Monroe that the enlisted men held prisoner at Belle Isle were dying at the rate of ten per day. Butler forwarded the data to

*When the Van Lews freed their slave Mary Elizabeth Bowser, she went to Philadelphia where she received an education at a Quaker school. Returning to Richmond, Bowser got a job as a maid at the White House of the Confederacy (above left) through the influence of Elizabeth. As she cleaned Jefferson Davis's office, Bowser could read dispatches and orders waiting to be sent out, the contents of which she relayed to her former mistress.*

*Van Lew was involved with the breakout from Libby Prison (above right) by Federal officers in the winter of 1864. A handful of conspirators dug beneath the street to a vacant lot, keeping their work a secret from other prisoners. On the night of the escape, however, the secret got out and hundreds of prisoners scrambled over each other for a chance to crawl to freedom. Before the Rebel guards caught on, 109 men escaped, some of whom spent that night in Elizabeth Van Lew's home.*

WCD

*In her old age, Elizabeth Van Lew was shunned by Richmond society. "I live here in perfect isolation," she wrote. "No one will walk with us on the streets, no one will go with us anywhere. And it grows worse and worse as the years roll on and those I love go to their long rest." Federal intelligence chief Col. George Sharpe said of Elizabeth Van Lew, "For a long, long time, she represented all that was left of the power of the U.S. Government in Richmond."*

the secretary of war, Edwin M. Stanton, who took the information to Lincoln. A plan was formulated to send thirty-five hundred cavalrymen under Gen. Judson Kilpatrick and Col. Ulric Dahlgren to free the prisoners. According to documents found later, Dahlgren may have prepared orders of his own to kidnap or kill Jefferson Davis and members of his cabinet, and torch the city. The raid failed and Dahlgren was killed, and his body was sent to Richmond and buried in an unmarked grave. One of Van Lew's contacts observed the secret interment, and a month later Van Lew, perhaps feeling responsible for his death, supervised the removal and reburial of Dahlgren. After the war she informed the family of the actual burial site, and they retrieved it.

Like most Civil War spies, °Van Lew could be indiscreet. Had anyone in the provost marshal's office been paying careful attention, she would have been arrested. Her eccentric behavior prevented her arrest, but she was always under suspicion.• In mid-1864 a woman on the street gave Van Lew a letter requesting information on Confederate supplies, but Van Lew was suspicious and did nothing with the request. The woman apparently worked for the provost marshal's office and was seeking to entrap Van Lew.

When Grant's army broke through the Petersburg line on April 2, 1865, the Confederates abandoned Richmond. The Union army entered the city and found the Stars and Stripes flying at the Van Lew mansion and found Van Lew picking through the ruins of the Confederate War Department.

When the war ended, Van Lew was without funds, having spent everything she had on her spying efforts for the Union. Several attempts were made by former Union prisoners to compensate her for her service to them, but nothing came of them. Just two weeks after his inauguration, however, a thankful Ulysses S. Grant appointed Van Lew postmaster of Richmond with an annual salary of twelve hundred dollars. "You have sent me the most valuable information received from Richmond during the war," he said. She managed the Richmond post office for eight years. Nevertheless, she was a social outcast for the rest of her life. When her mother died in 1875 there were not enough friends on hand to serve as pall bearers.

BP In her later years °Van Lew became a pitiful figure who never received credit for the real courage that it took to be behind enemy lines and to be an enemy of her own people for what she believed was right.• As a last resort she solicited funds from soldiers and the families of soldiers she had assisted during the war, and they responded with gifts that allowed her to live out the rest of her life in relative comfort.

Van Lew died on September 25, 1900, in her family home, and she was buried upright in the family cemetery because of lack of space. No stone marked her grave until years later. In closing her journal, she wrote: "If I am entitled to the name of 'Spy' because I was in the secret service, I accept it willingly; but it will hereafter have to my mind a high and honorable significance. For my loyalty to my country, I have two beautiful names—here I am called, 'traitor,' farther North a 'spy'—I am called 'a spy' instead of the honored 'Faithful.'"

*During the four long years of the war, Van Lew's success as a Union agent was a result of her fooling Richmond society and the Confederate government, including Gen. John Winder (above), provost marshal of Richmond, who, like everyone else, dismissed her as an eccentric.*

*When Allan Pinkerton returned to civilian life, Col. Lafayette Baker (below) took over command of the Secret Service. Enthusiastic but not always effective, Baker was embarrassed when one of his men failed to guard President Lincoln the night of the assassination.*

Van Lew was successful in her work in no small part because she used blacks in her information-gathering enterprise. In fact, slaves and former slaves made ideal EGM spies because °Southerners throughout the war maintained a stereotypical perception of African Americans that refused to recognize their value in conveying information to the enemy. As long as slaves appeared happy and carefree and showed due deference, they were not suspected of duplicity. Southerners assumed blacks were neither intelligent enough nor capable of independent thought to spy for the Yankees. This unrealistic assessment of the capabilities of African Americans only enhanced their value as spies.• Furthermore, DWG °Southerners were convinced that their slaves knew little about what was going on, when in actuality the slaves, particularly house servants, probably knew far more than their owners.•

One of the first men to recognize and take advantage of this Southern prejudice was Pinkerton, and one of his most successful black operatives was John Scobell.

*Beautiful actress Pauline Cushman's best role was playing a Southern sympathizer while actually being a Federal agent named Harriet Wood. Throughout Tennessee and Kentucky she became the darling of Confederate troops as she gathered valuable information for the advancing Federal army. Eventually suspicions were aroused, secret papers were found, and she was tried and sentenced to hang. Pauline was dramatically saved when the Union army invaded the region and the retreating Confederates left her behind. Too well known to be useful as a spy, she returned to the stage, wearing a uniform (above) and telling about her exploits that became more and more thrilling as time passed.*

In his memoirs, Pinkerton recalled: "Scobell was a remarkably gifted man. He could read and write and was full of music. The manner in which he performed his duty was always a source of satisfaction to me, and apparently of gratification to himself."

Scobell was a Virginia slave whose owner perceived his intelligence and taught him to read and write beyond the rudimentary level. In addition, Scobell had an aptitude for music and learned the Scottish songs his owner sang and even sang them in a Scottish brogue. Both Scobell and his wife were freed before the war, but she remained in Richmond as a cook while he went north.

Pinkerton recruited Scobell and recalled, "He had only to assume the role of a light-hearted darky and no
EGM one would suspect his real role." °Scobell returned to the South as a Union spy, operating alone and serving in a variety of capacities—selling snacks, day laborer, and cook—among various Confederate camps where he collected information about troop strength, unit identification, and troop movements. He was always successful because he was unassuming, playing the role of the average African American in the South. Scobell was with Timothy Webster and Hattie Lawton, both Pinkerton operatives, when Webster and Lawton were apprehended in March 1862. Webster was hanged and Lawton imprisoned for a year before she was paroled; Scobell, in the meantime, was left to continue his work without being questioned.

Most African Americans who served as spies during the war remained nameless after the war.• One notable exception was Harriet Tubman. Prior to the war, the former slave from Maryland helped to establish the Underground Railroad, a clandestine network of safe houses that sheltered runaway slaves and assisted them
NIP in escaping from the South to the North. °Known as the "Moses of her people" or as "General Tubman," she helped hundreds to gain their freedom before she became so well known that she lost her effectiveness.•
CC °When the war broke out, she returned to Virginia to work for the Union cause.•

*In the group portrait (left), Harriet Tubman stands at the extreme left with seven unidentified persons. She helped hundreds of African Americans travel North to freedom before becoming too well known for clandestine operations. However, she was effective working within the Union army debriefing runaway slaves and recruiting candidates for spying.*

*John Scobell, shown below shooting his Confederate pursuers, was Pinkerton's best-known black operative, but others also risked their lives obtaining information for the Union. Furney Bryant, an escaped slave, controlled a large ring of black spies in the Carolinas and was instrumental in helping Federals snag a large cache of Confederate silver coins. In 1863 Bryant enlisted in a black regiment and served out the war in uniform. Alfred Wood, who passed for white, enlisted in a Texas Ranger unit, then deserted when he had gleaned enough information. A husband and wife team named Dabney kept Union General Hooker informed by an ingenious method. The wife, who worked for a Southern woman at Fredericksburg, sent messages to her husband across the Rappahannock by hanging laundry a certain way.*

Initially, Tubman assisted runaway slaves who entered Union camps from behind enemy lines, but her role quickly expanded. She accompanied the Union army to the Carolinas and worked with Col. James Montgomery and the Second South Carolina Volunteers, a regiment of black soldiers raised from freed South Carolina slaves. Tubman acted as liaison between the military and the slaves, interviewing slaves for information about Confederate troop positions and strengths and relaying that information to Montgomery.

When the war ended, Tubman received little compensation from the Union for all the risks she had endured for the cause. She was paid two hundred dollars for her three years of war service, but many of the officers under whom she worked lobbied that Congress should award her a pension and greater compensation. It was a long, frustrating political struggle. Tubman died in 1913 an indigent, running a veterans home. Although it was little consolation, she was given a military funeral.

Part of the allure of spying was the severity of the penalty for failure. One either succeeded or one was caught, and to be

*This Edwin Forbes sketch entitled "The Reliable Contraband" shows a slave being interviewed by soldiers. Union Col. Rush Hawkins, stationed in North Carolina, said, "If I want to find out anything hereabouts, I hunt up a Negro; and if he knows or can find out, I'm sure to get all I want." The African-American leader Frederick Douglass wrote in 1862, "It will be shown that they have been the safest guides to our army and the best pilots to our navy, and the most dutiful laborers on our fortifications, where they have been permitted to serve."*

caught was to be condemned to die, although the Victorian sensibilities of the era did not condone such a verdict against women. For the first two years of the war the death penalty was rarely invoked, but later, as life seemed less precious, it became easier to render the ultimate penalty against men caught spying. The raw heroism of the battlefield paled in comparison to heroism on the gallows. One such portrait of courage was that of Sam Davis in 1863.

In November 1863 Braxton Bragg's Confederates commanded the heights around Chattanooga and laid siege to the town below. Grant had just replaced William S. Rosecrans, and he expected reinforcements. Bragg was anxious to know the strength and disposition of the Northern troops rushing to Grant's aid, so he dispatched bands of scouts into the countryside. One of these groups was known as Coleman's Scouts—although the unit was led by Capt. Henry Shaw who used the pseudonym E. C. Coleman—and it had earned a notorious reputation among the Federals.

BP °Coleman's Scouts infiltrated the Union lines in Tennessee, using whatever disguises were necessary—Yankee uniforms or civilian clothing—to collect the information they needed. Twenty-one-year-old Sam Davis was one of the most intrepid and daring of

*When Gen. George B. McClellan was relieved of command in 1862, Allan Pinkerton returned to his detective agency. Thereafter, the U.S. Secret Service and the system of military intelligence were increasingly staffed by soldiers, particularly cavalrymen, who had an aptitude for the work, as opposed to civilian detectives favored by Pinkerton. Among the most noted of the scouts and guides of the Army of the Potomac were the men shown here with their leader, Lt. Robert Klein of the Third Indiana Cavalry. He is seated in the center with his young son sitting on the ground next to him.*

WCD Coleman's Scouts.• On November 19 °he was returning to Bragg's headquarters with information sewn into his saddle and in his boots when two Union soldiers in Confederate garb encountered him about fifteen miles south of Pulaski, Tennessee. When they attempted to conscript Davis for Southern service, he claimed to be on a mission for General Bragg and produced a pass signed by E. Coleman. The two riders took Davis prisoner and searched him. It was obvious he was carrying information beyond what a Confederate soldier should be carrying, thus they determined he was a spy.•

Davis was brought before Brig. Gen. Grenville Dodge, the thirty-one-year-old head of Union intelligence operating from Memphis to Mobile and from Atlanta to Richmond. After questioning the Confederate BP scout, °Dodge respected Davis's bravery and gave him an opportunity to save himself in return for identifying the leader of the Coleman Scouts.• What Dodge did not know was that the elusive Captain Coleman (Henry Shaw) was already in custody in the same jail in which Davis was being held. Shaw had been captured by Federal scouts who doubted his story that he was a former Confederate surgeon.

Davis adamantly refused to identify Shaw or reveal any other secrets. "I would die a thousand deaths before

*E. C. Coleman, head of Coleman's Scouts, was actually Capt. Henry Shaw, the bearded man seated in the center of the photograph at right. Shaw's intrepid Rebel operatives, including the martyred Sam Davis, the "Boy Hero of the Confederacy," worked behind the lines in Tennessee ferrying information to Confederate Gen. Braxton Bragg.*

*Union Gen. Grenville Dodge was in charge of intelligence operations in the western theater. A good organizer, Dodge was also an innovator, recruiting and training Northern sympathizers and runaway blacks for espionage, using numbers instead of names for his operatives, and having his agents track down and either confirm or quash damaging rumors which periodically swept the army.*

I would betray a friend or my country," he said. A court-martial board convened on November 24 and sentenced the young courier to be hanged on November 27.

JIR °Up until the moment of his execution, Union soldiers and Dodge pleaded with Davis, but he would not betray his commander. In a final letter to his mother, Davis wrote: "I have got to die tomorrow morning. . . . Mother, I do not hate to die." One of the last things he said on the scaffold was that he forgave the executioner for what he was about to do. Davis then turned and said, "I am ready."• An eyewitness reported: "The trap was sprung. There was a convulsive drawing up of the knees, a whirling of the body, and Davis was gone." In relating the story of Davis's hanging in 1893, one admirer wrote in the *Confederate Veteran* magazine: "No one ever awakened greater sympathy. His youth, his courage, his coolness under trying circumstances endeared him to all." Shaw watched the execution from his jail cell and lived under a cloud for the rest of his life as the man who lived because another had died.

AA °SPYING IN the Civil War should have been important, but because there was no coordinated system of interpreting intelligence and forwarding that information to the field quickly, Civil War espionage was not nearly as important as the volume of spying might suggest.• Nevertheless, it was clear, even before the war commenced, that clandestine activities would impact both sides, and so espionage—the gathering of sensitive information—experienced an extraordinary evolution on the American continent between 1861 and 1865.

JIR At the beginning of the war °there had been no rules for covert operations, so Civil War spies were forced to learn their jobs the hard way—by doing them. They bumbled and improvised and suffered and died.• For WCD these reasons °spying had a substantial impact on only a few operations and probably did not affect the course of the war because so many of the spies or would-be BP spies were unreliable.• Yet °whether or not these people made a difference in the course of the war, those who went behind enemy lines and risked their lives for their cause, be it Union or Confederate, should be honored for their bravery and dedication.• They performed an invaluable service to their country by establishing a basis on which all U.S. intelligence activities were eventually based. In 1885 the War Department formally authorized the individual military services to organize their own intelligence services.

# BANNERS OF GLORY

The FLAGS OF THE CIVIL WAR WERE far more than colorful strips of cloth; they were tangible symbols of everything for which the soldiers fought and inspired countless acts of heroism and bravery in battle. When a regiment's flag advanced, it meant that the regiment was winning and gave inspiration; when a flag was captured it meant the regiment was defeated. Brightly colored regimental flags graphically demonstrated for each soldier the direction in which his unit was to march and where it would stand to fire on the enemy. Flags communicated where a commander was to position his cavalry, indicated the fate of his men on the field, and warned of the advance of the enemy. The number of flags on the field often demonstrated how the battle was going; the men watched to see if their flags were surging forward or if they were falling back. Yet, in the heat and smoke of battle, a flag's greatest power was emotional, and banners became a binding force.

Although the three million men who fought the Civil War did so for many reasons, they held one thing in common: Each was prepared to die for his flag. Even if his carrying the flag made him a target, he would not leave that fabric behind willingly. "The colors bear the same relation to the soldier as honesty and integrity do to manhood," wrote Union Col. C. K. Hawkes. "It is the guiding star to victory. When in the smoke and din of battle the voice of the officer is drowned by the roar of artillery, the true soldier turns his eye to the colors that he not stray too far from it. And while it floats, he is conscious of his

| | |
|---|---|
| **WCD** | William C. Davis |
| **SH** | Steven Hill |
| **MJM** | Michael J. McAfee |
| **HMM** | Howard Michael Madaus |
| **BP** | Brian Pohanka |
| **DT** | Don Troiani |

*A Confederate color sergeant grasps the staff of his Army of Northern Virginia battle flag and stares with thoughtfulness and defiance at a distant Union picket line. He has been entrusted with immense responsibility, for if he falters in his duty, it will undoubtedly cause his regiment to hesitate also. If he carries the beloved symbol of his regiment toward the enemy position, he will gain honor and glory. However, such accolades will likely be purchased at the expense of death or painful wounds, for his standard will quickly become the target for Union fire.*

right and strength. Take it, guard it as you would the honor of the mother, wife, or friend you leave behind."

There are thousands of stories about soldiers on both sides who acted courageously to either advance their colors or capture the enemy's flag. At the December 13, 1862, battle of Fredericksburg, the color guard of the Twenty-first Massachusetts was killed. Sgt. Thomas Plunkett took up the fallen colors. William S. Clark recalled: "Sergeant Plunkett carried the colors proudly forward to the farthest point reached by our troops. A shell was thrown with fatal accuracy at the colors which again brought them to the ground, wet with the life blood of the brave Plunkett. Both of his arms were carried away."

°Rather than fall back and let the colors drop to the ground, Plunkett clutched the colors to his chest with the stumps of his arms and continued to march until he was relieved by another bearer. Many thought that his wounds were fatal and that he would die, but against everybody's expectations, he survived.•

This flag, stained with Plunkett's blood, was displayed at the Massachusetts State House as an inspirational symbol for years after the war. °When Plunkett died in 1884, the flag that he had carried at Fredericksburg, still stained with his blood, was sent to Worchester, Massachusetts, for his funeral. It was the only instance in the history of the Bay State in which any flag on display was allowed out of the state house.•

At Gettysburg, Confederate Col. Henry King Burgwyn Jr. of the Twenty-sixth North Carolina perished after taking up his regiment's fallen colors in an engagement with the Twenty-fourth Michigan. During the fierce fighting thirteen color-bearers in Burgwyn's regiment were killed one after another in the span of forty minutes. Similarly, Union Col. James P. McMahon of the 164th New York continued to advance his regiment's flag at Cold Harbor, Virginia, despite being riddled by Confederate fire. When he finally fell, his Southern adversaries honored his bravery with cheers.

Late in the war, during the one-sided fighting at Sayler's Creek on April 6, 1865, the Federal army seized more than fifty Confederate flags, and each captor later received the Medal of Honor. Pvt. Charles A. Taggart of the Thirty-seventh Massachusetts raced into the midst of a squad of Rebels, firing his weapon, grabbed their flag, and returned to his own lines. Taggart's comrades, however, saw the Southern banner racing toward them and believing they were being charged, fired on him, but he was wounded only slightly before reaching the safety of the Federal line.

During the same engagement, Lt. Thomas Custer, younger brother of Gen. George Armstrong Custer, encountered a Rebel color-bearer. Although the Southerner shot him in the face, Custer returned the man's fire, killing the standard bearer, and wrestled the banner from his grasp, capturing his second Confederate banner within five days of his first, a distinction that made him one of a handful of U.S. soldiers in military history to receive two Medals of Honor.

BP °The flags of both sides became more than just symbols and took on an importance of their own in that men in uniform valued them more than their own lives. This commitment was not just because they were patriotic, not just because they wanted to be the first to plant their flag on the enemy's earthworks, but because their national banners were intrinsic to everything they stood for as soldiers and as persons. To the men who fought the Civil War, their flags were almost living things.•

DT °National and regimental banners were fiercely defended in battle. Capturing an opponent's banner—if the soldier survived—was one of the most glorious battlefield accomplishments a man could experience. That achievement was every soldier's dream.•

Conversely, losing its flag was the greatest calamity
BP a regiment might experience. °When a battle turned against a unit and it seemed the flag might be captured, the soldiers often preferred to tear it into small pieces and hide the fragments inside their coats or under their shirts. They protected their flag so it would never be touched by an enemy and never be carried off as a trophy.•

The banner of the Fourteenth Mississippi was a beautiful painted flag that had been presented to the Shubuta Rifles by a group of patriotic women at the

*"Much depends upon the courage and daring of the color-sergeant," proclaimed a Civil War manual written by a Union officer. "Wherever he will carry the flag, the men will follow to protect and defend it; and no non-commissioned officer occupies a post that is so likely to bring distinction and promotion if he does his duty; whilst none is more certain to bring disgrace if he proves recreant to his trust." The two determined color bearers of the national (foreground) and regimental banners of the Third U.S. Regular Infantry appear to know full well the critical importance of their role in the impending battle.*

*Throughout the conflict, Northern and Southern women made flags for regiments from their local regions. Here, ladies of Philadelphia work on what appears to be a national banner while surrounded by paintings from the collection of the Pennsylvania Academy of Fine Arts. Virginian Constance Cary Harrison recalled that during the "autumn of '61," she worked with her female cousins to produce Confederate battle flags: "They were jaunty squares of scarlet, crossed with dark blue, edged with white, the cross bearing stars to indicate the number of the seceded States. We set our best stitches upon them, [and] edged them with golden fringes."*

beginning of the war. It had been entrusted to Andrew S. Payne who vowed that he would never surrender the flag to the Yankees. The regiment had fought with distinction, but in February 1862 it was among the units captured at Fort Donelson, Tennessee, by a Federal force under Ulysses S. Grant. Payne refused to dishonor his comrades by surrendering the flag, so he cut out the center of the banner, preserving two emblems—on one side, Liberty holding a portrait of Jefferson Davis in one hand and a sword in the other, and on the other side an eagle gripping a snake that had invaded its nest in a magnolia tree—and sewed it into the lining of his coat. The prisoners were sent to Camp Douglas, near Chicago, and paroled eight months later. When he returned to Mississippi, Payne returned the emblems to his regiment.

At the September 17, 1862, battle of Antietam, following the early morning attack on the Confederate line from the East Woods, seventeen-year-old Pvt. William Paul of the Ninetieth Pennsylvania convinced ten comrades to charge with him and retrieve the regimental flag. A group of Confederates were also rushing to secure the colors when Paul's band collided with them. A hand-to-hand struggle ensued, seven Union soldiers fell, but Paul wrung the flag from a Southerner's grasp and returned to his lines. The young private was awarded the Medal of Honor for his actions.

During the assault on Fort Harrison, Virginia, in September 1864, Color Sgt. J. R. Barnhardt of the Eighth North Carolina ripped his flag to pieces rather than surrender it. Other color-bearers tried to pull flags from their staffs and conceal them. For example, when Sgt. William N. Cameron of the Twenty-fifth Tennessee faced capture at the December 1862 battle of Murfreesboro, Tennessee, he tore his regiment's flag from its staff and stuffed it under his coat. The banner was never discovered during Cameron's captivity. The color sergeant of the Fourth Virginia, however, was not so fortunate. Just before he was captured at Spotsylvania Court House, Virginia, he stuffed the regimental colors under his jacket. The flag was discovered and became a trophy for the victorious Union regiment.

After he was captured with his regiment, the color-bearer of the Seventh Louisiana burned his flag rather than see it surrendered. Likewise, during the retreat following the Petersburg breakthrough, Sgt. George Barbee of the Forty-fourth North Carolina took his regiment's battle flag, wrapped it around a rock, and hurled it into the Appomattox River with the promise, "No enemy can ever have the flag of the Forty-fourth North Carolina."

In addition to being inspirational symbols, the colors served practical purposes. SH °The war was fought by regiments, individual units made up of one thousand men but typically numbering as few as five hundred. The regimental flag kept the men together in the field and vividly communicated to the field commander where his units were on the field. For these reasons the flags were made large so they could be seen despite the smoke and haze of battle.•

DT °When a regiment fired a volley, five hundred to one thousand muskets emitted huge clouds of white smoke. Individuals disappeared in the fog of battle, but flags were designed to be seen above the smoke from any point on the field. Thus soldiers were trained to focus on their regimental flag so they would know where they were supposed to be.• SH °As long as the flag went forward, they would be expected to advance with it, but if the flag withdrew to the rear, then they could fall back in good conscience and with honor.•

HMM °The banners on the battlefield also functioned as rallying points for a regiment. If a regiment broke and began to fall back, the officers focused on the flags and tried to rally their men around the colors. If a regiment pushed too far forward and the battle line became disorganized, the colors would become the rallying point around which the troops organized to reform their line.•

*Yankees and Rebels alike claimed they were fighting to uphold the ideals of their Revolutionary forefathers, and therefore both sides venerated George Washington. The image of the Father of His Country appears (above left) in the canton—the term for the blue portion in the upper left-hand corner of the banner—of the national color of the Seventeenth Massachusetts. Citizens of Baltimore presented this colorful flag to the Bay Staters in early 1862. The color with an eagle-bedecked canton (above right) belonged to the Twenty-fourth Massachusetts Infantry. The regiment's extensive battle honors cover every red stripe and much of the canton. These national colors illustrate the differing designs and the lack of conformity of such emblems during the Civil War.*

One dramatic instance of this occurred when the Irish Brigade, with its distinctive regimental green flags, spearheaded the Union assault against the middle of the Confederate line at the Sunken Road during the second phase of the battle of Antietam. The Irishmen advanced on the Rebel position until an opening volley struck the color-bearer of the Sixty-ninth New York and both he and the flag fell to the ground. The brigade commander, Thomas Francis Meagher, called out, "Raise the colors and follow me!" Seven more men fell while carrying the banner. Capt. James McGee then retrieved the flag, but as he moved forward a bullet snapped the staff and another passed through McGee's cap. Nevertheless, McGee continued to wave the banner and lead his men toward the Sunken Road although they never breached it. The brigade held out as best it could until ordered to fall back.

WCD °Carrying the flag was viewed as a position of great honor. Men vied for the position even though they knew that going into battle around the colors drastically shortened their life expectancy. Whenever a color-bearer fell on the battlefield, another man eagerly picked up the flag. For a few moments the new color-bearer would be a hero to his fellow soldiers in the regiment. If he survived he could be a hero for posterity, but his survival was never assured.•

The color guard typically consisted of six to nine of the regiment's steadiest men. When going into battle,

*The Twenty-second Pennsylvania Cavalry's flag (above left) displays the seal of the Keystone State in the canton. The flag also displays battle honors denoting the Twenty-second's participation in numerous obscure, but important, actions that took place on the fringes of their army's path during various campaigns. The regiment lost thirty-three men during three years of war. The national color above right belonged to the Second Battalion of the Eighteenth U.S. Regular Infantry, which fought in the western theater. The banners on these two pages all have different arrangements of stars because no design was mandated by law, and flag manufacturers chose layouts that suited their own purposes.*

they were positioned in the center of the regiment. When attacking, the color guard stepped in front of the regiment. When the line halted and the time came to fire, the color guard pulled back into the line.

Daniel G. McNamara of the Ninth Massachusetts described the drill: "Through the hail of shot and shell, the faithful guard marched with their precious colors onto the line of battle. Closely aligned by the right and left wings of the regiment. To waver for a moment, to break or retreat while death itself confronts them, would bring rout and disaster. If the color bearer be shot down, the flag is seized by the bravest man and again borne aloft, and onward."

The regimental flag was carried by color sergeants; the men around them were corporals who formed the color guard. The sergeants who bore the flags were not armed with muskets; their primary duty was to ensure the flag flew high in the center of the regimental line. The color guard carried their weapons at shoulder arms, even when the regiment fired on the enemy; the color guard were not authorized to discharge their weapons or engage the enemy unless the flags were threatened. The color guard's primary duty was to protect the unit's flags.

In March 1863 Peter Welch proudly accepted the post of color-bearer for the Twenty-eighth Massachusetts—a

*In addition to their flag shown on page 329, the Eighteenth U.S. Regulars carried the national flag pictured above left. In contrast to the other color, the canton of this flag contains five horizontal rows of stars, an indication it was made by Alexander Brandon under contract by the U.S. Quartermaster Department and issued by the New York Quartermaster Depot. The deep blue infantry regimental flag (above right) also conforms to the style issued by the New York Depot. No regimental numeral has been inserted in the scroll beneath the eagle as each regiment was to fill in its number. This flag did see action, and a Confederate sergeant captured it during the Union retreat on the first day of the battle of Stones River.*

regiment of the Irish Brigade—but he had to convince his wife that it was not a position of great danger: "I am sorry that you feel so uneasy about my carrying the flag. But it is not so bad as you think. There is no such thing as taking sure aim on the battlefield. The smoke of powder, the noise of firearms, and cannon, and the excitement of the battlefield makes it impossible so that if the colors are fired at, those on either side of the colors are more likely to get struck than the color bearer." On May 28, 1864, Welch died from wounds suffered during the battles for Spotsylvania Court House, Virginia.

BEFORE MANY flags ever saw battle, they were presented to their regiments in elaborate ceremonies. Entire towns both North and South bade farewell to their soldiers with parades, banquets, and eloquent tributes prior to
WCD the flag presentation. °The ritual was a symbolic farewell ceremony. As the men marched away with their new banner, the sight was often the last glimpse the townspeople would have of their sons and husbands.•

At one such ceremony in April 1861, Idelea Collens presented a regimental flag—proudly sown by the women of New Orleans—to the DeSoto Rifles of Louisiana: "Receive then, from your mothers and sisters, from those whose affections greet you, these colors woven by our feeble but reliant hands; and when this bright flag shall float before you on the battlefield, let it not only inspire you with the brave and patriotic ambition of a soldier aspiring to his own and his country's honor and glory, but also may it be a sign that cherished ones appeal to you to save them from a fanatical and a heartless foe."

The color sergeant accepted the flag and in response addressed first the flag and then his comrades: "May the god of battles look down upon us as we register a soldier's vow that no stain shall ever be found upon thy sacred folds, save the blood of those who attack thee or those who fall in thy defense. Comrades, you have heard the pledge, may it ever guide you on the tented field. In smoke, glare, and din of battle, amidst carnage and death, there let its bright folds inspire you with new strength, nerve your arms and steel your hearts to deeds of strength and valor."

*Regular organizations of the U.S. Army had lineages longer than those of volunteer units, and they often proudly displayed honors from previous wars upon their flags. The red battle flag above, most likely made of silk, was carried by Battery K, First U.S. Artillery and boasts battle honors from its involvement in the Mexican War. The Civil War designations indicate the gunners of Battery K fired at Confederates in many of the major engagements of the eastern theater.*

When he recalled a similar presentation ceremony for the First Tennessee Infantry, Pvt. Sam Watkins wrote: "To hear the young orators tell of how they would protect the flag, and that they would come back with the flag or come back not at all, and if they fell they would fall with their backs to the field and their feet to the foe, would fairly make our hair stand on end with intense patriotism, and we wanted to march right off and whip twenty Yankees."

In the South groups of patriotic women stitched and embroidered flags for their local companies. At first, so many companies were determined to carry their own flags that some newly formed regiments marched off to war with as many as ten distinct flags.

In the North most of the flags presented in these ceremonies were not the handiwork of the women left behind; they were finely crafted banners produced by general contractors, including some as respected as Tiffany and Company in New York City. The women of a town sometimes raised funds to purchase a flag by holding bake sales and quilting bees. In the South, when the supply of silk was exhausted, Chief Quartermaster William L. Cabell substituted cotton and then, in the spring of 1862, wool bunting, most of which had been seized when the Gosport naval facility had fallen into Confederate hands at the beginning of the war.

For the most part, each Federal regiment, following the old British system, carried two flags. One was the Stars and Stripes, and the second was a regimental or state flag. Regimental colors were generally one of two basic patterns. Artillery units were denoted by a yellow flag with two gold crossed cannon in the center. Infantry units carried a dark blue flag with the coat of arms of the United States in the center. Both flags were often edged in yellow silk and bore a red scroll displaying the unit's designation beneath the central emblem.

While it might be expected that there would be several variations of state flags, there were also numerous versions of the Stars and Stripes. The blue area (also called the canton or union) varied from flag to flag. At the time, army regulations required only: "In the upper quarter, next to the staff, in the Union, composed of a number of white stars, equal to the number of States, on a blue field, one-third the length of the flag, extending to the lower edge of the fourth red stripe from the top." °While no pattern had been standardized for the stars, the practice of aligning the stars in rows was traditional for naval banners and had been used to some extent in the army prior to the war, but the design was not mandated by law. Flag manufacturers therefore chose layouts for the stars that best suited their purposes. Some stars might be round, some might have five points and others six.•

The volunteer regiments of the Union states created various flag designs. Some conformed to U.S. Army regulations, others incorporated state motifs, and others combined the two. In addition, the Union army sometimes carried supplemental colors, such as corps flags (a corps might be composed of two divisions, totaling as many as thirty thousand men), guidons (smaller, dovetail flags usually carried by cavalry companies), and

*At the battle of Fredericksburg, a Confederate artilleryman reported that his fieldpieces were so well placed that their fire would cover the area in front of Marye's Heights "as with a fine-tooth comb." He was right. As the men of the Union Ninth Corps struggled forward, cannon shot hammered their ranks and two color bearers of the Twenty-first Massachusetts were shot down. Irish-born Sgt. Thomas Plunkett (below) quickly snatched up the now-frayed banner and moved to the front of his regiment. He held the treasured standard only a short time before he also fell victim to a Southern shell that ripped off both of his forearms. Sergeant Plunkett somehow held on to his flag and prevented it from hitting the ground until another man relieved him of his duty. Plunkett survived, and in 1866 he received the Medal of Honor for his bravery.*

signal flags. Some individual commanders, such as flamboyant George Armstrong Custer, had personal flags designed.

MJM °The fact that Custer had his own guidon conveys more about him than it does the army. His guidon, designed for his cavalry, placed crossed sabers over two colors. Union Gen. Philip H. Sheridan also had his own guidon, which placed general's stars over two colors. Most generals, however, did not go to that extreme. The unpretentious Grant did not have a personal flag.• In fact, after taking command of all Union armies in March 1864, when Grant first entered George Gordon Meade's headquarters at Brandy Station, he looked on Meade's elegant white-and-gold banner, which posed an eagle within a wreath of laurel leaves, turned to the general and asked, "What's this!—Is Imperial Caesar anywhere about here?"

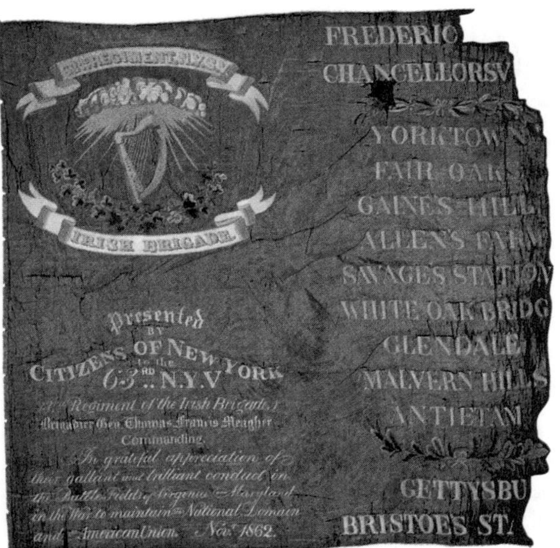


*The Sixty-third New York of the Irish Brigade carried this luxuriant green silken banner. The flag was presented to the regiment as a token of esteem from the "Citizens of New York" just after the battle of Fredericksburg. It bears the Irish symbols of a sunburst and harp over a spray of shamrocks, as well as an inscription in the lower left-hand corner that reads, "In grateful appreciation of their gallant and brilliant conduct on the Battlefields of Virginia and Maryland in the War to maintain the National Domain and the American Union. Nov. 1862." The original battle honors were contained between the wreaths on the standard's right side. The other engagements were added at the top and bottom later.*

Unlike their Union counterparts, Confederate regiments typically carried a single flag, a square battle flag in the East and a rectangular one in the West, but the familiar Rebel battle flag was never the official national flag of the Confederate States. The first flag to represent the seceding Southern states, before the Confederacy had time to design an official flag, was called the Bonnie Blue Flag. A simple blue rectangular flag with a single white star in the center, the flag was first used as a symbol of independence in 1810 when the Republic of West Florida (later parts of Mississippi and Alabama) rebelled against its Spanish rulers. It was revived twenty-five years later when the Republic of Texas was formed.

The Bonnie Blue Flag was displayed again during the Convention of the People of Mississippi on January 9, 1861, as the flag of the Republic of Mississippi. A songwriter, Harry Macarthy, was inspired by the banner to compose a song describing the way in which the South "Was a band of brothers native to the soil, / Fighting for the liberty we gained by honest toil." The lyrics listed all the states of the Confederacy, and the tune became the second most popular song—after "Dixie"—

*Both flags above incorporate the Pennsylvania state seal. The state flag on the left was issued to the Seventeenth Pennsylvania Cavalry at the close of the war. Note that the banner also designates the regiment as the 162d Pennsylvania. All Pennsylvania regiments were given a consecutive line number, while the cavalry and artillery units were additionally numbered by their branch of service. Therefore, the Seventeenth Cavalry was both the 162d regiment overall and the Seventeenth Cavalry unit raised by the Keystone State. The banner on the right belonged to the Eighty-fifth Pennsylvania Infantry; its fine condition makes it doubtful the standard saw much field use. The Eighty-fifth fought in the Peninsula campaign and in bitter, little-known actions in the Carolinas before returning to Virginia for the operations around Petersburg.*

in the South during the war and imbued the banner with a spirit of legitimacy to symbolize secession. Yet the Bonnie Blue Flag was not adopted or even considered as the official Confederate flag, probably because it had meaning only in Texas and along coastal Louisiana, Mississippi, and Alabama.

One of the first acts of the South's provisional congress was to appoint a six-member committee to select a flag for the country with the goal of finalizing the decision by March 4, the day of Abraham Lincoln's inauguration. WCD °Several high-ranking Confederates, including President Jefferson Davis, favored keeping the Stars and Stripes since the flag itself had never offended them. In their view, it was only the Northern stars on the flag that had caused problems for the South. Others, such as William Porcher Miles from South Carolina, maintained that the new country should have a new flag. Miles, who chaired the flag committee, pointed out in his final report to the congress that Liberia and the Sandwich Islands both had flags at that time that were adaptations of the Stars and Stripes:• "We feel no inclination to borrow it second hand, what had been pilfered and appropriated by a free Negro community and a race of savages."

Miles's committee considered several designs, including a design submitted by the chairman incorporating a

Scottish design on the theory that most Southerners had a common Celtic heritage. It featured a blue Saint Andrew's cross (or saltire) edged in white on a red field with a white star representing each Confederate state on the saltire. His design was initially dismissed as "a pair of suspenders."

HMM °Of the remaining designs submitted for consideration, the committee eventually selected the one that was most similar to the Stars and Stripes. On March 4, 1861, the flag known as the Stars and Bars was adopted as the new national flag of the Confederacy.• It consisted of three equal horizontal bars—red, white, red—and a blue canton bearing a circle of five-pointed stars equal to the number of states within the Confederacy. Two men claimed to have designed the flag. Nicola Marschall, a Prussian artist living in Montgomery, Alabama, said that he had based the new banner on the Austrian flag and had offered several variations on canton placement. Orren R. Smith of North Carolina also claimed to have designed the flag, basing it on the trinity of state, church, and press. The three were then bound by the blue canton with the circle of stars depicting mutual defense.

*Color-bearers were not the only soldiers to lose their lives defending the sacred flags of their regiments. During the second day of the battle of Gettysburg, Col. Harrison H. Jeffords's Fourth Michigan Infantry entered the Wheat Field to support fellow regiments. Within moments, attacking Southerners swarmed about the Wolverines, shooting down the color-bearer and capturing the banner. Jeffords, who had pledged in the presence of Michigan's governor to be the "special defender and guardian" of his regiment's flags, rushed with drawn sword into the fray (below). Cutting and slashing his foes, he freed the banner, but while he was doing so, a Confederate soldier bayoneted him through. The desperate remnants of the Fourth managed to retreat with the rescued flag and their gored colonel, but Jeffords soon died.*

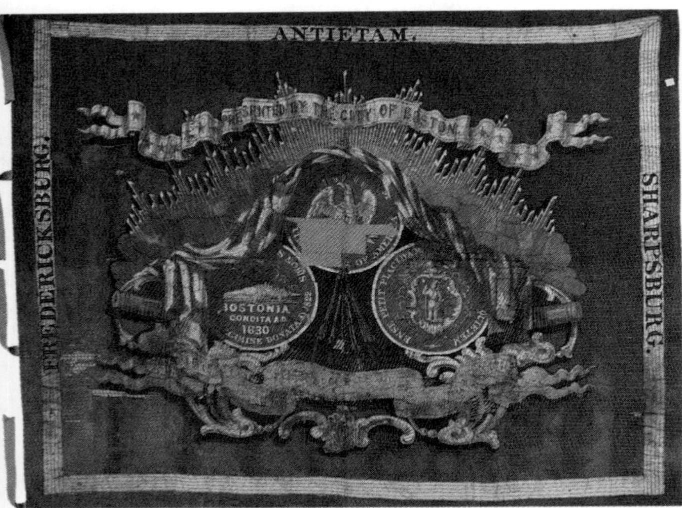


*Perhaps the most famous Union banners were the green regimental flags carried by the infantrymen of the Irish Brigade, a contingent made up of the Sixty-third, Sixty-ninth, and Eighty-eighth New York, Twenty-eighth Massachusetts, and the 116th Pennsylvania. The city of Boston presented the green and gold flag above, covered with the seals of the United States, Massachusetts, and Boston, to the members of the Twenty-eighth Massachusetts, who joined the Irish Brigade in November 1862. This particular flag, presented on May 5, 1864, was the third such color given to the regiment; the others had been shot to tatters in battle. By war's end, the Twenty-eighth had suffered so many casualties it was reorganized as a five-company battalion rather than a full regiment.*

The recommendation of the committee was adopted by the Congress, and a proclamation was passed praising the new banner: "Long may this flag wave over a brave, a free and a virtuous people. And may the career of the Confederacy be such as to endure this to our children as a flag of a just government. The cherished symbol of its cherished truth." When it was first adopted, the stars in the canton numbered seven. Two more were added by the third week of May 1861 with the secession of Virginia and Arkansas. In July two stars were added with the admission of North Carolina and Tennessee to the Confederacy. Eventually a twelfth and thirteenth star were added to represent the Secessionists who left Missouri and Kentucky to fight with the South.

Taken into battle for the first time in July 1861 at First Manassas, the similarity of the Stars and Bars to the Stars and Stripes created deadly problems in the smoke and chaos of combat. HMM °Confusion reigned on both sides. When either flag hung limp, each looked like a mass of red, white, and blue. Innumerable times Northerners and Southerners fired on their own men because they could not distinguish who was who. As a result, the Confederates decided to keep the Stars and Bars as a national flag and to devise a new battle flag.•

In the eastern theater of the war Confederate Gen. P. G. T. Beauregard championed the idea of a distinctive battle flag and chose the design originally submitted by Miles to the provisional congress in March 1861. Beauregard reviewed the matter with Joseph E. Johnston, his departmental commander, and the design was adopted after a decision that the flag would be square rather than rectangular to conserve material. The Saint Andrew's cross design became the standard battle flag used by the Army of Northern Virginia.

During the early years of the war, Confederate flags were not standardized in the western theater. Nevertheless, several flags gained distinction, such as the

*A Federal general wrote that the sergeant chosen to carry a regimental flag should be "selected for his gallantry and military bearing. . . . All the romance and heroism of the regiment center in the color-guard and the emblem with which they are intrusted." At Gettysburg, on July 1, Sgt. Benjamin Crippen of the 143d Pennsylvania Infantry personified this description. When his regiment, fighting in its first battle, began to break in the face of a Confederate onslaught, Crippen stood fast, gripping the national colors with one hand and shaking his fist at his foes with the other. His audacity rallied his fellow Pennsylvanians, but the 143d soon had to withdraw in the face of overwhelming numbers. In the process, Crippen was shot dead, one of forty-two of his regiment killed or mortally wounded that bloody day.*

Army of Tennessee corps flag of Gen. William J. Hardee, which was a blue rectangular flag with a white disk in the center. Lt. Gen. Leonidas Polk chose a red and white Saint George's cross—adapted from the British flag—on a blue field for his corps flag. Maj. Gen. Earl Van Dorn preferred a red rectangular flag bordered in yellow with a white crescent moon in the upper staff corner and thirteen white stars representing the Confederacy and its border states scattered across the field.

Officially, the Confederate War Department never approved a basic battle flag. The matter was left to the discretion of unit commanders. The eastern battle flag migrated into the western theater as eastern commanders were given commands in the West. When Beauregard arrived in the West in early 1862, he found that Polk's, Hardee's, and Van Dorn's troops were determined to keep their distinctive banners. Only Braxton Bragg's army, from the Southern coastal regions, had no banner of its own, and it was issued battle flags patterned after the Army of Northern Virginia.

Even the Native American tribes who fought for the Confederacy had their own flags. The Cherokees used an adaptation of the Stars and Bars with the addition of five red stars in the blue canton to represent the five Cherokee tribes fighting for the Confederacy. The Choctaws used a blue flag with a circle in the center, and inside the circle were a tomahawk, a bow, and crossed arrows.

*The laurel-wreath pattern shown in these flags proved to be popular with many artillery units. At top is the banner of Battery L, First U.S. Artillery; at bottom is the banner of Batteries B and L, Second U.S. Artillery. The flags are scarlet with the crossed cannons and lettering embroidered in yellow.*

When Johnston took command of the Army of Tennessee during the winter of 1863–64, he dictated the adoption of his version of the battle flag of the Army of Northern Virginia, which was rectangular and borderless. Only the men of Patrick Cleburne's division refused to accept Johnston's battle flag. They had always carried Hardee's blue flag, and they were allowed to retain their longtime banner.

HMM °Meanwhile, in May 1863, after two years' debate in the Confederate Congress, the Stars and Bars was replaced with a new flag, called the Stainless Banner. The new flag adopted the battle flag in the upper staff corner against a white field.• Unofficially, it was called the Jackson Flag since it debuted draped over the coffin of Lt. Gen. Thomas J. "Stonewall" Jackson in May 1863.

The new flag, also called the Second National Flag, was supposed to fly only over Confederate camps and was not a replacement for the battle flag. Even so, it HMM still caused problems. °When it hung limp, the battle-flag canton was obscured and it looked like a white flag of surrender or truce. Notwithstanding this confusion, the Confederacy used this flag until March 1865 when a red bar was added to the outside edge (or fly) of the banner. This last flag, introduced just one month before the surrender at Appomattox, was called the Third National Flag.•

During the war regiments both North and South decorated their flags with battle honors—listing the engagements in which the unit had participated. Union regiments tended to paint these battle honors on the stripes of the American flag; Confederates itemized them in the four areas created by the Saint Andrew's cross.

The devastation of war also showed itself in these flags. Tattered by bullets and torn by shells, these banners were tangible displays of the bravery of the men MJM who carried them. °If a flag were clean and lacked any holes, it had never been in danger. The more holes in the flag, the more battle scars, the braver the regiment was and the men in it.•

"Torn, riddled, or bloody as the old rag may be, to the soldier it is all the more beautiful in its tatters," wrote Union Lt. Robert S. Robertson. "For it is the emblem of all he loves with a love that impels him to die if need be for the object of his love." After the battle of Chickamauga, officers of the Twenty-eighth Tennessee noted that their flag was "riddled with bullets, being pierced not less than 30 times." At the same time, the battle flag of Hilliard's Alabama Legion had "the marks of over 80 bullets" and its bearer had been "thrice wounded and the flagstaff thrice shot away."

*Veterans of the Irish Brigade's Sixty-third, Sixty-ninth, and Eighty-eighth New York Infantry sail into New York Harbor in 1865, a scene captured in this 1869 oil painting by Thomas W. Wood. Just a few years earlier, these soldiers had marched out of New York to fight for the Union, their crisp, new flags brightening the cityscape and exciting cheering crowds. Now, as the handful of survivors prepare to disembark, the color guard holds aloft their war-weary, tattered flags, their evocative symbols of victory.*

FLAGS THEMSELVES may have been simple pieces of cloth, but within that cloth was an incredible power to rally the wounded to press on, to inspire the timid to bravery, and to bring the hard hearted to tears. Nowhere was this power better demonstrated than on July 1 at Gettysburg, Pennsylvania, along McPherson's Ridge.

Robert E. Lee's army was on the offensive, and the Twenty-sixth North Carolina was poised to enter the battle, following twenty-one-year-old Col. Henry King BP Burgwyn Jr. °He was the youngest regimental commander in the Army of Northern Virginia, a very proud young man who had not seen a great deal of combat. Thus he was eager to prove himself as well as his regiment.• The nine hundred men of the Twenty-sixth North Carolina had crossed Willoughby Run and started up a slope when they ran into the five hundred men of the Twenty-fourth Michigan of the famed Iron Brigade, a battle-toughened unit made up of midwestern farmers.

DT °As the Twenty-sixth advanced, color-bearer after color-bearer was shot down until the regiment's entire color guard was wiped out.• "At this time the colors

*"Hurrah! Hurrah! For Southern Rights; Hurrah! Hurrah for the Bonnie Blue Flag that bears a single star!" So went a portion of the lyrics celebrating the first banner to represent portions of the fledgling Confederate nation (above left). Inspired by the flag of the former Lone Star Republic of Texas, the Bonnie Blue was adopted by several Deep South states upon their secession. The First National Flag (above right), however, was the first standard formally adopted by the Confederate States of America. Although national flags were designed to be flown over government buildings or garrisons, Confederate troops also carried this banner, often called the Stars and Bars, into the opening engagements of the Civil War. This flag was generally replaced in battle when it was found that it too closely resembled the U.S. flag.*

had been cut down ten times," recalled Lt. Col. John R. Lane. "We have now struck the second line of the enemy where the fighting is fierce as the killing deadly. Captain McCreary seizes the following flag, waves it aloft and advancing to the front is shot through the heart and falls bathed in the flag at his last breath. Lieutenant George Wilcox now rushes forward and pulling the flag from under the dead hero advances with it a few steps. He also falls with two wounds in his body. The line hesitates. The crisis is reached. The colors must advance."

DT °Burgwyn himself rushed over, seized the flag, pointed his sword at the opposing Union line, and urged his regiment forward, but he was shot through the lungs before he could take a step. The boy colonel spun and fell with the flag wrapped around his body, staining it with his blood. Before the day ended, the Twenty-sixth lost thirteen color-bearers in the fight with the Michiganders at Willoughby's Run.• The North Carolina regiment took 895 men into the battle of Gettysburg; 697 were casualties after this fight.

For two hours after the assault, Burgwyn lay dying until he uttered his final words. "I know my gallant regiment will do their duty. Where's my sword?" he whispered. His men buried him in a gun case on the field until his body could be recovered for later burial in Raleigh. The loss of the Tar Heel regiment in this battle

was one of the highest regimental losses of the entire war, but the Michiganders also suffered grievous losses.

BP °The color guard of the Twenty-fourth Michigan was similarly slaughtered, losing nine color-bearers in the fight. Their flag took twenty-three bullets, but as was the case with the North Carolinians, the banner was borne safely off the field.•

During the first day at Gettysburg there were numerous desperate struggles for the colors of opposing regiments. The Sixth Wisconsin, another unit of the Iron Brigade, counterattacked the Second Mississippi. The Wisconsin regiment suffered heavy casualties, losing 175 men to gain just 130 yards of ground.

DT °The Mississippi troops occupied an unfinished railroad bed that had been excavated from the side of a hill and concentrated their fire on the attacking Wisconsin soldiers. The color-bearer of the Second Mississippi, Sgt. W. B. Murphy, waved the Confederate battle flag defiantly from the rim of the railroad cut. Soldier after soldier of the Sixth Wisconsin tried to get the Southern banner but was shot down.• Murphy recalled: "My color guards were all killed and wounded in less than five minutes and also my colors were shot more than one dozen times. They still kept rushing for my flag and there over a dozen men [were] shot down like sheep in their mad rush for the colors. It was one of the most deadly struggles that was ever witnessed during any battle of the war."

*By the second year of the war, the Confederate government recognized the needed to replace the Stars and Bars with a flag more distinctive to the Rebel cause. In May 1863 the Second National Flag (above left) was put into use. Nicknamed the "Stainless Banner," it incorporated the Saint Andrew's Cross of the battle flag as its canton, with a body of white cloth. This design also proved problematical, for without a breeze to expose the canton, the Second National often resembled a flag of surrender or became invisible against the smoke of battle. To rectify this problem, a red band was added to the fly edge to create the Third National Flag (above right). However, it was not formally adopted until March 1865, and saw relatively little use.*

*Early in the conflict, Confederate Gen. William J. Hardee developed the "Hardee," or "full moon," flag that was carried by some elements of the Army of Tennessee, a white disk on a white-bordered blue background. In the spring of 1864, Gen. Patrick Cleburne's soldiers vigorously protested the order they received to replace this flag with a version of the Confederate battle flag, and they were allowed to continue to fly the Hardee flag—the only Confederate troops permitted to do so. The decision was a wise one, for Cleburne's division, already considered by many to be the best warriors in the Army of Tennessee, seemed to acquire an even more enthusiastic spirit while fighting under their unique banner. "The Yanks was all afraid of the blue flag division," boasted one of Cleburne's infantrymen.*

DT °At that point Cpl. Francis Waller of the Sixth Wisconsin rushed Murphy. In a hand-to-hand struggle, Waller wrested the flag from the Confederate while the rest of the Iron Brigade unit poured into the railroad cut. Enough Federals surrounded the position to annihilate the Mississippians, but instead the Northerners called for the Southerners to drop their weapons and surrender. More than one thousand Rebels complied.• Corporal Waller was awarded the Medal of Honor for his bravery.

On the second day at Gettysburg, July 2, 1863, the area known as the Wheat Field earned the nickname the "Whirlpool of Death," because BP °no part of the battlefield was more contested. The line swayed back and forth across the trampled wheat. A brigade of Georgians and a brigade of South Carolinians came charging in on troops from the Union Fifth Corps. One Union regiment, the Fourth Michigan, was cut off and surrounded. Its flag-bearer fell. The Confederates rushed forward, and a Georgian seized the banner. Seeing the Confederate with the banner, the commander of the Fourth Michigan, Col. Harrison Jeffords, rushed forward with his sword in his hand. He struck down the Southerner and seized the flag, but no sooner had he recovered the flag than he was run through with a bayonet and killed by a charging Confederate. Jeffords's Michiganders were reinforced by another division, counterattacked, and retrieved their banner.• Jeffords was the only regimental commander killed by a bayonet during the war.

The Twenty-sixth North Carolina rested on the second day at Gettysburg, but on the third it marched all the way to the stone wall during Pickett's Charge. There their flag was captured after almost all of the color guard were killed. The Twenty-sixth marched to Gettysburg as the largest regiment in Lee's army and departed Pennsylvania with fewer than ninety men. The flag lost inside the Federal wall was difficult to identify.

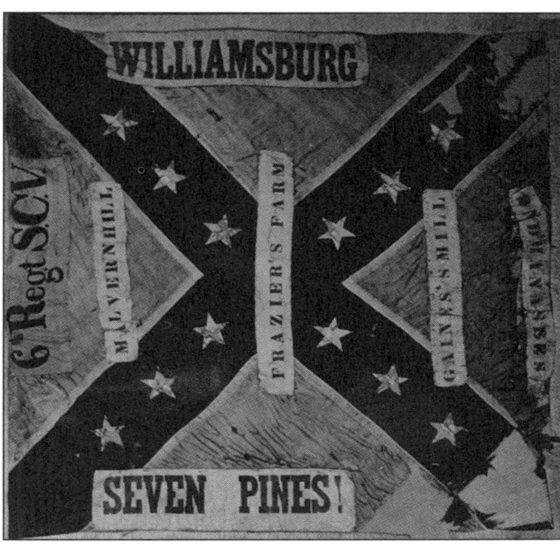


It had been recently issued, and no one had had time to sew "26 N.C." above and below the center star as was the custom among Confederate regiments.

SH °ETHNIC GROUPS within the Union army formed their own regiments either purposely or by law, and these units often carried flags that reflected their origin.•
MJM One of the more colorful regiments, °the Thirty-ninth New York, called the Garibaldi Guard, was an amalgam of many nationalities from New York City. The unit carried three colors: the Stars and Stripes; an Italian green-white-and-red flag that allegedly had been carried by Giuseppe Garibaldi during his campaign to unify Italy as a single nation-state; and a Hungarian flag inscribed "Victory or Death."•

Perhaps the most flamboyant colors carried by any ethnic regiment were those of the Irish Brigade, composed of emigrants from the Emerald Isle who had settled in Boston, New York City, and Philadelphia.
SH °Virtually all Irish regiments carried Irish flags, made of silk at great expense and using the traditional Irish symbols of a harp, a shamrock, and often a cloud with a sunburst. Given the restriction of carrying only two flags per regiment, when the troops had to choose between

*Still a powerful icon of the Confederacy is the battle flag of the Army of Northern Virginia (above). The design—incorporating a blue Saint Andrew's cross edged in white on a red field with a white star for each state—had been originally submitted for the national flag of the new country. Its design was dismissed as looking like "a pair of suspenders." Wishing a distinctive battle flag, Gen. P. G. T. Beauregard chose the design but made the flag square instead of rectangular to conserve cloth. The Confederate War Department never approved an official battle flag, leaving choices to unit commanders. In 1862 Beauregard brought his flag to the western theater but found that Hardee's, Van Dorn's, and Polk's troops wanted to keep their own flags. Only Braxton Bragg's army had no banner and so it was issued battle flags patterned after that of the Army of Northern Virginia. Polk's flag (left) had a red Saint George's cross—adapted from the English flag—on a blue field.*

*Maj. Gen. Earl Van Dorn chose as his battle flag this red rectangular flag bordered in yellow with a white crescent moon in the upper staff corner and thirteen white stars representing the Confederacy and its border states scattered across the field.*

carrying a national flag and a state flag or a national flag and an Irish flag, the state flag was usually sent home.•

At Fredericksburg, Virginia, on December 13, 1862, only one Irish banner—that of the Twenty-eighth Massachusetts—was carried into the field against an impenetrable Confederate position on the heights overlooking the town. The rest of the regimental flags had been torn to shreds during previous engagements, and new flags were en route. As the men marched through the town, many placed sprigs of green boxwood in their caps to remind them of their heritage. They charged the Southern position along the stone wall at the base of the heights, shouting the Gaelic battle cry "Faugh a Ballagh" ("Clear the Way").

The Irishmen charged toward the center of the Southern line, and despite the murderous fire unleashed by the Rebel defenders, the line of the Irish Brigade never wavered. The Confederate commanders were impressed by the sight. James Longstreet called the assault, "the handsomest thing in the whole war"; Lee commented, "Never were men more brave."

Thomas F. Galwey, a Union officer, wrote: "In glorious style their green sunbursts waving, every man has a sprig of green in his cap, and a half-laughing, half-murderous look in his eye. They reach a point within a stone's throw of the stone wall. They try to go beyond but are slaughtered. Nothing could advance further, and live."

DT °Of the brigade's 1,300 men, only 280 emerged unscathed. One company had only 3 survivors. After the fight, patrols for the dead and wounded also looked for the missing Stars and Stripes of the Sixty-ninth New York. The Irishmen feared it had been captured, which would dishonor the regiment. The patrol finally found the regiment's color sergeant dead and sitting propped up against a tree with his arms clasped across his chest. When they moved his body they found he had stuffed the battle flag under his coat. There was a bullet hole through his coat and the flag; he had died saving the colors.•

The bravery of such men inspired even the Confederates who had been forced to shoot them down. George Pickett observed: "Our hearts almost stood still as we watched those sons of Erin fearlessly rush to their deaths. The brilliant assault . . . was beyond description. . . . We forgot they were fighting us, and cheer after cheer at their fearlessness went up along our lines."

*Although his identity is lost to history, the proud countenance of this color sergeant of the 108th U. S. Colored Infantry indicates the dedication of African-American troops to the Northern cause. Black flag bearers, such as the one above, carried their banners toward the Rebel battle lines at numerous engagements, risking their lives for the honor of carrying the symbols of freedom and respect. In 1900 Sgt. William Carney of the Fifty-fourth Massachusetts became the first black soldier to be awarded the Medal of Honor for picking up the Fifty-fourth's flag after the regiment's color sergeant fell during the attack on Fort Wagner.*

Ethnic units like the Irish Brigade were segregated by choice; however, in the last two years of the war there were nearly two hundred thousand African-American soldiers in the Union army whose regiments were segregated by law. Eventually these black soldiers were organized into 166 regiments: 145 infantry, 7 cavalry, 12
SH heavy artillery, 1 field artillery, and 1 engineer. °When the first black regiments were mustered into service in 1863, it was understood that they would be separated from the white soldiers. Beginning in 1864, when African Americans volunteered in great numbers, they were mustered directly into the U.S. Army rather than into state regiments. The black regiments were not issued flags that distinguished them as such, but special flags were often presented to them.

A series of seven Pennsylvania regimental flags was created by David Bustill Bowser, a black artist in Philadelphia, who decorated them with allegorical scenes from the black experience and a motto on one side and the unit designation on the reverse. The flag of the 3d Pennsylvania U.S. Colored Troops (USCT) showed Columbia, the personification of liberty, presenting a flag to a black soldier with the motto "Rather

*Banners of the U. S. Colored Troops (USCT) often contained inspirational inscriptions and images. Those shown on these two pages belonged to regiments raised in Pennsylvania. The motto (top left) "Sic Semper Tyrannis"—"Thus Always to Tyrants"—was intentional irony, as it was also the state motto of Virginia. Other inspira-*

Die Freemen than Live to Be Slaves." The banner of the 6th Pennsylvania USCT showed Columbia speaking to a black soldier while a black girl applauds in the background with the motto "Freedom for All." The standard for the 22d Pennsylvania USCT showed a black soldier bayoneting a Rebel corporal with the motto "Sic Semper Tyrannis" (Thus Always to Tyrants—the motto of Virginia). The regimental colors for the 24th Pennsylvania USCT showed a black soldier on a hilltop receiving emancipation from God with the motto "Let Soldiers in War be Citizens in Peace." The flag of the 25th Pennsylvania USCT showed a slave receiving a rifle from the hand of Columbia with the motto "Strike for God and Liberty." The banner for the 45th Pennsylvania USCT showed a black soldier holding a U.S. flag and leaning in front of a bust of George Washington with the motto "One Cause, One Country." The regimental colors for the 127th Pennsylvania USCT showed a black soldier waving good-bye to Columbia with the motto "We Will Prove Ourselves Men."•

Twenty-nine black soldiers and sailors received the Medal of Honor during the Civil War, many of those for bravery related to the flag. They included heroes like Sgt. Major Christian Fleetwood and Sgt. William Carney of the Fifty-fourth Massachusetts who took to heart the admonition of Massachusetts Gov. John J. Andrew: "Hold on to the staff. If every thread is blown away your glory will be the same. Take this, sir, in behalf of the colored ladies of Boston and the Commonwealth, for the Fifty-fourth regiment Massachusetts volunteers. May you and your men prove that this emblem was never carried by worthier hands."

THE SOLDIERS of the nineteenth century demonstrated absolute loyalty to and devotion for their flags, be they Confederate battle flags or the Stars and Stripes. They carried their flags into the jaws of death, knowing that they would die. They wanted the responsibility and the honor of carrying their flag as far as they could get before they were struck down.

At the June 27, 1862, battle of Gaines's Mill, Virginia, Confederate Color Sgt. Jimmy Taylor had just celebrated his sixteenth birthday. His commander told the youngster he was not required to carry the flag into battle, but Taylor gallantly replied, "Sir, you gave the colors to me, I shall bear them." Taylor was shot once and continued forward. He was struck a second time and continued to advance. Finally, a third bullet hit him and he said: "I can go no further. I must give up my flag."

*tional phrases shown were: "We Want to Prove Ourselves Men" (over Columbia presenting a flag, bottom left); "Let Soldiers in War Be Citizens in Peace" (top right);and "Rather Die Freemen, Than Live to Be Slaves" (bottom right). All the regiments represented on these two pages were raised in Pennsylvania.*

It was also at the battle of Gaines's Mill that the colorful Fifth New York Zouaves, carrying both the Stars and Stripes and a flag presented to them by the City of New York, displayed outstanding gallantry in following their color bearers into the face of the Confederates, recounted elsewhere on pages 160–163 At Fredericksburg, another Zouave unit, the 114th Pennsylvania, rallied after their flag was taken up by their commander, Col. Charles Collis. When he saw the flag go down, Collis, an Irish-born lawyer, spurred his horse forward and seized it. Raising the flag over his head, he urged his Zouaves to counterattack and saved a Union artillery battery that was about to be captured. For his actions, Collis received the Medal of Honor.

In fact, during the war more than half the Medals of Honor awarded in the Union army were for bravery related to the flag. Southerners did not have an equiva-

*David Bustill Bowser, who lived in Philadelphia from 1820 to 1900, was a painter of emblems and banners for fireman's companies and fraternal organizations. He painted all of the banners of the U.S. Colored Troops pictured on pages 346 and 347. Bowser also painted landscapes, which the* New York Herald *called "excellent," and portraits, including several of Abraham Lincoln. Bowser's descendants are said to possess an uncashed check made out to the artist from Lincoln himself.*

lent medal, but their stories of saving their flag or capturing the enemy's flag were as numerous.

BP °In the course of the four years of war, the regiments, both Union and Confederate, had come to vest their respective flags with meanings that went far beyond the mere object. The flag represented the regiment. It represented their cause. Above all, the flags represented their comrades who had fallen trying to carry those flags into victory and those who had fallen trying to follow the flags.•

On April 12, 1865, at Appomattox Court House, Confederate troops reluctantly surrendered their weapons, their equipment, and their flags. Joshua Lawrence Chamberlain observed the reverence with which the Confederates furled their flags for the last time: "The emotion of the conquered soldiery was really sad to witness. Some of the men who had carried and followed those ragged standards through the four long years of strife, rushed, regardless of all discipline from their ranks, bent about their old flags, and pressed them to their lips." The Southerners relinquished seventy-one unit flags that day.

Not every flag was given up, however. Rather than surrender the flag of the Twenty-first Virginia, John H. Cumbia, the unit's longtime color-bearer, tore it from its staff, cut the flag into pieces, and gave them to the members of the regiment.

The captured Confederate flags were kept in the War Department. In 1868 they were identified and cataloged, and between 1874 and 1882 they were exhibited in the Washington Ordnance Museum, after which they were placed in storage. In 1888 President Grover Cleveland proposed to return the flags to the South, but the wounds of war were still sensitive, and Union veterans groups protested. Lucius Fairchild, a former colonel of the Second Wisconsin, condemned the plan, saying: "May God palsy the hand that wrote that order. May God palsy the brain that conceived it, and may God palsy the tongue that dictated it."

HMM °When the furor abated, the government decided not to return the flags. Seventeen years later, during Theodore Roosevelt's administration, Congress passed a resolution allowing all flags that could be identified to be returned to those southern states from which the units had originated.• Those which remained unidentified were given to the Confederate Memorial Literary Society in Richmond.

*On a cold winter day in 1863, Rebel soldiers of the Eighth Georgia gather about their regiment's battle flag as an infantryman paints "Fredericksburg" on it. Perhaps they are thinking of friends dead or mangled in combat or perhaps they are longing for home, safety, and comfort, and to stand once again on the red clay soil of the Peach State. The flag before them embodies both such sentiments. It is a physical affirmation of the sacrifices they have made and the ideals that keep them in combat. Soon, they will join the marching column in the background to fight with the Army of Northern Virginia.*

The flags of the Union army were retired in glory at war's end. After the Washington Review parade in May 1865, units were mustered out of the service, and the War Department allowed each regimental flag to return to the state from which the regiment was formed. Several states conducted formal ceremonies during which the banners were deposited in the capitols. There they were preserved by many veterans who had protected them with their lives and knew every tatter, rip, and bullet hole.

"The sentiment of the old soldier for the flag cannot be described," said Isaac H. Elliot of the Thirty-third Illinois. "In battle it is the symbol of courage and honor of those who follow it. The soldier will desert the wounded and die in combat to go with it to certain death. And there it will be passed from one dying grasp to another, and then another, and still another as long as a single thread of silk remains, or until the last drop of blood has been spilled. It is to him the glory and majesty of his country. It is the emblem of his native land."

In his poem "Those Rebel Flags," John Howard Jewett wrote: "Call it sentiment, call it misguided / To fight to death for a rag. / Yet trailed in the dust, derided, / The true soldier loves his flag." Today these flags, some nearly rags, are the only remaining witnesses to the momentous days of the Civil War. In them are forever woven the passions of victory and the pain of death.

# ARTILLERY

The HIGH CASUALTIES INCURRED during the Civil War were directly attributable to improving technologies that increased the effectiveness of many weapons, particularly artillery, while battlefield tactics remained unchanged. In supporting an attack, enhanced cannon fired an assortment of projectiles into fortified positions and enemy formations. On the defensive, updated artillery blasted oncoming infantry like oversized shotguns. Large-bore guns roared and their shells whistled and screamed through the air, terrifying soldiers long after the discharged rounds had passed. No other weapons of the war spoke with the fury of artillery.

"There is one thing that our government does that suits me to a dot," said one Union soldier in a letter to his mother in 1863. "That is, we fight mostly with artillery. The rebels fight mostly with infantry. They fight as though a man's life was not worth one cent or, in other words, with desperation."

Only about 6 percent of the soldiers in the Civil War were enrolled in the artillery branches of the two armies, but artillery played a pivotal role in almost every engagement of the war. From the massed Union batteries on Malvern Hill to the intrepid display of flying batteries at Fredericksburg to the devastating artillery duel at Gettysburg, the heavy weapons were always a factor and often decisive. Union Gen. William Tecumseh Sherman once observed, "A battery of field artillery is worth a thousand muskets."

| | |
|---|---|
| **TGC** | Thomas G. Clemens |
| **WCD** | William C. Davis |
| **GWG** | Gary W. Gallagher |
| **BP** | Brian Pohanka |
| **CWS** | Charles W. Smithgall |

*Federal artillery dominated the outcome of the July 1, 1862, battle of Malvern Hill, the final engagement of the Seven Days' battles. Yankee gunners, like this crew sketched by Alfred Waud in the act of firing a Parrott rifle, shredded the attacking Southern infantry. Union shells also blanketed the Confederates' batteries, preventing them from effectively returning fire. Robert Stiles, a member of the Richmond Howitzers, later wrote, "McClellan's majestic aggregation of batteries" unleashed a "storm of projectiles and [an] overwhelming cataclysm of destruction." Within moments, wrote Stiles, his battery's guns had been "crushed, smashed, and splintered" beyond use, and the gray-clad artillerymen were forced to abandon their positions.*

According to Col. Charles Wainwright, chief of artillery of the Union First and Fifth Corps, most battles followed the same pattern of attack: Confederate infantry attacked Union infantry, advancing over grasslands and woods, until the Federal artillery maneuvered into position and began to shell the Rebel force, disrupting their charge. When Yankee field commanders massed their artillery in the right place at the right time, the effect was devastating. There is no greater illustration of this than the performance of the Union batteries on July 1, 1862, at Malvern Hill.

George B. McClellan and his army were within sight of the spires of Richmond when a brilliant series of counterattacks by Robert E. Lee's reorganized Army of Northern Virginia thwarted the Yankee advance. McClellan ordered his battered army to retreat, and only one thing kept the Confederate commander from wiping out the entire Union force—Col. Henry Hunt and the artillery of McClellan's rear guard.

A native of Michigan and an 1839 graduate of West Point, Hunt was considered the foremost expert on light artillery tactics at the beginning of the Civil War. During the Mexican War he had learned the value of maneuvering his batteries on the battlefield for maximum effect. More recently Hunt had been one of the few bright spots among the Union commanders at First Bull Run when he used his guns to turn back a Confederate assault on the collapsing left flank of the Union line. BP °He recognized the value of artillery on the battlefield and knew that the concentrated firepower of well-trained gunners could turn the tide of battle.•

While Lee was harassing the retreating Union army, the Federals took up defensive positions at Malvern Hill, a 150-foot slope with deep ravines and swamps on its flanks and an open field of fire to its front. Hunt ordered his battery commanders to rim the slope with 100 guns in front and another 150 in reserve and on the flanks, placing the weapons wheel to wheel so his gunners could command the approaches and the surrounding terrain with concentrated fire.

*Known for his skill in handling cannon during the Mexican War, Henry J. Hunt (above) was responsible for the masterful deployment of the Union artillery at Malvern Hill. By the battle of Antietam, he was a brigadier general and chief of artillery of the Army of the Potomac. In this capacity Hunt distinguished himself in many later engagements.*

*The artillerymen of the First Massachusetts Battery (below), posing with their bird mascot perched on a sponge-staff, typified the cocky, well-equipped, and well-trained soldiers Hunt commanded.*

Five Confederate divisions positioned themselves along the Federals' front, with two more in reserve. James Longstreet proposed that Southern artillery be placed on the hills across from the Federal positions so their fire would disrupt the Yankee artillery long enough for the Rebels to assault. Lee approved and ordered the bombardment to precede the attack, but many of his cannon became bogged down in mud and in the surrounding woods. When the attack began at 1 P.M., most of the Rebel batteries were out of position, and only a handful of brave cannoneers opened fire on the Federal artillery.

TGC °The Confederate guns were committed piecemeal, one at a time, allowing the Union artillery to concentrate all of its fire on four or six guns at a time and knock them out of action. As soon as another Southern battery opened up, the Yankee gunners shifted their sights to that battery and rendered it useless.• For more than two hours the Federal batteries systematically cleared the field of Rebel artillery.

BP °Despite the terrible rain of shells from Malvern Hill, one intrepid Confederate captain, William Johnson Pegram,

*The Tredegar Iron Works, on the bank of the James River in Richmond, produced the majority of the Confederacy's Southern-made artillery pieces. Joseph Reid Anderson, Tredegar's superintendent and an 1836 graduate of West Point, and his work force of whites, free blacks, and slaves turned out bronze and iron smoothbores and rifles despite being plagued by scanty stocks of raw materials and transportation problems. Foundries in Tennessee, Georgia, Louisiana, Alabama, Mississippi, and South Carolina also made guns for the Rebel cause. The South's armies, however, always had to rely in part on using captured Federal artillery pieces and ammunition to resupply their war-torn batteries.*

positioned his guns as close as he could to the Union batteries and opened fire.• At twenty-one Pegram was one of Lee's youngest battery commanders. °He was short, extremely nearsighted, and wore very thick glasses. The enlisted men who served under him said that he was so nearsighted he never engaged the enemy until they were within his eyesight, and his eyesight was so bad he could see no more than a few hundred yards.•

°While Pegram lacked the dash and swagger of most officers, there was no better battery commander in Lee's army. He possessed those qualities that officers need to command: a will of iron, devotion to his cause, and the ability to inspire men. He used all of these skills to hold his gunners to their task at Malvern Hill. Five of his six guns were destroyed by Federal artillery fire. Nevertheless, with his only remaining gun, Pegram continued to fire into the Union line while his men were shot down around him.

The Yankee artillery commanded the field, but Lee was committed and ordered a frontal assault. "As each brigade emerged from the woods, from fifty to one hundred guns opened upon it, tearing great gaps in its ranks," Confederate Gen. D. H. Hill recalled. "But the heroes reeled on and were shot down by the reserves of the guns. Most of them had an open field half a mile wide to cross under fire of field artillery. It was not war, it was murder."

Hunt held his position on Malvern Hill despite having three horses shot from under him. One of his sections exhausted its ammunition, so the crews cut the harnesses and chains from the horses used to haul the cannon and fired them at the enemy. Darkness finally ended the attack. Pegram and the surviving Confederate artillerists pulled their remaining guns from the field and retreated with Lee's army.

Lee lost more than five thousand men at Malvern Hill, more than half of whom were victims of artillery fire. McClellan suffered three thousand casualties. °The

*Unlike the agricultural South, the North's industrial infrastructure was well established in 1861 and capable of the quick growth and rapid production necessary to supply the needs of war. The West Point Foundry at Cold Spring, New York (left), produced the Parrott gun, one of the most widely used rifled cannon in the Civil War. It was invented by Robert P. Parrott, a graduate of the U.S. Military Academy, who resigned his commission in 1836 to become superintendent of the private firm. During the war the foundry made 10-, 20-, and 30-pounders and reached a weekly production of twenty-five guns and seven thousand projectiles. By war's end it had produced more than seventeen hundred Parrott guns and 3 million projectiles. In 1862 Abraham Lincoln visited the foundry and called it, "A wonderful place!" The 1866 painting by John Ferguson Weir, called* The Gun Foundry *(left), depicts workers at the pouring pit, where molten iron ore was poured into the cannon mold. One writer of the time said of this painting, "We know of no picture which so deftly celebrates our industrial economy."*

Union artillery's performance saved McClellan's army on the battlefield. Hunt, by massing his guns, held off the Confederates long enough for the infantry to continue its retreat.•

FROM THE beginning of the war, the Federal artillery was the Union army's most powerful asset. Southern infantry was at least on equal terms with its Northern counterpart, and the Confederate cavalry exploited a two-year period of marked superiority over the awkward Yankee horse soldiers, but Rebel artillery remained outtrained, outgunned, and outmaneuvered throughout the war. The superiority of the Federal artillery was a legacy of the small but well-trained regular army artillery that had its roots in the West Point curriculum which exposed every cadet to the science of artillery. This elite group was the foundation of the Union artillery during the war and provided expert guidance in gunnery and battlefield tactics.

The power of Yankee artillery was also rooted in the industrial strength of the North, which had numerous machine shops and foundries that could manufacture

*Both sides used large cannon capable of firing shells 30-pounds or heavier to defend forts and cities. The Confederate guns pictured above appear to be 32-pounders and are part of a water battery—a stronghold positioned to fire on hostile ships—protecting Pensacola Bay, Florida. The large wheels on the cannon carriages made it easier for the gunners to move the heavy weapons forward to their firing positions. Two soldiers were needed to ram and swab the large barrels of garrison artillery pieces.*

cannon. When the war broke out, these foundries worked around the clock to produce 3-inch ordnance rifles and 12-pounder smoothbore Napoleons.

TGC °Made of iron and therefore cheaper than most artillery pieces, more than one thousand 3-inch rifles were cast during the war, giving the Union army a reliable, deadly accurate weapon.• One Southerner said that the 3-inch rifle was "a dead shot at any distance under a mile" and that Yankee gunners "could hit the end of a flour barrel more often than miss."

The most effective piece of the war TGC made by Northern foundries, however, was °the bronze 1857 light 12-pounder howitzer named after Napoleon III, who had helped develop the design for the French army. The Napoleon was the apogee of smoothbore cannon.• Smoothbores fired heavy projectiles and were the primary defensive and close-range weapon in the Union arsenal. They were called 12-pounders because the ammunition they fired weighed approximately twelve pounds. The Napoleon's barrel, commonly called the tube, weighed 1,227 pounds, about 500 pounds less than other 12-pounders of the day.

These 12-pounders were effective on the battlefield because they were mobile. The Napoleon was hitched to a limber—a two-wheeled wagon that carried ammunition—and pulled by a team of four or six horses with two men riding two of the horses to control the team. Once the gun crew arrived at its position, they would unhitch the gun, pull the limber a safe distance away from the line, unhitch it, and then move the horses to safety.

Napoleons fired a variety of ammunition: solid shot, CWS spherical case, or canister. °Solid shot was used for long-range shelling or for its smashing power. If enemy troops were sheltered in heavy woods, cannoneers used solid shot to splinter the trees. The rounds might not hit any soldiers, but the trees shattering overhead would terrify whatever troops were below them.•

When firing on soldiers in the open, gunners might use spherical case. Invented by Henry Shrapnel, an Englishman, this shell was a hollow sphere filled with musket balls. It was designed so that the friction of the shell traveling through the tube as it was being fired would ignite a fuse in the shell. The shell would explode over the heads of infantry, showering the soldiers with the musket balls and broken pieces of the shell.

A detail of the Seventeenth New York Infantry stands proudly beside a 6-pounder Confederate cannon and limber which they captured at the battle of Hanover Court House in May 1862. Capturing a fieldpiece was nearly as desirable an honor as taking an enemy's flag. Although 6-pounders saw a good deal of action in many of the battles during 1861 and 1862, artillerymen soon found that these relatively small guns were overpowered by more advanced smoothbores and rifles. Both Northern and Southern armies replaced 6-pounders with heavier guns as soon as possible. Only one 6-pounder, for example, is recorded to have taken part in the battle of Gettysburg. It belonged to a North Carolina battery in the Army of Northern Virginia.

To stop infantry at close range, gunners used canister, CWS °the most devastating antipersonnel ammunition of the war. Canisters were made of tin cans containing several stacked rows of twenty-seven round balls that were one and one half inches in diameter. Such canister rounds transformed cannon into giant shotguns.• It was fired as a last recourse to prevent an enemy from overrunning a cannon's position. At very close range, cannoneers loaded double canister—two canisters rammed together down the barrel on top of a strong charge of black powder. Double canister devastated entire ranks of men.

Early in the war, weapons makers experimented with rifled cannon. The technology had been developed decades earlier with muskets. Smoothbore cannon, like smoothbore muskets, could fire their shells only as far as the power charge allowed. As soon as the round was fired, it began to lose momentum and direction. Cannoneers could aim smoothbores generally, but their range was limited and could be shortened by crosswinds. To improve distance and accuracy, grooves were machined inside the barrel to cause the shell to spin as it left the muzzle. Spin increased a shell's velocity, range, and punching power once it reached its target.

TGC °One of the first and most successful Northern cannon makers to add rifling to his gun tubes was Robert Parker Parrott, a New Yorker. Parrott had graduated from West Point in 1824 and had been assigned to the artillery, which included a stint as an inspector at

*Big mortars, like the 10-inch variety seen at right awaiting assembly in a Union battery at Dutch Gap, Virginia, were specialized cannon that could lob shells over high walls into enemy-held positions. Visible in the background is a lookout tower from which spotters could gauge the accuracy of the mortar fire.*

*The William Trego painting below shows Federal gunners loading a 10-inch mortar in the foreground while huge 13-inch mortars belch forth fire and shot in the background. Such 13-inch behemoths needed the support of cast-iron carriages and could fling a two hundred-pound shell for more than two miles.*

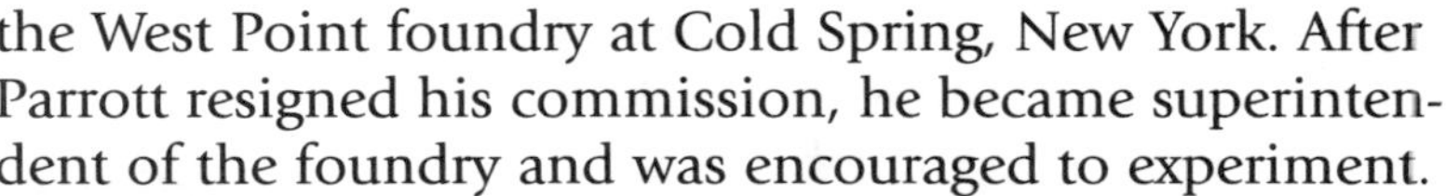

the West Point foundry at Cold Spring, New York. After Parrott resigned his commission, he became superintendent of the foundry and was encouraged to experiment.

When he found that rifled bronze cannon tubes wore out quickly, Parrott began using cast iron in making his gun tubes. Worried that the breech might not withstand repeated powder explosions, Parrott reinforced it with a wrought-iron band so that the explosion of the powder bag and the pressure generated by the explosion would not burst the cannon apart. The use of iron—which was less expensive than bronze—also reduced the weight of the weapon, allowing the reliable and effective cannon to travel with the army as field artillery.•

Parrott no doubt sensed the coming war in the late 1850s because he continued his experiments until it started. His first effort was a 10-pounder cannon, followed by 20- and 30-pounders, all of which were patented in 1860. The weapons were not perfect—they were not as accurate as many claimed they were and the heavier guns had a tendency to burst—but they were practical in that they were relatively inexpensive, could be produced quickly and in quantity, and could be operated by inexperienced crews. Furthermore, the weapons held up under extreme conditions; gun crews found that if the muzzle broke it could be sawed smooth and returned to action.

At the start of the war, the Union's adoption of the Napoleon, the 10-pounder Parrott rifle, and the 3-inch ordnance rifle gave the Federals the most advanced weapons available to any army of the period. In addition to these, Union Adm. John A. Dahlgren developed three types of cannon to be used on naval vessels (bronze boat howitzers and rifles, iron smoothbore shellguns, and iron rifles), and Confederate John Mercer Brooke developed a rifled cannon similar to the Parrott that could be single, double, or triple banded.

In addition to the overwhelming industrial strength of the North, the Union also had a wealth of technicians with an aptitude for these weapons. "While the South had at the beginning of the war the better raw material for infantry and cavalry, the North had the best for artillery," observed General Hunt in his capacity as chief of artillery for the Army of the Potomac. "A battery requires many mechanics with their tools and stores, and also what are called handy men. No country furnishes better men for the artillery proper than our Northern, and particularly our New England, states."

*Like a dead beast brought in from the hunt, a Confederate 8-inch Brooke rifle hangs from a sling cart, a vehicle used for transporting extremely heavy guns. Cannon tubes were suspended from the cart by ropes that ran under the cascabel—the ball at the breach—and the trunnions—the cylindrical projections on each side of the barrel that were used to attach a tube to its carriage. Another suspension rope was attached to a wooden pole inserted into the muzzle. Federal troops are hauling this Brooke gun from its position along the James River after the end of the war. Like Parrott rifles, this Confederate weapon had reinforcing bands shrunk onto its breach.*

*A row of 12-pound Napoleon cannon (above) sits at the U.S. arsenal at Washington awaiting shipment to the front. This versatile gun was developed by Emperor Napoleon III in 1853 and adopted by the U.S. Army a few years later. Only five Napoleon guns were in Federal service when the Civil War began, but hundreds were hurriedly produced by both Northern and Southern factories.*

Having the finest cannon and gun crews, however, did not guarantee that the Union commanders knew how to use their artillery on the battlefield. Even though the military academies across the country had tried to impress their students with Napoleonic tactics and strategies, they tended to ignore that in his march across Europe forty years earlier, Napoleon had turned his artillery into a powerful branch of his army by giving it mobility and using it aggressively. These innovations, however, were not widely accepted in the United States.

BP °America was not on the cutting edge of military theory in the mid-nineteenth century. Most European powers viewed the United States as a backwater and its military as unsophisticated. Although many branches of the service were backward by European standards, the Union artillery was an exception. Some brilliant men had been associated with the American artillery, particularly during the Mexican War. Principal among them was Samuel Ringgold.•

TGC °Ringgold developed what were called "flying batteries" during the Mexican War. He harnessed six or sometimes eight horses to a cannon and its limber and used that horsepower to gallop more than a ton of hardware across broken ground. This mobility added a new dimension to previously static artillery tactics.• Up until that time, most field commanders stationed their batteries in one specific spot and left them there to act like siege guns. The flying battery concept allowed a commander to move his guns rapidly to wherever they were needed as the battle progressed.

*The Confederacy not only supplemented its production of cannon with captured Union guns, but also with those imported from England. This fearsome-looking English weapon is a garrison-sized Armstrong rifle, named for its inventor, Sir William G. Armstrong. The rope and pulley apparatus attached to the barrel hoisted the projectile to the muzzle opening during the loading procedure. The South also imported smaller rifled fieldpieces designed by Armstrong. The famous Confederate artilleryman Edward Porter Alexander saw them tested and marveled at their accuracy. Alexander considered them to be "the most effective field-rifles yet made." Unfortunately for the Rebels, these guns arrived at the end of the war and never saw field service.*

West Point cadets studied Ringgold's dynamic use of artillery during the Mexican War, and when the Civil War war began, this group of trained officers demonstrated for the volunteer artillery crews how to fight effectively with these tactics. The expert guidance of these professional artillerists proved invaluable in battle after battle.

Sometimes old gunners who had moved into other branches of the service could not resist exercising what BP they had learned at the military academy. °During the September 17, 1862, battle of Antietam, Union Gen. John Gibbon, who had written *The Artillerist's Manual* in 1860, was at the head of the Western or "Black Hat" Brigade (renamed the Iron Brigade shortly after Antietam) and had been given the task of spearheading the assault through the Cornfield. He positioned a six-gun battery, Battery B of the Fourth U.S. Artillery, on a knoll to protect his right flank. The exposed battery drew heavy fire from the Confederates, and soon forty of the TGC battery's one hundred men were casualties.• °Gibbon noticed that the guns, which were firing canister at the charging Southerners, were discharging the deadly shot BP over the Rebels' heads.• °He shouted at the sergeant in command of the weapons to depress the gun tubes, but the man could not hear Gibbon above the noise of the battle, so the general jumped down from his horse, ran to one of the guns, and adjusted the elevating screw to depress the muzzle of the Napoleon. When it fired

*A portion of Pennsylvania's Keystone Independent Battery deploys for the camera (opposite page). Union batteries were usually made up of six cannon, while Confederate artillery units often had only four. At full strength, a six-gun contingent could have more than one hundred men and even more horses.*

*Although the rifled guns put in position by Union Capt. Quincy Gillmore (shown above as a major general) were a mile away from Fort Pulaski near Savannah, Georgia, in April 1862, they quickly tore apart and pockmarked the fort's brick walls, causing damage that smoothbores could never achieve. The plumes of red dust rising in the air with each shell strike signaled the sudden obsolescence of masonry forts. The sketch of Fort Pulaski below right indicates the severe damage that was caused. The earthen mounds on the fort's parade ground had been designed to stop and absorb the impact of bouncing round shot.*

again, the canister wreaked incredible havoc among the Confederates coming through the field and prevented the battery from being overrun.•

Most Federal commanders knew that artillery, if used well, could stave off defeat and that the big guns were a key ingredient to success on the battlefield. Yet while few quibbled over the effectiveness of artillery, too many failed to appreciate the tactical advantage of the weapons. When McClellan reorganized the army after the July 1861 disaster at Manassas, Virginia, he assigned his batteries to individual divisions and required each division to allocate two batteries as reserves for its corps. Unfortunately, command of the guns became confused. Some divisions maintained command of their artillery directly, others placed control with the corps commander, elsewhere command was divided between the two. In battle, this confusion was compounded when batteries received contradictory, confused, and countermanded orders. As a result, the Federal artillery was not always utilized to its potential.

In 1863 the artillery of the Army of the Potomac was again reorganized and its command centralized under a newly appointed chief of artillery, Henry Hunt. Batteries were grouped into brigades and placed under a corps chief of artillery. The reserve of one hundred guns was reorganized into five brigades, which Hunt dispatched piecemeal or en masse to reinforce weakened batteries in the field as situations developed in combat.

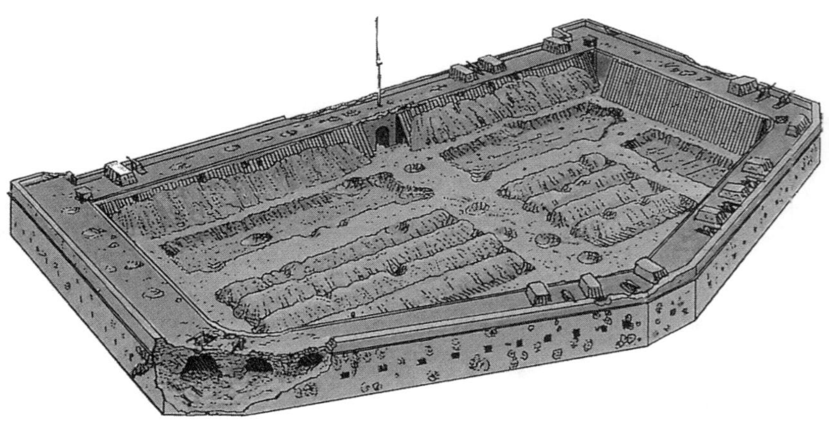

When it came to artillery, the agricultural South was at a logistical disadvantage. At the beginning of the war, the seceded states had only a meager number of smoothbore howitzers, 6-pounder guns, and assorted mortars, all of which were prewar surplus. In 1860 Virginia had purchased a few large-bore rifled Parrott guns from the West Point foundry. The rest of the Confederacy's weaponry consisted of thirty-five cannon captured during the takeover of the Harpers Ferry arsenal and several guns seized by the seceding states from the federal coastal forts and naval yards in the South.

To supplement this sparse assortment of cannon the Confederacy turned to imports and the best the states could manufacture. The South engaged in a brisk trade with Britain to acquire a number of Armstrong, Blakely, Clay, and Whitworth artillery rifles. These were used sparingly because the number of imports was never sufficient to meet the Rebels' needs.

Southern industrial strength was only one twentieth that of the North, which severely limited efforts by the Confederate states to manufacture cannon. At the start of the war the South had only one foundry—the Tredegar Iron Works in Richmond, Virginia—that could produce cannon in the numbers needed to equip its army. Brooke rifles, patterned after the Parrott gun, were produced there as well as smoothbore 12-pounder Napoleons. Other foundries were established in Alabama, Georgia, Mississippi, and South Carolina. Despite the shortage of raw materials, these armories produced more weapons than many believed possible.

Southerners also devoted their ingenuity to the design and manufacture of ammunition. As the war progressed ordnance engineers concentrated on rifled ammunition, believing that longer range and greater accuracy on the battlefield would offset smaller numbers of cannon.

Aside from the modest materials devoted to Confederate artillery, the South also suffered from a lack of men schooled

*The damage caused to Fort Pulaski by Union shells is graphically demonstrated by this picture of a clutch of Yankee troops posing in one of the holes blasted through the garrison's seven-foot-thick layer of bricks. The Southern commander of Pulaski, Col. Charles Olmstead, surrendered the fort and 385 men after enduring thirty hours of chaotic shellfire. The end came when Federal projectiles began to threaten the powder magazine. Olmstead later wrote, "Shots were shrieking through the air in every direction, while the ear was deafened by tremendous explosions."*

*U.S. Navy sailors and a marine wearing a white cross-belt serving on the U.S.S.* Miami *ready a 9-inch Dahlgren naval gun for firing. Invented by Union Adm. John A. Dahlgren, Dahlgren guns were easily distinguished by their sleek, smooth contours. Sailors nicknamed them "soda bottle cannon" because of their shape. These smoothbores came in a variety of sizes and were highly touted by those who served them. Launched in 1862, the* Miami *originally carried only one Dahlgren gun but added five more of the popular weapons to its arsenal in 1863. The ship served on both western and eastern rivers and dueled with the Confederate ironclad* Albemarle *on North Carolina's Roanoke River. During this fight the* Miami's *Dahlgren cannon proved unable to rupture the* Albemarle's *iron-plated sides—a case of weapon technology being outpaced by advances in ship design.*

WCD in the use of artillery. °Every major city in the Confederacy, however, had local, privately funded militia groups, and a number of these were artillery units, because many young men found the experience of riding alongside and firing the imposing weapons rather dashing and romantic.• When the war started, naturally these groups were mustered into the artillery branch.

BP °The best equipped Confederate artillery unit at the start of the war was the Washington Artillery of New Orleans, the oldest militia organization in Louisiana. Made up of aristocrats, it meant more to be a private in the Washington Artillery than to be a lieutenant or a captain in many other militia units. These men carried themselves well and were acquainted with the finer things in life. They had their own French chefs who accompanied them into the field.• At the beginning of the war the five companies were distributed between the two main fronts: four went east to fight with the Army of Northern Virginia and one went west as a unit within the Army of Tennessee.

GWG °The social pedigree of the men in the Washington Artillery did not guarantee that they would do better on the battlefield than other units, but the record shows that they achieved a high reputation on a number of battlefields during the war.• In the East, from First Manassas to Gettysburg, the Washington Artillery served with distinction using equipment they had seized from the Baton Rouge arsenal. Col. James Walton, an able and experienced officer, commanded the volunteer unit, but in combat he took his orders, like other artillery commanders, from Lee's most gifted artillery officer, twenty-six-year-old Edward Porter Alexander.

GWG °Alexander was a Georgian and an 1857 graduate of West Point. By far he was the best Confederate artillerist in the war; his only equal was his Northern counterpart, Henry Hunt.• Known to his friends as Porter, Alexander was an outstanding engineer and student of artillery who had helped develop a semaphore signal system before the war.

*Weathered Union artilleryman stand next to their iron 10-pound Parrott rifle in this photograph taken at Fair Oaks, Virginia, in June 1862. Parrott rifles were recognized by the extra layer of metal that reinforced the breach. This band, forced on the cannon when it was red-hot, shrank and fused itself to the barrel as it cooled. Unfortunately, the weapons had a tendency to rupture just forward of the breech band during firing and therefore were not as reliable as other cannon models. Nevertheless, the Parrott design was cheap and easy to mass-produce, and many of these weapons were made during the Civil War. Several Confederate foundries made their own versions of the Parrott rifle.*

When the war began, Alexander resigned his commission and was made a signal officer on P. G. T. Beauregard's staff. GWG °His career in the Southern signal corps, however, did not last long. After the battle of First Manassas he was made chief of ordnance for the Army of Northern Virginia. He was fascinated with two aspects of artillery: developing better ammunition (a problem that plagued the Confederacy throughout the war) and effectively organizing his batteries to mass their firepower better in battle.• BP °Alexander exemplified everything that Napoleon and Ringgold had demonstrated about artillery tactics. He saw the artillery as an offensive arm of the service, and he used it brilliantly in that way.• Alexander rose quickly in rank, moving from captain to colonel in less than a year. The Confederate army needed talented men in command and promoted gifted officers rapidly.

Another promising artillerist was Stephen D. Lee, who was two years older than Alexander and distantly related to Robert E. Lee. Lee was a South Carolinian and an 1854 graduate of West Point. He also began the war as a captain after relinquishing his commission as an artillery captain in the U.S. Army. Present at the firing on Fort Sumter where he helped direct unskilled gunners, Lee too was made a colonel within a year.

Lee attracted the attention of the Confederacy on August 30, 1862, at the battle of Second Manassas, when James Longstreet's and Thomas J. "Stonewall" Jackson's infantry failed to turn back a Union assault. Twice the Union lines crumbled and reformed and attacked. GWG °Jackson's line was beleaguered for most of the battle, almost breaking several times; then the Federals attacked again. There was no time for Longstreet's infantry to reinforce Jackson, but Lee's artillery was available.•

TGC °Lee saw that the Union flank was going to be exposed to his guns, which allowed him to fire down the length of the enemy line, enfilading the Federal columns. The situation called for the use of solid shot, which would smash everything in its path.• With only eighteen guns, Lee commenced firing.

"In a moment, the heavy fire of shot and shell was being poured into the thick columns of the enemy," Longstreet recounted. "In ten minutes, [the Union] stubborn masses began to waiver and give back. For a moment, there was chaos, then order returned, and they reformed. As the cannon thundered, their ranks broke, only to be formed again with dogged determination. A third time the batteries tore the Federals to pieces, and they fell back under this terrible fire."

Southern artillery had learned this lesson from the battle of Malvern Hill two months earlier: Massed artillery achieved maximum casualties. Lee's batteries at the battle of Second Manassas enjoyed one of the few times Confederate artillery had the advantage over the Federals.

GWG °Confederate artillery was almost always at a disadvantage on the battlefield. Yankee armies generally had more weapons, better weapons, and almost always better ammunition, and so the common experience for Rebel gunners was to try to hold their own against extremely long odds.•

The brilliance and bravery of the Southern artillerists almost made up for what they lacked in numbers of

*The term* heavy artillery *was generally applied to the cannon used in forts, although Union armies sometimes trundled large artillery pieces to the front to bombard besieged cities. The soldiers working the weapons in the image at right are members of the First Connecticut Heavy Artillery, a unit that took its heavy guns on several campaigns and bombarded Richmond and Fredericksburg, as well as taking part in the investment of Petersburg. Heavy artillery regiments were trained to serve the big guns and to fight as infantry. This picture was taken when the First was stationed at Fort Richardson, one of the garrisons protecting Washington, D.C.*

*Three of the Confederacy's finest artilleryman were Edward Porter Alexander (far left), John Pelham (near left), and William Pegram (not pictured). By far the best Southern artillerist, Alexander, a graduate of West Point, worked to develop better ammunition and organize his batteries to mass their firepower more effectively. He saw the artillery as an offensive arm of the service, and he used it brilliantly. His use of massed artillery at Fredericksburg and Chancellorsville, in particular, devastated Union attacks. At Fredericksburg, in full view of the Union's massed artillery and with only two pieces of artillery—one of which became disabled—Pelham controlled the whole scene, earning him the sobriquet "the Gallant Pelham." Noted for his good looks, courage, and dashing service in Jeb Stuart's cavalry, he was killed at age twenty-five at the March 17, 1863, battle of Kelly's Ford. Pegram lacked dash and swagger, but he had necessary qualities of command: will of iron, devotion to cause, ability to inspire men. Although nearsighted, he had no equal as a battery commander in Lee's army.*

men and cannon. One of the bravest was also one of the youngest. John Pelham, a twenty-three-year-old Alabama native, had excelled in artillery studies at West Point under his mentor, Henry Hunt. When war came, Pelham left the academy without graduating and joined the Confederate cause, quickly rising to command Jeb Stuart's horse artillery. Pelham devised new tactics for the horse artillery to improve its speed, movement, and accuracy.

BP °Pelham always moved his guns to the point of greatest threat and always placed these weapons where they could cause the greatest damage to the enemy regardless of the firepower directed against him. His combination of youth and dash generated a romantic aura of fearlessness on the battlefield.•

TGC °His greatest, most dramatic moment occurred during the December 13, 1862, battle of Fredericksburg. Pelham, with only two pieces of artillery, drove them onto a plain next to the Rappahannock River. In full view of the Union's massed artillery, he unlimbered his weapons and opened fire, bringing to a halt an assault by more than a division of Yankee infantry. By rapidly moving these two pieces from one position to another, he avoided most of the Federals' fire but eventually saw one of his cannon disabled. Pelham continued moving and firing his only operational gun around this vast

*The same fieldpieces that struck fear into the hearts of opponents with their deadly salvos were extremely vulnerable when limbered up and on the move. During fighting related to the battle of Chancellorsville that occurred on Fredericksburg's Marye's Heights, Union soldiers came upon retreating elements of the Washington Artillery. Yankee volleys killed or wounded twenty-nine of the battery's horses, resulting in the capture of six cannon and the wrecked caisson and limber pictured at right. A caisson was a two-wheeled cart that carried two ammunition chests, a spare wheel, and tools, while a limber held a single ammunition chest.*

amphitheater in the valley of the Rappahannock with Union troops watching on one side and Confederates watching from higher ground on the other. He and a handful of men controlled the whole scene.•

BP When he was informed of Pelham's action, °Robert E. Lee remarked, "It is good to see such courage in one so young." This action at Fredericksburg also bestowed the young Alabamian the sobriquet "the Gallant Pelham," which was used in official reports to describe his conduct.•

Pelham was killed in the spring of 1863 at the age of twenty-five at Kelly's Ford, Virginia, when he joined a cavalry charge and ironically was struck by a piece of an exploding artillery shell. The body of the fallen artillerist, escorted by a guard of honor, was laid in state at the capitol in Richmond. At least three women claiming to be his fiancée went into mourning when they heard of his death. George Schreef, one of the men who served with the Gallant Pelham, said: "Pelham's death cast a great gloom over us. We came to realize no one could fill his place as brilliantly as he had done."

IN ADDITION to field artillery used on the battlefield between two colliding armies, heavy artillery utilized large, big bore guns and mortars, including siege and garrison cannon, that were designed to demolish or to defend forts and earthworks. The advancing technology of artillery firepower, when applied to larger caliber weapons, quickly showed that the time of masonry and brick fortifications had passed.

In the United States, forts had been built near major ports of entry during times of immediate threat, first during the American Revolution (called first-system fortifications) and then during the War of 1812 (called second-system fortifications). The ease with which the British torched Washington, D.C., in 1814 clearly pointed to the weakness of many of these coastal defenses. Wanting to avoid a large standing army, the country's early military planners devised a defensive system of fortifications that did not require huge numbers of men for garrison duty. A special board of officers was appointed in 1816, headed by French military engineer Simon Bernard, to create a system of coastal defenses.

Constructed in the 1830s and 1840s, these forts were called the third system and formed a ring of stone and brick fortifications along the coastal United States. They were believed to be impregnable, but they had been built anticipating attack only by smoothbore cannon from ships, not by rifled cannon mounted on land or by siege mortars that could lob shells over the walls.

Brick forts like Sumter in South Carolina, Macon in North Carolina, Pulaski and Jackson in Georgia, Monroe in Virginia, Pickens and Taylor in Florida, and Morgan and Gaines in Alabama were already obsolete when the Civil War started, but few military planners conceded the point. Normally armed with seacoast cannon—smoothbore 24-pounders—none of the forts had ever been attacked, most were not manned fully, and some were as yet unfinished.

BP ○In the war's first days at Fort Sumter, it was clear that masonry fortifications were outdated. Forts like the third-system Sumter could not withstand the high-caliber shells of modern artillery.• Just a year after Sumter fell, the death knell of brick forts was sounded.

In February 1862, Union Capt. Quincy A. Gillmore brought rifled siege guns—cannon capable of firing projectiles weighing as much as eighty pounds—within range of Fort Pulaski, a Confederate stronghold at the mouth of Georgia's Savannah River. At first, the Confederates showed no concern. TGC °Several months earlier Robert E. Lee, prior to taking command of the Army of Northern Virginia, had made an inspection tour of the coastal forts in South Carolina and Georgia. As a young U.S. Army engineer, he had helped design and build Pulaski, and so he was confident that the fort's seven-foot-thick walls would withstand any Union attack. Lee's assessment, however, was based on his knowledge of smoothbore weapons.•

On April 10, 1862, Gillmore's guns opened fire on Pulaski and in just five hours punched through the brick walls of the fort. WCD °The Union gunners concentrated their fire on one specific point, which they were able to do because of the increased accuracy of rifled cannon, and simply fired time after time after time into the same spot. Eventually, they blasted a hole through the wall. The next day the gunners continued to focus on the breach in the wall and began shelling the wall of the fort's powder magazine. At that point, fearing that the magazine would explode, there was nothing the defenders inside the fort could do but surrender.•

For proving the effectiveness of rifled cannon, Gillmore was promoted to general and a year later was assigned the task of taking Charleston, South Carolina. He devised a three-part plan, but the heart of his attack was the bombardment of Fort Sumter and the city. In the marsh between James and Morris islands, in August 1863, Gillmore's engineers began building one of the most distinctive batteries ever constructed. Pilings were driven into the marsh and topped with a platform of logs two layers thick. A parapet was created using thirteen thousand sandbags standing independent of the gun platform, with both parts floating on the marsh. The gun deck was made of compacted marsh grass, canvas, and sand in the rectangular area formed by the parapet. On top of this base, engineers erected a close-fitting wooden platform.

On August 17 an 8,000-pound carriage was ferried to the site, and then a 16,300-pound 8-inch, 200-pounder Parrott was floated to the platform. Four days later, on

August 21, the gun was mounted and ready for service. Within a short time the crew dubbed the battery the "Swamp Angel." The site was seventy-nine hundred yards (nearly five miles) from Charleston. Gillmore sent a message demanding the evacuation of Morris Island and Fort Sumter or he would fire on the city. At 1:30 A.M. on August 22, 1863, the first of sixteen rounds was fired into Charleston, targeted toward Saint Michael's church steeple. On the next day twenty rounds were fired, but the last shot disabled the gun. The damage was not due to a weakness in the Parrott but rather due to unstable, experimental incendiary ammunition.

The Swamp Angel was not replaced but later a siege gun was mounted in the battery and finally two mortars were installed. Gillmore declared the Swamp Angel an experiment in artillery techniques, noting that the weapon was aimed using compass readings and the distance covered by the weapon's shells was greater than any previous bombardment. The siege of Charleston continued until the last month of the war when Sherman's army threatened to occupy the city and the Confederates evacuated. After the war the remains of the Swamp Angel were sold for scrap in Trenton, New Jersey, but when the parts were identified, city officials decided to display it as part of a war memorial.

When large-caliber siege guns proved that brick and mortar were undefensible, new fortifications were

*Massive 100-pounder Parrott rifles (above left), well protected by sandbags and woven baskets filled with earth known as gabions, await the order to fire upon Charleston, South Carolina. These guns could hurl their shells up to six miles, although accuracy was hardly guaranteed at that distance. Stands of projectiles are visible at the far left of the photograph. Despite their impressive size, such cannon were not invulnerable and the great stress placed on the barrels during firing sometimes led to irreversible damage. The Parrott gun pictured above right fractured its muzzle during a discharge.*

*The Swamp Angel was a 200-pounder Parrott rifle on a platform built in the marsh between James and Morris islands that helped to bombard Charleston. This cannon fired shells filled with Greek fire, an incendiary fluid, into the "Cradle of Secession." The Confederate commander in the city, Gen. P. G. T. Beauregard, wrote to the Union gunners that the firing of such "missiles . . . into the midst of a city . . . filled with women and children will give you a bad eminence in history." His warning was to no avail, however, for the Federal batterymen continued to fire the unstable rounds until one exploded inside the barrel, cracking the giant tube, throwing it onto its sandbag revetment, and rendering it useless. The Swamp Angel is shown as it appeared after the accident.*

erected utilizing an ancient technology to absorb the BP force of rifled artillery shells. °The Confederates turned to sand and sandbags and logs covered with earth and erected defensive structures at Forts Fisher, Anderson, and Branch in North Carolina and Fort McAllister outside of Savannah, Georgia. Sand absorbed the shock of exploding shells, and sand forts could be easily repaired,• but men seeking cover behind the walls of earthen forts were vulnerable to one of the oldest forms of artillery: the mortar—which had changed little in more than three hundred years of warfare.

TGC °Mortars did not have a long range, but they threw an explosive into the air and dropped it over an enemy wall where it would explode among the troops inside or possibly inside the fort's magazine. The North used huge siege mortars, sometimes with bores as large as ten or thirteen inches, that could hurl shells weighing several hundred pounds.

One of the most famous mortars of the war was the "Dictator," a seacoast mortar weighing several thousand pounds and mounted on a railroad flatcar. A spur line was built to run it into a ravine close to the enemy lines at Petersburg, Virginia, so it could fire its thirteen-inch payload high up over and into the city. Confederate defenders said they could track the shells at night by watching the burning glow of the fuse, which indicated whether they needed to seek shelter or not.• The Dictator dropped only forty-five two-hundred-pound shells on Petersburg during the summer of 1864. It was withdrawn from the battle after three months.

BP ○Probably the most dramatic use of mortars occurred during the July 30, 1864, battle of the Crater at Petersburg. The operation began as an attempt by the Union army to break through the Confederate earthworks by tunneling beneath them, planting a huge concentration of powder under the Southerners, and then igniting the explosives to create a gap in the Rebel works. Once the breach was created, Federal infantry would charge into Petersburg.

The attack, however, was a disaster for the Union. Although the Federals succeeded in blowing a gigantic crater in the Confederate lines that obliterated dozens of Southern soldiers in the explosion, when the Union infantry charged, the Rebels reacted quickly. The Yankee infantry was pinned down inside the crater while Confederate artillerymen brought up small so-called Coehorn mortars. Once in place the miniature mortars lobbed shells into the crater packed elbow to elbow with Union troops pinned down by Southern fire from above. The carnage was unbelievable when the rounds exploded among the exposed Northern troops who could only hug the ground or the walls of the crater.•

*The panorama below shows the men of Battery D, Second U.S. Artillery, at work on their 12-pound Napoleons. For many years this picture was thought to show the battery in action, but the clearness of the photograph and the precise stance of the gunners make it evident that this shot was staged for the photographer, most likely during a drill session. The soldiers seen at the muzzles of the cannons are the "number one men" of their crews. Their job was to use the sponge-rammer to push the charge down the barrel, then to swab the gun after each discharge. Swabbing the gun not only helped keep the barrel cool, but it also extinguished sparks that might accidentally set off the next round.*

*Lt. Alonzo Cushing (second from right) poses with the staff of Union Gen. Edwin V. Sumner (at the top of the steps) in 1862. At Gettysburg, an ammunition limber of Cushing's battery was struck and a spectacular explosion resulted. When the Federals ceased firing and pulled some of their guns back, Lee and his ordnance chief, Porter Alexander, thought that the Confederate barrage was successful, and so Pickett's Charge was launched. Cushing's battery wound up in some of the most savage fighting when the Rebels rushed the stone wall where it was stationed. Every Southerner was killed or captured. All that remained of Cushing's battery were six dismounted ordnance rifles, their carriages in splinters. Cushing was killed.*

THE LARGEST artillery duel of the war occurred at Gettysburg. For three days in July 1863 Lee's Army of Northern Virginia and George Gordon Meade's Army of the Potomac maneuvered, attacked, and counterattacked across the rolling meadows around the small Pennsylvania town. The effectiveness—and ineffectiveness—of artillery was a decisive factor in the outcome of the battle.

The first day of battle involved mostly infantry clashes between the two sides, but on the second day the southern end of the Union line, marked by a hill called Little Round Top, was in jeopardy
BP of falling into Confederate hands. °The boulder-strewn hill was not wooded on its western face and was empty of troops from either side. It was there for the taking. If the Confederates seized it, they would be able to enfilade the flank of the entire Union army. If the Federals occupied the hill, they would be able to protect their flank and command the southern regions of the battlefield.• Among the many officers taking positions on the hill was Lt. Charles Hazlett, a twenty-five-year-old commander of a battery of six Parrott rifles.

WCD °Little Round Top was a rugged, rocky hill. Only by superhuman effort did Hazlett and his men manhandle
BP their guns to the hill's summit,• °using sheer muscle power. Once their guns were in position, Hazlett's men played a conspicuous part in repulsing the ensuing Confederate attack. At one point during the attack, the Rebels were so close the guns could not be bought to bear on them. While there was little Hazlett's battery could do at that moment, his guns served a greater psychological purpose. Knowing that Federal artillery was deployed on Little Round Top infused the Union defenders with the will to hold their positions.•

By nightfall at the end of the second day, the two armies had consolidated their lines. Lee and his army were in the west, spread out along Seminary Ridge while the Union army occupied Cemetery Ridge, just a

*Although dramatic and exciting, this tableau of the last moments of Lieutenant Cushing in a detail from artist Paul Philippoteaux's Gettysburg Cyclorama, contains several factual errors. Cushing's battery was equipped with 3-inch rifles, not the 10-pound Parrott pictured here, and the guns were positioned farther to the front, along the famous stone wall. Although Philippoteaux portrayed the wounded battery commander lying along the trail of the cannon's carriage, and his first sergeant, Frederick Fuger, holding the battery guidon, Cushing actually was supported by Fuger until he received his fatal head wound. Additionally, with the exception of Fuger, Cushing's gun crew had been shot down or fled by the time the Rebel charge momentarily pierced the Union line. Nonetheless, this rendering captures well the chaos and carnage caused by the storied Confederate attack.*

mile to the east. Henry Hunt, the chief of the Union artillery, placed his seventy-seven cannon along the crest of the mile-long ridge.

After two days of fighting, Lee believed he had only one option: to attack the center of the Union line. On July 3 Lee and Longstreet devised a plan of attack calling for an infantry charge to smash the Union center in concert with a cavalry attack on the Union rear.

GWG ○Lee reasoned the only way the attack would succeed would be if his artillery could pave the way for the infantry by disrupting the Union defenders along Cemetery Ridge. He ordered a preassault bombardment by his massed artillery before noon on July 3. The chief of artillery, Edward Porter Alexander, was charged with seeing that the bombardment accomplished its end.•

Alexander massed nearly 170 guns to launch the largest bombardment of the war. For two hours he hurled a firestorm of shot and shell at the Union defenders. "The most horrific cannonade any of us had ever experienced was kept up, and it seemed as if neither man nor horse could possibly live under it," recalled Lt. George Finley of the Fifty-sixth Virginia Infantry. "Our gunners stood to their pieces and handled them with such splendid courage as to wait the admiration of the infantry crouching on the ground behind them."

*Members of the Fifth Company of the Washington Artillery of New Orleans, a unit that traced its lineage to the Mexican War, pose for a photograph just a few weeks before their participation in the battle of Shiloh. The Fifth Company stayed and fought in the western theater of the Civil War, while the other four companies of this famous battery bolstered the ranks of the Army of Northern Virginia. The well-dressed aristocratic artillerymen, whose French chef accompanied them, even had their own distinctive badge which they often wore on their caps or coat breasts that bore the challenging words, "Try Us."*

Longstreet asked Alexander to judge the effect of his bombardment on the Yankees and to send word when he thought the time was right to launch the attack. When it looked as if the Union line had weakened, Longstreet would order his division commanders—Gens. Isaac Trimble, James Johnston Pettigrew, and George Pickett—to begin their attack.

GWG °Alexander, however, had a difficult time seeing what was happening on Cemetery Ridge and gauging the effect of his fire because the exchange between the Confederate and Union artillery generated immense clouds of smoke, obscuring much of the battlefield.• What the Rebel artillerist could not see was that many of his shells flew harmlessly over the Yankees because his guns were aimed too high. One shot, however, struck an ammunition limber for a Union battery commanded by Lt. Alonzo Cushing, a twenty-two-year-old West Point graduate from Wisconsin. The explosion was spectacular.

WCD °Lee and Alexander both mistook the blast as a sign that the Confederate barrage was successful. When the Federals ceased to return fire and then pulled some of their guns back, Lee and Alexander believed the cannonade had done its job. The moment looked right to launch the assault• known afterward as Pickett's Charge.

"The rustle of thousands of feet amid the stubble stirs a cloud of dust like the spray at the bow of a vessel," Randolph Sharpwell of the Eighth Virginia Infantry recounted. "The two armies, for a moment, look on, apparently spellbound. Then the spell was broken by the crash of a hundred guns trained upon the advancing troops. Shot, shell, spherical case, shrapnel and canister—thousands of deadly missiles racing through the air thin our ranks."

*The 13-inch seacoast mortar shown above was nicknamed the "Dictator." It first lobbed shells into Petersburg while mounted on a railcar, but it was moved to the stationary position seen here in August 1864. Two gunners using special tongs called shell hooks were required to handle the mortar's 200-pound shells during loading.*

*To hide from the ever-present shelling, both Northern and Southern soldiers dug into the Virginia earth for protection. Yankee troops nicknamed the shell-scarred Confederate earthworks below "Fort Damnation" because the Rebel cannon posted there seemed to be constantly in action.*

The Federals were impressed with the martial display as the Confederates marched across the mile-wide field. The Rebels rushed the stone wall and the guns of Cushing's battery in the angle where the wall fell back several dozen yards. This battery of three-inch ordnance rifles stood in the vortex of the most savage fighting of the charge. Nevertheless, Cushing decided that his guns should be moved closer to the wall so they could meet the Confederate attack head on. As the Rebel infantry advanced, the Yankee gunners switched to canister shot and began delivering shotgunlike blasts into the Southern ranks.

At the height of the fighting Cushing was struck in the groin. Terribly wounded and facing certain death, the twenty-two-year-old battery commander could barely

speak, but he stayed by his guns,• refusing to leave the battlefield. ○First Sgt. Frederick Fuger held up his stricken commander, relaying the orders Cushing whispered, and the battery continued to fire as the Confederate infantry drew closer and the Union infantry began to return fire.• Another bullet struck Cushing, this one in his mouth, and he fell dead beside one of his guns.

○As the Confederates were about to leap over the wall into what was left of Cushing's battery, Fuger fired a final round of double canister point-blank into the Rebel ranks and fell back before the guns were overwhelmed. Within minutes, however, every Southerner who had crossed the wall was either killed or captured, and Cushing's guns were reclaimed.•

All that remained of Cushing's battery were six dismounted ordnance rifles and their carriages in splinters. Nothing of the limbers survived; they had either exploded or been shot to pieces. Twenty-nine horses

*At the January 15, 1864, battle of Fort Fisher, a Southern crew readies its huge Armstrong rifle to fire upon the attacking U.S. sailors and marines. Although the overall Federal attack was successful in taking the fort, the hapless naval column was thrown back with the loss of nearly three hundred men, a predictable result when pitting troops armed with pistols and cutlasses against the formidable firepower of the Armstrong rifle. Unlike forts erected of brick and stone, Fort Fisher had walls made of earth and sand and therefore was better able to withstand the impact of the pre-assault bombardment delivered by the naval warships in the background.*

had been killed, and thirty-six were wounded or otherwise unfit for service. The fifty used to pull the baggage wagons and forge were still healthy. Seven of the battery's officers and enlisted men had been killed and thirty-three wounded. One enlisted man was reported missing and presumed dead. Four men carried Cushing's body to the bivouac site beyond the field hospital, where it was claimed by Cushing's brother Milton.

A correspondent on the battlefield, in his description of Cushing's death, concluded, "Heaps of corpses and wounded in front of his battery this morning told a terrible tale of the effectiveness of its fire." Sergeant Fuger reported that he and the surviving cannoneers counted more than six hundred dead in front of Cushing's battery, all of them from Pickett's division.

*A fieldpiece sits on top of the battered outer wall of Fort Sumter at the end of the war. Intentionally or not, the composition of this photograph symbolically portrays the triumph of artillery over supposedly impregnable brick fortifications. But the reign of muzzle-loading cannon as lords of the battlefield was destined to be brief. Within the decades following the Civil War, breechloading artillery pieces would gain ascendancy. By World War I, the sound of horses' hooves pulling a gun into combat was replaced by the sound of an internal combustion engine. Nevertheless, the artillerymen of the American Civil War left a legacy of bravery and deadliness.*

As decisive a victory as Gettysburg was for the Union, °the North did not defeat the South on just one battlefield or in just one aspect of the fighting. The North defeated the South at every juncture, but ultimately it was the North's ability to take iron from the ground and turn it into weapons and ammunition that helped seal the fate of the Southern rebellion.•

WCD

From the beginning of the war, Federal artillery was the Union army's greatest asset, rooted in the industrial superiority of the North over the South. Yet despite their shortcomings in materiél, Confederate cannoneers compensated to some degree with incredible spirit and dedication. Unfortunately for the South, the ingenuity and unflagging grit of the disadvantaged Rebel artillerists did little to gain the victory they so earnestly sought. Thus, when Confederate artillerists faced the massed firepower of their Union counterparts, they responded by standing to their guns, returning shot for shot for as long as they could. While this practice failed to move the South closer to victory, it was a discipline that occasionally took on heroic, tragic proportions and elevated men like Pegram, Pelham, and Alexander to glory.

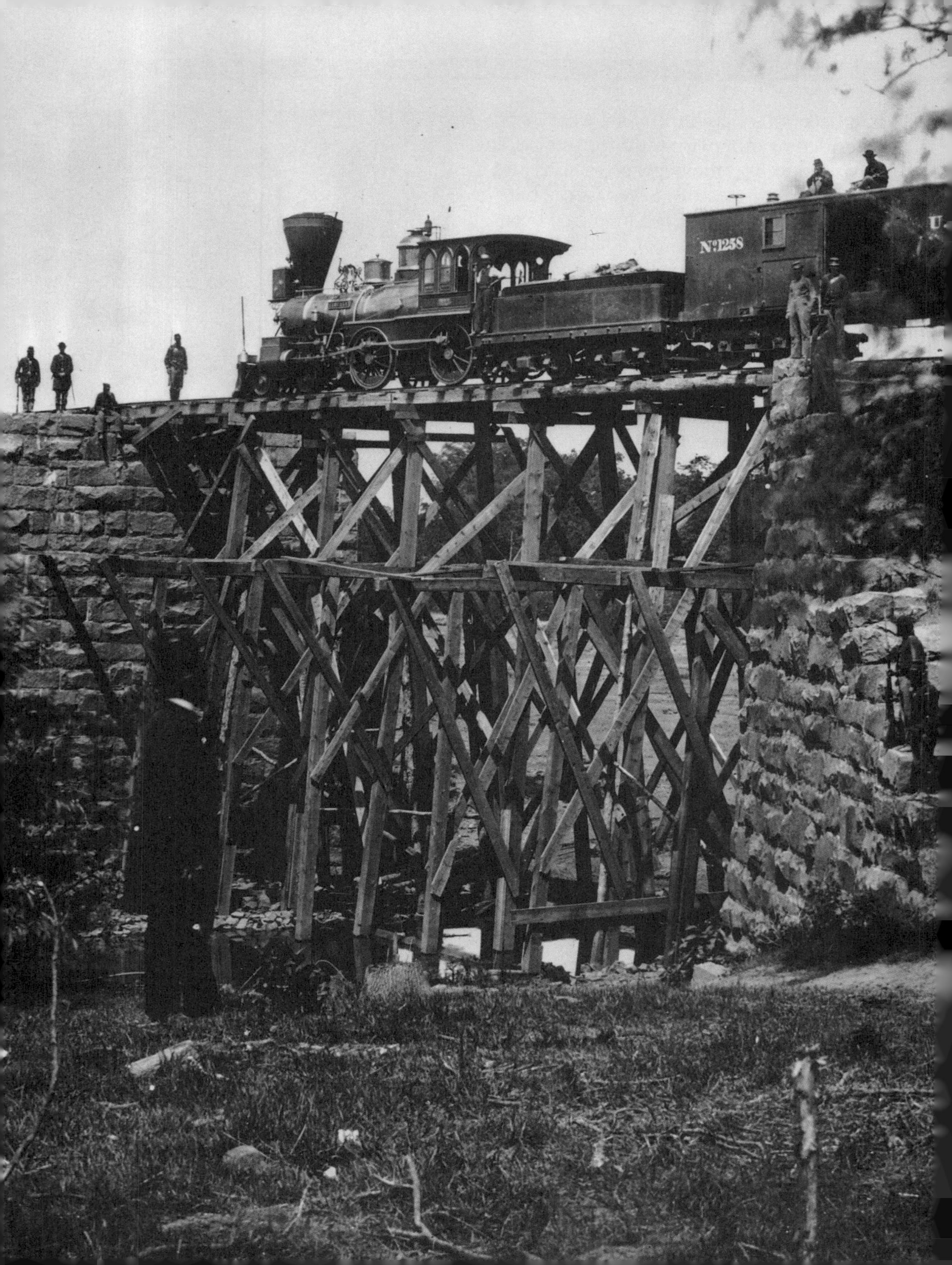
Nº1258

# TRAINS AT WAR

The CIVIL WAR WAS THE FIRST LARGE-scale conflict in which railroads played a major role, but many commanders were slow to grasp the possibilities offered by the comparatively new mode of transportation. When both sides began to utilize their rail lines to transport troops, supplies, wounded, and other materiél, the advantages soon became apparent, and railroads thereafter bore an ever-increasing load. Campaign strategy came to be based on the availability and capacity of railway lines, and the construction, maintenance, and defense of these vital links involved considerable numbers of men and equipment. As a result rail lines became military targets of prime importance, and the tide of battle often turned on the ability of railroads to rush reinforcements to the battlefield and maintain a steady flow of supplies.

Both North and South understood that destroying the other's railroads stemmed the flow of supplies to the battlefront, weakening armies faster and more effectively than any single weapon. As the war progressed, leaders on both sides realized that trains were the most effective nonfiring ordnance in their arsenals. Moreover, one did not have to attack trains themselves to render them useless; tearing up track and burning bridges effectively slowed the wheels of the iron horse.

Although railroads were of vital importance in the Civil War, their development occurred not very many years before. The Baltimore and Ohio, the first chartered railroad to operate in America, began carrying passengers and freight only in 1830, barely one generation

| | |
|---|---|
| WCD | William C. Davis |
| WPG | Walter P. Gray |
| JPH | John P. Hankey |
| JIR | James I. Robertson Jr. |
| JAW | James A. Ward |

*Before the war, the United States had the highest railroad accident rate in the world. An American passenger was nine times more likely to be killed in a train wreck than a French one and thirty-five times more likely than an Englishman. At a time when the average prewar passenger train speed was a sluggish fifteen miles per hour, the Louisville and Nashville Railroad offered some routes at a daring forty miles per hour. One L&N passenger stated after an 1860 journey that his trip had made him exceedingly nervous and that "the rocking and dancing and jumping of the cars" did little to allay his fears. The Chicago and Northwestern collision shown at right occurred in the 1850s.*

before the war. Its first cars were pulled by horses. The first steam-powered passenger-and-freight train ran between Charleston and Hamburg, South Carolina, in late 1830. At the close of that year, there were only twenty-three miles of operating railway lines in the United States: ten miles out of Charleston and thirteen out of Baltimore. By 1860, however, the nation had more than thirty thousand miles of rail, nearly half the world's total at the time.

The rolling stock developed quickly also. Early passenger trains were little more than stagecoaches coupled together and pulled by small engines. By the mid-1840s, though, the locomotives had grown to as much as fifteen tons, were the pride of the engine crews assigned to them, and stood as the most visible symbol
WCD of the Industrial Revolution in the United States. °They were huge, powerful, and fast, and they represented everything in which Americans prided themselves.•

Love of the machines, however, did not translate uniformly into love for the railroad industry. In the decade preceding the war, American rail lines were an uncoor-
JAW dinated tangle of track and commerce °supporting approximately three hundred independent, chartered railway companies, each of which was dedicated to its own bottom line.• Cooperation and standardization
WPG meant little to those who owned these businesses. °In communities where railroads intersected, the lines either failed to connect or connected haphazardly. Each

*Earlier in his career, Simon Cameron had helped settle disputes between the government and the Winnebago Indians and then made a fortune by adjusting their claims with notes drawn on his own bank. An 1860 presidential contender, he was appointed secretary of war in the Lincoln cabinet in return for throwing the Pennsylvania vote to Lincoln. He directed that all troops going to Washington should travel on a railroad in which he had a financial interest. The railroad then overcharged the government.*

railroad set its own gauge—the distance between the rails—which meant that one company's locomotive and cars might not fit another company's rails• and long-distance freight might have to be handled by several railroad companies, incurring separate charges with each line.

The early railroads were not only inefficient, they were dangerous. WCD °Rail companies usually built only a single line of track between two stations, eliminating the possibility for simultaneous two-way traffic. If a station master failed to telegraph ahead to check for unscheduled traffic, collisions were almost inevitable. This lack of coordination meant that there was a tremendous nascent transportation infrastructure ready for the war, but it was not yet ready for the demands of a large-scale modern war.•

*President-elect Abraham Lincoln was speaking in New York en route to his inauguration when he learned of a Baltimore plot to assassinate him. After completing his announced stops at Philadelphia and Harrisburg, Lincoln slipped aboard a different train. All other rail traffic was waved off the line to make room for this late night special train with its secret cargo. Telegraph linemen were ordered to cut the telegraph wires so that word of Lincoln's departure from Harrisburg would be blacked out. The train's crew, unaware that Lincoln was on board, were told only that they were carring an "important package." As a result, Lincoln passed through Baltimore while his assassins were sleeping. He is shown above, in a painting by H. D. Stitt, arriving at the Baltimore and Ohio station in Washington on February 23, 1861.*

Just before hostilities broke out between North and South, the most discussed and anticipated rail journey was Abraham Lincoln's trip from Springfield, Illinois, to Washington, D.C., prior to his inauguration as the sixteenth president. Because many threats were directed toward the president-elect's train, the trip foreshadowed the need to protect railroads that would become necessary during the war.

JIR °Various security arrangements were made for Lincoln's train. Guards were posted along bridges, crossings, and other strategic points to prevent sabotage or seizure. Most of the bridges were whitewashed with a mixture of salt and alum to fireproof them.•

In Baltimore, which was a hotbed of Secessionist activity, Allan Pinkerton, one of the men charged with the president-elect's security, detected a possible assassination plot and urged Lincoln to change his route. JPH °After discussing the matter with his advisers, Lincoln decided to travel through Baltimore ahead of his announced plans, so as to avoid whatever plot there might be.• He was in the capital before the conspirators learned that the schedule had been changed.

In early 1861, Southern sympathizers attacked troops from the Sixth Massachusetts who were traveling to Washington through Baltimore (above). When Maryland Gov. Thomas Hicks ordered the Northern Central Railroad into Baltimore cut, Secessionists tore up the line, damaging track, structures, and rights of way. This act prompted enraged secretary of war Simon Cameron—who owned a major share of the Northern Central—to order troops to fight their way through the town if necessary. President Lincoln, not wanting to aggravate Maryland into leaving the Union, rescinded Cameron's order.

Daniel C. McCallum (below) was appointed director and superintendent of military railroads for the North in February, 1862. A Scottish immigrant, he was an excellent railroader and shrewd administrator.

After the fall of Fort Sumter, Lincoln called for seventy-five thousand volunteers to converge on Washington to protect the capital and quash the rebellion. Most came by rail, but the confusion and disorder spawned by the president's request showed how disorganized, competitive, and corrupt both the railroad industry and the Federal government were at the time.

Wartime opportunists sprang up everywhere, including Lincoln's secretary of
WCD war, Simon Cameron, who °held a major investment in the railroads running through his native state of Pennsylvania. As secretary of war and the man most responsible for the mobilization of the volunteer army, Cameron was in a perfect position to profit personally. He channeled all troops en route to Washington via a rail line in which he had a personal interest and then overcharged the government for their transportation.•

Volunteers traveling to Washington by rail from the north had to transfer in Baltimore from one station to another, making their way across town to the Washington station at great peril. Southern sympathies were high in the city, as they were throughout Maryland. Usually, the rail cars were pulled by horses to the Washington connection at Camden Station, but frequently the volunteer soldiers marched to Camden Station, sometimes through a gauntlet of taunting spectators.

On April 19, 1861, just five days after the surrender of Fort Sumter, the situation in Baltimore got out of hand. Crowds turned against the Sixth Massachusetts Infantry while the Bay Staters were marching to the con-
JIR necting station. °The hostile citizens were not pleased with the prospect of Yankee soldiers waging war on the seceded states which Maryland supported. As the troops proceeded through the street, the crowd grew more hostile. Somebody threw a stone, somebody fired a gun, and a melee erupted between the citizens and the soldiers. Four Massachusetts men were killed and thirty-six were wounded, and at least twelve citizens were killed.•

*When Federal forces seized Virginia's Orange and Alexandria Railroad, they made its shop and yards in northern Virginia—just across the Potomac River from Washington—into the headquarters for the U.S. Military Railroad. The yard (left) was the hub of a series of rail routes reaching out to Lynchburg, Gordonsville, and Charlottesville. Crisscrossing Virginia, the Orange and Alexandria lines were continually fought over, destroyed, and rebuilt throughout the war.*

While these logistical problems annoyed Northern railroad companies, the South could only look on its Federal counterpart with envy. The Yankee rail lines were far superior to those of the Confederates. Not only were the Union railroads better supplied by the North's huge industrial base, they also served more of their WPG region than the Rebel lines covered in the South. °At the start of the war, there were approximately 31,100 miles of railroad in service in the United States. Of this, 22,400 miles were in the North and 8,700 were in the South.• During the war, no additional railroad construction occurred in the Confederacy.

At the beginning of the war, neither side was sure of how to take advantage of what their railroads offered;

*Just before the battle of Second Bull Run, Stonewall Jackson's foot cavalry marched fifty miles in thirty-six hours through Thoroughfare Gap to sweep first into Bristoe Station and then into Manassas Junction. They destroyed cars and engines belonging to the Orange and Alexandria Railroad, leaving a scrapheap (below left) of the remains. The view below right shows a derailed locomotive and the burned depot and storehouse that supplied Gen. John Pope's army. Before setting the fires, Jackson's weary Rebels found a bonanza of new saddles, blankets, and overcoats, as well as chocolate, tins of lobster, and barrels of whiskey.*

*A U.S. Military Railroad crew works with block and tackle to right an engine derailed by Stonewall Jackson's men on the Manassas Gap Railroad. Manassas Junction, site of two major engagements during the war, stood at the intersection of the Orange and Alexandria Railroad and the Manassas Gap Railroad. The Manassas Gap connected the Tidewater with the Blue Ridge and the agricultural bounty of Virginia's Shenandoah Valley.*

military planners had to learn as they went along. For its part, the North blundered spectacularly early in the war by not using trains to support fully its armies in battle. Union Maj. Gen. George B. McClellan could have scored enormous victories over his Southern adversaries in the battles fought in western Virginia during the late summer of 1861, but his forces were hobbled by breakdowns in telegraph communication and poorly scheduled troop and supply trains. Afterward, McClellan, a railroad president in the prewar years, wrote Lincoln: "It cannot be ignored. . . . The construction of railroads has introduced a new and very important element in war . . . for concentrating at particular positions, large masses of troops from remote sections . . . creating new strategic points and lines of operation."

Five weeks later, McClellan's observations on the strategic use of railroads came to pass on the battlefield, but it was for the South that trains delivered the first victory, when railroads made the difference between winning and losing at First Manassas. Confederate Gen. Joseph E. Johnston had ordered Brig. Gen. Edmund Kirby Smith's troops from the Shenandoah Valley to Manassas, and they arrived just in time to turn the battle in the Rebels' favor.

JPH °If Smith's troops had not appeared when they did, had they not been rested from the train ride rather than tired from marching across the countryside, the battle would have gone the other way. That lesson, however, was not really learned until similar events happened several times over during the next year or so to suggest how useful railroads could be in combat.•

Railroads even determined where the war would be fought. Without the railroads, the Civil War would have been fought primarily along the eastern seaboard and the nation's inland waterways. Trains changed all of that, transporting men and materiél to any spot on the map where track had been laid.

*Union Brig. Gen. Herman Haupt (above right) is shown overseeing a line crew near Bull Run (above left). He is standing on the right in the picture. Haupt, condsidered to be the greatest railroad construction engineer in the world, was chief of construction and transportation for the U.S. Military Railroad. At the beginning of the battle of Second Bull Run, Haupt barely escaped capture as his locomotive outraced the Confederate advance to Manassas Junction. He repeatedly telegraphed up the line to warn Washington, but Federal response was slow because many Union officers were enjoying themselves in the Capital, twenty miles away. Such occasions only reinforced Haupt's mistrust and disdain for the Union command. Only a few weeks earlier, Haupt had demanded—and received—extraordinary powers to overrule the orders of any Federal officer, regardless of rank, in matters pertaining to the railroad.*

FOLLOWING THE Southern success at First Manassas, and after almost a year of mismanaging its railroads, the North acted to bring order to the chaos of so many private lines. On January 31, 1862, Congress
WPG passed the Railways and Telegraph Act, °giving the Federal government the ability to impress or seize as necessary any communications and transportation systems it required, including railroads and telegraph systems. This established the structure for what would become the U.S. Military Railroad system. The military was now free to use railroads at established rates of payment and compensation. At the same time, the system helped eliminate the personal animosities, organizational antagonisms, and competitive efforts of the various independent railroads of the North.•

In addition, Lincoln replaced the controversial Cameron with Edwin M. Stanton, formerly an attor-
JAW ney for the Illinois Central Railroad. °Stanton was a good secretary of war—certainly by comparison with Cameron. Stanton hired the best technicians he could find to run the railroads for him. As long as they did their jobs and kept the trains running and on schedule, he let them spend whatever was necessary.•

On February 10, 1862, Lincoln wisely appointed Daniel C. McCallum as the director and superintendent

*Described by President Lincoln as the "most remarkable structure that human eyes ever rested upon. . . . There is nothing in it but beanpoles and cornstalks," this span over the Potomac Creek was truly remarkable. Herman Haupt built the bridge—ninety feet high and four hundred feet long—in less than two weeks, using soldiers who had never before built a bridge. It was constructed entirely of green timber because, as Haupt commented, "Timber at this time is very scarce." The bridge was demolished in the fall of 1862 by Federal troops, an action that warranted an investigation because it was a mistake. However, the investigation was dropped when Gen. Ambrose Burnside said that he had given the order to destroy the bridge "on the advice of others."*

of military railroads. McCallum was a Scottish immigrant and JPH °an excellent railroader who brought military discipline to operating more than two thousand miles of track, scheduling four hundred engines and six thousand cars, and supervising thousands of men detailed to run the railroad. He was also the kind of hardheaded, shrewd administrator needed to acquire the materials required by the railroads, fend off self-serving politicians, and make the military railroad function as an independent operation within the larger military apparatus.•

During the early years of the war the North's primary military attention focused on the Confederate Orange and Alexandria Railroad and the powerful Baltimore and Ohio line, both of which had strategically important tracks in hotly contested battle zones near Washington and throughout northern Virginia. After Federal troops occupied Alexandria in mid-1861, the U.S. Military Railroad took over the former headquarters of the Orange and Alexandria. As Federal forces muscled their way into Virginia, retreating Confederate troops developed a policy of taking with them all the railroad equipment they could and destroying whatever had to be left behind. This became an important strategy for both sides as the war continued.

WPG °Railroads quickly became strategic targets. The moment the fortunes of war shifted and it seemed likely that a rail line might fall into the hands of the Yankees, a Rebel commander's first obligation was to destroy whatever rail equipment he could not haul with his troops and to ensure that the Federals would not be able to utilize the line against the South.• Thus track was torn up, bridges were burned, and equipment was destroyed.

The destruction by the South of the North's bridges, rolling stock, and rails required a massive rebuilding program to keep Northern trains rolling. Having addressed the smooth running of the military railroad with the McCallum appointment, Lincoln made another brilliant move by appointing Herman Haupt as chief of construction and transportation for the U.S. Military Railroad. While McCallum worked wonders in the office and with Congress, Haupt handled matters in the field.

*As Federal troops pressed into the South, they often put liberated slaves to work at railroad construction. Here contraband laborers repair a section of track near Murfreesboro, Tennessee, after the battle of Stones River. There were fewer miles of track in the South than in the North but they used a greater variety of gauges. Often when a rail line was captured by the Federal troops, the first necessity was to realign the rails to conform to the standard gauge used by the rolling stock of the U.S. Military Railroad.*

JIR °Haupt was a Pennsylvanian, a child prodigy, and a mechanical genius. He graduated from West Point at the age of eighteen and went into railroad construction and civil engineering. By the age of forty he was considered the greatest railroad construction engineer in the world.•
JAW °Although extremely bright and well trained, Haupt was also a domineering, stubborn officer. When he decided on a course of action, nothing distracted him until he had finished it. By the outbreak of the Civil War, he had a wealth of experience in overseeing and managing men although many of his men might not have enjoyed the experience. One never contradicted or questioned Haupt. He was considered a railroader's railroader and the perfect man to ramrod the U.S. Military Railroad.•

WPG °Haupt's tremendous skills as an organizer were rooted in his abilities to identify a problem, select the best solution, secure the most qualified people, and obtain the material necessary to do the job. He was a driver of men and pushed people to the limit or inspired the best performance possible.• His first assignment was to rebuild a three-mile section of track near Belle Plain that had been destroyed by the Confederates as they backtracked into Virginia—part of which was the Richmond, Fredericksburg, and Potomac Railroad—taking the rails with them.

*Confederate cavalry used hit-and-run tactics against the U.S. Military Railroad near Washington. The locomotive Commodore lies on its side after a successful Confederate raid. In the foreground are the chemical jug, developing tray, and negative rack of the photographer who took the picture.*

At Belle Plain, the men assigned to Haupt as a work force had no experience in laying track and had cut the cross ties into varying lengths. Complicating the situation even more, he had to accomplish his task during drenching downpours. Haupt nevertheless drew out the most qualified men as assistant engineers and improvised several tools for the work. He worked these men around the clock and completed the three-mile stretch of track in three days.

"It was a hard-looking track when first laid," Haupt noted, "and when the General [Irvin McDowell] rode out the first morning to inspect it, he expressed an opinion that an engine could never run over it." When the repairs were finished, "He . . . expressed surprise to find the track in good line and surfaced and ballasted with earth."

One of Haupt's singular achievements was in building bridges seemingly overnight. After rebuilding the three-mile stretch of track near Belle Plain, he had to reerect a 150-foot bridge over Pohick Creek. The work began on the morning of May 3, and fifteen hours later trains were using the structure. Later the reconstruction work fell to a group of twenty-four thousand civilians known as the Construction Corps who built trestles, repaired bridges, and laid track, usually while under fire from Confederate guerrillas, partisans, and scouting patrols.

Immediately after rebuilding the Pohick Creek bridge, Haupt faced a particularly unusual bridge restoration project. The span over Potomac Creek was JAW °ninety feet high and four hundred feet long, and Haupt rebuilt the bridge entirely of green timber using soldiers from the Sixth and Seventh Wisconsin and the Nineteenth Indiana—men who had never built a bridge before. When it was finished in mid-May, the locomotive *Washington* was run across the structure to test it, and it did not collapse. Within days Haupt was running trains across the bridge hourly.

When Lincoln and several members of the cabinet visited McDowell's headquarters, they viewed the

Potomac Creek bridge.• After the president returned to Washington, he commented to the War Committee: "A most remarkable structure that human eyes ever rested upon. That man Haupt has built a bridge across Potomac Creek, . . . over which loaded trains are running every hour, and, upon my word, gentlemen, . . . There is nothing in it but beanpoles and cornstalks."

It was inevitable that a man as competent and headstrong as Haupt would clash with his superiors whenever they meddled with matters concerning the railroads. On one occasion, Haupt resigned rather than submit to orders he considered detrimental to the rail service. The results were disastrous. Soon, the government was pleading for his return. "Come back immediately," begged Peter H. Watson, assistant secretary of war. "Cannot get along without you. Not a wheel moving on any of the roads."

With his return, the government issued Order No. 23 providing Haupt with even more authority in running the railroads his way. WPG °There was no more eloquent example of the necessity with which Haupt's energies were viewed then the fact that after he left he was invited back and his position was reestablished.• Although they may have been temperamental and difficult to work with, men like McCallum and Haupt had the skill, knowledge, and drive to provide the Union with significantly better railroads than the South's, an advantage that contributed much to the North's ultimate victory.

*The Orange and Alexandria bridge across Bull Run was destroyed and rebuilt seven times during the war. One of the structures was wrecked by a flood which washed away the supporting timbers but left the rails intact. As the war progressed, General Haupt's bridge builders began replacing this and other damaged bridges with prefabricated structures made of one-size-fits-all trusses that could be assembled on-site by relatively untrained personnel.*

THE SOUTH was at a disadvantage in that it had fewer than half of the track miles the North had, which was further compounded by the lack of railroad men with the skill and talents of McCallum and Haupt to oversee its railroads. Confederates, however, were no less passionate than their Union counterparts in defense of their rail system.

One of the Civil War's most legendary behind the-lines raids focused

WPG

*James J. Andrews led the daring operation now known in American folklore as "The Great Locomotive Chase." A Union spy who had masqueraded in the South as a quinine salesman, Andrews, along with twenty-four Union soldiers, managed to steal the Confederate locomotive* General *while it was stopped in Big Shanty, Georgia, for its crew and passengers to eat breakfast. They did this in spite of four thousand Confederate troops camped nearby. The plan had been for Union Gen. Ormsby McKnight Mitchell to strike at Huntsville, Alabama, while Andrews's raiders headed to Chattanooga burning bridges, tearing up track, and cutting telegraph wires as they went. The two actions would isolate Chattanooga and make it vulnerable to Federal attack. However, after a successful start, the plan hit many snags. Mitchell took Huntsville, but then, incredibly, began destroying tracks and bridges, wrecking his own route to Chattanooga.*

*The drawing at right by Wilbur G. Kurtz shows the General delayed at Kingston, Georgia, for ninety minutes because Mitchell's raid had congested the tracks ahead with trains fleeing the fight. The raiders pulled away from the Kingston station just four minutes ahead of their pursuers.*

on the railroad in the South. History has come to call this daring operation "The Great Locomotive Chase." The raid was simple in theory but extremely dangerous in practice. Northern raiders disguised as Southerners traveled to Georgia intent on stealing a locomotive. Their plan was to head to Chattanooga, burning bridges, tearing up track, and cutting telegraph wires as they went. If successful, the mission would disrupt Confederate rail service and, at the same time, isolate Chattanooga, making it vulnerable to Federal attack.

°The leader of the raid was James J. Andrews, a Union spy masquerading as a quinine salesman who had traveled extensively through Georgia and Alabama in the first year of the war accumulating information for the North. He and twenty-four Union soldiers infiltrated the South, and on the morning of April 12, 1862, they found their way along the line of the Western and Atlantic Railroad to a station called Big Shanty, near present-day Kennesaw, Georgia. While the crew and passengers detrained for breakfast, leaving the train untended, and despite there being a camp of four thousand Confederate troops across the tracks, Andrews and his men stole the locomotive *General* and three boxcars,• leaving behind the passenger coaches.

The conductor, William Fuller, was startled by the sound of his train's sudden departure and believed that Confederate deserters were trying to escape from the

nearby camp, but he was not about to let anyone steal
WCD his train. °A man of tremendous determination, Fuller pursued his stolen train, first on foot, then by handcar, then by a commandeered locomotive.•

The raiders were occupied with cutting telegraph wires and tearing up track, so Andrews was unaware of Fuller's relentless pursuit. Andrews's main concern was what lay ahead. In his guise as a Southerner, he explained to station masters along the way that his train was on a special mission carrying ammunition to P. G. T. Beauregard.

JPH °Andrews was unflappable and managed to talk himself out of several difficult situations at numerous junction points where the *General* and its three-car train encountered other passing trains. The Western and Atlantic line was typical of the single-track railroads of the time, with regularly placed turnouts and sidings to permit trains to run in both directions, scheduled to pass each other at given times and places. Likewise, Andrews was delayed a number of times. Although he had a copy of the line's schedule, several of his anticipated delays were made longer by a Yankee raid on Huntsville, Alabama, which had congested the tracks with trains fleeing the fight. His last delay, at Kingston, held up the train for ninety minutes. The raiders pulled away from the station just four minutes before Fuller came through in a commandeered locomotive with a detail of Confederate soldiers.•

*Andrews's nemesis was William Fuller, conductor of the stolen* General. *Determined to retrieve his locomotive, Fuller pursued the absconders, first on foot, then by handcar, and finally with a commandeered locomotive, the* Texas. *The* Texas *was facing the wrong way, but Fuller was undeterred and ran the engine in reverse at speeds up to ninety miles an hour.*

*Shown at left is the* Texas, *with steam billowing behind its front, approaching a covered bridge containing a burning boxcar. Fuller simply pushed the car onto a siding and continued on his way. Andrews tore up the tracks behind him three times to derail Fuller. The first time Fuller and his engineer Jeff Cain derailed on a handcar, but quickly recovered. The second time, engineer Cain spotted the break in the track and reversed the engine. The third time, just minutes behind the* General *and running at full speed, the* Texas *sailed over the break without derailing. The many thrilling—and often farcical—events in the chase have made at least two exciting movies. In a silent classic made in 1927,* The General, *comedian Buster Keaton played Fuller. Fuller was portrayed by Jeffrey Hunter in the 1956 Walt Disney movie* The Great Locomotive Chase.

*After the fall of Atlanta, a photographer pictured the* General *with its cab shot away, its headlight gone, and almost every surface riddled with shot. The locomotive, a 4-4-0 built by Rogers, Ketchum, and Grosvenor in 1855, was one of the many that the Confederates attempted to destroy as they fled Atlanta. Refitted in 1868, the engine ran in revenue service until 1886. It was later fully restored and is today on display at Big Shanty Museum in Kennesaw, Georgia. The* Texas *can be seen at the Atlanta Cyclorama.*

Amazingly, Fuller had overcome all the obstacles Andrews had left behind to hinder any pursuit. The conductor had appropriated several locomotives along the way, and when those were stopped by torn-up tracks, Fuller ran ahead on foot until he could find another engine. Finally, he found a locomotive that seemed unstoppable, the *Texas,* one of the best engines on the line and the same model as the *General.* The only problem was the *Texas* was headed in the wrong direction when Fuller found it. Lacking a turnaround, the Southern railroader used it anyway, shifting the engine into reverse.

JPH °Andrews's raiders desperately fled their pursuer, running for their lives because they were dressed in civilian garb. If caught they would be hanged or shot as spies. They were now trying to elude a determined crew of experienced railroaders with a good engine on their own tracks. For their part, Fuller and his men knew that if Andrews and his raiders completed their mission, they would wreak havoc on the railroad and potentially the course of the war.•

The *Texas,* even though it was running in reverse,
WCD slowly gained on the *General.* °Andrews could now see his pursuers, and what added insult to injury was the fact that they were speeding toward him backward.

The raiders tried to wreck the *Texas* by releasing their boxcars in the hope that one would crash into the pursuing engine, but Fuller slowed his engine to allow the boxcar to couple with it and then pushed the car along in front of him. When Andrews threw back a second car, Fuller repeated the maneuver. The raiders gained the time it took the Southerners to handle both cars and the time it took for Fuller to release the two cars into a siding at Resaca.

Andrews decided to outrace his pursuer, opening the throttle and at times reaching speeds of ninety miles an hour. The raiders then attempted to derail the *Texas* by dropping the stringers they carried as fuel for bridge burning, but that too failed. They placed a rail across the tracks on a blind curve, but the *Texas* stayed on track even though it hit the rail head on.

Near Dalton the raiders erected a barrier across the track. Farther north they set fire to a boxcar and left it in a covered bridge, hoping that the fire would burn down the bridge and end the pursuit. Although the roof of the bridge caught fire, Fuller slowly pushed the burning car into the open and onto a siding.

Everything Andrews tried was countered by Fuller, who would not let anything prevent him from getting back his engine. Eventually, the raiders ran out of fuel• near Ringgold, Georgia. The chase had covered eighty-seven miles—the last fifty of which had been covered in sixty-five minutes. The Yankees jumped from the train and scattered into the woods.

WPG °Ultimately, Andrews and eight raiders were captured, court-martialed as spies, and hanged on June 7, 1862, in Atlanta. The rest were sent to prison camps.• Although it was a small affair and a failure, the raid itself has become a part of popular culture. The North JPH saw it as one of the great heroic acts of the war. °To recognize the raiders and their daring but hopeless railroad venture, Congress created the Medal of Honor, the highest award that American soldiers can receive.•

The South's foiling the raid was one of the few bright spots the Confederates enjoyed concerning the railroads during the war. In most other cases, the North simply outmaneuvered, outspent, and outmanufactured them. Before the war the South had been dependent on the North for most of its rolling stock, locomotives, and railroad iron. When that supply was ended, Southern railroads began to deteriorate on their own, especially when Federal armies waged war on them. As early as January 1862 the Confederate quartermaster general, Abraham C. Myers, complained that some railroads were only operating two trains a day, averaging six miles an hour.

Generally described as "two streaks of rust and a right of way," Southern railroads played a vital role throughout the war in relaying troops from one theater to

another. After the battle of First Manassas in July 1861, perhaps the most significant relocation of troops occurred during the fall of 1863, when James Longstreet's corps of eighteen thousand men was rushed from Virginia to Georgia by various routes and railroads, arriving in time to sway the outcome of the September 19–20, 1863, battle of Chickamauga.

Despite their timely arrival, G. Moxley Sorrel, one of Longstreet's staff, observed: "Never before were so many troops moved over such worn-out railways, none first-class from the beginning. Never before were such crazy cars—passenger, baggage, mail, coal, box, platform, all and every sort wobbling on the jumping strap-iron—used for hauling good soldiers."

*As the war went on, Confederate railway systems and rolling stock continued to deteriorate, but the railroad might of the North increased. Shown in an 1864 photograph above is a brightly decorated 4-4-2 engine named for Edwin M. Stanton, the North's secretary of war. Unlike modern engines, locomotives of the period connected to a load only at the rear. The cowcatcher was still very useful for clearing animals and debris from the track. To turn an engine around so it could run "head out," a gear-driven turntable was used, like the one on which the* Stanton *sits at the Orange and Alexandria yard in Alexandria.*

The Confederacy's ability to maintain its railroads was further hampered when the government preempted all foundries and iron manufacturers for military purposes. Thereafter Southern railroaders cannibalized minor rail lines to repair main lines, which gradually reduced the number of areas from which Rebel forces might draw their supplies. Because Confederate armies could not rely on Southern railroads to accumulate supplies, field commanders such as Robert E. Lee were unable to exploit their victories, which doomed them to win battles while they lost the war.

*After the battle of Shiloh, the Confederates retreated to the railhead at Corinth, Mississippi, whose Tishomingo Hotel is shown at right. Learning that the Union army had amassed a force of nearly 135,000, Confederate Gen. P. G. T. Beauregard decided to evacuate the town rather than fight. On the night of May 29, 1862, the Rebels stoked their campfires bright along the front and created noisy demonstrations. At the railway station, trains blew their whistles all night long in an attempt to make the Yankees believe Beauregard was being reinforced. The ruse worked. Cautious Federals entered the town the next morning to find the Confederates gone.*

*The easiest way to destroy a railroad was to set fire to a stack of ties with the rails placed over the stack (above left). Heat from the fire caused the rails to bend, rendering them nearly useless. General Haupt encouraged his rail crews to recycle bent rails when possible by picking them up and dropping them over an object until they were straight enough to be reused. However, heated rails bent around a tree or twisted lengthwise could never be reused.*

*The smoldering ruins of the bridge across the North Anna River (above right) resulted from a raid on Richmond by Union Gen. Philip Sheridan in May 1864. Sheridan got close enough to the Confederate capital to see the lights of the city and hear dogs bark. This span on the Richmond, Fredericksburg and Potomac Railroad was wrecked and rebuilt several times. Before the war, the line listed assets of ten locomotives, one switcher, eighty-eight slaves, and a bay horse.*

WPG °Perhaps the most important reason for the failure of the Confederacy's private railroads to organize and support Southern military campaigns was the laissez-faire philosophy of the South toward business. The government tended not to meddle in private businesses• or to force private businesses to behave in certain ways.

WITH EACH passing year of the war, Union attacks against Confederate railroads intensified and became more sophisticated. The sabotage of rail lines had WCD become a new chapter in the book of warfare. °Both sides knew that the most effective way to stop a train was not to attack the locomotive itself, but to tear up the track or burn a bridge. The loss of a bridge over a major river could effectively stop rail traffic for weeks or months or maybe even years, depending on the ability of the enemy to reconstruct the bridge. Some bridges destroyed during the Civil War were never reconstructed during the course of the war.•

Even though bridges and track were usually destroyed in areas out of sight from rail workers and soldiers, train JAW crews faced extremely hazardous duty. °Even in peacetime, railroading was a dangerous job, but it became doubly so during war. Railroad workers often went days

*With the Union capture of forts Henry and Donelson early in 1862, the Confederacy abandoned Nashville, the first state capital to be occupied by the North. It became a bastion of Federal power and, after Washington, perhaps the most fortified city in America during the war. Typical was this bridge across the Cumberland River. With its heavily timbered sides, guardhouses, and thick wooden gates, the structure provided a formidable defense against attack and sabotage.*

without sleep, then they repeatedly found themselves in the middle of the fighting and unarmed. It was a dangerous profession with armies shooting at them, shooting at their locomotives, then trying to knock their locomotives off the tracks, destroy their rails, and capture the goods that they were carrying.•

Bridges were built with guardhouses, and the protection of certain key lines and trestles became imperative, although there never seemed to be enough protection to go around. JAW °Bridges were vulnerable because of their length and frequently their remoteness. Troops on both sides tried to guard only the most vital parts of the railroad, those segments that would cost the most and take the longest time to repair. These troops, however, tended to be elderly men not fit for battle or green troops who had never been blooded. The simple fact was that nobody anywhere could protect an entire railway.•

Sometimes friendly troops themselves stopped the trains from running. Vandalism was rampant, and trains were stopped when soldiers in camp used railroad equipment and supplies against orders. Shortly after the September 17, 1862, battle of Antietam, Haupt found that the majority of problems he encountered while trying to restore the Manassas Gap and the Orange and Alexandria railroads were caused by Union troops.

"Camps had been established near the roads, and near the stations," Haupt reported, "and the soldiers would tear up sidings and switch stands, burn the wood provided for engines, wash clothes and their persons with soap in the streams and springs which supplied the water stations . . . and many of the engines were stopped on the road by foaming boilers caused by soapy water."

Haupt was noted for rebuilding railroads in record time, but as the war went on he also turned his attention to destroying them. His golden touch continued here, and he even wrote a book on the subject suc-

*In December 1864, Federal soldiers of the Fifth Corps, Army of the Potomac, under Maj. Gen. Gouverneur Warren make a Maltese cross, the badge of their corps, by heating rails from the Weldon Railroad near Petersburg, Virginia, and wrapping them around a tree. Iron rails so treated could not be salvaged. When William Tecumseh Sherman's men destroyed rail lines this way during their March to the Sea, the bent rails were called Sherman neckties.*

cinctly titled *How to Destroy Locomotives and Bridges.* JPH °He realized there was a very simple way to bring down most railroad bridges, and he designed a small bomb, basically a pipe bomb, that could be fitted into a hole in a wooden beam drilled with a hand auger. In just a few minutes, a skilled man could bring down a major bridge of any size.•

For damaging locomotives most effectively, Haupt recommended the simplest and most direct method: JPH °sending a cannonball through the boiler. The boiler could be fixed, but it took thousands of hours. Wrecking the boiler was easier than trying to bend the axles or tip the engine off the tracks.•

In previous wars, it was common for battles to be fought over control of rivers, harbors, farmland, and industry. With the Civil War, for the first time, battles were fought for rail lines. One of the bloodiest of these occurred in Corinth, Mississippi, on October 3–4, 1862. The Confederate objective was to regain control of the railroad intersection of the Mobile and Ohio and the Memphis and Charleston railroads at Corinth, which had been in Federal hands for several months.

JAW °The Yankees wanted to maintain control of the railhead in Corinth because to do so would effectively cut off supplies to the western and southern parts of the Confederacy. The result was a battle fought north of Corinth, not over the town, which had no strategic value, but over the intersection of the two rail lines.•

"The history of this war contains no bloodier page, perhaps, than that which will record this fiercely contested battle," wrote Confederate Maj. Gen. Sterling Price. He also might have written that the battle must have been one of the most frightening for the participants. Before it was over, both sides noted three earthquakes that shook the spirits of the men.

JPH °Corinth was one of the bloodiest battles in the first half of the war, but ironically the railroads played no direct part in it. The armies that engaged over the railroad junction arrived on foot or by horse. After two days

*Counterattack, raids, and sabotage of Federal property were always a possibility in heavily contested northern Virginia. Therefore, to protect its rolling stock, the U.S. Military Railroad moved a large number of locomotives from the captured Alexandria yards across the Potomac into Washington where they are shown here parked in view of the recently completed Capitol dome.*

of fighting had taken a thousand casualties on each side, the Confederates withdrew from Corinth. They never regained control of the railroad junction.•

AT THE start of the war, the railroads had been plodding, mismanaged military entities, but slowly they evolved into the main supply arteries of the war machine. By 1863 they began to accomplish incredible feats, a crowning moment of which was the rescue of Union Maj. Gen. William Rosecrans during the siege of Chattanooga, Tennessee.

WPG °Rosecrans's army was trapped, cut off from any reinforcements. Secretary of War Stanton proposed a long-distance relief and resupply by rail. In response, Maj. Gen. Joseph E. Hooker's corps was transported from Alexandria, Virginia, to Alabama by rail and then marched on to Chattanooga to relieve Rosecrans. It was the largest resupply and transportation of a military division by rail up to that time.•

JPH The logistics of the move were incredible. °Within three or four days of the proposal, equipment was being gathered in Washington and northern Virginia. The trains consisted of caravans of a locomotive and ten to twenty cars of all descriptions—freight cars, passenger cars, baggage cars, and flatcars. Each regiment traveled with its own supplies, artillery, weapons, ammunition, and horses. Previously, such a relocation would have divided the resources of the army into troop and supply trains. This maneuver to relieve Rosecrans was complete, a tactical innovation and a good move for an army that would have to go into battle soon. Within eleven and a half days the bulk of Hooker's army had traveled halfway across the country to relieve the Army of the Cumberland at Chattanooga. The siege was broken, and from that point on there was no doubt the Union controlled the western theater of war and that the North could move its troops by rail wherever they were needed.•

The operation covered twelve hundred miles over several lines that had been sabotaged at various times during the war. The first fifty miles of the Baltimore and Ohio track had been disabled and rebuilt the previous year. In the western segment of the journey, the final three hundred miles of track had been wrecked and repaired eighteen months prior to the movement. Even more remarkable, the operation suffered no mechanical difficulties, and afterward the equipment was returned quickly to the original railroads, which resumed normal operations.

At the completion of the relocation of Hooker's corps, W. P. Smith recorded: "So far, not one of thirty trains of six hundred cars has been delayed improperly. The only thing we have to regret is that the actual movement exceeds the requisitions by nearly 20 percent in men and more than 50 percent in horses."

The impressive ability of the Northern construction crews to build and repair railroads quickly was also demonstrated by Maj. Gen. Grenville Dodge who became a key architect in constructing the railroads that supplied William Tecumseh Sherman's army as the war WCD headed toward Atlanta. °Dodge devised rapid, almost overnight ways in which to lay new track to replace track that had been torn up. He designed strong, yet lightweight bridges that could be erected quickly over streams and rivers. He laid more than a hundred miles of track and put up more than a hundred bridges of one variety or another during Sherman's Atlanta campaign.• His procedures were modeled after Haupt's techniques developed early in the war, and demonstrated that within two years of their inception they had become standard practice within the military.

*By mid-1864 the U.S. Military Railroad Construction Corps had become adept at major bridge projects. Construction of the bridge below began at 5:00 A.M. on Friday, May 20, 1864, and rail traffic passed over it at 4:00 P.M. on Sunday, May 22. It was 414 feet long, 82 feet high, and contained 204,000 feet of timber. This was the fourth bridge to be built at this point over the Potomac Creek to carry trains of the Richmond, Fredericksburg and Potomac Railroad. The second one was the "beanpole and cornstalk" bridge (see photo page 388).*

*City Point landing on the James River in Virginia became the Union army's all-purpose rail-sea link during the final stages of the war.* The General Dix, *a locomotive weighing 59,000 pounds, is unloaded at the City Point docks. The tender piled high with wood used for fuel is behind the engine. A little more than twelve miles from Petersburg, City Point was built up over the winter of 1864-65 to funnel the might of the Northern war machine onto Richmond's doorstep.*

Northern construction crews became so adept at rebuilding wrecked rail lines that their accomplishments demoralized Southern troops. One disgruntled Rebel soldier said that he would not be surprised if the Yankees carried their own tunnels with them.

One innovation that allowed rebuilding miracles was the prefabricated bridge. Once again Haupt was behind
JAW the ingenious solution. °In 1862 Haupt reasoned that he could save time rebuilding bridges if he premanufactured them. During slack periods at the Orange and Alexandria yard, he had his crews create the bridge parts. They built them in pieces so they could be assembled in the field according to the length necessary to span the obstacle.

When the Federal army captured a railway on which the Confederates had burned or destroyed the bridges, Haupt noted how many bridges were needed and how long each should be. He then sent word to his storage depot to load a train with the necessary supplies and the right number of prefabricated bridges. He would put them in place, lay track on them, and begin running trains across the new structures until another obstacle was encountered.•

In May 1864 the war in the western theater focused on Georgia. Atlanta's role as a major Southern railroad
JIR and manufacturing center made it a prime target. °Five rail lines intersected at the city, and its seizure would cripple the Deep South commercially and economically.• Ironically, the retreating Confederate Army of Tennessee in Atlanta, under the leadership of Lt. Gen. John Bell

Hood, began destroying the city's railroad facilities long before Sherman's army could appropriate them.

JPH °When Hood evacuated Atlanta, one of the last things he did was to destroy systematically the city's railroad facilities. He burned his ammunition trains and what shop buildings and equipment he could. It was an evacuation under stress, but Hood did not want his ammunition or the city's railroad equipment to fall into Federal hands.•

After taking control of the city, Sherman resupplied himself by rail and then finished what Hood had started.
WPG °Over and above the destruction inflicted by Hood's own forces as they retreated from Atlanta, Sherman's troops paid particular attention to the railroad facilities in Atlanta. They burned the shops, the yards, and anything they could get their hands on to forever keep them from being used by anybody for railroad purposes.•

Sherman then turned eastward, toward the sea, for his epic march across Georgia from Atlanta to Savannah. The stated reason for the march was, in his words, "To make Georgia howl." He had readied his men for this moment. "The condition of the army is all that could be desired," Sherman observed. "They seem so full of confidence. Whether called on to fight, or to build bridges, make roads, or tear up railroads, they have done it with alacrity, and a degree of cheerfulness unsurpassed."

*Material for the Union Petersburg campaign had to be transported by water to the U.S. Military Railroad depot at City Point. On August 9, 1864, an explosion on a barge laden with munitions rocked Virginia for miles around. Close to 600 feet of warehouses were blown up, along with 180 feet of the wharf. Casualties included 70 killed and more than 250 injured. General Grant, whose headquarters were at City Point, was unharmed. Rebel saboteurs were blamed for the explosion.*

*With five major railroad lines intersecting in Atlanta, the city was a major rail center and thus a prime target whose capture would cripple the South both commercially and economically. Shown below (left) is a car shed of the Western and Atlantic Railroad, which, as Sherman drew near to Atlanta, was a principal support line for the Army of Tennessee under Gen. John Bell Hood. As the city's fall became imminent, Hood prepared to withdraw. Unable to take his trains, he ran seven locomotives, eighty-one freight cars filled with ammunition, and thirteen siege guns to the railroad yards. He then evacuated every building for half a mile around, and a cavalry rear guard set torches to the rolling stock and supplies. For five hours the ground heaved like an earthquake under the detonations, windows were shattered, and nearby buildings were pierced by shells as thousands of explosions rocked the darkness. To the north, Union General Slocum wondered if Hood was attacking Sherman. In Jonesboro, Sherman wondered if Hood was destroying Slocum. In the morning Federal troops found Hood's army gone and were confronted with scenes of desolation such as that of the Atlanta rail depot (below right).*

On the March to the Sea, Sherman destroyed everything that might have some use for the Confederate military. The most prized trophies, of course, were the JIR rail lines. °Sherman was the best general in the Civil War at tearing up railroads. He created a technique that became notorious as the war went along. His men would tear up the tracks, use the crossties for firewood, then take the metal rails themselves and lay them atop the burning wood until the middle of the rails became malleable. Soldiers would then take each rail and wrap it around a tree, creating a Sherman bow tie. Once the rails cooled, they were absolutely unusable and could never be straightened again. Meanwhile, the crossties had been incinerated, too, and so all that was left was the empty rail bed. Sherman's army employed this tactic across Georgia and into the Carolinas.•

While Sherman was tearing up Georgia railroads, in the rail center of Petersburg, twenty miles south of Richmond, the war was heading toward its conclusion on the Virginia front. In an effort to hurry the process along, the Federals unveiled a new weapon—one that delivered its punch via the railroad. It was a weapon of terror known as the "Dictator"—allegedly because it JPH "would dictate the terms of surrender"—°a huge, 13-inch seacoast mortar normally used to throw explosive shells into forts.

*In the final stages of the war, the industrial might of the North began to make all the difference. At Alexandria, Virginia, the U.S. Military Railroad's prefabricated bridge parts (above left) are ready for shipping and easy installation (above right) in a few hours by trained or untrained crews. The mills of the North spit out miles of rails (below). Such manufacturing capacity was nearly absent in the beleaguered South.*

The seventeen-thousand-pound weapon was capable of firing a three-hundred-pound shell five miles with a seventy-five-pound charge of black powder. The North used it to spook the defenders of Petersburg. It was one of the most modern weapons of war because the Confederates could never find the range on where the mortar's shells were originating because the Dictator was mounted on a railroad car. When Rebel shelling came close, Union forces simply moved the train. At the same time, as a war-making machine, the Dictator had a good deal more value as a psychological weapon than it did as offensive ordnance. The mortar was only capable of firing its projectiles at slow intervals, and its shells were not particularly effective, but the ability to throw a shell that size over a distance of five miles stuck in the minds of several artillery officers. It was a precedent for many later weapons.•

By April 1865 the conflict was all but over. Confederate troops were abandoning their capital at Richmond. Their president and his cabinet boarded the last train to leave the city. One last chore of the evacuation was the destruction of the remaining railroad equipment. Photographs of the railroad debris at Richmond are poignant, symbolic of the fundamental strategic role that railroads had played during the war. The

*In 1864 Sherman's men ripped up rails (above right) on The March to the Sea, and in Virginia Grant's troops rail-mounted a seventeen-thousand-pound seacoast mortar nicknamed the "Dictator" (above left) to terrorize Petersburg. The mortar was constantly moved, frustrating Confederate batteries trying to return its fire.*

*In April 1865 the old locomotive below, a victim of the fire that ravaged fallen Richmond's Burnt District, symbolized the end of the Confederate States of America.*

fact that the South destroyed so much of its own property indicated that those locomotives were viewed as critical resources. The railroads were so valuable that the Confederates could not allow them to fall into Northern hands at any cost.•

The tatters of Lee's Army of Northern Virginia fell back across the Virginia countryside with the goal of finding trains on the Richmond and Danville Railroad to take it to North Carolina to link up with the remnants of Joseph E. Johnston's Army of Tennessee. Federal cavalry, however, cut the rail line, and the Confederates marched toward Lynchburg, hoping to find supplies on the South Side Railroad station at Appomattox Station. Union horsemen again appeared and seized these supplies, forcing Lee to surrender to Ulysses S. Grant. Afterward, in providing rations for the Southern prisoners awaiting parole, the Northerners dispensed the supplies they had seized from the South Side train.

On April 12, 1865, the war ended, and American railroads looked forward to resuming their peacetime commerce, but there remained one last role before they could put the Civil War behind them.

*On Friday morning, April 21, 1865, the last train of the U.S. Military Railroad departed Washington, D.C. It traveled over the same rails that had brought Abraham Lincoln to his inauguration as president of the United States a little more than four years earlier. Now the martyred president was returning home for burial. During those four years, trains had changed the way wars would be fought. With the coming of the locomotive, warfare would never be the same again.*

After Lincoln's assassination on April 15, it was decided that his body would be returned by funeral train to Springfield, Illinois, for interment. On Friday morning, April 21, 1865, the last train of the U.S. Military Railroad departed Washington, D.C., for the journey over the same rails the president-elect had traveled when he
WCD entered Washington more than four years earlier. °There was an outpouring of grief and sadness all along the route. It was a last chance to pay tribute to the man called Father Abraham, who had freed the slaves, who had saved the Union, and who had given his own life.•

By the war's end, one thing was clear to military men: Trains had changed the way in which wars would
JIR be fought. °Generals who had made railroads a part of their overall logistics enjoyed great success; those who ignored or lacked them failed. Railroads came to have an overwhelming impact on the way wars were conducted because they provided a vehicle that could transport tremendous numbers of men, heavy loads of equipment, and do both faster than any other mode of transportation up to that time. The whole logistical aspect of war changed with the coming of the locomotive,• and warfare would never be the same again.

# BATTLEFIELD MEDICINE

While NO ONE WAS PREPARED FOR the enormous scale or duration of the Civil War, the least prepared were the medical departments of the armies of the North and the South. More than six hundred thousand men died during the war, and the terrible task of caring for the sick and wounded and hundreds of thousands of other casualties fell to the medical officers on the battlefield. With imagination, courage, and skill, these doctors joined their brothers in the line of fire, but their war was against disease and their battle was to save lives. To the men who survived the ministrations of battlefield medicine, these doctors and nurses would be both heroes and fiends rolled into one. Although they were fighting to save lives, they were often forced to torture their patients because they lacked sufficient anesthetic, time, or knowledge of how to care better for the horrible wounds they tried to treat.

WCD °The art of medicine in the United States was still primitive in the mid-nineteenth century. The education of doctors was basic and general because they learned their trade by observation. Surgery was practiced much as it had been at the beginning of the century, and operating techniques were crude and unsanitary.• The existence of microbes and germs had not as yet been accepted. Sicknesses were treated mostly at home—hospitals being rarely used—and local medicines were preferred over unknown and untested pharmaceuticals. There were advances in public health in cities such as New York, Philadelphia, and Chicago, but in rural areas things were as they had been for centuries.

| | |
|---|---|
| **GED** | Gordon E. Damman |
| **WCD** | William C. Davis |
| **PJD** | Peter J. D'Onofrio |
| **BP** | Brian Pohanka |
| **PSS** | Paul S. Sledzik |

*An Army of the Potomac directive on cooking bacon advised that it be washed and scraped, then soaked all night. The next day the bacon was to be boiled, and then simmered for three hours, after which time "the rind comes off easily, and the meat tastes fresh and sweet." Such instructions might be useful during winter quarters or between campaigns, but during battle or on the march soldiers had little time for such fuss. Food—unsanitarily handled and improperly cooked—was but one of the many ways soldiers fell prey to illness. Campsites such as that of the Eighteenth Pennsylvania Cavalry pictured here provided conditions for the development and spread of disease.*

Little was known about the causes of disease. The most popular, accepted view was rooted in the ancient theory of "humors" or miasma odors that emanated from the earth. Many diseases were common: typhoid, typhus, measles, mumps, smallpox, malaria, yellow fever, and smallpox. The last was the worst and most dreaded disease of the era, but a vaccine had been developed and had even been used during the Revolutionary War to inoculate Washington's army. European armies used discipline to deter the spread of diseases by strictly enforcing regulations on bathing and delousing.

At the beginning of the Civil War, for the first time in its history, the United States mobilized not one but two large armies, and there was little precedent for organizing the medical department of either. In the Union army at the beginning of the war, only one assistant surgeon was assigned to a regiment of one thousand men, and the qualifications for the position were so general as to allow almost anyone to hold the job.

Many believed that any competent civilian physician was capable of being a competent military medical surgeon, and so the regular army medical service recruited doctors from the medical schools. The regiments organized by the states appointed their own doctors, but frequently these men were elected to the position without regard for their qualifications. Massachusetts, Ohio, and Vermont were the only states to screen these positions.

"Physicians taken suddenly from civil life, with little knowledge of their duties . . . had to be taught them from the very alphabet," observed Dr. Charles S. Tripler, the first surgeon appointed to the Army of the Potomac. "It was the duty of the doctor to physic every man who chose to report sick, and to sign such papers as the colonel directed him to sign. To superintend the sanitary condition of the regiment, to call upon the commanding officers to abate nuisances, to take measures for the prevention of disease, was, in many instances, considered impertinent and obtrusive."

*The humorous painting above by Winslow Homer is titled* The Malingerer, *later called* Playing Old Soldier *(old soldier was a slang term for a malingerer). As the soldier shows his tongue to the field doctor, his eyes reveal that he is trying to be excused from his responsibilities. Surgeons developed a hard attitude toward shirkers, often discounting their complaints and returning them to duty. Occasionally, a truly sick soldier was mistaken for a malingerer and sent back into the line. After one such soldier died of typhoid, Surgeon Alfred L. Castleman of the Fifth Wisconsin was outraged. He complained to fellow doctors that it was better to "excuse ten 'seeds' (shirkers) who are worthless, even when in rank, than sacrifice one good man."*

When the fighting began, doctors faced not only thousands of wounded men at a time, but the worst wounds inflicted in the history of warfare. Military technology had created the percussion rifle, which fired a .58-caliber Minié bullet—a lead projectile more than one-half inch in diameter. Regardless of where a Minié bullet hit a man, it did a great deal of damage. If it struck a bone, the bone shattered. Any arm or leg wound that also destroyed a segment of bone essentially meant that the arm or leg had to be amputated because there was no technology for bone reconstruction. At the same time, surgical techniques were such that internal wounds could not be addressed because there was no such thing as internal surgery.

Three out of every four surgeries performed in the field during the war were amputations. Most were conducted under crude conditions in primitive surroundings, often on a kitchen table in an open shed by surgeons fatigued from overwork. "The shattering, splintering, and splitting of a long bone by the impact of the Minié or Enfield ball were, in many instances, both remarkable and frightful," observed Confederate physician D. J. Roberts, "and early experience taught surgeons that amputation was the only means of saving life."

*Wounded Union soldiers from the battle of the Wilderness were photographed outside the Marye house at Fredericksburg, Virginia, by a Mathew Brady photographer in May 1864. Fredericksburg was the nearest town where soldiers injured in this battle could be sorted before being given more treatment or shipped out for recuperation. They were left outside to wait their turn for help or were placed in the shade of a tree to recover from surgery that often rivaled their wounds in destructiveness.*

GED °The mortality rate of an amputee increased if the wound occurred closer to the midline of the trunk of the body. Amputation around the ankle had a mortality rate of 10 percent. Amputation of the leg around the knee increased the mortality rate to about 30 to 40 percent. Upper thigh amputations had a mortality rate of 65 percent. If the wound caused an amputation at the hip area, the mortality rate was 80 to 90 percent.•

PJD °Photographs of amputees who survived the war convey the wounded soldiers' sense of relief that they were still alive and also a sense of pride in having made a great sacrifice by the loss of a leg, an arm, or both because they knew they had done so in the name of the cause. They gave as much as they could in defense of the honor of the country they proudly served.• These men were also often proud of the work their surgeons had performed. "Dear Surgeon Ebersoll, my limb causes much curiosity among the surgeons here," wrote Alexander Ivy of the Seventh Wisconsin. "They say it is the best amputation they ever saw. They wonder how it was ever done, and wish to know how you did the work. Thanks to you for your skill in taking off my limb."

PSS °Photographs of these men also convey something of the whole experience of their wounding, their surgery, and their convalescence. It is communicated in their eyes, their faces, and the stump of their leg or arm. These were debilitating injuries with legs shortened two or three inches, arms or legs missing, portions of bone, tissue, and faces missing. The incredible thing was that men survived these kinds of injuries.•

GED °For the men awaiting treatment, the experience was horrifying, but for the doctors, not only did they face wounds they had never treated before, they were overcome by the sheer logistics of treating hundreds and thousands of patients within a short time.• "It was horrible to look upon ghastly wounds. To live amid fever, contagion, and the groans of the dying, to hear the

*The death of Union Gen. John Sedgwick illustrates the destructiveness of the advance of weapons technology. The accuracy and distance of the rifled Minié ball far exceeded that of the round musket projectiles from earlier wars and created fierce damage. Sedgwick, at the front directing the positioning of his troops at Spotsylvania, declared, "They couldn't hit an elephant at this distance." Seconds later, a sniper's round hit him in the cheek below the left eye. Death was instantaneous. When death did not come to soldiers hit by Minié balls, such destructiveness caused a tremendous amount of work for surgeons.*

cries of agony we were powerless to relieve," recalled Dr. J. R. Weist, a Federal physician. "We saw the lives of brave men ebb slowly away and watched them die before the cause in which they had sacrificed themselves was won."

The sights and sounds of the battlefield were like nothing anyone had ever seen before. Some wounds were so far beyond the skills of the surgeons, they could only leave the men under the comforting shade of a tree, a practice that eventually led to the determination of the "dying tree" after almost every battle. Often men of both sides found themselves under the tree, subtly aware that nothing could be done for them. Men who had been trying to kill each other only hours before now consoled each other while they waited to die.

A major problem early in the war was the gathering and transportation of the wounded from the battlefield to the rear. The men usually detailed for this kind of work were those the company commanders could best spare, namely, the malingerers and other undependables in addition to the company band members. Sometimes wounded men were left on the field unattended for days.

At first, the transportation of the wounded was delegated to the quartermaster corps. Few commanders

*Dr. Samuel Preston Moore (above) resigned his commission with the U.S. army to serve as surgeon general of the Confederacy. Always asked to do more with less, Moore made the best of it. He developed hospitals built around the concept of "huts" or wards of twenty-five to fifty patients with similar needs, a forerunner of today's general hospital.*

*Dr. Charles S. Tripler (below), the first medical director of the Army of the Potomac, was overwhelmed by the demands of a one-hundred-thousand-man army and was replaced in July 1862 by Dr. Jonathan Letterman.*

made a priority of caring for the wounded, and ambulance horses frequently were taken as mounts for the cavalry. In 1862 Kentucky Sen. William E. Simms complained: "Soldiers are allowed to lie on railway platforms for three days and are dying on the cars, in the hospitals, and on the streets for the want of a little attention. Medical officers have slain our troops."

The sheer number of casualties and the understaffing of the medical corps prolonged the treatment of the wounded for days after the fighting had stopped. "We have given out all our rags and bandages, and God knows what we shall do without these articles to dress wounds," reported Dr. A. B. Isham of the Seventh Michigan Cavalry. "I worked until one last night assisting and dressing wounds. Disabled men are still being brought in and set upon tents in the wet straw, for you must know it rains and has rained steadily since last Sunday."

Battlefield injuries, as horrible as they were, did not claim the majority of lives lost during the war. Field sanitation was a major problem. Most of the troops from the western states and those from the South were from farms, and for some their understanding of personal hygiene and use of latrines was somewhat lacking. BP °They did not understand how dirt could spread infection, not only in the hospital but among the camps themselves. They did not understand about purification of water, and that water that happened to look clean might in fact be deadly. They did not know that mosquitoes carried malaria and yellow fever.• Sanitation, however, was not a significant problem for those units commanded by current or former regular army officers; these men immediately indoctrinated their junior officers in the use of field latrines and demanded enforcement of good hygiene.

GED °The soldiers of both armies were accustomed to their mothers' cooking. They were accustomed to being clean and well clothed. Now they lived in tents, exposed to mud, rain, heat, cold, and poor food. When they were not engaged with the enemy, reveille was sounded at 5:30 in the morning, and they would drill throughout the day. There was little regard for adequate sleep, and if the company were on the march, the men were fortunate to get an hour or two of sleep a day. Moreover, sleep deprivation could debilitate the men and make them susceptible to disease.• Complicating matters even more, when the regiment was on the move, the men had to bathe in streams that were filled with all kind of bacteria, including the offal from their horses and the men themselves. No one yet knew that germs could be far deadlier than bullets.

WCD °For the vast majority of men in both armies, this was the first time they had ever associated with large numbers of other men. The health of easterners was better than those from the western and southern states with regard to communicable diseases. The latter group had come from smaller cities and rural towns and villages where the majority of the population lived in isolated or mostly isolated areas. The men from the larger eastern cities had survived the so-called childhood diseases that self-immunized their populations, but a significant percentage of the noneasterners had never been exposed to these diseases, and so when they reported to the training camps and then to the armies, where tens, twenties, hundreds of thousands of men were gathered in a single place, things like measles, mumps, chicken pox, and whooping cough ran rampant through entire regiments. Because these ailments hit the men when they were no longer children, they could be deadly. Measles alone probably killed one hundred thousand.•

In June 1862, Union Maj. S. C. Gordon noted: "I do not exaggerate when I say that more than a thousand cases of diphtheria occurred in these regiments. It seems to select the finest most able bodied men." He went on to add: "The death march could be heard at almost any hour of the day or night. That mournful roll of the drum or fife became so dismal, adding to the deadly homesickness, the fear of death, that a general order forbade any music at a funeral."

WCD °Many doctors had little consciousness of sterilization and sanitation. Soiled and contaminated blankets and bandages often went from one soldier to another after the first man had died. Surgeons cleaned their instruments on their pants legs, leather aprons, or the soles of their shoes. A surgeon suturing a wound might

*Union Surgeon General William A. Hammond brought efficiency and order to the army medical service, created a general hospital service, and tried to form an efficient ambulance corps. His foresight about the lasting importance of surgeons' medical records resulted in the publication of the* Medical and Surgical History of the War of the Rebellion, *the first publication by American physicians that was recognized as worthwhile in Europe. Unfortunately, he disagreed with Secretary of War Edwin M. Stanton on policy matters, was court-martialed on an insignificant charge, and was dismissed from the army in 1864. Vindicated after the war, he was placed on the retired list as a brigadier general in 1879.*

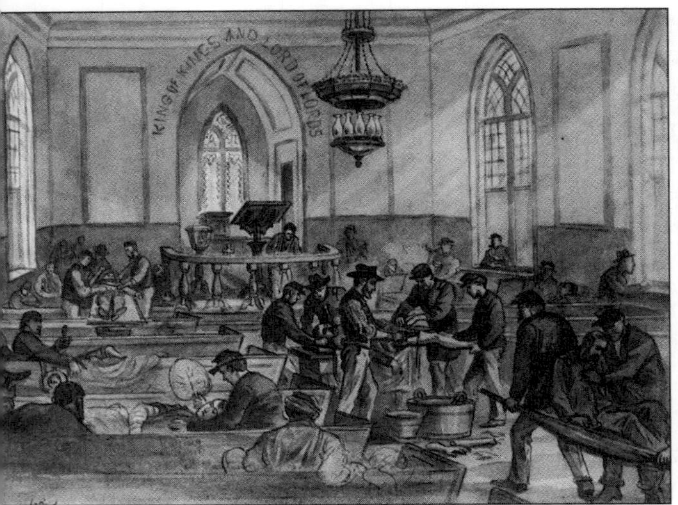

*Almost any building could be turned into a hospital on short notice. Throughout the South churches—like the Episcopal church in Middletown, Virginia, after the battle of Cedar Creek (above left)—or homes (above right) were used as surgical centers. Yankee troops often caused severe damage to churches and other public buildings by using them, not only for hospitals, but to stable horses and for target practice. To this day many antebellum homes in the South contain rooms with dark stains on the floors caused by the blood from Civil War amputations.*

lick the thread to get it through the eye of his needle, which meant that if he happened to have a cold or some other condition, he could infect his patients.• Surgeons rinsed out blood-stained sponges with the same filthy water that had stood by the operating table all day.

Dr. C. H. Tebault, a Confederate surgeon, observed: "One blessing we enjoyed, due to the blockade, was the absence of sponges, clean rags being substituted for them with telling advantage. These rags could be washed, as was done, and used over and over again. It is next to impossible at all, to wash an infected sponge."

After the first year of the war, physicians knew they had to improve their organization and their skills. Out of desperation came knowledge, and as the war proceeded, they amazed themselves at the gains they made. "Inexperience caused the sacrifice of thousands of lives," J. R. Weist recalled. "No department of the army demonstrated the evil consequences of imperfect knowledge in a greater degree than the Medical Department, and in none was complete knowledge of the art more quickly gained."

THERE WERE fifteen hundred casualties after the battle of First Manasass, and for the few men who practiced medicine on that battlefield, their experience was a baptism by fire. "At the time of the Battle of Bull Run," noted John D. Billings of Massachusetts, "there was no plan in operation by which the wounded in that battle were cared for. So general was the opinion that the war would be speedily ended, no one thought of such a thing, but this condition soon after changed. Preparations for war were made on a grander scale."

In July 1861 the Union army had no plan for evacuating the wounded from the regimental aid stations of the battle front to the general hospitals in Washington. There were no ambulances, and so the wounded had to walk back to their camps near the capital, a distance of twenty-seven miles.

PJD °The early years of the war were probably the worst moments for the medical departments of both armies because they were disorganized and too focused on individual units. Regimental surgeons worked only on the soldiers of their own regiment, which meant that one surgeon might be overwhelmed with casualties from a regiment that had been in action while a surgeon a few hundred yards away did nothing because his regiment had been held in reserve.• Some surgeons were also reluctant to treat the wounded of another regiment. When brigaded with other regiments there was duplication of equipment and supplies.

WCD °If the armies were maneuvering for a set-piece battle, the surgeons prepared as best they could. They

*A barn near the battlefield at Antietam is shown at left being used as a Union hospital. After the battle, a member of the U.S. Sanitary Commission wrote, "Indeed, there is not a barn or farmhouse, or store or church or schoolhouse between Boonsboro, Sharpsburg or Smoketown that is not gorged with wounded—Rebel and Union. Even the corncribs, and in many cases the cow stables, and in one place the mangers were filled. Several thousands lie in the open air upon straw."*

*An ambulance (above) was sometimes nothing more than a wooden covered wagon. Without springs, it could cause excruciating pain—or even death—for a badly wounded soldier as it jolted over rough terrain. However, the Federal ambulance system developed by Jonathan Letterman and manned by soldiers with specific training combined with the establishment of field hospitals set up near battlefields was a vast improvement over the previous haphazard treatment of the wounded.*

polished their instruments, sharpened their knives, and arranged their medicines. They would prepare a great deal of morphine, laudanum, and other opiates as painkillers and chloroform to use as an anesthesia. After that the surgeon waited.•

In August 1861, when George B. McClellan restructured the army, he also reorganized the medical department. As it was finally adopted, the plan called for field dressing stations, divisional field hospitals, and general hospitals. GED °The wounded either walked or were carried to a field dressing station, which was set up as close to the firing line as possible, in most cases fifty to one hundred yards behind the main battle lines, away from the line of fire, either behind trees or rocks or in a low area. This station would be manned by a surgeon, an assistant surgeon, and possibly a hospital steward. If a soldier was grievously wounded, the field dressing station performed only basic first aid and stopped any bleeding with tourniquets. Stretcher bearers would take the wounded man to an ambulance, which would then proceed to a field hospital, set up a mile or more behind the battle lines.•

Field hospitals were improvised just out of artillery range in nearby railway stations, barns, or private homes. The doctors needed water, light, and a flat surface for their operations. PJD °As the soldiers were brought to the hospital, a surgeon would perform a quick examination to determine the order of treatment for the most seriously wounded or those most likely to survive. One room might be set up for minor operations, such as suturing lacerations; others would be used for major operations, such as amputations.•

WCD °Any man taken to a field hospital, if he was conscious and not blind, probably felt a mortal terror the moment he

*Wounded men were often collected on battlefields by means of collapsible stretchers (below). A standard stretcher had folding legs which turned it into a low bed, keeping the wounded off the wet ground.*

*A train of ambulances (above left) is parked awaiting the wounded. City Point, Virginia, served as a processing point for wounded Federals late in the war. A steady stream of Northern supplies came into City Point's hospital, while injured men were placed on river transports and ferried north for more treatment or convalescence. In other theaters, men were shipped by train when rail was available. Army doctors were given control over the operation of such trains to ensure that the wounded were promptly delivered to the next stage of their care.*

*Union ambulance drivers of the First Division, Ninth Corps of the Army of the Potomac pose (above right) near Petersburg in 1864. Records kept by these soldiers became the basis for granting pensions to veterans long after the war.*

saw it. The first thing he was likely to see was a pile of arms and legs that had already been amputated from the men who had gone before him. He would hear moaning, groaning, crying, and screams of pain. He would see the surgeons covered with blood. One man described the terror of a wounded man who saw the reflected gleam of the steel instruments when a surgeon opened his medical case, because all of the instruments meant pain. Field hospitals were a bedlam—dying men and blood everywhere and chaos. The surgeons themselves were overworked, terrified, exasperated, and often disgusted at what was going on around them and what they had to do. It was like a scene from Dante's *Inferno.*•

"As the patient recovered from the effects of the ether, the thought of his wounded arm returned to him, and turning his eyes towards it, they met only the projecting stub," recalled John D. Billings. "As the awful reality dawned on him, he fell backwards in a swoon. Many men like him came to consciousness only to miss an arm or a leg which they had begged in the last moments to have spared."

A special kind of courage was needed to endure the sights and sounds of a field hospital. One of these physicians was Dr. Robert McMeans, who, on a cold and dark night after the October 8, 1862, battle of Perryville, Kentucky, wrote his last letter home to his wife: "My dear wife, I feel some better this morning, but still very weak. Doctor Weber would give me an order home

*During the Peninsula campaign, March through August 1862, many Union wounded were left behind on the battlefield. At Second Bull Run, ambulances broke down and poorly trained civilian drivers fled. Some of the wounded lay on the field for almost a week, enduring the summer heat and thunderstorms. Citizens were enraged. In July 1862 Jonathan Letterman (above) was appointed medical director of the Army of the Potomac and, with General McClellan's approval, established a distinct ambulance corps. The first critical test of the new corps came in September at Antietam, the bloodiest day in American history. The improvement was significant. By the night after the battle all the wounded had been carried away. Letterman's plan to treat the wounded first at field hospitals and then at improvised hospitals farther back also worked well.*

*In February 1863 a bill was introduced for Congress to establish an army-wide standardized ambulance corps like Letterman's, but it was defeated. Finally in March 1864 the Ambulance Corps Act was passed establishing the corps as a regular unit for all Federal armies. This legislation gave the Medical Department authority to train men, and it prohibited soldiers from quitting the field to help their wounded comrades, leaving that job to medical personnel.*

on furlough, but so long as my life holds out I feel it is my duty to follow my friends in their fate. My shirt is stiff with blood. I can say no more. My blessings on you." McMeans died of a heart attack the next morning while ministering to his troops.

There were three thousand wounded men in Perryville, and all of them had to be transported by ship, train, or carriage to larger hospitals after the battle. "I took on board our steamer 218 sick, more than our boat could accommodate," an official in Nashville recalled. "I left behind on the banks of the Tennessee a tottering, woebegone crowd. I had to say, 'I cannot take you.' God help them . . . for I feel they will never receive the warm welcome that awaits them at home."

GED °Large general hospitals were set up in the North and South. Washington, D.C., had sixteen general hospitals, and each had a bed capacity between three thousand and four thousand.• One of the largest Civil War hospitals was at City Point, Virginia, which was comprised of five corps hospitals and accommodated six thousand to ten thousand patients.

The hospital system in the South was perhaps the greatest achievement of the Southern medical service. By mid-1863 it oversaw a system of 154 hospitals in Alabama, Florida, Georgia, North Carolina, South Carolina, Tennessee, and Virginia. The largest of these was Chimborazo Hospital, a complex of 150 one-story buildings on 125 acres on a hill overlooking Richmond. The hospital housed more than 4,800 patients at a time, and over the course of the war treated 76,000 patients. The bakery daily generated 10,000 loaves and was supplemented with an ice house, soup kitchens, and a farm with more than 200 cows and a large goat herd.

The number of patients entering and released from the Confederate hospitals equaled the number in the North and in many ways surpassed it. Between September 1862 and December 1863 the thirty-nine hospitals in Virginia treated 293,165 patients, a number equal to every member of Robert E. Lee's Army of Northern Virginia being admitted to the hospital three times.

*Wounded soldiers on Marye's Heights after the battle at Spotsylvania in May, 1864, wait for treatment at a field hospital. Stretcher bearers would take a wounded man to an ambulance, which would then proceed to a field hospital set up just out of artillery range in a nearby railway station, barn, or private home. As the soldiers were brought in, a surgeon would perform a quick examination to determine the order of treatment for the most seriously wounded or those most likely to survive.*

Hospitals were designed with much thought given to ventilation. Fresh air was considered the best way to counter the humors and miasmas that many believed carried and spread disease. Insects were considered a nuisance, and so attempts were made to protect patients from them, which inadvertently reduced the spread of disease by flies and mosquitoes. Open latrines, however, were still used, but the widespread use of disinfectants and deodorants contributed to better sanitation.

One of the wounded who survived due to the hospital system was Columbus Rush, a Confederate soldier with the Twenty-first Georgia who was wounded at the battle of Fort Stedman, near Petersburg, Virginia.
PSS °He was twenty-two years old when his lower legs were shattered by a cannonball; both limbs were amputated just above the knee. Afterward he was taken to a hospital in Washington to convalesce. Rush went on to live in New York City, and after the war he was outfitted with a pair of artificial limbs. Thereafter he walked with the aid of two canes, one example of how men survived serious injuries and medical treatments.•

THROUGHOUT THE war the suffering of soldiers was horrible. They endured brutal conditions. They were plagued by hunger, exhaustion, and disease. They suffered loss of limbs, loved ones, and hope. Alongside them, doctors in blue and gray struggled to keep them alive, but not all of their efforts were successful. In many instances doctors were able to prolong life for only a short time, allowing a dying soldier time enough to send some last word to his parents, wife, family, or sweetheart.

A dying Confederate wrote: "My dear father, this is my last letter to you. I've been struck by a piece of shell, and my right shoulder is horribly mangled. I know that death is inevitable. I will die far from home, but I have friends here who are kind to me. May we meet again in

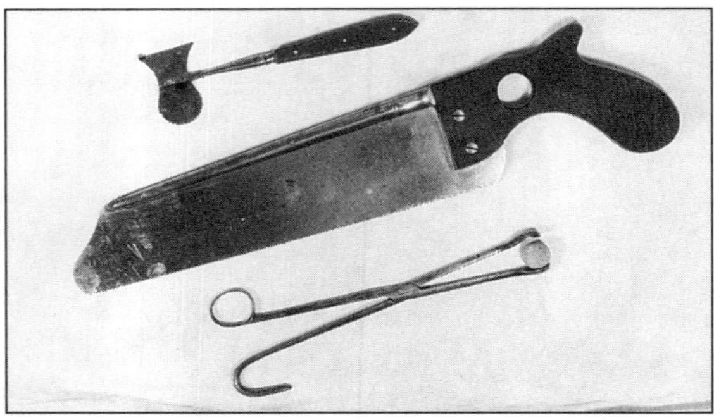

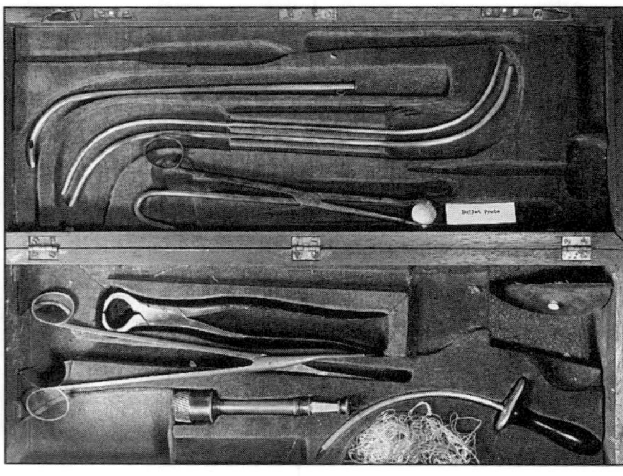

*Surgical tools always included the oft-used bone saw for amputations (top). From the beginning of the war Confederate surgeons were faced with a shortage of instruments. Moreover, one report noted that surgeons using tools made in the South "might as well be without any, for those they have are entirely useless." Dr. Letterman of the Army of the Potomac regretfully noted after Gettysburg that surgical tools belonging to the First and Eleventh Corps had been captured by the Rebels—a welcome haul for the Confederates.*

heaven. Your son, J. R. Montgomery, Spotsylvania Company, Virginia."

In July 1862 Jonathan Letterman was named medical director of the Army of the Potomac. An army surgeon for more than ten years, when he witnessed the huge number of casualties and the shortcomings of the medical service in conveying the wounded from dressing stations to field hospitals to general hospitals, he devoted himself to the establishment of an ambulance system and to expediting the flow of critical supplies.

Previously, ambulances had been driven by civilians who were likely to bolt for the rear at the sound of the first shot. Under Letterman, ambulances were manned by soldiers who received specific training for their positions. He set up division hospitals and regimental hospitals that merged into divisional units. The wounded were arranged so as to transport those less severely wounded to general hospitals, thereby clearing the overcrowding and allowing the worst cases to receive care in the field hospitals. The first critical test of the new system occurred during the September 17, 1862, battle of Antietam.

Before the battle, Letterman rode across the countryside looking for hospital sites. After selecting eight sites and setting up seventy-one field hospitals, he noted the shortage of medical supplies and ambulances and sent for these from Frederick, Maryland. Color-coded flags were used to guide ambulance drivers from the battlefield to the various hospitals set up several miles away. The ambulance corps system also allowed each division to have its own supply depot nearby to replenish supplies.

GED °With twenty-three thousand casualties in twelve hours, the battle of Antietam was the bloodiest day in American history. When night fell on the battlefield and the fighting ceased, Letterman's hospitals were just beginning to do their work. For the most part the wounded were removed from the field within several

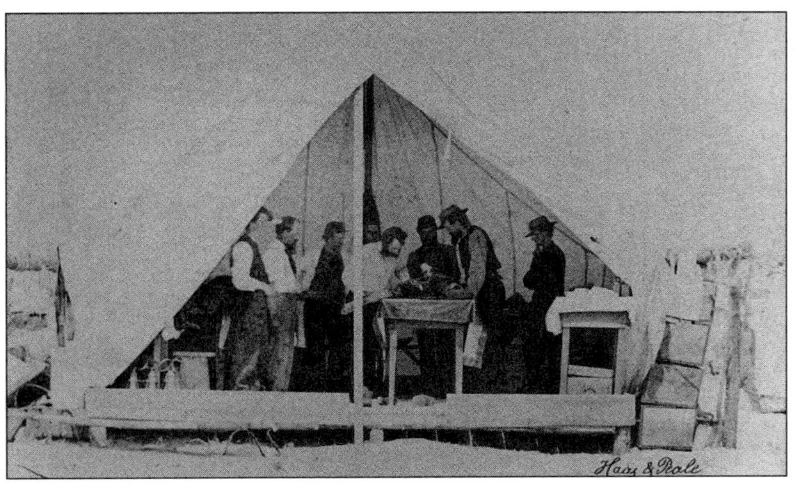

*Federal surgeon John J. Craven operates on a soldier at Morris Island, South Carolina. Craven would serve as physician to Jefferson Davis during the Confederate president's imprisonment after the war. Doctors were not immune from disease and the dangers of war. Federal records indicate 42 were killed in battle, 83 wounded, 290 died of disease or accidents, and four died in prison. Reliable records of Confederate casualties in the medical corps are not available.*

hours to a barn, house, or tent hospital. The surgeons worked straight through the night. Some operated for seventy-two hours without relief, working quickly over their tables, their aprons splattered with blood, and their hands covered with blood. An amputation procedure required an average of fifteen minutes. A surgeon would finish one and yell out, "Next!" The preparation for the next man would be little more than washing down the table with some water. The wounded man would be brought in, and the surgeon returned to his saw. Those kinds of operations went on for days after the battle.•

Four doctors were killed during the battle of Antietam; three were Federals and one was Confederate. One of these was Edward Revere, a physician with the Twentieth Massachusetts and the grandson of Revolutionary patriot Paul Revere.

The Dunker Church was used as a field dressing station. Two days after the last shots were fired, it was converted into a private embalming station so next of kin could claim the bodies of the dead already prepared for burial.

"I visited, after the battle, every hospital in the rear of our lines, and in no instances did I find any undue suffering for lack of medical supplies," Letterman reported. "Not only were the wounded of our own army supplied, but all the Confederate wounded, which fell into

*A surgeon and his assistant pretend to prepare for an amputation in a staged picture (right). Everything about this photograph seems unreal. The surgeon wears no apron, no bucket sits below the table to await the inevitable torrent of blood, and no other tools or medicines are visible. There is, however, nothing unreal about the picture below: a stack of severed feet and legs.*

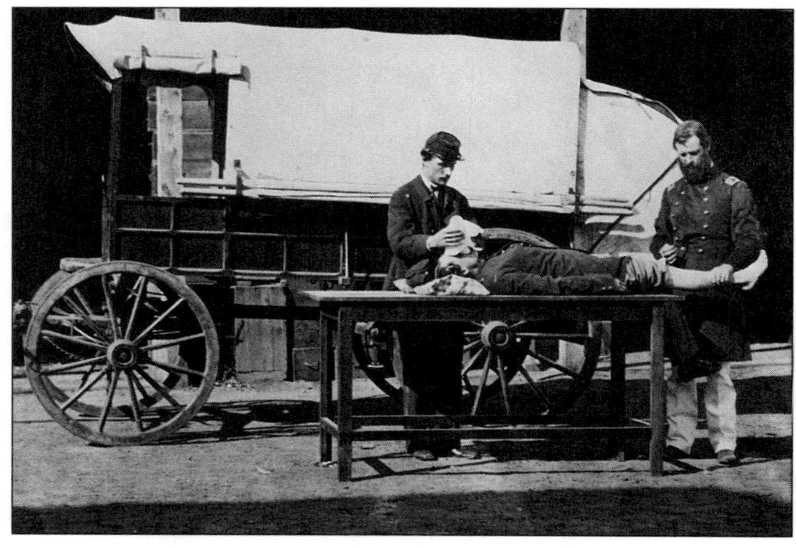

our hands, were furnished with all the medicines, . . . required for their use."

One civilian who came to Antietam to offer her assistance was Clara Barton, a native of Massachusetts who had worked in the Patent Office at the beginning of the war. She became interested in nursing, and although she was not affiliated with any formal organization at the time, she resigned her position and raised funds for food, medicines, and supplies. When she heard of the fighting in Maryland, she went to Sharpsburg with her own wagonload of bandages, food, and clothing.

Arriving at the northern edge of the infamous Corn Field at midmorning, Barton was welcomed to the Sam Poffenberger farmhouse by Dr. James Dunn and watched as harried surgeons dressed the soldiers' wounds with cornhusks. Most of the army's medical supplies were still en route from Frederick, so Barton donated her wagonload of supplies and joined the surgeons in their work. While the fighting continued around her, she cradled the heads of suffering soldiers, prepared food for them, brought water to the wounded men, and closed the eyes of the dead.

GED °The house was near enough to the fighting that it seemed to be under fire all afternoon. In the yard, a man asked Barton for a drink of water. As she raised his head with her right hand and held a cup to his lips with the other, a stray bullet clipped her sleeve and struck the man in the chest, killing him instantly.• So affected was Barton by the incident that she never repaired the hole in her dress. Nevertheless, the unlikely figure in a bonnet, red bow, and dark skirt continued moving from one wounded man to the next.

Working nonstop until dark, Barton comforted the men, performed impromptu surgery on some, and assisted the surgeons with their work—for a while being the only one to assist a surgery during a nearby artillery duel. When night fell, she produced four boxes of lanterns from her wagon. Two days after the battle, Barton collapsed from lack of sleep and a budding case of typhoid fever. She returned to Washington in the back of her wagon, exhausted and delirious. "In my feeble estimation," Dr. Dunn wrote to his wife, "General McClellan, with all his laurels, sinks into insignificance beside the true heroine of the age, the angel of the battlefield."

Barton's face was often blackened with gunpowder later as she followed the fighting. "I saw two hundred wagons crowded with wounded men," she noted during the battle of the Wilderness. "The dark spot in the mud told all too plainly where some poor fellow's life had dripped out in those dreadful hours. While our soldiers fight, I can stand and feed and nurse them. My place is anywhere between the bullet and the battlefield."

Her work did not stop when the wounded recovered, and Barton often talked with them during their convalescence and made inquiries regarding missing men. When prisoners were exchanged, she interviewed the freed soldiers for information on those who were still in Southern prisons. Despite the work of people like Barton, the politicians in Washington did

*The maiming caused by amputation was inevitably dramatic, and more so when the injury required disarticulation—removal of the limb at the joint. The more of a limb that was removed, the higher the chance of mortality. Disarticulation of the leg at the hip had the highest death rate at over 80 percent. Confederate General John Bell Hood survived such an operation.*

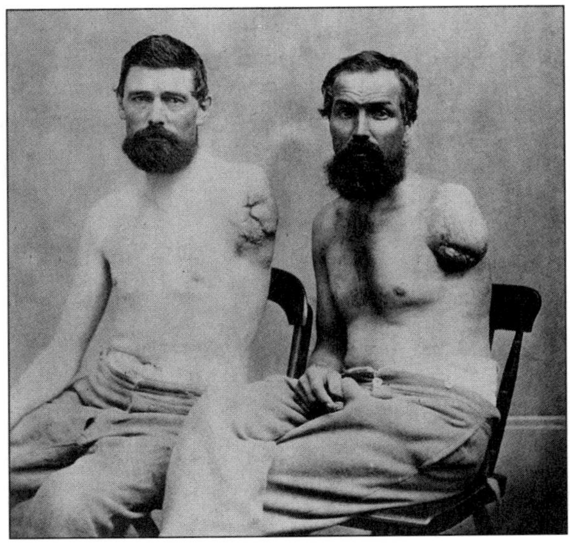

*Wounded Federal soldiers were photographed outside a U.S. Sanitary Commission station at Fredericksburg, Virginia, after the battle of the Wilderness in 1864. The commission was involved with ambulance service, nursing, and hospital service. Of the women who volunteered to work for the Sanitary Commission, Abraham Lincoln said, "If all that has been said by orators and poets since the creation of the world in praise of women applied to the women of America, it would not do them justice for their conduct in this war."*

not perceive the need for any further efforts to help the Union wounded.

Letterman's ambulance corps was standardized within the Army of the Potomac and approved by McClellan, but it could not be formally adopted by the army until it was approved by Congress. In February 1863 Letterman submitted his proposal to Congress, and it passed in the House but was defeated in the Senate as impractical.

In testifying for the need for the ambulance corps, Dr. Henry Bodich reported what he had seen on the Gettysburg battlefield: "My son lay helpless on the ground for some days by the side of his dead horse. After my son was assisted to the carriage, there was no water to be found. The driver was wholly ignorant of the names of those dying men he was carrying. When in sight of the mangled dead body of a first-born son, I would plead that such enormities shall never be permitted hereafter." The ambulance corps was finally approved on April 12, 1864, at which time it was mandated for all Federal armies.

During the battle of Gettysburg, Letterman's medical department was stationed well beyond the town, and the commanding general, George Gordon Meade, ordered that only ammunition wagons and ambulances be allowed nearer. The medical trains were allowed only as close as Union Mills and Westminster, about twenty-five miles from the fighting, which deprived the medical teams of the means of caring for the wounded. The corps and divisional medical staffs were with their troops, which afforded basic first aid to the wounded, but the major elements of the medical service were not on the battlefield until July 5.

"I had an interview with the commanding general on the evening of the 3d of July," Letterman reported, "to obtain permission to order up the wagons containing tents, etc. This request he did not think expedient to grant but in part, allowing one-half of the wagons to come to the front; the remainder were brought up as soon as it was considered by him proper to permit it."

GED ○A surgeon in a hospital behind Little Round Top recounted that he had exhausted his bandages and painkillers because Meade had decided that hospital supplies were a low priority when scheduling supply wagons. Ammunition had to be brought up first.•

*This 1864 print from* Frank Leslie's Illustrated Newspaper *was titled "Hospital Steward Filling Surgeon's Orders at the Army Drug Store." Pharmaceuticals were crude by today's standards, and in general, the South was more inventive with medicine because it had to be. Confederate physician F. Peyre Porcher produced a book on indigenous medicines which boasted "upwards of four hundred substances, possessing every variety of useful quality." Quinine was the drug most sorely missed by the Confederates, and alcohol was the one most universally dispensed by both sides. Painkillers such as laudanum, a tincture of opium, were effective but addictive. Because the level of dosage was not controlled, many soldiers suffered from drug addiction for the rest of their lives.*

The delay in medical treatment was the same for the Confederates who faced similar obstacles in getting their supplies in and their injured out. Pvt. J. W. Lokey of the Twentieth Georgia recalled: "Every ambulance and empty ordnance wagon was loaded with wounded and sent back to the Potomac at Williamsport. When loading the last wagon they said there was room for another man if he could sit up and ride, and I told them I could. . . . Language would fail me should I try to tell what those poor wounded men suffered on this trip."

Gen. John D. Imboden was charged with guarding the wagon train of Confederate wounded during the retreat back into Virginia. During the first four hours of his task, he claimed to hear and see more of "the horrors of war than I had witnessed from the Battle of Bull Run up to that day. In the wagons were men wounded and mutilated in every conceivable way. . . . Scarcely one in a hundred had received adequate surgical aid. Many of them had been without food for thirty-six hours. Their ragged, bloody, dirty clothes, all clotted and hardened with blood, were rasping the tender, inflamed lips of their gaping wounds."

A farmer in New Franklin, Pennsylvania, described his encounter with the train of injured men: "The large hall of my house and the yard in front were filled with wounded Confederate soldiers. They at once set up the clamor to my wife and other members of my family, '*Water! Water!! Give us water!!*' They also begged to have their wounds dressed." The Reverend J. C. Smith of New Franklin recalled: "All who were wounded in the head, the arms, the shoulders, the

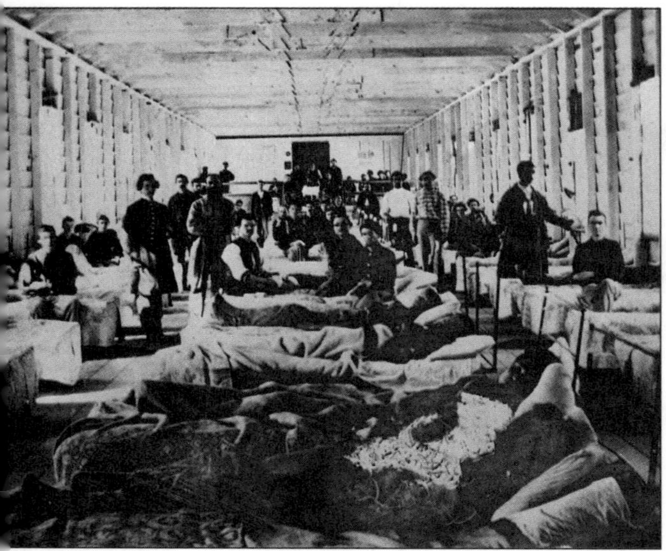

*As soldiers recovered, they were moved from hospitals to convalescent camps such as the Federal camp shown above at Alexandria, Virginia, where they could continue to heal. The nature of the camps varied, depending upon the condition of the soldiers sent there. Some were like extensions of hospitals, while others were more like a regular duty camp. Ambulatory men had great freedom in those camps. They still received necessary treatment but were expected to do modest chores—all part of getting ready to return to the front.*

nonvital parts of the body were compelled to walk through the ankle-deep mud. . . . When they came to a pump, one would place his wounded member under the spout while another would pump cold water on the sore. Then he would do a like service to his comrade. Thus the pumps were going all day." Smith concluded: "We estimated the number of wounded that passed through our town at twelve to fifteen thousand. It was an easy matter to trace their route of flight. Dead horses, broken-down and abandoned wagons, cannons, carriages and caissons, new-made graves were everywhere to be seen. It was simply a road covered with wrecks."

Initially, Southern planning had paralleled that of the North in that little thought had been given to the medical service. The Confederate medical corps consisted of former U.S. Army personnel and volunteers. WCD °The South had the benefit of Surgeon General Samuel P. Moore, an able administrator, but Moore suffered from a woeful shortage of materials and supplies, a problem that his counterparts in the North lacked. Moore's system was excellent when it worked, and was not markedly different from the system set up in the North for handling wounded men, but the Union had the luxury of better transportation, better facilities, and better supply. Once every element was in place in 1863, the Union system operated much more smoothly than the Confederate medical system.•

By 1864 the U.S. Congress had finally passed Letterman's ambulance act, which provided a Federal system for ambulances, stretcher-bearers, and medical treatment throughout the evacuation of the wounded. "It was necessary to park the ambulances under fire, and although the shells came close, each driver kept his team in place," wrote Lt. William F. Drum of the Twelfth U.S. Infantry. "It is a very brave man with a high sense of duty, who willingly goes under fire without arms. During the campaign, the Fifth Corps ambulance train removed more than eight thousand desperately wounded men from the field."

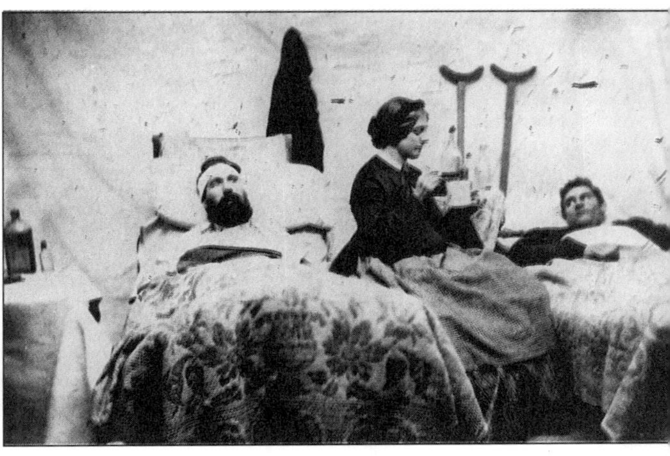

*This photograph of Federal nurse Anne Bell tending her patients is thought to have been taken at a hospital in Union-occupied Nashville, Tennessee. In the South the only trained group of women nurses came from the Catholic sisterhoods, but their numbers were few. The Confederate Congress officially recognized that women made excellent nurses and passed legislation in September 1862 providing pay, rations, and lodging for matrons and nurses at Southern hospitals. Still, recruiting nurses was difficult. Confederate nurse Kate Cumming wrote, "There is a good deal of trouble about the ladies in some of the hospitals. . . . Our friends have advised us to go home, as they say it is not considered respectable to go into one."*

ONCE THE wounded were removed from the battlefield, treated at the field station, and then operated on at the field hospital, they were allowed to convalesce. That often came at a facility back home or through care sent or paid for by the patient's family. At first, the nurses who staffed these hospitals were men, but as the war wore on, more and more women stepped forward.

Initially, women donated their services through various agencies that augmented the standard supplies issued the men in the field. Clothing of all kinds was contributed and occasionally included notes from the maker, such as New Englander Ellen Sprig's insertion: "My dear friend and brother in our country's cause, to your care and keeping I commit these socks. In every stitch is knit a prayer for peace. Some say our gifts never reach our soldiers, so it would be very gratifying to know who may receive my socks. I am most truly your friend."

As the U.S. government struggled to improve its medical systems on the battlefield, convalescent hospitals were sustained more and more by women who formed a nursing corps and dedicated themselves to saving lives. One of the first of these was founded by Dorothea Dix, a sixty-year-old crusader for the destitute and insane, who had visited Washington following the Baltimore riot of April 1861 to inspect the condition of the Massachusetts soldiers who had been injured in the melee. Afterward she met with the acting surgeon general, R. C. Wood, and announced her intention to found an army nursing corps made up of women volunteers. The secretary of war eventually responded by declaring that Dix would assist the chief surgeon in organizing military hospitals in Washington and appointing nurses to aid the suffering soldiers.

Dix enlisted the assistance of Dr. Elizabeth Blackwell, the first woman to earn a medical degree in

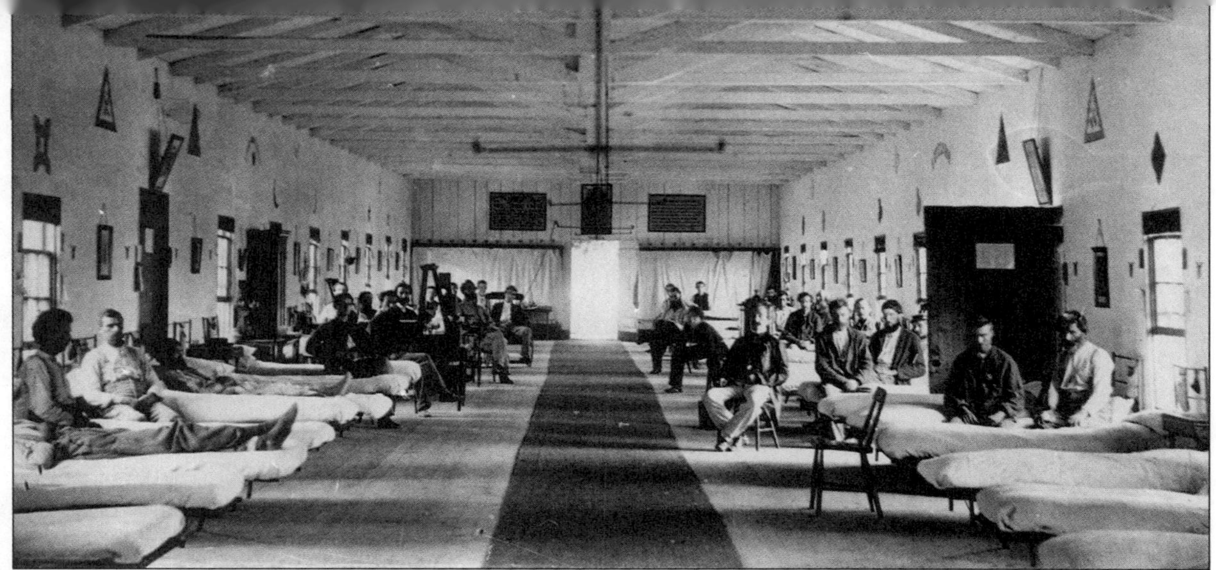

*A frequent visitor to Armory Square Hospital in Washington (above) was poet Walt Whitman, who spent many hours visiting the sick, bringing them jars of jam, writing paper and envelopes, tobacco, oranges, apples, and other items. He also gave them money. "Found several cases I thought good subjects for small sums of money," Whitman wrote in his diary. "The wounded men often come up broke, and it helps their spirits to have even the small sum I give them." When his brother was wounded at Fredericksburg in 1862, Whitman went there to care for him. In May 1865 his volume of poetry* Drum-Taps *showed his feelings about the horrors of war.*

America, who was then in charge of New York's Infirmary for Women and Children, along with the Women's Central Association for Relief in New York City. Applicants were screened through these two agencies and then trained at Bellevue Hospital. Only "sober, earnest, self-sacrificing, and self-sustained" women were interviewed. The response was overwhelming, but Dix was put off by the number of young, attractive unmarried women who volunteered. She promptly issued a statement: "No women under thirty need apply to serve in government hospitals. All nurses are required to be plain looking women. Their dresses must be brown or black, with no bows, no curls, no jewelry, and no hoops." The restrictions earned her the nickname "Dragon Dix," but she established and maintained a high standard of care within the Washington hospitals and worked tirelessly for no pay for the duration of the war.

Mary Ann Bickerdyke, a widow with two children, traveled with the Union armies in the western theater and nursed their wounded for four years and through nineteen battles. By the end of the war more than three thousand Northern women had volunteered as nurses. GED ○Many diaries of wounded soldiers compared these nurses and matrons to their mothers because they were often the only women around. The nurses wrote letters for them, read letters from home to them, held their hands as they lay dying, and performed many services that the men needed.•

*Douglas and Stanton Hospital was one of twenty-five hospitals in the Washington, D.C., area. Although a system of directories was established to help friends and relatives locate patients, it often failed in the confusion of war and with nearly 20,000 patients in the twenty-five hospitals. Walt Whitman wrote of a New York farmer who came to Washington seeking an injured brother. After searching diligently for a week, the frustrated man went back home, only to find a letter from his brother informing the man that the brother was at a hospital on Seventh Street.*

Women in the North who had loyally sent their husbands and sons off to war decided to fight their own war against death and disease on the battlefield by
BP working for the U.S. Sanitary Commission. °The organization allowed men who were too old to fight to join with thousands of women to hold fund-raisers to benefit the troops in the field, so that soldiers could have extra food and extra supplies. The Sanitary Commission also helped acquire the medicines to be used at the front. Many volunteered to work in the hospitals.• They provided the extra touches that comforted the wounded and assured worried families. Fanny Titus Hazen, one such Sanitary Commission nurse, noted in her diary, "I never failed to place by the heart of each silent soldier a bouquet of the choicest flowers that [his] dear mother might feel assured that an earnest, sympathetic heart had ministered to her son."

Whether purchased by the Sanitary Commission or the U.S. Army, surgeons used huge amounts of painkillers. While there were plenty of stories about injured soldiers biting a bullet in pain while an amputation was performed, most serious operations were done under heavy doses of chloroform with morphine or opium. The painkillers were crude but effective. They were also addictive.
WCD Thus °the war created a tremendous number of drug addicts as a result of the medications used particularly during and following amputations. Because no one knew proper dosages, surgeons administered enough to make a wounded man comfortable. That often led to overdosing

*Burial details followed closely after all battles. By common consent, the army holding the ground at the end of a fight buried the dead of both armies. During and after the war, the U.S. government exhumed the Union dead from hastily dug battlefield graves and reinterred them in national cemeteries. Confederate national cemeteries were established by the states, by communities, and even by private donors. Many Confederate soldiers were reinterred in sections reserved for them in private cemeteries or church yards. The embalmer became a common sight when the armies slowed down or entered a siege, as they did at Petersburg. Soldiers whose remains were suitably intact could be embalmed for shipment back home, with the cost usually borne by relatives.*

with the result that by the end of a three- or four-month period of convalescence, these men were often addicted to the drugs. Some of them carried the addiction with them well into the early days of the twentieth century.• It became so common that the condition was known as Old Soldiers disease.

Julius Hubray became addicted to opium following the amputation of his left PSS leg. °His final years were spent in the Soldiers Home in Washington. He never overcame his addiction, but he survived his injury by twenty-three and a half years before he died of an overdose of the drug.•

FOR THE surgeons, the war was an opportunity to improve their skills and to create new procedures. In their need to improvise and experiment, PJD important new discoveries were often made. °One of the classic tales told of the Southern medical corps was that because of the blockade, surgeons could not get the silk ligatures or sutures they normally used to close a wound. A doctor decided to substitute hairs from a horse's tail. Because horse hair is stiff, it was boiled to make it more pliable. What the doctor did not realize was that he was sterilizing the horse hairs, which was why he and his colleagues discovered that when they used boiled horse hairs the infection rate dropped tremendously among their patients.•

In addition to sterilization, the doctors rediscovered a forgotten cure for hospital gangrene, the infectious spread PSS of dead tissue following an amputation. °Both sides noted that flies would lay their eggs in the wounds of soldiers. The hatching larvae, called maggots, did not disturb living tissue, but they fed on dead tissue, which included infected tissue. Thus, the men whose wounds carried maggots survived more often than men whose wounds were cleaned of maggots. The latter developed gangrene and often died.

By trial and error, medicine moved forward. Quite by accident, the doctors discovered that men healed more quickly in ventilated, sunlit hospital wards. This brought

GED about a new hospital design based on °a spoke system where barracks were set up around a central corridor, like the spokes of a wheel. This design allowed good ventilation into these barracks, and it allowed doctors to isolate cases so that the gangrenous cases were placed in certain barracks and measles cases in another. For their time, these were significant medical advances.•

Short on medical supplies due to the GED Northern blockade, °the Confederates utilized home remedies and herbal medicine. They reverted to what they had learned from nature and revived many textbooks on herbal medicine, experimenting with roots, leaves, and bark from various plants and trees.• The July 1864 issue of *The Confederate States Medical and Surgical Journal* included a table of indigenous remedies for field service and the sick in general hospitals. Stimulants were derived from calamus, Virginia snakeroot, partridgeberry, sassafras, lavender, tulip tree, and Seneca snakeroot plants. Astringents were made from bearberry, marsh rosemary, sumac, and white oak leaves and bark. Tonics were extracted from dogwood, persimmon, American colombo, American gentian, hop, Georgia bark, wild cherry, white oak, blackberry, white willow, and sage.

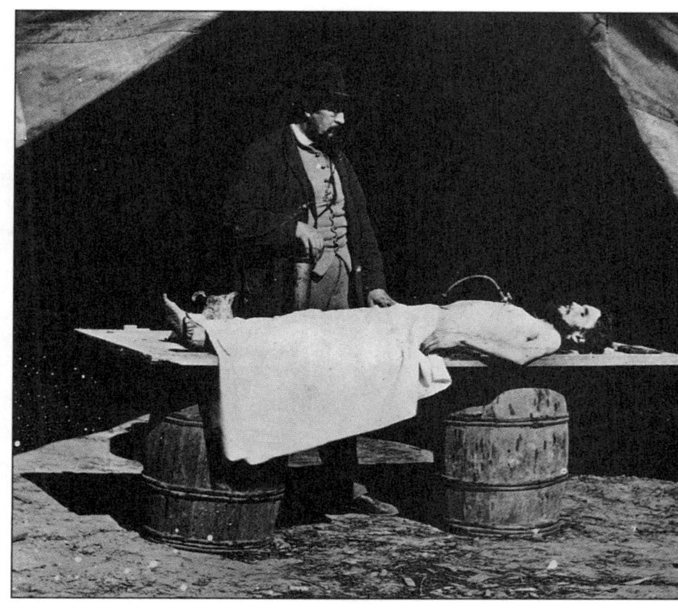

*A Dr. Burr, an embalming surgeon, was photographed as he began to prepare the body of a soldier so it could be sent home. Although embalming was an ancient practice, dating back thousands of years, the method of modern embalming essentially began with the Civil War. The cadaver was pumped free of blood and gasses and the circulatory system was then filled with a liquid to arrest or prevent decay.*

Soldiers with bowel problems were often dosed with soups made of roots such as blackberry or dogwoods, or teas made of fruits such as persimmons. Malaria was best treated with quinine, a popular all-around medicine, or with mashed dogwood roots made palatable with whiskey. Of course, the universal tonic for all maladies was alcohol, with whiskey, rum, and brandy being the most common. When lacking a proper anesthetic, surgeons would give the wounded several swallows to desensitize them to the pain before a saw was applied to their limbs.

BP In some instances °some rather clever resections were performed during the war. Splintered bone would be removed and that which remained would be drawn together, shortening the limb but allowing the patient to

*The largest hospital on each side was Chimborazo, the Confederate Hospital in Richmond (above), and the Union field hospital at City Point, Virginia (below). A matron at Chimborazo, Mrs. Phoebe Pember, recalled that one of the more interesting surgeries at the hospital wasn't performed by a surgeon. A Confederate soldier had a fearful wound in the instep of his left foot from which a tangled mass of flesh protruded. Doctors feared nerve damage if they removed the mass. One morning Nurse Pember found the formerly fretful soldier all smiles. The mass was gone, and in its place was a large but clean hole, rapidly healing, the result of a procedure performed during the night—by a rat.*

retain the use of his fingers or toes. Many officers endured resection operations and were able to return to duty.•

The field surgeons who lived and worked together on
the battlefield also shared ideas. Union Surgeon General
William Hammond recognized the importance of the
surgeons' medical records and insisted they be pub-
PJD lished for future study. °The result of this foresight was
the creation and publication in the 1870s and 1880s of
*The Medical and Surgical History of the War of the Rebel-
lion.* It was the first publication by American physicians
BP that was recognized as worthwhile in Europe.• °This
monograph was an example of the medical fraternity
striving to make the breakthroughs necessary to prevent
such a terrible waste of life in the future, and so the
Civil War became a great learning experience for doctors and surgeons. This vast collection of specimens, photographs, and case studies was assembled after the war to educate the military surgeons of the future because the doctors who had practiced during the war had gathered some hard-earned insights at great cost, and they wanted them to be remembered for future conflicts.•

"For many of the surgeons, the last call to duty has been sounded, and their names are already nearly forgotten,"

Wiest wrote in 1888. "Those who survive hold no great honor or profit under the government they helped to save, yet they are content with the memory of work well done and to be recognized as fellow soldiers and equal companions of those to whom the world has rendered the highest honors."

Throughout the Civil War, great advances were made in medicine, although most of these had to do with amputations. The makers of artificial limbs had no shortage of clients in the postwar years. Those who began the war as unschooled country doctors were mustered out and returned home as skilled surgeons with new medicines and new techniques to share with their colleagues. The hard-fought battles won in hospital organization and administration were applied in communities across the country by discharged doctors, overriding the stigma of hospital treatment. Furthermore, the field of nursing opened to women, and the standard of care increased in the country.

PJD ○If walls could talk, whether they be the walls of a house or a field hospital, they would cry over the horrors they witnessed. But at the same time, seeing the dedication and humanity of the doctors, those walls would say, "Considering your training and considering the adverse conditions under which you worked, it was a job well done."•

While the lessons of war are never worth the price, thousands of sacrificed lives allowed the medical community in both the North and the South to gain knowledge, experience, and confidence that permitted millions of others in the generations that followed to live.

*Doctors of the Army of the Potomac pose in front of a makeshift hospital. It is sometimes difficult to realize how far medical science has advanced since the Civil War. Antitoxins, antibiotics, and the science of bacteriology did not exist then. Sanitation was crude and the relationship between impure water and insects to disease was largely unknown. There was little local manufacture of drugs. The North imported much of its supply, but the South had to rely on blockade-runners for its imports. Civil War doctors had to make do and improvise. In spite of it—or perhaps because of—these difficulties, great advances in medicine were made throughout the war. By recording their successes and failures doctors and medical personnel furthered the development of medical science which has benefited future generations.*

*Union prisoners at Andersonville, August 17, 1864.*

# PRISON CAMPS

In A BLOODY WAR FILLED WITH countless battlefield horrors, the one thing every soldier feared most was capture and imprisonment.
GWG °Especially in the latter years of the war, the men who were captured and subsequently taken to prison camps had to endure far worse hardships than any they had seen or encountered on the battlefield.• While more than six hundred thousand men died during the conflict, hundreds of thousands were captured and subjected to horrible conditions, and approximately fifty thousand men died in Northern and Southern prisons.
BP °Over the years, the war has been romanticized, but the story of the prison camps and how Americans inflicted such suffering and torment on fellow Americans has been masked within the dark side of the war—the side that is filled with agony, suffering, shame, and even criminality.•

The tragedy of the prisoner-of-war system lay in the shortsighted way in which North and South went to
JIR war in 1861, making the situation a °sad and tragic one rather than one of brutality and atrocity. Indeed, many of the problems in handling prisoners of war were due to incompetency and ignorance• rather than hate and cruelty.

JMM °In the early days of the war, both sides believed the conflict would be brief. Few perceived the war would last for years, and those who did were ridiculed. Consequently, neither side made significant preparations for establishing prisoner-of-war camps or allocations for the logistical and medical facilities needed to care for

| | |
|---|---|
| **ECB** | Edwin C. Bearss |
| **FLB** | Frank L. Byrne |
| **WCD** | William C. Davis |
| **GWG** | Gary W. Gallagher |
| **JMM** | James M. McPherson |
| **WM** | William Marvel |
| **BP** | Brian Pohanka |
| **JIR** | James I. Robertson Jr. |

*As the war began, both sides believed the conflict would be brief, and so neither had thought much about where prisoners would be housed. Various forts, stockades, converted warehouses, and other makeshift facilities were used as prisons early in the war. Known in 1861 as the San Antonio Barracks, the Alamo, the site of the rally cry for Texas independence, was one of the first Southern prisons to hold Union captives.*

prisoners,• and so both sides hastily constructed ill-conceived prison camps.

The first prisoners of the war were taken early in 1861 in Texas, shortly after the Lone Star State seceded. In a single act, Gen. David E. Twiggs surrendered one-fifth of the U.S. Army to nine hundred unarmed Secessionist volunteers. Several officers signed paroles and were allowed to return home, but 2,648 Union prisoners spent the next two years awaiting exchange in makeshift detention camps in Bexar County.

The parole-and-exchange system implemented in Texas was modeled after a European tradition that was based on the integrity of the warring governments. Captured soldiers were released and allowed to return home to await orders to rejoin their units, which came after a comparable number of prisoners had been captured and "exchanged" on paper by the opposing side. In the first months of the Civil War, any prisoner not exchanged within ten days of his capture was usually released after signing a pledge that he would not bear arms against the enemy until he was notified that he had been exchanged.

Union soldiers in the South were not the only individuals to be incarcerated during the chaotic first weeks and months of the war. Deserters, stragglers, and civilians whose loyalty was questionable were also arrested and held in provost prisons in several sections of the country. Local jails were often used, but then old forts were renovated to accommodate prisoners, and most of these became prisoner-of-war facilities. Eventually 150 military prisons were established North and South. Of this number, only Fort Warren in the North and Raleigh Barracks in the South were regarded as bearable. The other 148 were distinguished by degrees of filth, disease, illness, and death.

These 150 prisons fell into seven categories: existing jails and prisons (city and county jails and state prisons); former coastal fortifications (used mostly in the North; Castle Pinckney in Charleston Harbor was the

*Winslow Homer's 1866 painting* Prisoners from the Front *(left) shows three Confederate prisoners under guard being brought before a dignified young Federal officer. This painting was widely acclaimed when exhibited at the 1867 Exposition Universelle in Paris. The Union officer on the right receiving the prisoners is thought to be based upon Gen. Francis C. Barlow, one of the North's "boy generals."*

only such structure to be used as a prison in the South); old buildings converted into prisons (primarily a Southern innovation but also used in the Union West); barracks enclosed by high fences (former training camps and fairgrounds mostly in the North); tents enclosed by high fences (one of the least expensive arrangements used by both sides); open stockades (mostly implemented in the South; no structures were provided for the prisoners); and open ground (guards posted around a mass of prisoners). As the number of prisoners increased, the captors moved sequentially from one category of prison to the next.

When it became evident that the war would last beyond a battle or two, the first men to grasp the need for prison facilities were Confederate President Jefferson Davis and Union Q.M. Gen. Montgomery C. Meigs. Davis directed his secretary of war, Leroy P. Walker, to make inquiries of the states regarding places where prisoners might be held, but the South did not assign a commander over the prisons until 1864. Despite being ignored at first, Meigs was more successful in seeing a system established in the North.

Lt. Col. William H. Hoffman was named in October 1861 to oversee the Federal prisons. He had been a prisoner in Texas and had been released upon signing an
WCD oath not to bear arms against the Confederacy. °He had a methodical mind, and he saw his mission as running

*The penny-pinching management style of Brig. Gen. William Hoffman (on the right below) cut to the bone rations and services for Confederate prisoners. At war's end, he returned an astounding $1.8 million in unused funds to the Federal treasury.*

*During the war 150 military prisons were established by the Federal and Confederate governments. Some were created from existing jails and prisons such as the Virginia State Penitentiary in Richmond.*

the Northern prison camps as efficiently and inexpensively as possible.• By insisting that money be spent only on the absolute necessities needed to live and by cutting back on the meager food rations provided for prisoners, Hoffman actually returned prison funds to the Federal budget every WCD month. °He reasoned that prisoners led sedentary lives as opposed to the vigorous, hard, active life of soldiers in the field, and thus inmates did not need as many calories as fighting men on the front. As a result of Hoffman's decision, many prisoners suffered malnutrition.• Similarly, he instructed his subordinates, "So long as a prisoner has clothing upon him, however much torn, issue nothing to him."

In the South, because most of the prisoner-of-war facilities were in and around Richmond, the city's provost marshal, John H. Winder, was placed in charge of them. When Yankee prisoners were transferred to other camps across the Confederacy, Winder remained responsible for them. Prior to the war, Winder had been an officer of artillery, but after hostilities began he resigned his commission and was appointed a brigadier general and provost of the Southern capital by his longtime friend, President Davis. Winder was an unflinching disciplinarian given to high-handed methods that were antagonistic to the Richmond population. Unfortu-

*Other military prisons were made from former coastal fortifications such as Castle Pinckney, which sat in the mouth of the Cooper River on a mud flat known as Shute's Folly near Charleston, South Carolina. Here Yankees were housed in the lower batteries and casemates while reasonably friendly Rebels walked patrol on the upper ramparts. Although no Civil War prison was pleasant, Pinckney's thick masonry caverns and cool sea breezes offered a respite from the South Carolina sun.*

*In addition to existing jails and coastal fortifications, warehouses, hotels, and commercial buildings were hurriedly converted into prisons. The first private building confiscated by the Confederacy to house captives was the Ligon Tobacco Warehouse at Twenty-fifth and Main in Richmond, the tall structure in the center of the picture (above left). The adjoining buildings were also soon taken over for prison use.*

*As the number of prisoners increased, prisons were created in open air camps. A photographer for Mathew Brady made the picture above right of Rebel prisoners under guard.*

WCD nately, °he was also a bumbling incompetent, and as a result, he paid little attention to what was going on in Confederate prisons.•

THE 150 PRISONS used during the war were established as far north as Boston, as far south as Dry Tortugas, Florida, and as far west as Fort Riley, Kansas, and Fort Craig, New Mexico. The largest prison in the war was Point Lookout in Maryland, a Federal prison where the Potomac River enters Chesapeake Bay. "The only possible way to avoid freezing was by devotion to the blankets," wrote Anthony M. Kiley, a prisoner at Point Lookout. "This became impossible when everything was afloat."

One of the rare good prisons on either side was Fort Warren, an old stone fort several miles out in Boston's harbor. Fewer than twenty Confederates died here, likely because its thick walls helped insulate them from the cold northern winters. In the South, Castle Pinckney, a small fort near Fort Sumter, was cooled by ocean breezes, so it was relatively comfortable for the Yankee prisoners sent there after the battle of First Manassas.

Conditions in other prisons were less bearable and even deadly. On Lake Erie, near Sandusky, Ohio, Johnson's Island held more than three thousand Confederate officers. The menu was not enough to keep the prisoners satisfied; thus "Rats are found to be very good for food, and every night many are captured and slain," wrote Forrest Carpenter from the prison. While the death rate on Johnson's Island was officially low, the guards played a deadly game, shooting into the barracks

*Gen. John H. Winder (above), provost marshall of Richmond, was placed in charge of Confederate prison camps and clumsily attempted throughout the war to provide adequate conditions for prisoners in the Confederate system. However, unlike his frugal Union counterpart General Hoffman, Winder never had the money or manpower to properly run the Southern prisons.*

at night and then listening to hear if anyone screamed after being shot.

As bad as prison conditions were in the North, they were worse in the South. Beautiful Belle Isle on the James River near Richmond held enlisted Union soldiers. It was one of the first Confederate prisons and held Federal soldiers after the battle of First Manassas in July 1861. It was in the middle of the river, with rapids all around, so it was unlikely that any prisoners who tried to escape would get out alive. Eventually more than seven thousand Union soldiers were imprisoned there. "Our men at Belle Isle are suffering the slowest starvation," wrote Union Gen. Neal Dow. "After a cold night, some of them are found dead. They lie in a trench that surrounds the camp."

At Salisbury, North Carolina, things began pretty well in a prison that was once a textile factory. The prisoners even played baseball. Within weeks, however, the facility was flooded with new prisoners, and within five months, more than three thousand of them died as the summer heat became unbearable. While conditions were oppressive, the guards had it little better. They were issued the same food rations as the prisoners.

Conditions varied from prison to prison, but captives
BP all faced the same ordeals. ○As soon as a man was taken prisoner, he would be disarmed and hustled to the rear. Once he was well behind enemy lines, he would be robbed of any valuables.• Southerners might be deprived of tobacco and personal items, and Northerners might be relieved of their shoes and winter over-

*The southernmost Union prison was Fort Jefferson in the Dry Tortugas beyond Key West, Florida. Its most famous inmate was the postwar prisoner Dr. Samuel Mudd, who set John Wilkes Booth's broken leg and therefore was sentenced to life imprisonment as a conspirator in the Lincoln assassination. When yellow fever swept the prison in 1867, killing the post's doctor, Mudd stepped in to provide medical help. As a result, members of the garrison petitioned President Andrew Johnson for Mudd's release and Johnson pardoned him.*

*When prisons could no longer hold the influx of prisoners, Federal officials turned to whatever might be used. Camp Douglas, a onetime army training camp in Chicago, became a popular site for photographers. Here a group of Confederate prisoners pose behind what appears to be a fire hydrant.*

coats, since these were in very short supply in the
JMM South. °Captors would take watches, money, or anything of value, stripping their prisoners of all dignity.•
BP °By the time the prisoners arrived at a camp, they were debilitated, dirty, depressed, and dispirited. As they passed into the place of confinement, they would be greeted by shouts of "Fresh fish!"—the nickname for a new arrival—from the prisoners already there.•

By 1862 the Northern and Southern prisons were fill-
JMM ing up fast. °The Lincoln administration came under mounting pressure to come to an agreement with the Confederates for a formal policy on the exchange of prisoners.• In July 1862 both sides agreed to a policy called
GWG the Dix-Hill Cartel. °If the North captured ten Confederates and the South captured ten Federals, they would simply exchange men of equal rank and allow them to go back into the service.• The cartel established a rate of exchange for prisoners of varying ranks, such as one lieutenant for two privates or one general for sixty privates.
GWG °If one side had more prisoners than the other, they would exchange an equal number and the balance would be paroled, meaning that they would not fight until the other side had captured a number of prisoners for whom they would be exchanged.•

JMM °This exchange program virtually emptied the prisons by the fall of 1862, and the system worked well for about a year.• The makeshift camps were abandoned, the prisoners of war were concentrated in specific camps, and exchange points were established. The Union

Some of the war's earliest prisoners, members of New York's famous "Fighting Sixty-Ninth" and of the Eleventh New York Fire Zouaves, pose for the camera at Castle Pinckney in Charleston Harbor (right). These men were captured at the battle of First Bull Run, July 21, 1861. The sign above their casemate door that reads "Musical Hall 444 Broadway" reminds them of home.

moved all prisoners to Johnson's Island, Camp Chase, and Alton in the west and Fort Delaware in the east. Prisoners for exchange were sent to the Gratiot Street Prison in Saint Louis in the west and the Old Capitol Prison in Washington, D.C., in the east. The Confederacy grouped its prisoners at Danville and Salisbury and used Libby Prison in Richmond as a distribution center.

FLB Eventually, °the officers on both sides who were in charge of these arrangements quibbled about whether or not prisoners were being properly exchanged. Each side charged the other with putting men back into combat before they had been properly exchanged.• The operation of the cartel was further complicated by the Emancipation Proclamation, which allowed former slaves and free African Americans to enlist in the Federal forces. Many were captured on the battlefield, but compared to their white comrades, blacks taken captive were less likely to see a Confederate prison because the South refused to treat African-American soldiers the same as
GWG whites for the purpose of exchange. °One of the most barbaric elements in the prisoner-of-war issue was that many prisoners were killed in the field. Although that was not limited to either side, it was especially prevalent when Rebel forces captured blacks in Yankee uniforms.•
WCD °To the Confederates it was inconceivable that a black man could be a soldier. They officially regarded all African-American soldiers as escaped slaves who ought to be killed or returned to slavery if they were captured.•

Maj. Gen. Ethan Allen Hitchcock was in charge of the Federal side of the prisoner exchange program. His hard-headed attitude was one factor that contributed to the demise of the program in 1864.

JMM °The most notorious massacre of black troops by Confederate soldiers occurred in the spring of 1864 at Fort Pillow, Tennessee, by cavalry under Nathan Bedford Forrest. Several dozen, perhaps as many as a hundred, black soldiers tried to surrender and were shot down by Forrest's troopers.• One of the Southerners, Sgt. Achilles Clark, recounted: "The poor, deluded Negroes would run up to our men, fall upon their knees and with uplifted hands scream for mercy, but they were ordered to their feet and then shot down. The white men fared little better."

*The Confederacy's Salisbury Prison in North Carolina became a central collection point for Northern enlisted men who were prisoners. Early in the war the converted cotton mill had housed Confederate deserters, criminals, and other rejects from the Southern army. Still in residence when Union troops began to arrive, these hard-boiled Rebels roved the prison in packs, preying on any Yankee who had the misfortune to find himself away from his friends. A similar situation at Andersonville involving Union "raiders" ended when the inmates tried and hanged the ringleaders. By 1864 the inmates at Salisbury were climbing the prison's numerous oak trees to gather acorns to eat.*

Similarly, on August 1, 1864, at Petersburg, Confederate soldier W. J. Pegram wrote that a few of the men in his unit had been wounded by black Union troops. "We'd exasperated them very much," he observed. "As soon as we got upon them, they threw down their arms to surrender, but were not allowed to. This was perfectly right, a matter of policy."

The War Department in Washington demanded that African-American prisoners be treated the same as whites in uniform and threatened to discontinue the exchange of prisoners. Otherwise, Southern prisoners would be held without parole. JMM °The Confederacy refused to back down, and the cartel was rescinded.•

As is often the case, there were ulterior motives behind the voiding of the cartel. Officially, the breakdown in the exchange agreement was attributed to the Confederacy's cruel treatment of blacks taken prisoner, but beyond that was the realization by Washington that the greatest weakness of the South was its limited manpower. WCD °Northerners knew that they had more men than the Confederates and believed that by stopping the exchange of prisoners, they would have vastly superior numbers against the Rebels.• On August 19, 1864, Ulysses S. Grant gave a final word on the matter of prisoner exchanges: "We ought not to make a single exchange until the war closes. We've got to fight until the military power of the South is exhausted, and if we

*After the British destroyed the Capitol during the War of 1812, Congress sat for a while in a temporary facility that was later known as the Old Capitol. The building became a fashionable boarding house where Congressmen such as South Carolina's John C. Calhoun lived. Rose O'Neal lived there with her aunt when she first came to Washington. By 1861 the Old Capitol had become dilapidated and so it was turned into a Federal prison that housed Confederates ranging from generals to blockade-runners to people only thought to be disloyal to the Union. When Rose O'Neal Greenhow was captured as a spy, she was incarcerated in her former home as was spy Belle Boyd. All of the prisoners had to endure bedbugs and meals of half-spoiled meat. Those who could afford it purchased better food at exorbitant prices from the commissary as well as a card to the "sinks," toilets used by officials that were clean and private. The gallows in the yard of the Old Capitol was the site of the hanging of Heinrich Wirz, the commandant of Andersonville Prison.*

release or exchange prisoners captured, it simply becomes a war of extermination."

With the suspension of prisoner exchanges, the prisons filled up again. By August 1864 the South held 50,000 prisoners, the North held 67,500. Fierce campaigning by Grant at Petersburg and William Tecumseh Sherman in Georgia and the Carolinas added thousands to the prisons. At the same time, the South was gripped by numerous shortages, not the least of which were food, clothing, and medicine. The Confederacy could no longer afford to meet the needs of its prisoners, but it had no choice. When all hope of reestablishing the exchange cartel was gone, Richmond decided to relocate its Yankee prisoners to areas that had more supplies. Winder dispatched two officers to select a site in southern Georgia, and within weeks a rough stockade had been erected near the village of Andersonville.

In the North, similar new camps were being opened. Hoffman selected a former recruitment camp in Elmira, New York, and another at Hart's Island, New York, and had fences installed around the camp barracks. With the founding of these basic facilities in Georgia and New York, the stark transformation of prison camp to concentration camp began.

UNLIKE THE majority of prisoner-of-war facilities around the country, Elmira did not begin as a tolerable compound and then degenerate into a squalid hellhole under the weight of overcrowding and poor treatment; Elmira began as one from the moment the first prisoners arrived.

G. T. Taylor of Alabama stated, "Elmira was nearer Hades than I thought any place could be." F. S. Wade added, "If there was ever a hell on earth, Elmira was [it]." Perhaps one prisoner summarized the situation best when he said that he found the camp to be not only a hellhole but a hellhole under siege.

Rupert W. Grambling of the Fifth Florida Infantry was captured on May 6, 1864, at the battle of the

Wilderness, Virginia. He kept a diary of his ordeal and imprisonment at Elmira. "We went into battle at two o'clock," he recalled. "Wounded in right arm and taken prisoner. Sent to rear in great pain. Had ball out and wound dressed. About six hundred prisoners with me." The trip to Elmira was not immediate. Two months after his capture, Grambling noted: "Sunday, July 24, 1864. Traveled through the Catskill Mountains up the Susquehanna River. Crossed it twenty times." After arriving at the camp, Grambling observed: "Elmira Prison is about ten acres square. Weather is very unpleasant and cold. I only have one blanket, and it is quite thin. Don't see how I am to live this winter without more cover."

*In Petersburg, Virginia, tobacco warehouses were converted to prison use. By design, such buildings had plenty of windows, good ventilation, and little machinery to move, making them better than average facilities as prisons. However, because these warehouses were beneath the guns of both armies and subject to the occasional shell that fell within the city, Union soldiers housed here during the 1864-1865 siege named the place "Castle Thunder."*

Although Northerners living near the prisons never suffered for lack of food as the people in the South did, there never seemed to be enough food to feed Confederate prisoners. Much of this was attributed to the frugal-mindedness of Hoffman. Needing an increase in his operating budget, Hoffman approved withholding part of the regular rations at each prison and placing the savings into a prison fund that was supposed to be used to purchase vegetables and fruits for the prisoners. This fund grew to amazing amounts at most prisons, but its use was never authorized. After the war Hoffman returned $1.8 million to the government from what he had saved by reducing prisoner rations. Of course, some Federal prison commandants used their camp's fund for their own purposes.

Another factor influencing the poor treatment of Southern prisoners was the reports of hunger and deprivation among Yankee prisoners in Confederate hands. A policy of retaliation was implemented by Hoffman and approved by Meigs and the secretary of war, Edwin M. Stanton. Rations were further reduced, sutlers were denied access to the prisoners, and food packages from home were confiscated. As a result, Rebel prisoners not only endured starvation rations, they also faced a greater risk of disease due to malnutrition.

*The notorious Elmira, New York, prison camp, called "Hellmira" by its wretched inmates, was a frigid nightmare under siege. Confederate prisoners, enduring starvation rations, faced a greater risk of disease due to malnutrition. The main water source was a pond that had become a cesspool. Because of overcrowding, half of the inmates had to endure cold New York winters in tents or in the open without adequate blankets or clothing. The view above was taken from an observation deck built just outside the compound so that well-fed, warmly dressed townspeople could pay a small admission fee and look at the suffering inhabitants. The death rate at Elmira, 25 percent of the total prison population, ranked it on a par with the most famous Confederate prison, Andersonville.*

A Confederate soldier from Maryland wrote home from Elmira: "I am almost starved to death. For breakfast I get one-third pound of bread and a small piece of meat, and for supper not any meat, but a small plate of warm water called soup." On December 26, 1864, Grambling recorded: "Quite sickly in camp again. From fifteen to twenty-five die a day."

GWG °Elmira was just six miles above the Pennsylvania border. The camp held twelve thousand Confederate prisoners of war over the course of the conflict, but one out of four Confederates who entered Elmira never left.• Built in 1864, it housed twice as many prisoners as it was intended to accommodate. When prisoners continued to arrive, with no time to build additional barracks, tents were erected. During the New York winters, half the prisoners were forced to stay in tents or in the open. Overcrowding in drafty barracks led to a host of other evils. Called "Hellmira" by those who were there, Elmira had all the problems of the worst prison camps.

The camp's main water source was a pond that quickly became a cesspool. "The drainage of the camp is into this pond or pool of standing water, and one large sink used by the prisoners stands directly over the pond which receives its fecal matter hourly," noted the camp surgeon, E. F. Sanger. "Seven thousand men will pass 2,600 gallons of urine daily, which is highly loaded with nitrogenous material. A portion is absorbed by the earth, still a large amount decomposes on the top of the earth or runs into the pond to purify."

BP °Epidemics raced through Elmira's crowded barracks. Disease claimed dozens, even hundreds until they ran their course.• Since the best medical teams were needed on the front lines, the prison hospital staff was usually
GWG underqualified and overworked. °The testimony about doctors and hospitals in most prisons was almost uni-

versally negative, and prisoners believed that a visit to the hospital was like receiving a death certificate.•

In a formal letter to the surgeon general, Sanger reported: "Since August, the date of my assignment to this station, there have been 2,011 patients admitted to the hospital [and] 775 deaths out of a mean strength of 8,347 prisoners of war, or 24 per-cent admitted and 9 per-cent died. [We] have averaged daily 451 in hospital and 601 in quarters. . . . At this rate the entire command will be admitted to the hospital in less than a year and 36 per-cent [will] die."

Nevertheless, Sanger was accused of killing more Confederates than any Union soldier at the front. "Sanger was simply a brute," charged Virginia newspaperman A. M. Kiley. "If he had not avoided a court-martial by resigning, even a military commission would have found it impossible to screen his brutality to the sick." And yet Sanger may have been an improvement because the doctor who had preceded him was described as being a "virgin in his knowledge of medicine."

As the dead bodies piled up at Elmira, former slave John W. Jones was paid forty dollars a month to bury them. He did a meticulous job and kept accurate death records throughout the camp's existence. No doubt, with the high death rate, Jones must have felt overworked and underpaid. At the rate prisoners were dying, he averaged sixteen cents per burial. The 25 percent death rate at Elmira ranked on a par with the worst

*Sgt. Berry Benson and nine other Confederates escaped Elmira prison (above) in October 1864 by tunneling out. Benson, a South Carolinian in the Army of Northern Virginia, then began a long trek across New York and Pennsylvania to reach Rebel lines. He stole a suit of clothes and was able to find or beg food from Northerners who believed his various stories. While riding a train south from Harrisburg, Benson saw the conductor coming for tickets. Quietly, he went to the platform and, grabbing a railing, hung onto the outside of the car until the conductor passed by. Moments later, the conductor returned and discovered him. When Benson told him a sad tale about not having a ticket, the sympathetic conductor had him come inside before the rocks brushed him off the train. Once safely behind Southern lines, Benson made his way back to his old unit. As he passed through camp, with soldiers crying out, "Look, it's Sergeant Benson," his own brother failed to recognize him because he and everyone back home thought Berry Benson was dead.*

*In 1873 artist Julian Scott, who received the Medal of Honor as a drummer boy in a Vermont regiment, painted this scene of a Union guard bringing meager rations to ragged Confederate prisoners. The fruit rinds and an empty bottle suggest that guards callously enjoyed luxuries denied starving Rebels. Later the artist painted a sympathetic view of a Confederate guard in a similar situation entitled* The Compassionate Enemy.

Confederate prison, Camp Sumter, Georgia, better known as Andersonville.

In December 1864 Elmira was smitten with smallpox. Within a week, a separate group of tents was erected far from the main prisoner barracks to quarantine the sick. Those who were ill shared cots, lying in reverse order with their heads at opposite ends of the cot. Pneumonia next swept through the camp, killing an average of fifteen men a day.

While most of the men who died at Elmira were the victims of disease, some simply froze to death in the winter. Prisoners stood ankle-deep in snow for roll call. Newer buildings proved inadequate for the weather. One prisoner complained that the camp was covered with several feet of snow and ice from December 6, 1864, to March 15, 1865.

The Confederates suffered in full view of the citizens of the nearby town. Enterprising townspeople built an observation deck outside the compound so curious Yankees could see the filthy Rebels. The voyeurs were charged fifteen cents to observe the Southerners in rags. Business must have been good because a second tower was built twenty feet taller, admission was reduced to ten cents, and concessions were sold. While the observation deck and tower were profitable, they also inspired humanitarian efforts from many townspeople. A school was established, books were donated, religious services were conducted, and clothing was collected (although prison officials chose not to distribute it).

Prior to the founding of the prison camp at Elmira, perhaps the most dreaded Northern prison was Fort Delaware. It was up the coast from Baltimore's Fort McHenry and was one of the newest forts in the chain of coastal fortifications protecting the country's Atlantic and Gulf coasts. Erected in the 1850s under the direction of Capt. George B. McClellan while he was assigned to the Corps of Engineers, the fort was a huge pentagonal structure of solid granite, with walls as much as thirty feet thick and thirty-two feet high. Within the structure were two three-story Georgian brick buildings, used to house the fort's garrison, and a parade ground. Massive arches supported three tiers of gun emplacements, and a drawbridge was used over the wide moat that surrounded the facility. The fort stood on the southeast corner of Pea Patch Island, which was a mud shoal in the Delaware River. The island measured 178 acres, but 128 of these were useless bogs. It had been formed in the 1700s when a ship loaded with peas wrecked on a sandbar. The peas sprouted, caught drifting debris and sediment, and became an island over the years.

*The reputation of Fort Delaware (above) as a dying ground was well known to Confederate soldiers. "The place was a bed of mud and filth. . . . The prisoners were half-fed and almost naked," wrote Lt. D.U. Barziza of Hood's Texas Brigade. There were also rumors that some prisoners at Fort Delaware were tortured.*

*Far away, Camp Ford at Tyler, Texas, seemed to be a place the war forgot. Prisoners and guards maintained a friendly if cautious relationship. Supplies were adequate, the water clean, and fuel plentiful. After 1864, conditions deteriorated, just as they did for civilians in the South. When the war ended, the Rebel guards simply fled, leaving the Yankees such as the men of the Nineteenth Iowa (below) to find their own way home.*

The fort was garrisoned in 1860 and was used to detain prisoners of state as early as February 1861. The first prisoners of war arrived in late July 1861, eight Confederates captured near Harpers Ferry and Martinsburg, and were kept in the fort's guardhouse until they were exchanged in the fall. Afterward and throughout the following spring, only political prisoners were housed in the facility.

In April 1862 Fort Delaware became an official prison when 250 men from Stonewall Jackson's brigade

*Fort McHenry, whose star-spangled banner waving in the War of 1812 inspired the national anthem, was another holding pen that quickly became overcrowded. Its tiny stockaded stables were renovated to accommodate six hundred men but by late summer of 1863 they held more than fifteen hundred Confederates. More than seven thousand men were housed at Fort McHenry during its brief life as a prison, with its first inmates coming from the field at Gettysburg. It also housed many political prisoners from pro-Confederate factions in Baltimore.*

arrived. The commanding officer moved his troops to the third floor of the fort's quarters, placed 200 of the prisoners on the second floor over the sally port, and confined the remaining 50 to the lower quarters. By June 15 the fort held 600 prisoners, and by July 1 that number had grown to 3,434. By mid-1863 no other Federal facility was as bad as Fort Delaware. Because it had the highest mortality rate of any prison, the prisoners dubbed it the "Fort Delaware Death Pen." After a succession of commanders, command was given in April 1863 to Albin F. Schoepf, a Hungarian immigrant, who was aptly nicknamed "General Terror" by the prisoners.

"The place was a bed of mud and filth. The filth mingled with the water they drank, and hundreds died of disease. The prisoners were half-fed and almost naked," wrote Lt. D. U. Barziza of Hood's Texas Brigade. As wretched as the conditions were, Fort Delaware was more notorious for the punishments meted out to the prisoners, which often crossed the line into torture. Inmates were bucked and gagged and hung by their thumbs for the slightest infraction of the rules. The prisoners were also used as forced labor to load and unload ships and erect housing for Federal officers.

GWG °Approximately thirty thousand Confederate soldiers were sent to Fort Delaware at one time or another
JIR during the war.• °It was a typical prison in that it was isolated and the men received very poor rations. Their only clothing was what they had on when they entered the prison. Overcrowding was always a way of life. Medical treatment was scarce and of limited quality. Fort Delaware came to be the epitome of a Civil War prison.•

BP °Sanitary conditions were terrible. The typical Civil War prisoner, not only in Fort Delaware, but in other Northern and Southern prisons as well, was covered with lice and other parasites. Some men's bodies were covered with sores, and when the camp was frequently

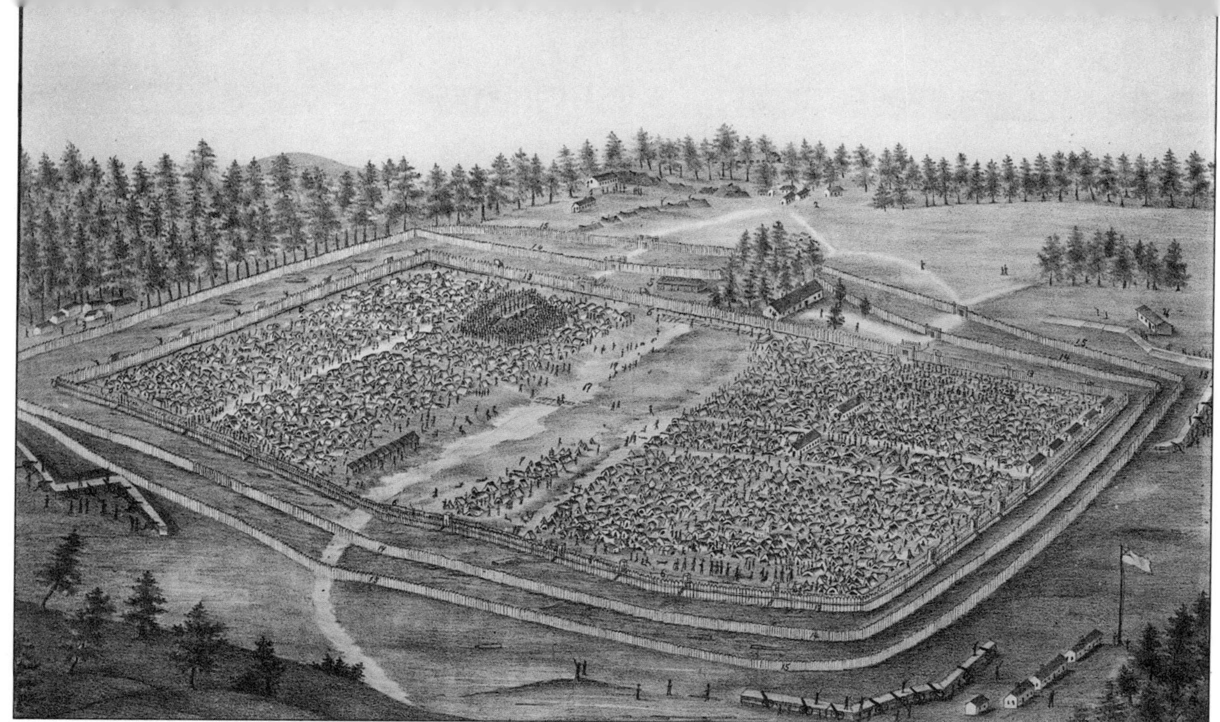

little more than a fetid pool of polluted water, open sores could easily develop into gangrene.•

By mid-1864 Fort Delaware's barracks, erected since the beginning of the war, had become dilapidated and were torn down, although additional housing had been ordered to be constructed on three separate occasions. It now held nine thousand prisoners and averaged eighty-eight deaths a month. Disease was rampant—smallpox, scurvy, dysentery, measles, and chronic diarrhea. Food was sparse. Each prisoner received two meals a day, the first usually consisted of two hardtack biscuits and a square inch of pickled meat; the second was the same as the first but supplemented with weak bean soup. Most prisoners enlarged their diet by catching and eating rats.

One of the basic problems with housing vast numbers of men in the fort was the fact that the facility was six feet below sea level and surrounded by a dike, which limited drainage. The camp grounds became a quagmire after a rain. A prison regulation also forbade more than a few prisoners to go to the latrines after dark. One prisoner recalled seeing a line of as many as five hundred men waiting their turn, and ultimately many never made it to the latrine. Eventually, the runoff mingled with the fort's drinking water supply, and disease broke out among the inmates.

**Andersonville,** *the name by which Camp Sumter is usually known, has been seared into America's consciousness as a symbol of man's inhumanity to man. It was a "notorious hell hole" in southwestern Georgia where the population grew rapidly from the time the first prisoner arrived in February, 1864, to 10,000 in May, and 33,000 in August, 1864. "One-third of the enclosure was swampy, a mud of liquid filth, voidings from the thousands seething with maggots," wrote an inmate. Food was scarce and housing almost non-existent. In spite of being forbidden to construct shelters, many prisoners built their own huts, lean-tos, or dug holes over which they would stretch a blanket. The stench was so bad that townspeople twelve miles away could smell the prison camp.*

*Living conditions were horrendous in Andersonville. Men died from starvation; from diseases such as dysentery, scurvy, and malaria; from beatings by other prisoners; and from punishment by the guards. By war's end Andersonville had 12,912 graves. Open trenches four feet deep like the one above were kept ready for the dead. On the worst day at Andersonville, a death occurred every eleven minutes.*

In the North, many blamed the bad conditions on Hoffman's tight purse strings, but neither Hoffman nor anyone else on either side could handle the huge problems festering in the prison camps. FLB ○As with everything else in the Civil War, the numbers of people involved were unprecedented. The sheer size of these camps presented problems that most officers were not prepared to deal with. Prison officials simply did not realize how difficult it would be to get rid of the sewage from that number of men in confinement.•

CONDITIONS IN Confederate prisons were no better and generally worse. The most notorious was Andersonville, which received its first prisoners early in 1864. Like Elmira, it was little more than a concentration camp from the time its first inmates arrived.

The site was selected by Capt. W. Sidney Winder, General Winder's son. The area was accessible by train, and the ground gradually sloped down to a wide stream known as Sweet Water Creek. A simple stockade was erected, enclosing almost seventeen acres with a fifteen-foot-high wall.

The first prisoners arrived on February 25, 1864, having been relocated from other prisons in Virginia. Thus they arrived already ill, half-starved, and half-naked. There were no structures within the stockade; prisoners were turned loose inside and left to themselves. The first inmates made huts of the wood that remained within the stockade. Later arrivals lived in tents, lean-tos, or in the open under scraps of blankets and rags. Some dug holes, covered the bottom with pine needles, and stretched a blanket over sticks.

When more prisoners arrived than had been anticipated in early 1864, the camp's first commandant, Col. Alexander W. Persons, enlarged the stockade to twenty-seven acres. A second stockade was built a half mile west of the main facility and used to confine officers.

°The layout of the camp was poorly conceived from the beginning,• and °the Confederate officials had trouble keeping the camp clean. They erected some latrines, called sinks, at the lower end of the creek that flowed through the middle of the stockade•—°the only source of water for the prisoners.• °Compounding the growing health problem, many prisoners had dug their living quarters far from the creek, and they were not willing to walk a great distance to use the latrine; thus the entire camp quickly grew filthy.•

"One-third of the enclosure was swampy, a mud of liquid filth, voidings from the thousands seething with maggots," wrote Charles Hopkins, an inmate at Andersonville. "Through this mass pollution passed the only water that found its way through the bullpen." Miraculously, during a violent summer storm, lightning struck the ground inside the camp and a second spring of water was released. It continued to flow during the rest of the war; the prisoners called it Providence Spring.

*Although the mortality rate at the Federal prison in Elmira, New York, were nearly as bad as that of Andersonville, outraged Northerners urged retribution for the atrocities of the Confederate camp. A postwar cartoon by Thomas Nast urges readers to compare the suffering of soldiers in Andersonville—characterized as "sickness, starvation, death"—with the ease of the "Rebel leader Jeff Davis" at Fortress Monroe—characterized as "health, plenty, luxury." Nast asks, "Soldiers! Have you fought in vain? Shall the Rebel leaders be restored to power?" Davis's situation was not as comfortable as portrayed here. He was manacled, confined to his cell, and given limited food and exercise.*

°By May 1, 1864, the camp accommodated ten thousand prisoners, but shortly after the stockade had been expanded, the population rose to twenty-nine thousand. In August 1864 the number of inmates reached an all-time high of thirty-three thousand,• which made Andersonville the fifth largest "city" in the Confederacy. Townspeople twelve miles away could smell the stench of the prison camp.

"The wretched prisoners burrowed in the ground like moles to protect themselves from the sun," observed Andersonville native Eliza F. Andrews. "These underground huts were alive with vermin and stank. Many of the prisoners were stark naked and lay on the ground in their own excrement. My heart aches for the poor wretches, Yankees though they are."

With overcrowding came diminished rations. At first they ran out of salt, then sweet potatoes, cornmeal,

*The engraving above, from an 1890 issue of* Century Magazine, *clearly shows Andersonville's dead-line, the boundary beyond which no soldier could go and live. Exaggerated reports of the number of prisoners killed for crossing the dead-line and photographs of survivors of starvation and dysentery like the one below inflamed the Northern public and eventually led to the hanging of Heinrich Wirz, commandant of the camp.*

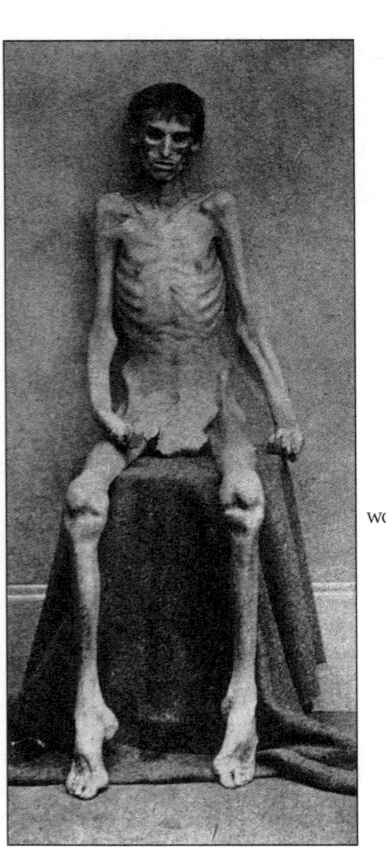

and meat. On one occasion, a bread wagon was rolled into the stockade, but before it could be issued to the prisoners, a mob rushed the wagon and took all the bread. As punishment, the commandant ruled that no more food would be distributed that day. Some inmates learned to catch low-flying swallows, and when they were successful, they ate the birds raw.

GWG °To the people of the North, Andersonville became the representative Confederate prison because it was one of the largest and because it hosted the most deaths—nearly thirteen thousand of the forty-one thousand men confined there during its fifteen months of operation. At the end of the war, when the prisoners from Andersonville came home, many of them were little more than living skeletons, and thus the horror associated with Andersonville came to define the horrors of Civil War prisons everywhere.•

The first escape attempt at Andersonville occurred shortly after the first inmates arrived, when fifteen men scaled the east wall using a rope made of rags. All of the men were recaptured within twenty-four hours, but as a result of the episode the commandant set up a dead-line around the inside perimeter of the stockade wall.
WCD °Almost every Civil War prison, North and South, had an equivalent of Andersonville's "dead-line"—a boundary beyond which no soldier could go.• The dead-line was clearly marked about twenty feet from the stockade wall, and the guards were ordered to fire on anyone touching or crossing this line.

On the same day that the dead-line was established, a man was killed by a guard when he reached inside the line to pick up a piece of rag. He was not the only man to lose his life over the line. Samuel Melvin recorded:

"July 27th, 1864. A man was shot for stepping over the dead-line. I call that murder."

WM °There were stories that as many as three hundred prisoners were killed for crossing the dead-line at Andersonville, but they proved to be inaccurate.• Perhaps as few as eleven men were killed at the dead-line. While reports in the Northern press and postwar accounts have distorted the situation at Andersonville, the truth itself was horrible enough.

One of the most incredulous aspects of prison life in Andersonville was the terror spread among the inmates by small groups of prisoners known as raiders. WM °The raiders were bands of thieves who preyed on the weaker prisoners, stealing food, clothing, money—whatever they could—from those who could ECB not resist.• They °shook down new prisoners for their money, beating them if necessary and taking what they wanted. They often attacked at night and frequently beat other prisoners to death. For a while, Andersonville became a jungle ruled by the raiders.•

The most ruthless raider gang was led by William "Mosby" Collins, formerly of the Eighty-eighth

*At Andersonville men who had no tent such as above lived in holes in the ground. One of the most incredulous aspects of prison life at Andersonville was the terror spread by small groups of prisoners known as raiders. These bands stole from the weak who could not resist and they frequently beat other prisoners to death. Finally, with the permission of Heinrich Wirz, a majority of the prisoners captured the miscreants, held a trial, and hanged six (below), with three others dying from beatings.*

*John Ransom, a brigade quartermaster with the Ninth Michigan Cavalry, kept a diary of his life as a prisoner at Andersonville. In July 1864 he wrote that he had "formed the habit of going to sleep as soon as the air got cooled off and before fairly dark. I wake up at two or three o'clock and stay awake. I then take in all the horrors of the situation. Thousands are groaning, moaning and crying with no bustle of the daytime to drown it." Ransom allowed himself the luxury of fantasies. "Have taken to building air castles of late, on being exchanged. Getting loony, I guess, same as all the rest." In September Ransom was shipped to a Confederate hospital. He wrote, "Hurrah! Hurrah! Hurrah! Can't holler, except on paper."*

*A former grocery warehouse of Richmond's Libby and Sons, Libby Prison (above left) housed Union officers. In the early days of the war, the prisoners were allowed to receive packages. Food, clothing, and blankets flowed in from home, from the U.S. Sanitary Commission, and from Northern citizens in general. The inmates were deluged with cakes, pies, hams, cookies, and canned goods. Union Gen. Neal Dow, a Maine abolitionist, wrote that he slept warmly under five blankets. Such comfort was not to last.*

*In 1862 prisoners crowd the windows of Libby Prison to watch Richmond photographer Charles Rees make the picture above right. By March 1864, following the embarrassing escape of 109 men, guards were ordered to shoot at anyone who came near a window. Prison rations were down to cornbread and an occasional potato. On some days there was no firewood for cooking because of a shortage of wood all over Richmond. Things were worse, however, at nearby Belle Isle, where enlisted men froze to death at night. General Dow noted in his diary that he had heard four hundred enlisted prisoners were being sent to Americus, Georgia, where the weather would be warmer. That new prison was Andersonville.*

Pennsylvania. They called themselves "Mosby's Rangers" and controlled life in the prison for some time. Finally, out of desperation and with the permission of the commandant, a majority of the prisoners took matters into their own hands. They arrested Collins and his men, held a trial, and hanged six of the twenty-four men. Three others died from beatings.

Samuel Melvin noted the incident in his diary: "Monday, July 11, 1864. Today, I saw six victims hung for murdering their fellow prisoners. They are the first ones I ever saw hung. They called them 'raiders.'" The prisoners refused to bury the raiders with the rest of the dead. Instead, the six were buried together in a separate part of the prison cemetery, where they rest today, segregated from the men they terrorized.

BOTH ENLISTED men and officers suffered hardships in prison camps, but enlisted men suffered more. If they were not placed in separate prisons, officers were usually kept in separate quarters. JMM °Officers usually received favors and occasionally better food, so their death rate in prison was much lower than that of the enlisted men.•

The most well known Southern prison for Union officers was Libby Prison in Richmond, Virginia. By the winter of 1863, one thousand officers were confined in the former grocery warehouse of Libby and Sons. By strictly enforcing a prison policy that forbade prisoners from coming within three feet of the windows, WCD °Libby became infamous because the guards would shoot anybody who

*Libby's open warehouse rooms were named for battles where the men who lived in them had been captured. This photo is of the Chickamauga Room. Here men slept, cooked, ate, and whiled away countless hours. As time passed, the Confederate jailers began to withhold packages from the North. When finally given to the prisoners, the parcels had been rifled and the food was usually spoiled because it was so old. Prison rations made bearable by supplements from home became subsistence fare.*

put his face into a window.• On March 5, 1864, Gen. Neal Dow wrote, "I have seen sentinels at the building opposite looking eagerly up at the windows in the hope to get a shot at a soldier." The guards called it "Sporting for Yan-
WCD kees." °A number of men lost their lives at Libby because they tried to look outside and get a view of the sun.•

Most civilians were appalled by the treatment prisoners received. Local sympathizer Julia Jefferson sent a gift to the prison commander at Fort Delaware and received a special pass to visit the prisoners and bring supplies. The Confederate prisoners were grateful for her efforts, and on April 15, 1864, they wrote: "We, the undersigned, confined in Fort Delaware, do appeal to your generosity. We are cut from all communication with our friends. We will be indebted to you for any kindness you may bestow upon us."

The vast majority of prisoners, however, had no visitors—only the brutal dullness of everyday life. By and
WCD large, °they had nothing to do. Mostly, they battled depression, which—combined with brutality, ignorance, and neglect—turned Civil War prison camps into killing camps.• From Fort Delaware, Wilbur Grambling wrote on August 2, 1864: "I'm getting tired of prison and grow more so every day. The thought of staying here all winter and perhaps 'til the war ends just makes the time a great deal longer."

BP °The Civil War soldier was not prepared for life in prison. No officer ever warned his regiment about what
WCD to do if they were taken prisoner.• °When prisoners

*This contemporary painting by David G. Blythe depicts life inside Libby Prison. Because the inmates were officers and mostly well educated, a large number of diaries exist that chronicle time spent there. Not surprisingly, most inmates' wartime accounts are bitter with outrage at the treatment given them by Rebel guards. Accounts tend to soften with time. Diaries published near the turn of the century reflect attitudes tempered by the spirit of sectional reconciliation that had swept the country.*

first arrived at a camp, they talked incessantly all day
long, much as they had when they were in camp with
BP the armies.• They would ask °who had won a recent
battle or what had happened to friends or relatives.•
When the excitement died down, however, they learned
it was time for survival.

To keep themselves sane, prisoners tried to follow
JMM some sort of routine. °They wore out the occasional
newspaper smuggled into the prison by passing it from
man to man. They reread letters from their families
until the paper wore out. They played chess and cards.•
Many carved or whittled objects that would later
WCD become treasured family heirlooms. °They kept diaries
if they had them. They wrote letters if they could write
or dictated to a fellow inmate who could. They sang
JMM and put on amateur dramatics.• °They tried to find
something to keep themselves busy because they realized that if they languished into depression, they might not ever recover.• "The uncertainty of our prospects of release," observed Alonzo Cooper from a Southern prison camp, "the strange sense of isolation, the absence of news, the many thoughts and desires that continually haunted us, the monotonous character of our daily life, the gradual but sure weakening of the body all had a depressing effect upon the mind, and, finally, men became insane."

To survive, prisoners had to keep busy, and their thoughts turned naturally to escape. In the words of one Yankee prisoner, "Freedom was more desired than salvation." At Andersonville, Samuel Morgan wrote: "How I long for liberty, how sick I am of corn meal. I dreamed last night of being paroled, and awoke to the disappointment of finding myself still in hell."

BP Methods of escape varied. °To get beyond the confining walls of their prison, some men lay in empty coffins to be carried out with the dead. They crawled out through latrines or tried to move underwater and surface a safe distance away from the camp. They tried everything. More often than not they failed, but sometimes the more harebrained and reckless the escape plan, the better it worked.•

Once outside the prison, the escaping soldier's hardship had only begun. In some cases, the fugitives had to WCD travel hundreds of miles to reach friendly lines. °Along the way, prisoners frequently had to depend on help from local people—white and black. It was not at all infrequent for slaves or free blacks in the South to hide an escaping Union soldier or to give him some food and some direction on where to go and how to find help along the way.•

The largest prison break took place at Libby Prison, in the heart of the Confederate capital at Richmond. One Union officer wrote: "We fumed and fretted, and our restraint grew more and more irksome. At last we settled down to the conviction that we were in for the war unless we effected escape."

Col. Thomas E. Rose had been captured at Chickamauga on September 20, 1863. After five months at JIR Libby Prison, he was ready to break free. °Rose was in his early thirties, heavyset, dark bearded, and energetic. When he found a way to get into the basement of the prison, he got the idea of digging a tunnel. Although Rose is credited with the idea and execution of the escape, the officer who masterminded the venture was Maj. Andrew G. Hamilton. "Masonry was removed from the fireplace to admit a man to the storeroom below," Rose wrote afterward. "Falling through and dropping down ten feet would bring a person to the empty basement under the adjoining room."•

*Col. Thomas E. Rose developed the plan that resulted in the largest prison break of the war. Twenty-five men took forty-seven days to dig a tunnel leading away from the basement of Libby Prison. When finished, the tunnel was sixty feet long and eight to nine feet underground. One hundred and nine men escaped; forty-eight were recaptured.*

*The most controversial incident of the war was the Fort Pillow Massacre on April 12, 1864. Fort Pillow, a Federal fort, was held by 262 African-American soldiers and 295 white troops. Nathan Bedford Forrest and 1500 Confederate troops assaulted the fort with small-arms fire in the morning. In the afternoon Forrest demanded surrender. William Bradford, in charge of the fort, asked for one hour to decide. When Forrest gave him twenty minutes, Bradford replied, "I will not surrender." Forrest's men charged the fort and drove the Union soldiers to the bank of the Mississippi River where they encountered more Confederates. In the ensuing battle 231 Federal troops were killed, eighty-six wounded, and 226 captured. Federal accounts claim that Bradford and his troops surrendered but were massacred in cold blood by Confederates who demonstrated a hatred of the African-American soldiers and animosity toward the whites who fought with them. Confederate accounts insist that the Federal troops refused to surrender and were killed in the course of fighting. The battle was investigated by the Joint Committee on the Conduct of the War, which issued a report containing appalling accounts of Confederate brutality. Whether Forrest ordered a slaughter or not, he was slow to stop it and he never apologized for the massacre.*

Hamilton believed they could dig under the basement wall and cross into freedom. Twenty-five men tunneled for forty-seven days using little more than clam shells and case knives. °They were armed with a kitchen knife, a discarded chisel, and a box with a sling on it for hauling the dirt out of the tunnel and into the basement where it was scattered about so that it would not be noticed.• The tunnel was eight to nine feet below the surface of the ground, and when it was completed it measured sixteen inches in diameter and nearly sixty feet long.

BP °The prisoners had a lot of close calls with the guards because word began to circulate that a tunnel was under construction. The more people who knew about the tunnel, the more dangerous it was, but Rose and the other officers persisted.• At one point, one of the diggers, Maj. B. B. McDonald, believed they had covered the necessary distance and broke through to the surface. When he emerged he saw that he was in an open lot near one of the guards. He turned back unnoticed, and someone stuffed a shirt in the opening. Four days later, the tunnel was finished. At first, only twenty-five men were involved in the plan. They were the first ones to use the tunnel early in the evening of February 9, 1864. Two hours after the last man had left, the rest of the prisoners were informed about the tunnel, and anyone strong enough was allowed to use it.

BP °The great breakout began under cover of darkness. One by one the Union officers went through the tunnel, into an alleyway, and then into the street. They slipped off into the city of Richmond.• Some of them made for the house of Elizabeth Van Lew, a Unionist sympathizer who had gotten word into the prison that she would hide and help any men who escaped. The breakout was not discovered until the next morning.

"When the Rebel officers counted the men, they found 109 too few," recalled L. W. Day, one of the men who remained in Libby. "They counted again. In a twinkling, the cavalry and hounds started in every direction. The prison guards were all arrested and charged with bribery." The tunnel was not discovered until late in the day.

JIR °Rose and 108 others made their escape from the prison and scattered in every direction. Of that number, 59 succeeded in getting to the Union lines. Two drowned in the effort. Among the 48 brought back to Libby Prison was Rose himself.• They were placed in irons in the darkest hole in the prison and given a diet of corn bread and water.

*Rock Island Prison was built in the Mississippi River between Rock Island, Illinois, and Davenport, Iowa, in the summer of 1863. The Union quartermaster general instructed that the barracks be "put up in the roughest and cheapest manner, mere shanties, with no fine work about them." The prisoners above are standing in line for roll call and rations.*

Those prisoners who escaped were few and lucky. Most were recaptured. The vast majority found prolonged captivity much as Samuel Melvin did at Andersonville: "Monday, June 6, 1864. Same as usual. Stayed in our humble dwelling most of the time. It is such. It is life and that is all. . . . How long must we stay here? None but the functionaries at Washington can tell." Wilbur Gambling was equally pensive in Elmira: "Friday, March 3, 1865. Weather remains the same. All quiet in camp. Almost crazy, I wanna go to Dixie so bad. Still live in hope, if I die in despair."

GWG °As the war went on through the summer of 1864 and into the fall, overcrowding placed ever-increasing burdens on all the services associated with the prisons,
WM from food to medical care to shelter.• °Throughout this time, the Federal government used prisoners as a propaganda tool. They publicized the poor condition of returning prisoners. They photographed men suffering from dysentery, portraying them as starved prisoners and implying that this starvation was deliberate. As a result, tremendous animosity was generated in the public toward all Confederates of high station and especially toward those officials who oversaw the prisoner-of-war camps.•

GWG Yet °there was no good evidence that the prisoners at Andersonville or at any other Confederate camp were systematically starved or mistreated on a large scale. Most of the problems that affected the treatment of Northern prisoners in Southern camps were problems

*Camp Douglas, built upon the former estate of Sen. Stephen A. Douglas near Chicago, was constantly flooded. Sanitation reached such lows in the prison barracks that H. W. Bellows of the U.S. Sanitary Commission thought nothing but fire could cleanse them. He urged the abandonment of the camp, but that was out of the question as long as the war continued to supply a steady stream of Confederate prisoners. In February 1863 the death rate at Camp Douglas reached 10 percent, the highest for any large prison during the war.*

that also affected the Southern population at large and
the Southern armies.• "The people of the North," wrote
Confederate officer McHenry Howard, "did not understand to what a condition our resources had fallen." The
Southern people were starving due to Federal raids that
JMM destroyed their crops and livestock. °Union soldiers suffered from malnutrition in overcrowded prison camps in
the South because Southern civilians and soldiers were
WCD suffering from malnutrition, too.• °The South simply
had no more to give to Federal prisoners.

On the other hand, Southern prisoners of war in the
North suffered far more from benign neglect than they
did from any kind of official attempt to harm their
GWG physical or their mental well-being.• °Civil War prisoner-of-war camps on both sides were only part of a
much larger awful situation in which thousands of
men were being shot down on battlefields or dying of
disease behind the lines.•

AS NORTHERN forces occupied more and more of the South, freed prisoners of war began returning home. In Washington, where he was working as a hospital orderly, Walt Whitman observed: "The released prisoners of war are now coming up from the Southern prisons. Can these be men? Were they really not mummied, dwindled corpses to endure the courses? They lay there with a horrible look in their eyes. Probably no more appalling sight was ever seen on this Earth."

On April 9, 1865, the Army of Northern Virginia surrendered at Appomattox Court House, Virginia. Five days later, President Abraham Lincoln was assassinated. On April 27, the paddle wheel steamboat *Sultana* churned up the Mississippi River carrying horses, pigs, cattle, and newly released Federal prisoners of war who were finally headed home.

GWG °The steamboat was grossly overloaded, crammed with more than twenty-two hundred men on a vessel that should not have been carrying half that many. The former prisoners occupied every available space on the ship, but they were willing to put up with it because they were headed home.• ECB °Some of them had been in Southern prison camps since 1863, and they were tired and weak. The overloaded steamer was several miles above Memphis, Tennessee, when its boiler exploded.•

"Some men were drowning, and some were burning, and some were crying for help," recalled Isaac Davenport, who was onboard the *Sultana*. "Some were killed instantly. Some blown away."

ECB °More than fifteen hundred men died in this great tragedy that went relatively unnoticed.• GWG °More men died on the *Sultana* than in any other ship-related disaster in American history, but because it occurred so close to the end of the war, so soon after the Lincoln assassination, these other events made the headlines, so the public never learned much about the disaster.•

The *Sultana* episode was not the final tragedy of Civil War prisons, because the issue of blame for the mistreatment of prisoners had yet to be resolved. WCD °The Northern public demanded that someone had to pay for the atrocities committed at Andersonville. The man behind the Andersonville tragedy, General Winder, however, had died in Florence, South Carolina, on February 8, 1865, overseeing the construction of another Southern prison. Thus the most immediate, visible culprit was the camp's commander, Maj. Heinrich H. Wirz.•

*When the war ended, Camp Fisk near Vicksburg, Mississippi, was established as an exchange point for prisoners captured in the western theater. Then a succession of boats began to carry the men north on the Mississippi River towards home, with the Federal government paying for their passage—five dollars for enlisted men and ten dollars for officers. The photograph above of the paddle-wheel steamboat* Sultana *was made the day before it sailed on April 27, 1865, carrying horses, pigs, cattle, and more than twenty-two hundred former prisoners of war. It was vastly overloaded, and when it was several miles north of Memphis, Tennessee, its boilers exploded. More than fifteen hundred men died in the greatest ship-related disaster in American history. The supreme irony of the tragedy was that these men had endured so much throughout the war, survived, and were so close to home.*

Wirz had deserted his family in Switzerland and moved to the United States in 1849. He lied about his background, claimed to be a doctor, and was employed as one in Louisiana. When the war started, he joined the army and was wounded, losing the use of his arm, which became a source of constant pain to him for the rest of his life. After serving two years on General Winder's staff and overseeing several prisons in Richmond, Wirz was ordered to Andersonville.

While he served as commandant, he
ECB was accused of deliberately abusing prisoners. °He would have the prisoners assembled and harangue them, telling them that he was more valuable to the Confederacy than Robert E. Lee. He would insult the men, making sure that they understood his authority. He was profane in his speech. Undoubtedly, he was the person to whom the prisoners easily attributed all their troubles.•

Wirz was arrested while processing the release of the last of the Andersonville prisoners. He could have escaped weeks before the Federals arrived at the camp, but Wirz believed that it was his duty to close the camp. He was taken to Washington and charged with conspiring with others to impair and injure the health and destroy the lives of the soldiers held under his authority. He was also charged specifically with the deaths of thir-
WCD teen prisoners. °The case against him was helped in that he was an unsympathetic character.• In the end,
JMM °he was the only person put on trial after the Civil War for war crimes.

During his two-month trial, starting in August 1865, a number of prisoners from Andersonville testified
BP against him.• °Unquestionably, he did not receive a fair trial. The military court was only interested in finding someone to blame for the large number of dead at Andersonville, and they found Wirz.• He was pronounced guilty and sentenced to death.

On November 10, 1865, Wirz was led to the same site at the Old Capitol Prison where the Lincoln conspirators had been hanged four months previously. He supposedly was told that his life would be spared if he implicated Confederate President Jefferson Davis. Wirz refused. On the gallows he turned to the hangman and forgave him, saying: "I know what orders are. I am being hung for obeying them."

BP ○The wall of the Old Capitol Prison was lined with Union soldiers. Even the trees had people in the limbs trying to get a good view. As an officer read the death sentence and prepared to drop Wirz through the trap, the soldiers surrounding the scaffold started chanting, "Wirz, remember Andersonville. Wirz, remember Andersonville. . . ." He died with those words ringing in his ears.•

*Alexander Gardner took this photograph of the execution of Heinrich Wirz, commandant of Andersonville Prison. Wirz was an unsympathetic character—caustic, quick-tempered, and profane—and some historians believe he was made a scapegoat for a deplorable situation. Wirz was arrested while processing the release of the last of the Andersonville prisoners. He could have left Andersonville earlier, but he believed it was his duty to close the camp. Wirz was the only person to be tried for war crimes after the Civil War, and his conviction seemed to be a foregone conclusion. He was hanged in the courtyard of the Old Capitol Prison.*

DURING THE war 647,000 soldiers were taken captive, which amounted to 16 percent of all enlistments—more than any war before or since. A third of these were exchanged or paroled, but 410,000 were held in the 150 prisoner-of-war camps erected across the country. Of that number, 56,014 died in confinement. The number of deaths in Confederate prisons totaled 30,218, approximately 15 percent of those incarcerated. In Federal prisons, 25,796 Southerners died, slightly more than 12 percent of those taken prisoner. Overall, the death rate in all prisons was about 13 percent of all those confined. The death rate on the battlefield was approximately 5 percent.

When the North ceased exchanging prisoners in 1863, although the Lincoln administration never admitted it, the Union prisoners in the South were sacrificed for greater gains on the battlefield. Northern prisoners were bitter about the breakdown of the exchange system, and they blamed their leaders for not pushing harder to liberate them. Grant came close to admitting the truth when he said, "It is hard on our men held in Southern prisons not to exchange them, but it is humanity to those left in the ranks to fight our battles."

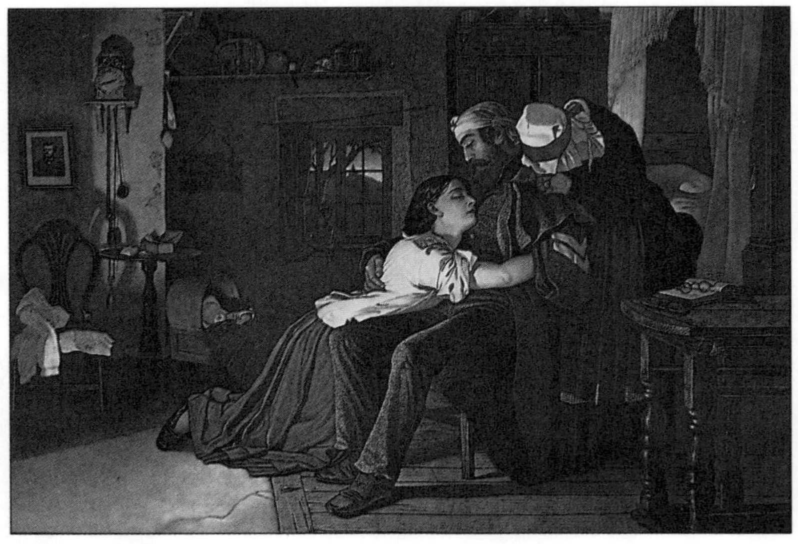

*William Sartain's sentimental painting* Home From Andersonville *portrays one of the lucky soldiers who eluded death on the battlefield and then overcame the cruel struggle of survival as a prisoner of war.*

ECB More than a century later, °the controversy surrounding Civil War prisons still causes rancor over the numbers who died and over which prison camps were worse. Both sides still point fingers for there is blame
JIR enough for each,• but °blaming the officials at one compound for shortcomings and failures does not lessen the shortcomings and failures at the other compounds. When one considers that every prisoner who died was an American, one sees that the loss was to the nation as a whole, whether they died at Elmira, Johnson's Island, Andersonville, or Libby.•

The dedication that some men had for their comrades can still be seen today. Dorance Atwater was a clerk of the dead at Andersonville. He recorded each of the 12,912 burials at the prison camp during the war. In 1865 Atwater and Clara Barton returned to Andersonville to paint and letter the original headboards for the dead. Today, Andersonville stands as a national memorial for all prisoners of war from the American Revolution to the present.

In the last entry in his diary at Andersonville, Samuel Melvin wrote: "Thursday, September 15th, 1864. Lay on my back all day. Eat not much. Cannot eat much. The rice I can't ford goes directly through me. I'm lying in a tent on my rubber blanket with an old Irishman next to me. He's most dead with the diarrhea. The next is a

Dutchman most dead with scurvy. The tents and blankets are just as full of lice and fleas as ever. As things look now, I stand a good chance to lay my bones in old Georgia, but I'd hate to. As bad as one can, I want to go home." Ten days later, Samuel Melvin died.

The war left a legacy of blood and controversy in the story of the treatment of prisoners of war. Soldiers held captive during the Civil War faced a cruel reality of suffering and death. Prisoners of war were a consequence of battle, and the atrocities perpetrated in prison camps both North and South reflected and magnified the greater tragedy of the war itself. The purpose in taking prisoners is to allow them to live while depriving the enemy of their service. For many who found themselves in Civil War prisons, death on the battlefield would have been more humane. As it was, once they were confined, prisoners of war found that the battle for survival was constant and perhaps the cruelest struggle that any of them would ever face.

# ARLINGTON

The NATIONAL CEMETERY AT ARLINGTON overlooks Washington, D.C., from across the Potomac River. Dominating the cemetery, a large house fronted by huge columns occupies the highest ground. At first glance the house looks out of place—a residence for the living, once the home of Confederate Gen. Robert E. Lee, in a military cemetery originally designed for Union soldiers. The structure is a tangible reminder of the sacrifices made during four years of civil war.

The selection of the Arlington estate for the national cemetery was not made solely because of its proximity to Washington, but also because it was the prewar home of Lee, then commander of the Army
AM of Northern Virginia. ○The Federal government could not have been ignorant of the fact that the estate was
BP beloved by Lee,• and ○there is evidence that the authorities wanted to impress upon him that if he ever chose to live at Arlington again, whenever he stepped out his front door, there would be the body of a Union soldier.•

Arlington had always been steeped in symbolism. Its builder and first owner was George Washington Parke Custis, the grandson of Martha Washington and the adopted son of George Washington and heir to his legacy. For Custis, Arlington was to be a national monument to the memory of the country's first president
AM and greatest hero. ○Custis was also the father of Lee's wife, Mary; thus he linked the generation that fought the American Revolution with the generation that fought the Civil War.•

| | |
|---|---|
| **WCD** | William C. Davis |
| **AM** | Agnes Mullins |
| **BP** | Brian Pohanka |
| **JIR** | James I. Robertson Jr. |
| **TLS** | Thomas L. Sherlock |

*George Washington Parke Custis, grandson of Martha Washington and the adopted son of George and Martha Washington, built a mansion on the heights overlooking the south side of the Potomac and named the property Arlington after the first Custis estate in America. Custis made Arlington a repository to the memory of the country's first president and dedicated himself to making the Revolution understandable to the next generation of Americans. In 1804, two years after construction on the mansion began, Custis married Mary "Molly" Lee Fitzhugh, and they had one daughter to survive to adulthood, Mary Anna Randolph Custis. As a child she played with her distant cousin Robert E. Lee on the grounds of the eleven-hundred-acre estate and in 1831 Robert and Mary were married in the home during a torrential rainstorm.*

Custis was only six months old when his father, John Parke Custis, died shortly after the battle of Yorktown. George and Martha Washington decided to adopt Martha's fatherless grandchildren, Washington
AM Custis and his sister, Eleanor. °Custis was a gifted if mischievous child. He admired his foster father and was awed by him, as was almost everyone. Custis had a sense of the dramatic, likely encouraged by the first president of the United States, who took him to theatricals and musicals in Philadelphia.•

Custis was a lackluster student and never graduated from any of the several schools in which he enrolled. In 1798 he returned to Mount Vernon and found that his father, apprised of the young man's scholastic shortcomings, had extensively outlined what was expected of him at the estate, detailing hourly and daily responsibilities. Washington's letter to his son suggested, "The hours allotted for study, if really applied to it, instead of running up & down stairs, & wasted in conversation with anyone who will talk with you, will enable you to make considerable progress in whatsoever line is marked out for you: and that you may do it, is my sincere wish."

Washington died the next year, and Martha died three years later. Custis inherited most of his father's personal belongings and a considerable amount of land from his mother, including land owned previously by his natural father and held in trust for him. He chose to build a home on eleven hundred acres on the south side of the Potomac and to make it a repository to the memory of the country's first president.

JIR Initially, °Custis called the property Mount Washington, but so many "Washingtons" appeared throughout the states after his father's death, he renamed it Arlington, which was the name of the first Custis estate in America on Virginia's eastern shore.• He commissioned George Hadfield, the architect of the Capitol, to design a classical revival–style mansion, modeling it after the Temple of Theseus in Athens. For financial reasons, the construction was undertaken in phases. The north wing was built in 1802, the south wing in 1804, and the building was completed in 1818. In the meantime, the estate was an active farm with an orchard, crops in the fertile fields closest to the Potomac, and a large grazing area for sheep herds.

A book published in 1859 described the mansion: "It is the most lovely spot, overlooking the Potomac; and from the noble portico, that adorns its front, so conspicuous from every point of the federal city and its vicinity, [Custis] saw that city grow into its present grand proportions, from a humble and uninteresting village."

*Efforts to foster the memory of George Washington, combined with Arlington's prominent location and beautiful surroundings, made the estate a tourist attraction for visitors to Washington and nearby Mount Vernon. Picnic parties liked to go there and Custis even "erected . . . various structures for accommodation of visitors," according to* Harper's Weekly *in 1853, which also reported that more than twenty thousand people visited Arlington "during the summer and autumn of 1852." Shown above is an 1853 souvenir plate with the Arlington mansion painted on it by Benson Lossing.*

AM To Custis, °Arlington was the home of a country squire or gentleman, a role in which he viewed himself in the English tradition. Because of his inherited wealth—his land—he knew that he would be a man of independent means for the rest of his life. Gifted with a privileged lifestyle and because of his unique exposure to the men who had fought the Revolution, he believed that he was called to make the Revolution understandable to the next generation of Americans.

He painted pictures of specific Revolutionary War battles that he believed demonstrated Washington's tactical skill. He chose battles that would have been defeats except for the presence of the commander in chief on the field, such as Germantown, Princeton, Trenton, Monmouth, and Yorktown. He wanted the paintings to be seen by the public because they carried an important historic message.•

AM Custis's artistic pursuits were °not limited to painting, however. He was also a musician and playwright.• His modest dramas, written around historic American events, themes, and settings, were performed throughout the eastern states and enjoyed a small measure of popularity.

His efforts to foster the memory of Washington, combined with Arlington's prominent location and beautiful surroundings, made the estate a tourist attraction for visitors to Washington and to nearby Mount

Vernon, Washington's home. In 1853 *Harper's Weekly* noted: "At the foot of a wooded slope, near the bank of the river is Arlington Springs, so well known to picnic parties. Actuated by that generous hospitality which is everywhere in the south, Mr. Custis erected several years ago, various structures for accommodation of visitors. It is estimated that during the summer and autumn of 1852, more than 20,000 people visited Arlington Springs."

In 1804 Custis married Mary "Molly" Lee Fitzhugh. Of the four children born to them, only one, Mary Anna Randolph Custis, survived to adulthood. A small, frail child prone to illness, °she was also a warm and loving person. Custis provided her with the kind of fine classical education he would have given a son, and her mother oversaw her religious training.•

Robert E. Lee was a distant cousin of Mary Custis, and as a boy he had spent many happy hours at Arlington. °The two had been childhood sweethearts. When he was twelve and she was ten, they had planted trees on the lawn as a symbol of their affection for each other.• In his maturity, he returned to Arlington as a lieutenant in the U.S. Army.

Lee's father, Henry "Lighthorse Harry" Lee, was a Revolutionary War hero and friend to Washington. In later life, Harry Lee was incarcerated in debtor's prison and finally forced to flee the country in disgrace. °His memory, however, was still sacred at Arlington. Here Robert learned of his father's contributions to the Revolution and of Washington's strong affection for his parents.•

Robert and Mary were married at Arlington on June 30, 1831, in the midst of a torrential thunderstorm. The marriage joined two of Virginia's most revered families.

Shortly after the ceremony, Lee and his bride left Arlington for Fort Monroe, Virginia, where Lee was then stationed. Mary Lee found the adjustment to military life difficult. "I am a wanderer on the face of the earth," she wrote, "with no place that I can call home." Adding to her unhappiness were frequent illnesses. Upon learning that she was expecting their first child, Mary Lee returned to the care of her parents at Arlington. It was a pattern to be repeated often over the next thirty years. Six of the seven Lee children were born at Arlington.

JIR °Lee was assigned to various posts across the country, returning to Arlington only to visit his family and to be with his children. While the estate was not a home to Lee in the literal sense that he lived there, he loved the place nonetheless.• From one of his various postings he wrote: "I want to see you all very much but have not the time. I hope our merciful Father in heaven will in His own time relieve us from our present troubles and enable us once more to enjoy the society of each other."

The only times Lee experienced feelings of peace were when he was at JIR Arlington. °He once made the statement that this was the place where his affections and attachments were more strongly placed than any other place in AM the world.• °The happiest times were at Christmas. Home for the holidays meant being at Arlington. When the Lee family drove up the carriage drive and made the last right-angle turn, the whole huge portico loomed in front of them and announced to the children that they were home. For years that would be where Grandpa and Grandma Custis would be waiting.•

*When he was in his thirties, Robert E. Lee was called the "handsomest man in the army." Married and a father, Lee was assigned to various posts around the country. Whenever possible he returned to his wife's family estate to be with her and their children. He once said Arlington was the place where his affection and attachments were more strongly placed than anywhere else in the world. Lee served in the Mexican War, a proving ground for many Civil War generals, and then was named superintendent of the U.S. Military Academy at West Point, where he served from 1852 to 1855. These were pleasant times for Lee, surrounded by his wife and seven children, all living together for the first time after a long career filled with distant postings and lonely separations. Lee next assumed the management of Arlington as well as its considerable debts when Mary inherited her father's estate. Before the war, all the debts were paid off and the Lees finally had a home they could call their own.*

In 1857, while Lee was serving in Texas, news arrived that Custis had died. On returning to Arlington, Lee found the estate dilapidated, his wife an invalid, and his children in mourning. Custis had left Arlington and the Washington treasures to Mary Lee in his will, but he had also left debts.

JIR °Arlington had fallen on hard times. As executor of the estate, Lee spent the next two years, as much time as furloughs would permit, overseeing the day-to-day operation of the plantation.• To assist in running the estate, Lee secured a commission for his eldest son, George Washington Custis Lee.

*In 1861 Gen. Winfield Scott was the U.S. Army's highest ranking officer and President Lincoln's chief military advisor. Before the war, Scott had been Lee's commander and he refused a Confederate commission to retain command of Union forces. Lee, on the other hand, declined Lincoln's offer of field command, a decision Scott told Lee was, "the greatest mistake of your life." Scott grasped the strategic significances of Lee's Arlington estate and ordered its seizure by the North as one of its first actions of the war.*

While pondering whether to return to active military service, Lee received an urgent request from the War Department in October 1859. He was charged with retaking the arsenal at Harpers Ferry, which had fallen into the hands of an abolitionist fanatic—John Brown. Lt. J. E. B. "Jeb" Stuart acted as Lee's aide during the affair, and after Lee's detachment had successfully quelled the takeover, the young lieutenant observed: "Colonel Robert E. Lee deserves a gold medal from Virginia. I presume no one but myself will ever know the immense but quiet service he tendered the state and country, for which I'll give praise."

Although his success at Harpers Ferry won Lee acclaim and notoriety, it was a hollow victory. On his return to Texas in December 1860, he encountered the specter of secession. Three months later he was ordered to Washington, barely escaping imprisonment when Texans began to seize federal property. At the War Department, Lee was promoted to colonel and given command of the First U.S. Cavalry. In other circumstances, it would have been the crowning achievement of a long and honorable military career, but for Lee, whose first allegiance was to Virginia, it created a crisis of conscience. When asked which way he would go if Virginia seceded from the Union, Lee

*In May 1861 Federal troops poured across the Chain Bridge (right) and others that crossed the Potomac to occupy the Virginia heights and take control of Lee's home. Later in the war, Federals would remove the planks of the Chain Bridge at night to ensure that no Rebels could have an easy approach to the capital from the Virginia side. Today's Arlington Memorial Bridge is an elegant design which visually links the mansion with the Lincoln Memorial across the river, underscoring the relationship of Lee, Arlington, and the government he chose to leave.*

replied, "If the Union is dissolved and the government disrupted, I shall return to my native state and share the miseries of my people, and save in defense, draw my sword on none."

On April 17, 1861, an ordinance of secession was introduced to the Virginia Convention. The following day, Lee was summoned to meet with Francis Blair, the newly appointed postmaster general. In Blair's home, across from the White House, Lee was offered the field command of the army that was being assembled to invade the South. He returned to Arlington to consider the offer.

Lee wrestled with his conscience as few people have ever had to do. On the one hand, he had the responsibility for his wife's estate, he had a duty to his ill wife, he had an obligation to his children, and he had a love for his native state. On the other hand, he had more than thirty years of service in the army and he had a certain dedication and devotion to his country.

Family members reported that he stayed up all night, pacing back and forth until dawn, before he sat down and composed a short note in which he resigned from the army: "General, since my interview with you on the 18th, I have felt that I ought no longer retain my commission in the Army. I therefore tender my resignation, which I request that you recommend for acceptance. I shall carry with me to the grave the most grateful recollection of your kind consideration, and your name and fame will always be dear to me. Save in defense of my native state, I never desire again to draw my sword."

Virginia did not wait long to call for Lee's services, and again duty required him to leave family, friends, and Arlington. On Monday, April 26, 1861, Lee left the majestic estate to catch a train to Richmond, Virginia.

*When Union Brig. Gen. Irvin McDowell established his headquarters at Arlington, he chose not to occupy the mansion but to live in a small tent on the lawn. He assured Mrs. Lee that he would "endeavor to have all things so ordered that on your return you will find things as little disturbed as possible." However, souvenir hunters pilfered some of the artifacts Custis had collected, and so McDowell had the contents of the house packed and shipped to the Patent Office for safekeeping.*

LEE'S DEPARTURE marked the end of an era for Arlington. He never again occupied the house and only years later did he even glimpse it. The Civil War was to transform Arlington from a shrine to the memory of Washington into a solemn memorial to the Civil War dead.

Shortly after assuming his duties in Richmond, Lee wrote his wife and daughters: "War is inevitable, and

*Brig. Gen. Irvin McDowell (on the second step, center, facing to his right) posed in front of Arlington with his staff in this 1861 photograph from the Brady collection, possibly made by Brady's chief assistant and Washington office manager, Alexander Gardner. Weeds grow up around the porch. The yard appears trampled to bare dirt. The army, hastily building barracks and fortifications on the property, had no intention of maintaining a lawn.*

there is no telling when it will burst around you. . . . You have to move and make arrangements to go to some point of safety which you must select. The Mount Vernon plate and pictures ought to be secured. Keep quiet while you remain, and in your preparations. . . . May God keep and preserve you and have mercy on all our people."

WCD °There were sound reasons for the Union to occupy the estate and Arlington heights as quickly as possible. First, because Arlington and Alexandria were enemy territory, lying just across the Potomac from Washington, it was important for the defense of the Federal capital that the Union army extend its lines as far south as possible. Second, because Arlington commanded some of the highest ground on the southern side of the Potomac, it was logical to occupy, defend, entrench, and fortify the area. Third, many also likely believed that by striking against Lee, occupying his home, and turning it to the purposes of the Yankee cause, they were also striking a blow against Confederacy morale.• Gen. Winfield Scott, Lee's former commander, had long grasped the strategic significance of the estate, and to preempt the Southerners' occupation of the grounds, Scott ordered its seizure.

AM °On May 24, 1861, at 2 A.M., fourteen thousand Union soldiers crossed the Potomac and occupied

*The choice of Arlington for defensive fortifications was a practical one. Left unguarded, the property might have afforded Southern cannoneers an excellent shot at Washington, which was spread out below and well within artillery range. Like dozens of other forts and gun emplacements ringing the Northern capital, Arlington sat through the war without an enemy engagement. This picture of the barracks for the headquarters guard was made in 1864 by Union Capt. A. J. Russell, the finest soldier-photographer on either side.*

Arlington and Alexandria.• The action was accomplished with only one casualty, Col. Elmer Ellsworth, who was killed by an irate Alexandria innkeeper incensed over Ellsworth's removal of a Confederate flag from the roof of his hotel. AM °Gen. C. W. Sanford of the New York Militia commanded the troops that reached the Arlington estate before dawn.• Only a few persons climbed the hill to see the house, one of whom was Sanford, who wanted to ensure that the home would not be disturbed. When he found only the servants there, Sanford decided to set up his headquarters nearby so as to safeguard the house and its furnishings.

JIR °Mary Lee had vacated Arlington about a week and a half prior to the occupation, thinking her absence would be only temporary, and traveled to Ravensworth with her daughter Agnes and then to Kinloch with her daughter Mary.• Concern for some family possessions, the Washington relics, and "her people" led her to request permission of the Union authorities to return to Arlington. When she learned that she would most likely be denied, she wrote a scathing letter on May 30, 1861, to the officer in charge: "It never occurred to me, . . . that *I* could be forced to sue for permission to enter my *own home,* and that such an outrage as its military occupation to the exclusion of me and my children, could ever have been perpetrated by anyone in the whole extent of this country." She went on to describe herself as "homeless," cut off from the family's funds in Alexandria banks, and thus deprived of "means for my support." She asked that a few of the elderly slaves from the estate be allowed to bring themselves and some of her belongings to her, concluding, "that God may ever spare you & yours the agony and inconvenience I am now enduring."

In the meantime, Maj. Gen. Irvin McDowell had taken over Sanford's headquarters at Arlington, and he responded tactfully: "With respect to the occupation of Arlington by the United States troops, I beg to say it has been done by my predecessor with every regard to the preservation of the place. . . . I assure you it has been, and will be my earnest endeavor to have all things so ordered that on your return you will find things as little disturbed as possible." Many observers thought it strange that McDowell, who was then the commanding general of the Union army, chose to live in a small tent, work at a rough table, and sleep on a camp bed while a large comfortable home was only a few feet away.

Arlington became a drill camp. Trees were felled to make barracks, a series of earthen defenses were dug, and plans were prepared to erect two defensive forts, later named Whipple and McPherson for fallen Union generals. A French observer traveling with the Union

*This photograph, also made by A. J. Russell, is entitled "Bird's-eye view of corrals on Cemetery Grounds." Photographed on June 29, 1864, two weeks after Arlington had been declared a national cemetery, Russell's assignment may have been to document the estate's condition as it switched from being a fortress to a cemetery.*

*Although there were sound strategic military reasons for the Union army to seize Arlington, other actions were more symbolic. For instance, the Federals constructed on the estate a refugee camp known as Freedman's Village, shown in these two photographs from 1863. When President Lincoln signed the Emancipation Proclamation, liberated slaves poured into Washington, D.C., and while housing could have been erected anywhere for them, Arlington was chosen. Freedman's Village included a school, a church, a hospital, and a home for the aged for the two thousand residents. Those who fell prey to illness or injury while there were buried on the grounds. The village remained intact until the 1890s.*

*Technically, Robert E. Lee did not own the 196 slaves living at Arlington before the war. Nonetheless, as master at Arlington, he was bound to fulfill his father-in-law's wish that they be freed within five years of Custis's death. Lee freed the last of them in 1862. This must have presented some hard choices for Lee because an easy solution to reducing his debt on the estate would have been to sell the slaves to plantations in the Deep South.*

army observed: "The tents of the guard and of the servants of the staff were set up in the gardens, trampled by men and animals. The park roads were deeply furrowed by the continual passage of artillery and ammunition wagons everywhere."

After the first battle at Manassas in July 1861, a defeated and dispirited Union army returned to Washington, but many fell back only as far as the Arlington defenses. McDowell was replaced by George B. McClellan but continued to maintain his headquarters at Arlington since McClellan preferred to live in Washington. During the reorganization of the Union army, McDowell found it necessary to occupy the mansion. McClellan ordered the defensive works enlarged and strengthened, including those around the Arlington estate. Roads were cut through the woods to connect the forts, and trees were removed to increase fields of

*A man of great passions, Secretary of War Edwin Stanton disliked career army officers because they felt they knew more about conducting a war than he did. Stanton accepted the recommendation of Montgomery Meigs and ordered Arlington to be appropriated for a military cemetery.*

fire. The wooded fields around Arlington were devastated, although a few stands were allowed to remain near the house.

Despite the ruination of the fields around the house, the old mansion maintained a strange, serene charm. In November 1861, an army surgeon described the home to his wife: "After the vandalism I have witnessed, it was a pleasurable relief to find here respect for the property and furniture. The garden, with its fences preserved, and the walls of almost every room in the immense old building are covered with rich paintings and old family pictures. The antique bureaus and sideboards, calling up impressions of generations long passed away, are still tenants of the building; and the halls recall [Sir Walter] Scott's description of the Halls of the Douglas, where the arms of hunters and the trophies of the hunt mingled with the trappings of the warrior."

In late 1861 Selina Gray, Mary Lee's housekeeper, apprised McDowell that several of the Washington relics and other family items had been pilfered. She had tried to safeguard them in the basement and the attic, but one morning she found the areas had been broken into and several of the boxes of artifacts had been opened. Gray turned her keys over to McDowell, hoping that she would be relieved of the responsibility for the heirlooms. McDowell sealed the areas and then had the contents of the house packed and shipped to the Patent Office for safekeeping.

Lee knew what was happening to his wife's house, and by Christmas 1861 he had resigned himself to never seeing Arlington again. In a letter to one of his daughters, he wrote: "Your old home, if not destroyed by our enemies, has been so desecrated that I cannot bear to think of it. I should have preferred it to have been wiped from this earth, its beautiful hill sunk, and its sacred trees buried, rather than have been degraded." Lee wrote to Mary: "It is better to make up our minds to a general loss. They cannot take away the remembrance of the spot, and the memories of those that to us rendered it sacred. That will remain to us as long as life will last, and that we can preserve."

*That the headquarters of the surveyor of the cemetery was placed in the back yard of the mansion (shown here in a June 29, 1864, photograph by A. J. Russell) indicates that army personnel did not intend to dig the first graves near the house. When the quartermaster general, Montgomery Meigs, visited Arlington in August, he was angered because unless graves were placed near the house, it would be possible for Lee to use it again as a private residence after the war. It is said that Meigs stood on the portico and ordered interment of soldiers just outside the fence in the flower garden. He then asked Secretary of War Stanton to order soldiers out of the house and to install civilian cemetery caretakers.*

During the first year of the war, the Arlington estate bustled with activity as the Union army established its defensive line around the capital. The second year was not as lively. The house and grounds no longer hosted McDowell's headquarters. Instead, several officers moved into the mansion as part of the coordination of the capital defenses, but the war itself became more distant. Elaborate galas and balls were hosted at Arlington, and the estate became a sightseeing attraction for Washington residents eager to visit the home of the suddenly legendary Lee who had stymied McClellan's Peninsula campaign and vanquished another Union army at a second battle near Manassas.

In 1863 a portion of the estate was confiscated by the Federal government and put to use as a refugee camp for large numbers of escaped slaves, or contrabands. Following the promulgation of the Emancipation Proclamation, a great number of these refugees had descended on Washington in search of food and shelter. Many of them were moved to a Freedman's Village erected in the southern section of the Arlington estate.

It was a model community and housed approximately two thousand freedmen in rows of two-and-a-half-storied white frame houses that lined streets named for prominent abolitionists. The village included a school, a church, a hospital, and a home for the aged.

*The barns and enlisted men's barracks (above left) show that garrison life at Arlington in June 1864 for these common soldiers was quite different from that of Yankee soldiers down the road at Petersburg, Virginia, where a bloody siege had begun a week earlier. The officers' quarters (above right) were large and airy and even boasted glass windows with divided lights.*

The able-bodied were taught various trades in the village's workshops or worked the land along the river. BP °Numbers of these people, however, died of illness and disease and were buried there.• The village remained intact until the late 1890s.

Meanwhile, the war became increasingly bitter, and Congress began seeking ways to exact financial hardship on the Rebel South. In July 1862 an act for collecting taxes in the insurrectionist districts was passed. "The rebellion will not be crushed out by offering olive branches or by the utterance of honeyed words from the lips of Congress," said Congressman Henry Wilson, chairman of the Judiciary Committee. "Traitors have no right to expect to be shielded from the consequences of WCD their crimes." °The tax was designed to penalize Confederates who owned property in the North. Men like Lee and other officers in the Confederate army were beyond the reach of Union authorities, but their property in the North was not.•

JIR °The tax on Arlington was $92.07 plus a 50 percent penalty, but the owner was required to appear in person before the proper official to pay the tax. Mary Lee was too crippled to make the journey to Alexandria even if she had been able to get a pass through the lines. She sent a relative, Philip R. Feudal, to pay the assessment, but the tax office refused to take payment from anyone but the owner of the estate. Arlington was therefore confiscated to be sold at public auction. On January 11, 1864, the Federal government was the high bidder and bought the estate for a little under $26,800.•

*Despite a daunting intelligence and a gift for backstage finagling, Montgomery Meigs was occasionally hobbled by his vanity and a penchant for pettiness. As quartermaster general, he was beset with problems of corruption, kickbacks, and poor supply contracts. His management of federal military hospitals and prisoner-of-war camps was less than stellar. Ultimately responsible for the disposition of the dead, he was ordered to find a suitable place for a national cemetery. The idea of burying soldiers near the Arlington mansion apparently originated with Meigs, who had little love for Robert E. Lee, his former superior officer. Although Meigs's motive may have been vindictive, the selection of Arlington as a national cemetery was publicly applauded. Meigs's written requisition suggesting Arlington for a military cemetery and its written approval by Secretary of War Stanton are dated the same day, indicating the two men had already made up their minds.*

By 1864 the human price exacted by three years of fighting was staggering. In the North, the public was growing weary of casualty lists and frustrated with the government's handling of burial arrangements. The Lincoln administration was aware of the shortcomings because JIR °Washington, D.C., had became a vast military hospital complex. Sickness killed two men for every man who died in battle, and the dead awaiting burial were piling up in enormous numbers. Moreover, conventional cemeteries were filling up, causing the military authorities to look for new sites in which to bury the nation's dead.•

The families of those who lost loved ones in the war had begun criticizing TLS °the government for the haphazard way that soldiers were being buried on the battlefields. Political pressure was building to bury the dead in a more honored and dignified manner. Ultimately, the man responsible for the final disposition of the dead was Montgomery C. Meigs, the quartermaster general, and he was ordered to conduct a survey of potential areas that might be used for a national cemetery.•

On June 15, 1864, Meigs reported to the secretary of war, Edwin M. Stanton: "I have visited and inspected the grounds now used as a cemetery upon the Arlington Estate. I recommend that interments in this ground be discontinued, and that the land surrounding the Arlington Mansion, now understood to be the property of the United States, be appropriated as a national military cemetery." Stanton presently replied: "The Arlington Mansion and the grounds immediately surrounding it are appropriated for a military cemetery. The Quartermaster General is charged with the execution of this order. He will cause the grounds, not exceeding two hundred acres, to be immediately surveyed, laid out and enclosed for this purpose."

Like Lee, Meigs was a southerner and an engineer. JIR °Meigs had graduated fifth in his class at West Point, which won him assignment to the Corps of Engineers.

*The first grave markers in Arlington were made of wood and had to be replaced every five years. In 1872 the quartermaster department adopted the more traditional white marble markers, and by 1880 marble had replaced all other headstones. Once the order was given, burial began in earnest, with more than fifteen hundred men a month being interred. Despite its reputation as the premiere shrine of the Civil War dead, by the century's end Arlington contained fewer graves than the national military cemeteries at Vicksburg and Nashville.*

He worked with Lee on various projects on the Mississippi River and was then assigned to Washington, where his tasks included the expansion of the Capitol's wings and the construction of a new dome.•

Despite being a southerner and having a brother on the Confederate side, Meigs's loyalty lay firmly with the North. Unlike Lee, whose family was part of the landed gentry of Virginia, Meigs's family was from the professional classes. His view of duty was utilitarian and pragmatic.

WCD °Both Meigs and Lee had grown up under the same flag and been educated at the expense of the same government at the same school. Both had served at the same posts for the same army. Yet Lee became a Confederate, and in the eyes of Meigs, Lee was a traitor.•

Even prior to getting official consent to use Arlington as a cemetery, Meigs had ordered interments on the property, specifying they be placed as close as pos-
TLS sible to the house. °The first military burial took place at Arlington on May 13, 1864, when the remains of Pvt. William Christman, a soldier with the Sixty-seventh Pennsylvania Infantry, were interred, but it was not until June 15, almost a month later, that the actual orders were cut establishing Arlington as a national cemetery.•

*Three unidentified men in civilian dress stand in the Custis family plot in another of Captain Russell's June 1864 photographs. Here are the graves of George Washington Parke Custis and his wife, Mary Lee Fitzhugh Custis, parents of Mrs. Robert E. Lee. The Federal cemetery was managed by civilian caretakers who were given the run of the Arlington mansion by Montgomery Meigs because he was angered that military officers had disregarded his orders to bury soldiers close to the house.*

The officer in charge of carrying out these orders was Gen. Gustavus DuRussy, the commanding officer at Arlington, whose quarters were in the mansion. Not wishing to see the graves of soldiers outside his headquarters, DuRussy instructed his men to begin interments in the far northeastern corner of the allotted two hundred acres—almost half a mile away from the mansion.

When Meigs visited Arlington in August 1864, he
AM was surprised to see no graves near the house. °He was angered because unless graves were placed near the house, the house could conceivably be used as a private residence by Lee after the war. Meigs stood on the portico and ordered the interment of soldiers just outside the old board fence to the flower garden.• To avoid any further confusion, he asked that Secretary of War Stanton order the soldiers out of the house so it could be used by civilian caretakers of the cemetery.

In October 1864, Meigs returned to Arlington, this time to bury his own son, who had been killed in
BP action near Harrisonburg, Virginia. °John Meigs had graduated at the top of his West Point class in 1863, just like his father. He had been assigned to the Corps of Engineers, like his father. In October 1864, he blundered into a fight with some Confederate scouts and was killed.• His father marked the grave with a monu-

ment showing the young lieutenant in full uniform lying on the ground, his revolver at his side, surrounded by hoofprints.

John Meigs was one of more than seven thousand Federal soldiers buried at Arlington by the end of 1864, and another eight thousand joined them before the end of hostilities in 1865. The once beautifully landscaped grounds of the estate were now scarred by rows of crude wooden markers that stretched the full width of the allotted land.

JIR °There was no honor attached to being buried at Arlington in the first few years of the cemetery's existence. The first graves were unknown soldiers or men whose parents were too poor to pay funeral costs. A few Confederate soldiers were buried there in the beginning, miles and miles from the land that they held so dear.• After the war, many of the Southern dead interred at Arlington were claimed by family members and reinterred in their native states.

For the Lees the dearest land was Arlington, but Arlington was more than an estate. Mary Lee had always regarded the responsibility of preserving and protecting Arlington and the Washington relics as a sacred duty. When she discovered what had happened to her home and that Federal soldiers were buried in the flower gardens that had been planted by her father, she was outraged: "I learned that my garden laid out with so much taste by my dear father's own hand has been all changed, the splendid forests levelled to the ground, the small enclosure allotted to his and my mother's remains surrounded closely by the graves of those who aided to bring all this ruin on the children and country. They are even planted up to the very door without regard to common decency." In a later letter, she added: "Even savages would have spared that place . . . yet they have done everything to debase and desecrate it."

After the war, there was talk about returning the land to the Lees. While the Lees were anxious about the estate and the mansion, the prospect of having the grounds returned to its previous owners was no less distressing for the relatives of those buried in Arlington. Meigs wrote to Stanton: "Inquiries have been

*The loss of Arlington was a terrible tragedy for both Lees. Mary Lee especially had felt a sacred duty to preserve and protect her family's Washington relics. However, Robert, who desired to see the reunification of the country after the war, would not allow his family or his property to become a point of dissension between North and South and so he never challenged the Federal government's seizure of the property. He died in 1870 as a man without country, without possessions, without a home, and without military honors. Today at Arlington National Cemetery the mansion has again become a tourist attraction, administered by the National Park Service, and its official name is Arlington House, The Robert E. Lee Memorial.*

made lately of members of Congress by their constituents, the bodies of whose kindred repose in the cemetery, suggesting a fear that the United States may yet restore to the original possessors the land consecrated by their remains. I respectfully recommend that the title be investigated by the legal adviser of the government and that if not perfect, steps be taken to make it entirely secure."

Many in the North approved of the confiscation of the estate and its use as a national cemetery. The *Washington Morning Chronicle* described the action as "a righteous use of the estate of the rebel General Lee," and charged him with murdering hundreds of Union soldiers. A visitor to the cemetery, however, commented: "To see the house of Robert Lee sacked and made into a cemetery, and to fancy the thoughts that would fill the great heart were so strange to me, and in their strangeness so painful, that I doubt whether I ever had a sadder walk than the visit to the heights of Arlington."

AM °Lee, whose greatest concern after the war was the reunification of the country, would not permit any

*In 1869 President Andrew Johnson quietly arranged for Mary Lee to recover some of the Custis family heirlooms from the time of George Washington, including a set of china given to Martha Washington by Lafayette, a punch bowl from Mount Vernon, a mirror, a dresser, and a set of tent poles and tent pegs used by George Washington during the Revolutionary War. The press discovered the presidential directive and branded it an outrage. The same Congress which had adopted articles of impeachment against Johnson prevented the return of the items to Mary Lee.*

family members to sue for Arlington. He would not allow himself, his family, or his property to become a focal point for dissension that would further separate the North from the South and delay reconstruction.•

While Lee did not press to regain his wife's estate, Mary received word that the Washington heirlooms might be returned if she were to apply for them. In 1868 President Andrew Johnson offered a general amnesty. As part of the amnesty, former Confederates were allowed to reapply for citizenship and the return of personal possessions. The Lees requested that the Washington relics be returned, and Johnson was willing to accommodate them, but word of the impending return caused a storm in Congress.

WCD °Lee himself was a symbol of the lost cause and therefore became a special case in the minds of the Radical Republicans of the postwar years. These men were the most vindictive toward former Confederates and were determined not to allow this great symbol of the rebellion to use the courts to reclaim his family's property. As a result, the Lee family faced several obstacles to recovering anything.•

Lee died in 1870 as a man without a country, without possessions, without a home, and without military honors. He had sacrificed everything to duty and conscience. In 1873, a few months before her death, Mary Lee made one last visit to Arlington, but she was so distressed by its appearance she never left her carriage. A former slave still living on the property brought her a drink of water and watched her carriage leave, noting that the former owner of the house never looked back. "My dear home was so changed that it seemed but a dream of the past," she later said.

JIR °The estate passed to her oldest son, George Washington Custis Lee, who sued the federal government for its return. The case eventually reached the Supreme Court, which ruled in 1882 that the government was guilty of illegal seizure.• The U.S. government, by an act of Congress in March 1883, returned the Washington relics and paid the Lee family $150,000 for the Arlington estate. Meigs did not witness the reversal of his actions; he had died in January 1882 and was buried next to his son at Arlington.

Custis Lee, the bachelor eldest son of Gen. and Mrs. Robert E. Lee, inherited Arlington, while his brothers "Rooney" and Robert inherited other Custis lands, called White House and Romancoke on the Pamunkey River in eastern Virginia. Rooney rebuilt White House, which had been destroyed in the war, and both sons farmed their properties. Custis sued the federal government for the return of Arlington. The case eventually reached the Supreme Court, which ruled in 1882 that Arlington had been illegally seized. By act of Congress in March 1883, the U.S. government returned the Custis family's Washington relics and paid the Lee family $150,000 for the Arlington estate. Beginning in 1865, Custis taught engineering at Virginia Military Institute and then succeeded his father as president of Washington and Lee College in 1871.

AFTER THE conclusion of the war and the end of battlefield casualties, cleanup operations were conducted on all the major battlefields because thousands of soldiers had been buried hastily in shallow, inadequate graves. Near Manassas, soldiers' remains were regularly discovered and transported to Arlington for burial. A vault was erected in the Lee rose garden to accommodate the partial remains of 2,111 unknown soldiers
TLS in a common grave. °The large circular vault was partitioned into areas for skulls, leg bones, and arm bones.• The *National Intelligencer* described the project: "At the time we looked into this gloomy cavern, a literal Golgotha, . . . they were dropping fragmentary skeletons into this receptacle daily." The vault was sealed in September 1866, and a granite monument was erected above it to commemorate the fallen soldiers.

In trying to exact some measure of revenge against Lee by making the mansion uninhabitable, Meigs unwittingly preserved Arlington as a monument to
AM heroes. °Instead of being an insult to the man who led the Army of Northern Virginia, Arlington National Cemetery became a public treasure dominated by the house which that man so dearly loved. It became the final resting place of people for whom he had great admiration for the services rendered to their country.•

So many people flocked to Arlington Cemetery after the war to pay their respects, the government was prompted to institute a national day of remembrance in
TLS 1868. °Decoration Day, currently observed as Memorial Day, was established by Gen. John A. Logan in General Orders No. 11 and was originally devoted only to the Union dead—only their graves were allowed to be decorated. The graves of Confederates who had died in nearby hospitals were expressly left out of the honor, and southern women who came to spread flowers on

*So many people flocked to Arlington Cemetery after the war to pay their respects that in 1868 the government instituted a day of remembrance for the Union dead, called Decoration Day (now observed as Memorial Day and honoring soldiers of all wars). A principal speaker on that first occasion was Congressman James A. Garfield, who had been a major general in the war and would be elected president of the United States in 1880.*

those graves were forbidden to enter Arlington cemetery. Thus, scattered around the cemetery were bare graves surrounded by flower-strewn graves. That evening, a windy thunderstorm swept through the area, and the next day the wind had blown flowers over all the graves so that visitors could not tell which were Union and which were Confederate.•

Speaking on the occasion of that first Decoration Day at Arlington, Gen. James A. Garfield said: "We do not know one promise these men made, one pledge they gave, one word they spoke. But we do know they summoned up and perfected by one supreme act the highest virtues of men and citizens. For love of country, they accepted death. That act resolved all doubts and made immortal their patriotism and their virtue."

During the early years of Arlington's use as a soldiers' cemetery, grave markers were made of wood and had to be replaced every five years. An experimental marker made of stone composed with a metal alloy was introduced into one of the sections, but in 1872 the quartermaster department adopted the more traditional white marble markers. By 1880 these had replaced all other headstones.

If time healed the wounds of war, recognition of the duty shown by Confederate soldiers to their vision of country slowly gained recognition. "For years I was face to face with some fragment of the Army of Northern Virginia, and had the intent to do it harm," wrote Col. Charles Francis Adams in 1902. "But now, looking back through the perspective of nearly forty years, I glory in it and in them. They were worthy of the best steel. I am proud to say that I was their countryman."

In 1906 Congress authorized the construction of a Confederate memorial in Arlington, and Moses Ezekiel, a Southern veteran of the battle of New Market, Vir-
BP ginia, was commissioned to design it. °He seemed the natural choice to execute the memorial• because he had been a cadet at the Virginia Military Institute and had participated at New Market in a charge that drove
BP the Yankees away from an artillery battery. °He never forgot the sight of his classmates being cut down around him.•

*Just as at picturesque Lookout Mountain, Tennessee, where men enjoyed dramatically posing atop spectacular crags, the front porch of Robert E. Lee's mansion became a favorite place for Union soldiers such as the officers of the 71st New York Infantry pictured here, to have their photo made.*

The memorial was dedicated on June 3, 1914, the JIR birthday of Jefferson Davis. °There is not an ounce of defiance in it. The figure atop the thirty-two-foot shaft is the figure of the South, but she looks down with sadness. A long leaf of peace adorns her head. In her hand are symbols representing an Old Testament prophecy about turning the tools of war into the tools of peace: "They shall beat their swords into plowshares, and their spears into pruning hooks; nation shall not lift up sword against nation, neither shall they learn war anymore." The figure looks down sadly on the four hundred Southern graves gathered around her.• An inscription reads: "Not for fame or reward, not for place or for rank, not lured by ambition or goaded by necessity, but in simple obedience to duty as they understood it these men suffered all, sacrificed all, dared all—and died." All 409 Confederate soldiers buried at Arlington were reinterred around the base of the memorial. The headstones vary slightly from those of their Union counterparts in that they come to a point at the top. Legend says that the points are to prevent Yankees from resting on the stones.

BP °These Southerners believed that what they were fighting for was right, just, and would affect not only their families and the people they cared about, but gen-

*The erection of the Confederate Memorial at Arlington, authorized by Congress in 1906, was in keeping with the spirit of sectional reconciliation that swelled at the end of the nineteenth century and was capped by the Spanish-American War. In that war, represented at Arlington by a monument to the USS Maine, Americans north and south fought once again under the same flag for a common cause. This photograph of Arlington was made in 1926.*

erations yet unborn. These were people who gave their lives with a sense of hope.• To the Civil War soldier, conflict was not an evil, but a necessity, because the ideals of freedom of government of the people and by the people came at a price.

"In our youth our hearts were touched by fire. It was given to us to learn at the outset that life is a profound and passionate thing," wrote Oliver Wendell Holmes Jr., a young officer with the Twentieth Massachusetts who
BP would later become a Supreme Court justice. °Holmes often came to Arlington to sit and meditate. He wrote eloquent passages on the meaning of the war and why the men of his generation gave everything. They even gave their names, sacrificed their identities for what they believed in. Every one of those headstones, every one of those memorials represents a person who should be meaningful to every American across the decades because each one of them gave more than he took from this country.•

In later years the burial of notable figures from the war enhanced Arlington's identity as a national cemetery. By the end of the nineteenth century it had become the most widely known of the country's eighty-three national cemeteries, reflecting the spirit of Confederate veteran Theodore O'Hara's poem, whose verses

*Today the 612-acre Arlington National Cemetery is the honored resting place of more than two hundred thousand Americans, including presidents, Supreme Court justices, astronauts, and soldiers—from privates to generals—from every major war. The mansion has been restored to its 1861 appearance and some of the original Custis and Lee family furnishings have been returned. Among other sites that draw visitors are the grave of President John F. Kennedy, marked by an eternal flame, and his wife, Jacqueline Kennedy Onassis; the Tomb of the Unknowns containing the remains of soldiers from World War I, World War II, Korea, and Vietnam; and, nearby, the Marine Corps War Memorial, a sculpture portraying the raising of the flag on Iwo Jima during World War II. There are also monuments to war correspondents, military nurses, the Seabees, the Rough Riders, the Coast Guard, and the 101st Airborne. A memorial slab honors fourteen unknown dead from the War of 1812. The earliest major monument is the tomb of the Unknown Dead of the Civil War.*

*Seemingly endless rows of simple white headstones are reminders of the sacrifices made by Americans for a country which is again united.*

were strategically placed on bronze plaques throughout the grounds: "On Fame's eternal camping-ground, / Their silent tents are spread, / And Glory guards, with solemn round, / The bivouac of the dead."

The American poet Walt Whitman remarked that the real war would never get in the books. For him, the true heroes were the foot soldiers under whose cautious hand was saved the Union of these states. They now lie without adornment, beside presidents and dignitaries, in honored glory at Arlington. It was the Greek poet Horace who said in 23 B.C., "It is sweet and honorable to die for one's country."

# Bibliography


Abdill, George B. *Civil War Railroads.* New York: Bonanza Books, 1961.

Acken, J. Gregory, ed. *Inside the Army of the Potomac: The Civil War Experience of Captain Francis Adams Donaldson.* Mechanicsburg, Penn.: Stackpole Books, 1998.

Axelrod, Alan. *The War Between the Spies: A History of Espionage During the American Civil War.* New York: Atlantic Monthly Press, 1992.

Bakeless, John. *Spies of the Confederacy.* Philadelphia: J. B. Lippincott Co., 1970.

Baker, Jean H. *Mary Todd Lincoln: A Biography.* New York: Norton, 1987.

Becker, Carl M., and Ritchie Thomas, eds. *Hearth and Knapsack: The Ladley Letters, 1857-1880.* Athens, Ohio: Ohio University Press, 1988.

Beller, Susan P. *Medical Practices in the Civil War.* Cincinnati: Betterway Books, 1992.

Berline, Jean V. *A Confederate Nurse — The Diary of Ada W. Bacot, 1860-1863.* Columbia, S.C.: University of South Carolina Press, 1994.

Bigla, Philip. *In Honored Glory: Arlington National Cemetery—The Final Post.* Rev. ed. Kingsport, Tenn.: van der Merwe, Cobus, 1998.

Blassingame, John. *The Slave Community.* New York: Oxford University Press, 1972.

Christ, Elwood. *The Struggle for the Bliss Farm at Gettysburg.* Baltimore: Butternut and Blue, 1993.

Clinton, Catherine. *Tara Revisited: Women, War, and the Plantation Legend.* New York: Abbeville Press, 1995.

Clinton, Catherine, and Nina Silber, eds. *Divided Houses: Gender and the Civil War.* New York: Oxford University Press, 1992.

Coco, Gregory A. *A Strange and Blighted Land — Gettysburg: The Aftermath of Battle.* Gettysburg: Thomas, 1994.

Coggins, Jack. *Arms and Equipment of the Civil War.* Garden City, N.Y.: Doubleday & Co., 1962.

Comings, Harrison H. *Personal Reminiscences of Co. E, N.Y. Fire Zouaves.* Malden, Mass.: J. G. Tilden, 1886.

Cunningham, H. H. *Doctors in Gray: The Confederate Medical Service.* Baton Rouge: Louisiana State University Press, 1958.

Davenport, Alfred. *Camp and Field Life of the Fifth New York Volunteer Infantry.* New York: Dick and Fitzgerald, 1879.

Davis, William C. *The Orphan Brigade: The Kentucky Confederates Who Couldn't Go Home.* Baton Rouge: Louisiana State University Press, 1980.

Denney, Robert E. *Civil War Medicine — Care and Comfort of the Wounded.* New York: Stirling Publishing, 1993.

Donald, David Herbert. *Lincoln.* New York: Simon & Schuster, 1995.

Dyer, Frederick H. *A Compendium of the War of the Rebellion.* 3 vols. Des Moines: Dyer, 1908. Reprint, Dayton, Ohio: Morningside Bookshop, 1978.

Eby, Cecil D., Jr., ed. *A Virginia Yankee in the Civil War: The Diaries of David Hunter Strother.* Chapel Hill: The University of North Carolina Press, 1961.

Emery, Edwin. *The Press and America: An Interpretive History of Journalism.* Englewood Cliffs, N.J.: Prentice-Hall, Inc., 1954, 1962.

Faust, Drew Gilpin. *Southern Stories: Slaveholders in Peace and War.* Columbia: University of Missouri Press, 1992.

Flood, Charles Bracelen. *Lee: The Last Years.* Boston: Houghton Mifflin, 1981.

Fox, William F. *Regimental Losses in the American Civil War, 1861-1865.* 1898. Reprint, Dayton, Ohio: Morningside Bookshop, 1985.

Fox-Genovese, Elizabeth. *Within the Plantation Household: Black and White Women of the Old South.* Chapel Hill: University of North Carolina Press, 1988.

Frassanito, William A. *Grant and Lee: The Virginia Campaigns, 1864-1865.* New York: Charles Scribner's Sons, 1983.

——— *Antietam: The Photographic Legacy of America's Bloodiest Day.* New York: Charles Scribner's Sons, 1978.

Gallagher, Gary W., ed. *The First Day at Gettysburg: Essays on Confederate and Union Leadership*. Kent, Ohio: The Kent State University Press, 1992.

Gardner, Alexander. *Gardner's Photographic Sketchbook of the Civil War*. Washington, D.C.: Philp & Solomons, 1866. Reprint, New York: Dover Publications, 1959.

Genovese, Eugene D. *Roll Jordan Roll: The World the Slaves Made*. New York: Pantheon Books, 1974.

Gibbons, Tony. *Warships and Naval Battles of the Civil War*. New York: Gallery Books, 1989.

Glatthaar, Joseph T. *Forged in Battle: The Civil War Alliance of Black Soldiers and White Officers*. New York: Free Press, 1990.

Gooding, Henry G. *On the Altar of Freedom: A Black Civil War Soldier's Letters from the Front*. Edited by Virginia M. Adams. Amherst: The University of Massachusetts Press, 1991.

Hague, Carthenia Antoinette. *A Blockaded Family: Life in Southern Alabama During the Civil War*. Lincoln: University of Nebraska Press, 1991.

Harrison, Constance Cary. "Virginia Scenes in '61," In *Battles and Leaders of the Civil War*, ed. Robert U. Johnson and Clarence C. Buel, 1:160-66.

Harwell, Richard Barksdale. *Kate: The Journal of a Confederate Nurse*. Baton Rouge: Louisiana State University Press, 1959.

Hazlett, James C., Edwin Olmstead, and H. Hume Parks. *Field Artillery Weapons of the Civil War*. Newark: University of Delaware Press, 1983.

Hesseltine, William B., ed. *Civil War Prisons*. Kent, Ohio: Kent State University Press, 1962.

Hine, Darlene Clark, Elsa Barkley Brown, and Rosalyn Terborg-Penn, eds. *Black Women in America*. 2 vols. Bloomington: Indiana University Press, 1993.

Hinkel, John V. *Arlington, Monument to Heroes*. Englewood Cliffs, N.J.: Prentice-Hall, 1965.

Holzer, Harold, and Mark E. Neeley, Jr. *Mine Eyes Have Seen the Glory: The Civil War in Art*. New York: Orion Books, 1993.

Horan, James D. *Brady: Historian with a Camera*. New York: Crown, 1955.

Johnson, Robert U. and Clarence C. Buel, eds. *Battles and Leaders of the Civil War*. 4 vols. New York: Century, 1884-88. Reprint, New York: Thomas Yoseloff, Inc., 1956.

Johnston, Angus James, II. *Virginia Railroads in the Civil War*. Richmond: Virginia Historical Society, 1959.

Jones, John B. *A Rebel War Clerk's Diary*. Edited by Earl S. Miers. Baton Rouge: Louisiana State University Press, 1993.

Katcher, Philip. *Flags of the American Civil War: Confederate*. Osprey Men-at-Arms Series, no. 252. London: Reed International Books, 1992.

———. *Flags of the American Civil War: State and Volunteer*. Osprey Men-at-Arms Series, no. 256. London: Reed International Books, 1993.

———. *Flags of the American Civil War: Union*. Osprey Men-at-Arms Series, no. 258. London: Reed International Books, 1993.

Katz, D. Mark. *Witness to an Era: The Life and Photographs of Alexander Gardner — The Civil War, Lincoln, and the West*. New York: Viking, 1991. Reprint, Nashville, Tenn.: Rutledge Hill Press, Inc., 1999.

Kautz, August V. *Customs of Service for Non-Commissioned Officers and Soldiers*. 1864. Reprint, Evansville, Ind.

Kennett, Lee. *Marching Through Georgia: The Story of Soldiers & Civilians During Sherman's Campaign*. New York: HarperCollins Publishers, 1995.

Kincaid, David. *The Irish Volunteer: Songs of the Irish Union Soldier, 1861-1865*. Ryko, RCD 10395.

Klotter, James C. *The Breckinridges of Kentucky, 1760-1981*. Lexington: University of Kentucky Press, 1986.

Lee, Agnes. *Growing Up in the 1850s: The Journal of Agnes Lee*. Edited by Mary Custis Lee DeButts. Chapel Hill: University of North Carolina Press, 1984.

Long, E. B., and Barbara Long. *The Civil War Day by Day, An Almanac 1861-1865*. Garden City, N.Y.: Doubleday, 1971.

Longacre, Edward G., ed. *From Antietam to Fort Fisher: The Civil War Letters of Edward King Wightman, 1862-1865*. Rutherford, N.J.: Farleigh Dickinson University Press, 1985.

Madaus, Howard M. *The Battleflags of the Confederate Army of Tennessee.*

Markle, Donald E. *Spies and Spymasters of the Civil War*. New York: Hippocrene Books, 1994.

Marvel, William, *Andersonville: The Last Depot*. Chapel Hill: University of North Carolina Press, 1994.

McAfee, Michael J. *Zouaves, The First and the Bravest*. Gettysburg, Penn.: Thomas Publications, 1991.

McGuire, Judith W. *Diary of a Southern Refugee During the War, by a Lady of Virginia*. Lincoln: University of Nebraska Press, 1980.

McHenry, Robert, ed. *Famous American Women: A Biographical Dictionary from Colonial Times to the Present*. New York: Dover Publications, Inc., 1980.

McPherson, James M. *For Cause and Comrades: Why Men Fought in the Civil War*. New York: Oxford University Press, 1997.

Meier, August, and Elliot Rudwick. *From Plantation to Ghetto*. New York: Hill and Wang, 1970.

Mellon, James. *Bullwhip Days: The Slaves Remember, an Oral History*. New York: Weidenfeld and Nicolson, 1988.

Meredith, Roy. *Mathew Brady's Portrait of an Era*. New York: Norton, 1982.

Meredith, Roy, and Arthur Meredith. *Mr. Lincoln's Military Railroads: A Pictorial History of United States Civil War Railroads*. New York: Norton, 1979.

Miller, Francis Trevelyan, ed. *Photographic History of the Civil War. Vol. 8*. New York: Review of Reviews, 1911. Reprint, New York: Thomas Yoseloff, 1957.

Mills, H. Sinclair, Jr. *The Vivandiere: History, Tradition, Uniform and Service*. Collingswood, N.J.: C. W. Historicals, 1988.

Neely, Mark E. Jr. *The Fate of Liberty: Abraham Lincoln and Civil Liberties*. New York: Oxford University Press, 1991.

Panzer, Mary. *Mathew Brady and the Image of History*. Washington, D.C.: Smithsonian Institution Press, 1997.

Porter, Horace. *Campaigning with Grant*. New York: Konecky & Konecky, 1992.

Pritzer, Barry. *Mathew Brady*. New York: Crescent Books, 1992.

Randall, Ruth Painter. Colonel Elmer Ellsworth. Boston: Little Brown, 1960.

Ransom, John L. *Andersonville Diary*. Philadelphia: Douglas Brothers, 1881.

Reef, Catherine. *Arlington National Cemetery*. New York: Dillon Press, 1991.

"Repelling Lee's Last Blow at Gettysburg." In *Battles and Leaders of the Civil War*, ed. by Robert U. Johnson and Clarence C. Buel, Vol. 3:387-92.

Robertson, James I., Jr. *Stonewall Jackson: The Man, The Soldier, The Legend*. New York: Macmillian Publishing Co. 1997.

———. *Soldiers Blue and Gray*. Columbia: University of South Carolina Press, 1988.

Ryan, David D., ed. *A Yankee Spy in Richmond: The Civil War Diary of "Crazy Bet" Van Lew*. Mechanicsburg, Penn.: Stackpole Books, 1996.

Sears, Stephen W. *To the Gates of Richmond: The Peninsula Campaign*. New York: Ticknor & Fields, 1992.

Small, Cindy L. *The Jennie Wade Story*. Gettysburg: Thomas, 1991.

Speer, Lonnie R. *Portals to Hell: Military Prisons of the Civil War*. Mechanicsburg, Penn.: Stackpole Books, 1997.

Starr, Louis M. *Bohemian Brigade: Civil War Newsmen in Action*. 1954. Reprint, Madison: University of Wisconsin Press, 1987.

Stevenson, R. R. *The Southern Side, or Andersonville Prison*. Baltimore: Turnbull Brothers, 1876.

Stiles, Robert. *Four Years Under Marse Robert*. New York: Neale, 1903.

Straubing, Harold Elk. *In Hospital and Camp: The Civil War Through the Eyes of Its Doctors and Nurses*. Harrisburg, Penn.: Stackpole Books, 1993.

Stryker, Colonel William S. "The 'Swamp Angel,'" In *Battles and Leaders of the Civil War*, ed. Robert U. Johnson and Clarence C. Buel, 4:72-74.

Styple, William B., ed. *Our Noble Blood: The Civil War Letters of Major-General Regis de Trobriand*. Kearny, N.J.: Belle Grove Publishing Co., 1997.

Sullivan, George. *Mathew Brady: His Life and Photographs*. New York: Cobblehill Books, 1994.

Summers, Festus P. *The Baltimore and Ohio in the Civil War*. 1939. Reprint, Gettysburg, Penn.: Stan Clark Military Books, 1993.

Tagg, Larry. *The Generals of Gettysburg: The Leaders of America's Greatest Battle*. Campbell, California: Savas Publishing Co., 1998.

Taylor, James E. *With Sheridan Up the Shenandoah Valley in 1864: Leaves From a Special Artist's Sketchbook and Diary*. Cleveland: The Western Reserve Historical Society, 1989.

Thomas, Dean S. *Cannons: An Introduction to Civil War Artillery*. Gettysburg: Thomas Publications, 1985.

Thompson, William F. *The Image of War: The Pictorial Reporting of the American Civil War*. 1959. Reprint, Baton Rouge: Louisiana State University Press, 1994.

Tidwell, William A., James O. Hall, and David Winfred Gaddy. *Come Retribution: The Confederate Secret Service and the Assassination of Lincoln*. Jackson: University Press of Mississippi, 1994.

Time-Life Books. *Arms and Equipment of the Confederacy*. Echoes of Glory. Alexandria, Va., 1991.

———. *Arms and Equipment of the Union*. Echoes of Glory. Alexandria, Va., 1991.

——— *Gettysburg*. Voices of the Civil War. Alexandria, Va., 1998.

———. *Shenandoah 1862*. Voices of the Civil War. Alexandria, Va., 1998.

Turner, Justin, and Linda Turner. *Mary Todd Lincoln: Her Life*. New York: Knopf, 1987.

U. S. War Department. *The War of the Rebellion: A Compilation of the Official Records of the Union and Confederate Armies*. 128 vols. Washington, D.C.: U.S. Government Printing Office, 1880-1901.

Van der Heuvel, Gerry. *Crowns of Thorns and Glory: Mary Todd Lincoln and Varina Howell Davis*. New York: Dutton, 1988.

Warner, Ezra J. *Generals in Blue: Lives of the Union Commanders*. Baton Rouge: Louisiana State University Press, 1964.

———. *Generals in Gray: Lives of the Confederate Commanders*. Baton Rouge: Louisiana State University Press, 1959.

Webber, Thomas L. *Deep Like the Rivers: Education in the Slave Quarter Community*. New York: Norton, 1978.

Whitman, Walt. *Memoranda During the War*. Boston: Applewood Books, 1990.

Wiley, Bell Irvin. *Confederate Women*. Contributions in American History, no. 38. Westport, Conn.: Greenwood Press, 1975.

———. *The Life of Billy Yank: The Common Soldier of the Union*. Baton Rouge: Louisiana State University Press, 1952.

———. *The Life of Johnny Reb: The Common Soldier of the Confederacy*. Baton Rouge: Louisiana State University Press, 1943.

Wilson, Douglas L., and Rodney O. Davis, eds. *Herndon's Informants: Letters, Interviews, and Statements about Abraham Lincoln*. Chicago: University of Illinois Press, 1998.

"Women in the War." *U.S. Service Magazine* 4, no. 3 (September 1865).

Woodward, C. Vann. *Mary Chesnut's Civil War*. New Haven: Yale University Press, 1981.

# Illustration Credits

THE SOURCES for the illustrations in this book are shown below. Credits from left to right are separated by semicolons, from top to bottom by dashes. The following abbreviations have been used throughout:

| | |
|---|---|
| LC | Library of Congress, Washington, D.C. |
| Miller | *The Photographic History of the Civil War,* Francis Trevelyan Miller, editor in chief, New York Castle Books. |
| NA | National Archives, Washington, D.C. |
| USAMHI | U.S. Army Military History Institute, Carlisle, Pennsylvania. |

**ii and iii:** *Thunder On Little Kennesaw* by Don Troiani, photograph courtesy of Historical Art Prints, Southbury, Conn. **2:** South Carolina Historical Society. **4:** LC (USZ62-28351); LC (USZ62-15392). **5:** LC (USZ62-41678). **6:** LC (USZ62-10293)—LC (USZ62-2582), *Harper's Weekly,* July 31, 1861. **7:** LC (B8171-2297). **8:** ©Collection of The New-York Historical Society, negative number 58244. **9:** LC (USZ62-067818). **10:** LC (USZ62-16178). **11:** LC (USZ62-67819). **12:** LC (USZ62-44265). **13:** South Carolina Historical Society. **14:** LC (USZC4-4575). **15:** LC (USZ62-16168). **16:** ©Collection of The New-York Historical Society, negative number 48099. **17:** The Museum of the Confederacy, Richmond, Virginia, copy photography by Katherine Wetzel. **18:** LC (USZ62-11341). **19:** ©Collection of The New-York Historical Society, negative number 27225. **20:** LC (USZ62-122077). **21:** LC (USZ62-38902). **22:** Courtesy of Webb Garrison. **23:** LC (USZ62-33468). **24:** LC (USZ62-28860). **25:** LC (USZ62-01283). **26:** LC (USZ62-31963). **27:** LC (USZ62-31963). **28:** LC (USZ62-1287). **29:** LC (B8184-440). **30:** LC (B8171-519). **31:** LC (USZC4-4608). **32:** The Metropolitan Museum of Art, Gift of Charles Stewart Smith, 1884. (84.12a); The Metropolitan Museum of Art, Gift of Charles Stewart Smith, 1884. (84.12b); The Metropolitan Museum of Art, Gift of Charles Stewart Smith, 1884. (84.12c). **33:** LC (8184-10061). **34:** LC (USZC4-44731). **35:** ©Collection of The New-York Historical Society, negative number 48163. **36:** LC (USZ62-089745). **37:** LC (USZ62-7357). **38:** Audio-Visual Archives, Special Collections and Archives, University of Kentucky Libraries. **40:** USAMHI, MOLLUS Collection (2:54). **41:** Lloyd Ostendorf Collection, Dayton, Ohio—LC (BH824-4575). **42:** Lloyd Ostendorf Collection, Dayton, Ohio. **43:** Lloyd Ostendorf Collection, Dayton, Ohio—Lloyd Ostendorf Collection, Dayton, Ohio. **44:** Lloyd Ostendorf Collection, Dayton, Ohio—Lloyd Ostendorf Collection, Dayton, Ohio; The Filson Club Historical Society, Louisville, Kentucky. **45:** Lloyd Ostendorf Collection, Dayton, Ohio; Lloyd Ostendorf Collection, Dayton, Ohio. **46:** The Museum of the Confederacy, Richmond, Virginia, copy photography Katherine Wetzel; The National Archives, photograph courtesy of The Museum of the Confederacy, Richmond, Virginia, copy photography Katherine Wetzel. **47:** The Virginia Historical Society—The Library of Congress, photograph courtesy of The Museum of the Confederacy, Richmond, Virginia, copy photography Katherine Wetzel. **48:** USAMHI, MOLLUS Collection (91:4694B); USAMHI, MOLLUS Collection (14:31630). **49:** The Library of Congress, photograph courtesy of The Museum of the Confederacy, Richmond, Virginia, copy photography Katherine Wetzel. **50:** Leib Image Archives. **51:** The Virginia Historical Society. **52:** The National Archives, photograph courtesy of The Museum of the Confederacy, Richmond, Virginia, copy photography Katherine Wetzel. **53:** Courtesy of the Stonewall Jackson Foundation, Lexington, Virginia. **54:** Audio-Visual Archives, Special Collections and Archives, University of Kentucky Libraries. **55:** *Frank Leslie's Illustrated History of The Civil War*—Civil War Photograph Album, Mss. 2828, Louisiana and Lower Mississippi Valley Collections, LSU Libraries, Louisiana State University, Baton Rouge, LA. **56:** Audio-Visual Archives, Special Collections and Archives, University of Kentucky Libraries. **57:** Audio-Visual Archives, Special Collections and Archives, University of Kentucky Libraries. **58:** Cook Collection, Valentine Museum, Richmond, Virginia—Audio-Visual Archives, Special Collections and Archives, University of Kentucky Libraries. **60:** Courtesy of Brian C. Pohanka; The Museum of the Confederacy, Richmond, Virginia, copy photography Katherine Wetzel. **62:** The Museum of the Confederacy, Richmond, Virginia, copy photography Katherine Wetzel; The Library of Congress, photograph courtesy of The Museum of the Confederacy, Richmond, Virginia, copy photography Katherine Wetzel. **64:** Lloyd Ostendorf Collection, Dayton, Ohio—Lloyd Ostendorf Collection, Dayton, Ohio. **65:** Audio-

Visual Archives, Special Collections and Archives, University of Kentucky Libraries. **66:** Lloyd Ostendorf Collection, Dayton, Ohio; Lloyd Ostendorf Collection, Dayton, Ohio. **67:** Lloyd Ostendorf Collection, Dayton, Ohio. **69:** Courtesy of Beauvoir, the Jefferson Davis Home and Presidential Library; National Portrait Gallery, Washington D.C./Art Resource, NY. **70:** Courtesy of Webb Garrison; Courtesy of Webb Garrison—Cook Collection, Valentine Museum, Richmond, Virginia. **71:** The Museum of the Confederacy, Richmond, Virginia, photography by Katherine Wetzel. **72:** The Museum of the Confederacy, Richmond, Virginia, copy photography by Katherine Wetzel. **73:** The Museum of the Confederacy, Richmond, Virginia, sketch by William Ludwell Sheppard, photography by Katherine Wetzel. **75:** Lloyd Ostendorf Collection, Dayton, Ohio. **76:** Lloyd Ostendorf Collection, Dayton, Ohio. **77:** Courtesy of the Illinois State Historical Library; Lloyd Ostendorf Collection, Dayton, Ohio; Lloyd Ostendorf Collection, Dayton, Ohio. **78:** Lloyd Ostendorf Collection, Dayton, Ohio. **79:** Lloyd Ostendorf Collection, Dayton, Ohio. **81:** LC (USZ62-12824). **82:** Courtesy of the Illinois State Historical Library. **83:** Lloyd Ostendorf Collection, Dayton, Ohio. **84:** The Museum of the Confederacy, Richmond, Virginia, copy photography Katherine Wetzel—Courtesy of Beauvoir, the Jefferson Davis Home and Presidential Library. **85:** The Old Court House Museum, Vicksburg, Mississippi; The Museum of the Confederacy, Richmond, Virginia, copy photography Katherine Wetzel. **86:** Courtesy of the Illinois State Historical Library. **87:** Lloyd Ostendorf Collection, Dayton, Ohio. **88:** Lloyd Ostendorf Collection, Dayton, Ohio. **89:** The Museum of the Confederacy, Richmond, Virginia, copy photography Katherine Wetzel—Courtesy of Beauvoir, the Jefferson Davis Home and Presidential Library. **90:** The Museum of the Confederacy, Richmond, Virginia, copy photography Katherine Wetzel—The Museum of the Confederacy, Richmond, Virginia, copy photography Katherine Wetzel. **91:** The Old Court House Museum, Vicksburg, Mississippi. **92:** The Library of Congress, photograph courtesy of Cowles Enthusiast Media. **94:** West Virginia and Regional History Collection, West Virginia University Libraries. **95:** Courtesy of Richard Williams. **96:** Courtesy of the Atlanta History Center—The Museum of the Confederacy, Richmond, Virginia, copy photography Katherine Wetzel. **97:** LC (B817-7122). **98:** *Frank Leslie's Illustrated Newspaper,* December 21, 1861; *Harper's Weekly,* September 19, 1863. **99:** Adams County Historical Society—Adams County Historical Society. **100:** *Battles and Leaders of the Civil War,* Clarence C. Buell and Robert U. Johnson, eds. **101:** LC (B8184-10573). **102:** Miller (9:67)—LC (USZ62-11596). **103:** *Harper's Weekly,* June 29, 1861. **104:** LC (B8171-742)—Miller (7:322-23). **105:** LC (B8171-2402). **106:** G. H. Suydam Collection, Louisiana and Lower Mississippi Valley Collections, LSU Libraries, Louisiana State University, Baton Rouge, LA. **107:** Private Collection, photography courtesy of Brandywine River Museum—The Library of Congress, General Collection. **108:** *Harper's Weekly,* September 5, 1863. **109:** Cincinnati Art Museum, The Edwin and Virginia Irwin Memorial. **110:** LC (USZ62-33005). **111:** Courtesy of South Caroliniana Library, University of South Carolina, Columbia. **112:** *Harper's Weekly,* December 24, 1864; The Western Reserve Historical Society, Cleveland, Ohio. **113:** The Western Reserve Historical Society, Cleveland, Ohio. **114:** Miller (9:309). **116:** State of South Carolina Confederate Relic Room and Museum, Columbia, South Carolina. **118:** *Frank Leslie's Illustrated Newspaper,* May 23, 1863. **119:** LC (USZ62-119343). **120:** Courtesy of Webb Garrison—Courtesy of Webb Garrison. **121:** The Museum of the City of New York, gift of Mrs. J. West Roosevelt—*Frank Leslie's Illustrated Newspaper,* May 11, 1861. **122:** LC (B8184-B445); LC (B8184-7721). **123:** LC (B8121-741). **124:** USAMHI, MOLLUS Collection (92:4734); The Western Reserve Historical Society, Cleveland, Ohio. **125:** LC (B8184-4092)—Miller (7:329). **126:** LC (USZ62-19319)—LC (USZ62-079788). **127:** *Frank Leslie's Illustrated Newspaper,* August 31, 1861—*Frank Leslie's Illustrated Newspaper,* June 21, 1862. **128:** LC (USZ62-9797)—Johnson-Jones family, near Richmond, Virginia [June 1862], Plan file (BVIII), Special Collections Department, Robert W. Woodruff Library, Emory University. **129:** LC (USZ62-8542)—LC (B8171-2405). **130:** NA (79-T-2148). **131:** USAMHI (RG980-CWP 4.30). **132:** Blaylock image from Misc. Photos #P-4090 (B), Southern Historical Collection, Wilson Library, The University of North Carolina at Chapel Hill. **133:** Courtesy of Lauren Cook Burgess—Courtesy of Lauren Cook Burgess. **134:** Courtesy of the Illinois State Historical Library—The State Archives of Michigan, negative number 02254. **135:** Courtesy of The Trustees of Boston Public Library; Courtesy of The Trustees of Boston Public Library. **136:** The Museum of the Confederacy, Richmond, Virginia, copy photography Katherine Wetzel. **137:** *The Southern Side* by R. Randolph Stevenson. **138:** LC (B8171-502)—*Harper's Weekly,* April 4, 1863. **139:** *Harper's Weekly,* February 3, 1866. **140:** *114th Pennsylvania Volunteer Infantry* by Don Troiani, photograph courtesy of Historical Art Prints, Southbury, Conn. **142:** *76th Pennsylvania Volunteer Infantry* by Don Troiani, photograph courtesy of Historical Art Prints, Southbury, Conn.; *146th New York Volunteer Infantry* by Don Troiani, photograph courtesy of Historical Art Prints, Southbury, Conn.; *165th New York Volunteer Infantry* by Don Troiani, photograph courtesy of Historical Art Prints, Southbury, Conn.; *33rd New Jersey Volunteer Infantry* by Don Troiani, photograph courtesy of Historical Art Prints, Southbury, Conn. **143:** *Harper's Pictorial History of The Civil War.* **144:** Chicago Historical Society (ICHi-10215). **145:** Chicago Historical Society (ICHi-13910). **147:** West Point Museum Collection, United States Military Academy. **148:** LC (B8184-10696).

**149:** *Frank Leslie's Illustrated Newspaper,* May 18, 1861. **150:** *Frank Leslie's Illustrated Newspaper,* May 25, 1861. **151:** Collection of Michael J. McAfee. **152:** USAMHI, MOLLUS Collection (55:2741); Courtesy of Brian Pohanka. **153:** Courtesy of Brian Pohanka. **154:** LC (B8184-4376)—Courtesy of Brian Pohanka. **155:** NA (111-B-5886)—*9th New York Volunteer Infantry* by Don Troiani, photograph courtesy of Historical Art Prints, Southbury, Conn. **156:** Louisiana Tiger Zouaves from Lockett Papers #P-432/60, Southern Historical Collection, Wilson Library, The University of North Carolina at Chapel Hill—*Gentle Tiger: The Gallant Life of Robardeau Wheat* by Charles L. Dufour. **158:** *Red Devils* by Don Troiani, photograph courtesy of Historical Art Prints, Southbury, Conn. **159:** The Rhode Island Historical Society, Providence, RI, photograph courtesy of Cowles Enthusiast Media. **160:** *10th New York Volunteer Infantry* by Don Troiani, photograph courtesy of Historical Art Prints, Southbury, Conn. **161:** Sketch by Alfred R. Waud—Courtesy of Brian Pohanka. **162:** Winslow Homer, American, 1836-1910. *The Brierwood Pipe,* 1864. Oil on canvas, 42.8 x 37.5 cm. © The Cleveland Museum of Art, 1998, Mr. and Mrs. William H. Marlatt Fund, 1944.524. **163:** *Photographic History of The Civil War* by William C. Davis and Bell I. Wiley where photograph was reproduced courtesy of Terrence P. O'Leary. **164:** *Excelsior: The 140th New York Zouave Brigade at Saunders' Field* by Don Troiani, photograph courtesy of Historical Art Prints, Southbury, Conn. **165:** LC (B8171-7198). **166:** Courtesy of Brian Pohanka. **167:** Courtesy of Brian Pohanka. **168:** *Captain Clooney's Charge* by Bradley Schmehl, photograph courtesy of Green Flag Productions, Williamsburg, VA. **170:** LC (USZ62-31649). **171:** Frank & Marie-Therese Wood Print Collections, Alexandria, VA. **172:** LC (BH831-971). **173:** LC (B8171-627). **174:** NA (111-B-5252)—Miller (1:343). **175:** Miller (8:100-101). **176:** LC (B8184-550); LC (B815-733). **177:** *Rock of Erin* by Don Troiani, photograph courtesy of Historical Art Prints, Southbury, Conn. **178:** *Cleburne* by David Wright, courtesy of Gray Stone Press and Gallery. **179:** LC (USZ62-42193). **180:** Courtesy of The Civil War Library and Museum, Philadelphia, PA, photograph by Blake A. Magner. **181:** LC (USZ62-7017), sketch by Alfred R. Waud. **182:** USAMHI, MOLLUS Collection (11:L542). **183:** LC (B8171-7517). **184:** NA (111-B-3876). **185:** LC (B812-3231)—USAMHI, MOLLUS Collection (9:417). **186:** *Harper's Pictorial History of The Civil War.* **187:** LC (B8171-638). **188:** LC (B813-1905). **189:** The Western Reserve Historical Society, Cleveland, Ohio; LC (B8172-1565). **190:** LC (B8171-2735)— The Library of Congress, photograph courtesy of Cowles Enthusiast Media. **191:** LC (B813-2117). **192:** LC (USZ62-6888). **193:** Courtesy of The Civil War Library and Museum, Philadelphia, PA. **194:** LC (B813-2184)—Collection of Michael J. McAfee, photograph courtesy of Cowles Enthusiast Media. **195:** LC (B8171-9552X). **196:** LC (B8171-617). **198:** NA (111-BA-1088). **199:** NA (111-B-3251)—*Frank Leslie's Illustrated Newspaper,* July 20, 1861. **200:** ©Collection of The New-York Historical Society, negative number 71909. **201:** *Frank Leslie's Illustrated Newspaper,* August 31, 1861; Historical Collections, Bridgeport Public Library. **202:** William Tappan Thompson, Joel Chandler Harris Papers #5 (Box 16:folder 14), Special Collections Department, Robert W. Woodruff Library, Emory University—LC (BH82-5172). **203:** Courtesy of the Atlanta History Center. **204:** The Museum of the Confederacy, Richmond, Virginia, photography by Katherine Wetzel. **205:** LC (USZ62-10356). **206:** *Frank Leslie's Illustrated Newspaper.* **207:** *Harper's Weekly*—USAMHI, MOLLUS Collection (91:4690A) **208:** LC (BH841-27). **209:** LC (B8171-7235). **210:** LC (B8171-4018); LC (B8184-B5077). **211:** *Photographic History of The Civil War* by William C. Davis and Bell I. Wiley where photograph was reproduced courtesy of Mrs. Albert McBride. **212:** LC (BH82401-4742)—Collection of Michael J. McAfee. **213:** LC (B8171-2351). **214:** LC (B8171-254)—LC (USZ62-160), sketch by Alfred R. Waud. **215:** Bowdoin College Museum of Art, Brunswick, Maine, gift of the Homer Family. **216:** LC (BH83-2571). **217:** LC (USZ62-178), *Harper's Weekly,* November 15, 1862. **218:** LC (USZ62-153). **219:** West Point Museum Collection, United States Military Academy. **220:** LC (B814-1378). **221:** *Photographic History of The Civil War* by William C. Davis and Bell I. Wiley where photograph was reproduced courtesy of Rinhart Galleries, Inc. **222:** *Frank Leslie's Illustrated Newspaper,* January 14, 1865—Buffalo & Erie County Historical Society. **223:** LC (B8171-2447)—The Ohio Historical Society. **224:** The Metropolitan Museum of Art, Gift of the friends of Mathew Brady, 1896, Charles Loring Elliott, oil on canvas. **226:** LC (USZ62-10991). **227:** LC (USZ62-31490). **228:** LC (USZ64-4885). **229:** LC (BH834-35)—LC (USZ62-110151). **230:** LC (USZ62-8963)—LC (USZ62-110152). **231:** Beinecke Rare Book and Manuscript Library, Yale University—Beinecke Rare Book and Manuscript Library, Yale University. **232:** Courtesy George Eastman House. **233:** Photographic History Collection, National Museum of American History/Smithsonian Institution. **234:** LC (USZ62-10556). **235:** National Portrait Gallery, Smithsonian Institution, Washington, D.C., photograph courtesy of D. Mark Katz. **236:** LC (USZ62-8929)—LC (BH838-84). **237:** ©Collection of The New-York Historical Society, negative number 56205. **238:** LC (USZ62-39409). **239:** NA (111-B-1074)—LC (USZ62-13357). **240:** LC (USZ62-13818). **241:** LC (USZ62-5803). **242:** LC (USZ62-13293)—NA (111-B-5737). **243:** National Portrait Gallery, Smithsonian Institution, Washington, D.C./Art Resource, NY. **244:** LC (B8184-651). **245:** LC (BH827701-550). **246:** USAMHI, MOLLUS Collection (43:L2133); LC (BH841-27). **247:** LC (B8171-2388); LC (B8184-B511). **248:** LC (USZ62-8046); The Library of Congress. **249:** LC (B8184-

144)—The Western Reserve Historical Society, Cleveland, Ohio. **250:** LC (B8171-7813). **251:** LC (BH826-2681)—LC (BH827-2102). **252:** LC (B8171-217)—LC (BH837-205); LC (B8171-7383). **253:** LC (B8172-1174); LC (BH827701-622)—NA (111-B-487)—LC (B8184-B528). **254:** LC (B8161-4100)—NA (111-B-250); LC (B8184-660). **255:** LC (B8184-B305)—LC (B8171-444); LC (B811-2448)—LC (B8184-B550). **256:** Collection of D. Mark Katz. **259:** *Witness to an Era* by D. Mark Katz where photograph was reproduced from the collection of Marshall Pywell. **260:** Collection of D. Mark Katz—*Witness to an Era* by D. Mark Katz where photograph was reproduced from the collection of Lawrence T. Jones III. **261:** Collection of D. Mark Katz; Collection of D. Mark Katz; Collection of D. Mark Katz; Collection of D. Mark Katz. **262:** *Witness to an Era* by D. Mark Katz where photograph was reproduced from the collection of David L. Hack. **263:** Collection of D. Mark Katz. **265:** Collection of D. Mark Katz. **266:** USAMHI, MOLLUS Collection (43:2141)—Massachusetts Commandery Military Order of the Loyal Legion and the US Army Military History Institute. **267:** USAMHI, MOLLUS Collection (43:L2141)—LC (B8184-558); LC (B8184-40497). **268:** LC (B8171-7934). **269:** USAMHI, MOLLUS Collection (43:L2126). **270:** Collection of D. Mark Katz. **271:** Collection of D. Mark Katz. **272:** Collection of D. Mark Katz. **274:** LC (USZ62-077870)—Collection of D. Mark Katz; LC (USZ62-098648). **275:** Collection of D. Mark Katz—LC (8184-7964). **276:** Collection of D. Mark Katz. **277:** LC (USZ62-36603). **278:** LC (B8171-7110); LC (B8171-886). **279:** *Witness to an Era* by D. Mark Katz where photograph was reproduced from the collection of Lloyd Ostendorf. **280:** LC (USZ62-8340)—LC (B8171-7951). **281:** LC (USZ62-8812); *Witness to an Era* by D. Mark Katz where photograph was reproduced from the collection of Lloyd Ostendorf—LC (BH8331-575); LC (USZ62-9794). **282:** LC (B8171-7765). **283:** *Witness to an Era* by D. Mark Katz where photograph was reproduced from the collection of the Lincoln Life Insurance Co.—*Harper's Weekly*, May 13, 1865. **284:** LC (B8171-7784); LC (B8171-7773); LC (B817-7789); LC (B817-7779)—LC (B8171-7757). **285:** LC (B8171-1287). **286:** LC (B8171-7753); The Western Reserve Historical Society, Cleveland, Ohio. **287:** *Witness to an Era* by D. Mark Katz where photograph was reproduced from the collection of the Kansas State Historical Society—*Witness to an Era* by D. Mark Katz where photograph was reproduced from the collection of Marshall Pywell. **288:** Collection of D. Mark Katz; LC (USZ62-11000). **289:** Collection of D. Mark Katz—*Witness to an Era* by D. Mark Katz where photograph was reproduced courtesy of the Smithsonian Institution, National Anthropological Archives. **290:** *Witness to an Era* by D. Mark Katz where photograph was reproduced courtesy of the Smithsonian Institution, National Anthropological Archives. **291:** *Witness to an Era* by D. Mark Katz where photograph was reproduced courtesy of the Acacia Life Insurance Co. **292:** With Permission. Pinkerton Inc. **294:** LC (USZ62-4916). **296:** *Harper's Weekly;* October 24, 1863. **297:** With Permission. Pinkerton Inc. **298:** With Permission. Pinkerton Inc.—Alonzo Chappel in *History of the War for the Union, Civil, Military & Naval,* New York: Johnson, Fry & Co. **299:** LC (B8171-7949). **300:** Miller (8:323)—Chicago Historical Society (ICHi-08280). **301:** LC (B8171-7202). **302:** Cook Collection, Valentine Museum, Richmond, Virginia—Special Collections Department, University Libraries, Virginia Tech, Blacksburg, Virginia. **303:** LC (BH83201-2492). **304:** With Permission. Pinkerton Inc.—*The Spy of the Rebellion* by Allan Pinkerton; *The Spy of the Rebellion* by Allan Pinkerton. **305:** *The Spy of the Rebellion* by Allan Pinkerton. **306:** *Harper's Weekly,* April 4, 1863. **308:** LC (BH82401-4864). **310:** USAMHI, MOLLUS Collection (94: 4841). **311:** Cook Collection, Valentine Museum, Richmond, Virginia. **312:** *On Hazardous Service* by William Gilmore Beymer. **313:** USAMHI, MOLLUS Collection (28: 1385); LC (B8184-10277). **314:** Cook Collection, Valentine Museum, Richmond, Virginia. **315:** LC (B8171-8967X)—LC (B812-2902). **316:** NA (111-BA-1897). **317:** Photographs and Prints Division, Schomburg Center for Research in Black Culture, The New York Public Library, Astor, Lenox and Tilden Foundations—*The Spy of the Rebellion* by Allan Pinkerton. **318:** LC (USZ62-15833). **319:** LC (B8171-7294). **320:** Tennessee State Library and Archives—LC (B8172-1672). **322:** *The Forlorn Hope* by Don Troiani, photograph courtesy of Historical Art Prints, Southbury, Conn. **324:** *Confederate Standard Bearer* by Don Troiani, photograph courtesy of Historical Art Prints, Southbury, Conn. **325:** *Union Standard Bearer* by Don Troiani, photograph courtesy of Historical Art Prints, Southbury, Conn. **326:** Lloyd Ostendorf Collection, Dayton, Ohio. **328:** 17th Massachusetts, First National (#1987.439), Courtesy Commonwealth of Massachusetts State House Flag Collection, photo by Douglas Christian; USAMHI, MOLLUS Collection (24: 1183). **329:** Pennsylvania Capitol Preservation Committee; West Point Museum Collection, United States Military Academy. **330:** West Point Museum Collection, United States Military Academy; West Point Museum Collection, United States Military Academy. **331:** West Point Museum Collection, United States Military Academy. **332:** USAMHI, MOLLUS Collection (187: 4376). **333:** The University of Notre Dame Archives. **334:** Pennsylvania Capitol Preservation Committee; Pennsylvania Capitol Preservation Committee. **335:** *Saving the Flag* by Don Troiani, photograph courtesy of Historical Art Prints, Southbury, Conn. **336:** 28th Massachusetts, Third Irish color (#1987.251), Courtesy Commonwealth of Massachusetts State House Flag Collection, photo by Douglas Christian. **337:** James E. Taylor drawing reproduced from *Campfires and Battlefields* by Rossiter Johnson. **338:** West Point Museum Collection, United States Military Academy—West Point

Museum Collection, United States Military Academy. **339:** West Point Museum Collection, United States Military Academy. **340:** Chicago Historical Society (1920.1668); Confederate Memorial Hall, New Orleans, Louisiana, photo by C. Levet. **341:** Confederate Memorial Hall, New Orleans, Louisiana, photo by C. Levet; The Museum of the Confederacy, Richmond, Virginia, photography by Katherine Wetzel. **342:** The Museum of the Confederacy, Richmond, Virginia, photography by Katherine Wetzel. **343:** State of South Carolina Confederate Relic Room and Museum, Columbia, South Carolina—Wisconsin Veterans Museum, Madison, Wisconsin. **344:** Confederate Memorial Hall, New Orleans, Louisiana. **345:** Collection of Michael J. McAfee. **346:** Photography Collections, University of Maryland Baltimore County—Photography Collections, University of Maryland Baltimore County. **347:** Photography Collections, University of Maryland Baltimore County—Photography Collections, University of Maryland Baltimore County. **348:** Moorland-Spingarn Research Center, Howard University, negative number 5221. **349:** *Emblems of Valor* by Don Troiani, photograph courtesy of Historical Art Prints, Southbury, Conn. **350:** *Washington Artillery of New Orleans* by Don Troiani, photograph courtesy of Historical Art Prints, Southbury, Conn. **352:** LC (USZ62-7011), sketch by Alfred R. Waud. **353:** Courtesy of The Civil War Library and Museum, Philadelphia, Pennsylvania, photograph by Blake A. Magner—Massachusetts Commandery Military Order of the Loyal Legion and the US Army Military History Institute. **354:** LC (B8171-862). **355:** Putnam County Historical Society, Cold Spring, New York. **356:** LC (B8184-10561). **357:** LC (B8171-2354). **358:** Miller (5:141)—West Point Museum Collection, United States Military Academy. **359:** Miller (5:141). **360:** Miller (5:127)—NA (111-B-5097). **361:** The Valentine Museum, Richmond, Virginia. **362:** The Western Reserve Historical Society, Cleveland, Ohio—Fort Pulaski National Monument. **363:** ©Collection of The New-York Historical Society, negative number 50486. **364:** LC (B8184-B504). **365:** LC (B8171-476). **366:** LC (B8171-2311). **367:** Cook Collection, Valentine Museum, Richmond, Virginia; Cook Collection, Valentine Museum, Richmond, Virginia. **368:** NA (B-74). **371:** LC (B8184-8013); LC (B8178-12). **372:** LC (B8184-10397). **373:** LC (B8184-10396). **374:** LC (B8171-7211). **375:** National Park Service. **376:** Courtesy of Cowles Enthusiast Media. **377:** LC (B8171-7463)—NA (111-B-391). **378:** Beverly R. Robinson Collection, US Naval Academy Museum, Annapolis, Maryland. **379:** LC (B8171-3048). **380:** LC (B184-B185). **382:** Union Pacific Museum Collection (46-22-A)—Reproduced from People's Pictorial Edition of *Battles and Leaders of The Civil War.* **383:** The Hays T. Watkins Research Library, B & O Railroad Museum. **384:** *Harper's Weekly*—LC (B8172-1926). **385:** NA (64-CV-293)—Miller (5:283); LC (B8184-10091). **386:** LC (B8184-B4787). **387:** LC (B8184-622); LC (B8172-1567). **388:** LC (B8184-4071). **389:** LC (B8171-2663). **390:** Miller (8:27). **391:** NA (111-B-3347). **392:** Courtesy of the Atlanta History Center—Courtesy of the Atlanta History Center. **393:** Courtesy of the Atlanta History Center—Courtesy of the Atlanta History Center. **394:** LC (B8184-B6328). **396:** LC (B8184-10163)—LC (B818-10043). **397:** LC (B8171-173); LC (B8171-762). **398:** LC (B8171-2642). **399:** LC (USZ62-14925), *Harper's Weekly.* **400:** Miller (3:145). **401:** Miller (5:272-73). **402:** Miller (5:289). **403:** USAMHI, MOLLUS Collection (70:3471). **404:** LC (B811-3665); LC (B8171-2715). **405:** NA (77-F-194-6-42); NA (111-BA-1764)—USAMHI, MOLLUS Collection (50:2487). **406:** LC (B8184-10212); USAMHI, MOLLUS Collection (54:2653)—LC (B8171-3258). **407:** The Hays T. Watkins Research Library, B & O Railroad Museum. **408:** LC (B8184-B462). **410:** USAMHI, MOLLUS Collection (35:1717). **411:** *Playing Old Soldier,* 1863, Winslow Homer, U.S., 1836-1910, oil on canvas, 16 x 12 in. (40.6 x 30.5 cm), Courtesy, Museum of Fine Arts, Boston, Ellen Kelleran Gardner Fund (43.129). **412:** LC (B8184-2507). **413:** The Historical Society of Plainfield, NJ and The Drake House Museum. **414:** Cook Collection, Valentine Museum, Richmond, Virginia—LC (B812-9289). **415:** LC (B8172-1558). **416:** The Western Reserve Historical Society, Cleveland, Ohio; USAMHI, MOLLUS Collection (43:L2123-D). **417:** Reproduced from People's Pictorial Edition of *Battles and Leaders of The Civil War.* **418:** The Minnesota Historical Society, St. Paul, Minnesota—Archive Photos, New York. **419:** LC (B8171-2585); LC (B8161-7538). **420:** Courtesy of The Civil War Library and Museum, Philadelphia, PA, photograph by Blake A. Magner. **421:** Miller (7:303). **422:** LC (B8151-10168)—LC (B8151-10169). **423:** USAMHI, MOLLUS Collection (4:169L). **424:** Lloyd Ostendorf Collection, Dayton, Ohio —Armed Forces Institute of Pathology, photograph courtesy of Cowles Enthusiast Media. **425:** The Library of Congress. **426:** LC (B8184-740). **427:** *Frank Leslie's Illustrated Newspaper,* November 12, 1864. **428:** LC (B8184-B390). **429:** USAMHI, MOLLUS Collection (79:3921). **430:** USAMHI, MOLLUS Collection (41:2014). **431:** LC (USZ62-122078). **432:** LC (B811-2529). **433:** LC (B8184-2531). **434:** LC (B8184-10369)—LC (B8171-7134). **435:** LC (B171-7442). **436:** The Western Reserve Historical Society, Cleveland, Ohio. **438:** The Daughters of the Republic of Texas Library at the Alamo (CN94.1). **439:** The Metropolitan Museum of Art, Gift of Mrs. Frank B. Porter, 1922. (22.207), negative number 51782—USAMHI, MOLLUS Collection (33:1626). **440:** USAMHI, MOLLUS Collection (17:813)—USAMHI, MOLLUS Collection (26:1264). **441:** *Harper's Weekly,* May 31, 1862; NA (111-B-497). **442:** Cook Collection, Valentine Museum, Richmond, Virginia—USAMHI, MOLLUS Collection (101:L5175). **443:** Chicago Historical Society (ICHi-01801). **444:** USAMHI, MOLLUS Collection (26:1265)—Archive Photos, New York. **445:**

North Carolina Collection, University of North Carolina Library at Chapel Hill. **446:** USAMHI, MOLLUS Collection (44:L2197). **447:** LC (B8184-B-570). **448:** The Museum of the Confederacy, Richmond, Virginia, copy photography by Katherine Wetzel. **449:** LC (USZ62-15596). **450:** West Point Museum Collection, United States Military Academy. **451:** Delaware Public Archives, *Harper's Weekly,* June 27, 1863—LC (B816-3028). **452:** Enoch Pratt Free Library, Baltimore, Maryland. **453:** LC (USZ62-17090). **454:** LC (B8171-8221). **455:** LC (USZ62-059398). **456:** LC (USZ62-51085)—LC (B8184-5526). **457:** LC (B816-8219)—*The Southern Side* by R. Randolph Stevenson. **458:** LC (B8171-7557); Chicago Historical Society (ICHi-22083). **459:** Chicago Historical Society. **460:** *Libby Prison,* 1863, David Gilmour Blythe, U.S., 1815-1865, oil on canvas, 24 1/8 x 36 1/8 in. (61.3 x 91.8 cm), Courtesy Museum of Fine Arts, Boston, Bequest of Martha C. Karolik for the M. and M. Karolik Collection of American Paintings, 1815-1865 (48.414). **461:** LC (B812-9614). **462:** LC (98-131-816459). **463:** Department of the Army, The Rock Island Arsenal Museum, Rock Island, IL. **464:** LC (B8184-10180). **466:** The Library of Congress, photograph courtesy of Cowles Enthusiast Media. **467:** LC (B171-7752). **468:** The Lincoln Museum, Fort Wayne, IN #4148. **470:** NA (165-C-518). **472:** LC (USZ62-92330). **473:** Courtesy of Arlington House, the Robert E. Lee Memorial, National Park Service. **475:** LC (USZ62-21849). **476:** Alonzo Chappel in *History of the War for the Union, Civil, Military & Naval,* New York: Johnson, Fry & Co.—LC (B8171-7656). **477:** Reproduced from People's Pictorial Edition of *Battles and Leaders of the Civil War.* **478:** NA (111-B-6246). **479:** NA (165-C-513). **480:** NA (165-C-1078). **481:** LC (B8184-B350)—LC (B8184-B1163). **482:** LC (USZ62-40603). **483:** NA (165-C-516). **484:** NA (165-C-1076); NA (165-C-515). **485:** Reproduced from People's Pictorial Edition of *Battles and Leaders of the Civil War*). **486:** USAMHI, MOLLUS Collection (57:2826). **487:** NA (165-C-514). **489:** LC (USZ62-85378); LC (BH834-68). **490:** LC (USZ62-13017). **491:** LC (USZ62-2487). **492:** LC (BH826-1480). **493:** NA (111-B-4446). **494:** Reproduced from People's Pictorial Edition of *Battles and Leaders of the Civil War*). **495:** Courtesy of Arlington House, the Robert E. Lee Memorial, National Park Service..

# Index

Page numbers in *italics* refer to illustrations or material in captions.
An illustration of a subject discussed in the text on the same page is not indexed separately.
Regiments are listed by state.
Locations are listed by state.

abolitionist movement, *12*, 17
abolitionists
Douglass, Frederick, 18
Garrison, William Lloyd, 16–17, *198*
Greeley, Horace, 198–99
Howe, Julia Ward, 121–22
Jacobs, Harriet, 119
Stanton, Elizabeth Cady, 120
Stowe, Harriet Beecher, 120–21
Truth, Sojourner, 120
Tubman, Harriet, 121
Adams, Charles Francis, 492
addiction, 431–32
African cooking, *16*
Alabama, Athens, 193–94
Alamo, *438*
Alcott, Louisa May, 124
Alexander, Edward Porter, *361*, 364–65, *367*, 375–76
Allen, E. J. (Pinkerton, Allan) J., 298
Allison, Andrew B., *158*, 160, 162
ambulance corps, 426
ambulances, 418, *419*, 422
American Colonization Society, 14
ammunition, 356–57
amputations, 411–12, 418–19, 421, *424*, *425*
Anderson, Joseph Reid, *354*
Anderson, Robert, 39–40
Andersonville prison, *437*, 446, 454–58, 468–69
Andrews, Eliza Frances Fanny, *111*, 455
Andrews, James J., 392–95
Anthony, Susan B., 130
Antietam battlefield, *176*, *266–67*
Antietam, battle of,
care of wounded, 422–25
documentary photos, 265, 268–69
Archer, Frederick Scott, *244*
Arlington
*Locations*
Confederate memorial at, 492–93
confiscated, 484–85
construction, 472–73
Freedman's Village, 483–84
and Robert E. Lee, 474–75, 477, 482, 488–90
military cemetery, 485, 486–88, 491
occupation by Union, 478–82, 483
Arlington cemetery, *486*
Armstrong rifle, *361*, *378*
Armstrong, William G., *361*
Army of the Northern Virginia, *343*
Army of the Potomac
Fifth Corps, *399*
First Division, Ninth Corps, *419*
Arnold, Laura Jackson, 52–54
Arnold, Samuel, *284*
artillerists
Alexander, Edward Porter, 364–65
Gibbon, John, 361–62
Gillmore, Quincy A., *362*, 369–71
Hazlett, Charles, 374
Hunt, Henry, 352–53
Hunt, Henry, *353*, 354–55, 362, 375
Lee, Stephen D., 365–66
Pegram, William Johnson, 353–54, *367*, 445
Pelham, John, 367–68
Ringgold, Samuel, 360–61
artillery
Dahlgren naval gun, *364*
Dictator, *377*, 404–405, *406*
Napoleon cannon, *360*, *373*
Parrott rifle, *352*, *355*, *365*, *371*, *372*
Swamp Angel, 370–71
power of Federal, 355–56
South's disadvantage in, 363–64
field, 356–68, 374–79
heavy, *366*, 368–73
mortars, *358*, 372–73, *377*
Ashby, Turner, 186
assassination, of Lincoln, 82
*Atlanta Daily Intelligencer*, *203*
Atwater, Dorance, 468
Atzerodt, George, *285*
Aubrey, Cullen B., 222

Baker, Edward, 43
Baker, Lafayette C., *283*, *315*
Baker, Luther, *283*
Baker, Mrs. E. H., *306*
Baltimore and Ohio Railroad, *383*
Barbee, George, 327
Barnhardt, J. R., 326
Barton, Clara, 118, 124–26, *126*
Beauregard, P. G. T., 301–302, 336, *372*, *396*
Beauvoir, *89*
Belknap, William, 247
Bell, Anne, *429*
Belle Isle prison, 442
Bennett, James Gordon, 198
Benson, Berry, *449*
Berger, Anthony, *242*
Berrian, John H., *158*, 160
Bickerdyke, Mary Anne, 124, *126*
Billings, John D., 416–17, 419
Bingham, Anthony, *5*

Bingham, George Caleb, 109
black soldiers, 28–34
Black, William, *102*
Blackwell, Elizabeth, 429–30
Blalock, Malinda (Sam), 131, *132*
Bland, James, *20*
Bodich, Henry, 426
Bogy, Lewis V., *289*
Bohemian Brigade (war reporters), 202–204, 218–22, 223
Booth, John Wilkes, 82, *83*, 84, 284–85
Booth, Lionel F., 32
Border Slave States, 25–26
*Boston Journal*, *207*
Botts, John Minor, *97*
Bowser, David Bustill, *345–46*, 348
Bowser, Mary Elizabeth, 135, 312–13
Boyd, Belle, 307–11, *308*
Bradford, William, *462*
Bradwell, Myra, 87
Brady, Julia, *235*
Brady, Mathew, *208*, 216, *224*, 225–35, 243–51, 257–58, *259*, 260–65, 273, 276, 287–89
    photos of Lincoln, 235–36, 244
Breckenridge, John C., 56, 58–59
Breckenridge, Joseph, 57
Breckenridge, Melissa DeShay, 58
Breckenridge, Robert J., 56–58
Breckenridge, Robert Jr., 57–58
Breckenridge, Willie, 57, *58*
*Bridgeport Farmer*, 201
Brooke gun, *359*
Brooks, Preston, 20
Brown, Henry "Box", *25*
Brown, John, 20–21
Brownell, Francis E., 149, *151*
Brownell, Kady, 128, *131*
Bryant, Furney, *317*
Buchanan, James, 71, 300
Buford, John, 96
Bureau of Military Information, *301*
Burgwyn, Henry King, 324, 339–40
Burns, John, 105–107
Burnside, Ambrose, *254*
Burr, Dr., *433*
Butler, Benjamin, 28, 114

Cadwallader, Sylvanus, 213–14
Cain, Jeff, 393
caisson, *368*
Calhoun, John C., *234*
Cameron, Simon, *382*, 384, 387
Cameron, William N., 326
Canadian soldiers, 187–88
cannon
    Dahlgren naval gun, 364
    Napoleon, 356
    rifled, 357–59
    smoothbore, 356–57
Carney, William, *345*
Carry Me Back to Ol' Virginny, *20*
cartes de visite, 237–38, *261*, *265*
Cartwright, Samuel, 11–12
Cashier, Albert (Jennie Hodgers), 132–33, *134*
Castle Pinckney prison, 441
Castleman, Alfred L., *411*
casualty lists, 203, *211*
Cavadra, Adolfo, 194
Cavadra, Federico, 194
Celestrino, Joao M., *284*
censorship, 208–10
Chain Bridge, *476*
Chamberlain, Joshua Lawrence, 348
Chambers, William H., 163
Chancellorsville, *186*
Chapman, Frank G., *221*
Chesnut, Mary, 136–37
Chicago and Northwestern Railroad, *382*
child soldiers, 101, *102*
children, in wartime, 101, *102*, 103–105
Clalin, Frances L., *135*
Clark, Achilles, 445
Clay, Edward W., *38*
Clay, Henry, 65
Cleburne, Patrick, 33, 176–77, *178*
Clem, John, *102*, 104–105
Coats, Andrew, 162
Cobb, Howell, 33
Cofer, Willis, *6*
Coffin, Charles C., 205, *207*
Coffin, Levi, 17
Coleman, E. C. (Henry Shaw), 318–20
Collins, Charles, 347
Collins, Idelea, 330–31
Collins, Septima, 139
Collins, William Mosby, 457–58
color guard, 328–29
color sergeants, 329
Confederate railroad, *392–95*
Congor, Everton J., *283*
Connecticut
  *Regiment*
    First Heavy Artillery, *366*
  *Location*
    Bridgeport, *201*
Conrad, Thomas Nelson, *302*
contrabands, 28–29, 34–35, *106*, 137, *329*, *389*, *481*
convalescent camps, *428*
Cooke, John Rogers, 47–48
Cooke, Philip St. George, *46*, 47–48
Cooley, Sam A., *210*
Cooper, Alonzo, 460
Coppens, Gaston, 157, 190
Copperhead societies, *294*
Corinth, battle of, 399–40
Corby, William, *173*, 174
Corcoran, Michael, 171–72
correspondence, wartime, 107–108
correspondents, special, 206
cotton, *2*, 15, *36*
cotton engine, 7–8
Crater, battle of, 373
Craven, John J., *423*
Crippen, Benjamin, *337*
Crittenden, George, 54–55
Crittenden, John J., 54–55
Crittenden, Thomas, 54–55
Culp, Wesley, 108–109
Culver, Mary, 107
Cumming, Kate, 124, *429*
Cushing, Alonzo, *374*, *375*, 376–79
Cushman, Pauline, *316*
Custer, George Armstrong, 129, *253*, 333
Custer, Thomas, 325
Custis, George Washington Parke, 471–74, *487*
Custis, Mary Anna Randolph, 474
Custis, Mary Lee Fitzhugh, *487*

D'Avignon, Francis, *233*, *234*
D'Epineuil, Lionel J., 185, *192*
D'Utassy, Frederic, 192, *194*
Daguerre, Louis, 227
daguerreotypy, 227–31
Dahlgren naval gun, *364*
Dahlgren, John A., *364*
Dahlgren, Ulric, 314
Davenport, Alfred, 162
Davis, Jefferson, (President of Confederacy), 26, 63, 67–75, 83–85, 88, 135, *455*
Davis, Jefferson C., (Union Major General),35
Davis, Jefferson Jr., *85*
Davis, Joseph, 67
Davis, Margaret, *85*, *90*
Davis, Sam, 318–20

Davis, Varina Anne "Winnie", *84*, *85*, *90*
Davis, Varina Howell, 63–64, 67–75, 77, 79, 80, 83–85, 88–91
Davis, William, *85*
de Polignac, Camille Armand, 190–91
de Trobriand, Phillippe Régis, 191–92
dead-line, 456–57
death rates, 467
Decoration Day, 491–92
Dennis, Mary W., *135*
Denroche, E. S., *104*
Dictator, 372–73, *377*, 404–405, *406*
disease, infectious, 414–15
Dix, Dorothea Lynde, *128*, 429–30
Dix-Hill Cartel, 443–44
Dodge, Grenville, 319–29, *320*, 401
Donaldson, Francis A., *220*
Dorsey, Sarah, 84–85, 88
Douglas, Stephen A., 19
Douglass, Frederick, 17, 27, 35–36
Dow, Neal, *458*
Doyle, James, 20
Drayton, Percival, 48–49
Drayton, Thomas, *48*, 49
Dred Scott decision, 15
drug addiction, 431–32
Drum, William F., 428
Duffié, Alfred Alexander, 185–86, *189*
Dunn, James, 424–25
DuRussy, Gustavus, 487
Duryée, Abram, 150–51, *152*, *153*
Duvall, Betty, 301

Early, Jubal, 94
Edmonds, Sarah, 133, *134*, 188, *306*
Edward, Prince of Wales, 171, 235, *239*
Edwards, Lucy, *17*
elderly, in war, 105–107
Elliot, Isaac H., 349
Ellsworth, Elmer Ephraim, 43, 143–51, 215
Emancipation Proclamation, 24–27
embalming, *432*, *433*
engravings, *216*
epidemics, 448, 450
espionage, 293–95
Ewell, Richard, 94
Ewing, Thomas, *109*
executions, 285–87, 466–67
Ezekiel, Moses, 492–93

Farnham, Noah, 151
Ferrandini, Cypriano, 297
Finley, George, 375
flags
  Army of Northern Virginia, *343*
  Batteries B and L, Second U.S. Artillery, *338*
  Battery K, First U.S. Artillery, *331*
  Battery L, First U.S. Artillery, *338*
  Bonnie Blue Flag, 333–34, *340*
  Eighteenth U.S. Regular Infantry, *329*, *330*
  Eighth Georgia, *349*
  Eighty-fifth Pennsylvania Infantry, *334*
  First National (Confederate), *340*
  Irish Brigade, *336*
  Native American, 337
  Polk, *343*
  Second National Flag (Confederate), *341*
  Seventeenth Massachusetts, *328*
  Seventeenth Pennsylvania Cavalry, *334*
  Sixty-third New York, *333*
  Stainless Banner (Second National Flag), 338, *341*
  Stars and Bars, *335–36*
  Third National, 338, *341*
  Third U.S. Regular Infantry, *325*
  Twenty-eighth Massachusetts, *336*
  Twenty-fourth Massachusetts Infantry, *328*
  Twenty-second Pennsylvania Cavalry, *329*
  U.S.C.T. Pennsylvania, *346*, *347*
  Van Dorn, Earl, *344*
  108th U.S. Colored Infantry, *345*
flags, confusion between, 336
Fleetwood, Christian A., *34*
Florida
  *Locations*
    Dry Tortugas, Fort Jefferson, *442*
    Pensacola Bay, water battery, *356*
Floyd, John B., 39
Forbes, Edwin, *219*, *318*
Forrest, Nathan Bedford, 32–33, 445, *462*
Forsyth, John, *202*
Fort Delaware prison, 450–54
Fort Fisher, *378*
Fort Gaines, *255*
Fort McHenry, prison camp, *452*
Fort Pillow massacre, 32–33, 445, *462*
Fort Pulaski, *362*, *363*, 369–70
Fort Richardson, *366*
Fort Sumter, *379*
Fort Totten, 253
Fort Warren prison, 441
forts, design of, 369
    earth , *378*
    masonry, *362*, *363*
    sand, 372
Fox, Lydia Mantle, 248
*Frank Leslie's Illustrated Newspaper*, *206*, *219*, *427*
Freedman's Village, *481*
Freedmen's Bureau, 36, *37*
French Mary, 129, *130*
French soldiers, 189–92
Fritchie, Barbara, *113*
Fuger, Frederick, *375*, 378–79
Fugitive Slave Act of 1850, 15–16, 28
Fuller, William, 392–95

Galwey, Thomas F., 344
Gambling, Wilbur, 463
gangrene, 432
Garde Lafayette, 191–92
Gardner, Alexander, 218, 233–34, 237–38, 243, 246, 257–65, *266–67*, 268–73, *274–75*, 276–79, 282–91, *467*
Gardner, Eliza, *265*
Gardner, James, *260*, *268*
*Gardner's Photographic Sketch Book of the War*, 277–78
Garfield, James A., 492
Garrison, William Lloyd, 16, 198
*General* locomotive, *392*, 394–95, 402

Georgia
  *Regiment*
    Eighth, *349*
  *Locations*
    Andersonville, prison camp, *453*, 454–58, 468–69
    Atlanta
      *Intelligencer* office, *203*
      rail yard, *404*
    Ebenezer Creek, 34–35
    Fort Pulaski, 362, 363
    Kingston, rail station, *392*
    Savannah, *98*
    Savannah, Hermitage Plantation, *10*

German immigrants, 178–84
Gettysburg, *99*, *214*
Gettysburg Cyclorama, *375*

Gettysburg, battle of, 94–102, *177*
artillery, 374–79
Pickett's Charge, 376–79
report of battle, 218–22
Gettysburg, battlefield photos, 271–73, 274–75, 276
Gibbon, John, 361–62
Gibson, James F., 26, *263*, 264–69, *276*
Gillmore, Quincy A., *362*, 369–71
Gooding, James H., *32*
Gordon, S. C., 415
Grambling, Rupert W., 446–48
Grant, Julia, 89–90
Grant, Ulysses S., *81*, 135, *232*, 245, *248*, 276, 314, 467
Grapevine Bridge, *252*
Great Locomotive Chase, 392–95
Greeley, Horace, 198–99, 204–205
Greenhow, Little Rose, *303*
Greenhow, Robert, 299–300
Greenhow, Rose O'Neal, 135–36, 299–305
*Gun Foundry, The*, *355*

Hamilton, Andrew G., 461
Hamlin, Hannibal, *261*
Hammond, William A., *415*
Hanscom, Simon P., *221*
Hardee, William J., *342*
Hardinge, Samuel Wylde, 310
*Harper's Weekly*, *218*
Harrison, Constance Cary, 100, *326*
Haupt, Herman, *387*, *388*, 389, 398–99, 402
*Haverhill Democrat*, *201*
Hawkes, C. K., 323
Hawkins, Rush C., 154–155, *318*
Haywood, Felix, *30*
Hazen, Fanny Titus, 431
Hazlett, Charles, 374
Helm, Benjamin Hardin, 42, *44*
Helm, Emilie Todd, 42–44
Henson, Cy, 11
Herold, David E., 284–85
Heth, Henry, 96
Hicks, Thomas, *384*
Hitchcock, Ethan Allen, *444*
Hodgers, Jennie, 132–33, *134*
Hoffman, William H., 439–40, 446, 447
Holmes, Oliver Wendell, Jr., 494
Holmes, Oliver Wendell, Sr., 269–70
Homer, Winslow, *162*, *215*, *217*, *411*, *439*
Hood, John Bell, 402–403, *404*
Hopkins, Charles, 455
hospitals, field, 418–21, 422–24
hospitals, Southern, 420–21
Howard, Oliver O., 181–82, *185*, 36
Howe, Julia Ward, 121–22
Howe, Orion P., *101*
Howell, Margaret Graham, *84*
Howell, Varina. *See* Davis, Varina Howell
Hubray, Julius, 432
Hunt, Henry J., 352–53, 354–55

Illinois
*Regiments*
Nineteenth, 193
Ninety-fifth, 132
*Location*
Chicago, Camp Douglas, *443*, *464*
illustrations, 214–15
Imboden, John D., 427
immigrants
Canadian, 187–88
French, 189–92
German, 178–84
Irish, 170–78
Indiana
*Regiment*
Eleventh (Wallace's Zouaves), 154
Indians, *289–90*
intelligence operatives, 320. *See also* spies
Iowa
*Regiment*
Nineteenth, 451
Irish Brigade, 172–75, *336*, *339*, 343–45
sacrifice of, 173–75
Irish immigrants, 170–78
Irish nationalism, 170–73
ironclad, *254*
Isham, A. B., 414
Ivy, Alexander, 412

Jackson, James W., 149
Jackson, Thomas Jonathan "Stonewall," 52–53, 309, *385*
Jacobs, Harriet, 119
Jefferson, Julia, 459
Jeffords, Harrison H., *335*
Jewett, John Howard, 349
Jim Crow laws, 37
Johnson's Island prison, 441–42
Johnson, Andrew, 36, *490*
Johnson, Charles, 29
Johnson, Eastman, *19*, *20*
Johnson, Hannah, 26–27
Jones, Anna, 128–29
Jones, John W., 449
Jordan, Thomas, 300–301
Julian, George, 34

Kansas
*Locations*
Fort Leavenworth, 287
Lawrence, *108*
Kansas–Nebraska Act of 1854, 19–20
Keckley, Elizabeth, 76, 82–83
Kendall, Amos, 198
Kentucky
*Location*
Lexington, *65*
Kiley, Anthony M., 441
Kilpatrick, Judson, 128–29
Klein, Robert, *319*
Knox, J., *221*
Knox, Thomas, *222*
Kryzanowski, Waldimir, *193*
Kurtz, Wilbur G., *392*

Lane, John R., 340
Lane, Joseph S., *211*
Lawton, Hattie, *305*
Le Mere, Thomas, *242*
Lee, Custis, *249*, *491*
Lee, George Washington Custis, *73*
Lee, Henry "Lighthorse Harry," 474
Lee, Mary Custis, 51–52, 474–75, 479–80, 484, *489*, 490
Lee, Robert E., 50–52, 245–46, *249*, 370, 374–76, 471, 474–78, 482, 489–90
Lee, Samuel Phillips, *51*
Lee, Stephen D., 365–66
Leslie, Frank, *206*
Lester, Charles Edwards, 232
Letterman, Jonathan, *262*, *420*, 422–24, 426–27
Lewis, Pryce, 306
Libby Prison, 458–59, 461–63
*Liberator*, *198*
Liberia, 14–15
Life of a Spy, *296*
Lincoln, Abraham, 5, *28*, 30, 32, 34, 40–43, 63, 65–67, 72, 78–82, 143, *201*, *205*, 210–11, 222–27, 235–36, *240–42*, 278–83, *299*
assassination attempt, 297–98, *383*

assassination of, *83*
first inaugural, *248*
funeral procession, *250*
funeral train, *407*
photos of, 278–79, *280–81*, 282–83
Lincoln, Mary Todd, *41*, 42–46, 63–67, 72, 74–83, *78*, 85–88, 91, 123–24
Lincoln, Robert Todd, 42, *77*, 85–87, *88*
Lincoln, Tad (Thomas), *75*, *77*, 78, 85, *242*
Lincoln, Willie, *75*, *77*, 78
Lind, Jenny, *230*
lithography, *234*
Livermore, Mary, 93–94
locomotives,
*Commodore*, *390*
*General*, *392*, *394*
*General Dix*, *402*
*Stanton*, *396*
*Texas*, *393*, *394*
Lokey, J. W., 427
Lossing, Benson, *472*
Louisiana
*Units*
First Battalion (Gaston Coppens's Zouaves), *156–57*, 189
First Special Battalion (Wheat's Tigers), 156
Washington Artillery, 364, *376*
*Locations*
Baton Rouge, *106*
New Orleans, 114
Louisville and Nashville Railroad, *382*

Macarthy, Harry, 333–34
Madison, Dolley, *229*, 231
*Malingerer, The*, 411
Mallard, Mary, 111–12
Malvern Hill, battle of, 352–55
Manassas Gap Railroad, *386*
March to the Sea, 111–13, 137, *406*
Marschall, Nicola, 335
Maryland
*Locations*
Baltimore, train station, *384*
Fredericksburg, *123*, *300*
Point Lookout prison, 441
Massachusetts
*Regiments*
Fifty-fourth, 30, 346
sacrifice of, 31
First Battery, *353*
Ninth Infantry, *174*, *175*
Seventeenth, *328*
Sixth, *384*
Tenth, 131
Twenty-eighth, *336*
Twenty-fourth Infantry, *328*
*Locations*
Boston, Fort Warren prison, 441
Haverhill, *201*
massacres
black troops,444–45
Fort Pillow, 32–33, 445, *462*
Pottawatomie, 20–21
McCallum, Daniel C., *384*, 387
McClellan, George B., 29, 142, *205*, *280*, 296, 298–99, 362, 386, 418, 450–51
McClernand, John A., *299*
McCulloch, Henry E., *31*
McDonald, B. B., 462
McDowell, Irvin, *477*, *478*, 480–83
McGee, James, 328
McMahon, James P., 324
McMeans, Robert, 419–20
McNamara, Daniel G., 329
Meade, George Gordon, 100, 333, 426–27
Meagher, Thomas Francis, 172, *174*, 175–76, 328
Medal of Honor, *34*
*Medical and Surgical History of the War of the Rebellion*, 434
medical treatment, delays in, 426–28
medicine, herbal, 433
Meigs, John, 487–88
Meigs, Montgomery C., 485–89
Melvin, Samuel, 463, 468–69
Michigan,
*Regiments*
Fourth Infantry, 335, 342
Twenty-fourth, 339–41
Michigan State Relief Association, *125*
Middle Passage, *5*
Miles, William Porcher, 334–35
Miller, Mary, *113*
Minié bullet, 411
Mississippi
*Regiment*
Second, 341–42
*Locations*
Biloxi, *89*
Corinth, Tishomingo Hotel, *396*
Vicksburg, 107
Mitchell, Ormsby McKnight, *392*
Montgomery, J. R., 421–22
Montgomery, William, 166
Moore, Samuel Preston, *414*, 428
Morgan, Sarah, 118
Morse, Samuel F. B., 227
mortars, *358*, 372–73, *377*
Mosby, John, 189
Mudd, Samuel, *442*
multinational regiments, 192–94
Murphy, W. B., 341

Napoleon cannon, *360*, *373*
Nast, Thomas, *216*, *455*
Nat Turner revolt, *21*
National Portrait Gallery, *237*
Native Americans, *289–90*
*Negro Life at the South*, *19*, *20*
New Jersey
*Regiment*
Thirty-third, *142*
New York
Eleventh Corps, *186*
*Regiments*
Eleventh Volunteers (Fire Zouaves), 146–50, 152–53, *154*, *443*
Fifth (Duryee's Zouaves), 150, *152–54*, *158*, 159–64, *254*
Fifty-fifth, 191–92, 255
Fifty-third Zouaves, 192
Fighting Sixty–Ninth, 443
Forty-first, *183*
Ninth (Hawkins's Zouaves), 154–55
Seventeenth Infantry, *357*
Seventy-ninth Highlanders, 192–93
Sixth State Militia, *145*
Sixty-ninth, 171
Sixty-third, *333*
Tenth National Zouaves, *160*
Thirty-ninth (Garibaldi Guard), 192, *194*, 343
140th Zouave, *164*
146th Zouave, 142
153rd Volunteers, 131–32
164th Infantry, *255*
165th Zouave, *142*, *166*
*Locations*
Cold Spring, West Point Foundry, *355*
Elmira, prison camp, 446–47, 448–50, *448*, *449*

New York City, *121*
Battery, 170
Broadway & Fulton Streets, *228*
Printing House Square, *200*
Riverside Drive, *166*
*New York Herald*, 199, 209
*New York Tribune*, *199*, *200*, 203, 204–06
news media, 40, 76, 79
newspaper vendor, *220*, 222
Newton, Solomon, 131
Norris, William, *302*
North Carolina
*Regiment*
Twenty-sixth, 131, 339–41, 342–43
*Location*
Salisbury Prison, 442, *445*
North Central Railroad, *384*
nurses, 429–30
Alcott, Louisa May, 124
Barton, Clara, 125–26, 424–25
Bell, Anne, *429*
Bickerdyke, Mary Ann, 124–26
Cumming, Kate, 124, *429*
Hazen, Fanny Titus, 431

O'Hara, Theodore, 494–95
O'Kane, Dennis, *177*
O'Sullivan, Timothy, 26, *30*, *260*, *269*, 276
Ohio
*Location*
Sandusky, Johnson's Island prison, 441–42
*Old Kentucky Home*, *19*, *20*
Old Man Afraid of His Horses, *290*
Old Soldiers disease, 431–32
Olmstead, Charles, *363*
Orange and Alexandria Railroad, *385*, *386*, *391*, *396*

Packs His Drum, *290*
Paine, Lewis, *284*, 285–86
Parrott rifle, *352*, *355*, *365*, *371*, *372*
Swamp Angel, 370–71
Parrott, Robert Parker, *355*, 357–59
Paul, William, 326
Payne, Andrew S., 326
Pegram, William Johnson, 353–54, *367*, 445
Pelham, John, 367–68
Pelham, William, 188
Pember, Phoebe, 434
Pennsylvania
*Regiments*
Eighteenth Cavalry, *410*
Eighty-fifth, *334*
Keystone Independent Battery, *360*
Ninety-sixth Infantry Regulars, *253*
Seventeenth Cavalry, *334*
Sixty-ninth, *177*
Twenty-second Cavalry, *329*
Seventy-second (Baxter's Fire Zouave), 163
Seventy-sixth Zouave, *142*
114th (Collis's Zouave), *165*, 347
143d Infantry, *337*
*Locations*
Emmitsburg, Farmers' Inn, *276*
Gettysburg, *99*, *177*, *214*, *274–75*, 94–103
cemetery, 247
Philadelphia, *326*
Pittsburgh, *211*
pharmaceuticals, *427*
Philippoteaux, Paul, *375*
Phoenix, Katie, *35*
photography, 215–18
field, *209–10*, *223*, *244*, *269*
invention of, 227–28
of rich and famous, 229–36, 244–45
war, 236–44, *246–47*, *252–55*, 263–78
wet plate process, 244, 265, 268
physicians, 409–11, 415–16
Billings, John D., 416–17, 419
Blackwell, Elizabeth, 429–30
Dunn, James, 424–25
Isham, A. B., 414
Letterman, Jonathan, 422–24, 426–27
McMeans, Robert, 419–29
Revere, Edward, 423
Roberts, D. J. , 411
Sanger, E. F., 448–49
Tebault, C H., 416
Weist, J. R., 412–13, 416, 434–35
Pickett's Charge, 376–79
Pickett, George, 345
Pierce, Tillie, 95–103
Pinkerton, Allan J., 263–64, 295–99, 302–303, 315–16
*Pittsburgh Dispatch*, 211
plantations, *2*, *8–11*, *13–16*, *18*
Plunkett, Thomas, 324, *332*
Point Lookout prison, 441
Porcher, F. Peyre, *427*
Pottawatomie massacre, 20–21
Potter, Robert B., *246*
press, 40, 76
abolitionist, 198–99
criticizes Mrs. Lincoln, *76*, *79*
rumors carried by, 199
Press Association of the Confederate States, 201–202
Prince of Wales, 171, 235, 239
printing press, 198, *199*
prison conditions, 440–43, 448–50, 452–61, 463–64, 468–69
for officers, 458–59
prison escapes, 461–63
prisoner-of-war
statistics, 467
facilities, 438–39
Andersonville (Camp Sumter), 446, 454–58, 468–69
Belle Isle, 442
Castle Pinckney, *154*, 441
Elmira, 446–47, 448–50, *455*
Fort Delaware, 450–54
Fort Warren, 441
Johnson's Island, 441–42
Libby Prison, 458–59, 461–63
Point Lookout, 441
Salisbury, 442
prisoner-of-war policy, 438, 443–46
prisoner-of-war system, 437–69
prostitution, 114–15, 128–29

Quakers, 16
Quantrill, William Clarke, *108*

railroad bridges, *380*, *388*, 390–91, *393*, *397*, *398*, *401*
railroads
advantage of Federal, 385
confederate, *392–95*, 395–97
early history, 381–82
lack of coordination, 382–83, 386
rebuilding of, 401–402
sabotage of, 392–95, 397–99
troop relocation, 400–401
Baltimore and Ohio, *383*
Chicago and Northwestern, *382*
Louisville and Nashville, *382*
Manassas Gap, *386*
North Central, *384*

Orange and Alexandria, *385*, *386*, *391*, *396*
Richmond, Fredericksburg and Potomac, *388*, *397*, *401*
U.S. Military, *385*, *386*, *400*
Weldon, *399*
Western and Atlantic, *404*
Railways and Telegraph Act, 387
Ransom, John, *457*
Red Bear, *290*
refugees, 34–35, 114, 137
Reid, Whitelaw, *209*
religion, slaves and, *13*
Rembert, James, *26–27*
reporters, 76, 211–13
war, 218–22
Republican party, 22
resections, 433–34
Reynolds, John, 97
Rhode Island
*Regiments*
Burnside Zouaves, 159
First Volunteers, 254
Richmond, Fredericksburg and Potomac Railroad, *388*, *397*, *401*
Ringgold, Samuel, 360
Roberts, D. J., 411
Rock Island Prison, *463*
Rorty, James McKay, 194–95
Rose, Thomas E., 461–63
Rosecrans, William, 400–401
rumors, carried by press, 199
Rush, Columbus, 421
Russell, A. J., *483*, *487*
Russell, William Howard, 204, 212
Ryan, George, *164*

Salisbury prison, 442
Sanger, E. F., 448–49
sanitary fairs, *121*
sanitation, lack of, 414–16, 432–33
Sartain, William, *468*
Schoepf, Albin, *185*
Schriver, Henrietta, 96–97
Schurz, Carl, 179–80
Scobell, John, 315–16, *317*
Scott, Dred, 15, *22*
Scott, Joseph R., 145
Scott, Julian, *450*
Scott, Winfield, *229*, *476*
Scully, Father, *175*
Scully, John, 306
Second Bull Run, battle of, *387*
Secret Service bureau (Confederate), *302*
secret societies, *294*
Sedgwick, John, *413*
Seller, Henry, 126
Seymour, Truman, 31
Sharpe, George H., *301*
Sharpwell, Randolph, 377
Shaw, Henry (E. C. Coleman), 318–20
Shaw, Robert Gould, 30
Sheppard, William Ludwell, *204*
Sheridan, Philip H., 134
Sherman, William Tecumseh, *101*, *222*
March to the Sea, 34–35, *110–113*, *137*, 209–10, 211–13, 403–404
Shrapnel, Henry, 357
Sickles, Daniel E., 43
Sigel, Franz, 180–81, *182*
Simms, William E., 414
Skelley, Jack, 108–110
slave auction, *10*
slave cabins, *8–10*, 14, 16, 35
slaves, *2*, *4–6*, *8–12*, *14*, *16–25*, *27–28*, *38*
children, *18*
control of, 9–11
cooks, *16*
family, *14*
religion and, 13
slavery, economics of, 4
slavery, prevailing view of, 4–5
slave pens, *7*
slave revolts, 12–13, 199–200
slave songs, 12
slave trading, *4–7*
sling cart, *359*
smallpox, 450
Smart, Frederick, *154*
Smith, J. C., 427–28
Smith, Orren R., 335
Society of Friends, 16
soldiers of fortune, 184–87
Sorrel, G. Moxley, 396
South Carolina, *26–27*, 113
*Regiments*
First Volunteers (Union), 29–30
Second Volunteers (Union), 29–30
*Locations*
Beaufort, *11*
Charleston, siege of, 370
Charleston Harbor, *371*, *372*
Castle Pinckney, *154*, *440*, 441
Edisto Island, *124*
Port Royal, *9*
Spelman, Francis, 163
spies
Andrews, James J., 392–95
Bowser, Mary Elizabeth, 312–13
Boyd, Belle, 307–11, *308*
Coleman's Scouts, 318–20
Davis, Sam, 318–20
Greenhow, Rose O'Neal, 299–305
Lewis, Pryce, 306
Pinkerton, Alan, 295–99, 302–303
Scully, John, 306–307
van Lew, Elizabeth, 310, 311–15
Webster, Timothy, *304*, 305–308
Army of the Potomac, *300*
black, 312–13
Scobell, John, 315–16
Tubman, Harriet, 316–17
female, 134–36, 307. (*See also* individual names above)
spiritualism, 79, *87*
spy rings, 294–95
Stahel, Julius, *184*
Stanford, C. W., 479
Stanton, Elizabeth Cady, 120
Stanton, Edwin M., 387, *482*
Stanton locomotive, *396*
starvation, *456*
sterilization, 432
Stiles, Robert, *352*
Stitt, H. D., *383*
Stowe, Harriet Beecher, *23*, 120–21
stretcher, *418*, *421*
Strother, David Hunter, *182*
Stuart, Flora Cooke, 47
Stuart, James Ewell Brown "Jeb", *46*, 47–48, 152, 476
*Sultana* steamboat, *466*
disaster, 465
Sumner, Charles, 20
Sumner, Edwin V., *374*
surgical tools, *422*
Surratt, Mary, 285–86
Sutler, Johnson the, *255*
Swain, Lucien B., 163
Swamp Angel, 370–71, *372*
Taggart, Charles A., 325
Taney, Roger Brooke, 15, *231*
Tarleton, Susan, *178*
Taylor, George, *105*
Taylor, Jimmy, 347
Taylor, Sarah Knox, 67

Taylor, Susie King, 127–28
Taylor, Walter, *249*
Taylor, Zachary, 67, *231*
Taylor, Zachary, cabinet of, *230*
Tebault, C. H., 416
telegraph, 198, *213*
Tennessee
  *Locations*
    Fort Pillow, *32–33*, *462*
    Knoxville, *95*
    Murfreesboro, *389*
    Nashville, Cumberland River bridge, *398*
Tepe, Marie, 129, *130*
Terrill, James B., 59–60
Terrill, William Sr., 59–60
*Texas* locomotive, *393*, 394–95
Texas
  *Location*
    Tyler, Camp Ford, *451*
*The Gallery of Illustrious Americans*, 233, 234
Thirteenth Amendment, 34
Thomas, George H., 49–50
Thompson, Franklin (Sarah Edmonds), 133, *134*, 188
Thompson, William Tappan, *202*
Tibbals, Laura, *17*
Todd, Alexander, *43*, 44
Todd, David, *43*
Todd, Elizabeth Humphries, *64*
Todd, Elody, 45–46
Todd, Emilie, *44*
Todd, Mary Ann. See Lincoln, Mary Todd
Todd, Robert S., *64*
total war, 111–13
Townsend, George Alfred, 203
Tredegar Iron Works, *354*
Trego, William, *358*
Tripler, Charles S., *414*
Truth, Sojourner, *119*, 120
Tubman, Harriet, 18, *120*, 121, 316–17
Turchin, Ivan V., 193–94
Turchin, John Basil, *195*
Turner, Nat, 13, *21*
Twiggs, David E., 438

U S. Military Telegraph Service, *213*
U.S. Artillery
    First, Battery K, *331*
    First, Battery L, *338*
    Second, Batteries B and L, *338*
    Second, Battery D, *373*
U.S. Christian Commission, *104*, *122*
U.S. Colored Troops, *31*, *33*
  108th Infantry,*345*
  Pennsylvania, *346*, *347*
    Forty-fifth, 346
    Sixth, 346
    Third, 345–46
    Twenty-fifth, 346
    Twenty-fourth, 346
    Twenty-second, 346
    127th, 346
U.S. Military Railroad, *385*, *386*, 387–91, *400*, *405*, *407*
U.S. Military Railroad Construction Corps, *391*, *401*
U.S. Navy, *364*
U.S. troops
  Artillery
    Second, Horse Battery A, *263*
  Regular Infantry
    Eighteenth, 329, 330
    Third, 325
  Second Division, Ninth Corps, *255*
  Eleventh Corps, 181–84
  Signal Corps, *300*
U.S. Sanitary Commission, *104*, *121*, *122*, *123*, *125*, *426*, 431
U.S.S. *Miami*, *364*
*Uncle Tom's Cabin*, *23*
Underground Railroad, 17–18, *24*
United States Zouave Cadets, 143–45

Van Lew, Elizabeth, 135, *310*, 311–15, 462
Van Wagener, Isabella (Sojourner Truth), 119
ventilation, 432–33
Virginia
  *Locations*
    Alexandria, *405*
      Freedman's Village, *481*
      rail yard, *385*, *396*
    Bull Run, *387*, *391*
    Cedar Mountain, *138*
    Chickahominy Creek, *252*
    City Point, Union field hospital, *434*
    City Point landing, U.S. Military Railroad depot, *402*, *403*
    Dutch Gap, *358*
    Fair Oaks, *365*
    Fort Damnation, 377
    Fredericksburg
      Marye house, *412*
      Marye's Heights, *368*, *412*
    Middletown, Episcopal church, *416*
    Morgantown (now West Virginia), *94*
    Norfolk, *124*
    North Anna River, *397*
    Petersburg, *247*, 373
      warehouse prison, *447*
    Potomac Creek, *388*
    Rappahannock River, *30*
    Richmond, *70*, *100*, *249*, *406*
      abandonment of, 405–406
      Belle Isle prison, 442
      Burnt District, *278*
      Chimborazo Hospital, 420, *434*
      Gallego Flour Mill, *278*
      Libby Prison, 313, 458–59, *460*, 461–63
      Ligon Tobacco Warehouse, *441*
      State Penitentiary, *440*
      Tredegar Iron Works, *354*
      Van Lew mansion, *310*
      White House of the Confederacy, *313*
    Southampton County, *21*
    White House Landing, 125
vivandiéres, 129–30
Vizetelly, Frank, *212*

Wade, Jennie, 108–110
Wainwright, Charles, 352
Wakeman, Edwin (Sarah Rosetta), 131–32, *133*
Walker, Mary Edwards, 126, *129*
Wallace, Lew, 154
Waller, Francis, 342
Walton, James, 364
war crimes trial, 466–67
war, romantic images of, 141, 143, 145, 167
Washington, D.C., 19
  *Locations*
    Armory Square Hospital, *430*
    Douglas and Stanton Hospital, *431*
    F Street, *250*
    Ford's Theater, *282*
    Fort Richardson, *366*
    Fort Totten, *253*
    Old Arsenal Prison, *284*
    Old Capitol Prison, 303, 446, 467
    7th & D Streets, *270*

train station, *383*
U.S. arsenal, *360*
U.S. Capitol, *147*, *248*, *252*, *281*, *294*, *400*
Washington, George, 472
Washington, Martha, 472
Watkins, Sam, 331
Watson, Sam, 200
Waud, Alfred R., *139*, *214*, *221*, *352*
Webb, Alexander, *375*
Webb, Varina Howell Hayes, *90*
Webb, Varina Margaret, *90*
Webster, Daniel, *233*
Webster, Timothy, *304*, 305–307
Weed, Stephen, 101–102
Weikert, Jacob, 96, 98
Weir, John Ferguson, *355*
Weist, J. R., 412–13, 416
Welch, Peter, 329–30
Weldon Railroad, *399*
West Point Foundry, *355*
West Virginia
*Locations*
Harpers Ferry, *246*
Martinsburg, *113*
Morgantown, *94*
Western and Atlantic Railroad, *404*
Wheat, Chatham Roberdeau, 156–57
White House of the Confederacy, *70*
White, Martha Todd, 44–45
Whitman, Walt, 222, 271, *430*, 464–65, 495
Whitney, Eli, 7
Whytal, James, 164
Wilcox, George, 340
Wilkeson, Bayard, 220–21
Wilkeson, Samuel, 220–22, *223*
Williams, Lawrence Orton, *296*
Wilson, Henry, 310
Winder, John H., *315*, 440–41, *442*
Winslow, Cleveland, *161*, 163
Wirz, Heinrich H., *286*, 287, 465–67
Wisconsin
Sixth, 341–42
Women's Central Association of Relief, 121
women
abolitionists, 118–22
nurses, 124–26
physicians, 126, 429–30
soldiers, 130–34
Southern, 110–12
spies, 134–36
vivandiéres, 120–30
in war, 95–103, 108–110
war effort at home, *103*, 122–23
Wood, Alfred, *317*
Wood, Harriet (Pauline Cushman), *316*
Wood, Thomas W., *32*, *339*
World's Fair of 1851, *236*
wounded, *412*, *416*, *421*, *426*
in Wilderness Campaign, 408
transportation of, 413–14, 420
Wyndham, Percy, 186–87, *188*
Wyoming
*Location*
Fort Laramie, *290*

Zouaves
romantic image of, 141, 143–45
*Regiments*
Baxter's Seventy-second Pennsylvania Fire, *163*
Burnside Rhode Island, *159*
Collis's 114th Pennsylvania, 165
Coppens' Louisiana, *156–57*, 189–90
Duryée's Fifth New York, 150, *152–54*, 159–64
Ellsworth's Eleventh New York Fire, 146–50, 148–50, *154*
Ellsworth's United States Cadets, *144*
Fifth New York, *152–54*, *158*, *161*
First Louisiana Special Battalion (Wheat's Tigers), 156
French, *167*
Hawkins's Ninth New York, 154–155
Seventy-sixth Pennsylvania Keystone, *142*
Tenth New York National, *160*
Thirty-third New Jersey, 142
Wallace's Eleventh Indiana, *154*
114th Pennsylvania, *165*
140th New York, *164*
146th New York, *142*
165th New York Infantry, *142*, *166*